# CRIMINOLOGICAL PERSPECTIVES

*A Reader*

This book is the third in a series published by Sage in association with The Open University.

*The Problem of Crime*
edited by John Muncie and Eugene McLaughlin

*Controlling Crime*
edited by Eugene McLaughlin and John Muncie

*Criminological Perspectives: A Reader*
edited by John Muncie, Eugene McLaughlin and Mary Langan

The books are one component of The Open University course D315 *Crime, Order and Social Control*. Details of this and other Open University courses can be obtained from the Central Enquiry Service, P.O. Box 200, The Open University, Milton Keynes, MK7 6YZ. For availability of other course components, including video- and audio-cassette materials, contact Open University Educational Enterprises Ltd, 12 Cofferidge Close, Stony Stratford, Milton Keynes, MK11 1BY.

# CRIMINOLOGICAL PERSPECTIVES

## *A Reader*

*edited and introduced by*
John Muncie
Eugene McLaughlin and
Mary Langan

SAGE Publications
London • Thousand Oaks • New Delhi
in association with

The Open
University

SAGE Publications Ltd
6 Bonhill Street
London EC2A 4PU

SAGE Publications Inc
2455 Teller Road
Thousand Oaks, California 91320

SAGE Publications India Pvt Ltd
32, M-Block Market
Greater Kailash – I
New Delhi 110 048

**British Library Cataloguing in Publication data**

A catalogue record for this book is available
from the British Library.

ISBN 0 7619 5002-8
ISBN 0 7619 5003-6 (pbk)

**Library of Congress catalog record available**

Typeset by Mayhew Typesetting, Rhayader, Powys
Printed in Great Britain by The Cromwell Press,
Trowbridge, Wiltshire

# Contents

# Acknowledgements

The authors and publishers wish to thank the following for permission to reprint copyright material.

University of Pittsburgh Press for 'Causes of criminal behaviour' by Enrico Ferri, abridged from *The Positive School of Criminology: Three Lectures by Enrico Ferri*, Stanley E. Grupp (ed.), copyright © 1968.

Heinemann Publishers (Oxford) Ltd for extracts from *Criminality and Economic Conditions* by Willem Bonger, 1916.

Black Rose Books for 'Law and authority' by Peter Kropotkin, from *Words of a Rebel*, translated by G. Woodcock, Montreal/New York, 1992.

Oxford University Press and the author for 'British criminology before 1935' by David Garland, abridged from *The British Journal of Criminology*, Vol. 28, No. 2, 1988.

Cambridge University Press and the authors for 'Genetic factors in the etiology of criminal behaviour' by Sarnoff A. Mednick, William F. Gabrielli Jr and Barry Hutchings, from *The Causes of Crime: New Biological Approaches*, S. Mednick, T. Moffit and S. Stack (eds), Cambridge University Press, 1987.

HMSO for 'Personality theory and the problem of criminality' by H.J. Eysenck, abridged from *Applying Psychology to Imprisonment*, B. McGurk, D. Thornton and M. Williams (eds), 1987; and for 'Crime and consumption' by Simon Field, from *Trends in Crime and their Interpretation*, Home Office Research Study No. 119, 1990. Crown copyright is reproduced with the permission of the Controller of HMSO.

Routledge, the authors and editors for 'Explanations of crime and place' by Anthony E. Bottoms and Paul Wiles, abridged from *Crime, Policing and Place: Essays in Environmental Criminology*, David Evans, Nicholas Fyfe and David Herbert (eds), 1992; for extracts from *The New Criminology* by Ian Taylor, Paul Walton and Jock Young, 1973; and for extracts from 'The power of law' by Carol Smart, from *Feminism and the Power of Law*, 1989.

Tavistock Publications for 'Crime, power and ideological mystification' by Steven Box, from *Power, Crime and Mystification*, 1983.

The Institute of Economic Affairs' Health and Welfare Unit for 'The underclass' by Charles Murray, abridged from *The Emerging Underclass* by Charles Murray, the main part of which first appeared in *The Sunday Times Magazine* in November 1989.

Penguin Books Ltd for 'Relative deprivation' by John Lea and Jock Young, from *What is to be Done about Law and Order?*, 1984. Copyright © John Lea and Jock Young, 1994.

BasicBooks, a division of HarperCollins Publishers, Inc. for selected excerpts from pp. 310–24 of 'Seductions and repulsions of crime' by Jack Katz, in *Seductions of Crime: Moral and Sensual Attractions in Doing Evil*, © 1988 by Jack Katz; and for selected excerpts from pp. 117–23 and 142–4 of 'On deterrence' by James Q. Wilson, from *Thinking About Crime*, © 1975, 1983, Basic Books, Inc.

The author for 'The etiology of female crime: a review of the literature' by Dorie Klein, from *Issues in Criminology*, Vol. 8, No. 2, 1973.

McGraw-Hill, Inc. and the author for 'Afterword: Twenty years ago . . . today' by Dorie Klein, from *The Criminal Justice System and Women*, B.R. Price and N.J. Sokoloff (eds), 1995.

Rutgers University Press (US rights) and Virago Press (rest of world) for 'Explaining Male Violence' by Lynne Segal abridged from *Slow Motion: Changing Masculinities, Changing Men*, © 1990 by Lynne Segal.

The Free Press, a Division of Simon & Schuster Inc. for extracts from *Outsiders: Studies in the Sociology of Deviance* by Howard S. Becker, © 1963 by The Free Press.

Kluwer Academic Publishers and the author for 'Toward a political economy of crime' by William J. Chambliss, abridged from *Theory and Society*, Vol. 2, 1975; for 'Critical criminology and the concept of crime' by Louk H.C. Hulsman, abridged from *Contemporary Crises*, Vol. 10, No. 1, 1986; and for 'The punitive city' by Stanley Cohen, from *Contemporary Crises*, Vol. 3, No. 4, 1979.

The Civil Liberties Trust and the author for the extract from *Drifting into a Law and Order Society* by Stuart Hall, 1980 (Cobden Trust).

UCL Press Ltd for 'Criminalisation and racialisation' by Michael Keith, abridged from *Race, Riots and Policing*, 1993.

The author for 'Giving criminals their just deserts' by Andrew von Hirsch, abridged from *Civil Liberties Review*, No. 3, 1976.

Anderson Publishing Co. for 'The value of rehabilitation' by Francis T. Cullen and Karen E. Gilbert, abridged from *Reaffirming Rehabilitation*, 1982.

Oxford University Press and the author for '"Situational" crime prevention: theory and practice' by Ronald V.G. Clarke, from *British Journal of Criminology*, Vol. 20, No. 2, 1980.

NACRO and the author for 'Social crime prevention strategies in a market society' by Elliott Currie, abridged from *International Developments in Crime and Social Policy*, NACRO Crime and Social Policy, 1991.

The American Society of Criminology and the authors for 'The new penology' by Malcolm M. Feeley and Jonathan Simon, from *Criminology*, Vol. 30, No. 4, 1992.

Cambridge University Press and the author for 'Crime, authority and the policeman state' by V.A.C. Gatrell, from *Cambridge Social History of Britain*,

*1750–1950*, F.M.L. Thompson (ed.), Vol. 3, 1990; and for 'Reintegrative shaming' by John Braithwaite, from *Crime, Shame and Reintegration*, 1989.

Georges Borchardt, Inc. (US rights) and Penguin Books Ltd (UK and Commonwealth rights) for extracts from 'The Caracel' by Michel Foucault, from *Discipline and Punish: The Birth of Prison*, translated by Alan Sheridan (first published by Éditions Gallimard 1975, published by Allen Lane 1977, reprinted in North America by permission of Georges Borchardt, Inc.; copyright © Éditions Gallimard 1975, translation copyright © Alan Sheridan 1977).

Canada Law Book Inc. for 'From the Panopticon to Disney World: the development of discipline' by Clifford D. Shearing and Philip C. Stenning, abridged from *Perspectives in Criminal Law*, A. Doob and E. Greenspan (eds), 1985.

Open University Press and the author for 'Feminist approaches to criminology or postmodern woman meets atavistic man' by Carol Smart, abridged from *Feminist Perspectives in Criminology*, A. Morris and L. Gelsthorpe (eds), 1990.

Academic Press London, a Division of Harcourt Brace & Co. Inc. for 'Towards transgression: new directions in feminist criminology' by Maureen Cain, from *International Journal of the Sociology of Law*, 1990.

Collective Press for 'Postmodernism and critical criminology' by Alan Hunt, from *New Directions in Critical Criminology*, B.D. Maclean and D. Milanovic (eds), 1991.

Butterworths, the Australian and New Zealand Society of Criminology and the author for 'Human rights and crimes of the state: the culture of denial' by Stanley Cohen, abridged from the *Australian and New Zealand Journal of Criminology*, Vol. 26, No. 2, 1993.

Every effort has been made to trace all copyright holders, but if any have been inadvertently overlooked the publishers will be pleased to make the necessary arrangements at the first opportunity.

# Preface

It became commonplace in the late 1960s and early 1970s to assert that the end of criminology was imminent. According to the emergent common wisdom, the whole criminological project was fatally flawed. A generation of 'young radicals' confidently informed us that we should concern ourselves with new developments in social, political and legal theory rather than the empiricist claims of criminology. We were urged not only to leave a sinking ship but to celebrate its going down. And yet somewhat bizarrely, in the 1990s, despite what seemed like a devastating deconstruction, criminology is not only still with us, it is flourishing: important new criminology departments have been established, reflecting the student demand for criminology courses and degrees; criminology conferences of a variety of hues are burgeoning; most academic presses have at least one thriving criminology series and a generation of young criminologists has been told that they have never had it so good in terms of university posts and research opportunities. We are also being offered a bewildering and stimulating choice of criminological discourses and story lines, some old, some re-works, some genuinely new, some reassuring and some troubling, about what criminology is and should be in the late twentieth century and the fragmented pathways criminology will take in the new century. Some are (yet again) looking beyond criminology, others believe that we are in need of a major criminological reinvention and redrawing of boundaries, yet others are endeavouring to get to grips with various aspects of the archaeology of criminological and indeed *pre*-criminological knowledge, and professional criminologists, who have learned to live with or ignore passing fads, continue to pursue criminology's historic empirical project. It would seem that the deconstruction of criminology has resulted not in its demise, but reconstruction.

It is therefore, we feel, an appropriate moment to assemble a collection of readings which both reflects and re-presents the numerous and diverse lines of theoretical enquiry that constitute criminology. The overall aim of *Criminological Perspectives* is two-fold: to provide an accessible set of edited readings which introduces undergraduate students to the eclectic nature of 'criminological knowledge' and to prompt readers to gaze critically upon, not only its constituent elements, but the very soul of the criminological enterprise. In compiling this collection we recognize that we have been unable (not least because of the constraints of space) to cover every aspect of criminology. Like all editors, we have been forced to make some difficult choices and uneasy compromises. Uppermost in our minds were the needs of our primary audience, Open University students studying the undergraduate course *Crime, Order and Social Control*. This book is a principal component of the course and the selection, relevance and indeed the editing can only be truly understood in that context. By choosing original readings, rather than depending on existing textbook summaries, commentaries and reviews, we hope to encourage our students to acquire a critical appreciation of criminology 'in the raw'. As far as possible, we have chosen readings for each part which are to some extent in dialogue and deliberation with each other. To do so, we have concentrated on pieces which provide expositions of key theoretical positions. We ask our students to pay due homage to the complicated multiple origins of criminological theory, but to avoid reading or mapping subsequent developments as some readily identifiable linear, uncontested progression. We prefer them to see the ever-present historical traces, thematic survivals, empirical residues, generative narratives, unresolved lines of dispute and to reflect upon the reality that no one theoretical perspective can legitimately lay sole claim to the empirical referents of crime. Criminology in our view is a classic 'site' of contested meaning where competing theoretical perspectives meet. Sometimes they are able to speak to, listen to and understand each other, at others they appear not to share any common discourse. There is, therefore, no one criminology to be found in this Reader but a multitude of often contradictory criminological perspectives which in the main depend and draw upon knowledges and concerns generated from elsewhere. To illustrate this point we have included pieces that depart from traditional agendas, transgress conventional boundaries and suggest new points of departure and fruitful avenues for cross-discipline development.

The book is in six parts. Part One (Chapters 1–8) focuses on the origins of criminology as expressed through a wide variety of subject positions and theoretical arguments. It reveals a number of 'starting-points' from classicist interpretations of the function of law, positivist interrogations of the causes of crime and quantitative studies of crime statistics, through to Marxist, sociological and anarchist critiques of the problems of crime, law, the state and social order. The impact of such intellectual traditions – emanating from continental Europe – on penal policy and practice in late nineteenth and early twentieth century Britain is also addressed.

Part Two (Chapters 9–17) concentrates on criminology's historic concern to discover the causes of crime. Again, a wide variety in type of explanation and level of analysis is notable. The readings illustrate some of the key *contemporary* attempts to tackle the issue of crime causation and include discussion of genetic factors, personality traits, social disorganization, consumption patterns, illegitimacy and the underclass, relative deprivation, masculinity and the moral and expressive attractions of the preference for crime over non crime. A number of competing theoretical positions and paradigms are at work in these chapters, from individual and sociological variants of positivism to neo-classicism, left realism and gender studies. Also included is a feminist critique of criminology's traditional representation of female criminality.

Part Three (Chapters 18–26) reveals that understanding the 'problem of crime' does not simply involve trying to account for why certain individuals transgress moral and legal codes whilst others do not, but also necessitates interrogation of how and why it is that only certain behaviours seem to be subjected to criminal sanction whilst other harmful acts may go unnoticed, unpoliced or are even socially approved. Key readings from interactionist, labelling, Marxist and critical criminological perspectives are included to show how the subject matter of criminology has been significantly broadened to encompass issues of social order, power, criminalization and the ability of the state and powerful groups in society to confer and enforce the label of criminality on others. Collectively these readings encourage a critical reading and deconstruction of traditional and populist notions of what constitutes 'crime', 'criminality' and 'criminal behaviour'.

Part Four (Chapters 27–33) examines a number of competing rationales for systems of crime control, from deterrence, just deserts and rehabilitation to crime prevention. Critiques of existing justice systems – emanating from left realist and abolitionist perspectives – are also included. The part concludes by asking how far the contemporary concern to create cost-effective and efficient control systems has only served to disguise and circumvent broader issues and debates about philosophical justification through a more pragmatic and narrow focus on matters of crime management.

Part Five (Chapters 34–39) explores how individuals and populations are controlled not simply through the formal processes of criminal justice, but through the imposition of forms of regulation and surveillance in non-judicial 'community' settings. Foucault's vision of a 'carceral society' is assessed through interrogations of how community-based corrections, private security, urban design, as well as the law, are implicated in creating disciplinary societies. The part concludes by looking at how far alternative informal systems of control – based on notions such as shaming – can offer a more equitable and less repressive vision of the future of social control.

Part Six (Chapters 40–46) poses a number of questions concerning the futures of criminology and its potential for theoretical development. A range of critical perspectives – left realist, feminist, postmodern, human rights – are explored and compared. Some of these appear to herald new openings for criminological study; others are a reversion to more traditional forms of analysis. At one and the same time they underline the past failings of criminology, its continuing diversity and fragmentation and yet the remaining potential to shed new light on such issues as crime and criminalization, harm and harm reduction and state and social control. In important respects this current uncertainty and eclecticism is born not just from the contemporary inability of criminology clearly to define the parameters of its own discourse, but is derived from the historically problematic and contested nature of the concepts of 'crime', 'law' and 'justice' themselves.

We are indebted to many people in putting this text together, not least the thousands of students who have studied criminology with The Open University over the past sixteen years. Their response to, and ability to engage with, previous course materials has been central in our decisions of what to include and what to omit and in guiding our assessment of what is accessible and appropriate for undergraduate study. We have also had the benefit of working with a team of assessors, academics and tutors at the University who have continually reminded us to keep the needs of students uppermost in our minds. Informal discussions with Pat Carlen (Keele), Stan Cohen (Jerusalem), Richard Sparks (Keele), Loraine Gelsthorpe (Cambridge), Gordon Hughes (Northampton) and Karim Murji (Roehampton) have been more influential than they may have realized. Hilary Canneaux and Sue Lacey at The Open University have been invaluable in providing administrative and secretarial support and we are indebted to Gillian Stern at Sage for her unwavering belief that this project was both feasible and worthwhile.

John Muncie
Eugene McLaughlin
Mary Langan

*September 1995*

# *Criminological Perspectives*: an introduction

Whilst the transgression of moral and legal codes has probably always raised concerns for the maintenance of social order, 'crime' and 'criminology' have not always been with us. The first generally recognized school of criminology, the classical school of the eighteenth century, was less concerned with understanding the nature of 'the criminal' and more with developing rational and systematic means of delivering justice (Beccaria, 1764 – Chapter 1). In essence, classicism was, and remains, a plea for the supremacy of law, rather than of religion, superstition and arbitrary justice. Crime is understood as a product of a rational free will; a course of action freely chosen through calculations of the pain and pleasure involved. Its control is assumed to lie in better and more efficient means of punishment. Establishing specific causes of crime or trying to understand its meaning is of little or no concern (Wilson, 1983 – Chapter 27).

It was not until the early nineteenth century that crime was perceived as a major social problem and became an object of enquiry in its own right. In important respects, a concept of 'crime' only came to replace a concept of 'sin' when a burgeoning legal apparatus, designed to protect property and the interests of the nation-state, evolved out of the social and economic transformations of the industrial revolution (Gatrell, 1990 – Chapter 34). As concern over the 'problem of crime' intensified, so crime became the object of more systematic observance and measurement. Analysis of its extent and causes was first made possible through the publication of national criminal statistics in France in the 1820s. Regularities in the occurrence of crime were then explained with reference to such factors as age, sex, climate and economic conditions (Quetelet, 1842 – Chapter 2). If crime rates were regular and predictable, it was assumed that the causes of crime must lie outside of each individual's control. It was not a simple matter of individual choice.

Such was the cornerstone of a *positivist* criminology which radically proposed that crime was a non-rational and determinate product of undersocialization and could be studied, via clinical and statistical methods, in much the same way as scientists studied the natural world (Ferri, 1901 – Chapter 4). Typically, positivist conceptions of crime – whether they be individually or socially based – focus on isolating specific causes. The Italian *scuola positiva* of the late nineteenth century maintained that criminality had multi-factor explanations. In its earliest form, biological causes were prioritized. The criminal, it was argued, was a throwback to a more primitive form of human being, distinguishable through such physiological characteristics as large jaw and ears and facial asymmetry (Lombroso and Ferrero 1895 Chapter 3). Such a conclusion was based on the careful and painstaking measurement of the skulls and skeletons of 'known criminals'. As a result it has been heralded as the first *scientific* study of crime. And it is probably no coincidence that it is also from this time that the term *criminology* is widely assumed to have originated.

The impact of positivism on subsequent developments within criminology cannot be overstated. By searching for the causes of *criminal* behaviour as opposed to other human behaviours, positive criminology assumes that such behaviour has its own peculiar set of characteristics. The aim is to isolate key differences between criminals and non-criminals. Some theorists focus on biological and psychological factors, attempt to isolate specific genetic or personality causes and thus locate the sources of crime primarily within the individual (Mednick, Gabrielli and Hutchings, 1987 – Chapter 9; Eysenck, 1987 – Chapter 10). Other theorists argue that more insights can be gained by studying the social context external to individuals and maintain that crime is better explained with reference to such factors as levels of economic consumption (Field, 1990 – Chapter 12), sites of social disorganization and types of urban structure (Bottoms and Wiles, 1992 – Chapter 11). The origins of all such social approaches can be traced to the insistence that social phenomena, such as crime and law, have an objective existence of their own and exist independently of the individuals who experience them (Durkheim, 1895 – Chapter 6).

Positivist criminologies – whether individual or sociological in focus – remain influential because they prolong the modernist concern to account for crime with reference to some quantifiable and objective criteria. They also hold on to the hope that because people are propelled into crime through a range of determining factors, then it will always remain possible to treat or neutralize the underlying causes. Such treatments may range from individual rehabilitation (Cullen and Gilbert, 1982 – Chapter 29) through to social and welfare reform (Currie, 1991 – Chapter 31).

Positivism, however, has always stood uneasily against the key principle of classicism that every individual is, and should be made, responsible for their actions. The development of criminology as a practical science in early twentieth century Britain, for example, has meant that the advocacy of positivist treatment methods has always been contested by dominant classicist assumptions of free will and the pragmatic concerns of penal administrators (Garland, 1988 – Chapter 8).

Almost from its inception, scientific positivism was also under attack from some anarchists (Kropotkin, 1898 – Chapter 7) and Marxist-inspired authors (Bonger, 1916 – Chapter 5) for failing to take a more critical stance towards the nature of the social order in which crime and criminality are located. They warned that crime cannot be analysed outside of the social and economic circumstances in which it occurs. The propositions that law is a tool of state repression and that crime is a product of exploitative labour relations challenged the key positivist assumptions that crime is something abnormal and only practised by identifiable, pathological 'others'. Rather, such analyses (with differing ideological and political emphases) maintained that crime was widespread and ubiquitous – a defining characteristic of a social order based on inequality and social division.

Despite such pragmatic, theoretical and political misgivings, it was not until the mid twentieth century that the conventional wisdom of positivism was subjected to sustained intellectual challenge. Whilst positivism tends to deny that criminality involves any element of choice, creativity or meaning, interactionism and ethnographic research is more concerned to grant authenticity to deviant actions by recording the motives and meanings of the deviant actors themselves (Sykes and Matza, 1957 – Chapter 18; Katz, 1988 – Chapter 15). Interactionism produced an epistemological break by radically shifting the object of criminological inquiry away from trying to isolate the presumed factors propelling a pathological few to break the rules of an assumed social consensus, to an analysis which rested on a conflict or pluralist conception of society in which deviance was ubiquitous and where 'crime' was constructed through the partial and pernicious practices of social reaction and social control. The adages of social reaction theory that 'there can be no crime without law' and that 'social control leads to deviance' effectively turned the time-honoured premises of positivism on their head (Becker, 1963 – Chapter 19). By the early 1970s this critical paradigm effectively placed a number of counter propositions on the criminological agenda. Criminology was under challenge from a more comprehensive sociology of crime and deviance. Here questions of social control, rather than crime causation, are the central matters of concern. A determination to 'appreciate' (and some would say 'celebrate') deviance in terms of its subjective meaning for particular actors takes precedence over the scientific assertions that criminal behaviour is determined by a mix of innate, genetic or physiological incapacities (born bad) or instances of ineffective child rearing, family pathology and social disorganization (made bad). By focusing on processes of criminalization and law formation, rather than crime and criminal behaviour, whole new areas of research and empathies have been opened up, in which definitional rather than behavioural issues are central.

It is in this context that we can account for the emergence in the 1970s of *The New Criminology*, (Taylor, Walton and Young, 1973 – Chapter 21). Despite its title, its originality lay not so much in innovation, but in the attempt to synthesize several different old traditions. The concern to respect the authenticity of the diverse and unique worlds of everyday life continued a tradition established by the Chicago School of the 1930s and the social interactionists; whilst dimensions of power and social control were appropriated from social reaction theory. The New Criminology, however, attempted to ground this anti-positivist radicalization by taking the world of personal meanings and social reaction back into a critique of the history and structure of society. This was achieved through locating definitions of crime and modes of control in the precise context of the social relationships and institutional arrangements emanating from particular modes of economic production. Clearly what this work was advocating was that the key subject of the new criminology was not crime and deviance as behaviours, but a critical understanding of the social order and the power to criminalize and control. When the task of criminology was defined as one of creating a society 'in which the facts of human diversity are not subject to the power to criminalize', it was clear that the aim was to transform criminology from a science of social control and into a fully politicized struggle for social justice. Part of this also relied on a reworking of the theoretical premises of Marxism (Chambliss, 1975 – Chapter 20). Following the supposition that laws perpetuate a particular mode of economic production, it is argued that bourgeois law not only acts to preserve existing unequal forms of property ownership, but also punishes the property offences of the poor whilst maintaining stable conditions for the exploitation of their labour. The subject matter of criminology has, as a result, been considerably broadened from its previous narrow focus of attempting to discover why those lowest in the social order appeared to exhibit the highest rate of criminality. Investigating the policies and crimes of the powerful (Box, 1983 – Chapter 22) and the human rights violations of the state (Cohen, 1993 – Chapter 45), for example, have become legitimate forms of enquiry. Similarly, it is argued that more can be discovered about crime by examining how certain individuals and communities become subject to processes of state criminalization, rather than by trying to identify particular causes (Scraton and Chadwick, 1991 – Chapter 25; Keith, 1993 – Chapter 24).

In this way criminology has also become more critical of the agencies of criminal justice, and suggests that law and its enforcement are the key instruments by which 'race', class and gender power can be 'legitimately' exercised (Hall, 1980 – Chapter 23). The scientific objectivity and political neutrality of previous criminology is called into question; and the complex question of the relationship between knowledge and power is posed. Reliance on official statistics as 'real' indicators of where in society crime is committed and the rate at which it is committed is summarily dismissed (Box, 1983 – Chapter 22). A critical approach not only argues that a greater number of 'crimes' are committed than official statistics suggest, but also that criminality is to be found at all points in the social formation. The key questions are directed not so much at the criminal act in isolation but at the dynamics of social institutions which construct crime and their ability to convey such social constructions to the public. The study of crime necessitates a much wider study of the agencies, processes and structures of social control (Cohen, 1979 – Chapter 36).

These theoretical developments, originating from the mid 1970s, however, took place against the political backdrop of a resurgence in popular law and order politics and authoritarianism. In Britain and the United States the rhetoric of a resurgent radical Right revived a neo-classical vision of criminality as voluntaristic – a course of action willingly chosen by calculating individuals, lacking in self-control and with a potential for communal contamination and moral degeneracy (Murray, 1990 – Chapter 13). New 'realist' theorists of the Right disengaged from existing criminological agendas – whether they be positivist or critical – by simply claiming that crime emanates from wicked evil people who are insufficiently deterred from their actions by a criminal justice system deemed to be chaotic and ineffective (Wilson, 1983 – Chapter 27) or lacking in 'just deserts' (von Hirsch, 1976 – Chapter 28). Both remind us of the potency and endurance of classicist and neo-classicist formulations of the 'crime problem'. The key concern is with developing efficient means of judicial control rather than with questions of causality. Against a backdrop of perennially growing official statistics of crime and the presumption of increases in a rational public fear, the extension of police powers, the erosion of civil liberties and the expansion of imprisonment to unprecedented levels have all been justified (Hall, 1980 – Chapter 23). The public/political debate has come to be dominated by images of violent crime, lawlessness and a declining morality. In the late twentieth century it seems that authoritarianism, retribution and vindictive punishment are continually reproduced to the almost total exclusion of welfare and rehabilitative goals (Cullen and Gilbert, 1982 – Chapter 29). However, the discourse of the New Right has also been significantly tempered by an apparent failure of its policies to prevent escalating crime rates. Within the developing ethos of cost-effectiveness in all public services, it appears to be acknowledged that all that can be realistically hoped for is to implement more pragmatic means of managing crime through situational preventative measures (Clarke, 1980 – Chapter 30) and developing ever more cost-effective and efficient methods of managing the criminal justice system (Feeley and Simon, 1992 – Chapter 33).

The New Right colonization of almost the whole terrain of law and order politics in the late 1970s also forced sections of the Left to rethink their position and to move closer to the mainstream in a pragmatic attempt to counter some of its more reactionary policies. In a peculiarly British development, the self-styled left realists have gradually disassociated themselves from the 'new' and 'critical' criminologies and attempt to impact on Labour Party politics in an effort to find a new criminology for new times (Young, 1986 – Chapter 40). Left realism, however, initiated its programme through virulent attacks directed as much to the Left as to the Right. Labelling its former bed fellows as idealist, it argues that the Left has traditionally either romanticized or underestimated the nature and impact of crime and largely 'speaks to itself' through its lack of engagement with the day-to-day issues of crime control and social policy. With empirical support from a series of victim surveys carried out through the 1980s, left realism is able to assert that the problem of crime is indeed growing and that, in particular, property and street crimes are real issues that need to be addressed, rather than dismissed as social constructions. In short it concurs with right realism that people's fear of crime is rational and a reflection of inner city social reality. However, it differs from the Right in its insistence that the causes of crime need to be once more established and theorized; and a social justice and welfare programme initiated to tackle social and economic inequalities, under the rubric of 'inclusive citizenship' (Currie, 1991 – Chapter 31).

Clearly this marks a distinct break with the critical agenda of *The New Criminology*. It invokes many themes (such as crime causation) which are grounded in positivist criminology, with, for example, street crime being portrayed as caused by relative deprivation (Lea and Young, 1984 – Chapter 14). In this respect it appears to reflect and indeed mirror New Right and media-driven definitions of what constitutes serious crime and consequently downplays corporate crime and crimes of the state. Analyses of the relationship between the public, criminal justice agencies, offenders and victims are largely restricted to street crime and fail to capture the harm caused, for example, by workplace injury, occupation-related diseases and environmental pollution (Box, 1983 – Chapter 22). Left realism's dismissal of critical criminology as idealist also seems to provide a ready alliance with the Right in its denigration of the critical Left. In particular, it ignores the interventionist role that critical criminologists in Britain have played since the 1970s in developing a politics of support for marginalized groups such as black youth, prisoners, gypsies and women, as well as establishing independent enquiries into aspects of state authoritarianism and monitoring police practices (Scraton and Chadwick, 1991 – Chapter 25).

Equally, critical criminology has not ignored the necessity of developing new theoretical frameworks in which to further an understanding of processes of criminalization. It believes that the para-Marxist heritage need not be abandoned in total but can be refined and developed; to deliver not a sealed doctrine, but a new set of provisional hypotheses or frames of conceptual resources/deposits. For example, it has become common to find a more complex set of analyses which move away from a restricted chain of criminological references – state, law, crime, criminals – to the examination of other arenas of social regulation such as medicine, welfare and sexuality. By recognizing and working within Foucauldian concepts of 'knowledge', 'governance' and the 'order of things' it has become possible to acknowledge how networks of power and resistance are diffuse and governed more by their own internal logics and knowledges than by the definite intentions of particular classes or oppressive states (Foucault, 1977 – Chapter 35). This direction in turn has opened up work on a variety of semi-autonomous realms, such as informal justice, local communities, privatized organizations and families in which notions of policing and control are present, but whose relation to the state is by no means direct and unambiguous (Shearing and Stenning, 1985 – Chapter 37; Smart, 1989 – Chapter 38). It is in these areas too that interest in the potential of often neglected processes of informal networks of order and control has been awakened, albeit sometimes from different theoretical starting points (Braithwaite, 1989 – Chapter 39).

In this context the issue of idealism vs realism becomes something of a red herring. It is surely just as 'real' to unearth the complexities of processes of criminalization, resistance and control, as it is to be bound to public perceptions and victim surveys. The urge to 'become real' has taken many guises. Whilst the mainstream of criminology increasingly appears to be simply involved in a technocratic exercise to evaluate the effectiveness of criminal justice procedures, the critical paradigm continues to expose the discriminatory powers and outcomes of such procedures and retains a space in which alternative visions of social justice can be created (De Haan, 1991 – Chapter 32). Such visions remain important for they enable us to rethink social conditions in terms of them not simply being made bearable (as in left realism or social democratic reformism) but transformed into a vehicle for emancipation.

A key failing of all criminologies up to the 1970s was to acknowledge the 'presence of absence' in the form of any critical analysis of gender relations and women and crime. The development of feminist inroads into the male bastion of criminology initially took the form of a comprehensive critique of the discipline firstly for its neglect even to study women's involvement in crime and criminal justice and secondly for its total distortion of women's experiences as essentially biologically driven (Klein, 1973 – Chapter 16). Since the mid 1970s a burgeoning literature has revealed that women's crimes are committed in different circumstances to men's and that the response to women's lawbreaking is constituted within sexist assumptions of femininity which have only further added to women's oppression. This body of knowledge has now successfully demonstrated how criminology has traditionally been driven by male assumptions and interests, how criminalized women are seen as doubly deviant and how assumptions about appropriate gender roles mean that women are judged less on the nature of their offences and more on their 'deviant' lifestyles. As a result some feminists have drawn more on sociologies of gender, than any pre-existing criminological knowledge, to explore their subject matter, with the important message for male criminology that the object of their enquiry is essentially 'masculine' and that as much can be learned about processes of control and criminalization by focusing on those structures and processes that create conformity and social order, as on a sole concern with those that produce deviance and criminality (Segal, 1990 –

Chapter 17). Others have gone further by questioning whether the focus on female lawbreakers is a proper concern for feminism and indeed whether a feminist criminology is theoretically possible or even politically desirable (Smart, 1990 – Chapter 41). Latterly this relation between feminism and criminology has been further problematized by a deconstructionist or postmodern twist which claims that the unifiers of 'women', 'crime' and 'criminology' trap any investigation in essentialist categories that obstruct the production of new knowledge. It is perhaps no surprise that the deconstruction of criminology has gathered most strength in some feminist perspectives, for it is they that were first alerted to the need for criminology to deconstruct itself if it was to break out of its gender essentialism.

The tendency of the social sciences to deconstruct and question their own internal logic is slowly permeating the discipline of criminology. As some feminist critics have warned, the discipline will remain forever self-justifying unless it is prepared to adopt a more critical stance towards the key referents of 'crime' and 'deviance' (Cain, 1990 – Chapter 42). The process of deconstruction also has its origins in the work of Foucault and his location of the discourse of criminology in the combination of knowledge and power that evolved with the modern state and the emergence of the social sciences. Foucault's acknowledgement of a multiplicity of power relations and the diverse settings in which they are activated, in particular, questioned the ability of any total theory (Marxism, for example) to answer all questions. For example, talk of such totalities as 'the state', 'working class' and 'capitalism' were for Foucault misleading because 'power is everywhere'. This disenchantment with a priori claims to the 'truth', as represented in stark form by the way criminology has progressed through paradigmatic construction and contestation, is substantiated in the postmodern insistence that we should break with the rational and totalizing (modernist) intellectual movements of the past. Whilst modernism (of which criminology is but one element) attempts to ratify knowledge so that the social can be made an ordered totality, postmodernism views the world as replete with an unlimited number of models of order, each generated by relatively autonomous and localized sets of practices. Modernism strives for universality, postmodernism accepts relativity as a lasting feature of the world. In essence postmodernism challenges the logic of 'referential finalities' as the foundation of western society. Rather it stresses the diversity and particularity of social life and accordingly asserts that no one theoretical paradigm is capable of making sense of the social world (Hunt, 1991 – Chapter 44).

This post-criminological sensibility implies an abandonment of the concept of crime and its replacement by a new language to designate objects of censure and codes of conduct (Hulsman, 1986 – Chapter 26). By definition this would mean that criminology would lose its very *raison d'être*. Exactly what form such a project might take remains unclear, but the challenge of postmodernism is one that urges us continually to address the limitations of accepted knowledges, to avoid dogmatism and to recognize the existence of a wide variety of subjectivities.

Unsurprisingly, this rejection of totalizing theory and of 'objective' criteria for establishing truth and meaning, can be viewed as intellectually liberating or as intrinsically nihilistic and conservative. For example, at present it is far from clear how a total rejection of established concepts might further an understanding of the relations between criminalization, poverty, inequality, racism, sexual violence and repressive state practices. The failure to replace existing concepts with alternative visions may only leave us with a series of dislocated and fragmented positions (Ericson and Carriere, 1994 – Chapter 46). Whilst we may sympathize with the postmodernist objection to the colonization of the intellectual world by a single all-encompassing meta-narrative, does this also mean that we can dispense with the imaginative purchase provided by critical and Utopian visions?

The place of critical criminology within these new discourses and theoretical dilemmas remains somewhat ambivalent. In attempting to overcome the mantle of 'determinism', it has to move to a more complex understanding of an ever-changing social order, and also face the potentially devastating vagaries of deconstructionist discourse. However, for some the key task remains that of constructing a framework which is capable of locating discrete and specific instances of criminalization within a general theory of the social order. For them, if critical criminology is to remain relevant and ensure that theoretical production and political practice act in tandem, it must remain true to a Marxist heritage and continue to reassert the centrality of primary determining contexts: 'race', class and patriarchy as being crucial to understanding the meaning of new social formations and post-industrial relations of production (Scraton and Chadwick, 1991 – Chapter 25). Alternatively, others would argue that a critical realist policy agenda must be formulated which retains some purchase with the principles of idealism but remains capable of identifying realizable ways of empowering those groups – such as women in prison – that are subject to some of the worst excesses of state regulation (Carlen, 1992 – Chapter 43).

Another fruitful line of enquiry may lie in the argument that much more needs to be done to explore and keep pace with the effects of ever-increasingly sophisticated means of technological surveillance and control in the postmodern landscape. Again this will mean that criminology is forced to move beyond its traditional boundaries and in this instance to confront the insights offered by a radical social geography (Keith, 1993 – Chapter 24). All such developments move us further from criminology's traditional and myopic search for 'causes and solutions' and into yet more complex and reflexive frames of understanding.

By taking account of all these perspectives, it is increasingly apparent that there is, and always will be, an inherent tension in criminology. There will always remain those who, attuned to the limited and limiting nature of criminological discourse, seek continually to expand and transgress its boundaries with the ultimate aim of collapsing the meta-narrative of criminology itself. Others – albeit with their own divergent agendas – will remain content to operate within criminology's self-imposed constraints and prefer to see criminology as an ongoing and unfinished project. What is remarkable and ironic is that, in the final instance, this tension between 'the within' and 'the beyond', rather than signalling criminology's demise, may indeed be its greatest strength. Criminology will always appear to be in a process of 'becoming'. Its work will never seem to be complete.

# PART ONE
# CRIMINOLOGICAL FORMATIONS

## Introduction

This collection of essays is designed to introduce the reader to the disparate and diverse origins of the study of crime and the law. It includes some of the now classic formulations of the nature and problem of crime as expressed by such eighteenth century philosophers as Cesare Beccaria, early nineteenth century mathematicians such as Adolphe Quetelet, late nineteenth century physicians such as Cesare Lombroso and sociological theorists such as Emile Durkheim. The seven classic readings reproduced here cover a period that stretches from 1764 to 1916. It is a period in which many of the debates about the function of law, the nature of crime, the causes of crime and the extent of crime, with which we are now familiar, were first given intellectual and public expression. The readings are not simply of historical curiosity. Each, in different ways, continues to influence contemporary understandings and formulations of the 'crime problem'.

It is perhaps of some significance that the origins of modern criminological theory can be traced, not to the study of crime and criminals, but to Enlightenment philosophers, particularly in France and Italy, reflecting on the nature and functions of criminal law. Beccaria's *On Crimes and Punishments* (1764) set out a then controversial programme for criminal law reform. Critical of the barbarism, irregularity and ad hoc nature of eighteenth century criminal justice, he urged that social order be based on law, rather than religion or superstition; that the machinery of justice be answerable to rules of due process; that sentencing policies be formulated to 'fit the crime'; and that punishment be prompt and certain. At the time, Beccaria's work was condemned for its extreme rationalism, but within his recommendations are the seeds of policies present in most criminal justice systems around the world today. Above all he is now recognized as the founding father of a *classical* school of criminology (a term he never himself used, but was so described by later theorists) characterized by the key doctrines of rationality, free will and the social contract.

In contrast a *positivist* criminology, which emerged from the mid nineteenth century onwards, was concerned less with the content and implementation of criminal law and more with establishing the causes of law breaking. In 1827 the French government published the first national statistical tables of crime, the annual *Compte général*. Whilst acknowledging the limitations of such statistics in revealing the true extent of crime in society, Quetelet discovered a remarkable constancy in recorded crime in France between 1826 and 1829. He thus argued that, even if individuals have free will, criminal behaviour appears to obey the same scientific laws that govern the natural world. Of note was the regularity with which young males and those in lowly employment had a greater propensity towards crime. The two factors most strongly associated with criminality were age and sex, but the rates of property and personal crime were also found to fluctuate according to the seasons and with the state of the economy. As a result, Quetelet formulated the then remarkable proposition that criminality is not freely chosen or that it is a sign of human wickedness, but that it is an inevitable and resultant feature of social organization. It was thus society that caused crime.

By the 1870s the impact of positivism on the doctrine of free will was underlined in Lombroso's key text *Criminal Man*. After studying anatomy and pathology, Lombroso argued that a significant proportion of criminals had cranial and other physiological defects which suggested that they were born to criminality and represented a throwback to primitive forms of social evolution. The extract reproduced here from his work with fellow collaborator William Ferrero applies this reasoning to establish a criminal type in women. Although female criminality increases with advances in civilization, most women are deemed non-criminal because biological factors predispose them to be more conservative and socially withdrawn. The physical characteristics of female criminals, such as prostitutes, however, resemble those of male criminals, and their criminality is often more cruel, wicked and vindictive. In an exceptional, and subsequently highly controversial, series of statements Lombroso and Ferrero claimed that 'the female born criminal, when a complete type, is more terrible than the male'.

Lombroso's insistence on the accurate and deliberate measurement of the physical anomalies of known criminals has for many established him as the first 'scientific' criminologist. And whilst his particular theory of crime causation was eventually to be discredited through the weight of counter argument, the principles of the Italian school of positivism (of which Lombroso is usually lauded as the founder) were gradually to become influential not only in intellectual circles but in the development of less uniform and more individually oriented forms of penal treatment. By the turn of the century classicists and positivists were engaged in a series of bitter arguments about the nature of criminal responsibility and the objectives of punishment. The extract from one of three lectures given by Enrico Ferri at the University of Naples in 1901 clearly illustrates the divergencies between these two schools of thought and the depth of feeling by which the exponents of positivism sought to deliver their message.

In contrast the extracts from Bonger and Durkheim, whilst sharing some features with the fundamentals of positivism, mark something of a return to the principles of Quetelet in the insistence that the causes of crime lie not in individual abnormalities, but in the nature of economic conditions and social structures. Bonger was the first to apply the Marxist inspired notions of class conflict and capitalist exploitation to the concept of crime. In a scathing attack on the egoistic and competitive tendencies of capitalism, Bonger argued that most crime could be accounted for by a lack of common ownership of property and the brutalized conditions of existence endured by all classes in a society characterized by unfettered forms of capitalist exchange and labour exploitation. Durkheim's work in general adopts a less conflict-based analysis of society, preferring to view the social structure as characterized above all by consensus or a collective conscience. Durkheim, who is lauded as the founder of a sociological criminology, once more remarked on the regularity and constancy of crime rates in particular societies, and insisted that social phenomena (such as crime and law) have an objective existence irrespective of how they are experienced by individuals. This led to the now famous and perpetually controversial propositions that crime is normal, crime is inevitable and that crime is useful to society. The extract reproduced here from his 1895 work *The Rules of Sociological Method* marks a radical departure from the then prevailing notions of classical free will and positivist ideas of individual abnormality. Rather crime performs a vital function for society in establishing clear moral boundaries and in paving the way for social innovation and change.

Kropotkin's contribution, originally published in 1898, offers a more strident critique of bourgeois law from an anarchist perspective. In terms echoed some seventy years later by some abolitionist and critical criminologists (see Parts Three and Four), Kropotkin roundly condemns the role of law in facilitating the accumulation of property in the hands of the few and in perpetuating barbaric forms of repression and control. For him the real criminals in society are not those 'unfortunates' who populate the prisons, but those figures of authority who, through their self-interested formulation and implementation of criminal law, have served to put them there.

It is now commonplace to assume that the origins of criminology lie fundamentally within the classic statements of such 'founding fathers'. However, we conclude this part by reproducing Garland's more sober reflections on the origins of criminology in Britain. Certainly, whilst key theoretical paradigms, such as the Italian positivism of Lombroso made some impact, he argues that of more importance was an indigenous tradition of applied medico-legal science. British criminology developed as a much more policy and institutionally based affair. It would be misleading always to assert that criminology was born out of grand and competing theoretical ideas. It was also, more mundanely, intimately tied to key institutions – particularly those associated with medicine and penal administration – of criminal justice.

# 1

# On crimes and punishments

## Cesare Beccaria

[. . .]

If we glance at the pages of history, we will find that laws, which surely are, or ought to be, compacts of free men, have been, for the most part, a mere tool of the passions of some, or have arisen from an accidental and temporary need. Never have they been dictated by a dispassionate student of human nature who might, by bringing the actions of a multitude of men into focus, consider them from this single point of view: the *greatest happiness shared by the greatest number*. Happy are those few nations that have not waited for the slow succession of coincidence and human vicissitude to force some little turn for the better after the limit of evil has been reached, but have facilitated the intermediate progress by means of good laws. And humanity owes a debt of gratitude to that philosopher who, from the obscurity of his isolated study, had the courage to scatter among the multitude the first seeds, so long unfruitful, of useful truths.

The true relations between sovereigns and their subjects, and between nations, have been discovered. Commerce has been reanimated by the common knowledge of philosophical truths diffused by the art of printing, and there has sprung up among nations a tacit rivalry of industriousness that is most humane and truly worthy of rational beings. Such good things we owe to the productive enlightenment of this age. But very few persons have studied and fought against the cruelty of punishments and the irregularities of criminal procedures, a part of legislation that is as fundamental as it is widely neglected in almost all of Europe. Very few persons have undertaken to demolish the accumulated errors of centuries by rising to general principles, curbing, at least, with the sole force that acknowledged truths possess, the unbounded course of ill-directed power which has continually produced a long and authorized example of the most cold-blooded barbarity. And yet the groans of the weak, sacrificed to cruel ignorance and to opulent indolence; the barbarous torments, multiplied with lavish and useless severity, for crimes either not proved or wholly imaginary; the filth and horrors of a prison, intensified by that cruellest tormentor of the miserable, uncertainty – all these ought to have roused that breed of magistrates who direct the opinions of men.

The immortal Montesquieu has cursorily touched upon this subject. Truth, which is one and indivisible, has obliged me to follow the illustrious steps of that great man, but the thoughtful men for whom I write will easily distinguish my traces from his. I shall deem myself happy if I can obtain, as he

Abridged from *On Crimes and Punishments*, pp. 8–19; 55–9; 62–4; 93–9. (New York: Bobbs-Merrill, 1963. First published 1764.)

did, the secret thanks of the unknown and peace-loving disciples of reason, and if I can inspire that tender thrill with which persons of sensibility respond to one who upholds the interests of humanity.
[. . .]

## The origin of punishments, and the right to punish

[. . .]
No man ever freely sacrificed a portion of his personal liberty merely in behalf of the common good. That chimera exists only in romances. If it were possible, every one of us would prefer that the compacts binding others did not bind us; every man tends to make himself the centre of his whole world.

The continuous multiplication of mankind, inconsiderable in itself yet exceeding by far the means that a sterile and uncultivated nature could offer for the satisfaction of increasingly complex needs, united the earliest savages. These first communities of necessity caused the formation of others to resist the first, and the primitive state of warfare thus passed from individuals to nations.

Laws are the conditions under which independent and isolated men united to form a society. Weary of living in a continual state of war, and of enjoying a liberty rendered useless by the uncertainty of preserving it, they sacrificed a part so that they might enjoy the rest of it in peace and safety. The sum of all these portions of liberty sacrificed by each for his own good constitutes the sovereignty of a nation, and their legitimate depositary and administrator is the sovereign. But merely to have established this deposit was not enough; it had to be defended against private usurpations by individuals each of whom always tries not only to withdraw his own share but also to usurp for himself that of others. Some tangible motives had to be introduced, therefore, to prevent the despotic spirit, which is in every man, from plunging the laws of society into its original chaos. These tangible motives are the punishments established against infractors of the laws. I say 'tangible motives' because experience has shown that the multitude adopt no fixed principles of conduct and will not be released from the sway of that universal principle of dissolution which is seen to operate both in the physical and the moral universe, except for motives that directly strike the senses. These motives, by dint of repeated representation to the mind, counterbalance the powerful impressions of the private passions that oppose the common good. Not eloquence, not declamations, not even the most sublime truths have sufficed, for any considerable length of time, to curb passions excited by vivid impressions of present objects.

It was, thus, necessity that forced men to give up part of their personal liberty, and it is certain, therefore, that each is willing to place in the public fund only the least possible portion, no more than suffices to induce others to defend it. The aggregate of these least possible portions constitutes the right to punish; all that exceeds this is abuse and not justice; it is fact but by no means right.

Punishments that exceed what is necessary for protection of the deposit of public security are by their very nature unjust, and punishments are increasingly more just as the safety which the sovereign secures for his subjects is the more sacred and inviolable, and the liberty greater.

*Cesare Beccaria*

### Consequences

The first consequence of these principles is that only the laws can decree punishments for crimes; authority for this can reside only with the legislator who represents the entire society united by a social contract. No magistrate (who is a part of society) can, with justice, inflict punishments upon another member of the same society. But a punishment that exceeds the limit fixed by the laws is just punishment plus another punishment; a magistrate cannot, therefore, under any pretext of zeal or concern for the public good, augment the punishment established for a delinquent citizen.

The second consequence is that the sovereign, who represents the society itself, can frame only general laws binding all members, but he cannot judge whether someone has violated the social contract, for that would divide the nation into two parts, one represented by the sovereign, who asserts the violation of the contract, and the other by the accused, who denies it. There must, therefore, be a third party to judge the truth of the fact. Hence the need for a magistrate whose decisions, from which there can be no appeal, should consist of mere affirmations or denials of particular facts.

The third consequence is this: even assuming that severity of punishments were not directly contrary to the public good and to the very purpose of preventing crimes, if it were possible to prove merely that such severity is useless, in that case also it would be contrary not only to those beneficent virtues that spring from enlightened reason which would rather rule happy men than a herd of slaves in whom a timid cruelty makes its endless rounds; it would be contrary to justice itself and to the very nature of the social contract.

### Interpretations of the laws

A fourth consequence: Judges in criminal cases cannot have the authority to interpret laws, and the reason, again, is that they are not legislators. Such judges have not received the laws from our ancestors as a family tradition or legacy that leaves to posterity only the burden of obeying them, but they receive them, rather, from the living society, or from the sovereign representing it, who is the legitimate depositary of what actually results from the common will of all [. . .]

Nothing can be more dangerous than the popular axiom that it is necessary to consult the spirit of the laws. It is a dam that has given way to a torrent of opinions. This truth, which seems paradoxical to ordinary minds that are struck more by trivial present disorders than by the dangerous but remote effects of false principles rooted in a nation, seems to me to be fully demonstrated. Our understandings and all our ideas have a reciprocal connection; the more complicated they are, the more numerous must the ways be that lead to them and depart from them. Each man has his own point of view, and, at each different time, a different one. Thus the 'spirit' of the law would be the product of a judge's good or bad logic, of his good or bad digestion; it would depend on the violence of his passions, on the weakness of the accused, on the judge's connections with him, and on all those minute factors that alter the appearances of an object in the fluctuating mind of man. Thus we see the lot of a citizen subjected to frequent changes in passing through different courts, and we see the lives of poor wretches become the victims of the false ratiocinations or of the momentary seething ill-humours of a judge who mistakes for a legitimate interpretation that vague product of the jumbled series of notions which his mind stirs up. Thus we see the same crimes differently punished at different times by the same court, for having consulted not the constant fixed voice of the law but the erring instability of interpretation.

The disorder that arises from rigorous observance of the letter of a penal law is hardly comparable to the disorders that arise from interpretations. The temporary inconvenience of the former prompts one to make the rather easy and needed correction in the words of the law which are the source of uncertainty, but it curbs that fatal licence of discussion which gives rise to arbitrary and venal controversies. When a fixed code of laws, which must be observed to the letter, leaves no further care to the judge than to examine the acts of citizens and to decide whether or not they conform to the law as written; when the standard of the just or the unjust, which is to be the norm of conduct for the ignorant as well as for the philosophic citizen, is not a matter of controversy but of fact; then only are citizens not subject to the petty tyrannies of the many which are the more cruel as the distance between the oppressed and the oppressor is less, and which are far more fatal than those of a single man, for the despotism of many can only be corrected by the despotism of one; the cruelty of a single despot is proportioned, not to his might, but to the obstacles he encounters. In this way citizens acquire that sense of security for their own persons which is just, because it is the object of human association, and useful, because it enables them to calculate accurately the inconveniences of a misdeed. It is true, also, that they acquire a spirit of independence, but not one that upsets the laws and resists the chief magistrates; rather one that resists those who have dared to apply the sacred name of virtue to that weakness of theirs which makes them yield to their self-interested and capricious opinions.

These principles will displease those who have assumed for themselves a right to transmit to their inferiors the blows of tyranny that they have received from their superiors. I would, indeed, be most fearful if the spirit of tyranny were in the least compatible with the spirit of literacy.

## Obscurity of the laws

If the interpretation of laws is an evil, another evil, evidently, is the obscurity that makes interpretation necessary. And this evil would be very great indeed where the laws are written in a language that is foreign to a people, forcing it to rely on a handful of men because it is unable to judge for itself how its liberty or its members may fare – in a language that transforms a sacred and public book into something very like the private possession of a family. When the number of those who can understand the sacred code of laws and hold it in their hands increases, the frequency of crimes will be found to decrease, for undoubtedly ignorance and uncertainty of punishments add much to the eloquence of the passions. What are we to make of men, therefore, when we reflect that this very evil is the inveterate practice of a large part of cultured and enlightened Europe?

One consequence of this last reflection is that, without writing, a society can never acquire a fixed form of government with power that derives from the whole and not from the parts, in which the laws, which cannot be altered except by the general will, are not corrupted in their passage through the mass of private interests. Experience and reason have shown us that the probability and certainty of human traditions diminish the further removed they are from their source. For, obviously, if there exists no enduring memorial of the social compact, how are the laws to withstand the inevitable pressure of time and of passions?

[. . .]

## Promptness of punishment

The more promptly and the more closely punishment follows upon the commission of a crime, the more just and useful will it be. I say more just, because the criminal is thereby spared the useless and cruel torments of uncertainty, which increase with the vigour of imagination and with the sense of personal weakness; more just, because privation of liberty, being itself a punishment, should not precede the sentence except when necessity requires. Imprisonment of a citizen, then, is simply custody of his person until he be judged guilty; and this custody, being essentially penal, should be of the least possible duration and of the least possible severity. The time limit should be determined both by the anticipated length of the trial and by seniority among those who are entitled to be tried first. The strictness of confinement should be no more than is necessary to prevent him from taking flight or from concealing the proofs of his crimes. The trial itself should be completed in the briefest possible time. What crueller contrast than the indolence of a judge and the anguish of a man under accusation – the comforts and pleasures of an insensitive magistrate on one side, and on the other the tears, the squalor of a prisoner? In general, the weight of punishment and the consequence of a crime should be that which is most efficacious for others, and which inflicts the least possible hardship upon the person who suffers it; one cannot call legitimate any society which does not maintain, as an infallible principle, that men have wished to subject themselves only to the least possible evils.

I have said that the promptness of punishments is more useful because when the length of time that passes between the punishment and the misdeed is less, so much the stronger and more lasting in the human mind is the association of these two ideas, *crime and punishment*; they then come insensibly to be considered, one as the cause, the other as the necessary inevitable effect. It has been demonstrated that the association of ideas is the cement that forms the entire fabric of the human intellect; without this cement pleasure and pain would be isolated sentiments and of no effect. The more men depart from general ideas and universal principles, that is, the more vulgar they are, the more apt are they to act merely on immediate and familiar associations, ignoring the more remote and complex ones that serve only men strongly impassioned for the object of their desires; the light of attention illuminates only a single object, leaving the others dark. They are of service also to more elevated minds, for they have acquired the habit of rapidly surveying many objects at once, and are able with facility to contrast many partial sentiments one with another, so that the result, which is action, is less dangerous and uncertain.

Of utmost importance is it, therefore, that the crime and the punishment be intimately linked together, if it be desirable that, in crude, vulgar minds, the seductive picture of a particularly advantageous crime should immediately call up the associated idea of punishment. Long delay always produces the effect of further separating these two ideas; thus, though punishment of a crime may make an impression, it will be less as a punishment than as a spectacle, and will be felt only after the horror of the particular crime, which should serve to reinforce the feeling of punishment, has been much weakened in the hearts of the spectators.

Another principle serves admirably to draw even closer the important connection between a misdeed and its punishment, namely, that the latter be as much in conformity as possible with the nature of the crime. This analogy facilitates admirably the contrast that ought to exist between the inducement to crime and the counterforce of punishment, so that the latter may deter and lead the mind toward a goal the very opposite of that toward which the seductive idea of breaking the laws seeks to direct it.

Those guilty of lesser crimes are usually punished either in the obscurity of a prison or by transportation, to serve as an example, with a distant and therefore almost useless servitude, to nations which they have not offended. Since men are not induced on the spur of the moment to commit the gravest crimes, public punishment of a great misdeed will be regarded by the majority as something very remote and of improbable occurrence; but public punishment of lesser crimes, which are closer to men's hearts, will make an impression which, while deterring them from these, deters them even further from the graver crimes. A proportioning of punishments to one another and to crimes should comprehend not only their force but also the manner of inflicting them.

**The certainty of punishment: Mercy**

One of the greatest curbs on crimes is not the cruelty of punishments, but their infallibility, and, consequently, the vigilance of magistrates, and that severity of an inexorable judge which, to be a useful virtue, must be accompanied by a mild legislation. The certainty of a punishment, even if it be moderate, will always make a stronger impression than the fear of another which is more terrible but combined with the hope of impunity; even the least evils, when they are certain, always terrify men's minds, and hope, that heavenly gift which is often our sole recompense for everything, tends to keep the thought of greater evils remote from us, especially when its strength is increased by the idea of impunity which avarice and weakness only too often afford.

Sometimes a man is freed from punishment for a lesser crime when the offended party chooses to forgive – an act in accord with beneficence and humanity, but contrary to the public good – as if a private citizen, by an act of remission, could eliminate the need for an example, in the same way that he can waive compensation for the injury. The right to inflict punishment is a right not of an individual, but of all citizens, or of their sovereign. An individual can renounce his own portion of right, but cannot annul that of others.

As punishments become more mild, clemency and pardon become less necessary. Happy the nation in which they might some day be considered

pernicious! Clemency, therefore, that virtue which has sometimes been deemed a sufficient substitute in a sovereign for all the duties of the throne, should be excluded from perfect legislation, where the punishments are mild and the method of judgment regular and expeditious. This truth will seem harsh to anyone living in the midst of the disorders of a criminal system, where pardons and mercy are necessary to compensate for the absurdity of the laws and the severity of the sentences. This, which is indeed the noblest prerogative of the throne, the most desirable attribute of sovereignty, is also, however, the tacit disapprobation of the beneficent dispensers of public happiness for a code which, with all its imperfections, has in its favour the prejudice of centuries, the voluminous and imposing dowry of innumerable commentators, the weighty apparatus of endless formalities, and the adherence of the most insinuating and least formidable of the semi-learned. But one ought to consider that clemency is a virtue of the legislators and not of the executors of the laws, that it ought to shine in the code itself rather than in the particular judgments. To make men see that crimes can be pardoned or that punishment is not their necessary consequence foments a flattering hope of impunity and creates a belief that, because they might be remitted, sentences which are not remitted are rather acts of oppressive violence than emanations of justice. What is to be said, then, when the ruler grants pardons, that is, public security to a particular individual, and, with a personal act of unenlightened beneficence, constitutes a public decree of impunity? Let the laws, therefore, be inexorable, and inexorable their executors in particular cases, but let the legislator be tender, indulgent, and humane. Let him, a wise architect, raise his building upon the foundation of self-love and let the general interest be the result of the interests of each; he shall not then be constrained, by partial laws and tumultuous remedies, to separate at every moment the public good from that of individuals, and to build the image of public well-being upon fear and distrust. Wise and compassionate philosopher, let him permit men, his brothers, to enjoy in peace that small portion of happiness which the grand system established by the First Cause, by that *which is*, allows them to enjoy in this corner of the universe.
[. . .]

## Proportion between crimes and punishments

It is to the common interest not only that crimes not be committed, but also that they be less frequent in proportion to the harm they cause society. Therefore, the obstacles that deter men from committing crimes should be stronger in proportion as they are contrary to the public good, and as the inducements to commit them are stronger. There must, therefore, be a proper proportion between crimes and punishments.

If pleasure and pain are the motives of sensible beings, if, among the motives for even the sublimest acts of men, rewards and punishments were designated by the invisible Legislator, from their inexact distribution arises the contradiction, as little observed as it is common, that the punishments punish crimes which they themselves have occasioned. If an equal punishment be ordained for two crimes that do not equally injure society, men will not be any more deterred from committing the greater crime, if they find a greater advantage associated with it.

Whoever sees the same death penalty, for instance, decreed for the killing of a pheasant and for the assassination of a man or for forgery of an important writing,will make no distinction between such crimes, thereby destroying the moral sentiments, which are the work of many centuries and of much blood, slowly and with great difficulty registered in the human spirit, and impossible to produce, many believe, without the aid of the most sublime of motives and of an enormous apparatus of grave formalities.

It is impossible to prevent all disorders in the universal conflict of human passions. They increase according to a ratio compounded of population and the crossings of particular interests, which cannot be directed with geometric precision to the public utility. For mathematical exactitude we must substitute, in the arithmetic of politics, the calculation of probabilities. A glance at the histories will show that disorders increase with the confines of empires. National sentiment declining in the same proportion, the tendency to commit crimes increases with the increased interest everyone takes in such disorders; thus there is a constantly increasing need to make punishments heavier.

That force, similar to gravity, which impels us to seek our own well-being is restrained in its operation only to the extent that obstacles are set up against it. The effects of this force are the confused series of human actions. If these clash together and disturb one another, punishments, which I would call 'political obstacles', prevent the bad effect without destroying the impelling cause, which is that sensibility inseparable from man. And the legislator acts then like an able architect whose function it is to check the destructive tendencies of gravity and to align correctly those that contribute to the strength of the building.

Given the necessity of human association, given the pacts that result from the very opposition of private interests, a scale of disorders is distinguishable, the first grade consisting of those that are immediately destructive of society, and the last, of those that do the least possible injustice to its individual members. Between these extremes are included all the actions contrary to the public good that are called crimes, and they all descend by insensible gradations from the highest to the lowest. If geometry were applicable to the infinite and obscure combinations of human actions, there ought to be a corresponding scale of punishments, descending from the greatest to the least; if there were an exact and universal scale of punishments and of crimes, we would have a fairly reliable and common measure of the degrees of tyranny and liberty, of the fund of humanity or of malice, of the various nations. But it is enough for the wise legislator to mark the principal points of division without disturbing the order, not assigning to crimes of the first grade the punishments of the last.
[. . .]


## How to prevent crimes

It is better to prevent crimes than to punish them. This is the ultimate end of every good legislation, which, to use the general terms for assessing the good and evils of life, is the art of leading men to the greatest possible happiness or to the least possible unhappiness.

But heretofore, the means employed have been false and contrary to the end proposed. It is impossible to reduce the turbulent activity of mankind to a geometric order, without any irregularity and confusion. As the constant and very simple laws of nature do not impede the planets from disturbing one another in their movements, so in the infinite and very contrary attractions of pleasure and pain, disturbances and disorder cannot be impeded by human laws. And yet this is the chimera of narrow-minded men when they have power in their grasp. To prohibit a multitude of indifferent acts is not to prevent crimes that might arise from them, but is rather to create new ones; it is to define by whim the ideas of virtue and vice which are preached to us as eternal and immutable. To what should we be reduced if everything were forbidden us that might induce us to crime! It would be necessary to deprive man of the use of his senses. For one motive that drives men to commit a real crime there are a thousand that drive them to commit those indifferent acts which are called crimes by bad laws; and if the probability of crimes is proportionate to the number of motives, to enlarge the sphere of crimes is to increase the probability of their being committed. The majority of the laws are nothing but privileges, that is, a tribute paid by all to the convenience of some few.

Do you want to prevent crimes? See to it that the laws are clear and simple and that the entire force of a nation is united in their defence, and that no part of it is employed to destroy them. See to it that the laws favour not so much classes of men as men themselves. See to it that men fear the laws and fear nothing else. For fear of the laws is salutary, but fatal and fertile for crimes is one man's fear of another. Enslaved men are more voluptuous, more depraved, more cruel than free men. These study the sciences, give thought to the interests of their country, contemplate grand objects and imitate them, while enslaved men, content with the present moment, seek in the excitement of debauchery a distraction from the emptiness of the condition in which they find themselves. Accustomed to an uncertainty of outcome in all things, the outcome of their crimes remains for them problematical, to the advantage of the passions that determine them. If uncertainty regarding the laws befalls a nation which is indolent because of climate, its indolence and stupidity are confirmed and increased; if it befalls a voluptuous but energetic nation, the result is a wasteful diffusion of energy into an infinite number of little cabals and intrigues that sow distrust in every heart, make treachery and dissimulation the foundation of prudence; if it befalls a brave and powerful nation, the uncertainty is removed finally, but only after having caused many oscillations from liberty to slavery and from slavery back to liberty.

Do you want to prevent crimes? See to it that enlightenment accompanies liberty. Knowledge breeds evils in inverse ratio to its diffusion, and benefits in direct ratio. A daring impostor, who is never a common man, is received with adorations by an ignorant people, and with hisses by an enlightened one. Knowledge, by facilitating comparisons and by multiplying points of view, brings on a mutual modification of conflicting feelings, especially when it appears that others hold the same views and face the same difficulties. In the face of enlightenment widely diffused throughout the nation, the calumnies of ignorance are silenced and authority trembles if it be not armed with reason. The vigorous force of the laws, meanwhile, remains immovable, for no enlightened person can fail to approve of the clear and useful public compacts of mutual security when he compares the inconsiderable portion of useless liberty he himself has sacrificed with the sum total of liberties sacrificed by other men, which, except for the laws, might have been turned against him. Any person of sensibility, glancing over a code of well-made laws and observing that he has lost only a baneful liberty to injure others, will feel constrained to bless the throne and its occupant.

[. . .]

Another way of preventing crimes is to direct the interest of the magistracy as a whole to observance rather than corruption of the laws. The greater the number of magistrates, the less dangerous is the abuse of legal power; venality is more difficult among men who observe one another, and their interest in increasing their personal authority diminishes as the portion that would fall to each is less, especially in comparison with the danger involved in the undertaking. If the sovereign, with his apparatus and pomp, with the severity of his edicts, with the permission he grants for unjust as well as just claims to be advanced by anyone who thinks himself oppressed, accustoms his subjects to fear magistrates more than the laws, [the magistrates] will profit more from this fear than personal and public security will gain from it.

Another way of preventing crimes is to reward virtue. Upon this subject I notice a general silence in the laws of all the nations of our day. If the prizes offered by the academies to discoverers of useful truths have increased our knowledge and have multiplied good books, why should not prizes distributed by the beneficent hand of the sovereign serve in a similar way to multiply virtuous actions? The coin of honour is always inexhaustible and fruitful in the hands of the wise distributor.

Finally, the surest but most difficult way to prevent crimes is by perfecting education – a subject much too vast and exceeding the limits I have prescribed for myself, a subject, I venture also to say, too intimately involved with the nature of government for it ever to be, even in the far-off happy ages of society, anything more than a barren field, only here and there cultivated by a few sages. A great man, who enlightens the world that persecutes him, has indicated plainly and in detail what principal maxims of education are truly useful to men: they are, that it should consist less in a barren multiplicity of things than in a selection and precise definition of them; in substituting originals for the copies of the moral as well as physical phenomena which chance or wilful activity may present to the fresh minds of youths; in leading them toward virtue by the easy way of feeling, and in directing them away from evil by the infallible one of necessity and inconvenience, instead of by the uncertain means of command which obtains only simulated and momentary obedience.

## Conclusion

From what has thus far been demonstrated, one may deduce a general theorem of considerable utility, though hardly conformable with custom, the usual legislator of nations; it is this: *In order for punishment not to be, in every instance, an act of violence of one or of many against a private citizen, it must be essentially public, prompt, necessary, the least possible in the given circumstances, proportionate to the crimes, dictated by the laws.*

# 2

# Of the development of the propensity to crime

## *Adolphe Quetelet*

### Of crimes in general, and of the repression of them

Supposing men to be placed in similar circumstances, I call the greater or less probability of committing crime, the *propensity to crime*. My object is more especially to investigate the influence of season, climate, sex, and age, on this propensity.

I have said that the circumstances in which men are placed ought to be similar, that is to say, equally favourable, both in the existence of objects likely to excite the propensity and in the facility of committing the crime. It is not enough that a man may merely have the intention to do evil, he must also have the opportunity and the means. Thus the propensity to crime may be the same in France as in England, without, on that account, the *morality* of the nations being the same. I think this distinction of importance.

There is still another important distinction to be made; namely, that two individuals may have the same propensity to crime, without being equally *criminal*, if one, for example, were inclined to theft, and the other to assassination.

Lastly, [. . .] our observations can only refer to a *certain number of known and tried offences, out of the unknown sum total of crimes committed*. Since this sum total of crimes committed will probably ever continue unknown, all the reasoning of which it is the basis will be more or less defective. I do not hesitate to say, that all the knowledge which we possess on the statistics of crimes and offences will be of no utility whatever, unless we admit without question that *there is a ratio, nearly invariably the same, between known and tried offences and the unknown sum total of crimes committed*. This ratio is necessary, and if it did not really exist, every thing which, until the present time, has been said on the statistical documents of crime, would be false and absurd. We are aware, then, how important it is to legitimate such a ratio, and we may be astonished that this has not been done before now. The ratio of which we speak necessarily varies according to the nature and seriousness of the crimes: in a well-organized society, where the police is active and justice is rightly administered, this ratio, for murders and assassinations, will be nearly equal to unity; that is to say, no individual will disappear from the society by murder or assassination, without its being known: this will not be precisely the case with poisonings. When we look to thefts and offences of

Abridged from *A Treatise on Man*, pp. 82–96; 103–8. (Edinburgh: Chambers, 1842.)

smaller importance, the ratio will become very small, and a great number of offences will remain unknown, either because those against whom they are committed do not perceive them, or do not wish to prosecute the perpetrators, or because justice itself has not sufficient evidence to act upon. Thus, the greatness of this ratio, which will generally be different for different crimes and offences, will chiefly depend on the activity of justice in reaching the guilty, on the care with which the latter conceal themselves, on the repugnance which the individuals injured may have to complain, or perhaps on their not knowing that any injury has been committed against them. Now, if all the causes which influence the magnitude of the ratio remain the same, we may also assert that the effects will remain invariable. This result is confirmed in a curious manner by induction, and observing the surprising constancy with which the numbers of the statistics of crime are reproduced annually – a constancy which, no doubt, will be also reproduced in the numbers at which we cannot arrive: thus, although we do not know the criminals who escape justice, we very well know that every year between 7,000 and 7,300 persons are brought before the criminal courts, and that 61 are regularly condemned out of every 100; that 170,000 nearly are brought before courts of correction, and that 85 out of 100 are condemned; and that, if we pass to details, we find a no less alarming regularity; thus we find that between 100 and 150 individuals are annually condemned to death, 280 condemned to perpetual hard labour, 1,050 to hard labour for a time, 1,220 to solitary confinement (*à la réclusion*), etc.; so that this budget of the scaffold and the prisons is discharged by the French nation, with much greater regularity, no doubt, than the financial budget; and we might say, that what annually escapes the minister of justice is a more regular sum than the deficiency of revenue to the treasury.

I shall commence by considering, in a general manner, the propensity to crime in France, availing myself of the excellent documents contained in the *Comptes Généraux de l'Administration de la Justice* of this country; I shall afterwards endeavour to establish some comparisons with other countries, but with all the care and reserve which such comparisons require.

During the four years preceding 1830, 28,686 accused persons were set down as appearing before the courts of assize, that is to say, 7,171 individuals annually nearly; which gives 1 accused person to 4,463 inhabitants, taking the population at 32,000,000 souls. Moreover, of 100 accused, 61 persons have been condemned to punishments of greater or less severity. From the remarks made above with respect to the crimes which remain unknown or unpunished, and from mistakes which justice may make, we conceive that these numbers, although they furnish us with curious data for the past, do not give us any thing exact on the propensity to crime. However, if we consider that the two ratios which we have calculated have not sensibly varied from year to year, we shall be led to believe that they will not vary in a sensible manner for the succeeding years; and the probability that this variation will not take place is so much the greater, according as, all things being equal, the mean results of each year do not differ much from the general average, and these results have been taken from a great number of years. After these remarks, it becomes very probable that, for a Frenchman, there is 1 against 4,462 chances that he will be an accused person during the course of the year; moreover, there are 61 to 39 chances, very nearly, that he will be condemned at the time that he is accused. These results are justified by the numbers of the following table [Table 2.1]:

[Table 2.1]

| Years | Accused persons present | Condemned persons | Inhabitants to one accused person | Condemned in 100 accused persons | Accused of crimes against | | Ratio between the numbers of the two kinds of crime |
|-------|------|------|------|------|------|------|------|
| | | | | | Persons | Property | |
| 1826 | 6,988 | 4,348 | 4,557 | 62 | 1,907 | 5,081 | 2.7 |
| 1827 | 6,929 | 4,236 | 4,593 | 61 | 1,911 | 5,018 | 2.6 |
| 1828 | 7,396 | 4,551 | 4,307 | 61 | 1,844 | 5,552 | 3.0 |
| 1829 | 7,373 | 4,475 | 4,521 | 61 | 1,791 | 5,582 | 3.1 |
| Total | 28,686 | 17,610 | 4,463 | 61 | 7,453 | 21,233 | 2.8 |

Thus, although we do not yet know the statistical documents for 1830, it is very probable that we shall again have 1 accused person in 4,463 very nearly, and 61 condemned in 100 accused persons; this probability is somewhat diminished for the year 1831, and still more for the succeeding years. We may, therefore, by the results of the past, estimate what will be realized in the future. This possibility of assigning beforehand the number of accused and condemned persons which any country will present, must give rise to serious reflections, since it concerns the fate of several thousand men, who are driven, as it were, in an irresistible manner, towards the tribunals, and the condemnations which await them.

These conclusions are deduced from the principle [. . .] that effects are proportionate to their causes, and that the effects remain the same, if the causes which have produced them do not vary. If France, then, in the year 1830, had not undergone any apparent change, and if, contrary to my expectation, I found a sensible difference between the two ratios calculated beforehand for this year and the real ratios observed, I should conclude that some alteration had taken place in the causes, which had escaped my attention. On the other hand, if the state of France has changed, and if, consequently, the causes which influence the propensity to crime have also undergone some change, I ought to expect to find an alteration in the two ratios which until that time remained nearly the same.

It is proper to observe, that the preceding numbers only show, strictly speaking, the probability of being accused and afterwards condemned, without rendering us able to determine any thing very precise on the degree of the propensity to crime; at least unless we admit, what is very likely, that justice preserves the same activity, and the number of guilty persons who escape it preserves the same proportion from year to year.

In the latter columns of the preceding table [Table 2.1], is first made the distinction between crimes against persons and crimes against property: it will be remarked, no doubt, that the number of the former has diminished, whilst the latter has increased; however, these variations are so small, that they do not sensibly affect the annual ratio; and we see that we ought to reckon that three persons are accused of crimes against property to one for crimes against person.

[. . .]

**Of the influence of knowledge, of professions [. . .] on the propensity to crime**

It may be interesting to examine the influence of the intellectual state of the accused on the nature of crimes: the French documents on this subject are such, that I am enabled to form the following table [Table 2.2] for the years 1828 and 1829; to this table I have annexed the results of the years 1830 and 1831, which were not known when the reflections which succeed were written down.

[Table 2.2]

| Intellectual state of the persons accused | 1828–9: accused of crimes against | | Ratio of crimes against property to crimes against persons | 1830–1: accused of crimes against | | Ratio of crimes against property to crimes against Persons |
|---|---|---|---|---|---|---|
| | Persons | Property | | Persons | Property | |
| Could not read or write | 2,072 | 6,617 | 3.2 | 2,134 | 6,785 | 3.1 |
| Could read and write but imperfectly | 1,001 | 2,804 | 2.8 | 1,033 | 2,840 | 2.8 |
| Could read and write well | 400 | 1,109 | 2.8 | 408 | 1,047 | 2.6 |
| Had received a superior education to this 1st degree | 80 | 206 | 2.6 | 135 | 184 | 1.4 |
| | 3,553 | 10,736 | 3.0 aver. | 3,710 | 10,856 | 2.9 aver. |

Thus, all things being equal, the number of crimes against persons, *compared with the number of crimes against property*, during the years 1828 and 1829, was greater according as the intellectual state of the accused was more highly developed; and this difference bore especially on murders, rapes, assassinations, blows, wounds, and other severe crimes. Must we thence conclude that knowledge is injurious to society? I am far from thinking so. To establish such an assertion, it would be necessary to commence by ascertaining how many individuals of the French nation belong to each of the four divisions which we have made above, and to find out if, proportion being considered, the individuals of that one of the divisions commit as many crimes as those of the others. If this were really the case, I should not hesitate to say that, since the most enlightened individuals commit as many crimes as those who have had less education, and since their crimes are more serious, they are necessarily more criminal; but from the little we know of the diffusion of knowledge in France, we cannot state any thing decisively on this point. Indeed, it may so happen, that individuals of the enlightened part of society, while committing fewer murders, assassinations, and other severe crimes, than individuals who have received no education, also commit much fewer crimes against property, and this would explain what we have remarked in the preceding numbers. This conjecture even becomes probable, when we consider that the enlightened classes are presupposed to possess more affluence, and consequently are less frequently under the necessity of having recourse to the different modes of theft, of which crimes against property almost entirely consist; whilst affluence and knowledge have not an equal power in subduing the fire of the passions and sentiments of hatred and vengeance. It must be remarked, on the other hand, that the results contained in the preceding table only belong to two years, and consequently present a smaller probability of expressing what really is the case, especially those results connected with the most enlightened class, and which are based on very small numbers. It seems to me, then, that at the most we can only say that the ratio of the number of crimes against persons to the number of crimes against property varies with the degree of knowledge; and generally, for 100 crimes against persons, we may reckon fewer crimes against property, according as the individuals belong to a class of greater or less enlightenment.

[. . .]

The following details, which I extract from the *Rapport au Roi* for the year 1829, will serve to illustrate what I advance:

'The new table, which points out the professions of the accused, divides them into nine principal classes, comprising,

The *first*, individuals who work on the land, in vineyards, forests, mines, etc., 2,453.

The *second*, workmen engaged with wood, leather, iron, cotton, etc., 1,932.

The *third*, bakers, butchers, brewers, millers, etc., 253.

The *fourth*, hatters, hairdressers, tailors, upholsterers, etc., 327.

The *fifth*, bankers, agents, wholesale and retail merchants, hawkers, etc., 467.

The *sixth*, contractors, porters, seamen, waggoners, etc., 289.

The *seventh*, innkeepers, lemonade-sellers, servants, etc., 830.

The *eighth*, artists, students, clerks, bailiffs, notaries, advocates, priests, physicians, soldiers, annuitants, etc., 449.

The *ninth*, beggars, smugglers, strumpets, etc., 373.

Women who had no profession have been classed in those which their husbands pursued.

Comparing those who are included in each class with the total number of the accused, we see that the first furnishes 33 out of 100; the second, 26; the third, 4; the fourth, 5; the fifth, 6; the sixth, 4; the seventh, 11; the eighth, 6; the ninth, 5.

If, after that, we point out the accused in each class, according to the nature of their imputed crimes, and compare them with each other, we find the following proportions:

In the first class, 32 of the 100 accused were tried for crimes against persons, and 68 for crimes against property. These numbers are 21 and 79 for the second class; 22 and 78 for the third; 15 and 85 for the fourth and fifth; 26 and 74 for the sixth; 16 and 84 for the seventh; 37 and 63 for the eighth; 13 and 87 for the ninth.

Thus, the accused of the eighth class, who all exercised liberal professions, or enjoyed a fortune which presupposes some education, are those who, relatively, have committed the greatest number of crimes against persons; whilst 87-hundredths of the accused of the ninth class, composed of people without character, have scarcely attacked any thing but property.'

These results, which confirm the remark made before, deserve to be taken into consideration. I shall observe that, when we divide individuals into two classes, the one of liberal professions, and the other composed of journeymen, workmen, and servants, the difference is rendered still more conspicuous.

[. . .]

## On the influence of seasons on the propensity to crime

The seasons have a well-marked influence in augmenting and diminishing the number of crimes. We may form some idea from the following table [Table 2.3], which contains the number of crimes committed in France against persons and property, during each month, for three years, as well as the ratio of these numbers. We can also compare the numbers of this table with those which I have given to show the influence of seasons on the development of mental alienation, and we shall find the most remarkable coincidences, especially for crimes against persons, which would appear to be most usually dependent on failures of the reasoning powers:

[Table 2.3]

| Months | Crimes against Persons | Property | Ratio: 1827–28 | Crimes against Persons | Property | Ratio 1830–31 |
|---|---|---|---|---|---|---|
| January | 282 | 1,095 | 3.89 | 189 | 666 | 3.52 |
| February | 272 | 910 | 3.35 | 194 | 563 | 2.90 |
| March | 335 | 968 | 2.89 | 205 | 602 | 2.94 |
| April | 314 | 841 | 2.68 | 197 | 548 | 2.78 |
| May | 381 | 844 | 2.22 | 213 | 569 | 2.67 |
| June | 414 | 850 | 2.05 | 208 | 602 | 2.90 |
| July | 379 | 828 | 2.18 | 188 | 501 | 2.66 |
| August | 382 | 934 | 2.44 | 247 | 596 | 2.41 |
| September | 355 | 896 | 2.52 | 176 | 584 | 3.32 |
| October | 285 | 926 | 3.25 | 207 | 586 | 2.83 |
| November | 301 | 961 | 3.20 | 223 | 651 | 2.95 |
| December | 347 | 1,152 | 3.33 | 181 | 691 | 3.82 |
| Total | 3,847 | 11,205 | 2.77 | 2,428 | 7,159 | 2.94 |

First, the epoch of maximum (June) in respect to the number of crimes against persons, coincides pretty nearly with the epoch of minimum in respect to crimes against property, and this takes place in summer; whilst, on the contrary, the minimum of the number of crimes against persons, and the maximum of the number of crimes against property, takes place in winter. Comparing these two kinds of crimes, we find that in the month of January nearly four crimes take place against property to one against persons, and in the month of June only two to three. These differences are readily explained by considering that during winter misery and want are more especially felt, and cause an increase of the number of crimes against property, whilst the violence of the passions predominating in summer, excites to more frequent personal collisions.
[. . .]

## On the influence of sex on the propensity to crime

[. . .]
At the commencement, we may observe that, out of 28,686 accused, who have appeared before the courts in France, during the four years before 1830,

there were found 5,416 women, and 23,270 men, that is to say, 23 women to 100 men. Thus, the propensity to crime in general gives the ratio of 23 to 100 for the sexes. This estimate supposes that justice exercises its duties as actively with regard to women as to men; and this is rendered probable by the fact, that the severity of repression is nearly the same in the case of both sexes; in other words, that women are treated with much the same severity as men.

We have just seen that, in general, the propensity to crime in men is about four times as great as in women, in France; but it will be important to examine further, if men are four times as criminal, which will be supposing that the crimes committed by the sexes are equally serious. We shall commence by making a distinction between crimes against property and crimes against persons. At the same time, we shall take the numbers obtained for each year, that we may see the limits in which they are comprised [Table 2.4]:

[Table 2.4]

| Years | Crimes against persons | | | Crimes against property | | |
|---|---|---|---|---|---|---|
| | Men | Women | Ratio | Men | Women | Ratio |
| 1826 | 1,639 | 268 | 0.16 | 4,073 | 1,008 | 0.25 |
| 1827 | 1,637 | 274 | 0.17 | 4,020 | 998 | 0.25 |
| 1828 | 1,576 | 270 | 0.17 | 4,396 | 1,156 | 0.26 |
| 1829 | 1,552 | 239 | 0.15 | 4,379 | 1,203 | 0.27 |
| Averages | 1,601 | 263 | 0.16 | 4,217 | 1,091 | 0.26 |
| 1830 | 1,412 | 254 | 0.18 | 4,196 | 1,100 | 0.26 |
| 1831 | 1,813 | 233 | 0.13 | 4,567 | 993 | 0.22 |
| Averages | 1,612 | 243 | 0.15 | 4,381 | 1,046 | 0.24 |

Although the number of crimes against persons may have diminished slightly, whilst crimes against property have become rather more numerous, yet we see that the variations are not very great; they have but little modified the ratios between the numbers of the accused of the two sexes. We have 26 women to 100 men in the accusations for crimes against property, and for crimes against persons the ratio has been only 16 to 100. In general, crimes against persons are of a more serious nature than those against property, so that our distinction is favourable to the women, and we may affirm that men, in France, are four times as criminal as women. It must be observed, that the ratio 16 to 26 is nearly the same as that of the strength of the two sexes. However, it is proper to examine things more narrowly, and especially to take notice of individual crimes, at least of those which are committed in so great a number, that the inferences drawn from them may possess some degree of probability. For this purpose, in the following table [Table 2.5] I have collected the numbers relating to the four years before 1830, and calculated the different ratios; the crimes are classed according to the degree of magnitude of this ratio. I have also grouped crimes nearly of the same nature together, such as issuing false money, counterfeits, falsehoods in statements or in commercial transactions, etc.

[Table 2.5]

| Nature of crimes | Men | Women | Women to 100 men |
|---|---|---|---|
| Infanticide | 30 | 426 | 1,320 |
| Miscarriage | 15 | 39 | 260 |
| Poisoning | 77 | 73 | 91 |
| House robbery (vol domestique) | 2,648 | 1,602 | 60 |
| Parricide | 44 | 22 | 50 |
| Incendiarism of buildings and other things | 279 | 94 | 34 |
| Robbery of churches | 176 | 47 | 27 |
| Wounding of parents (blessures envers ascendans) | 292 | 63 | 22 |
| Theft | 10,677 | 2,249 | 21 |
| False evidence and suborning | 307 | 51 | 17 |
| Fraudulent bankruptcy | 353 | 57 | 16 |
| Assassination | 947 | 111 | 12 |
| False coining (fausse monnaie, counterfeit making, false affirmations in deeds etc. | 1,669 | 117 | 11 |
| Rebellion | 612 | 69 | 10 |
| Highway robbery | 648 | 54 | 8 |
| Wounds and blows | 1,447 | 78 | 5 |
| Murder | 1,112 | 44 | 4 |
| Violation and seduction | 685 | 7 | 1 |
| Violation on persons under 15 years of age | 585 | 5 | 1 |

As we have already observed, to the commission of crime the three following conditions are essential – the will, which depends on the person's morality, the opportunity, and the facility of effecting it. Now, the reason why females have less propensity to crime than males, is accounted for by their being more under the influence of sentiments of shame and modesty, as far as morals are concerned; their dependent state, and retired habits, as far as occasion or opportunity is concerned; and their physical weakness, so far as the facility of acting is concerned. I think we may attribute the differences observed in the degree of criminality to these three principal causes. Sometimes the whole three concur at the same time: we ought, on such occasions, to expect to find their influence very marked, as in rapes and seductions; thus, we have only 1 women to 100 men in crimes of this nature. In poisoning, on the contrary, the number of accusations for either sex is nearly equal. When force becomes necessary for the destruction of a person, the number of women who are accused becomes much fewer; and their numbers diminish in proportion, according to the necessity of the greater publicity before the crime can be perpetrated: the following crimes also take place in the order in which they are stated – infanticide, miscarriage, parricide, wounding of parents, assassinations, wounds and blows, murder.

With respect to infanticide, woman has not only many more opportunities of committing it than man, but she is in some measure impelled to it, frequently by misery, and almost always from the desire of concealing a fault, and avoiding the shame or scorn of society, which, in such cases, thinks less unfavourably of man. Such is not the case with other crimes involving the destruction of an individual: it is not the degree of the crime which keeps a woman back, since, in the series which we have given, parricides and wounding of parents are more numerous than assassinations, which again are more frequent than murder, and wounds and blows generally; it is not simply weakness, for then the ratio for parricide and wounding of parents should be the same as for murder and wounding of strangers. These differences are more especially owing to the habits and sedentary life of females; they can only conceive and execute guilty projects on individuals with whom they are in the greatest intimacy: thus, compared with man, her assassinations are more often in her family than out of it; and in society she commits assassination rather than murder, which often takes place after excess of drink, and the quarrels to which women are less exposed.

If we now consider the different kinds of theft, we shall find that the ratios of the propensity to crime are arranged in a similar series: thus, we have successively house robbery, robbery in churches, robberies in general, and, lastly, highway robbery, for which strength and audacity are necessary. The less conspicuous propensity to cheating in general, and to fraudulent bankruptcy, again depend on the more secluded life of females, their separation from trade, and that, in some cases, they are less capable than men – for example, in coining false money and issuing counterfeits.

If we attempt to analyse facts, it seems to me that the difference of morality in man and woman is not so great as is generally supposed, excepting only as regards modesty; I do not speak of the timidity arising from this last sentiment, in like manner as it does from the physical weakness and seclusion of females. As to these habits themselves, I think we may form a tolerable estimate of their influence by the ratios which exist between the sexes in crimes of different kinds, where neither strength has to be taken into consideration, nor modesty – as in theft, false witnessing, fraudulent bankruptcy etc.; these ratios are about 100 to 21 or 17, that is to say, about 5 or 6 to 1. As to other modes of cheating, the difference is a little greater, from the reasons already stated. If we try to give a numerical expression of the intensity of the causes by which women are influenced, as, for example, the influence of strength, we may estimate it as being in proportion to the degree of strength itself, or as 1 to 2 nearly; and this is the ratio of the number of parricides for each sex. For crimes where both physical weakness and the retired life of females must be taken into account, as in assassinations and highway robberies, following the same plan in our calculations, it will be necessary to multiply the ratio of power or strength ½ by the degree of dependence 1–5, which gives 1–10, a quantity which really falls between the values 12–100 and 8–100, the ratios given in the table [Table 2.5]. With respect to murder, and blows and wounds, these crimes depend not merely on strength and a more or less sedentary life, but still more on being in the habit of using strong drinks and quarrelling. The influence of this latter cause might almost be considered as 1 to 3 for the sexes. It may be thought that the estimates which I have here pointed out, cannot be of an exact nature, from the impossibility of assigning the share of influence which the greater modesty of woman, her physical weakness, her dependence, or rather her more retired life, and her feebler passions, which are also less frequently excited by liquors, may have respectively on any crime in particular. Yet, if such were the characters in which the sexes more particularly differ from each other, we might, by analyses like those now given, assign their respective influence with some probability of truth, especially if the observations were very numerous.

[. . .]

## Of the influence of age on the propensity to crime

Of all the causes which influence the development of the propensity to crime, or which diminish that propensity, age is unquestionably the most energetic. Indeed, it is through age that the physical powers and passions of man are developed, and their energy afterwards decreases with age. Reason is developed with age, and continues to acquire power even when strength and passion have passed their greatest vigour. Considering only these three elements, strength, passion, and judgment (or reason), we may almost say, a priori, what will be the degree of the propensity to crime at different ages. Indeed, the propensity must be almost nothing at the two extremes of life; since, on the one hand, strength and passion, two powerful instruments of crime, have scarcely begun to exist and, on the other hand, their energy, nearly extinguished, is still further deadened by the influence of reason. On the contrary, the propensity to crime should be at its maximum at the age when strength and passion have attained their maximum, and when reason has not acquired sufficient power to govern their combined influence. Therefore, considering only physical causes, the propensity to crime at different ages will be a property and sequence of the three quantities we have just names, and might be determined by them, if they were sufficiently known. But since these elements are not yet determined, we must confine ourselves to seeking for the degrees of the propensity to crime in an experimental manner; we shall find the means of so doing in the *Comptes Généraux de la Justice*. The following table [Table 2.6] will show the number of crimes against persons and against property, which have been committed in France by each sex during the years 1826, 27, 28, and 29, as well as the ratio of these numbers; the fourth column points out how a population of 10,000 souls is divided in France, according to age; and the last column gives the ratio of the total number of crimes to the corresponding number of the preceding column; thus there is no longer an inequality of number of the individuals of different ages.

[Table 2.6]

| Individuals' age | Crimes against | | Crimes against property in 100 | Population according to age | Degrees of the propensity to crime |
|---|---|---|---|---|---|
| | Persons | Property | | | |
| Less than 16 years | 80 | 440 | 85 | 3,304 | 161 |
| 16 to 21 | 904 | 3,723 | 80 | 887 | 5,217 |
| 21 to 25 | 1,278 | 3,329 | 72 | 673 | 6,816 |
| 25 to 30 | 1,575 | 3,702 | 70 | 791 | 6,671 |
| 30 to 35 | 1,153 | 2,883 | 71 | 732 | 5,514 |
| 35 to 40 | 650 | 2,076 | 76 | 672 | 4,057 |
| 40 to 45 | 575 | 1,724 | 75 | 612 | 3,757 |
| 45 to 50 | 445 | 1,275 | 74 | 549 | 3,133 |
| 50 to 55 | 288 | 811 | 74 | 482 | 2,280 |
| 55 to 60 | 168 | 500 | 75 | 410 | 1,629 |
| 60 to 65 | 157 | 385 | 71 | 330 | 1,642 |
| 65 to 70 | 91 | 184 | 70 | 247 | 1,113 |
| 70 to 80 | 64 | 137 | 68 | 255 | 788 |
| 80 and upwards | 5 | 14 | 74 | 55 | 345 |

This table gives us results conformable to those which I have given in my *Recherches Statistique* for the years 1826 and 1827. Since the value obtained for 80 years of age and upwards is based on very small numbers, it is not entitled to much confidence. Moreover, we see that man begins to exercise his propensity to crimes against property at a period antecedent to his pursuit of other crimes. Between his 25th and 30th year, when his powers are developed, he inclines more to crimes against persons. It is near the age of 25 years that the propensity to crime reaches its maximum.

[. . .]

If, instead of taking crimes collectively, we examine each in particular in proportion to age, we shall have a new proof that the maximum of crimes of different kinds takes place between the 20th and 30th years, and that it is really about that period that the most vicious disposition is manifested. Only the period of maximum will be hastened or retarded some years for some crimes, according to the quicker or slower development of certain qualities of man which are proportioned to those crimes. These results are too curious to be omitted here: I have presented them in the following table [Table 2.7], according to the documents of France, from 1826 to 1829 inclusively, classing them according to the periods of maxima, and taking into account the population of different ages. I have omitted the crimes which are committed in smallest number, because the results from that alone would have been very doubtful.

Thus the propensity to theft, one of the first to show itself, prevails in some measure throughout our whole existence; we might be led to believe it to be inherent to the weakness of man, who falls into it as if by instinct. It is first exercised by the indulgence of confidence which exists in the interior of families, then it manifests itself out of them, and finally on the public highway, where it terminates by having recourse to violence, when the man has then made the sad essay of the fullness of his strength by committing all the different kinds of homicide. This fatal propensity, however, is not so precocious as that which, near adolescence, arises with the fire of the passions and the disorders which accompany it, and which drives man to violation and seduction, seeking its first victims among beings whose weakness opposes the least resistance. To these first excesses of the passions, of cupidity, and of strength, is soon joined reflection, plotting crime; and man, become more self-possessed and hardened, chooses to destroy his victim by assassination or poisoning. Finally, his last stages in the career of crime are marked by address in deception, which in some measure supplies the place of strength. It is in his decline that the vicious man presents the most hideous spectacle; his cupidity, which nothing can extinguish, is rekindled with fresh ardour, and assumes the mask of swindling; if he still uses the little strength which nature has left to him, it is rather to strike his enemy in the shade; finally, if his depraved passions have not been deadened by age, he prefers to gratify them on feeble children. Thus, his first and his last stages in the career of crime have the same character in this last respect: but what a difference! That which was somewhat excusable in the young man, because of his inexperience, of the violence of his passions, and the similarity of ages, in the old man is the result of the deepest immorality and the most accumulated load of depravity.

[. . .]

[Table 2.7]

| Nature of the crimes | Under 16 years | 16–21 | 21–25 | 25–30 | 30–35 | 35–40 | 40–45 | 45–50 | 50–55 | 55–60 | 60–65 | 65–70 | 70–80 | 80 and upwards |
|---|---|---|---|---|---|---|---|---|---|---|---|---|---|---|
| Violations on children under 15 years | 4 | 120 | 71 | 96 | 73 | 39 | 34 | 45 | 22 | 18 | 26 | 17 | 21 | 2 |
| House robbery | 54 | 965 | 845 | 766 | 528 | 351 | 249 | 207 | 112 | 56 | 61 | 34 | 14 | – |
| Other thefts | 332 | 2,479 | 2,050 | 2,292 | 1,716 | 1,249 | 1,016 | 707 | 433 | 263 | 190 | 98 | 65 | 10 |
| Violation and seduction | 9 | 155 | 156 | 148 | 99 | 38 | 40 | 27 | 9 | 5 | 3 | 1 | 2 | – |
| Parricide | 6 | 13 | 12 | 13 | 6 | 3 | 2 | 1 | 4 | 2 | – | – | – | 1 |
| Wounds and blows | 6 | 180 | 300 | 359 | 219 | 129 | 101 | 95 | 55 | 35 | 23 | 10 | 7 | 1 |
| Murder | 15 | 139 | 198 | 275 | 172 | 103 | 84 | 49 | 48 | 30 | 25 | 17 | 9 | – |
| Infanticide | 1 | 40 | 99 | 134 | 76 | 44 | 30 | 8 | 7 | 1 | 8 | 4 | 2 | – |
| Rebellion | 5 | 67 | 129 | 156 | 115 | 51 | 51 | 35 | 29 | 16 | 16 | 5 | 5 | – |
| Highway robbery | 21 | 80 | 111 | 149 | 107 | 60 | 62 | 46 | 22 | 21 | 8 | 6 | 4 | – |
| Assassination | 10 | 90 | 144 | 203 | 183 | 100 | 104 | 89 | 53 | 32 | 24 | 13 | 15 | 1 |
| Wounding parents | 2 | 47 | 64 | 73 | 72 | 40 | 30 | 16 | 8 | 2 | 1 | – | – | – |
| Poisoning | 5 | 6 | 17 | 30 | 27 | 15 | 20 | 12 | 6 | 2 | 5 | 4 | 1 | – |
| False witnessing and suborning | 2 | 23 | 46 | 48 | 44 | 42 | 42 | 35 | 23 | 15 | 15 | 11 | 7 | – |
| Various misdemeanours | 8 | 86 | 202 | 276 | 312 | 244 | 207 | 185 | 129 | 78 | 75 | 28 | 28 | 2 |

**Conclusions**

In making a summary of the principal observations contained in this chapter,
we are led to the following conclusions.

(1) Age (or the term of life) is undoubtedly the cause which operates with
most energy in developing or subduing the propensity to crime.

(2) This fatal propensity appears to be developed in proportion to the
intensity of the physical power and passions of man: it attains its maximum
about the age of 25 years, the period at which the physical development has
almost ceased. The intellectual and moral development, which operates more
slowly, subsequently weakens the propensity to crime, which, still later,
diminishes from the feeble state of the physical powers and passions.

(3) Although it is near the age of twenty-five that the maximum in number
of crimes of different kinds takes place, yet this maximum advances or
recedes some years for certain crimes, according to the quicker or slower
development of certain qualities which have a bearing on those crimes. Thus,
man, driven by the violence of his passions, at first commits violation and
seduction; almost at the same time he enters on the career of theft, which he
seems to follow as if by instinct till the end of life; the development of his
strength subsequently leads him to commit every act of violence – homicide,
rebellion, highway robbery still later, reflection converts murder into assassination and poisoning. Lastly, man, advancing in the career of crime,
substitutes a greater degree of cunning for violence, and becomes more of a
forger than at any other period of life.

(4) The *difference of sexes* has also a great influence on the propensity to
crime: in general, there is only one woman before the courts to four men.

(5) The propensity to crime increases and decreases nearly in the same
degrees in each sex; yet the period of maximum takes place rather later in
women, and is near the thirtieth year.

(6) Woman, undoubtedly from her feeling of weakness, rather commits
crimes against property than persons; and when she seeks to destroy her kind,
she prefers poison. Moreover, when she commits homicide, she does
not appear to be proportionally arrested by the enormity of crimes which, in
point of frequency, take place in the following order: infanticide, miscarriage,
parricide, wounding of parents, assassination, wounds and blows, murder: so
that we may affirm that the number of the guilty diminishes in proportion as
they have to seek their victim more openly. These differences are no doubt
owing to the habits and sedentary life of woman; she can only conceive and
execute guilty projects on individuals with whom she is in constant relation.

(7) The *seasons*, in their course, exercise a very marked influence on crime:
thus, during summer, the greatest number of crimes against persons are
committed, and the fewest against property; the contrary takes place during
winter.

(8) It must be observed that age and the seasons have almost the same
influence in increasing or diminishing the number of mental disorders and
crimes against persons.

(9) *Climate* appears to have some influence, especially on the propensity to
crimes against persons: this observation is confirmed at least among the races
of southern climates, such as the Pelasgian race, scattered over the shores of
the Mediterranean and Corsica, on the one hand; and the Italians, mixed with
Dalmatians and Tyrolese, on the other. We observe, also, that severe climates,

which give rise to the greatest number of wants, also give rise to the greatest number of crimes against property.

(10) The countries where frequent mixture of the people takes place; those in which industry and trade collect many persons and things together, and possess the greatest activity; finally, those where the inequality of fortune is most felt, all things being equal, are those which give rise to the greatest number of crimes.

(11) Professions have great influence on the nature of crimes. Individuals of more independent professions are rather given to crimes against persons; and the labouring and domestic classes to crimes against property. Habits of dependence, sedentary life, and also physical weakness in women, produce the same results.

(12) *Education* is far from having so much influence on the propensity to crime as is generally supposed. Moreover, moral instruction is very often confounded with instruction in reading and writing alone, and which is most frequently an accessory instrument to crime.

(13) It is the same with *poverty*; several of the departments of France, considered to be the poorest, are at the same time the most moral. Man is not driven to crime because he is poor, but more generally because he passes rapidly from a state of comfort to one of misery, and an inadequacy to supply the artificial wants which he has created.

(14) The higher we go in the ranks of society, and consequently in the degrees of education, we find a smaller and smaller proportion of guilty women to men; descending to the lowest orders, the habits of both sexes resemble each other more and more.

(15) Of 1,129 murders committed in France, during the space of four years, 446 have been in consequence of quarrels and contentions in taverns; which would tend to show the fatal influence of the use of *strong drinks*.

(16) In France, as in the Low Countries, we enumerate annually 1 accused person to 4,300 inhabitants nearly; but in the former country, 39 in 100 are acquitted, and in the second only 15; yet the same code was used in both countries, but in the Low Countries the judges performed the duty of the jury. Before correctional courts and simple police courts, where the committed were tried by judges only, the results were nearly the same for both countries.

(17) In France, crimes against persons were about one-third of the number of crimes against property, but in the Low Countries they were about one-fourth only. It must be remarked, that the first kind of crimes lead to fewer condemnations than the second, perhaps because there is a greater repugnance to apply punishment as the punishment increases in severity.

I cannot conclude this chapter without again expressing my astonishment at the constancy observed in the results which the documents connected with the administration of justice present each year.

'Thus, as I have already had occasion to repeat several times, we pass from one year to another, with the sad perspective of seeing the same crimes reproduced in the same order, and bringing with them the same punishments in the same proportions.' All observations tend likewise to confirm the truth of this proposition, which I long ago announced, that *every thing which pertains to the human species considered as a whole, belongs to the order of physical facts*: the greater the number of individuals, the more does the influence of individual will disappear, leaving predominance to a series of general facts, dependent on causes by which society exists and is preserved. These causes we now

want to ascertain, and as soon as we are acquainted with them, we shall determine their influence on society, just in the same way as we determine effects by their causes in physical sciences.
[. . .]
[M]an commits crime with at least as much regularity as is observed in births, deaths, or marriages, and with more regularity than the receipts and expenses of the treasury take place. [. . .] since the crimes which are annually committed seem to be a necessary result of our social organization, and since the number of them cannot diminish without the causes which induce them undergoing previous modification, it is the province of legislators to ascertain these causes, and to remove them as far as possible: they have the power of determining the budget of crime, as well as the receipts and expenses of the treasury. Indeed, experience proves as clearly as possible the truth of this opinion, which at first may appear paradoxical, viz., that *society prepares crime, and the guilty are only the instruments by which it is executed*. Hence it happens that the unfortunate person who loses his head on the scaffold, or who ends his life in prison, is in some manner an expiatory victim for society. His crime is the result of the circumstances in which he is found placed: the severity of his chastisement is perhaps another result of it. [. . .]

# 3

# The criminal type in women and its atavistic origin

## Cesare Lombroso and William Ferrero

[. . .] [A] comparison of the criminal skull with the skulls of normal women reveals the fact that female criminals approximate more to males, both criminal and normal, than to normal women, especially in the superciliary arches in the seam of the sutures, in the lower jaw-bones, and in peculiarities of the occipital region. They nearly resemble normal women in their cheek-bones, in the prominence of the crotaphitic line, and in the median occipital fossa. There are also among them a large proportion (9.2 per cent) of virile crania.

The anomalies more frequent in female criminals than in prostitutes are: enormous pterygoid apophisis; cranial depressions; very heavy lower jaw; plagiocephalia; the soldering of the atlas with the occiput; enormous nasal spine; deep frontal sinuses; absence of sutures; simplicity of sutures; wormian bones.

Fallen women, on the other hand, are distinguished from criminals by the following peculiarities: clinoid apophisis forming a canal; tumefied parietal prominences; median occipital fossa of double size; great occipital irregularity; narrow or receding forehead; abnormal nasal bones; epactal bone; prog-nathous jaw and alveolar prognathism; cranial sclerosis; a virile type of face; prominent cheek-bones.

[. . .] More instructive than a mere analytical enumeration of the charac-teristics of degeneration is a synthesis of the different features peculiar to the female criminal type.

We call a *complete type* one wherein exist four or more of the characteristics of degeneration; a *half-type* that which contains at least three of these; and *no type* a countenance possessing only one or two anomalies or none.

Out of the female delinquents examined 52 were Piedmontese in the prison of Turin, and 234 in the Female House of Correction were natives of different Italian provinces, especially from the South. In these, consequently, we set aside all special characteristics belonging to the ethnological type of the different regions, such as the brachycephali of the Piedmontese, the dolicho-cephali of the Sardinians, the oxycephali.

We studied also from the point of view of type the 150 prostitutes whom we had previously examined for their several features; as well as another 100 from Moscow whose photographs Madame Tarnowsky sent us.
[. . .]

Abridged from *The Female Offender*, pp. 28; 103–13; 147–52; 190–1. (London: Fisher Unwin, 1895.)

The results of the examination may be thus summarized:

1   The rarity of a criminal type in the female as compared with the male delinquent. In our homogeneous group (286) the proportion is 14 per cent, rising, when all other observations are taken into account, to 18 per cent, a figure lower almost by one-half than the average in the male born criminal, namely, 31 per cent.

In normal women this same type is only present in 2 per cent.

[. . .]

2   Prostitutes differ notably from female criminals in that they offer so much more frequently a special and peculiar type. Grimaldi's figures are 31 per cent (of anomalies), Madame Tarnowsky's 43 per cent, our own 38 per cent; making a mean of 37.1 per cent. These results harmonize with the conclusions to which we had already arrived in our study of particular features, and our survey of the various types of born prostitutes as distinguished from ordinary female offenders.

3   In the differentiation of female criminals, according to their offences, our last observations on the 286 criminals (made first without knowing the nature of their crimes and classified afterwards) give the prevalence of the criminal type among thieves as 15.3 and 16 per cent; among assassins as 13.2 per cent, and as rising to 18.7 per cent in those accused of corruption, among whom were included old prostitutes.

The least frequency was among swindlers, 11 per cent, and infanticides, 8.7 per cent, such women being indeed among the more representative of occasional criminals.

[. . .]

Here we see the crescendo of the peculiarities as we rise from moral women, who are most free from anomalies, to prostitutes, who are free from none, and we note how homicides present the highest number of multiple anomalies.

All the same, it is incontestable that female offenders seem almost normal when compared to the male criminal, with his wealth of anomalous features.

[. . .]

The remarkable rarity of anomalies (already revealed by their crania) is not a new phenomenon in the female, nor is it in contradiction to the undoubted fact that atavistically she is nearer to her origin than the male, and ought consequently to abound more in anomalies.

We saw, indeed, that the crania of male criminals exhibited 78 per cent of anomalies, as against 27 per cent in female delinquents and 51 per cent in prostitutes; but we also saw that the monstrosities in which women abound are forms of disease, consequent on disorder of the ovule. But when a departure from the norm is to be found only in the physiognomy, that is to say, in that portion of the frame where the degenerative stamp, the type declares itself, then even in cases of idiotcy, of madness, and, what is more important for our purpose, of epilepsy, the characteristic face is far less marked and less frequent in the woman. In her, anomalies are extraordinarily rare when compared with man; and this phenomenon, with a few exceptions among lower animals, holds good throughout the whole zoological scale.

[. . .]

Atavism helps to explain the rarity of the criminal type in woman. The very precocity of prostitutes – the precocity which increases their apparent beauty – is primarily attributable to atavism. Due also to it is the virility underlying the female criminal type; for what we look for most in the female is femininity, and when we find the opposite in her we conclude as a rule that there must be some anomaly. And in order to understand the significance and the atavistic origin of this anomaly, we have only to remember that virility was one of the special features of the savage women.

[. . .]

The criminal being only a reversion to the primitive type of his species, the female criminal necessarily offers the two most salient characteristics of primordial woman, namely, precocity and a minor degree of differentiation from the male – this lesser differentiation manifesting itself in the stature, cranium, brain, and in the muscular strength which she possesses to a degree so far in advance of the modern female.

[. . .]

The analogy between the anthropology and psychology of the female criminal is perfect.

Just as in the mass of female criminals possessing few or unimportant characteristics of degeneration, we find a group in whom these features are almost more marked and more numerous than in males, so while the majority of female delinquents are led into crime either by the suggestion of a third person or by irresistible temptation, and are not entirely deficient in the moral sense, there is yet to be found among them a small proportion whose criminal propensities are more intense and more perverse than those of their male prototypes.

'No possible punishments,' wrote Corrado Celto, an author of the fifteenth century, 'can deter women from heaping up crime upon crime. Their perversity of mind is more fertile in new crimes than the imagination of a judge in new punishments.'

'Feminine criminality,' writes Rykère, 'is more cynical, more depraved, and more terrible than the criminality of the male.'

'Rarely is a woman wicked, but when she is she surpasses the man' (Italian Proverb).

'The violence of the ocean waves or of devouring flames is terrible. Terrible is poverty, but woman is more terrible than all else' (Euripides).

'The perversity of woman is so great,' says Caro, 'as to be incredible even to its victims.'

[. . .] Another terrible point of superiority in the female born criminal over the male lies in the refined, diabolical cruelty with which she accomplishes her crime.

[. . .] We may assert that if female born criminals are fewer in number than the males, they are often much more ferocious.

What is the explanation? [. . .] [T]he normal woman is naturally less sensitive to pain than a man, and compassion is the offspring of sensitiveness. If the one be wanting, so will the other be.

We also saw that women have many traits in common with children; that their moral sense is deficient; that they are revengeful, jealous, inclined to vengeances of a refined cruelty.

In ordinary cases these defects are neutralized by piety, maternity, want of passion, sexual coldness, by weakness and an undeveloped intelligence. But when a morbid activity of the psychical centres intensifies the bad qualities of women, and induces them to seek relief in evil deeds; when piety and maternal sentiments are wanting, and in their place are strong passions and intensely erotic tendencies, much muscular strength and a superior intelligence for the conception and execution of evil, it is clear that the innocuous semi-criminal present in the normal woman must be transformed into a born criminal more terrible than any man.

What terrific criminals would children be if they had strong passions, muscular strength, and sufficient intelligence; and if, moreover, their evil tendencies were exasperated by a morbid psychical activity! And women are big children; their evil tendencies are more numerous and more varied than men's, but generally remain latent. When they are awakened and excited they produce results proportionately greater.

Moreover, the born female criminal is, so to speak, doubly exceptional, as a woman and as a criminal. For criminals are an exception among civilized people, and women are an exception among criminals, the natural form of retrogression in women being prostitution and not crime. The primitive woman was impure rather than criminal.

As a double exception, the criminal woman is consequently a monster. Her normal sister is kept in the paths of virtue by many causes, such as maternity, piety, weakness, and when these counter influences fail, and a woman commits a crime, we may conclude that her wickedness must have been enormous before it could triumph over so many obstacles.

[. . .]

M. R., a case described by Ottolenghi, was a thief, a prostitute, a corrupter of youth, a blackmailer, and all this at the age of 17. When only 12 she robbed her father in order to have money to spend among her companions. At 15 she fled from home with a lover, whom she left almost at once for a career of prostitution. With a view to larger gains, when only 16 she organized a vast system of prostitution, by which she provided young girls of 12 and 15 for wealthy men, from whom she exacted large sums, of which only a few sous went to the victims. And by threats of exposure she managed to levy costly blackmail on her clients, one of whom, a highly placed functionary, was dismissed from his post in consequence of her revelations. She was extremely vindictive, and committed two crimes of revenge which serve to show the strange mixture of ferocity and cunning composing her character. One of her companions having spoken evil of her, she (who was then only 16 years of age) let a little time pass, then coaxed her enemy to accompany her outside the gates of the town. They reached a deserted spot as evening fell, and M. R. suddenly threw the other girl on the ground, and while recalling her offence proceeded to beat her violently with a pair of scissors and a key, nor desisted until her victim had fainted; after which she quietly returned to town. 'You might have killed her,' somebody said. 'What did that matter?' she replied; 'there was nobody to see.' 'You might have employed a hired assassin.' 'I am afraid of those,' was the answer. 'Besides, on principle one should do things oneself.' 'But with a key you could never have killed her' (went on the other). 'If one beats the temples well,' M. R. replied, 'it is quite possible to kill a person even with a key.'

She conceived on another occasion such a violent hatred to a brilliant rival that, enticing her into a café, she furtively poisoned her coffee and thus caused her death.

It would be difficult to find greater wickedness at the service of a vindictive disposition and an unbridled greed. We may regard M. R. as an instance in which the two poles of depravity were united. That is to say, she was sanguinary (for she went about always with a dagger in her pocket, and stabbed anybody who offended her in the least) and at the same time inclined to commit the more cautious and insidious crimes, such as poisoning, blackmail, etc. And we consequently find in her an example of the law we have already laid down, to the effect that the female born criminal, when a complete type, is more terrible than the male.

# 4

# Causes of criminal behavior

## *Enrico Ferri*

When a crime is committed in some place, attracting public attention either through the atrocity of the case or the strangeness of the criminal deed – for instance, one that is not connected with bloodshed, but with intellectual fraud – there are at once two tendencies that make themselves felt in the public conscience. One of them, pervading the overwhelming majority of individual consciences, asks: How is this? What for? Why did that man commit such a crime? This question is asked by everybody and occupies mostly the attention of those who do not look upon the case from the point of view of criminology. On the other hand, those who occupy themselves with criminal law represent the other tendency, which manifests itself when acquainted with the news of this crime. This is a limited portion of the public conscience, which tries to study the problem from the standpoint of the technical jurist. The lawyers, the judges, the officials of the police, ask themselves: What is the name of the crime committed by that man under such circumstances? Must it be classed as murder or patricide, attempted or incompleted manslaughter, and, if directed against property, is it theft, or illegal appropriation, or fraud? And the entire apparatus of practical criminal justice forgets at once the first problem, which occupies the majority of the public conscience, the question of the causes that, led to this crime, in order to devote itself exclusively to the technical side of the problem, which constitutes the juridical anatomy of the inhuman and antisocial deed perpetrated by the criminal.

In these two tendencies you have a photographic reproduction of the two schools of criminology. The classic school, which looks upon the crime as a juridical problem, occupies itself with its name, its definition, its juridical analysis, leaves the personality of the criminal in the background and remembers it only so far as exceptional circumstances explicitly stated in the law books refer to it: whether he is a minor, a deaf-mute, whether it is a case of insanity, whether he was drunk at the time the crime was committed. Only in these strictly defined cases does the classic school occupy itself theoretically with the personality of the criminal. But ninety times in one hundred these exceptional circumstances do not exist or cannot be shown to exist, and penal justice limits itself to the technical definition of the fact. But when the case comes up in the criminal court, or before the jurors, practice demonstrates that there is seldom a discussion between the lawyers of the defense and the judges for the purpose of ascertaining the most exact definition of the fact, of determining whether it is a case of attempted or merely projected crime, of

Abridged from *The Positive School of Criminology; Three Lectures by Enrico Ferri* (ed. S.E. Grupp), pp. 70–94. (Pittsburgh, PA: University of Pittsburgh Press, 1968. First published 1901.)

finding out whether there are any of the juridical elements defined in this or that article of the code. The judge is rather face to face with the problem of ascertaining why, under what conditions, for what reasons, the man has committed the crime. This is the supreme and simple human problem. But hitherto it has been left to a more or less perspicacious, more or less gifted, empiricism, and there have been no scientific standards, no methodical collection of facts, no observations and conclusions, save those of the positive school of criminology. This school alone makes an attempt to solve in every case of crime the problem of its natural origin, of the reasons and conditions that induced a man to commit such and such a crime.

For instance, about 3,000 cases of manslaughter are registered every year in Italy. Now, open any work inspired by the classic school of criminology, and ask the author why 3,000 men are the victims of manslaughter every year in Italy, and how it is that there are not sometimes only as many as, say, 300 cases, the number committed in England, which has nearly the same number of inhabitants as Italy; and how it is that there are not sometimes 300,000 such cases in Italy instead of 3,000?

It is useless to open any work of classical criminology for this purpose, for you will not find an answer to these questions in them. No one, from Beccaria to Carrara, has ever thought of this problem, and they could not have asked it, considering their point of departure and their method. In fact, the classic criminologists accept the phenomenon of criminality as an accomplished fact. They analyse it from the point of view of the technical jurist, without asking how this criminal fact may have been produced, and why it repeats itself in greater or smaller numbers from year to year, in every country. The theory of a free will, which is their foundation, excludes the possibility of this scientific question, for according to it the crime is the product of the fiat of the human will. And if that is admitted as a fact, there is nothing left to account for. The manslaughter was committed, because the criminal wanted to commit it; and that is all there is to it. Once the theory of a free will is accepted as a fact, the deed depends on the fiat, the voluntary determination, of the criminal, and all is said.

But if, on the other hand, the positive school of criminology denies, on the ground of researches in scientific physiological psychology, that the human will is free and does not admit that one is a criminal because he wants to be, but declares that a man commits this or that crime only when he lives in definitely determined conditions of personality and environment which induce him necessarily to act in a certain way, then alone does the problem of the origin of criminality begin to be submitted to a preliminary analysis, and then alone does criminal law step out of the narrow and arid limits of technical jurisprudence and become a true social and human science in the highest and noblest meaning of the word. It is vain to insist with such stubbornness as that of the classic school of criminology on juristic formulae by which the distinction between illegal appropriation and theft, between fraud and other forms of crime against property, and so forth, is determined, when this method does not give to society one single word which would throw light upon the reasons that make a man a criminal and upon the efficacious remedy by which society could protect itself against criminality.

[. . .]

The method which we, on the other hand, have inaugurated is the following. Before we study crime from the point of view of a juristic phenomenon, we must study the causes to which the annual recurrence of crimes in all countries is due. These are natural causes, which I have classified under the three heads of anthropological, telluric and social. Every crime, from the smallest to the most atrocious, is the result of the interaction of these three causes, the anthropological condition of the criminal, the telluric environment in which he is living, and the social environment in which he is born, living, and operating. It is a vain beginning to separate the meshes of this net of criminality. There are still those who would maintain the one-sided standpoint that the origin of crime may be traced to only one of these elements, for instance, to the social element alone. So far as I am concerned, I have combatted this opinion from the very inauguration of the positive school of criminology, and I combat it today. It is certainly easy enough to think that the entire origin of all crime is due to the unfavorable social conditions in which the criminal lives. But an objective, methodical, observation demonstrates that social conditions alone do not suffice to explain the origin of criminality, although it is true that the prevalence of the influence of social conditions is an incontestable fact in the case of the greater number of crimes, especially of the lesser ones. But there are crimes which cannot be explained by the influence of social conditions alone. If you regard the general condition of misery as the sole source of criminality, then you cannot get around the difficulty that out of one thousand individuals living in misery from the day of their birth to that of their death only one hundred or two hundred become criminals, while the other nine hundred or eight hundred either sink into biological weakness, or become harmless maniacs, or commit suicide without perpetrating any crime. If poverty were the sole determining cause, one thousand out of one thousand poor ought to become criminals. If only two hundred become criminals, while one hundred commit suicide, one hundred end as maniacs, and the other six hundred remain honest in their social condition, then poverty alone is not sufficient to explain criminality. We must add the anthropological and telluric factor. Only be means of these three elements of natural influence can criminality be explained. Of course, the influence of either the anthropological or telluric or social element varies from case to case. If you have a case of simple theft, you may have a far greater influence of the social factor than of the anthropological factor. On the other hand, if you have a case of murder, the anthropological element will have a far greater influence than the social. And so on in every case of crime, and every individual that you will have to judge on the bench of the criminal.

The anthropological factor. It is precisely here that the genius of Cesare Lombroso established a new science, because in his search after the causes of crime he studied the anthropological condition of the criminal. This condition concerns not only the organic and anatomical constitution, but also the psychological, it represents the organic and psychological personality of the criminal. Every one of us inherits at birth, and personifies in life, a certain organic and psychological combination. This constitutes the individual factor of human activity, which either remains normal through life, or becomes criminal or insane. The anthropological factor, then, must not be restricted, as some laymen would restrict it, to the study of the form of the skull or the bones of the criminal. Lombroso had to begin his studies with the anatomical conditions of the criminal, because the skulls may be studied most easily in the museums. But he continued by also studying the brain and the other physiological conditions of the individual, the state of sensibility, and the circulation of matter. And this entire series of studies is but a necessary scientific introduction to the study of the psychology of the criminal, which is precisely the one problem that is of direct and immediate importance. It is this problem which the lawyer and the public prosecutor should solve before discussing the juridical aspect of any crime, for this reveals the causes which induced the criminal to commit a crime. At present there is no methodical standard for a psychological investigation, although such an investigation was introduced into the scope of classic penal law. But for this reason the results of the positive school penetrate into the lecture rooms of the universities of jurisprudence, whenever a law is required for the judicial arraignment of the criminal as a living and feeling human being. And even though the positive school is not mentioned, all profess to be studying the material furnished by it, for instance, its analyses of the sentiments of the criminal, his moral sense, his behavior before, during, and after the criminal act, the presence of remorse which people, judging the criminal after their own feelings, always suppose the criminal to feel, while, in fact, it is seldom present. This is the anthropological factor, which may assume a pathological form, in which case articles 46 and 47 of the penal code remember that there is such a thing as the personality of the criminal. However, aside from insanity, there are thousands of other organic and psychological conditions of the personality of criminals, which a judge might perhaps lump together under the name of extenuating circumstances, but which science desires to have thoroughly investigated. This is not done today, and for this reason the idea of extenuating circumstances constitutes a denial of justice.

This same anthropological factor also includes that which each one of us has: the race character. Nowadays the influence of race on the destinies of peoples and persons is much discussed in sociology, and there are one-sided schools that pretend to solve the problems of history and society by means of that racial influence alone, to which they attribute an absolute importance. But while there are some who maintain that the history of peoples is nothing but the exclusive product of racial character, there are others who insist that the social conditions of peoples and individuals are alone determining. The one is as much a one-sided and incomplete theory as the other. The study of collective society or of the single individual has resulted in the understanding that the life of society and of the individual is always the product of the inextricable net of the anthropological, telluric and social elements. Hence the influence of the race cannot be ignored in the study of nations and personalities, although it is not the exclusive factor which would suffice to explain the criminality of a nation or an individual. Study, for instance, manslaughter in Italy, and, although you will find it difficult to isolate one of the factors of criminality from the network of the other circumstances and conditions that produce it, yet there are such eloquent instances of the influence of racial character, that it would be like denying the existence of daylight if one tried to ignore the influence of the ethnical factor on criminality.

In Italy there are two currents of criminality, two tendencies which are almost diametrically opposed to one another. The crimes due to hot blood and muscle grow in intensity from northern to southern Italy, while the crimes against property increase from south to north. In northern Italy, where movable property is more developed, the crime of theft assumes a greater intensity, while crimes due to conditions of the blood are decreasing on account of the lesser poverty and the resulting lesser degeneration of the people. In the south, on the other hand, crimes against property are less frequent and crimes of blood more frequent. Still there also are in southern Italy certain cases where criminality of the blood is less frequent, and you cannot explain this in any other way than by the influence of racial character. If you take a geographical map of manslaughter in Italy, you will see that from the minimum, from Lombardy, Piedmont, and Venice, the intensity increases until it reaches its maximum in the insular and peninsular extreme of the south.

[. . .]

Let this be enough so far as the anthropological factor of criminality is concerned. There are, furthermore, the telluric factors, that is to say, the physical environment in which we live and to which we pay no attention. It requires much philosophy, said Rousseau, to note the things with which we are in daily contact, because the habitual influence of a thing makes it more difficult to be aware of it. This applies also to the immediate influence of the physical conditions on human morality, notwithstanding the spiritualist prejudices which still weigh upon our daily lives. For instance, if it is claimed in the name of supernaturalism and psychism that a man is unhappy because he is vicious, it is equivalent to making a one-sided statement. For it is just as true to say that a man becomes vicious because he is unhappy. Want is the strongest poison for the human body and soul. It is the fountain head of all inhuman and antisocial feeling. Where want spreads out its wings, there the sentiments of love, of affection, of brotherhood, are impossible. Take a look at the figures of the peasant in the far-off arid Campagna, the little government employe, the laborer, the little shopkeeper. When work is assured, when living is certain, though poor, then want, cruel want, is in the distance, and every good sentiment can germinate and develop in the human heart. The family then lives in a favorable environment, the parents agree, the children are affectionate. And when the laborer, a bronzed statue of humanity, returns from his smoky shop and meets his white-haired mother, the embodiment of half a century of immaculate virtue and heroic sacrifices, then he can, tired, but assured of his daily bread, give room to feelings of affection, and he will cordially invite his mother to share his frugal meal. But let the same man, in the same environment, be haunted by the spectre of want and lack of employment, and you will see the moral atmosphere in his family changing as from day into night. There is no work, and the laborer comes home without any wages. The wife, who does not know how to feed the children, reproaches her husband with the suffering of his family. The man, having been turned away from the doors of ten offices, feels his dignity as an honest laborer assailed in the very bosom of his own family, because he has vainly asked society for honest employment. And the bonds of affection and union are loosened in that family. Its members no longer agree. There are too many children, and when the poor old mother approaches her son, she reads in his dark and agitated mien the lack of tenderness and feels in her mother heart that her boy, poisoned by the spectre of want, is perhaps casting evil looks at her and harboring the unfilial thought: 'Better an open grave in the cemetery than one mouth more to feed at home!'

It is true that want alone is not sufficient to prepare the soil in the environment of that suffering family for the roots of real crime and to develop it. Want will weaken the love and mutual respect among the members of that family, but it will not be strong enough alone to arm the hands of the man for a matricidal deed, unless he should get into a pathological mental condition, which is very exceptional and rare. But the conclusions of the positive school are confirmed in this case as in any other. In order that crime may develop, it is necessary that anthropological, social and telluric factors should act together.

[. . .]

We have now surveyed briefly the natural genesis of crime as a natural social phenomenon, [. . .] which in any determined moment [acts] upon a personality standing on the cross road of vice and virtue, crime and honesty. This scientific deduction gives rise to a series of investigations which satisfy the mind and supply it with a real understanding of things, far better than the theory that a man is a criminal because he wants to be. No, a man commits crime because he finds himself in certain physical and social conditions, from which the evil plant of crime takes life and strength. [. . .]

[. . .] To sum up, crime is a social phenomenon, due to the interaction of anthropological, telluric, and social factors. This law brings about what I have called criminal saturation, which means that every society has the criminality which it deserves, and which produces by means of its geographical and social conditions such quantities and qualities of crime as correspond to the development of each collective human group.

Thus the old saying of Quetelet is confirmed: 'There is an annual balance of crime, which must be paid and settled with greater regularity than the accounts of the national revenue.' However, we positivists give to this statement a less fatalistic interpretation, since we have demonstrated that crime is not our immutable destiny, even though it is a vain beginning to attempt to attenuate or eliminate crime by mere schemes. The truth is that the balance of crime is determined by the physical and social environment. But by changing the condition of the social environment, which is most easily modified, the legislator may alter the influence of the telluric environment and the organic and psychic conditions of the population, control the greater portion of crimes, and reduce them considerably. It is our firm conviction that a truly civilized legislator can attenuate the plague of criminality, not so much by means of the criminal code, as by means of remedies which are latent in the remainder of the social life and of legislation. And the experience of the most advanced countries confirms this by the beneficent and preventive influence of criminal legislation resting on efficacious social reforms.

We arrive, then, at this scientific conclusion: in the society of the future, the necessity for penal justice will be reduced to the extent that social justice grows intensively and extensively.

# 5

# Criminality and economic conditions

## *Willem Bonger*

[. . .] [I]t is certain that man is born with social instincts, which, when influenced by a favorable environment can exert a force great enough to prevent egoistic thoughts from leading to egoistic acts. And since crime constitutes a part of the egoistic acts, it is of importance, for the etiology of *crime in general*, to inquire whether the present method of production and its social consequences are an obstacle to the development of the social instincts, and in what measure. We shall try in the following pages to show the influence of the economic system and of these consequences upon the social instincts of man.

After what we have just said it is almost superfluous to remark that the egoistic tendency does not *by itself* make a man criminal. For this something else is necessary. It is possible for the environment to create a great egoist, but this does not imply that the egoist will necessarily become criminal. For example, a man who is enriched by the exploitation of children may nevertheless remain all his life an honest man from the legal point of view. He does not think of stealing, because he has a surer and more lucrative means of getting wealth, although he lacks the moral sense which would prevent him from committing a crime if the thought of it occurred to him. We shall show that, as a consequence of the present environment, man has become very egoistic and hence more *capable of crime*, than if the environment had developed the germs of altruism.

*The present economic system* is based upon exchange. [. . .] such a mode of production cannot fail to have an egoistic character. A society based upon exchange isolates the individuals by weakening the bond that unites them. When it is a question of exchange the two parties interested think only of their own advantage even to the detriment of the other party. In the second place the possibility of exchange arouses in a man the thought of the possibility of converting the surplus of his labor into things which increase his well-being in place of giving the benefit of it to those who are deprived of the necessaries of life. Hence the possibility of exchange gives birth to cupidity.

The exchange called simple circulation of commodities is practiced by all men as consumers, and by the workers besides as vendors of their labor power. However, the influence of this simple circulation of commodities is weak compared with that exercised by capitalistic exchange. It is only the exchange of the surplus of labor, by the producer, for other commodities, and hence is for him a secondary matter. As a result he does not exchange with a

Abridged from *Criminality and Economic Conditions*, pp. 402–5; 667–72. (London: Heinemann, 1916.)

view to profit (though he tries to make as advantageous a trade as possible), but to get things which he cannot produce himself.

Capitalistic exchange, on the other hand, has another aim – that of making a profit. A merchant, for example, does not buy goods for his own use, but to sell them to advantage. He will, then, always try, on the one hand, to buy the best commodities as cheaply as possible, by depreciating them as much as he can; on the other hand, to make the purchaser pay as high a price as possible, by exaggerating the value of his wares. *By the nature of the mode of production itself* the merchant is therefore forced to make war upon two sides, must maintain his own interests against the interests of those with whom he does business. If he does not injure too greatly the interests of those from whom he buys, and those to whom he sells, it is for the simple reason that these would otherwise do business with those of his competitors who do not find their interest in fleecing their customers. Wherever competition is eliminated for whatever cause the tactics of the merchant are shown in their true light; he thinks only of his own advantage even to the detriment of those with whom he does business. 'No commerce without trickery' is a proverbial expression (among consumers), and with the ancients Mercury, the god of commerce, was also the god of thieves. This is true, that the merchant and the thief are alike in taking account *exclusively* of their own interest to the detriment of those with whom they have to do.

The fact that in our present society production does not take place generally to provide for the needs of men, but for many other reasons, has important effects upon the character of those who possess the means of production. Production is carried on for profit exclusively; if greater profits can be made by stopping production it will be stopped – this is the point of view of the capitalists. The consumers, on the other hand, see in production the means of creating what man has need of. The world likes to be deceived, and does not care to recognize the fact that the producer has only his own profit in view. The latter encourages this notion and poses as a disinterested person. If he reduces the price of his wares, he claims to do it in the interest of the public, and takes care not to admit that it is for the purpose of increasing his own profits. This is the falsity that belongs inevitably to capitalism.

In general this characteristic of capitalism has no importance for the morality of the consumer, who is merely duped, but it is far otherwise with the press, which is almost entirely in the power of the capitalists. The press, which ought to be a guide for the masses, and is so in some few cases, in the main is in the hands of capitalists who use it only as a means of making money. In place of being edited by men who, by their ability and firmness, are capable of enlightening the public, newspapers are carried on by persons who see in their calling only a livelihood, and consider only the proprietor of the sheet. In great part the press is the opposite of what it ought to be; it represents the interests of those who pay for advertisements or for articles; it increases the ignorance and the prejudices of the crowd; in a word, it poisons public opinion.

Besides this general influence upon the public the press has further a special place in the etiology of crime, from the fact that most newspapers, in order to satisfy the morbid curiosity of the public, relate all great crimes in extenso, give portraits of the victims, etc., and are often one of the causes of new crimes, by arousing the imitative instinct to be found in man.

As we have seen above the merchant capitalist makes war in two directions; his interests are against those of the man who sells to him, and of the man who buys from him. This is also true of the industrial capitalist. He buys raw materials and sells what he produces. But to arrive at his product he must buy labor, and this purchase is 'sui generis.'

Deprived as he is of the means of production the working-man sells his labor only in order not to die of hunger. The capitalist takes advantage of this necessitous condition of the worker and exploits him. [. . .] Little by little one class of men has become accustomed to think that the others are destined to amass wealth for them and to be subservient to them in every way. Slavery, like the wage system, demoralizes the servant as well as the master. With the master it develops cupidity and the imperious character which sees in a fellow man only a being fit to satisfy his desires. It is true that the capitalist has not the power over the proletarian that the master has over his slave; he has neither the right of service nor the power of life and death, yet it is none the less true that he has another weapon against the proletarian, a weapon whose effect is no less terrible, namely enforced idleness. The fact that the supply of manual labor always greatly exceeds the demand puts this weapon into the hands of every capitalist. It is not only the capitalists who carry on any business that are subjected to this influence, but also all who are salaried in their service.

Capitalism exercises in still a third manner an egoistic influence upon the capitalistic 'entrepreneur'. Each branch has more producers than are necessary. The interests of the capitalists are, then, opposed not only to those of the men from whom they buy or to whom they sell, but also to those of their fellow producers. It is indeed claimed that competition has the effect simply of making the product better and cheaper, but this is looking at the question from only one point of view. The fact which alone affects criminality is that competition forces the participants, under penalty of succumbing, to be as egoistic as possible. Even the producers who have the means of applying all the technical improvements to perfect their product and make it cheaper, are obliged to have recourse to gross deceits in advertising, etc., in order to injure their competitors. Rejoicing at the evil which befalls another, envy at his good fortune, these forms of egoism are the inevitable consequence of competition.

[. . .]

What are the conclusions to be drawn from what has gone before? When we sum up the results that we have obtained it becomes plain that economic conditions occupy a much more important place in the etiology of crime than most authors have given them.

First we have seen that the present economic system and its consequences weaken the social feelings. The basis of the economic system of our day being exchange, the economic interests of men are necessarily found to be in opposition. This is a trait that capitalism has in common with other modes of production. But its principal characteristic is that the means of production are in the hands of a few, and most men are altogether deprived of them. Consequently, persons who do not possess the means of production are forced to sell their labor to those who do, and these, in consequence of their economic preponderance, force them to make the exchange for the mere necessaries of life, and to work as much as their strength permits.

This state of things especially stifles men's social instincts; it develops, on the part of those with power, the spirit of domination, and of insensibility to the ills of others, while it awakens jealousy and servility on the part of those who depend upon them. Further the contrary interests of those who have property, and the idle and luxurious life of some of them, also contribute to the weakening of the social instincts.

The material condition, and consequently the intellectual condition, of the proletariat are also a reason why the moral plane of that class is not high. The work of children brings them into contact with persons to associate with whom is fatal to their morals. Long working hours and monotonous labor brutalize those who are forced into them; bad housing conditions contribute also to debase the moral sense, as do the uncertainty of existence, and finally absolute poverty, the frequent consequence of sickness and unemployment. Ignorance and lack of training of any kind also contribute their quota. Most demoralizing of all is the status of the lower proletariat.

The economic position of woman contributes also to the weakening of the social instincts.

The present organization of the family has great importance as regards criminality. It charges the legitimate parents with the care of the education of the child; the community concerns itself with the matter very little. It follows that a great number of children are brought up by persons who are totally incapable of doing it properly. As regards the children of the proletariat, there can be no question of the education properly so-called, on account of the lack of means and the forced absence of one or both of the parents. The school tends to remedy this state of things, but the results do not go far enough. The harmful consequences of the present organization of the family make themselves felt especially in the case of the children of the lower proletariat, orphans, and illegitimate children. For these the community does but little, though their need of adequate help is the greatest.

Prostitution, alcoholism, and militarism, which result, in the last analysis, from the present social order, are phenomena that have demoralizing consequences.

As to the different kinds of crime, [. . .] the very important group of economic criminality finds its origin on the one side in the absolute poverty and the cupidity brought about by the present economic environment, and on the other in the moral abandonment and bad education of the children of the poorer classes. Then, professional criminals are principally recruited from the class of occasional criminals, who, finding themselves rejected everywhere after their liberation, fall lower and lower. The last group of economic crimes (fraudulent bankruptcy, etc.) is so intimately connected with our present mode of production, that it would not be possible to commit it under another.

The relation between sexual crimes and economic conditions is less direct; nevertheless these also give evidence of the decisive influence of these conditions. We have called attention to the four following points.

First, there is a direct connection between the crime of adultery and the present organization of society, which requires that the legal dissolution of a marriage should be impossible or very difficult.

Second, sexual crimes upon adults are committed especially by unmarried men; and since the number of marriages depends in its turn upon the economic situation, the connection is clear; and those who commit these crimes are further almost exclusively illiterate, coarse, raised in an environment almost without sexual morality, and regard the sexual life from the wholly animal side.

Third, the causes of sexual crime upon children are partly the same as those of which we have been speaking, with the addition of prostitution.

Fourth, alcoholism greatly encourages sexual assaults.

As to the relation between crimes of vengeance and the present constitution of society, [. . .] it produces conflicts without number; statistics have shown that those who commit them are almost without exception poor and uncivilized, and that alcoholism is among the most important causes of these crimes.

Infanticide is caused in part by poverty, and in part by the opprobrium incurred by the unmarried mother (an opprobrium resulting from the social utility of marriage).

Political criminality comes solely from the economic system and its consequences.

Finally, economic and social conditions are also important factors in the etiology of degeneracy, which is in its turn a cause of crime.

Upon the basis of what has gone before, we have a right to say that the part played by economic conditions in criminality is preponderant, even decisive.

This conclusion is of the highest importance for the prevention of crime. If it were principally the consequence of innate human qualities (atavism, for example), the pessimistic conclusion that crime is a phenomenon inseparably bound up with the social life would be well founded. But the facts show that it is rather the optimistic conclusion that we must draw, that where crime is the consequence of economic and social conditions, we can combat it by changing those conditions.

However important crime may be as a social phenomenon, however terrible may be the injuries and the evil that it brings upon humanity, the development of society will not depend upon the question as to what are the conditions which could restrain crime or make it disappear, if possible; the evolution of society will proceed independently of this question.

What is the direction that society will take under these continual modifications? This is not the place to treat fully of this subject. In my opinion the facts indicate quite clearly what the direction will be. The productivity of labor has increased to an unheard of degree, and will assuredly increase in the future. The concentration of the means of production into the hands of a few progresses continually; in many branches it has reached such a degree that the fundamental principle of the present economic system, competition, is excluded, and has been replaced by monopoly. On the other hand the working class is becoming more and more organized, and the opinion is very generally held among working-men that the causes of material and intellectual poverty can be eliminated only by having the means of production held in common.

Supposing that this were actually realized, what would be the consequences as regards criminality? Let us take up this question for a moment. Although we can give only personal opinions as to the details of such a society, the general outlines can be traced with certainty.

The chief difference between a society based upon the community of the means of production and our own is that material poverty would be no longer known. Thus one great part of economic criminality (as also one part of infanticide) would be rendered impossible, and one of the greatest demoralizing forces of our present society would be eliminated. And then, in this way those social phenomena so productive of crime, prostitution and alcoholism would lose one of their principal factors. Child labor and overdriving would no longer take place, and bad housing, the source of much physical and moral evil, would no longer exist.

With material poverty there would disappear also that intellectual poverty which weighs so heavily upon the proletariat; culture would no longer be the privilege of some, but a possession common to all. The consequences of this upon criminality would be very important, for [. . .] even in our present society with its numerous conflicts, the members of the propertied classes, who have often but a veneer of civilization, are almost never guilty of crimes of vengeance. There is the more reason to admit that in a society where interests were not opposed, and where civilization was universal, these crimes would be no longer present, especially since alcoholism also proceeds in large part from the intellectual poverty of the poorer classes. And what is true of crimes of vengeance, is equally true of sexual crimes in so far as they have the same etiology.

A large part of the economic criminality (and also prostitution to a certain extent) has its origin in the cupidity excited by the present economic environment. In a society based upon the community of the means of production, great contrasts of fortune would, like commercial capital, be lacking, and thus cupidity would find no food. These crimes will not totally disappear so long as there has not been a redistribution of property according to the maxim, 'to each according to his needs', something that will probably be realized, but not in the immediate future.

The changes in the position of woman which are taking place in our present society, will lead, under this future mode of production, to her economic independence, and consequently to her social independence as well. It is accordingly probable that the criminality of woman will increase in comparison with that of man during the transition period. But the final result will be the disappearance of the harmful effects of the economic and social preponderance of man.

As to the education of children under these new conditions it is difficult to be definite. However, it is certain that the community will concern itself seriously with their welfare. It will see to it that the children whose parents cannot or will not be responsible for them, are well cared for. By acting in this way it will remove one of the most important causes of crime. There is no doubt that the community will exercise also a strict control over the education of children; it cannot be affirmed, however, that the time will come when the children of a number of parents will be brought up together by capable persons; this will depend principally upon the intensity that the social sentiments may attain.

As soon as the interests of all are no longer opposed to each other, as they are in our present society, there will no longer be a question either of politics ('a fortiori' of political *crimes*) or of militarism.

Such a society will not only remove the causes which now make men egoistic, but will awaken, on the contrary, a strong feeling of altruism. [. . .] In a larger measure this will be realized under a mode of production in common, the interests of all being the same.

In such a society there can be no question of crime properly so called. The eminent criminologist, Manouvrier, in treating of the prevention of crime expresses himself thus: 'The maxim to apply is, act so that every man shall always have more interest in being useful to his fellows than in harming them.' It is precisely in a society where the community of the means of production has been realized that this maxim will obtain its complete application. There will be crimes committed by pathological individuals, but this will come rather within the sphere of the physician than that of the judge. And then we may even reach a state where these cases will decrease in large measure, since the social causes of degeneracy will disappear, and procreation by degenerates be checked through the increased knowledge of the laws of heredity and the increasing sense of moral responsibility.

'It is society that prepares the crime', says the true adage of Quetelet. For all those who have reached this conclusion, and are not insensible to the sufferings of humanity, this statement is sad, but contains a ground of hope. It is sad, because society punishes severely those who commit the crime which she has herself prepared. It contains a ground of hope, since it promises to humanity the possibility of some day delivering itself from one of its most terrible scourges.

# 6

# The normal and the pathological

## Emile Durkheim

[. . .]

If there is any fact whose pathological character appears incontestable, that fact is crime. All criminologists are agreed on this point. Although they explain this pathology differently, they are unanimous in recognizing it. But let us see if this problem does not demand a more extended consideration.

[. . .] Crime is present not only in the majority of societies of one particular species but in all societies of all types. There is no society that is not confronted with the problem of criminality. Its form changes; the acts thus characterized are not the same everywhere; but, everywhere and always, there have been men who have behaved in such a way as to draw upon themselves penal repression. If, in proportion as societies pass from the lower to the higher types, the rate of criminality, i.e., the relation between the yearly number of crimes and the population, tended to decline, it might be believed that crime, while still normal, is tending to lose this character of normality. But we have no reason to believe that such a regression is substantiated. Many facts would seem rather to indicate a movement in the opposite direction. From the beginning of the [nineteenth] century, statistics enable us to follow the course of criminality. It has everywhere increased. In France the increase is nearly 300 per cent. There is, then, no phenomenon that presents more indisputably all the symptoms of normality, since it appears closely connected with the conditions of all collective life. To make of crime a form of social morbidity would be to admit that morbidity is not something accidental, but, on the contrary, that in certain cases it grows out of the fundamental constitution of the living organism; it would result in wiping out all distinction between the physiological and the pathological. No doubt it is possible that crime itself will have abnormal forms, as, for example, when its rate is unusually high. This excess is, indeed, undoubtedly morbid in nature. What is normal, simply, is the existence of criminality, provided that it attains and does not exceed, for each social type, a certain level [. . .]

Here we are, then, in the presence of a conclusion in appearance quite paradoxical. Let us make no mistake. To classify crime among the phenomena of normal sociology is not to say merely that it is an inevitable, although regrettable phenomenon, due to the incorrigible wickedness of men; it is to affirm that it is a factor in public health, an integral part of all healthy societies. This result is, at first glance, surprising enough to have puzzled even ourselves for a long time. Once this first surprise has been overcome,

Abridged from *The Rules of Sociological Method*, pp. 65-73. (New York: Free Press, 1964. First published 1895.)

however, it is not difficult to find reasons explaining this normality and at the same time confirming it.

In the first place crime is normal because a society exempt from it is utterly impossible. Crime [. . .] consists of an act that offends certain very strong collective sentiments. In a society in which criminal acts are no longer committed, the sentiments they offend would have to be found without exception in all individual consciousnesses, and they must be found to exist with the same degree as sentiments contrary to them. Assuming that this condition could actually be realized, crime would not thereby disappear; it would only change its form, for the very cause which would thus dry up the sources of criminality would immediately open up new ones.

Indeed, for the collective sentiments which are protected by the penal law of a people at a specified moment of its history to take possession of the public conscience or for them to acquire a stronger hold where they have an insufficient grip, they must acquire an intensity greater than that which they had hitherto had. The community as a whole must experience them more vividly, for it can acquire from no other source the greater force necessary to control these individuals who formerly were the most refractory. For murderers to disappear, the horror of bloodshed must become greater in those social strata from which murderers are recruited; but, first it must become greater throughout the entire society. Moreover, the very absence of crime would directly contribute to produce this horror; because any sentiment seems much more respectable when it is always and uniformly respected.

One easily overlooks the consideration that these strong states of the common consciousness cannot be thus reinforced without reinforcing at the same time the more feeble states, whose violation previously gave birth to mere infraction of convention – since the weaker ones are only the pro-longation, the attenuated form, of the stronger. Thus robbery and simple bad taste injure the same single altruistic sentiment, the respect for that which is another's. However, this same sentiment is less grievously offended by bad taste than by robbery; and since, in addition, the average consciousness has not sufficient intensity to react keenly to the bad taste, it is treated with greater tolerance. That is why the person guilty of bad taste is merely blamed, whereas the thief is punished. But, if this sentiment grows stronger, to the point of silencing in all consciousnesses the inclination which disposes man to steal, he will become more sensitive to the offenses which, until then, touched him but lightly. He will react against them, then, with more energy; they will be the object of greater opprobrium, which will transform certain of them from the simple moral faults that they were and give them the quality of crimes. For example, improper contracts, or contracts improperly executed, which only incur public blame or civil damages, will become offenses in law.

Imagine a society of saints, a perfect cloister of exemplary individuals. Crimes, properly so called, will there be unknown; but faults which appear venial to the layman will create there the same scandal that the ordinary offense does in ordinary consciousnesses. If, then, this society has the power to judge and punish, it will define these acts as criminal and will treat them as such. For the same reason, the perfect and upright man judges his smallest failings with a severity that the majority reserve for acts more truly in the nature of an offense. Formerly, acts of violence against persons were more frequent than they are today, because respect for individual dignity was less strong. As this has increased, these crimes have become more rare; and also, many acts violating this sentiment have been introduced into the penal law which were not included there in primitive times.

In order to exhaust all the hypotheses logically possible, it will perhaps be asked why this unanimity does not extend to all collective sentiments without exception. Why should not even the most feeble sentiment gather enough energy to prevent all dissent? The moral consciousness of the society would be present in its entirety in all the individuals, with a vitality sufficient to prevent all acts offending it – the purely conventional faults as well as the crimes. But a uniformity so universal and absolute is utterly impossible; for the immediate physical milieu in which each one of us is placed, the hereditary antecedents, and the social influences vary from one individual to the next, and consequently diversify consciousnesses. It is impossible for all to be alike, if only because each one has his own organism and that these organisms occupy different areas in space. That is why, even among the lower peoples, where individual originality is very little developed, it nevertheless does exist.

Thus, since there cannot be a society in which the individuals do not differ more or less from the collective type, it is also inevitable that, among these divergences, there are some with a criminal character. What confers this character upon them is not the intrinsic quality of a given act but that definition which the collective conscience lends them. If the collective conscience is stronger, if it has enough authority practically to suppress these divergences, it will also be more sensitive, more exacting; and, reacting against the slightest deviations with the energy it otherwise displays only against more considerable infractions, it will attribute to them the same gravity as formerly to crimes. In other words, it will designate them as criminal.

Crime is, then, necessary; it is bound up with the fundamental conditions of all social life, and by that very fact it is useful, because these conditions of which it is a part are themselves indispensable to the normal evolution of morality and law.

Indeed, it is no longer possible today to dispute the fact that law and morality vary from one social type to the next, nor that they change within the same type if the conditions of life are modified. But, in order that these transformations may be possible, the collective sentiments at the basis of morality must not be hostile to change, and consequently must have but moderate energy. If they were too strong, they would no longer be plastic. Every pattern is an obstacle to new patterns, to the extent that the first pattern is inflexible. The better a structure is articulated, the more it offers a healthy resistance to all modification; and this is equally true of functional, as of anatomical, organization. If there were no crimes, this condition could not have been fulfilled; for such a hypothesis presupposes that collective sentiments have arrived at a degree of intensity unexampled in history. Nothing is good indefinitely and to an unlimited extent. The authority which the moral conscience enjoys must not be excessive; otherwise no one would dare criticize it, and it would too easily congeal into an immutable form. To make progress, individual originality must be able to express itself. In order that the originality of the idealist whose dreams transcend his century may find expression, it is necessary that the originality of the criminal, who is below the level of his time, shall also be possible. One does not occur without the other.

Nor is this all. Aside from this indirect utility, it happens that crime itself plays a useful role in this evolution. Crime implies not only that the way remains open to necessary changes but that in certain cases it directly prepares these changes. Where crime exists, collective sentiments are sufficiently flexible to take on a new form, and crime sometimes helps to determine the form they will take. How many times, indeed, it is only an anticipation of future morality – a step toward what will be! According to Athenian law, Socrates was a criminal, and his condemnation was no more than just. However, his crime, namely, the independence of his thought, rendered a service not only to humanity but to his country. It served to prepare a new morality and faith which the Athenians needed, since the traditions by which they had lived until then were no longer in harmony with the current conditions of life. Nor is the case of Socrates unique; it is reproduced periodically in history. It would never have been possible to establish the freedom of thought we now enjoy if the regulations prohibiting it had not been violated before being solemnly abrogated. At that time, however, the violation was a crime, since it was an offense against sentiments still very keen in the average conscience. And yet this crime was useful as a prelude to reforms which daily became more necessary. Liberal philosophy had as its precursors the heretics of all kinds who were justly punished by secular authorities during the entire course of the Middle Ages and until the eve of modern times.

From this point of view the fundamental facts of criminality present themselves to us in an entirely new light. Contrary to current ideas, the criminal no longer seems a totally unsociable being, a sort of parasitic element, a strange and unassimilable body, introduced into the midst of society. On the contrary, he plays a definite role in social life. Crime, for its part, must no longer be conceived as an evil that cannot be too much suppressed. There is no occasion for self-congratulation when the crime rate drops noticeably below the average level, for we may be certain that this apparent progress is associated with some social disorder. Thus, the number of assault cases never falls so low as in times of want. With the drop in the crime rate, and as a reaction to it, comes a revision, or the need of a revision in the theory of punishment. If, indeed, crime is a disease, its punishment is its remedy and cannot be otherwise conceived; thus, all the discussions it arouses bear on the point of determining what the punishment must be in order to fulfil this role of remedy. If crime is not pathological at all, the object of punishment cannot be to cure it, and its true function must be sought elsewhere.

[. . .]

# 7

# Law and authority

*Peter Kropotkin*


If one studies the millions of laws that rule humanity, one can see easily that they are divisible into three main categories: protection of property, protection of government, protection of persons. And in analysing these three categories one comes to the same conclusion regarding each of them: *the uselessness and harmfulness of the law*.

As for the protection of property, the socialists know what that means. Laws regarding property are not fashioned to guarantee either individuals or society the fruits of their labour. They are made, on the contrary, to pilfer from the producer part of what he produces and to assure to the few whatever they have pilfered, either from the producers or from society as a whole. When the law established the right of Sir Such-and-Such over a house, for example, it established his right, not over a cabin that he might have built himself, nor over a house he might have erected with the help of a few friends; nobody would dispute his right if such had been the case. The law, on the contrary, established his rights over a mansion that *is not* the product of his labour, first because he has had it built by others, whom he has not paid the true value of their work, and next because his mansion represents a social value he could not produce on his own: the law establishes his rights over a portion of that which belongs to everybody and not to anyone in particular. The same house, built in the beautiful heart of Siberia, would not have the value it has in a large city. Its value derives, as we know, from the works of fifty generations who have built the city, adorned it, provided it with water and gas, with fine boulevards, universities, theatres and shops, with railways and roads radiating in all directions.

Thus in recognizing the rights of Sir Such-and-Such over a house in Paris, in London, in Rouen, the law appropriates to him – unjustly – a certain part of the products of the work of all humanity. And it is precisely because that appropriation is a crying injustice (all other forms of property have the same character) that it has needed a whole arsenal of laws and a whole army of soldiers, policemen and judges to sustain it, against the good sense and the feeling of justice that is inherent in humanity.

Thus the greater part of our laws – the civil codes of all countries – have no other object than to maintain this appropriation, this monopoly to the profit of a few against the whole of humanity. Three-quarters of the cases judged by the tribunals are merely quarrels that have cropped up among monopolists; two robbers quarrelling over the booty. And a great part of our

From *Words of a Rebel* (trans. G. Woodcock), pp. 159–64. (Montreal/New York: Black Rose Books, 1992. First published 1898.)

criminal laws have the same aim, since their object is to keep the worker in a position subordinate to the employer, to assure to one the exploitation of the other.

As to guaranteeing the producer the product of his work, there are not even any laws that provide it. That is so simple and so natural, so much in accordance with human customs and habits that the law has not even dreamed of it. Open brigandage, with arms in hand, no longer exists in our century; a worker need no longer dispute with another worker over the products of their toil; if there is some failure of understanding between them, they deal with it without having recourse to the law, by calling in a third party, and if there is anyone who insists on requiring from another person a part of what he has produced, it can only be the property-owner, coming to claim his lion's share. As to humanity in general, it respects everywhere the right of each person over what he has produced, without the need to have any special laws to cover it.

All these laws about property, which make up the great volumes of codes and are the delight of our lawyers, have no object but that of protecting the unjust appropriation of the work of humanity by certain monopolists, and thus have no reason to exist; and socialist revolutionaries are determined to make them vanish on the day of the revolution. We can, in fact and in full justice, make a great bonfire of *all* the laws that are related to the so-called 'rights of property', of all the property titles, of all the archives – in brief, of all that has reference to an institution which soon will be considered a blot on the history of humanity as humiliating as slavery and serfdom in past centuries.

What we have just said about the laws concerning property applies completely to the second category of laws – the laws that maintain the government – constitutional laws, in other words.

Once again there is a whole arsenal of laws, decrees, or ordinances, this time serving to protect the various forms of representative government – by delegation or usurpation – under which human societies struggle for existence. We know very well – the anarchists have often demonstrated it by their incessant criticism of the various forms of government – that the mission of *all* governments, monarchical, constitutional and republican, is to protect and maintain by force the privileges of the owning classes: aristocracy, priesthood and bourgeoisie. A good third of our laws, the 'fundamental' laws, laws on taxes, customs duties, on the organization of ministries and their chancelleries, on the army, the police, the church, etc. – and there are tens of thousands of them in every country – have no other end but to maintain, keep in repair and develop the governmental machine, which in its turn serves almost entirely to protect the privileges of these possessing classes. Analyse all these laws, observe them in action from day to day, and you will see that there is not a single one worth keeping, beginning with those that bound the communes hand and foot to the parson, the local merchant and the governmental boss, and ending with that famous constitution (the nineteenth or twentieth since 1789), which gives us a chamber of dunces and petty speculators ready for the dictatorship of any adventurer who comes along, for the rule of some crowned cabbage-head.

Briefly, regarding these laws there can be no doubt. Not only the anarchists, but also the more or less revolutionary middle class are in agreement on this: that the best use one can make of the laws concerning the organization of government is to burn them in a bonfire celebrating their end.

There remains the first category of laws, the most important, because most of the prejudices cluster around them; the laws regarding the protection of persons, the punishment and prevention of 'crimes'. If the law enjoys a certain consideration, it is because people believe this category of laws absolutely indispensable for the security of the individual in society. Laws have developed from the nucleus of customs that were useful for human societies and were exploited by the rulers to sanction their domination. The authority of the chiefs of the tribes, of the rich families of the communes, and of the kind, were supported by the function of judges which they exercised, and even to the present, when people talk of the need for government, it is its function of supreme judge that is implied. 'Without government, people would strangle each other', says the village wiseacre. 'The ultimate end of society is to give every accused person twelve honest jurors', said Edmund Burke.

But despite all the presuppositions that exist on this subject, it is high time the anarchists loudly declared that this category of the laws is as useless and harmful as the rest.

First of all, when we consider the so-called 'crimes', the attacks against the persons, it is well known that two-thirds or even three-quarters of them are inspired by the desire to lay hold of somebody's wealth. That immense category of so-called 'crimes and misdemeanours' would disappear on the day private property ceased to exist.

'But', we shall be told, 'there will still be the brutes who make attempts on the lives of citizens, who strike with the knife in every quarrel, who avenge the least offence by a murder, if there are not laws to restrain them and punishments to hold them back.' This is the refrain that has been sung to us ever since we expressed doubt of society's right to punish. Yet one fact has been clearly established: the severity of punishments in no way diminishes the number of crimes. You can hang, draw and quarter the murderers as much as you like, but the number of murders will not diminish. On the other hand, if you abolish the death penalty there will not be a single murder more. Statisticians and legists know that when the severity of the penal code is lessened there is never an increase in the number of attempts against the lives of citizens. On the other hand, when the crops are abundant, when bread is cheap and the weather is good, the number of murders decreases at once. It is proved by statistics that the number of crimes increases and declines in relation to the price of necessities and to good or bad weather. Not that all murders are inspired by hunger. Far from it; but when the harvests are good and necessities are affordably priced, people are happy and less wretched than usual, and they do not let themselves be led away by dark passions that tempt them to stick knives into the chests of their neighbours for futile reasons.

Besides, it is well known that fear of punishment has not halted a single murderer. Whoever is about to kill his neighbour for vengeance or poverty does not reflect a great deal on the consequences; there has never been a murderer who lacked the firm conviction that he would escape from prosecution. Let anyone think about this subject, let him analyse crimes and punishments, their motives and consequences, and if he knows how to reason without letting himself be influenced by preconceived ideas, he is bound to reach this conclusion:

'Without considering a society where people will receive a better education, where the development of all their faculties and the possibility of using them will give men and women so much pleasure that they would not risk it all by indulging in murder, without considering that future society, and taking into account only our present society, with the sad products of poverty we see everywhere in the low taverns of the cities, the number of murders would not increase in any way if one day it were decided that no punishment be inflicted on murderers; indeed it is very likely there would be a fall in the number of cases involving recidivists, brutalized in the prisons.'

We are told constantly of the benefits of the law and of the salutary effects of punishment. But has anyone ever tried to establish a balance between the benefits that are attributed to the law and its penalties, and the degrading effect of those penalties on humanity? One has merely to consider the accumulation of evil passions that are awakened among the spectators by the atrocious punishments inflicted publicly in our streets and squares. Who is it that has thus fostered and developed the instincts of cruelty among humanity (instincts unknown to the animals, man having become the most cruel animal on earth), if it is not the king, the judge and the priest, armed by the law, who had flesh torn away by strips, with burning pitch poured into the wounds, had limbs dislocated, bones broken, men sawn in two, so as to maintain their authority? You need merely consider the torrent of depravity let loose in human societies by spying and informing, encouraged by judges and paid for by the government in hard cash under the pretext of assisting the discovery of crimes. You need only to go into prisons and observe there what the man becomes who is deprived of liberty and thrust among other depraved beings permeated with all the corruption and vice that breed in our prisons today, to realize that the more they are 'reformed', the more detestable the prisons become, our modern and model penitentiaries being a hundred times more corrupting than the dungeons of the Middle Ages. Finally, you need only consider what corruption and deprivation of the mind is generated among humankind by these ideas of *obedience* (essence of the law), of punishment, of authority having the right to punish and judge apart from the urgings of conscience, by all the functions of executioners, jailers and informers – in brief by all that immense apparatus of law and authority. You have only to consider all that, and you will certainly be in agreement with us, when we say that law and its penalties are abominations that should cease to exist.

Meanwhile, people who are not ruled by police, and because of that are less imbued by authoritarian prejudices, have perfectly understood that someone called a 'criminal' is simply an unfortunate; that it is not a question of whipping or chaining him, or causing his death on the scaffold or in prison, but of succouring him by the most brotherly care, by treating him as an equal and taking him to live among honest people. And we hope the coming revolution will resound with this call:

'Burn the guillotines, demolish the prisons, drive away the judge, the policeman, the spy – an impure race if ever there was one – but treat as a brother him who has been led by passion to do ill to his kind; above all deprive the truly great criminals, those ignoble products of bourgeois idleness, of the possibility of parading their vices in seductive form, and you can be sure that we shall no longer have more than a very small number of crimes to point to in our society. Apart from idleness, what sustains crime is law and authority; the laws on property, the laws on government, the laws with their penalties and punishments. And Authority, which takes on itself to make these laws and apply them.

'No more laws! No more judges! Freedom, Brotherhood and the practice of Solidarity are the only effective bulwark we can raise to the anti-social instincts of a few among us.'

# 8

# British criminology before 1935

## David Garland

### I

[. . .]

By convention, modern scientific criminology is said to have begun with Lombroso's criminal anthropology in the 1870s, and in one sense this is true enough, since it was the impact of Lombroso which sparked off the international congresses and debates of the 1880s and brought the idea of a criminological science to public prominence for the first time. But criminology in Britain did not develop out of the Lombrosian tradition. Nor did it derive from the European movement, despite the way in which Edwardian penal reforms appeared to follow its lead – even despite the fact that it would later be a group of European *émigrés* who did most to establish an academic profession of criminologists in this country. In fact the scientific approach to crime and punishment was not something which Britain reluctantly imported from abroad. On the contrary, there existed in Britain, from the 1860s onward, a distinctive, indigenous tradition of applied medico-legal science which was sponsored by the penal and psychiatric establishments, and it was this tradition which formed the theoretical and professional space within which 'criminological science' was first developed in this country. If we are to understand criminology and its social foundations it is important not to confuse these two traditions, or to collapse one onto the other. In particular, we should avoid assuming that any criminological work which is 'positivist' in style is somehow derived from the 'Scuola Positiva' of Lombroso. Much of the early British criminology which I will describe falls into the broad epistemological and methodological categories which we nowadays call 'positivist' – but it had little to do with Lombroso's Positivism, nor indeed with that of Comte.

Lombrosian criminology grew, somewhat accidentally, out of an anthropological concern to study man and his natural varieties. The identification of human types led Lombroso and others to isolate such types as the genius, the insane, the epileptoid and the criminal, and to subject them to scientific scrutiny and categorization. To some extent this was effectively the redescription in scientific language of distinctions which were already established in cultural terms, and certainly the excitement which followed Lombroso's identification of 'the born criminal' occurred because his work allowed a spectacular convergence between human science and the concerns of social policy. His differentiation of 'the criminal type' chimed with deep-rooted

Abridged from *The British Journal of Criminology*, 1988, 28(2): 1–17.

cultural prejudice and also with the real processes of differentiation which were then being established by the expanding prison system, so that the apparent policy implications of Lombroso's work immediately became a focus for widespread attention. But although Lombroso was well aware of the social policy relevance of his anthropology, and took pains to promote it, he was not, at first, particularly well informed about the practical realities of crime and punishment. In consequence, his penology was not just radical and at odds with current practices: it was also naive and uninformed, demonstrating a lack of familiarity with the normal range of offenders and with the institutions which dealt with them. In fact it is clear that Lombroso had developed his conception of the criminal type more out of theoretical commitment than from practical experience or observation. And although exposure to criticism and his increasing involvement in penal affairs eventually led him to amend his initial framework, and to tone down his more outrageous propositions, it was the clear and unqualified claims of his early work which continued to define the Lombrosian tradition, particularly for those who viewed it from afar.

The psychiatric and medico-legal framework within which Britain developed its early criminological science was different from the Lombrosian tradition in a number of important respects. Unlike anthropology, psychiatry was not concerned to isolate discrete types of human individuals and classify them by means of racial and constitutional differences. Instead, it was a therapeutically oriented discipline based upon a classification system of psychiatric disorders which, like the disease model of nineteenth century medicine, discussed the condition separately from the individual in whom it might be manifested. Within the classification system of morbid psychology there were a variety of conditions which criminals were typically said to exhibit – insanity, moral insanity, degeneracy, feeble-mindedness, etc. But generally speaking, *the* criminal was not conceived as *a* psychological type. Instead the spectrum of psychiatric conditions might be usefully applied to a part of the criminal population: there was no separate criminal psychology or psychiatry, based upon ontological difference.

But more important than this *theoretical* difference was the way in which British psychiatry contrasted with Lombrosian anthropology in its *practical* commitments and its relationship to the institutions of criminal justice. Theorizing about the condition of criminals was not done in the abstract, but instead was linked to professional tasks such as the giving of psychiatric evidence before a court of law, or the decisions as to classification, diagnosis and regimen which prison medical officers made on a daily basis. This practical experience was crucial in shaping the psychiatric approach to criminological issues because it ensured that psychiatrists and prison medics were well aquainted with the day to day realities of criminal justice and with the need to bring psychiatric propositions into line with the demands of courts and prison authorities.

[. . .]

The British tradition of scientific thinking about criminals was thus, from an early age, situated within an institutional framework which had the support of the prison establishment and the prestige of medicine behind it. Partly in consequence, it was generally modest in its claims, and very respectful of the requirements of institutional regimes and legal principles. As far as most prison doctors and experienced psychiatrists were concerned, the majority of criminals were more or less normal individuals; only a minority required psychiatric treatment, and this usually involved removing them from the penal system and into institutions for the mentally ill or defective. And although the diagnostic and therapeutic claims of psychiatry changed over time, from an early stage there was a recognition that, for the mainstream of offenders, the normal processes of law and punishment should apply. Compared to the sweeping claims of criminal anthropology, the psychiatric tradition was, by the 1880s, somewhat conservative in appearance.

But conservative or not (and here it depends on point of view) it was within this framework that most scientific-criminological work was done in Britain up until the middle of the twentieth century. It is, for example, almost exclusively within the Reports of the Medical Commissioner of Prisons and of the various Prison Medical Officers that one will find any official discussion of criminological science in the period before 1935. Similarly, most of the major scientific works on crime, written in Britain before 1935, were written by medics with psychiatric training and positions within the prison service, among them J.F. Sutherland (1908), R.F. Quinton (1910), J. Devon (1912), M. Hamblin Smith (1922), W.C. Sullivan (1924) and W. Norwood East (1927).

The first university lectures in 'Criminology' delivered in this country – given at Birmingham by Maurice Hamblin Smith from the 1921/1922 session onwards – were directed to postgraduate medical students within a course entitled 'Medical Aspects of Crime and Punishment', and long before Mannheim began teaching at the London School of Economics (LSE) in 1935 there were courses on 'Crime and Insanity' offered at London University by senior prison medical officers such as Sullivan and East.

As for professional journals, although there was no specialist periodical devoted to criminology before 1950 (if one excludes the crime enthusiast's magazine *The Criminologist*, one issue of which appeared in 1927), a variety of medical and psychiatric journals devoted regular sections to issues of criminological science, above all the *Journal of Mental Science* (JMS), which had a criminological review section and regular articles, and the *Transactions* of the Medico-Legal Association, which from 1933, was renamed *The Medico-Legal and Criminological Review*. In contrast, journals such as *The Sociological Review*, which would later become an important outlet for criminological publications, carried nothing substantial on the subject from its inception in 1908 until the first British publications of Mannheim and Radzinowicz in the late 1930s.

[. . .]

## II

The British tradition of institutionally based, administratively oriented criminology was, by its nature, a dynamic, evolving tradition. The 'criminological' texts which it generated grew out of practical contexts which were forever changing, since institutions continually redefined their operations and took on new concerns, and also because new methods, theories and techniques became available to the professionals responsible for administering them.

Much of the nineteenth century criminology, in this sphere, had grown out of the reclassification of selected offenders as being primarily psychiatric cases, rather than criminal ones, either because of moral insanity, or later, because of the less severe but more widespread diagnosis of feeble-mindedness. Underlying this process and the theoretical texts it produced was, of course, the institutional division between the asylum and the prison, or more broadly, between medicine and law. After about 1895 this simple division began to be reformulated to accommodate the much more complex world of penal-welfare institutions, with its more refined classifications and selection procedures, and the allocation of offenders to a greatly extended range of institutions and regimes. One result of this was an important extension of the specialist's role within the system, and a corresponding increase in the production of criminological literature which theorized those new diagnostic and classificatory tasks and the principles upon which they should be based. Such work as *Alcoholism* (1906) by W.C. Sullivan, *Recidivism* (1908) by J.F. Sutherland, *The Psychology of the Criminal* (1922) by M. Hamblin Smith and 'The Psychology of Crime' (1932) by H.E. Field are significant examples of criminological work derived from this developing context.

In 1919, the new penological emphasis upon individual character and specialized treatment – together with concerns about the large numbers of shell-shocked and mentally disturbed men returning from the War – led the Birmingham Justices to establish a permanent scheme for the clinical examination of adult offenders who came before the courts. Previously such work had been done on an occasional, *ad hoc* basis, and depended upon the skill and interest of the local prison doctor. By appointing M. Hamblin Smith and W.A. Potts, both psychiatrically trained prison medics, and charging them with these new duties, the Justices (together with the Prison Commission) effectively created a new specialism for applied criminology. Before long, Potts, and particularly Hamblin Smith, were adapting the standard forms of mental tests for use in this specialist area, publishing the results of their clinical studies, and writing extensively about the need for this kind of investigation and its implications for the treatment and prevention of crime. In *The Psychology of the Criminal* (1922) and in a series of articles in the JMS, The Howard Journal and elsewhere, Smith emphasized the importance of criminological study, though for him this meant the kind of clinical examination of individuals which the Birmingham scheme employed. As Britain's first authorized teacher of 'criminology', and the first individual to go under the title of 'criminologist', it is significant that Smith, too, rejected the search for 'general theories' in favour of the 'study of the individual'. Significantly too, the centres of criminological research and teaching, which he called to be set up in each university town, were envisaged as places where 'young medical graduates' would be trained to become expert in the medical examination and assessment of offenders.

Hamblin Smith was also one of the first criminological workers in Britain to profess an interest in psycho-analysis, which he utilized as a means to assess the personality 'make-up' of offenders, as well as proposing it as a technique for treating the mental conflicts and abnormalities which, he claimed, lay behind the criminal act. In this respect, Smith met with much official opposition, particularly from W. Norwood East, but there were others, outside the establishment, who were more enthusiastic about the role of psycho-analysis. In the winter of 1922–3 Dr Grace Pailthorpe voluntarily assisted Smith in the psycho-analytic investigation of female offenders at Birmingham, and went on to complete a 5-year study at Holloway, funded by a grant from the Medical Research Council (MRC). Her Report – completed by 1929, but delayed by the MRC until 1932 – and its claim that crime was a symptom of mental conflict which might be psycho-analytically resolved, met with some consternation in official circles (see East, 1936: 319) but it excited the interest of a number of analysts and medical psychologists who formed a group to promote the Report and its approach. Out of their meetings emerged the Association for the Scientific Treatment of Criminals (1931), which, in 1932, became the Institute for the Scientific Treatment of Delinquency (ISTD).

In fact most of the founder members of this group were in some way or other involved in the new and expanding out-patient sector of psychiatric work, made possible by the opening of private clinics such as the Tavistock (1921), the Maudsley (1923), the new child guidance centres, and eventually, the ISTD's own Psychopathic Clinic (1933) (later moved and renamed the Portman Clinic (1937)). Once again this new field of practice gave rise to its own distinctive brand of criminological theory. The early publications of the ISTD emphasize the clinical exploration of individual personality, and in that sense are continuous with much previous work. But they also manifest a new preventative emphasis, which reflected the fact that the new clinics operated outside the formal penal system, and could deal with individuals before their disturbed conduct actually became criminal. Eventually the group's emphasis upon psycho-analysis, and its open hostility to much official penal policy, ensured that the ISTD remained essentially outsiders, usually operating at arms length from the Home Office and the Prison Commission. This outsider status forms an important background to the later decision of the Home Office to establish a criminological institute at Cambridge, rather than under ISTD auspices in London, for although 'the formation of such a body was one of the original aims of the ISTD' (Glover, 1950–51: 161–3) the Home Office appears not to have even considered such an option.

Despite its subsequent neglect, the work of W. Norwood East – particularly *Forensic Psychiatry* (1927) and *The Medical Aspects of Crime* (1936) – better represents the mainstream of British criminology in the 1920s and 1930s. East was a psychiatrically trained prison medical officer who became a leading figure in the 1930s as Medical Director on the Prison Commission, and President of the Medico-Legal Society, and his views dominated official policy-making for a lengthy period. East was himself a proponent of a psychological approach to crime, but he viewed its scope as being sharply delimited, and consistently warned against the dangers and absurdities of exaggerating its claims. In 1934, he established an extended experiment at Wormwood Scrubs, whereby those offenders deemed most likely to respond to psychological therapy – particularly sex offenders and arsonists – were subjected to a period of investigation and treatment by Dr W.H. de B. Hubert. At the end of five years, East and Hubert's *Report on the Psychological Treatment of Crime* (1939) re-affirmed East's view that while 80 per cent of offenders were psychologically normal, and would respond to routine punishment, a minority might usefully be investigated and offered psychological treatment. The Report proposed a special institution to deal with such offenders – a proposal which was immediately accepted but not enacted until the opening of Grendon Underwood in 1962. East and Hubert also recommended that this proposed institution should function as a centre for criminological research, and it is significant that here, when a criminological centre is proposed for the first time in an official Report, it should be envisaged as a psychiatric institution, dealing only with a small minority of offenders.

An important departure from this series of clinically based, psychiatric studies, was *The English Convict: A Statistical Study*, by Dr Charles Goring (1913). This work also grew out of institutional routines, insofar as anthropometric measurement was used in prisons for the identification of habitual offenders during the 1890s, but it represented much more than the writing up of daily experience. In fact, in its final, expanded form, the study represents a major development because it signals the use of deliberately undertaken social science research to answer questions posed in institutional practice. The questions taken up here were numerous, and came from a variety of sources. Major Arthur Griffiths had previously suggested that data might be collected to test Lombroso's criminal type hypothesis against the evidence of English prisoners (Radzinowicz and Hood, 1986: 20) and this may have been the original motivation of his name-sake, Dr. G.B. Griffiths, who began the work at Parkhurst Prison in 1901. It was probably a belief that other, useful information could be generated – for example, about the numbers of feeble-minded persons in prison, or the effect of prison diet and conditions upon the physical and mental health of inmates – which led Sir Bryan Donkin and Sir Herbert Smalley, the senior medical staff of the prison system, to take up the research and extend it considerably. The work was completed by Dr Charles Goring, after a lengthy secondment at Karl Pearson's Biometrical laboratory, where he tabulated and analysed a vast quantity of data – motivated, no doubt, by a mixture of scientific curiosity and eugenist commitment.

As its sponsors intended, the study gave a definitive refutation of the old Lombrosian claim that the criminal corresponded to a particular physical type, thus confirming the position which the British authorities had held all along. However Goring's study went much further than this negative finding. In fact, in an important sense Goring's analysis *began* by assuming that there was no criminal type, as such, and although it was not much noticed at the time, his study is chiefly notable for demonstrating a quite new way of conceiving the criminal 'difference'. In the early part of the book, Goring set out extensive theoretical and methodological arguments which insisted that criminality should be viewed not as a qualitative difference of type, marked by anomaly and morbidity, but instead as a variant of normality, differentiated only by degree. Following the arguments of Manouvrier and Topinard, he pointed out that so-called criminal 'anomalies' are only 'more or less extreme degrees of character which in some degree are present in all men'. Moreover, he made it clear that his use of statistical method necessarily presupposed this idea of a criminal characteristic which is a common feature of all individuals, and he went on to name this hypothesized entity 'the criminal diathesis'.

This conception of criminality as normal, rather than morbid or pathological, implied a new basis for criminological science, which Goring vigorously set forth. From now on, criminology could no longer depend upon the clinical gaze of a Lombroso and its impressionistic identification of anomalies. (Goring had, in any case, provided a devastating critique of such methods.) Instead it must be a matter of large populations, careful measurement and statistical analysis, demonstrating patterns of differentiation in the mass which would not be visible in the individual or to the naked eye. His own study, he concluded, had revealed a significant, but by no means universal, association between criminality and two heritable characteristics, namely low intelligence and poor physique.

Although *The English Convict* made a massive impact abroad, and especially in the USA, in Britain it received a surprisingly muted response which dismayed both its author, and his mentor, Karl Pearson. On the one hand, Goring's attack had been centred upon theoretical positions which had little support in this country; and on the other, it appeared to have policy implications – eugenic and otherwise – which were not altogether welcome in official circles. The Prison Commission, while supporting the study's publication as a Blue Book, refused to endorse all of its conclusions. Sir Evelyn Ruggles-Brise provided a preface to the book which took care to render its findings compatible with the official brand of penal reform, while Sir Bryan Donkin (1917) distanced himself from the study altogether, arguing that 'even correct generalizations . . . concerning convicted criminals in the mass are not likely to be of much positive value in the study or treatment of individuals . . .'. In much the same way W.C. Sullivan, the medical superintendent of Broadmoor, argued in *Crime and Insanity* (1924) that clinical rather than statistical methods were the only reliable means to obtaining useful, policy relevant knowledge. Nevertheless, Goring's major argument – for the importance of statistical method in criminological research – was, in the long term, taken up by the British authorities. By the end of the 1930s, the Prison Commission and the Home Office had each embarked upon large-scale, statistically based projects – eventually published as East (1942) and Carr-Saunders *et al.* (1942) – and this became the characteristic form of government-sponsored research in the years after 1945.

*The English Convict* was a transitional work. Its conception of criminality as continuous with normal conduct, together with its statistical sophistication, opened up new research questions and methods for their solution, and gave British criminological work a scope and rigour which it had not possessed before. However its extensive engagement with older questions about 'criminal types' and 'physical anomalies' meant that for much of the book its language and concepts were those of a pre-modern idiom – an idiom which, even in 1913, was not much spoken in this country. A mark of the book's success is that this idiom quickly became archaic, even in places such as the USA where it had once been strong.
[. . .]


## III


[. . .]
This essay has concentrated upon some of the earlier work which helped prepare a social and institutional space for criminology in Britain. In particular it has discussed the institutionally linked psychiatric tradition, which can be seen as the crucial route by which the idea of a scientific approach to criminals became implanted – however marginally – in penal practice, in the courts, and in the policy thinking of governmental authorities. To some extent this might be seen as the 'official criminology' of the period. It did not represent a general theory of crime, or even a full research programme which might produce one, and it would later be unpopular with academics for precisely that reason. But, as I have stressed, this tradition had no such ambition. Its goal was not general theory but instead particular understanding for specific, practical purposes, and it was bound to conflict with the intellectual ambitions of academic criminology in the 1950s, just as it had done with the continental work of the 1880s.

Criminologists in Britain, before the development of a university-based profession, were characteristically practitioners. In so far as they had an expertise or a knowledge-base it was a detailed knowledge of the institutional terrain and its requirements, together with a general training in medicine or psychiatry, and later, psychology. It was this practical surface of emergence which largely accounts for the individualized, policy-based and theoretically limited criminology which was characteristic of Britain before 1935.
[. . .]

## References

Carr-Saunders, A., Mannheim, H. and Rhodes, E.C. (1942) *Young Offenders*. London.

Devon, J. (1912) *The Criminal and the Community*. London.

Donkin, H.B. (1917) 'Notes on mental defect in criminals', *JMS*, LXIII.

East, W. Norwood (1927) *An Introduction to Forensic Psychiatry in the Criminal Courts*. London.

East, W. Norwood (1936) *The Medical Aspects of Crime*. London.

East, W. Norwood (1936a) Obituary of M. Hamblin Smith, *JMS*, LXXXII.

East, W. Norwood and Hubert, W.H. de B. (1939) *Report on the Psychological Treatment of Crime*. HMSO, London.

East, W. Norwood (1942) *The Adolescent Criminal: a Medico-Sociological Study of 4,000 Male Adolescents*. London.

Field, H.E. (1932) 'The psychology of crime: the place of psychology in the treatment of delinquents', *British Journal of Medical Psychology*, 12: 241–56.

Glover, E. (1950–51) Obituary of Dr E.T. Jensen, *British Journal of Delinquency*, 1.

Goring, C. (1913) *The English Convict: A Statistical Study*. London.

Quinton, R.F. (1910) *Crime and Criminals 1876–1910*. London.

Radzinowicz, L. (1961) *In Search of Criminology*. London.

Radzinowicz, L. and Hood, R. (1986) *History of the English Criminal Law*, vol. 5.

Smith, M. Hamblin (1922) *The Psychology of the Criminal*. London.

Smith, M. Hamblin (1922) 'The medical examination of delinquents', *JMS*, LXVIII.

Sullivan, W.C. (1906) *Alcoholism*. London.

Sullivan, W.C. (1924) *Crime and Insanity*. London.

Sutherland, J.F. (1908) *Recidivism: Habitual Criminality and Habitual Petty Delinquency*. Edinburgh.

# PART TWO
# THE PROBLEM OF CRIME I:
# CAUSATION

---

# Introduction

The search for the causes of crime has formed the bedrock of most criminological studies, at least up to the 1970s. Since then, the question of causation has been critiqued by a variety of radical criminologies more concerned to reveal how 'crime' and 'the criminal' are constructed through processes of law creation and enforcement (see Part Three); and more recently has been dismissed as a fruitless and failed exercise which distracts attention away from the more pressing tasks of crime management, crime prevention and policy analysis (see Part Four). It is common for many contemporary criminologists to claim that studies of the aetiology of crime are in terminal decline.

However, this selection of readings should reveal that this is not necessarily the case. The selection has been governed by two main criteria. First, to illustrate the diverse schools of thought which make claim to the theorization of the causes of crime, and secondly, to establish that each of these schools has retained a strong contemporary presence. For this reason, rather than reprinting the classic statements of crime causation (such as Merton's anomie theory or the Chicago School's notion of social disorganization in the 1930s), we have chosen to focus upon a body of theoretical and empirical work which has emerged in the 1980s and 1990s. Some of this work is innovative; much of it marks a reworking or critical development of earlier positions.

If Lombroso's work established a need to examine the biological bases of criminality, then the extract reproduced here from Mednick, Gabrielli and Hutchings represents its modern and more sophisticated version. Based on a detailed study of adoptees, their biological parents and adoptive parents, they make the claim that some genetic and biological factors are transmitted through the generations of some families and that these factors must be involved in the aetiology of at least some criminal behaviour. Eysenck's reiteration and reinforcement of his 1964 theory, that certain personality traits are likely to lead to a greater propensity towards anti-social behaviour, shares some of these concerns. However, biology alone, he argues, is an insufficient explanation. Eysenck's work is more concerned to reveal the impact of interrelationships between genetic factors and processes of socialization.

Whilst Mednick et al. and Eysenck are included here to illustrate those theories concerned with the individual basis of criminality, the following extracts are more concerned to explore the relevance of geographical place and economic factors. Bottoms and Wiles suggest some ways in which micro (individual) and macro (social structure) levels of analysis might be combined (through the adoption of Giddens's structuration theory) in order to reach a more adequate understanding of the impact of space/time/sense of location on particular rates of crime. Field's work establishes that such rates appear to be dramatically influenced by cycles of economic growth and recession. In what was at the time a serious embarrassment to a Conservative administration intent on disclaiming any economic causes of crime, this Home Office research concludes that since 1950 the annual growth in property crime provides a mirror image of annual declines in personal consumption. Notwithstanding such a seemingly incontrovertible conclusion, the British government was (and remains) more persuaded by counter arguments from the likes of the American political adviser Charles Murray. He argues forcibly that rising crime rates are caused by the growth of an underclass – identified primarily by illegitimacy, family breakdown and welfare dependence. In his view the growth in crime is directly related to increasing numbers of barbaric young men who have grown up without the civilizing institution of marriage and without the moral awareness brought about through family responsibilities.

If Murray represents one strand (amongst many) of a contemporary conservative criminology, the extract from Lea and Young represents a response from some sections of the left. Adopting a position of left realism, they argue that the key to crime is not absolute deprivation, or unemployment, but relative deprivation. Crime occurs when there is an excess of expectations over opportunities for fulfilling them. The extract here from *What Is to Be Done about Law and Order?* explores how the Left can regain some of the political initiative on matters of law and order by adopting a middle ground which neither claims that crime is caused by abject poverty nor that it is a freely chosen activity on the part of the wicked. Rather it stems from economic and political discontent and an absence of economic and political opportunities.

The extract from Katz's *Seductions of Crime* eschews all reference to factors of individual or social structural causation. In what has emerged as one of the most controversial criminological texts of the 1990s, he explores (and exposes) our prevailing and continual fascination with crime; as news, as excitement, as lived experience. Critiqued by the Right for being overly concerned with the criminal's own point of view and by the Left for assuming the existence of some latent human evil, Katz's argument is likely to remain influential in his insistence that all of us (and especially governments) readily engage in activities which at other times and in other places we would unhesitatingly describe as being 'criminal'.

The final selections from Klein and Segal are designed to introduce the reader to an even more complex range of issues which are raised through interrogations of the relationship between crime and gender. Klein provides a thorough critique of many of the early criminologies (such as Lombroso – see Part One) not only for their relative neglect of the criminality of women but also for their implicit or explicit assumptions about the inherent nature of women. Thus traditionally female crime has been analysed in terms of sexuality, biological drives, inferiority, deceit and mental instability. Above all, many of the concepts applied to male crime, such as those derived from economic and social determinism, are notably lacking in analyses of female crime. For example, economic offences such as shoplifting have for women been traditionally explained as outlets for sexual frustration. When Klein published her critique in 1973, feminist work on crime and criminality was in its infancy. As she notes in an afterword, published some twenty years after her original work, the field has subsequently burgeoned in a variety of directions (see also Part Six). The extract from Segal is but one of those directions. She explores the connections between crime (particularly violent crime) and masculinity. As most crime is committed by men and much more remains hidden in the home and domestic sphere, Segal argues (in contrast to some other feminist authors) that the wider causes of male behaviour must be located in societies which construct 'masculinity' in terms of heterosexual power. But neither 'violence' nor 'masculinity' are unitary phenomena. Rather masculinity is mediated through class, race and economic context to produce a situation in which the increased barbarism of public life is reflected back into an increased barbarism in private life. The issue then is not simply one of masculinity.

Collectively these essays reveal that questions of aetiology remain fiercely debated. The issue remains, though, of how far any one theory is capable of winning all the arguments. It is more likely that *certain* theories will remain better placed to analyse *certain* behaviours and social events of which some may come to be defined as 'crime'. Numerous general theories of crime causation have also been advanced which amalgamate many of the specific propositions raised in these individual chapters. But whatever is gained in generality is certainly lost in an unfettered multi-dimensional eclecticism. Given the widespread nature of crime, it may be that no specific motivational theory is required, or is indeed possible. Crime, as Durkheim (see Part One) argued, is a social fact. It may require no more or less an explanation than is required for any other everyday activity.

# 9

# Genetic factors in the etiology of criminal behavior

*Sarnoff A. Mednick, William F. Gabrielli Jr and Barry Hutchings*

Human behavior patterns are generally ascribed to an interaction of life experiences and genetic predispositions, but the importance of genetic influences in shaping conduct has often been contested. This debate has been especially intense, and often emotional, in explaining criminal behavior (Sarbin and Miller, 1970). Reluctance to consider genetic factors in crime has had political overtones (Haller, 1968), but it may also reflect the fact that, until recently, the evidence for genetic influences consisted mainly of studies of twins, some of which were methodologically questionable.

Christiansen (1977a) reported on the criminality of a total population of 3,586 twin pairs from a well-defined area of Denmark. He found 52 per cent of the twins concordant for criminal behavior for (male–male) identical twin pairs and 22 per cent concordance for (male–male) fraternal twin pairs. This result suggests that identical twins inherit some biological characteristic (or characteristics) that increases their common risk of being registered for criminal behavior.

It has been pointed out, however, that identical twins are treated more alike than are fraternal twins (Christiansen, 1977b). Thus their greater similarity in criminal behavior may be partly related to their shared experience. This has produced a reluctance to accept in full the genetic implications of twin research. The study of adoptions better separates environmental and genetic effects; if convicted adoptees have a disproportionately high number of convicted biological fathers (given appropriate controls), this would suggest the influence of a genetic factor in criminal behavior. This conclusion is supported by the fact that almost none of the adoptees know their biological parents; adoptees often do not even realize they have been adopted.

Two US adoption studies have produced highly suggestive results. Crowe (1975) found an increased rate of criminality in 37 Iowan adoptees with criminal biological mothers. Cadoret (1978) reported on 246 Iowans adopted at birth. Antisocial behavior in these adoptees was significantly related to antisocial behavior in the biological parents. In a study of Swedish adoptees Bohman, Cloninger, Sigvardsson, and von Knorring (1982) found that criminal behavior in the biological parents was significantly related to criminal behavior in the adoptees. This relationship held only for property crimes.

The study to be described in this chapter was based on a register of all 14,427 non-familial adoptions in Denmark in the years 1924–47. This register

From *The Causes of Crime: New Biological Approaches* (eds S. Mednick, T. Moffit and S. Stack), pp. 74–91. (Cambridge: Cambridge University Press, 1987.)

Table 9.1    *Number of adoptions in five-year periods*

| Years | Male | Female | Total |
|---|---|---|---|
| 1924–8 | 578 | 1,051 | 1,629 |
| 1929–33 | 730 | 1,056 | 1,786 |
| 1934–8 | 832 | 1,092 | 1,924 |
| 1939–43 | 1,650 | 1,731 | 3,381 |
| 1944–7 | 2,890 | 2,782 | 5,672 |
| (4 years) | | | |
| year uncertain | 20 | 15 | 35 |
| Total | 6,700 | 7,727 | 14,427 |

was established at the Psykologisk Institut in Copenhagen by a group of American and Danish investigators (Kety et al., 1968). The register includes information on the adoptee and his or her adoptive and biological parents. We hypothesized that registered criminality in the biological parents would be associated with an increased risk of registered criminal behavior in the offspring.

## Procedures

Information on all non-familial adoptions in the Kingdom of Denmark between 1924 and 1947 ($n = 14,427$) was obtained from records at the Ministry of Justice. The distribution of adoptions by sex of adoptee for five-year periods appears in Table 9.1. Note the increase in adoptions with increasing population, especially during the war years, and the larger number of females adopted.

### Criminality data

Court convictions were used as an index of criminal involvement. Minors (below 15 years of age) cannot receive court convictions. Court convictions information is maintained by the chief of the police district in which an individual is born. The court record (Strafferegister) contains information on the date of the conviction, the paragraphs of the law violated, and the sanction. To obtain access to these records it is necessary to know the place of birth. When subjects' conviction records could not be checked, it was usually because of a lack of information or ambiguity regarding their date and/or place of birth. The court record was obtained for all of the subjects for whom date and place of birth were available ($n = 65,516$).

Information was first recorded from the adoption files of the Ministry of Justice. In these files, birthplace was then available for the biological and adoptive parents but not for the adoptees; birthplace for the adoptees was obtained from the Central Persons Register or the local population registers. The Central Persons Register was established in 1968; adoptees who died or emigrated before 1968 were thus excluded from the study. There were some difficulties in these searches. The criminal records of persons who have died or have reached the age of 80 are *sometimes* removed from the registers and archived in the Central Police Office in Copenhagen. Thus if an individual had a court conviction but had died before our search began, his or her record might have been transferred from the local police district to the Copenhagen

Table 9.2  *Conviction rates of completely identified members of adoptee families*

| Family member | Number identified | Number not identified | Number of criminal law court convictions | | | |
|---|---|---|---|---|---|---|
| | | | None | One | Two | More than two |
| Male adoptee | 6,129 | 571 | 0.841 | 0.088 | 0.029 | 0.040 |
| Female adoptee | 7,065 | 662 | 0.972 | 0.020 | 0.005 | 0.003 |
| Adoptive father | 13,918 | 509 | 0.938 | 0.046 | 0.008 | 0.008 |
| Adoptive mother | 14,267 | 160 | 0.981 | 0.015 | 0.002 | 0.002 |
| Biological father | 10,604 | 3,823 | 0.714 | 0.129 | 0.056 | 0.102 |
| Biological mother | 12,300 | 2,127 | 0.911 | 0.064 | 0.012 | 0.013 |

Central Police Office. There the record would be maintained in a death register. In view of this, the entire population (adoptees and parents) was checked in the death register. If an adoptee had died or emigrated before the age of 30, the adoptee and parents were dropped from the study since the adoptee had not gone through the entire risk period for criminal conviction. A small section of Denmark in southern Jutland belonged to Germany until 1920. If an individual from this area was registered for criminality before 1920 but not *after* 1920, that individual's record was lost to this study.

For each individual we coded the following information: sex, date of birth, address, occupation, place of birth and size of the community into which the child was adopted. The subjects' occupations permitted us to code socio-economic status (Svalastoga, 1959). For the adoptees we also coded marital status in 1976.

*Not fully identified cases*

It will be recalled that in order to check the court register it was necessary to have name, date and place of birth. A considerable number of cases were lost to this investigation for the following reasons. (a) There was no record of place and/or date of birth. (b) In Denmark the biological mother is required by law to name the biological father. In some few cases she refused, was unsure, or named more than one possible father. These cases were dropped from the population. (c) Among the adoptive parents, 397 were single women. This was because either the adoptive father died just before the formal adoption or the child was adopted by a single woman (not common in this era). (d) Because of additional difficulties involved in checking the criminal registers before 1910, individuals who were born before January 1, 1885, were excluded from the study.

In the case of exclusion of an *adoptee* for any of the above reasons the entire adoptive family was dropped. If a parent was excluded, the remaining subjects were retained for analysis. Table 9.2 presents the number of fully identified individuals in each of the subject categories.

*Results*

The data to be reported consist of convictions for violation of the Danish Criminal Code (Straffeloven). The levels of court convictions for each of the members of the adoption family are given in Table 9.2. The biological-father and male-adoptee conviction rates are considerably higher than the rates for the adoptive father. The rate for adoptive fathers is a bit below that (8 per cent) for men of this age group, in this time period (Hurwitz and Christiansen, 1971). Note also that most of the adoptive-father convictions are attributable to one-time offenders. The male adoptees and the biological fathers are more heavily recidivistic.

The rates of conviction for the women are considerably lower and there is considerably less recidivism than there is for men. The biological mothers and female adoptees have higher levels of court convictions than the adoptive mothers. The adoptive mothers are just below the population average for women of this age range and time period, 2.2 per cent. The individuals who gave up their children for adoption, and their biological offspring, show higher rates of court convictions than the general population and the adoptive parents.

In light of current adoption practices one might be surprised that adoptive parents with court convictions were permitted to adopt. It should be recalled, however, that many of these adoptions took place during the Great Depression and World War II. It was more difficult to find willing adoptive homes in these periods owing partly to the relative unavailability of adoptive parents and to the additional number of adoptees available. Adoptive parents were accepted if they had had a 5-year crime-free period before the adoption.

In most of the analyses that follow, we shall consider the relation between parents' criminal convictions and criminal convictions in the adoptees. If either mother or father (biological and/or adoptive) had received a criminal law conviction, the *parents* of that adoptee will be considered criminal. In view of the low level of convictions among the female adoptees, the analyses will concentrate on the criminal behavior of the male adoptees.

### Types of crime

Of the adoptive parents, 5.50 per cent were convicted for property crimes; 1.05 per cent committed violent acts; and 0.54 per cent were convicted for sexual offenses. Of the biological parents, 28.12 per cent were responsible for property crimes; 6.51 per cent committed violent crimes; and 3.81 per cent committed sexual offenses. Individuals could be registered for more than one type of crime.

### Cross-fostering analysis

Because of the size of the population it is possible to segregate subgroups of adoptees who have combinations of convicted and non-convicted biological and adoptive parents. Table 9.3 presents the four groups in a design that is analogous to the cross-fostering paradigm used in behavior genetics. As can be seen in the lower-right-hand cell, if neither the biological nor adoptive parents are convicted, 13.5 per cent of their sons are convicted. If the adoptive parents are convicted and the biological parents are not convicted, this figure rises to only 14.7 per cent. Note that 20.0 per cent of the sons are convicted if the adoptive parents are *not* convicted and the biological parents are convicted. If *both* the biological and adoptive parents are convicted, we observe the highest level of conviction in the sons, 24.5 per cent. The comparison analogous to the cross-fostering paradigm favors a partial genetic etiology. We must caution, however, that simply knowing that an adoptive parent has been convicted of a

Table 9.3  *Cross-fostering analysis:*
*percentage of adoptive sons convicted of*
*criminal law offenses*

| Have adoptive parents been convicted? | Have biological parents been convicted? | |
| --- | --- | --- |
| | Yes | No |
| Yes | 24.5 | 14.7 |
| | (of 143) | (of 204) |
| No | 20.0 | 13.5 |
| | (of 1,226) | (of 2,492) |

Note: Numbers in parentheses represent the total number
for each cell.

crime does not tell us how criminogenic the adoptee's environment has been.
(Recall the preponderance of one-time offenders in the adoptive parents and
the adoptive agency's condition that the adoptive parents not have a conviction for the 5 years preceding the adoption.) On the other hand, at
conception, the genetic influence of the biological father is already complete.
Thus this analysis does not yield a fair comparison between environmental
and genetic influences included in Table 9.3. However, this initial analysis
does indicate that sons with a convicted biological parent have an elevated
probability of being convicted. This suggests that some biological characteristic is transmitted from the criminal biological parent that increases the
son's risk of obtaining a court conviction for a criminal law offense.

A log-linear analysis of the data in Table 9.3 is presented in Table 9.4.
Adoptive-parent convictions are not associated with a significant increment in
the son's level of convictions. The effect of the biological parents' convictions
is marked. The model presented in Table 9.4 reveals that, considering only the
*additive* effect of the biological parent and the adoptive parent, the improvement in the chi-square value leaves almost no room for improvement by an
interaction effect.

The adoptive parents have a low frequency of court convictions. In order to
simplify interpretation of the relations reported below we have excluded cases
with adoptive-parent criminality. (Analyses completed that did include adoptive-parent criminality did not alter the nature of the findings to be reported.)

Table 9.4  *Log-linear analysis: influences of adoptive-parent and biological-*
*parent convictions on male-adoptee convictions*

| Model | Model $\chi^2$ | d.f. | $p$ | Improvement $\chi^2$ | d.f. | $p$ |
| --- | --- | --- | --- | --- | --- | --- |
| Baseline (S, AB) | 32.91 | 3 | 0.001 | | | |
| Adoptive parent (SA, AB) | 30.71 | 2 | 0.001 | 2.20 | 1 | n.s. |
| Biological parent (SB, AB) | 1.76 | 2 | 0.415 | 31.15 | 1 | 0.001 |
| Combined influence (SB, SA, AB) | 0.30 | 1 | 0.585 | 32.61 | 2 | 0.001 |
| Biological parent given adoptive parent (SB/SA, AB) | – | – | | 28.95 | 1 | 0.001 |
| Adoptive parent given biological parent (SA/SB, AB) | – | – | | 1.46 | 1 | n.s. |

Note: S denotes adoptee-son effect; A, adoptive-parent effect; B, biological-parent effect; n.s.,
not significant.

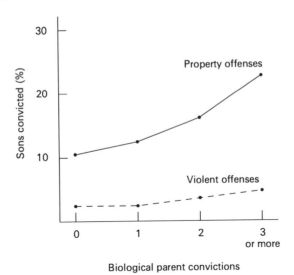

Figure 9.1   *Percentage of male adoptee property offenders and violent offenders by biological-parent convictions*

Figure 9.1 presents the relation between convictions in the sons and degree of recidivism in the biological parents. The relation is positive and relatively monotonic (with the scales utilized on the X and Y axes). Note also that the relation is highly significant for property crimes and not statistically significant for violent crimes.

### The chronic offender

The chronic offender is rare but commits a markedly disproportionate number of criminal offenses. This extremely high rate of offending suggested that genetic predisposition may play an important role in these cases. We examined the relation between convictions of the chronic adoptee offender and his biological parents.

In an important US birth cohort study (Wolfgang et al., 1972), the chronic offender was defined as one who had been arrested five or more times; these chronic offenders comprised 6 per cent of the males and had committed 52 per cent of the offenses. In our adoption cohort we recorded court convictions rather than arrest data. If we select as chronic offenders those with three or more court convictions, this includes 4.09 per cent of the male adoptees. This small group of recidivists accounts for 69.4 per cent of all the court convictions for all the male adoptees. This is a high concentration of crime in a very small fraction of the cohort.

Table 9.5 shows how the chronic offenders, the other offenders (one or two convictions), and the non-offenders are distributed as a function of level of crime in the biological parents. As can be seen, the proportion of chronic adoptee offenders increases as a function of level of recidivism in the biological parents.

Another way of expressing this concentration of crime is to point out that the chronic male adoptee offenders with biological parents with three or more

Table 9.5 *Proportion of chronic offenders, other offenders, and non-offenders among male adoptees as a function of convictions of biological parents*

| Number of male-adoptee convictions | Number of biological-parent convictions | | | |
|---|---|---|---|---|
| | 0 | 1 | 2 | 3 or more |
| Non-offenders (no convictions) | 0.87 | 0.84 | 0.80 | 0.75 |
| Other offenders (1 or 2 convictions) | 0.10 | 0.12 | 0.15 | 0.17 |
| Chronic offenders (3 or more convictions) | 0.03 | 0.04 | 0.05 | 0.09 |
| Number of adoptees | 2,492 | 547 | 233 | 419 |

Note: Data do not include cases in which adoptive parents were convicted of criminal law violation.

offenses number only 37. Although they comprise only 1 per cent of the 3,691 male adoptees in Table 9.5, they are responsible for 30 per cent of the male adoptee convictions. We should also note that the mean number of convictions for the chronic adoptee offenders increases sharply as a function of biological parent recidivism. The biological parents with zero, one, two, or three or more convictions have male adoptees (i.e., male children who are subsequently adopted by others) averaging 0.30, 0.41, 0.48 and 0.70 convictions, respectively.

We have presented evidence that there is an association between biological parents' convictions and the convictions of their (subsequently) adopted sons. The relation seems stronger for chronic offenders. The sons of chronic offenders account for a disproportionate number of the convictions in the cohort.

## Sibling analyses

There are a number of instances in which a biological mother and/or biological father contributed more than one child to this population. These offspring are, of course, full and half-siblings; they were sometimes placed in different adoptive homes. We would predict that the separated full siblings should show more concordance for criminal convictions than the separated half-siblings. Both of these groups should show more concordance than two randomly selected, unrelated, separately reared male adoptees.

The probability of any one male adoptee being convicted in 0.159. The probability of drawing a pair of unrelated, separated male adoptees with at least one having a conviction is 0.293. The probability that both of the pair will have been convicted is 0.025. Thus pairwise concordance for unrelated separated male adoptees is 8.5 per cent. This can be seen as a baseline. There were 126 male–male half-sibling pairs placed in separate adoptive homes. Of these, 31 pairs had at least one member of the sibship convicted; of these 31 pairs, 4 pairs were concordant for convictions. This yields a concordance rate for half-siblings of 12.9 per cent. There were 40 male–male full-sibling pairs placed in different adoptive homes. Of these, 15 pairs had at least one member of the sibship convicted; of these 15 pairs, three pairs were concordant for convictions. This yields a concordance rate for full siblings of 20 per cent. These numbers are very small, but the results are in the predicted direction. As the degree of genetic relation increases, the level of concordance increases.

Table 9.6  *Concordance for criminal law convictions in male siblings placed in separate adoptive homes*

| Degree of genetic relation | Pairwise concordance (%) |
| --- | --- |
| Unrelated, raised apart | 8.5 |
| Half-siblings, raised apart | 12.9 |
| Full siblings, raised apart | 20.0 |
| Half-siblings and full siblings, raised apart, criminal father | 30.8 |
| Unrelated 'siblings' raised together in adoptive home | 8.5 |

We also considered the level of concordance of the sibling pairs whose biological father was a criminal (had at least one conviction). Of 98 fathers with at least one pair of male–male, separated, adopted-away siblings, 45 had received at least one conviction. (It should be noted that this is a significantly higher rate of convictions (45.9 per cent) than the conviction rate (28.6 per cent) for the total population of biological fathers, $\psi^2(1) = 14.6$, $p < 0.01$.)

We combined full- and half-sibling pairs (because of the small number and because the siblings shared criminal biological fathers). Of the 45 sibling pairs, 13 had at least one member with a conviction; of these 13, four pairs were concordant for convictions. This yields a concordance rate of 30.8 per cent. Table 9.6 summarizes these sibling analyses. The pairwise concordance rates can be compared with the male–male rates for twins from a population twin study; Christiansen (1977a) reported 36 per cent pairwise concordance for identical twins and a 13 per cent rate for fraternal twins.

Although these numbers are very small, they represent all of the cases, as defined, in a total cohort of adoptions. The results suggest that a number of these separated, adopted siblings inherited some characteristic that predisposed both of them to being convicted for criminal behavior. As would be expected, in those instances in which the biological father was criminal, the effect was enhanced.

*Specificity of a genetic relation*

Earlier, we mentioned a study of a small sample of adoptees (Crowe, 1975). Crowe reported the impression that there was some similarity in the types of crime committed by the biological mother and the adoptee. This suggests specific genetic predispositions for different types of crime. In order to explore this possibility, we examined the rates of violent crimes in the adoptees as a function of violent crime in the biological parents. We completed similar analyses for property crimes. We also examined more specific types of crime (theft, fraud, assault, etc.) for similarity in the biological parent and the adoptee.

If the genetic predisposition was specific for type of crime, these 'specificity' analyses should have resulted in our observing a closer relation between adoptee and biological-parent levels of conviction for each of these types of crime. The best predictor of each type of adoptee crime, however, was number of biological-parent convictions rather than type of biological-parent offense. This suggests that the biological predisposition the adoptee inherits must be of a general nature, partly determining the degree of law abidance shown by the adoptee. It is also possible that the data of this study are too gross for the detection of a specificity relation. This may require careful coding of details of the criminal behavior. This was not possible in our study.

## Sex differences

As can be seen in Table 9.2, convictions of females for criminal law violations are very infrequent. It might be speculated that those women who do exhibit a level of criminal behavior that prompts a court conviction must have a severe predisposition for such behavior. Criminal involvement of many men, on the other hand, may tend to be more socially or environmentally inspired. These statements suggest that convictions in the biological mother are more closely related to the adoptee's conviction(s) than criminal behavior in the biological father.

In every analysis we conducted, the relation between biological-mother conviction and adoptee conviction is significantly stronger than the relation between biological-father conviction and adoptee conviction. In comparison with the relation between biological-father and adoptee convictions, convictions of the biological mothers are more closely related to convictions of the daughters. This result is statistically significant, but the relatively low frequency of female convictions forces us to interpret these findings with caution.

## Historical period

The period of these adoptions (1924–67) spans some important historical changes in Denmark, including a world war, the Great Depression, and industrialization. It is conceivable that the influence of genetic factors might be affected by these social upheavals. It is also possible that changes in level or type of crime during these years might influence the relations observed. Analyses conducted for the entire population were repeated for each of the 5-year periods. The results were virtually identical for all of the periods and virtually identical to the analyses of the total sample. The social changes during these years did not interact with the relation between biological-parent and adoptee crime.

## Controlling genetic influence in examining environmental effects

In many social science investigations genetic characteristics are not considered. In some analyses this may contribute error; sometimes omission may lead to incomplete conclusions. For example, separation from a father is associated with an increased level of delinquency in a son. This has been interpreted as a result of failure of identification or lack of consistent discipline. As we can see from Table 9.2, some fathers who permit themselves to be separated from their child have a relatively high level of criminal convictions. The higher level of delinquency found for separated children might be partially due to a genetic transmission of criminogenic predispositional characteristics from antisocial fathers. If this genetic variance were partially accounted for, the environmental hypotheses could be more precisely tested. We utilized such partial genetic control to study an important criminological variable, social status. We separated the variance ascribable to 'genetic' social class and 'rearing' social class (Van Dusen et al., 1983). We examined adoptee convictions as a joint function of biological parents' social class and adoptive parents' social class. It is clear from inspection of Table 9.7 that male-adoptee convictions vary as a function of both genetic and environmental social class; log-linear analyses reveal that both effects are statistically significant. Although the genetic effect is of interest here, we emphasize that,

Table 9.7    *Percentage of male adoptees with criminal convictions as a function of adoptive and biological parents' socioeconomic status*

| Adoptive parents' SES | Biological parents' SES | | | |
|---|---|---|---|---|
| | High | Middle | Low | Total |
| High | 9.30 | 11.52 | 12.98 | 11.58 |
| | (441) | (903) | (775) | (2,099) |
| Middle | 13.44 | 15.29 | 16.86 | 15.62 |
| | (320) | (870) | (795) | (1,985) |
| Low | 13.81 | 17.25 | 18.04 | 17.19 |
| | (210) | (568) | (787) | (1,565) |
| Total | 11.64 | 14.31 | 16.00 | 14.55 |
| | (971) | (2,341) | (2,337) | (5,649) |

Note: Numbers in parentheses represent total number for each cell.

to our knowledge, this is the first controlled demonstration that *environmental* aspects influence the social class–crime relation. This finding suggests that, regardless of genetic background, improved social conditions are likely to lead to a reduction in criminal behavior.

Table 9.7 is of interest in another regard. Careful inspection reveals a correlation between adoptive-parent socioeconomic status (SES) and biological-parent SES. This represents the attempt by the adoptive agency to match certain characteristics of the two sets of parents in order to increase the likelihood that the adoptee will fit into the adoptive home. In terms of the adoption research design, this correlation is undesirable because it reduces the independence of the genetic rearing and environmental influences on the adoptee. Since social class is not independent of convictions (Table 9.7), it is conceivable that the relation between biological-parent and adoptee convictions is, in part, mediated by social class. Inspection of Table 9.7 reveals, however, that this relation exists at each level of adoptive-parent social class. In addition we have conducted stepwise multiple regression analyses that varied the order of entry of biological-parent convictions and SES and adoptive-parent convictions and SES. These analyses indicate that, independent of SES, biological-parent convictions are significantly related to adoptee convictions.

## Methodological issues

### Not fully identified subjects

If we are to generalize from the results of this study, it is useful to consider what biases might be introduced by the loss of subjects in specific analyses. Table 9.2 indicates the total number of subjects who could not be fully identified (name, birthday and birthplace). We should note that we know the name, occupation, birthdate and other facts concerning most of the lost subjects; in almost all cases a subject could not be checked in the court conviction register because we were not certain of the subject's place of birth.

The information is relatively complete for the adoptive parents. In contrast, 26.5 per cent of the biological fathers and 14.7 per cent of the biological mothers are not fully identified. These differences probably reflect the relative importance of the adoptive and biological parents to the adoption agency. The agency's chief concern was with the placement and welfare of the adoptee. After the adoption, they had less reason to be concerned with the biological parents.

The most general characteristic of those not fully identified is that they tend *slightly* to come from areas outside Copenhagen. Perhaps the urban adoption offices followed more thorough recording procedures than did offices outside the city. The differences are very small. The sons of the biological fathers not fully identified have a rate of 10.3 per cent criminal law convictions; the identified biological fathers' sons have criminal law convictions in 11.4 per cent of cases. In cases in which the biological mother is not fully identified, slightly fewer of the sons have criminal law convictions (9.6 per cent). The adoptees who were not fully identified have biological mothers and biological fathers with slightly higher SES than those who were fully identified. Their rearing (adoptive) homes were of almost identical SES.

Our consideration of the characteristics of those not fully identified does not suggest that their inclusion would have altered the nature of the results presented above. Perhaps the most critical facts in this judgment are that the adopted-away sons of parents not fully identified have levels of criminal law convictions and rearing social status that are approximately the same as for the sons of those parents fully identified. The differences observed are small; it is difficult to formulate any manner in which the lost subjects might have an impact on the relations reported.

*Transfer history*

Most of these adoptions were the results of pregnancies of unwed women. The adoptive agency had a policy of taking newborns from their biological mothers and either immediately placing them in a previously arranged adoptive home (25.3 per cent of the adoptions) or placing them in an orphanage from which they were available for adoption. Of those placed in an orphanage, 50.6 per cent were placed with an adoptive family in the first year, 12.8 per cent were placed with an adoptive family in the second year, and 11.3 per cent were placed after the age of 2.

Within each of these age-of-transfer groups, analyses were conducted to ascertain whether the biological parents' convictions were related to male-adoptee conviction. Similar significant positive relations were observed at each transfer age. Age of transfer did not interact with genetic influence so as to alter significantly the relations observed with the full population. It should be noted that there was a statistically significant tendency for a high level of adoptee criminality to be associated with more time spent in an orphanage awaiting adoption. This effect was true for males only.

The operational definition of criminal behavior in this study included only court convictions for criminal law offenses. (We completed an analysis of police arrest data using a subsample of this adoption cohort and obtained very similar results; see Hutchings and Mednick, 1977.) Use of the conviction definition has some advantages. We are relatively certain that the individual actually committed the offense recorded. Court convictions imply a high threshold for inclusion; minor offenses are less likely to result in court conviction. There are also disadvantages. The subject's behavior goes through several screening points. Someone must make a complaint to the police, or the police must happen on the scene of the crime. The police must decide that a crime has been committed and apprehend the culprit. The prosecuting attorney must decide that the evidence is sufficient to warrant a court trial. The court must then find the culprit guilty. There are decision points all along the way that may result in the elimination of individuals who have actually committed offenses against the criminal code. Such individuals might then end up among our control subjects (assuming that they do not also commit offenses for which they are convicted). In this case they add error to the analyses. Data comparing self-reports of crimes and official records of crimes suggest, however, that whereas only a fraction of crimes committed by an individual are noted by the police, those who 'self-report' more crimes have more crimes recorded in the official registers. Those offenders who are not found in the official registers have typically committed very few and very minor offenses (Christie et al., 1965).

## Labeling of the adoptee

The advantage of the adoption method is the good separation of genetic and rearing contributions to the adoptee's development. But the adoptions were not arranged as controlled experiments. The adoption agency's prime concern was the welfare of the adoptee and the adoptive parents. Prospective adoptive parents were routinely informed about the criminal convictions of the biological parents. This could result in the labeling of the adoptee; this in turn might affect the likelihood that the adoptee would commit criminal acts. Thus the convictions of the biological parents might have had an environmental impact on the adoptee via the reactions of the adoptive parents.

We examined one hypothesis related to this possibility. If the biological parents received a criminal conviction before the adoption, it is likely that the adoptive parents were so informed; if the biological parents' first conviction occurred after the adoption, the adoptive parents could not have been informed. Of the convicted biological parents, 37 per cent had received their first conviction before the adoption took place. In these cases, the adoptive parents were likely to have been informed of this criminal record. In 63 per cent of the cases the first conviction occurred after the adoption; in these cases the conviction information could *not* have been transmitted to the adoptive parents. For all convicted biological parents, the probability of a conviction in their adopted-away son was 15.9 per cent. In cases in which the biological parent was first convicted before adoption, 15.6 per cent of the male adoptees were convicted. In cases in which the biological parent was convicted after the adoption, 16.1 per cent of the male adoptees were convicted. In the case of female adoptees, these figures were 4 per cent and 4 per cent.

These analyses utilized convictions. In a previous analysis with a large subsample of this population a very similar result was obtained by studying the effect of timing of the initial arrest of the biological father (Hutchings and Mednick, 1977). Additional analyses by type or severity of crime revealed no effect of the adoptive parents' having been informed of the convictions of the biological parents. The fact that the adoptive parents had been informed of the biological parents' convictions did not alter the likelihood that the adoptive son would be convicted. This result should not be interpreted as suggesting that labeling (as defined) had no effect on the adoptees' lives. It did not, however, affect the probability that the adoptee would be convicted for a criminal act.

## Denmark as a research site

This project was carried out in Denmark; on most crime-related social dimensions, Denmark must rank among the most homogeneous of the Western nations. This fact may have implications for the interpretation of this study. An environment with low variability permits better expression of existing genetic tendencies in individuals living in that environment. This factor probably magnifies the expression of any genetic influence. At the same time, however, the Danish population probably has less genetic variability than some Western nations; this, of course, would minimize the expression of genetic influence in research conducted in Denmark. It is very likely impossible to balance these two considerations quantitatively. We are reassured regarding the generality of our findings by similar results in adoption studies in Sweden and Iowa (Bohman et al., 1982; Cadoret, 1978; Crowe, 1975).

## Summary and conclusions

In a total population of adoptions, we noted a relation between biological-parent criminal convictions and criminal convictions in their adopted-away children. The relation is particularly strong for *chronic* adoptee and biological-parent offenders. There was no evidence that the type of biological-parent conviction was related to the type of adoptee conviction. A number of potentially confounding variables were considered; none of these proved sufficient to explain the genetic relation. We conclude that some factor is transmitted by convicted parents that increases the likelihood that their children will be convicted for criminal law offenses. This is especially true of chronic offenders. Because the transmitted factor must be biological, this implies that biological factors are involved in the etiology of at least some criminal behavior.

Biological factors and their interaction with social variables may make useful contributions to our understanding of the causes of criminal behavior.

## References

Bohman, M., Cloninger, C., Sigvardsson, S. and von Knorring, A.L. (1982) 'Predisposition to petty criminality in Swedish adoptees: genetic and environmental heterogeneity', *Archives of General Psychiatry*, 39(11): 1233–41.

Cadoret, R.J. (1978) 'Psychopathy in adopted away offspring of biological parents with antisocial behavior', *Archives of General Psychiatry*, 35: 176–84.

Christiansen, K.O. (1977a) 'A review of studies of criminality among twins', in S.A. Mednick and K.O. Christiansen (eds), *Biosocial Bases of Criminal Behavior*. New York: Gardner Press. pp. 45–88.

Christiansen, K.O. (1977b) 'A preliminary study of criminality among twins', in S.A. Mednick and K.O. Christiansen (eds), *Biosocial Bases of Criminal Behavior*. New York: Gardner Press. pp. 89–108.

Christie, N., Andenaes, J. and Skerbaekk, S. (1965) 'A study of self-reported crime', *Scandinavian Studies in Criminology*, 1: 86–116.

Crowe, R. (1975) 'Adoptive study of psychopathy: preliminary results from arrest records and psychiatric hospital records', in R. Fieve, D. Rosenthal and H. Brill (eds), *Genetic Research in Psychiatry*. Baltimore, MD: Johns Hopkins University Press.

Haller, M.H. (1968) 'Social science and genetics: a historical perspective', in D. Glass (ed.), *Genetics*. New York: Rockefeller University Press.

Hurwitz, S. and Christiansen, K.O. (1971) *Kriminologi*. Copenhagen: Glydendal.

Hutchings, B. and Mednick, S.A. (1977) 'Registered criminality in the adoptive and biological parents of registered male criminal adoptees', in S.A. Mednick and K.O. Christiansen (eds), *Biosocial Bases of Criminal Behavior*. New York: Gardner Press. pp. 127–42.

Kety, S.S., Rosenthal, D., Wender, P.H. and Schulsinger, F. (1968) 'The types and prevalence of mental illness in the biological adoptive families of adopted schizophrenics', in D. Rosenthal and S.S. Kety (eds), *The Transmission of Schizophrenia*, Oxford: Pergamon.

Sarbin, T.R. and Miller, J.E. (1970) 'Demonism revisited: the XYY chromosomal anomaly', *Issues in Criminology*, 5: 195–207.

Svalastoga, K. (1959), *Prestige, Class and Mobility*, Copenhagen: Gyldendal.

Van Dusen, K., Mednick, S.A., Gabrielli, W.F. and Hutchings, B. (1983) 'Social class and crime in an adoption cohort', *Journal of Criminal Law and Criminology*, 74(1): 249–69.

Wolfgang, M.E., Figlio, R.M. and Sellin, T. (1972) *Delinquency in a Birth Cohort*. Chicago: University of Chicago Press.

# 10

# Personality theory and the problem of criminality

*H.J. Eysenck*

## Introduction

In psychiatry generally, the diathesis–stress model is widely accepted; it postulates a *predisposition* to develop certain types of mental illness, such as neurosis or psychosis, which is activated by certain environmental stress factors. A similar conception can be applied to criminality; certain types of personality may be more prone to react with anti-social or criminal behaviour to environmental factors of one kind or another. To say this is not to accept the notion of 'crime as destiny', to quote Lange's famous monograph in which he showed that identical twins are much more alike with respect to criminal conduct than are fraternal twins. There is no predestination about the fact that heredity, mediated through personality, plays some part in predisposing some people to act in an anti-social manner. Environment is equally important, and, as we shall see, it is the interaction between the two which is perhaps the most crucial factor.

Much of the research in this field has been episodic and following the principles of benevolent eclecticism; in this chapter we will rather adopt the method of looking at a general theory of anti-social behaviour, which makes predictions as to the type of personality expected to indulge in such conduct, and summarize the evidence relating to the theory. Before turning to the evidence, it will therefore be necessary to present in brief outline the theory in question (Eysenck, 1960, 1977). The reason for singling out the theory is, in the first place, that it has attracted far more research than any other, and secondly, that it is the only one which has tried to link together genetic factors, a causal theory, and personality in one general theory.

## Statement of theory

Briefly and concisely, the theory tries to explain the occurrence of socialized behaviour suggesting that anti-social behaviour, being obviously egocentric and orientated towards immediate gratification, needs no explanation. It is suggested that the socialization process is essentially mediated by Pavlovian conditioning, in the sense that anti-social behaviour will be punished by parents, teachers, peers etc., and that such punishment constitutes the

Abridged from *Applying Psychology to Imprisonment* (eds B. McGurk, D. Thornton and M. Williams), pp. 30–1; 34–46. (London: HMSO, 1987.)

*unconditioned stimulus* (US), where the contemplation or execution of such behaviour constitutes the conditioned stimulus. The pain/anxiety properties of the US transfer through conditioning to the CS [conditioned stimulus], and as a consequence the person will desist from committing anti-social acts, or even contemplating them, because of the painful CRs [conditioned responses] which inevitably follow. The theory is elaborated in Eysenck (1977), where supportive evidence will be found.

Individual differences in the speed and strength of formation of conditioned responses would, in terms of the theory, be fundamental in accounting for the observed relations between personality and criminality. As Eysenck (1967, 1980) has shown, there is considerable evidence to suggest that introverts form conditioned responses more quickly and more strongly than extraverts, and accordingly one would expect extraversion to be positively correlated with anti-social conduct. Emotional instability or neuroticism would be expected to multiply with the habits of socialized or anti-social conduct, according to Hull's general theory in which performance is a multiplicative function of habit and drive, with anxiety in this case acting as a drive (Eysenck, 1973). The third major dimension of personality, psychoticism, comes into the picture because of the well-documented relationship between crime and psychosis (Eysenck and Eysenck, 1976), and because the general personality traits subsumed under psychoticism appear clearly related to anti-social and non-conformist conduct. The precise nature of these three major dimensions of personality will be discussed later on in this chapter; here we will only look at one particular problem which is closely related to the general theory of conditioning as a basis for anti-social conduct.

The theory suggests that conditioning produces socialized behaviour, and that introverts will show more socialized behaviour because they condition more readily. The same theory would also imply, however, that if the socialization process were inverted, i.e. if parents, teachers, peers, etc. praised the child for anti-social conduct, and punished him for socialized behaviour, then introverts would be more likely to show anti-social behaviour. Raine and Venables (1981) have shown that this is indeed so; children who showed better conditioning in a laboratory situation than other children were remarkably socialized in their behaviour when brought up in a favourable type of environment, and remarkably anti-social in their behaviour when brought up in a non-favourable type of environment. This experiment shows more clearly than almost any other the inter-relationship between genetic factors on the one hand, and environmental ones on the other.

[. . .]

## Dimensions of personality

We will now turn to personality factors as more narrowly defined. Our discussion will begin with the three major dimensions of personality, which emerge from hundreds of correlational and factor analytic studies in many different countries. Royce and Powell (1983) have summarized and reanalysed these data, and confirm the theory developed by Eysenck and Eysenck (1976) that these three factors deal essentially with social interactions (extraversion–introversion), emotional reactions and anxieties (neuroticism), and aggressive and egocentric impulses and their control (psychoticism). Many different

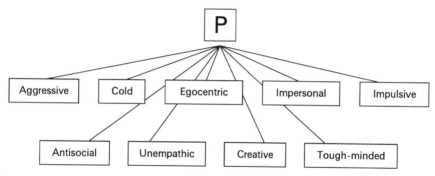

Figure 10.1 *Traits characterizing the psychoticism factor*

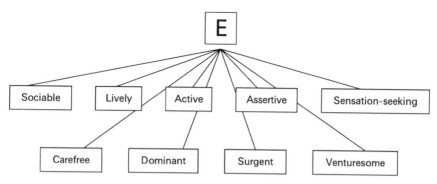

Figure 10.2 *Traits characterizing the extraversion factor*

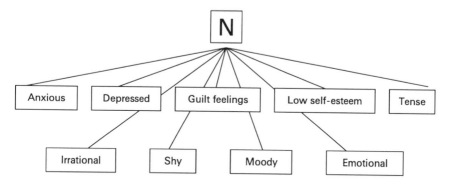

Figure 10.3 *Traits characterizing the neuroticism factor*

terms are of course used for these dimensions but Eysenck and Eysenck (1985) discuss the experimental literature which suggests the relevance of the terms proposed above.

The nature of these three major dimensions of personality can best be discerned from the data shown in Figures 10.1–10.3. These list the various traits, correlations between which have generated at the empirical level the three major dimensions of P, E and N. In this section we will simply look at descriptive studies involving the relationship between anti-social and criminal behaviour, on the one hand, and these major dimensions, and the traits relating thereto, on the other. [. . .] Here let us mainly stress that the personality traits and dimensions dealt with here have a strong genetic component [. . .]; this does not prove, but it does suggest that genetic factors may also play an important part in the genesis of anti-social and criminal behaviour.

Much of the early literature has been summarized by Passingham (1972), who found that while a number of studies supported Eysenck's hypothesis of a positive correlation between criminality and P, E and N, there were many exceptions, and occasional reversals. There are of course many reasons why results have not always been positive. Criminals are not a homogeneous group, and different investigators have studied different populations, specializing in different types of crime. Control groups have not always been carefully selected; some investigators, for instance, have used the usual students groups as controls, which is inadvisable. There has been a failure to control for dissimulation; there is evidence that high lie-scorers lower their neuroticism and psychoticism scores, and they seem to do the same for extraversion (McCue et al., 1976) [. . .] Some of the most negative reports contain evidence of high L scales, and are hence inadmissible. Other reasons refer to the incarceration of many delinquents; this would interfere with verbal responses on questionnaire items relating to sociability, and hence lead to an understatement of the delinquent's degree of extraversion. More important even than any of these reasons is probably the fact that many early investigations were done without any prior hypothesis being stated, and used questionnaires and other measures which bear only tangential relation to the Eysenck Questionnaires.

Eysenck (1977) lists many more recent investigations, most done from the point of view of testing the hypothesis linking criminality and P, E and N; these results are very much more positive. Some of the studies also strongly support the view that within the criminal fraternity different types of crimes are related to different personality patterns. Thus Eysenck, Rust and Eysenck (1977) studied five separate groups of criminals (conmen, i.e. confidence tricksters; criminals involved with crime against property; criminals specializing in violence; inadequate criminals, and a residual group, not specializing in one type of crime). Figure 10.4 shows the differential patterns of P, E and N of these various groups, with conmen for instance having a much lower P score than the other groups.

Mitchell et al. (1980) studied the difference between violent and non-violent delinquent behaviour and found that violence was more frequently associated with low trait anxiety than non-violent behaviour; their results agree with the Eysenck, Rust and Eysenck findings. Schwenkmezger (1983) subdivided his sample of delinquents into three major groups, corresponding to conmen, offences against property, and offences involving violence. As in the Eysenck, Rust and Eysenck study, conmen have much lower values on the various measures involved (impulsivity, risk taking, aggressiveness, dominance, and excitement) than the other two groups. Discriminant function analysis showed two significant functions, the first of which separates conmen from the other two groups. The second function involved mainly aggressive, dominant and risk taking behaviour, and has offences involving violence at one extreme.

The most recent study by Wardell and Yeudall (1980), specially concerned with this problem, used ten personality factors derived from an extensive psychological test battery administered to 201 patients on criminal wards at a

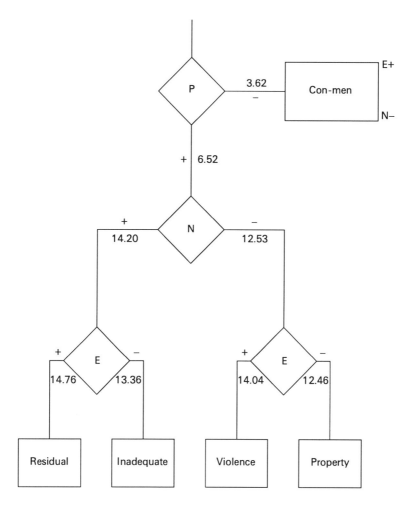

Figure 10.4 *P, E and N scores of different types of criminals (Eysenck et al., 1977)*

mental hospital and showed many important differences between patients involved with different types of crime. Other recent studies supporting this view are by McGurk (1978), McGurk and McDougall (1981), McGurk and McEwan (1983), and McGurk, McEwan and Graham (1981). To this list might be added some studies cited by Eysenck (1977) showing that murderers (i.e. mainly the usual type of family murder) tend to be significantly introverted. Professional gunmen, on the other hand, are exceedingly extraverted, thus showing that even a single category (murder) may require subdivision in order to give comprehensible and replicable correlations with personality.

Rahman and Hussain (1984), studying female criminals in Bangladesh, found them to have much higher P and N scores than controls; those engaged in prostitution, fraud, kidnapping and possession of illegal arms also had high E scores. Murderers, on the other hand, were significantly introverted.

Holcomb et al. (1985) have shown how complex motivation and personality even within a single category of crime may be. They studied a sample of 80 male offenders charged with premeditated murder, and found that these could be divided into five personality types using MMPI scores. The results were cross validated using a second sample of 80 premeditated murders. A discriminant analysis resulted in a 96.25 correct classification of subjects from the second sample into the five types. Clinical data from a mental status interview schedule supported the external validity of these types. There were significant differences among the five types in hallucinations, disorientation, hostility, depression and paranoid thinking.

**The Eysenck studies**

We may now turn to the work of the Eysencks in temporal order, as these were the major studies to try to obtain direct empirical evidence regarding the theory under discussion. In the first of these studies (Eysenck and Eysenck, 1970), 603 male prisoners were compared with a control group of over 1,000 males. Results supported strongly the hypothesis that prisoners would have higher P scores, moderately strongly the hypothesis that prisoners would have higher N scores, and rather more weakly the hypothesis that prisoners would have higher E scores. Similar results were found in a later study by Eysenck and Eysenck (1971), contrasting 518 criminals and 606 male trainee railmen. Significant differences were found on P and N, and on E the direction of the prediction was reversed, criminals having lower E scores than controls. In a later study of the personality of female prisoners (Eysenck and Eysenck, 1973) 264 female prisoners were found to be characterized by high P, high N and high E scores; for them therefore E agreed with the predicted direction.

In a study of personality and recidivism in Borstal boys (Eysenck and Eysenck, 1974), recidivists were insignificantly higher than non-recidivists on P and N, but significantly higher on E. In the last of this series of studies (Eysenck and Eysenck, 1977) over 2,000 male prisoners and over 2,400 male controls were given the Eysenck personality questionnaire, and then sub-divided into age groups, ranging from 16 to 69 at the extremes. It was found that the lie-scale disclosed little dissimulation in either group. Scores on psychoticism, extraversion and neuroticism fell with age for both prisoners and controls. Prisoners had higher scores than controls, as predicted, on all three scales.

A replication of some of this work was carried out by Sanocki (1969) in Poland, using the short form of the Maudsley Personality Inventory on 84 Polish prisoners and 337 Polish controls, matched for age, education and social class. Criminals were found to be significantly more extraverted, and non-significantly more neurotic. Sanocki also found that different types of prisoners in his study differed significantly with respect to the inventory scores, adding another proof to the hypothesis of criminal heterogeneity. He also showed that a prisoner's behaviour in prison correlated with E, extraverts offending significantly more frequently against prison rules.

Two further points about the Eysenck studies may be of relevance. The first is that Eysenck and Eysenck (1971) constructed an empirical criminality scale by bringing together all those items which showed the greatest differentiation between criminals and normals; this will later on be referred to as the 'C' scale. The other point is made by Burgess (1972), who pointed out that Eysenck's theory implies that criminals and normals would differ on a combination of N and E, not necessarily on one or the other in separation; he was able to show that even in studies which failed to show significance for one or the other variable, the combination did show highly significant differences.

The 'C' scale was constructed for adults; similar scales have been proposed by Allsop and Feldman (1975), and by Saklofske, McKerracher and Eysenck (1978) for children. Like the adult scale they use selected items from the P, E and N scales. The scales have been found to be very useful in discriminating different groups of children. The data demonstrate clearly that delinquent boys have higher extraversion, psychoticism and neuroticism scores, and that the criminal propensity (C) scale discriminates even better between them and non-delinquent boys. Similar differences were also observed between well-behaved and badly behaved non-delinquent boys.

## Other recent studies

Barack and Widom (1978) studied American women awaiting trial. Compared to a heterogeneous control group, these women scored significantly higher on the neuroticism and psychoticism scales, and on Burgess's $h$ scale $(h = E \times N)$. Singh (1982) compared 100 Indian female delinquents with 100 female non-delinquents, matched in terms of socioeconomic status, age and urban versus rural place of residence; he found that delinquents had higher scores on extraversion and neuroticism than did non-delinquents. Smith and Smith (1977) looked at the psychoticism variable in relation to reconviction, and found a very highly significant correlation between psychoticism and reconviction. Their finding supported the results obtained by Saunders and Davies (1976), who administered the Jesness Inventory to samples of young male offenders, and concluded that:

> one can . . . see a picture of the continuing delinquent as being unsocialised, aggressive, anti-authority and unempathic. This appears to present a somewhat similar pattern of characteristics to that described by Eysenck as 'psychotic'.

Of particular interest are some results of a follow-up of an investigation carried out by West and Farrington (1973). (See also Farrington et al., 1982.) In the original study 411 boys, aged 8 to 9, attending six adjacent primary schools in a working class area of London, were given the Junior Maudsley Inventory at age 10 to 11, and again at age 14 to 15; they were also given the Eysenck Personality Inventory at age 16 to 17. The original data did not provide very strong support for the theory, but more interesting are new data relating to delinquency as a young adult, i.e. convictions in court for offences committed between a boy's 17th and 21st birthdays. Eighty-four boys were classified as juvenile delinquents, 94 as young adult delinquents, and 127 as delinquents at any age (up to 21). This study is particularly important because the delinquents were almost all non-institutionalized at the time of testing. (The following data were communicated privately by D.P. Farrington on 10 June 1976.)

*Extraversion*  As regards juvenile delinquency, E scores were dichotomized into roughly equal halves, and 24 per cent of those with above average scores became juvenile delinquents, in comparison with 16 per cent of those with below average scores; so the lowest quarter of E scores at age 16 included significantly few juvenile delinquents – 12.6 per cent as opposed to 23.4 per cent. The tendency of above average E scorers at age 16 to become young adult delinquents was much clearer (30 per cent as opposed to 16 per cent). Farrington states that: 'Low E scores genuinely predicted a low likelihood of adult delinquency.' The major burden of these and other significant relationships was borne by the lowest quarter of E scorers; introverts were very unlikely to become delinquents.

*Neuroticism*   There was little overall relationship between neuroticism and criminality except that those on the lowest quarter of N scorers at age 10 tended not to become adult delinquents (12 per cent as opposed to 25 per cent), and not to be delinquents at any age (17 per cent as opposed to 34 per cent). Quadrant analysis, of the kind suggested by Burgess (1972) shows that neurotic extraverts at age 16 included significantly more adult delinquents, and significantly more delinquents at any age, than the remainder.

The data, as Farrington points out, suggest that the personality theory might apply to adult delinquency rather than to juvenile delinquency. It is notable that the adult offences included proportionately more aggressive crimes, more damaging offences and more drug offences than the juvenile offences.

For reasons to be discussed presently, this seems an unlikely hypothesis; in school-boys for instance very clear-cut relationships between personality and anti-social behaviour often of a not very serious kind, have been found. These studies are mainly based on self-reports (Gibson, 1971), a type of study which furnishes the child with a list of minor and not-so-minor misdemeanours frequently committed by school children, and asks him or her anonymously to endorse those items which they have been guilty of. There are two studies which have related self-reported offending to the three major dimensions of personality (Allsop and Feldman, 1975, 1976). In addition, these studies used an outside criterion (teacher's ratings) in order to check on the validity of self ratings; results were very similar for both types of measures. The ratings of the teachers were concerned with school behaviour ('naughtiness'). Scores on the anti-social behaviour scale (ASB) were positively and significantly related to P, E and N in descending order of significance, and 'naughtiness' (Na) scores to P and N, although only the former achieved statistical significance. The P, E and N scores were then divided at the median points and the mean ASB and Na scores plotted for those high (i.e. above the median) on all 3, 2 only, one only, or none out of P, E and N. The results, which are quite striking, are shown in Figure 10.5. They clearly suggest the usefulness of combining personality scores when analysing self-report data. These data come from the study of secondary schoolgirls (Allsop and Feldman, 1975); a similar study, done on schoolboys, has obtained very similar results (Allsop and Feldman, 1976).

The differential relationship between personality and type of offence has also been studied using self-reports. Hindelang and Weis (1972), using cluster analysis, formed 26 offences self-reported by 245 Los Angeles middle class high-school males into seven groups, and then correlated the scores on each of the seven clusters with the four possible combinations of E and N. They expected a descending order of frequency of offending–EN, either En or eN, and en; this was obtained for 'general deviance' and 'traffic truancy' and partially obtained for two other clusters, concerning 'drug-taking' and

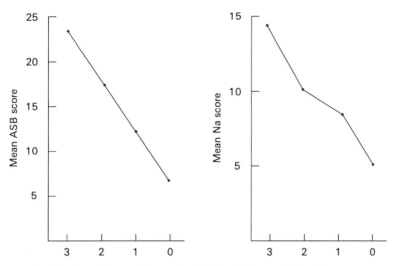

Figure 10.5 *Number of personality scales (P, E and N) on which subjects scored highly, as related to anti-social behaviour (ASB) score and naughtiness (Na) score (Allsop and Feldman, 1975)*

'malicious destruction', respectively. No difference between the combinations of E and N was found for theft and the second of two clusters concerning drugs. For the 'aggressive' clusters the En combination was the highest. These data again show the need to break down criminality into more homogeneous clusters, but of course the sample is a somewhat unusual one.

Allsop (1976) has reported one further study where he used 368 white boys between the ages of 13 and 16. Teachers were asked to rate the behaviour of the boys; on this basis they were divided into well and badly behaved. When these ratings were compared with the personality scale scores, the results indicated that:

> badly behaved boys predominate at the high level of P and at the low level of P where there is a combination of high E/high N scores; well-behaved boys predominate at the low level of P except where E and N are simultaneously high.

Using the ASB, he subdivided the total scale into ten sub-scales according to type of offence; this table sets out the correlations of P, E and N with each of the sub-scales as well as the total scale. It showed that all the correlations are positive, being highest with P and lowest with N.

Among non-incarcerated adolescents the pattern is much the same. R. Foggitt (1976) has studied a non-institutionalized sample of delinquent and non-delinquent adolescents. Factor analysis of the intercorrelations between the crimes and the personality scales of E and N showed that they were all positively intercorrelated and that a single general factor emerged from the analysis on which different crimes had loadings as follows. Truancy, 0.56; poor work history, 0.62; vagrancy, 0.71; attempted suicide, 0.56; frequency of violence, 0.74; destructiveness of violence, 0.72; heavy drinking, 0.45; excessive drugs, 0.52; theft, 0.71; fraud, 0.50; group-delinquency, 0.46; number of convictions, 0.59. For the personality variables the loadings were 0.44 for E and 0.42 for N.

Two interesting recent studies extend the scope of the work so far reviewed. Perez and Torrubia (1985) used Zuckerman's (1979) concept of sensation-seeking defined as the need for varied, novel and complex sensations and experiences, and willingness to take risks for the sake of such experiences. This scale, which is correlated with extraversion and defines one aspect of that dimension of personality (Eysenck and Eysenck, 1985) was measured in a Spanish translation of the scale published by Zuckerman, Eysenck and Eysenck (1978). Three hundred and forty-nine students were tested, using the sensation seeking scale as well as a 37-item Spanish version of a written self-report delinquency (SRD) scale. A correlation of 0.46 was obtained for the total of the sensation seeking scale, with the highest correlations going to the experience seeking (0.45) and disinhibition (0.43) scales. These are the values for males; for females they were 0.49 for the total scale, and 0.43 and 0.45 for the experience seeking and disinhibition scales. Correlations for the other two scales were smaller (in the neighbourhood of 0.20) but still significant.

Also using a self-report format, Rushton and Chrisjohn (1981) tested eight separate samples, obtaining significant positive correlations with extraversion, largely insignificant ones with neuroticism, and very positive and significant ones with psychoticism. Correlations with the lie scale were uniformly negative and mostly significant. Subjects of these experiments were high school and university students, totalling 410 in all. As the authors summarize their findings:

> The evidence showed clear support for a relationship between high delinquency scores and high scores on both extraversion and psychoticism. These relationships held up across diverse samples and different ways of analyzing the data. No support was found for a relationship between delinquency scores and the dimension of neuroticism. (1981: 11)

In another interesting study, Martin (1985) pointed out that:

> Attempts to verify Eysenck's theory of criminality have usually been concerned with the proportion by which delinquents differ from non-delinquents on the dimensions of extraversion, neuroticism and psychoticism. There are very few studies concerned with the proportion in which these dimensions are related to the acquisition of moral social rules, the real core of this theory. The current study examines the theory from a new approach, trying to show in what measures the value priorities of a group of 113 juvenile delinquents are related to the personality dimensions stated by Eysenck. (1985: 549)

It was found that extraversion and psychoticism showed the largest number of significant relationships. The youths who scored high and low on the E scale differed in six terminal values and six instrumental values out of a total of 36 values. Values concerned with morality, and those which imply an acceptance of the social norms, are considered the most important factors for the youths with low E scores.

Those who scored high on the psychoticism dimension consider the following values as the most important: 'An exciting life; pleasure; ability'; all these have clear personal significance. They gave less importance to values related to the social environment, such as 'world peace', 'equality' and 'social recognition'. As far as they go, these results are in good accord with the personality theory under discussion, and they also suggest a new approach to validating the theory.

Drug takers constitute a rather special sample of criminals, although the study just mentioned shows drug taking offences to be highly correlated with other types of criminality. Shanmugan (1979) compared 212 drug users and 222 non-drug users matched with respect to sex, age, educational qualification and socioeconomic status, and found that drug users were high on extraversion and neuroticism; stimulant-depressant drug users were found to be high on psychoticism as well as on the 'C' (criminal propensity) scale. Gossop (1978) studied the personality correlates of female drug addicts convicted of drug-related violent and other offences. Convicted subjects were more extraverted than non-convicted subjects. Another study, Gossop and Kristjansson (1977), investigated 50 drug takers and found that subjects convicted of non-drug offences scored higher on extraversion than subjects not convicted of such offences. Drug-dependent subjects altogether scored extremely highly on the 'C' (criminal propensity) scale. This reflects to some extent their high scores on the P and N dimensions.

### Specific traits and criminality

Before considering the large number of German-speaking studies using inventories derived from and similar to the Eysenck Questionnaires, it may be useful to consider quickly studies involving a number of specific traits which, as Figures 10.1–10.3 show, are involved in the three major dimensions of personality. Most work has been done on such factors as anxiety and depression, sensation-seeking, impulsiveness, impulse control, hostility and aggression, and lack of conformity. Typical and relatively recent studies only will be quoted; these usually have bibliographies referring to earlier studies.

Sensation or stimulation seeking has been studied by Farley and Sewell (1976) and Whitehill, De Myer-Gapin and Scott (1976), the former using a questionnaire, the latter a laboratory experimental technique. They found support for the hypothesis, which was formulated earlier by Quay (1965), that criminals would be sensation seekers. Robins (1972), can also be quoted in support.

Impulsiveness and lack of impulse control has frequently been suggested as a major component of criminality. Hormuth et al. (1977) using both questionnaires and experimental methods, were able to verify the prediction of less impulse control in delinquents with the former. The latter study also found positive results favouring the hypothesis. These data may be considered together with a related concept, namely that of risk-taking, which is often considered almost synonymous with impulsivity or lack of impulse control. A very thorough review of the literature is given by Lösel (1975), who found risk-taking more prominent among delinquents. The best available study on risk-taking, also giving a good summary of the literature, is by Schwenkmezger (1983); his conclusion is that results obtained by various investigators can best be interpreted in the sense that delinquent behaviour is favoured by impulsive, risky decision strategies, influenced more by hope of luck and chance than by realistic estimates of one's own abilities and possibilities.

Hostility and aggression are other traits frequently associated with criminality, and the Foulds scales (Foulds et al., 1960) have often been used as a measuring instrument. Data reported by Blackburn (1968, 1970), and Crawford (1977) suggest that positive relationships exist, with long-term prisoners generally having higher total hostility scores than normals, and violent offenders being more extra-punitive than non-violent offenders. Megargee's (1966) hypothesis contrasting over- and under-control would distinguish between extremely assaultive offenders (over-controlled) who would be expected to express less hostility than only moderately assaultive offenders. This theory was supported by Blackburn (1968) but not by Crawford (1977). Berman and Paisley (1984) compared juveniles convicted of assaultive offences with others convicted of other types of offences, and found that the former exhibited significantly higher psychoticism, extraversion and neuroticism scores; sensation seeking scores were also significantly lower for the non-assaultive group of property offenders.

A French Canadian group was studied by Coté and Leblanc (1982). Using the Jesness Inventory (Jesness, 1972) and the Eysenck Personality Inventory, they studied 825 adolescents from 14 to 19 years old, and correlated personality measures with self-reported indices of delinquency. They found the following traits very significantly correlated with delinquency; psychoticism (0.36), manifest aggressiveness (0.34), extraversion (0.32), bad social adjustment (0.32), alienation (0.25), repression (-0.25), and some traits showing even lower but still significant correlations.

The Jesness Inventory, just mentioned, consists of 155 items, scored on ten sub-scales (social maladjustment, value orientation, immaturity, alienation, autism, withdrawal, manifest aggression, social anxiety, repression and denial), and a predictive score, the Anti-social index. The relationships between the Eysenck and Jesness Personality Inventories have been explored by Smith (1974). Some of the observed correlations are quite high, e.g. between social maladjustment, autism, manifest aggression, withdrawal, on the one hand, and N and P, on the other. Social anxiety is negatively correlated with E, and highly positively with N. Saunders and Davies (1976) found evidence for the validity of the Jesness Inventory, as did Mott (1969). The scales most diagnostic appeared to be social maladjustment, value orientation, alienation, manifest aggression, and denial. In addition, Davies (1967) found some evidence in his follow-up studies for the validity of the autism, withdrawal and repression scales.

There are many studies using MMPI profiles, such as those of Davies and Sines (1971), and Beck and McIntyre (1977). The scales usually involved are the psychopathic deviate and hysteria scales, hypochondriasis, masculinity/femininity interest patterns, and mania; these suggest neurotic extraversion in the main. A more detailed account of work with the MMPI will be found in Dahlstrom and Dahlstrom (1980). As regards anxiety, a typical report is that by Lidhoo (1971), who studied 200 delinquent and 200 non-delinquent adolescents, matched for age, sex and socioeconomic status; all the subjects were Indian. The main and highly significant differences observed were with respect to emotionality, with the delinquents more tense, more depressed, and more easily provoked, and sexual maladjustment.

With only one or two exceptions, all the studies so far considered have been published in English and relate to English and American populations. It may be useful to summarize the major findings before going on to the large body of German-speaking studies investigating the major theories here considered. Replication is the life-blood of science, and here we would seem to have an ideal opportunity to compare two sets of data, not just collected by different investigators, but collected in different countries and by means of different inventories, although the German inventory used in all these studies was explicitly based on the Eysenck Personality Inventory. Thus we would here seem to have a cross-cultural replication, and if similar results are obtained, we could feel much more secure in regarding these conclusions as being firmly based.

The first conclusion which seems appropriate is that while the earlier studies summarized by Passingham were not theory centred, often used inappropriate questionnaires, and paid little attention to important methodological requirements, later studies summarized in Eysenck (1977), were methodologically much superior, and gave much more definitive and significant support to the personality theory in question. Studies carried out since then have maintained this improvement, and are nearly all equally positive in the outcome. Our first conclusion therefore must be that we now have good evidence for the implication of psychoticism, extraversion and neuroticism as predisposing factors in juvenile and adult criminality, and even in juvenile anti-social behaviour not amounting to legally criminal conduct. These correlations are based both on self-reported anti-social behaviour and criminal activity, and on legally defined criminality.

It would seem that different types of criminal activity may show differential relationships to personality, but too little has been done in that field to be very definitive to one's conclusions. Males and females seem to have similar personality patterns, as far as criminality is concerned, but little seems to have been done in making deliberate gender comparisons.

While P, E and N are related to criminality at all ages, there seem to be definite patterns suggesting that N is more important with older criminals, E with younger criminals. Why this should be so is not clear, but the data definitely tend in that direction. Possibly N, as a multiplicative drive variable, assumes greater importance with older people in whom habits have already been settled more clearly than is the case with younger persons. Another possibility is that the largely incarcerated adult samples cannot properly answer the social activity questions which make up a large part of the extraversion inventory. A study specifically directed to the solution of this problem would seem called for.

## Summary of German studies

A summary of 15 empirical German studies, using altogether 3,450 delinquents and a rather larger number of controls, has been reported by Steller and Hunze (1984). All these studies used the FPI (Freiburger Persönlichkeits Inventar) of Fahrenberg, Selg and Hampel (1978). In addition, Steller and Hunze report a study of their own, using a self-report device for the measurement of anti-social conduct. The FPI contains nine traits and three dimensional scales, the latter being extraversion, emotional ability or neuroticism, and masculinity. The nine trait scales relate to nervousness, aggressiveness, depression, excitability, sociability, stability, dominance, inhibition and openness. Typical of the general findings are those of the special study carried out by Steller and Hunze, where they found that delinquents showed higher scores on nervousness, depression, excitability, sociability, extraversion, and neuroticism. These results appeared separately on two alternative forms of the FPI.

In summarizing the results from all the other German studies, Steller and Hunze point out that for the trait scales there is a very clear picture. Delinquents are higher on depression, nervousness, excitability and aggression. Regarding the major dimensions, a great majority show excessive degrees of neuroticism, and to a lesser extent extraversion. Sociability, as a major trait involved in extraversion, was significantly elevated in 25 per cent of all the comparisons, with criminals being more sociable. If we can use aggressiveness as an important part of psychoticism, then it is clear that these results agree very well with those of the English-speaking samples.

German studies show a similar differentiation between older and younger subjects, as far as neuroticism and extraversion are concerned. For the younger groups, delinquents are characterized much more clearly by greater sociability, dominance and openness; extraversion is implicated in almost every comparison between young delinquents and non-delinquents. This agrees well with the English-speaking data.

The German data give evidence also for the fact that the different types of criminality may be related differentially to personality, but the data are not extensive enough to make any definitive summary possible. There is, however, an interesting summary of data relating personality to the duration of incarceration, suggesting an increase in emotional instability with incarceration. However, there is also evidence that prisoners on probation showed increases in emotional instability. Clearly a more detailed investigation of this question is in order, particularly as Bolton et al. (1976) report discrepant findings.

It is sometimes suggested that possibly the differences between criminals and non-criminals might be due to the process of incarceration itself. This is unlikely, because several of the studies discussed compared the anti-social and criminal activities of children and juveniles none of whom were incarcerated at any time. Even more relevant and impressive is work showing that long before anti-social acts are committed, children who later on commit them are already differentiated from those who do not. Consider as an example the work of Burt (1965) who reported on the follow-up of children originally studied over 30 years previously. Seven hundred and sixty-three children of whom 15 per cent and 18 per cent respectively later became habitual criminals or neurotics, were rated by the teachers for N and for E. Of those who later became habitual offenders, 63 per cent had been rated as high on N; 54 per cent had been rated as high on E, but only 3 per cent as high on introversion. Of those who later became neurotics, 59 per cent had been rated as high on N, 44 per cent had been rated as high on introversion, but only 1 per cent as high on E. Similar data are reported by Michael (1956), and more recently Taylor and Watt (1977) and Fakouri and Jerse (1976) have published data showing that prediction of future criminal behaviour is possible from early school records. Thus the future criminal, like the future neurotic, is already recognizable in the young child.

Several of the studies summarized by Steller and Hunze used self-reported delinquency, and found, very much as did the English-speaking studies, that very similar personality correlates were observed here as in the case of legally defined delinquency.

The authors conclude that:

in agreement with Eysenck's hypothesis and findings, it was found that in many samples emotional instability ('neuroticism') and high extraversion were found (in delinquents). The corresponding increases in the FPI dimensional scales were found most clearly in juvenile samples, but for grown-up delinquents were found in the FPI trait scales which represent major components of dimensional scales emotional instability and extraversion. (1984: 107)

We may thus conclude that this essay in replication has been eminently successful, in that identical findings are reported from the German literature as we have found to be representative of the English-speaking literature. There seems to be little doubt, therefore, that personality and anti-social and criminal behaviour are reasonably intimately correlated, and that these correlations can be found in cultures other than the Anglo-American. Eysenck (1977) has reported such confirmatory studies from widely different countries, including India, Hungary, Poland, and others, as well as the German and French-speaking samples mentioned in this chapter.
[. . .]

# References

Allsop, J.F. (1976) 'Investigations into the applicability of Eysenck's theory of criminality to the anti-social behaviour of schoolchildren'. Unpublished PhD thesis, University of London.

Allsop, J.F. and Feldman, M.P. (1975) 'Extraversion, neuroticism and psychoticism and anti-social behaviour in school girls', *Social Behaviour and Personality*, 2: 184–9.

Allsop, J.F. and Feldman, M.P. (1976) 'Item analyses of questionnaire measures of personality and anti-social behaviour in school girls', *British Journal of Criminology*, 16: 337–51.

Barack, L.I. and Widom, C.S. (1978) 'Eysenck's theory of criminality applied to women awaiting trial', *British Journal of Psychiatry*, 133: 452–6.

Beck, E.A. and McIntyre, C.S. (1977) 'MMPI patterns of shoplifters within a college population', *Psychological Reports*, 41: 1035–40.

Berman, T. and Paisley, T. (1984) 'Personality in assaultive and non-assaultive juvenile male offenders', *Psychological Reports*, 54: 527–30.

Blackburn, R. (1968) 'Personality in relation to extreme aggression in psychiatric offenders', *British Journal of Psychiatry*, 114: 821–8.

Blackburn, R. (1970) 'Personality types among abnormal homicides', Special Hospital Research, No. 1, London.

Bolton, N., Smith, F.V., Heskin, K.J. and Barister, P.A. (1976) 'Psychological correlates of long-term imprisonment', *British Journal of Criminology*, 16: 38–47.

Burgess, P.K. (1972) 'Eysenck's theory of criminality: a new approach', *British Journal of Criminology*, 12: 74–82.

Burt, C. (1965), 'Factorial studies of personality and their bearing in the work of the teacher', *British Journal of Educational Psychology*, 35: 308–28.

Coté, G. and Leblanc, M. (1982) 'Aspects de personalité et comportement delinquent', *Bulletin de Psychologique*, 36: 265–71.

Crawford, D.A. (1977) 'The HDHQ results of long-term prisoners: relationships with criminal and institutional behaviour', *British Journal of Social and Clinical Psychology*, 16: 391–4.

Dahlstrom, W.G. and Dahlstrom, L. (eds) (1980) *Basic Readings on the MMPI*. Minneapolis: University of Minnesota Press.

Davies, M.B. (1967) *The Use of the Jesness Inventory in a Sample of British Probationers*. London: HMSO.

Davies, K.R. and Sines, J.O. (1971) 'An anti-social behaviour pattern associated with a specific MMPI profile', *Journal of Consulting and Clinical Psychology*, 36: 229–34.

Eysenck, H.J. (1960) Symposium: 'The development of moral values in children. VII. The contribution of learning theory', *British Journal of Educational Psychology*, 30: 11–21.

Eysenck, H.J. (1967) *The Biological Basis of Personality*. Springfield, Ill.: C.C. Thomas.

Eysenck, H.J. (1970) *The Structures of Human Personality*, 3rd edn. London: Methuen.

Eysenck, H.J. (1973) 'Personality, learning and "anxiety"', in H.J. Eysenck (ed.), *Handbook of Abnormal Psychology*, 2nd edn. London: Pitman. pp. 390–419.

Eysenck, H.J. (1976) 'The biology of morality', in T. Lickona (ed.), *Moral Development and Behavior*. New York: Holt, Rinehart and Winston. pp. 108–23.

Eysenck, H.J. (1977) *Crime and Personality*, 3rd edn. London: Routledge and Kegan Paul.

Eysenck, H.J. (ed.) (1980) *A Model for Personality*. New York: Springer.

Eysenck, H.J. and Eysenck, M.W. (1985) *Personality and Individual Differences*. New York: Plenum.

Eysenck, H.J. and Eysenck, S.B.G. (1976) *Psychoticism as a Dimension of Personality*. London: Hodder and Stoughton.

Eysenck, H.J. and Eysenck, S.B.G. (1978) 'Psychopathy, personality and genetics', in R.D. Hare and D. Schalling (eds),*Psychopathic Behaviour*. London: John Wiley, pp. 197–223.

Eysenck, S.B.G. and Eysenck H.J. (1970) 'Crime and personality: an empirical study of the three-factor theory', *British Journal of Criminology*, 10: 225–39.

Eysenck, S.B.G. and Eysenck, H.J. (1971) 'A comparative study of criminals and matched controls on three dimensions of personality', *British Journal of Social and Clinical Psychology*, 10: 362–6.

Eysenck, S.B.G. and Eysenck, H.J. (1971) 'Crime and personality: item analysis of questionnaire responses', *British Journal of Criminology*, 11: 49–62.

Eysenck, S.B.G. and Eysenck, H.J. (1973) 'The personality of female prisoners', *British Journal of Psychiatry*, 122: 693–8.

Eysenck, S.B.G. and Eysenck, H.J. (1974) 'Personality and recidivism in Borstal boys', *British Journal of Criminology*, 14: 285–7.

Eysenck, S.B.G. and Eysenck, H.J. (1977) 'Personality differences between prisoners and controls', *Psychological Reports*, 40: 1023–8.

Eysenck, S.B.G., Rust, J. and Eysenck, H.J. (1977) 'Personality and the classification of adult offenders', *British Journal of Criminology*, 17: 169–79.

Fahrenberg, J., Selg, H. and Hampel, R. (1978) *Das Freiburger Persönlichkeits–inventar*. Göttingen: Hogrefe.

Fakouri, E. and Jerse, F.W. (1976) 'Unobtrusive detection of potential juvenile delinquency', *Psychological Reports*, 39: 551–8.

Farley, F.H. and Sewell, T. (1976) 'Test of an arousal theory of delinquency', *Criminal Justice and Behaviour*, 3: 315–20.

Farrington, P., Biron, L. and Leblanc, M. (1982) 'Personality and delinquency in London and Madrid', in J. Gunn and D.P. Farrington (eds), *Abnormal Offenders, Delinquency, and the Criminal Justice System*. New York: Wiley.

Foggitt, R. (1976) 'Personality and delinquency'. Unpublished PhD thesis, University of London.

Foulds, G.A., Caine, T.M. and Creasy, M.I. (1960) 'Aspects of extra- and intra-punitive expression in mental illness', *Journal of Mental Science*, 196: 599–610.

Gibson, H.B. (1971) 'The factorial structure of juvenile delinquency: a study of self-reported acts', *British Journal of Social and Clinical Psychology*, 10: 1–9.

Glueck, S. and Glueck, E. (1956) *Physique and Delinquency*. New York: Harper.

Gossop, M. (1978) 'Drug dependence, crime and personality among female addicts', *Drug and Alcohol Dependence*, 3: 359–64.

Gossop, M.R. and Kristjansson, I. (1977) 'Crime and personality', *British Journal of Criminology*, 17: 264–73.

Hindelang, M. and Weis, J.G. (1972) 'Personality and self-reported delinquency: an application of cluster analysis', *Criminology*, 10: 268–76.

Holcomb, W.R., Adam, N.A. and Ponder, H.N. (1985) 'The development and cross-validation upon MMPI typology of murderers', *Journal of Personality Assessment*, 49: 240–4.

Hormuth, S., Lamm, H., Michelitsch, I., Scheuermann, H., Trommsdorf, G. and Vogele, I. (1977) 'Impulskontrolle und einige Persönlichkeitscharakteristika bei delinquenten und nicht-delinquenten Jugendlichen', *Psychologische Beiträge*, 19: 340–59.

Jesness, C.F. (1972) *The Jesness Inventory: Manual*. Palo Alto, CA: Consulting Psychologist Press.

Lidhoo, M.L. (1971) 'An attempt to construct a psycho-diagnostic tool for the detection of potential delinquents among adolescents aged 14–19 years'. Unpublished PhD thesis, University of Panjab.

Lösel, F. (1975) *Handlungskontrolle und Jugend-delinquenz.* Stuttgart: Enke.

McCue, P., Booth, S. and Root, J. (1976) 'Do young prisoners under-state their extraversion on personality inventories?', *British Journal of Criminology*, 16: 282, 283.

McGurk, B.J. (1978) 'Personality types among "normal" homicides', *British Journal of Criminology*, 18: 146–61.

McGurk, B.J. and McDougall, C. (1981) 'A new approach to Eysenck's theory of criminality', *Personality and Individual Differences*, 2: 338–40.

McGurk, B.J. and McEwan, A.W. (1983) 'Personality types and recidivism among Borstal trainees', *Personality and Individual Differences*, 4: 165–70.

McGurk, B.J., McEwan, A.W. and Graham, F. (1981) 'Personality types and recidivism among young delinquents', *British Journal of Criminology*, 21: 159–65.

Martin, A.L. (1985) 'Values and personality: a survey of their relationship in the case of juvenile delinquency', *Personality and Individual Differences*, 4: 519–22.

Megargee, E.I. (1966) 'Undercontrolled and overcontrolled personality types in extreme anti-social aggression', *Psychological Monographs*, 80, Whole Number 611.

Michael, C.M. (1956) 'Follow-up studies of introverted children: IV. Relative incidence of criminal behaviour', *Journal of Criminal Law and Criminality*, 47, 414–22.

Mitchell, J., Rogers, R., Cavanaugh, J. and Wasyliw, O. (1980) 'The role of trait anxiety in violent and non-violent delinquent behavior', *American Journal of Forensic Psychiatry*.

Mott, J. (1969) *The Jesness Inventory: An Application to Approved School Boys.* London: HMSO.

Passingham, R.E. (1972) 'Crime and personality: a review of Eysenck's theory', in V.D. Nebylitsyn and J.A. Gray (eds), *Biological Bases of Individual Behaviour.* London: Academic Press.

Perez, J. and Torrubia, R. (1985) 'Sensation seeking and anti-social behaviour in a student sample', *Personality and Individual Differences*, 6: 401–3.

Quay, H.C. (1965), 'Psychopathic personality as pathological stimulation-seeking', *American Journal of Psychiatry*, 122: 180–3.

Rahman, A. and Hussain, A. (1984) 'Personality and female criminals in Bangladesh', *Personality and Individual Differences*, 5: 473–4.

Raine, A. and Venables, P. (1981) 'Classical conditioning and socialization – a biosocial interaction', *Personality and Individual Differences*, 2: 273–83.

Robins, L.N. (1972) 'Follow-up studies of behaviour disorders in children', in H.C. Quay and J.S. Werry (eds), *Psychopathological Disorders of Childhood.* New York: Wiley.

Royce, J.P. and Powell, A. (1983) *Theory of Personality and Individual Differences: Factors, Systems and Processes.* Englewood Cliffs, NJ: Prentice-Hall.

Rushton, J.F. and Chrisjohn, R.D. (1981) 'Extraversion, neuroticism, psychoticism and self-reported delinquency: evidence from eight separate samples', *Personality and Individual Differences*, 2: 11–20.

Saklofske, D.H., McKerracher, D.W. and Eysenck, S.B.G. (1978) 'Eysenck's theory of criminality: a scale of criminal propensity as a measure of anti-social behaviour', *Psychological Reports*, 43: 683–6.

Sanocki, W. (1969) 'The use of Eysenck's inventory for testing young prisoners', *Przeglad Penitencjarny* (Warszawa), 7: 53–68.

Saunders, G.R. and Davies, M.B. (1976) 'The validity of the Jesness Inventory with British delinquents', *British Journal of Social and Clinical Psychology*, 15: 33–9.

Schwenkmezger, P. (1983) 'Risikoverhalten, Risikobereitschaft und Delinquenz: Theoretische Grundlagen und differentialdiagnostische Untersuchungen'. *Zeitschrift für Differentielle und Diagnostische Psychologie*, 4: 223–39.

Shanmugan, T.E. (1979) 'Personality factors underlying drug abuse among college students', *Psychological Studies*, 24–35.

Singh, A. (1982) 'A study of the personality and adjustments of female juvenile delinquents', *Child Psychiatry Quarterly*, 13: 52–9.

Smith, D.E. (1974) 'Relationships between the Eysenck and Jesness Personality Inventories', *British Journal of Criminology*, 14: 376–84.

Smith, D.E. and Smith, D.D. (1977) 'Eysenck's psychoticism scale and reconvictions', *British Journal of Criminology*, 17: 387–8.

Steller, M. and Hunze, D. (1984) 'Zur Selbstbeschreibung von Delinquenten im Freiburger Persönlichkeitsinventar (FPI) – Eine Sekundäranalyse empirischer Untersuchungen', *Zeitschrift für Differentielle und Diagnostische Psychologie*, 5: 87–110.

98        *H.J. Eysenck*

Taylor, T. and Watt, D.C. (1977) 'The relation of deviant symptoms and behaviour in a normal population to subsequent delinquency and maladjustment', *Psychological Medicine*, 7: 163–9.

Wardell, D. and Yeudall, L.T. (1980) 'A multidimensional approach to criminal disorders: the assessment of impulsivity and its relation to crime', *Advances in Behaviour Research and Therapy*, 2: 159–77.

West, D. and Farrington, D.P. (1973) *Who Becomes Delinquent?* London: Heinemann.

Whitehill, M., De Myer-Gapin, S. and Scott, T.J. (1976) 'Stimulation seeking in anti-social preadolescent children', *Journal of Abnormal Psychology*, 85: 101–4.

Zuckerman, M. (1979) *Sensation Seeking: Beyond the Optimal Level of Arousal*. Hillsdale: NJ: Erlbaum.

Zuckerman, M., Eysenck, S.B.G. and Eysenck, H.J. (1978) 'Sensation seeking in England and America: cross-cultural, age and sex comparisons', *Journal of Consulting and Clinical Psychology*, 1: 139–49.

# 11

# Explanations of crime and place

## Anthony E. Bottoms and Paul Wiles

The opportunity for two criminologists to reflect, in the company of geographers, upon some aspects of the spatial distribution of crime produces something of a dilemma. On the one hand we want to give full weight to and to welcome the very real contributions which geographers have recently made to this subject (e.g. in Britain alone, Davidson, 1981; Herbert, 1982; Smith, 1986); on the other hand, there seems little point in producing yet another substantive overview of what these writers, and their criminological and sociological colleagues, have discovered to date.

We have chosen, therefore, to write largely in a methodological vein, though with reference where appropriate to substantive findings. Our framework of approach is the intimate relationship of social relations and spatial structures found within the theory of 'structuration', a framework which has attracted considerable recent attention and critical debate among general human geographers and social theorists (e.g. Gregory and Urry, 1985), but which has so far been given little consideration in discussions of the spatial dimensions of crime and offending. We adopt this approach because structuration theory offers a model for explanation which brings together, in a coherent fashion, a number of elements which we have been developing in our own work on residential areas and crime; it offers, in our view, both a framework within which previous research can be synthesized, and a valuable stimulus for future research.

[. . .]

## Statistical distributions and ethnography: history and problematic

The work of the pre-war Chicago researchers has justly remained important because they employed a wide variety of research methods, examining *inter alia* both the statistical data on offender distributions in the city (Shaw and McKay, 1942) and aspects of the ethnography of street life and crime (e.g. Cressey, 1932; Shaw, 1930). They established that offender residence in Chicago was not randomly distributed across the city but was quite clearly patterned, with the highest offender rate areas located in an inner city zone close to the central business district, and then a diminution of the offender rate as one moved outwards towards the periphery of the city. In order to explain this distribution they utilized a theory of the growth of the city in terms of a historical process of urban development radiating outwards from

Abridged from *Crime, Policing and Place: Essays in Environmental Criminology* (eds D.J. Evans, N.R. Fyfe and D.T. Herbert), pp. 11–35. (London: Routledge, 1992.)

the city's core. This theory seemed adequately to explain the distribution of land use they had found in Chicago, although it continued to be a matter of some debate as to how far the theory fitted other cities, and therefore whether it was a general theory. Their theory of urban development did not itself explain why offenders lived in some areas rather than others; however, from their ethnographic work the Chicagoans did develop an explanation of why and how offending occurred, based on the key concept of 'social disorganization'. Essentially their argument was that offending manifested itself in a lack of structurally located social bonds which encouraged legitimate and discouraged deviant behaviour. Such social disorganization was the result of new immigrant populations coming together and not having had the opportunity to develop a stable social structure with clear norms. Such populations were to be found in those areas of the city, immediately surrounding the inner core, which had been abandoned by more established groups and so offered the cheapest available housing for the new immigrants – the well-known 'interstitial areas' of the Chicago theory. The continuing process of immigration into Chicago meant that as immigrant groups developed more stable normative structures they moved out of the interstitial areas to be replaced, in their turn, by new immigrants. So the cycle was repeated, with new groups gradually developing from disorganization to more stable normative structures and at the same time moving their location gradually outward from the city's centre. In this way areas of the city continued to have patterned offender rates over time.

The Chicago theory of social disorganization has been very influential in the history of criminology. It appears to offer an answer to the problem of the relationship between studies of the areal statistical distribution of crime and offending, and studies of the ethnography of criminal behaviour. As a result much subsequent criminological research used the idea of social disorganization as a central concept. However, there are very real problems with the concept, and beginning with Whyte's (1943) classic *Street Corner Society*, it was subjected to a series of critiques. A number of writers pointed out that empirical studies of interstitial areas and/or deviant behaviour did not support the idea that illegal behaviour was always the result of 'disorganization' – rather, it might instead be the result of highly organized, but alternative sets of normative values. The fact that action is morally disapproved of does not mean that it is necessarily any less related to social organization (see e.g. Becker, 1963). The result, it was argued, was that the theory, like a number of other social theories of crime, was overdeterministic and therefore overpredictive of crime (Matza, 1964). Basically the concept of social disorganization was attacked as being at best a value judgement, and at worst empirically false.

Although the concept of social disorganization has been subject to so much criticism it has nevertheless lived on. For example, recent discussion in the United States has used the notion of an 'underclass', whose lack of a normative order is said to be demonstrated by the collapse of the (black) family, to explain the high crime rates of their cities' ghettos (for a discussion of how these ideas have been used in popular debate see e.g. *Chicago Tribune*, 1986). This renaissance of social disorganization is not entirely surprising since criminology has failed to develop any very satisfactory alternative concept to bridge the two levels of analysis. The alternative has all too often been simply to operate at just one level of analysis. Recent research in Britain has sometimes exemplified this approach. Janet Foster, in a study of crime on housing estates in south London, is most illuminating about the ethnography of crime but says little about the distribution of crime between or within estates (Foster, 1990). On the other hand, the analysis of the results of the British Crime Survey examined the distribution of crime across socially different types of areas (using the ACORN classifications) but said little about why these areas have such different crime rates or indeed whether the classification which was used captured socially similar areas within its categories (Mayhew et al., 1989). Of course, many problems of this kind may simply be due to the limitations of the particular research methods being used within a particular project, and in the end to the lack of the resources available to employ additional or alternative methods. However, the gap remains, and an adequate environmental criminology clearly needs a model of explanation which can link statistical analyses of the distribution of crime with ethnographic studies of criminal and social action.

## Structuration theory

In order to explore what might be an adequate explanatory model for environmental criminology, we need first to explore the more general question of what an adequate explanatory model in social science might look like.

Social science has always had a problem with what form explanation ought to take, given that it is concerned with the activity of human beings. The twin dangers are that explanations either operate with models of human action which are so deterministic that they deny any role for human agency, or they are so voluntaristic and particularistic that they deny any real possibility of social science explanations at all. The history of social science could be written in terms of the various attempts to overcome this problem. Social science, like other human activities, has its fashions and at different times fashion has pushed researchers towards one or other of these extremes. The result has been that at different times explanations have been dominated by structural accounts, which have stressed the extent to which human behaviour is a product of the constraints imposed by social structures which are external to the individual (such as the economy), or alternatively by accounts of action, which have emphasized the extent to which human action is a consequence of the creative understanding of particular individuals, and their interaction with other actors. Both approaches have had the advantage of highlighting, often with great clarity, certain aspects of the human condition, but the disadvantage is that they remain partial.

Research in environmental criminology has been prone to just these difficulties. Explanations of where offences occur, or where offenders live, can all too easily assume that place or design acts as a deterministic and monocausal variable. Alternatively, they may assume that place can stand as an operational construct for other aspects of social structure, such as class, or employment status, or family structure; or that it is simply a sorting mechanism which brings together in one place those individuals who possess criminogenic attributes (generally of a genetic or psychological kind). These latter formulations use place as a second order explanation, parasitic on separate explanations of criminal behaviour, which simply accounts for the distribution of crime in geographical space. Alternatively again, structural explanations of this kind may combine the influence of place and the influence of class/employment/family structure, yet remain straightforwardly deterministic. All of these approaches can be criticized as giving insufficient weight to human agency (see for example the work of Sally Merry (1981) on the limitations of a purely design-orientated approach to crime).

A very different approach has been the 'appreciative' one, which has produced a rich harvest of qualitative studies giving a vivid picture of life in a particular area, or the life history of individuals. The difficulty with this approach is that it can ignore the fact that there is a spatial patterning of crime which is in need of explanation, and/or that there are structural aspects in the wider society which powerfully shape the day-to-day lives of individual actors. One researcher who recognized just these difficulties was Owen Gill (1977), who set out to write an appreciative ethnography of the lives of a group of boys from a 'problem council estate' in Merseyside, but found himself successively drawn into social structural issues (and in particular the local housing market) in order to make adequate sense of his ethnographic data.

Writing on social theory and the methodology of the social sciences is replete with warnings against the partiality of 'structural' and 'action-based' approaches, and numerous attempts have been made, with varying degrees of success, to provide a framework for explanation which overcomes the problem. A particularly interesting recent approach to the issue has been made by Anthony Giddens in his 'theory of structuration', the very term combining the connotations of structure and action within a single theory (Giddens, 1984). Giddens has argued not simply that explanations ought to be adequate at both these levels (as for example Max Weber did) but rather that it is a fundamental mistake to conceive of them as separate levels at all. Instead Giddens proposes that:

> The basic domain of study of the social sciences, according to the theory of structuration, is neither the experience of the individual actor, nor the existence of any form of societal totality, but social practices ordered across space and time. (1984: 2)

Space and time are central to Giddens's model of explanation, and so it is especially appropriate to consider this approach in developing theories of environmental criminology. As Giddens puts the matter:

> [Most] social scientists have failed to construct their thinking around the modes in which social systems are constituted across time–space. . . . investigation of this issue is one of the main tasks imposed by the 'problem of order' as conceptualized in the theory of structuration. It is not a particular type of 'area' of social science which can be pursued or discarded at will. *It is at the very heart of social theory, as interpreted through the notion of structuration, and should hence also be regarded as of very considerable importance for the conduct of empirical research in the social sciences.* (1984: 110, italics added)

We shall not attempt to summarize all Giddens's arguments but merely to indicate the most important elements for our purposes. These include the following:

1   Human subjects are knowledgeable agents, though this knowledgeability is bounded on the one hand by the unconscious, and on the other hand by unacknowledged conditions and/or unintended consequences of action.

2   Human subjects largely act within a domain of 'practical consciousness' which often cannot be expressed in terms such as 'motives' or 'reasons' but which 'consist of all the things which actors known tacitly about how to "go on" in the context of social life without being able to give them direct discursive expression' (Giddens, 1984: xxiii). This 'practical consciousness' must, however, be understood and made plain by the researcher in explanation.

3   Structuration theory seeks to escape from the traditional dualism in social theory between 'objectivism' and 'subjectivism'. Thus the theory accepts concepts of 'structure' and 'constraint', normally associated with 'objective' social science, but insists that they be understood only through the actions of knowledgeable agents; on the other hand it believes that 'subjectivist' social science has overemphasized the degree to which everyday action is directly motivated.

4   Structures may act as constraints on individual action but they are also, and at the same time, the medium and outcome of the conduct they recursively organize – what Giddens refers to as the 'duality of structure'. Structures, therefore, do not exist outside of action, and they do not only constrain, but also enable social action.

5   'Routine' is a predominant form of agents' day-to-day activity: most daily practices are not directly motivated, and routinized practices are a prime expression of the 'duality of structure' in respect of the continuity of social life.

6   Structuration theory accepts and tries to elaborate Marx's famous dictum that human beings 'make history, but not in circumstances of their own choosing'. This is part of the duality of structure, and emphasizes that social change and social process, linked to the reflexivity of human action, is an intrinsic part of human social life, even though that social life also has considerable continuities.

Giddens insists that both action and structure exist only within the ongoing process of human existence, which is largely constituted in practical consciousness. Structures, for Giddens, are properties which both allow and result in a practical consciousness which is able to follow regular patterns over time/space. The same practical rules which guide the social action of individuals are at the same time the basis for the reproduction of social systems. Looked at in this way the 'structure' of place is not simply a constraint on action but instead is one part of the social system which informs the practical (and sometimes discursive) consciousness of social actors. Put more simply, if we want to understand the geography of crime we have to understand how place, over time, is part of the practical consciousness of social actors who engage in behaviour, including actions we define as criminal. The structure of place is central, but it is not external to human agency and must be understood as part of a historical process.

Giddens's theory, then, gives us a model of explanation which we can use to examine critically some recent environmental criminology. Place cannot be made epiphenomenal to the explanation of human activity (as some human geographers once, suicidally, seemed to want to suggest) because place, together with time, are intrinsic dimensions of human existence. In acting, agents have to come to terms with the intrinsicality of space/time – which [. . .] they frequently do through routines. How they do so, whether they do so in different ways, and how modernity has extended the possible ways in which different actors operate in space/time are all interesting and empirical questions. All of us use our sense of 'locale' (for definition see note 1) to guide our everyday actions, and this is no less true in relation to crime. As Reiss put it, in mercifully straightforward terms,

> our sense of personal safety and potential victimisation by crime is shaped less by knowledge of specific criminals than it is by knowledge of dangerous and safe places and communities. (1986: 1)

To this one might add, first, that the general public's sense of safety relates not only to place but also to different times of day in place, and second, that the everyday life of offenders, as well as of victims and potential victims, is shaped in part by understandings of the nature of particular areas and, within them, of specific locations – and those understandings are undoubtedly important in shaping the geographical distribution of offending behaviour.

## Structuration and environmental criminology

Let us now consider how structuration theory can help take forward the study of environmental criminology.

To assess this issue we shall examine a recent essay by Per-Olof Wikström (1990), written in an attempt to summarize the literature on crime, criminality and the urban structure as a background paper for a new and major empirical research project in Stockholm. Wikström's paper is both up-to-date and of high quality; it provides, therefore, a useful exemplar of the 'state of the art' in environmental criminology, and a way of testing whether the application of a structuration approach (which Wikström does not consider) might have something to offer to this field of study.

Like most environmental criminologists, Wikström draws a clear distinction between area offender rates and area offence rates [. . .] In summarizing the relationship between urban structure (especially housing) and area offender rates, Wikström postulates two main effects:

1   Housing and [offender-rate based] criminality are related because social groups with a greater propensity to crime are concentrated in certain types of housing. . . .
2   Housing can itself affect the resident's propensity to crime in that the local housing conditions are of importance both to the social life and the social control of the neighbourhood (the 'contextual' effect). This effect may be subdivided into
    (a)   situational influence on propensity to offend; and
    (b)   long-term influence on the development of the individual resident's person-ality and life-style, tending to reinforce a propensity to crime . . . (primarily applies to neighbourhood influences on children and young people). (1990: 17)

[. . .]

Turning to the relationship between urban structures and area offence rates, Wikström adopts an approach arising out of routine activities theory, and opportunity theory:

> Inter-district variations in the use of urban land generate different activities more or less frequently *at different times of the week and day in different parts of the city.* Segregation and the spatial variation in the pursuit of various activities, each of

which will be perceived as more or less attractive by different social groups, ensure that *the social make-up of residents and visitors at different times of day will show distinct inter-district variations.*

The type of activities being pursued and the social composition of the people in the district at any one time can be assumed to be related to

1  the availability of suitable criminal targets, the presence of motivated offenders and the presence of direct social control (capable guardians) [explanation of offence rates for instrumental crime];
2  the occurrence of encounters (environments) liable to provoke friction in the parochial and public orders [explanation of some expressive crime]. (1990: 23, italics added)

Wikström then offers a diagram (reproduced here as Figure 11.1) summarizing his approach to the explanation of offence rates.

These summary statements undoubtedly capture much of our present knowledge about the reasons for inter-area variation in offender rates and offence rates within cities.[2] They are a bold and interesting attempt at synthesis, though – as Wikström would, we think, be the first to agree – they incorporate within them both some points with solid support in empirical research, and others which in the present state of knowledge seem reasonable or even probable, but where the empirical support is much more slender.

From the perspective of structuration theory, two points stand out as interesting in Wikström's summaries. The first concerns the marked emphasis, in the offence rate summary, on the differential paths taken by different actors in space and time, linking with structuration theory's emphasis on space/time issues. The second and closely related point concerns the use of Cohen and Felson's routine activities theory (1979), emphasizing the extent to which offences either arise directly out of the routine (legal) activities of social actors, or how even a deliberately and consciously illegal activity (e.g. a planned burglary trip) may in practice be confined to areas or trunk roads already known to the offender(s) through their everyday lives (see Brantingham and Brantingham, 1981). Clearly, there is an intriguing link to be forged here

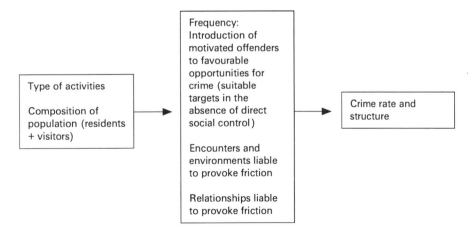

Figure 11.1  *Variation in crime (offence rate) and structure in the urban environment (after Wikström 1990)*

between the centrality of *routines* in Giddens's structuration theory (itself an interesting innovation in general sociological theory) and the emerging importance of routine activities theory in environmental criminology.

But while one can see important points of contact between structuration theory and Wikström's approach, a structuration perspective also suggests some weaknesses in his otherwise excellent paper. Two such weaknesses seem particularly apparent, and it is worth elaborating these by way of constructive criticism.

First, Wikström's approach markedly understates the importance of social process. In his offender-rate based analysis, for example, it can be argued that insufficient attention is paid to the constantly changing nature of the local housing market, in particular districts (often linked to more macro-level economic changes, or alterations in government housing policies). In structuration theory, structures are always simultaneously both enabling and constraining, and therefore never static. Similarly, Wikström's diagram for considering offence rate variations (Figure 11.1) gives inadequate attention to the changes (as opposed to the continuities) in the use by social actors of different districts within the city, or (at a more micro-level as highlighted by Sherman et al., 1989) to the constantly evolving character of, for example, particular streets or particular bars in city centre locations.

Second, Wikström's approach arguably pays too little attention to the perceptions, routine activities and decisions of individual actors (as opposed to aggregate patterns of social activity). In so doing, he risks missing the important distinction, central to structuration theory, between the intended and unintended consequences of individual action. Yet unintended consequences of action can be of central importance in, for example, the operation of housing markets (itself central to Wikström's framework for understanding offender rate variations); or the evolution of particular micro-level locations towards or away from being 'hot spots' of crime.

A more detailed consideration of the issues of process and unintended consequences may therefore help in the development of a more adequate approach to environmental criminology.

## Unintended consequences of action and processes of change

An important aspect of Giddens's structuration theory is that the structures which result from human action are not just a result of the intended consequences of such actions. Indeed, Giddens's notion that human action largely follows 'routines' precisely emphasizes the inadequacy of a fully intentional model of human action. The result is that not only may the consequences of rationally calculated action be unforeseen by actors (or foreseen but unintended), but also human action may frequently not be guided by conscious intention at all. In sum, the structural results of a series of human actions may be quite different from what the actors may have foreseen or intended.

Giddens gives as an example a model of how racial segregation in a city might occur:

A pattern of ethnic segregation might develop, without any of those involved intending this to happen, in the following way, which can be illustrated by analogy. Imagine a chessboard which has a set of 5-pence pieces and a set of 10-pence pieces.

These are distributed randomly on the board, as individuals might be in an urban area. It is presumed that, while they feel no hostility towards the other group, the members of each group do not want to live in a neighbourhood where they are ethnically in a minority. On the chessboard each piece is moved around until it is in such a position that at least 50 per cent of the adjoining pieces are of the same type. The result is a pattern of extreme segregation. The 10-pence pieces end up as a sort of ghetto in the midst of the 5-pence pieces. The 'composition effect' is an outcome of an aggregate of acts – whether those of moving pieces on the board or those of agents in a housing market – each of which is intentionally carried out. But the eventual outcome is neither intended nor desired by anyone. It is, as it were, everyone's doing and no one's. (1984: 10)

It is interesting that Giddens introduces the concept of a 'market' into this example, since this concept is used by economists to signify the summation of the consequences of individual economic decisions, regardless of whether those consequences were intended or foreseen by the actors. Taub et al. (1984), in their study of the decline of neighbourhoods in Chicago in both racial and crime terms, use a similar market-based model to explain the actions of individual householders (as opposed to corporations etc). They argue that such individual residents, when faced with signs of neighbourhood decline, can take decisions only in terms of their own purposes and in the context of their (limited) understanding of what other residents will do. The result can be that, in a similar way to Giddens's example, while none of the residents have an interest in the neighbourhood declining, the unintended consequence of their individual decisions can be precisely that.

The idea of a 'market', of course, is a model developed to help understand the aggregate results of action from an economic point of view and although, as Taub et al. have shown, it can be usefully employed to help explain the processes by which neighbourhoods decline it is not in itself wholly adequate to explain why a neighbourhood's crime or offender-rate pattern changes. What seems to be needed, then, is a model of neighbourhood activity which helps us to understand how changing crime or offending behaviour can be the result of a summation of individual actions, and their intended, unintended and unforeseen consequences: in other words, we need a construct which will fulfil for criminology some of the functions which the market fulfils for economists.

Some time ago Albert Reiss suggested that changes in neighbourhood crime patterns could be thought of as analogous to communities having crime careers (Reiss, 1986). Reiss did not develop this idea of 'community crime careers' much further, but in our view it is extremely suggestive. The term 'community crime career' in effect encompasses the notion that a neighbourhood's crime pattern is the summation of the consequences, whether intended or not, of the way a multitude of actors interact (which itself is linked to their practical consciousness of locale) in an historical process. As such it can equally be applied to offender changes in or offence-rate crime patterns, or to the relationship between the two. [. . .]

Some help in developing this concept may perhaps be obtained by considering again the work of Taub et al. (1984), although the writing of these authors predates that of Reiss. When they constructed a general theory of neighbourhood change out of their research, Taub et al. argued that

There are three types of social and ecological pressures that interactively determine the pattern of change in urban neighborhoods: (1) ecological facts; (2) corporate and institutional decisions; and (3) decisions of individual neighborhood residents. (1984: 182)

They pointed out that, traditionally, most urban theorists have concentrated on the 'ecological facts'[3] as the main explanatory variable as regards general social change in neighbourhoods, giving a strongly structural quality to such explanations. Such an emphasis, Taub and his colleagues believed,

> gives the wrong impression about the dynamics of neighborhood change. Individual residents and local corporate actors are, after all, the ones whose day-to-day decisions define the texture and quality of urban life. If ecological facts are overwhelming, it is because of the effect of these facts on the perceptions and actions of individual and corporate actors. In a neighborhood that goes up or down, it is ultimately the actions of these residents that make the outcomes real. (1984: 186)

Although their language is different these authors are essentially following the model of explanation proposed by Giddens in insisting that 'place' has to be considered always as it is constituted through human action. Their three-fold interactive model of ecological facts/individual decisions/corporate decisions also offers a valuable framework for analysis of area change,[4] even though the concept of 'ecological facts' needs some reinterpretation from the standpoint of structuration theory.[5]

Despite its merits, however, Taub et al.'s model is of limited value for present purposes because the analysis of individual and corporate actors' perceptions and decisions is applied only to the operations of the property market and its consequences. If we are to develop the notion of 'community crime career' more generally, then we need to extend this type of analysis to encompass all the structures which are relevant to the processes of change in offender and offence rates, as illustrated, for example, in Wikström's summaries. We return to this point, with examples, in the following section.

One other matter, of some importance for what we would regard as an adequate development of Taub et al.'s analysis, must be raised here. Even where actors appear to be operating in a market type situation, a model which focuses on their actions as motivated solely towards that market will have serious inadequacies. One only has to reflect momentarily on the reality of actors' behaviour in parts of the British housing market to see why this is so. Even after the changes of the 1980s a significant proportion of the British housing stock exists within a market of bureaucratic allocation, whose rules are very different from those of a price market. [. . .] In this sector actors need a very sophisticated understanding of the rules of the market in order adequately to foresee the consequences of their choices; yet there is some evidence to suggest that in some areas the allocation process is operated by the local authority in such a paternalistic way that actors do not even perceive that they have a choice. Even where actors do understand that they have a choice, and understand the rules of allocation, it does not necessarily follow that they will maximize the benefits available to them as the model of a rationally calculating market actor would suggest. In the 1980s replication stage of the Sheffield research tenants in a notorious high-rise block of flats had to be re-housed due to its impending demolition. Because of the rules of allocation in Sheffield, these 'clearance' tenants had priority in the allocation to vacant housing units in the local authority's stock, and they could therefore have secured transfers on to some of the most select council estates in the city. In fact few of them chose to do this even though advisers, ranging from community workers to police community constables, explained to them how to do so. Most of them instead chose to move to nearby (and by no means select) estates. The reason was because their bounded sense of location meant that they regarded the alternative select estates as inappropriate for them either in geographical terms (they did not 'belong' in a different sector of the city) or in class terms (the select estates were for the 'respectable'). Such a sense of locale is particularly powerful in Sheffield: one community constable, who was bemoaning the tenants' refusal to maximize the advantage available to them, was reminded by his colleague that he had himself declined a transfer to a different police division because he didn't feel at home in the area! However, a sense of location is merely one of the other aspects of structure which needs to be built in to the full development of a concept of community crime career, as should become clear from the final section of this chapter.

### Developing the community crime career concept: offender and offence rate variations reconsidered

The concept of a community crime career is, of course, a concept embodying the idea of social change at a meso-level. Structuration theory, as we have seen, places considerable emphasis on social process and social change, holding indeed that such matters are intrinsic to social life as lived out by human agents acting reflexively. But Giddens (1984: ch. 5) also argues, correctly in our view, that given the premisses of structuration theory no general theory of social change is possible:

> The reflexive nature of human social life subverts the explication of social change in terms of any simple and sovereign set of causal mechanisms. . . . To insist that social change be studied in 'world time' [i.e. examination of all social conjunctures in the light of reflexively monitored 'history'] is to emphasise the influence of varying forms of intersocietal system upon episodic transactions. If all social life is contingent, all social change is conjunctural. That is to say, it depends upon conjunctions of circumstances and events that may differ in nature according to variations of context, where context (as always) involves the reflexive monitoring by the agents involved of the conditions in which they 'make history'. (1984: 237, 245)

This does not mean, as Giddens goes on to emphasize (1984: 244f) that we cannot generalize at all about social change; it does mean, however, that there 'are no universal laws in the social sciences, and there will not be any' (1984: xxxii).

The implications of this for the concept of community crime careers are, first, that exact prediction of the precise course of such careers will be impossible, but secondly, that we should be able to analyse with some precision the general factors that may influence the development of such careers, in a probabilistic manner. At the present time our ability to specify these factors is rather rudimentary, but it should improve if more scholars develop empirical research specifically based upon the concept of community crime careers.

Let us take two particular examples, one focused upon an *offender-rate based* community crime career, and the other on an *offence-rate based* career. As to the former, Wikström's formulation (discussed earlier) carries considerable plausibility, provided that it is supplemented by an understanding of processes

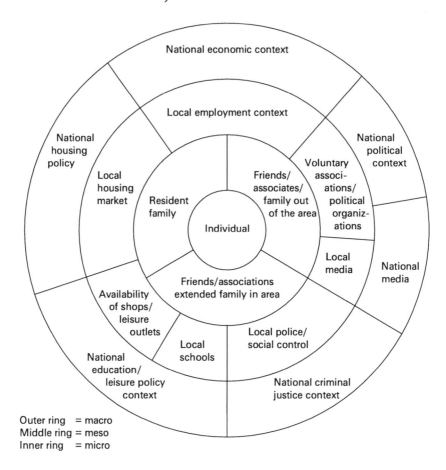

Figure 11.2  *Heuristic model of the context of offending*

of social change and of the unintended consequences of choices made by individuals and corporate actors within the housing market, as previously discussed [. . .]. Wikström highlights the allocative functions of the housing market, and the contextual effect of housing allocations (itself divided into 'situational' and longer-term effects) as the explanation of changing offender rates. A way of elaborating the issues relevant to this approach, modifying an idea originally suggested by Wikström's colleague Peter Martens (1990: 66), is shown in Figure 11.2. In considering this diagram, it should be noted that in our view the housing market context (on the left of the diagram) has to be especially prioritized in the explanation, for the reason that it is the housing market which is responsible for the allocation of families and individuals to particular areas; but all the other matters shown in the diagram also come into play by way of contextual effects [. . .].

Figure 11.2 explicitly employs the terminology of 'macro', 'meso' and 'micro' processes. We use these terms for heuristic purposes only. We are aware that Giddens (1984: 139–44) eschews them and insists that such distinctions are merely interconnected aspects of how the social phenomenon being examined is located in space/time. Certainly Giddens is right to make this point, and we agree with him that structure is as relevant to micro-sociology as to macro-sociological issues, while no macro-sociological structure can be adequately understood aside from an understanding of the purposive decisions and routine activities of human agents, and their interaction with the constraining and enabling features of the social and material contexts within which that action takes place. Having said that, it remains in our view the case that a micro/meso/macro distinction has a clear heuristic value in environmental criminology, and that Figure 11.2 offers a possible way of conceptualizing it with regard to offender-rate variations in space and over time.

Turning now to offence-rate based community crime careers, Wikström's approach (see Figure 11.1) again offers a valuable starting-point, though once more needing supplementation from concepts of process and unintended consequences. It is, however, worth elaborating this approach a little by way of a specific example, that of city centre crime, in order to develop its potential.

City centres have few residents, but a disproportionate incidence of criminal incidents relative to their land use area (Baldwin and Bottoms, 1976). Thus the city centre is a paradigm case of a high offence area which is not a high offender area. In the daytime, the city centre is of course a hive of commercial and other activity; much of the daytime crime consists of shop-lifting or auto-crime, but more personalized crime such as bag-snatching may also feature, considerably aided by the anonymity of the city centre crowd (Poyner, 1983; ch. 6). At night the city centre changes character in terms of both activities and its user population (the average age plummets as the centre is largely taken over by youths). Crimes of public violence and disorder occur disproportionately in city centres at night, often in or close to pubs, clubs or other places of entertainment: these crimes are highly focused upon Friday and Saturday evenings, with a special time focus on pub and club closing times (Hope, 1985; Ramsay, 1982; Wikström 1985). Such incidents are also highly localized, with a few locations providing a disproportionate share of the crimes (Hope, 1985; Sherman et al., 1989).

We immediately see here clear evidence of differential social activity in space/time by different groups, even in an area which is open to all. Further detailed research would probably show age, class and/or sex segregation in specific locations within the city centre both by day and by night – and would almost certainly show some city centre users to be anxious about groups of youths hanging about (Phillips and Cochrane, 1988) or vagrant alcoholics (Ramsay, 1989). Owners of specific premises may seek to achieve a degree of social segregation by manipulating the sense of location (elaborate entrance portals to an exclusive hotel; interior design deliberately calculated to make a particular age group, class or sex feel at home); others may seek to boost a sense of safety through the employment of private security companies (as, increasingly, in shopping malls with multiple retail outlets) or physical security devices (use of CCTV, and so on). There is clearly here a rich field of exploration in the patterning of use of the city centre, and, by those who do use it, in the patterning of the use of specific sites. Nor is any of this static. Perceptions of the desirability of a particular shop/café/bar can easily change over time, and individual decisions about custom can cumulatively have important long-term consequences. Add to this the fact that city centres themselves change over time, both in their land use and design (increasing use of pedestrianized streets, increasing development of multiple stores rather than small shops, and so on) and in their social use (the city centre in the evening in the early 1960s was much less predominantly a young person's domain), and we begin to see the complexity of the whole picture within which city centre crime must be understood. Wikström's model (Figure 11.1) is correct in so far as it goes, but needs a much greater understanding of the fluidity of social routines and practices before it can be fully adequate. [. . .]

These examples are no more than suggestive, and the concept of a community crime career clearly requires further elaboration. We hope, however, that the examples may help to bring alive some of the theoretical issues discussed in more abstract terms earlier in this chapter.

**Conclusion**

What we have tried to argue in this chapter is that a proper understanding of the spatial aspects of offences and offending is possible only if a model is employed which is capable of including the natural and built environment, the political, economic, social and cultural contexts and structures of areas and the actions of individuals and corporate bodies within areas, within a theory which accounts for the ongoing processes of interaction between them. We have used Giddens's structuration theory because we believe that it offers such a framework, and we have tried to show how the elements of this approach can illuminate current work within environmental criminology.

The task of developing a more adequate environmental criminology seems to us rather urgent at the present time, since for a variety of reasons the structures and understandings which underpin much existing scholarship are undergoing some rapid changes. [. . .] The tenure map of Britain is being redrawn, and this may well have significant consequences for the geography of crime. Perhaps more fundamental is the movement of the urban middle class into rural communities, and the consequential push of the less affluent rural young into the towns in search of affordable housing: the old rural/urban crime patterns will almost certainly be affected by this process. In the towns themselves, city centres are increasingly facing competition from large out-of-town shopping areas on the North American model, where rather different strategies of social control and segregation are being deployed. Industry and commerce, and even retailing, are also increasingly being segregated from residential areas and placed on industrial estates, technology parks, and so on. At the same time as the geography of Britain is being altered in these ways, so also technological innovations are constantly affecting the ability of social actors (both individuals and corporate bodies) to manipulate the constraints of both time and distance. If, as Giddens suggests, our sense of location is a key aspect of our social existence and is a product of our experience and interaction within space/time then the sense of location of many modern Britons is likely to be significantly changed. If it is, then the appropriateness of place to life-style, including the criminal, and to life experiences, including victimization, will also change. It is therefore vital that we should possess an adequate model for understanding these processes and their criminological consequences. We can at any rate confidently predict that there will be no shortage of interesting research topics for future environmental criminologists.

## Notes

1 Sherman et al. define 'place' as ' a fixed physical environment that can be seen completely and simultaneously, at least on its surface, by one's naked eyes' (1989: 31). Our own usage in this chapter, not least in the title, is of course considerably broader than this. It should be added, however, that Sherman et al. are not blind to what they call the 'sociological concept of place', defined as 'the social organization of behaviour at a geographic place'. This point is developed and strengthened by Giddens (1984) in his concept of 'locales', which, he insists, 'are not just places but *settings* of interaction, the settings of interaction in turn being essential to specifying its *contextuality*' (pp. xxv, 118). Giddens's formal definition of a locale is as follows: 'a physical region involved as part of the setting of interaction, having definite boundaries which help concentrate interaction in one way or another' (1984: 375).

2 Even within its own terms, however, it can be argued that Wikström's formulation pays too little attention to the implications of spatial form and design for offence rate distribution (see Newman, 1972). Although we are stressing (following Giddens) that it is actors' conceptions of 'locale' which are critical (either in direct awareness or more usually in practical consciousness), nevertheless the physical nature of the environment must place some limits on what these conceptions can consist of.

3 'Ecological facts', according to Taub et al., 'define the social and economic context for a neighborhood' (1984: 182). The ecological facts of particular importance for neighbourhood decline are said to be:

1 the potential employment base for neighbourhood residents;
2 demographic pressures on the neighbourhood housing market;
3 the age and original quality of the housing stock;
4 external amenities such as attractive physical locations (hills, views, and so on).

4 Taub et al.'s distinction between corporate and individual actors is important because it recognizes that in a market situation corporate actors have greater power to influence outcomes, whether such corporate actors are commercial corporations, non-commercial organizations such as universities (the University of Chicago features strongly in one of Taub et al.'s area case studies) or individual actors who band together in a political or community organization in order to derive the benefits of corporate power. Of course, in markets the ultimate corporate actors are either those who hold a monopoly, or those who can use the legislative and administrative power of the state to redefine the nature of the market.

5 Some of the 'ecological facts' as defined by Taub et al. (e.g. the local employment base) are of course themselves part of the social structures which are constituted and reproduced in human action.

## References

Baldwin, J. and Bottoms, A.E. (1976) *The Urban Criminal*. London: Tavistock.

Becker, H.S. (1963) *Outsiders*. New York: Free Press.

Brantingham, P.L. and Brantingham, P.J. (1981) 'Notes on the geometry of crime', in P.J. Brantingham and P.L. Brantingham (eds), *Environmental Criminology*, Beverly Hills, CA: Sage.

*Chicago Tribune* (eds) (1986) *The American Millstone*. Chicago: Contemporary Books.

Cohen, L.E. and Felson, M. (1979) 'Social change and crime rate trends: a routine activities approach', *American Sociological Review*, 44: 588–608.

Cressey, P.G. (1932) *The Taxi-Dance Hall*. Chicago: University of Chicago Press.

Davidson, N. (1981) *Crime and Environment*. London: Croom Helm.

Foster, J. (1990) *Villains: Crime and Community in the Inner City*. London: Routledge.

Giddens, A. (1984) *The Constitution of Society*. Cambridge: Polity.

Gill, O. (1977) *Luke Street*. London: Macmillan.

Gregory, D. and Urry, J. (1985) *Social Relations and Spatial Structures*. London: Macmillan.

Herbert, D.T. (1982) *The Geography of Urban Crime*. London: Longman.

Hope, T. (1985) *Implementing Crime Prevention Measures*. Home Office Research Study 86. London: HMSO.

Martens, P.L. (1990) 'Family, neighbourhood and socialisation', in P.-O.H. Wikström (ed.), *Crime and Measures against Crime in the City*. Stockholm: National Council for Crime Prevention.

Matza, D. (1964) *Delinquency and Drift*. London: Wiley.

Mayhew, P., Elliott, D. and Dowds, L. (1989) *The 1988 British Crime Survey*. Home Office Research Study 111. London: HMSO.

Merry, S. (1981) 'Defensible space undefended: social factors in crime prevention through environmental design', *Urban Affairs Quarterly*,16: 397–422.

Newman, O. (1972) *Defensible Space*. New York: Macmillan.

Phillips, S. and Cochrane, R. (1988) *Crime and Nuisance in the Shopping Centre*. Crime Prevention Unit Paper 16. London: Home Office.

Poyner, B. (1983) *Design Against Crime: Beyond Defensible Space*. London: Butterworths.

Ramsay, M. (1982) *City Centre Crime*. Home Office Research and Planning Unit Paper 10. London: Home Office.

Ramsay, M. (1989) *Downtown Drinkers: the Perceptions and Fears of the Public in a City Centre*. Crime Prevention Unit Paper 19. London: Home Office.

Reiss, A.J. (1986) 'Why are communities important in understanding crime?', in A.J. Reiss and M. Tonry (eds), *Communities and Crime*. Chicago: University of Chicago Press.

Shaw, C.R. (1930) *The Jack Roller*. Chicago: University of Chicago Press.

Shaw, C.R. and McKay, H.D. (1942) *Juvenile Delinquency and Urban Areas*. Chicago: University of Chicago Press.

Sherman, L.W., Gartin, P.R. and Buerger, M.E. (1989) 'Hot spots of predatory crime: routine activities and the criminology of place', *Criminology*, 27: 27–55.

Smith, S.J. (1986) *Crime, Space and Society*. Cambridge: Cambridge University Press.

Taub, R., Taylor, D.G. and Dunham, J.D. (1984) *Paths of Neighborhood Change*. Chicago: University of Chicago Press.

Whyte, W.H. (1943) *Street Corner Society*. Chicago: University of Chicago Press.

Wikström, P.-O.H. (1985) *Everyday Violence in Contemporary Sweden*. Stockholm: National Council for Crime Prevention.

Wikström, P.-O.H. (1990) 'Delinquency and urban structure', in P.-O.H. Wikström (ed.), *Crime and Measures against Crime in the City*. Stockholm: National Council for Crime Prevention.

# 12

# Crime and consumption

## Simon Field

The main finding of this study is that economic factors have a major influence on trends in both property and personal crime. 'Personal consumption *per capita'* is the amount that each person in the country spends, on average, during the year. 'Real' (after inflation) annual growth in personal consumption was found to be inversely related to growth in recorded property crime. Thus in years when people are increasing their spending very little – or even reducing it – property crime tends to grow relatively quickly, whereas during years when people are rapidly increasing their expenditure, property crime tends to grow less rapidly or even fall. In England and Wales, the relationship has held throughout the twentieth century, and has been particularly strong in the last twenty years (see Figure 12.1). A similar association between property crime and personal consumption can be demonstrated for the United States, Japan and France in the last 15 or 20 years, but is not apparent in Sweden, and the relationship takes a different form in West Germany. Economic factors in general, and consumption growth in particular, appear to be among the most important determinants of fluctuations in the growth of property crime in industrialized countries.

The evidence suggests that this effect is *short term,* rather than one which might explain the growth of property crime in the long term. Thus although property crime certainly tends to grow less quickly during years in which consumption grows rapidly, there is also evidence of compensating 'bounce-back' in the following years. Thus the long-term rate of property crime growth might be unaffected by a surge in consumption growth. While the full relation between long-run economic growth and growth in property crime is as yet unclear, it seems that the effects identified in this study have only a limited bearing on the issue.

Personal crime – sexual offences and violence against the person (but not robbery) – also shows a distinctive relation to personal consumption. It appears to increase in line with consumption, so that personal crime appears to increase more rapidly during periods of rapidly increasing consumption. This means that personal crime responds to consumption growth in the *opposite* manner to that of property crime: during periods of slow consumption growth, personal crime tends to grow more slowly than usual, whereas in periods of rapid consumption growth, personal crime also tends to grow more rapidly (see Figure 12.2).

These results provide a powerful explanatory framework against which trends in recorded crime can be assessed, and offer an immediate insight into

Abridged from *Trends in Crime and Their Interpretation,* Home Office Research Study No. 119, pp. 5-8; 19; 36; 58-9. (London: HMSO, 1990.)

*Simon Field*

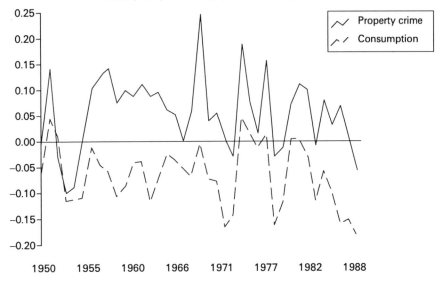

Figure 12.1 *Property crime and consumption, 1950–1988*

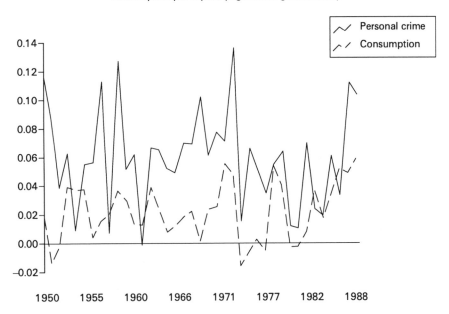

Figure 12.2 *Personal crime and consumption, 1950–1988*

the trends in recorded crime in England and Wales during the 1980s. The most striking feature of these trends has been the way in which during the first years of the decade in 1980 and 1981, recorded property crime of most types grew very rapidly, while personal crime grew very little. There followed a gradual reverse in this pattern, such that personal crime grew rapidly in 1987 and 1988, while property crime grew very little during the same period. This shift can now be attributed at least in part to the underlying effect of the business cycle: personal consumption actually fell during the 1980–81 recession – so that a high rate of property crime growth and low rate of personal crime growth might have been expected. Consumption grew extremely fast in 1987–8 underlying the observed reverse pattern of low (or negative) property crime growth and rapid growth in personal crime. Similar patterns are observable in previous economic cycles.

## Explaining the relation between crime and economic cycles

In principle, consumption growth might have three sorts of effect on crime:

1  It increases the goods available for theft or vandalism: the opportunity effect.
2  Consumption growth indicates an increasing capacity for the lawful acquisition of goods, thereby reducing the temptation of unlawful acquisition through theft: the motivation effect.
3  It alters the pattern of crime opportunities by precipitating an alteration in lifestyle or 'routine activities': the lifestyle effect.

Here it is argued that property crime is primarily affected by the second 'motivation' factor in the short run, so that rapid growth in consumption generates low growth in property crime. In the long run the other two factors appear to balance out the motivation effect, so that the long-run effect of economic growth on property crime may be small.

Why does only one factor dominate in the short run? Potential victims are very widely spread in society. Potential offenders however, are likely to be concentrated in particular social groups, whose position in the labour market is liable to be weak or marginal. Fluctuations in aggregate consumption growth will therefore tend to be amplified in the experience of potential offenders, since marginal labour market groups commonly experience aggregate fluctuations in such an amplified form. Better placed labour market groups tend to be more insulated from the vicissitudes of the economy. It follows that a surge in consumption growth will be amplified in the experience of potential offenders, and the 'motivation' effect on them will therefore outweigh the 'opportunity' and 'routine activity' effects on potential victims. Property crime will therefore be lower than it otherwise would be. Conversely a deep trough in consumption growth will result in more property crime. In addition, a sharp fall in consumption growth may trigger frustration as economic expectations are lowered. This could undermine social controls.

This theory provides an explanation of the observed relation of consumption and property crime, and explains why the effect is cyclical rather than long term.

Personal crime, in the form of violence against the person and sexual offences, responds positively to rapid consumption growth. Personal crime is not directly affected by the goods available to the victim or the offender, but is affected by the pattern of routine activities, which in turn is affected by consumption and income growth. There is good evidence that people who go out more often are much more likely to be the victims of personal crime than those who do not, and there is also evidence that when consumption increases some of that consumption goes on increased time spent outside the home. This suggests an explanation for the observed positive relation between personal crime and consumption: when spending rises, people spend more time outside the home, and as a result there are more opportunities for personal crime.

## Unemployment and crime

The idea that unemployment causes crime has long been discussed in criminology. Unemployment rises and falls over the business cycle. In the face of the powerful evidence of a relation between crime and the business cycle, what role can be attributed to unemployment?

(Offences of violence against the person turned out to have a distinctive relation with unemployment, which will be discussed separately.)

Although personal consumption and unemployment are both indicators of the business cycle, they behave somewhat differently; in particular, fluctuations in unemployment tend to lag behind consumption growth. As described, fluctuations in consumption growth are coincident with fluctuations in the growth of property crime. It is therefore no surprise that in practice, trends in personal consumption are tied much more closely to crime trends than are trends in unemployment. Once the effect of personal consumption on crime is taken into account, no evidence emerged, despite extensive statistical testing, that unemployment adds anything extra to the explanation of any type of crime. The whole relation between the business cycle and crime appears to be encapsulated in that between personal consumption and crime. Thus fluctuations in the total number of unemployed persons appear to be independent of fluctuations in the number of offences.

Both the power and limitations of this result deserve emphasis. A major drawback of many of the published time series studies of unemployment and crime is that unemployment is often the only economic indicator which has been used. As it has been demonstrated here that crime does have a strong relationship to the behaviour of the economy, it will be no surprise that some relation emerges when unemployment - alone of economic indicators - is compared with crime rates over time. The data used for the current study show such a relationship. The strength of the analysis conducted here is that it demonstrates an extremely strong relationship between crime and the business cycle, and demonstrates that unemployment adds nothing to the explanation of this pattern, once consumption growth - the key factor - is taken into account. It follows from this result that any simplistic theory of the aggregate relationship between unemployment and crime - for example one that claimed that for every extra ten unemployed persons there would be one extra offence per year - must be counted as disproved.

The qualification to this result is that it refers to aggregate data. Even if trends in national levels of unemployment are unrelated to trends in national levels of crime, it does not follow that unemployment cannot cause crime. For a potential or actual offender, the experience of unemployment might precipitate offending or an increase in offending. An increase in the rate of unemployment among this population sub-group will therefore increase the rate of offending by this sub-group. However, as potential and actual offenders are unlikely to have a labour market position representative of the population as a whole, fluctuations in the rate of unemployment among this group may follow a very different pattern from fluctuations in the national rate of unemployment. It follows that fluctuations in aggregate unemployment could be independent of fluctuations in crime, even though unemployment is causing crime.

[. . .]

Violence against the person, like the other 'personal' crime of sexual offences, seems to rise in response to rapid consumption growth. [. . .] Uniquely amongst crime, violence against the person is strongly related to unemployment during the preceding year and is also affected by the level of unemployment benefit. This strongly suggests that unemployment – perhaps long-term unemployment in particular – and the material deprivation that goes with it, may be a causal factor in crimes of violence against the person. During economic boom periods therefore, the positive effect of rapid consumption growth on violence against the person is subject to a countervailing influence – the decline in unemployment which tends to occur at such periods. This apparent paradox is probably explained by the heterogeneous nature of the 'violence against the person' category: it includes offences which range from domestic violence to pub brawls, whose causal basis will be diverse.

[. . .]

In explanation of the observed relation between property crime and consumption, it has been argued here that fluctuations in the national economy are amplified among potential offender groups because such groups may have a vulnerable position in the labour market. If this is so, it would follow that measures taken to reduce the vulnerability of such groups and improve their economic situation may help to reduce the level of property crime. More generally, the strong aggregate relationship between consumption and property crime must, at bottom, be explicable in terms of a relationship between the economic status of individuals and their propensity to become involved in crime. It may be that persons who face sudden reverses in their economic circumstances are particularly likely to become involved in crime. This study has identified aggregate indicators of this effect, and it would be consistent with these findings to suppose that such individual reverses are a continuous factor behind the level of property crime, and not simply an explanation which only has relevance to the impact of national economic trends.

Findings at this level of generality are at some remove from specific policy prescriptions, but they support the proposition that measures to support the economic position of individuals, social groups or localities who are identified as 'at risk' could reduce the total amount of property crime. The particular emphasis suggested by these findings lies with the pattern over time of the economic circumstances leading to crime. The implication is that sudden reverses in circumstances, rather than simply poor economic circumstances, may lie behind the commission of crime. This implies that economic interventions which aim (perhaps among other objectives) to reduce the level of property crime, should seek to *secure* as well as improve the economic position of individuals at risk.

The identified relation between personal crime and consumption does not lend itself as readily to policy prescription. The underlying factor is almost certainly for persons to spend increased income on leisure activities away from home where their risk of victimization is higher. [. . .]

In conclusion, the findings of this research study have immediate practical and theoretical application. On the practical side, there has emerged a novel means of looking at crime statistics in relation to trends in the economy. This provides a means of understanding some of the major features of crime trends and anticipating their course a few years into the future. This has great practical value as a means of forecasting demands on the criminal justice system.

On the theoretical side, strong evidence has emerged of economic causes of crime. The precise nature of these causes deserves to be further unravelled, and further research in this field could yield evidence of the scope for initiatives and policies designed to mitigate the criminogenic impact of these economic causes.

# 13

# The underclass

## Charles Murray

### The concept of 'underclass'

'Underclass' is an ugly word, with its whiff of Marx and the lumpen-proletariat. Perhaps because it is ugly, 'underclass' as used in Britain tends to be sanitized, a sort of synonym for people who are not just poor, but especially poor. So let us get it straight from the outset: the 'underclass' does not refer to degree of poverty, but to a type of poverty.

It is not a new concept. I grew up knowing what the underclass was; we just didn't call it that in those days. In the small Iowa town where I lived, I was taught by my middle-class parents that there were two kinds of poor people. One class of poor people was never even called 'poor'. I came to understand that they simply lived with low incomes, as my own parents had done when they were young. Then there was another set of poor people, just a handful of them. These poor people didn't lack just money. They were defined by their behaviour. Their homes were littered and unkempt. The men in the family were unable to hold a job for more than a few weeks at a time. Drunkenness was common. The children grew up ill-schooled and ill-behaved and contributed a disproportionate share of the local juvenile delinquents.

British observers of the nineteenth century knew these people. To Henry Mayhew, whose articles in the *Morning Chronicle* in 1850 drew the Victorians' attention to poverty, they were the 'dishonest poor', a member of which was

> distinguished from the civilised man by his repugnance to regular and continuous labour – by his want of providence in laying up a store for the future – by his inability to perceive consequences ever so slightly removed from immediate apprehensions – by his passion for stupefying herbs and roots and, when possible, for intoxicating fermented liquors . . . .

Other popular labels were 'undeserving', 'unrespectable', 'depraved', 'debased', 'disreputable' or 'feckless' poor.

As Britain entered the 1960s a century later, this distinction between honest and dishonest poor people had been softened. The second kind of poor person was no longer 'undeserving'; rather, he was the product of a 'culture of poverty'. But intellectuals as well as the man in the street continued to accept that poor people were not all alike. Most were doing their best under difficult circumstances; a small number were pretty much as Mayhew had described

---

Abridged from *The Emerging Underclass*, pp. 1–23; 33–5. (London: Institute of Economic Affairs, 1990.)

them. Then came the intellectual reformation that swept both the United States and Britain at about the same time, in the mid-1960s, and with it came a new way of looking at the poor. Henceforth, the poor were to be homogenized. The only difference between poor people and everyone else, we were told, was that the poor had less money. More importantly, the poor were all alike. There was no such thing as the ne'er-do-well poor person – he was the figment of the prejudices of a parochial middle class. Poor people, *all* poor people, were equally victims, and would be equally successful if only society gave them a fair shake.

### The difference between the US and the UK

The difference between the Unites States and Britain was that the United States reached the future first. During the last half of the 1960s and throughout the 1970s something strange and frightening was happening among poor people in the United States. Poor communities that had consisted mostly of hardworking folks began deteriorating, sometimes falling apart altogether. Drugs, crime, illegitimacy, homelessness, drop-out from the job market, drop-out from school, casual violence – all the measures that were available to the social scientists showed large increases, focused in poor communities. As the 1980s began, the growing population of 'the other kind of poor people' could no longer be ignored, and a label for them came into use. In the US, we began to call them the underclass.

For a time, the intellectual conventional wisdom continued to hold that 'underclass' was just another pejorative attempt to label the poor. But the label had come into use because there was no longer any denying reality. What had once been a small fraction of the American poor had become a sizeable and worrisome population. An underclass existed, and none of the ordinary kinds of social policy solutions seemed able to stop its growth. One by one, the American social scientists who had initially rejected the concept of an underclass fell silent, then began to use it themselves.

By and large, British intellectuals still disdain the term. In 1987, the social historian John Macnicol summed up the prevailing view in the *Journal of Social Policy*, [vol. 16, no. 3, pp. 293–318] writing dismissively that underclass was nothing more than a refuted concept periodically resurrected by Conservatives 'who wish to constrain the redistributive potential of state welfare'. But there are beginning to be breaks in the ranks. Frank Field, the prominent Labour MP, has just published a book with 'underclass' in its subtitle. The newspapers, watching the United States and seeing shadows of its problems in Britain, have begun to use the term. As someone who has been analysing this phenomenon in the United States, I arrived in Britain earlier this year, a visitor from a plague area come to see whether the disease is spreading.

With all the reservations that a stranger must feel in passing judgement on an unfamiliar country, I will jump directly to the conclusion: Britain does have an underclass, still largely out of sight and still smaller than the one in the United States. But it is growing rapidly. Within the next decade, it will probably become as large (proportionately) as the United States' underclass. It could easily become larger.

I am not talking here about an unemployment problem that can be solved by more jobs, nor about a poverty problem that can be solved by higher benefits. Britain has a growing population of working-aged healthy people who live in a different world from other Britons, who are raising their children to live in it, and whose values are now contaminating the life of entire neighbourhoods – which is one of the most insidious aspects of the phenomenon, for neighbours who don't share those values cannot isolate themselves.

There are many ways to identify an underclass. I will concentrate on three phenomena that have turned out to be early-warning signals in the United States: illegitimacy, violent crime, and drop-out from the labour force. In each case I will be using the simplest of data, collected and published by Britain's Government Statistical Service. I begin with illegitimacy, which in my view is the best predictor of an underclass in the making.

### Illegitimacy and the underclass

It is a proposition that angers many people. Why should it be a 'problem' that a woman has a child without a husband? Why isn't a single woman perfectly capable of raising a healthy, happy child, if only the state will provide a decent level of support so that she may do so? Why is raising a child without having married any more of a problem than raising a child after a divorce? The very word 'illegitimate' is intellectually illegitimate. Using it in a gathering of academics these days is a *faux pas*, causing pained silence.

I nonetheless focus on illegitimacy rather than on the more general phenomenon of one-parent families because, in a world where all social trends are ambiguous, illegitimacy is less ambiguous than other forms of single parenthood. It is a matter of degree. Of course some unmarried mothers are excellent mothers and some unmarried fathers are excellent fathers. Of course some divorced parents disappear from the children's lives altogether and some divorces have more destructive effects on the children than a failure to marry would have had. Being without two parents is generally worse for the child than having two parents, no matter how it happens. But illegitimacy is the purest form of being without two parents – legally, the child is without a father from day one; he is often without one practically as well. Further, illegitimacy bespeaks an attitude on the part of one or both parents that getting married is not an essential part of siring or giving birth to a child; this in itself distinguishes their mindset from that of people who do feel strongly that getting married is essential.

Call it what you will, illegitimacy has been sky-rocketing since 1979. I use 'sky-rocketing' advisedly. [. . .] From the end of the Second World War until 1960, Britain enjoyed a very low and even slightly declining illegitimacy ratio. From 1960 until 1978 the ratio increased, but remained modest by international standards – as late as 1979, Britain's illegitimacy ratio was only 10.6 per cent, one of the lowest rates in the industrialized West. Then, suddenly, during a period when fertility was steady, the illegitimacy ratio began to rise very rapidly – to 14.1 per cent by 1982, 18.9 per cent by 1985, and finally to 25.6 per cent by 1988. If present trends continue, Britain will pass the United States in this unhappy statistic in 1990.

The sharp rise is only half of the story. The other and equally important half is that illegitimate births are not scattered evenly among the British population. In this, press reports can be misleading. There is much publicity about the member of the royal family who has a child without a husband, or the socially prominent young career woman who deliberately decides to have a baby on her own, but these are comparatively rare events. The increase in illegitimate births is strikingly concentrated among the lowest social class.

## Municipal Districts

This is especially easy to document in Britain, where one may fit together the Government Statistical Service's birth data on municipal districts with the detailed socioeconomic data from the general census. When one does so for 169 metropolitan districts and boroughs in England and Wales with data from both sources, the relationship between social class and illegitimacy is so obvious that the statistical tests become superfluous. Municipal districts with high concentrations of household heads in Class I (professional persons, by the classification used for many years by the Government Statistical Service) have illegitimacy ratios in the low teens (Wokingham was lowest as of 1987, with only nine of every 100 children born illegitimate) while municipalities like Nottingham and Southwark, with populations most heavily weighted with Class V household heads (unskilled labourers), have illegitimacy ratios of more than 40 per cent (the highest in 1987 was Lambeth, with 46 per cent).

The statistical tests confirm this relationship. The larger the proportion of people who work at unskilled jobs and the larger the proportion who are out of the labour force, the higher the illegitimacy ratio, in a quite specific and regular numeric relationship. The strength of the relationship may be illustrated this way: suppose you were limited to two items of information about a community – the percentage of people in Class V and the percentage of people who are 'economically inactive'. With just these two measures, you could predict the illegitimacy ratio, usually within just three percentage points of the true number. As a statistician might summarize it, these two measures of economic status 'explain 51 per cent of the variance' – an extremely strong relationship by the standards of the social sciences.

In short, the notion that illegitimate births are a general phenomenon, that young career women and girls from middle-class homes are doing it just as much as anyone else, is flatly at odds with the facts. There has been a *proportional* increase in illegitimate births among all communities, but the *prevalence* of illegitimate births is drastically higher among the lower-class communities than among the upper-class ones.

## Neighbourhoods

The data I have just described are based on municipal districts. The picture gets worse when we move down to the level of the neighbourhood, though precise numbers are hard to come by. The proportion of illegitimate children in a specific poor neighbourhood can be in the vicinity not of 25 per cent, nor even of 40 per cent, but a hefty majority. And in this concentration of illegitimate births lies a generational catastrophe. Illegitimacy produces an underclass for one compelling practical reason having nothing to do with morality or the sanctity of marriage. Namely: communities need families. Communities need fathers.

This is not an argument that many intellectuals in Britain are ready to accept. I found that discussing the issue was like being in a time warp, hearing in 1989 the same rationalizations about illegitimacy that American experts used in the 1970s and early 1980s.

[. . .]

### 'Mainly a black problem'?

'It's mainly a black problem'. I heard this everywhere, from political clubs in Westminster to some quite sophisticated demographers in the statistical research offices. The statement is correct in this one, very limited sense: blacks born in the West Indies have much higher illegitimacy ratios – about 48 per cent of live births in the latest numbers – than all whites. But blacks constitute such a tiny proportion of the British population that their contribution to the overall illegitimacy ratio is minuscule. If there had been no blacks whatsoever in Britain (and I am including all blacks in Britain in this statement, not just those who were born abroad), the overall British illegitimacy ratio in 1988 would have dropped by about one percentage point, from 25 per cent to about 24 per cent. Blacks are not causing Britain's illegitimacy problem.

In passing, it is worth adding that the overall effect of ethnic minorities living in the UK is to *reduce* the size of the illegitimacy ratio. The Chinese, Indians, Pakistanis, Arabs and East Africans in Britain have illegitimacy ratios that are tiny compared with those of British whites.

### 'It's not as bad as it looks'

In the United States, the line used to be that blacks have extended families, with uncles and grandfathers compensating for the lack of a father. In Britain, the counterpart to this cheery optimism is that an increasing number of illegitimate births are jointly registered and that an increasing number of such children are born to people who live together at the time of birth. Both joint registration and living together are quickly called evidence of 'a stable relationship'.

The statements about joint registration and living together are factually correct. Of the 158,500 illegitimate births in England and Wales in 1987, 69 per cent were jointly registered. Of those who jointly registered the birth, 70 per cent gave the same address, suggesting some kind of continuing relationship. Both of these figures have increased – in 1961, for example, only 38 per cent of illegitimate births were jointly registered, suggesting that the nature of illegitimacy in the United Kingdom has changed dramatically.

You may make what you wish of such figures. In the United States, we have stopped talking blithely about the 'extended family' in black culture that would make everything okay. It hasn't. And as the years go on, the extended family argument becomes a cruel joke – for without marriage, grandfathers and uncles too become scarce. In Britain, is it justified to assume that jointly registering a birth, or living together at the time of the birth, means a relationship that is just as stable (or nearly as stable) as a marriage? I pose it as a question because I don't have the empirical answer. But neither did any of the people who kept repeating the joint-registration and living-together numbers so optimistically.

If we can be reasonably confident that the children of never-married women do considerably worse than their peers, it remains to explain why. Progress has been slow. Until recently in the United States, scholars were reluctant to concede that illegitimacy is a legitimate variable for study. Even as that situation changes, they remain slow to leave behind their equations and go out to talk with people who are trying to raise their children in neighbourhoods with high illegitimacy rates. This is how I make sense of the combination of quantitative studies, ethnographic studies and talking-to-folks journalism that bear on the question of illegitimacy, pulling in a few observations from my conversations in Britain.

### Clichés about role models are true

It turns out that the clichés about role models are true. Children grow up making sense of the world around them in terms of their own experience. Little boys don't naturally grow up to be responsible fathers and husbands. They don't naturally grow up knowing how to get up every morning at the same time and go to work. They don't naturally grow up thinking that work is not just a way to make money, but a way to hold one's head high in the world. And most emphatically of all, little boys do not reach adolescence naturally wanting to refrain from sex, just as little girls don't become adolescents naturally wanting to refrain from having babies. In all these ways and many more, boys and girls grow into responsible parents and neighbours and workers because they are imitating the adults around them.

That's why single-parenthood is a problem for communities, and that's why illegitimacy is the most worrisome aspect of single-parenthood. Children tend to behave like the adults around them. A child with a mother and no father, living in a neighbourhood of mothers with no fathers, judges by what he sees. You can send in social workers and school teachers and clergy to tell a young male that when he grows up he should be a good father to his children, but he doesn't know what that means unless he's seen it. Fifteen years ago, there was hardly a poor neighbourhood in urban Britain where children did not still see plentiful examples of good fathers around them. Today, the balance has already shifted in many poor neighbourhoods. In a few years, the situation will be much worse, for this is a problem that nurtures itself.

### Child-rearing in single-parent communities

Hardly any of this gets into the public dialogue. In the standard newspaper or television story on single-parenthood, the reporter tracks down a struggling single parent and reports her efforts to raise her children under difficult circumstances, ending with an indictment of a stingy social system that doesn't give her enough to get along. The ignored story is what it's like for the two-parent families trying to raise their children in neighbourhoods where they now represent the exception, not the rule. Some of the problems may seem trivial but must be painfully poignant to anyone who is a parent. Take, for example, the story told me by a father who lives in such a neighbourhood in Birkenhead, near Liverpool, about the time he went to his little girl's Christmas play at school. He was the only father there – hardly any of the other children had fathers – and his daughter, embarrassed because she was different, asked him not to come to the school anymore.

The lack of fathers is also associated with a level of physical unruliness that makes life difficult. The same Birkenhead father and his wife raised their first daughter as they were raised, to be polite and considerate – and she suffered for it. Put simply, her schoolmates weren't being raised to be polite and considerate – they weren't being 'raised' at all in some respects. We have only a small body of systematic research on child-rearing practices in contemporary low-income, single-parent communities; it's one of those unfashionable topics. But the unsystematic reports I heard in towns like Birkenhead and council estates like Easterhouse in Glasgow are consistent with the reports from inner-city Washington and New York: in communities without fathers, the kids tend to run wild. The fewer the fathers, the greater the tendency. 'Run wild' can mean such simple things as young children having no set bedtime. It can mean their being left alone in the house at night while mummy goes out. It can mean an 18-month-old toddler allowed to play in the street. And, as in the case of the couple trying to raise their children as they had been raised, it can mean children who are inordinately physical and aggressive in their relationships with other children. With their second child, the Birkenhead parents eased up on their requirements for civil behaviour, realizing that their children had to be able to defend themselves against threats that the parents hadn't faced when they were children. The third child is still an infant, and the mother has made a conscious decision. 'I won't knock the aggression out of her,' she said to me. Then she paused, and added angrily, 'It's *wrong* to have to decide that.'

## The key to an underclass

I can hear the howls of objection already – lots of families raise children who have those kinds of problems, not just poor single parents. Of course. But this is why it is important to talk to parents who have lived in both kinds of communities. Ask them whether there is any difference in child-raising between a neighbourhood composed mostly of married couples and a neighbourhood composed mostly of single mothers. In Britain as in the United States – conduct the inquiries yourself – the overwhelming response is that the difference is large and palpable. The key to an underclass is not the individual instance but a situation in which a very large proportion of an entire community lacks fathers, and this is far more common in poor communities than in rich ones.

## Crime and the underclass

Crime is the next place to look for an underclass, for several reasons. First and most obviously, the habitual criminal is the classic member of an underclass. He lives off mainstream society without participating in it. But habitual criminals are only part of the problem. Once again, the key issue in thinking about an underclass is how the community functions, and crime can devastate a community in two especially important ways. To the extent that the members of a community are victimized by crime, the community tends to become fragmented. To the extent that many people in a community engage in crime as a matter of course, all sorts of the socializing norms of the community change, from the kind of men that the younger boys choose as heroes to the standards of morality in general.

Consider first the official crime figures, reported annually for England by the Home Office. As in the case of illegitimacy, I took for granted before I began this exploration that England had much lower crimes rates than the United States. It therefore came as a shock to discover that England and Wales (which I will subsequently refer to as England) have a combined property crime rate apparently as high, and probably higher, than that of the United States. (I did not compare rates with Scotland and Northern Ireland, which are reported separately.) I say 'apparently' because Britain and the United States use somewhat different definitions of property crime. But burglaries, which are similarly defined in both countries, provide an example. In 1988, England had 1,623 reported burglaries per 100,000 population compared with 1,309 in the US. Adjusting for the transatlantic differences in definitions, England also appears to have had higher rates of motor vehicle theft than the United States. The rates for other kind of theft seem to have been roughly the same. I wasn't the only one who was surprised at these comparisons. I found that if you want to attract startled and incredulous attention in England, mention casually that England has a higher property crime rate than that notorious crime centre of the western world, the United States. No one will believe you.

*Violent crime*

The understandable reason why they don't believe you is that *violent* crime in England remains much lower than violent crime in the United States, and it is violent crime that engenders most anxiety and anger. In this regard, Britain still lags far behind the US. This is most conspicuously true for the most violent of all crimes, homicide. In all of 1988, England and Wales recorded just 624 homicides. The United States averaged that many every 11 days – 20,675 for the year.

That's the good news. The bad news is that the violent crime rate in England and Wales has been rising very rapidly. [. . .]

The size of the increase isn't as bad as it first looks, because England began with such a small initial rate (it's easy to double your money if you start with only a few pence – of which, more in a moment). Still, the rise is steep, and it became much steeper in about 1968. Compare the gradual increase from 1955 to 1968 with what happened subsequently. By 1988, England had 314 violent crimes reported per 100,000 people. The really bad news is that you have been experiencing this increase despite demographic trends that should have been working to your advantage. This point is important enough to explain at greater length.

The most frequent offenders, the ones who puff up the violent crime statistics, are males in the second half of their teens. As males get older, they tend to become more civilized. In both England and the United States, the number of males in this troublesome age group increased throughout the 1970s, and this fact was widely used as an explanation for increasing crime. But since the early 1980s, the size of the young male cohort has been decreasing in both countries. In the United Kingdom, for example, the number of males aged 15 to 19 hit its peak in 1982 and has subsequently decreased both as a percentage of the population and in raw numbers (by a little more than 11 per cent in both cases). Ergo, the violent crime rate 'should' have decreased as well. But it didn't. Despite the reduction in the number of males in the highest-offending age group after 1982, the violent crime rate in England from 1982 to 1988 rose by 43 per cent.

Here I must stop and briefly acknowledge a few of the many ways in which people will object that the official crime rates don't mean anything – but only briefly, because this way lies a statistical abyss.

*The significance of official crime rates*

One common objection is that the increase in the crime rate reflects economic growth (because there are more things to steal, especially cars and the things in them) rather than any real change in criminal behaviour. If so, one has to ask why England enjoyed a steady decline in crime through the last half of the nineteenth century, when economic growth was explosive. But, to avoid argument, let us acknowledge that economic growth does make interpreting the changes in the property crime rate tricky, and focus instead on violent crime, which is not so directly facilitated by economic growth.

Another common objection is that the increase in crime is a mirage. One version of this is that crime just seems to be higher because more crimes are being reported to the police than before (because of greater access to telephones, for example, or because of the greater prevalence of insurance). The brief answer here is that it works both ways. Rape and sexual assault are more likely to be reported now, because of changes in public attitudes and judicial procedures regarding those crimes. An anonymous purse-snatch is less likely to be reported, because the victim doesn't think it will do any good. The aggregate effect of a high crime rate can be to reduce reporting, and this is most true of poor neighbourhoods where attitudes toward the police are ambiguous.

The most outrageously spurious version of the 'crime isn't really getting worse' argument uses *rate* of increase rather than the *magnitude* of increase to make the case. The best example in Britain is the argument that public concern about muggings in the early 1970s was simply an effort to scapegoat young blacks, and resulted in a 'moral panic'. The sociologist Stuart Hall and his colleagues made this case at some length in a book entitled *Policing the Crisis* [London: Macmillan, 1978] in which, among other things, they blithely argued that because the rate of increase in violent crimes was decreasing, the public's concern was unwarranted. It is the familiar problem of low baselines. From 1950 to 1958, violent crime in England rose by 88 per cent (the crime rate began at 14 crimes per 100,000 persons and rose by 13). From 1980 to 1988 violent crime in England rose by only 60 per cent (it began at 196 crimes per 100,000 persons and rose by 118). In other words, by the logic of Hall and his colleagues, things are getting much better, because the rate of increase in the 1980s has been lower than it was during the comparable period of the 1950s. [. . .]

*The intellectual conventional wisdom*

The denial by intellectuals that crime really has been getting worse spills over into denial that poor communities are more violent places than affluent communities. To the people who live in poor communities, this doesn't make much sense. One man in a poor, high-crime community told me about his experience in an open university where he had decided to try to improve himself. He took a sociology course about poverty. The professor kept talking about this 'nice little world that the poor live in', the man remembered. The professor scoffed at the reactionary myth that poor communities are violent places. To the man who lived in such a community, it was 'bloody drivel'. A few weeks later, a class exercise called for the students to canvass a poor neighbourhood. The professor went along, but apparently he, too, suspected that some of his pronouncements were bloody drivel – he cautiously stayed in his car and declined to knock on doors himself. And that raises the most interesting question regarding the view that crime has not risen, or that crime is not especially a problem in lower-class communities: do any of the people who hold this view actually *believe* it, to the extent that they take no more precautions walking in a slum neighbourhood than they do in a middle-class suburb?

These comments will not still the battle over the numbers. But I will venture this prediction, once again drawn from the American experience. After a few more years, quietly and without anyone having to admit he had been wrong, the intellectual conventional wisdom in Britain as in the United States will undergo a gradual transition. After all the statistical artifacts are taken into account and argued over, it will be decided that England is indeed becoming a more dangerous place in which to live: that this unhappy process is not occurring everywhere, but disproportionately in particular types of neighbourhoods; and that those neighbourhoods turn out to be the ones in which an underclass is taking over. Reality will once again force theory to its knees.

## Unemployment and the underclass

If illegitimate births are the leading indicator of an underclass and violent crime a proxy measure of its development, the definitive proof that an underclass has arrived is that large numbers of young, healthy, low-income males choose not to take jobs. (The young idle rich are a separate problem.) The decrease in labour force participation is the most elusive of the trends in the growth of the British underclass.

The main barrier to understanding what's going on is the high unemployment of the 1980s. The official statistics distinguish between 'unemployed' and 'economically inactive', but Britain's unemployment figures (like those in the US) include an unknown but probably considerable number of people who manage to qualify for benefit even if in reality very few job opportunities would tempt them to work.

On the other side of the ledger, over a prolonged period of high unemployment the 'economically inactive' category includes men who would like to work but have given up. To make matters still more complicated, there is the 'black economy' to consider, in which people who are listed as 'economically inactive' are really working for cash, not reporting their income to the authorities. So we are looking through a glass darkly, and I have more questions than answers.

### *Economic inactivity and social class*

The simple relationship of economic inactivity to social class is strong, just as it was for illegitimacy. According to the 1981 census data, the municipal districts with high proportions of household heads who are in Class V (unskilled labour) also tend to have the highest levels of 'economically inactive' persons of working age (statistically, the proportion of Class V households explains more than a third of the variance when inactivity because of retirement is taken into account).

This is another way of saying that you will find many more working-aged people who are neither working nor looking for work in the slums than in the suburbs. Some of these persons are undoubtedly discouraged workers, but two questions need to be asked and answered with far more data than are currently available – specifically, questions about lower-class young males.

### Lower-class young males

First, after taking into account Britain's unemployment problems when the 1981 census was taken, were the levels of economic inactivity among young males consistent with the behaviour of their older brothers and fathers during earlier periods? Or were they dropping out more quickly and often than earlier cohorts of young men?

Second, Britain has for the past few years been conducting a natural experiment, with an economic boom in the south and high unemployment in the north. If lack of jobs is the problem, then presumably economic inactivity among lower-class healthy young males in the south has plummeted to insignificant levels. Has it?

The theme that I heard from a variety of people in Birkenhead and Easterhouse was that the youths who came of age in the late 1970s are in danger of being a lost generation. All of them did indeed ascribe the problem to the surge in unemployment at the end of the 1970s. 'They came out of school at the wrong time,' as one older resident of Easterhouse put it, and have never in their lives held a real job. They are now in their late twenties. As economic times improve, they are competing for the same entry-level jobs as people 10 years younger, and employers prefer to hire the youngsters. But it's more complicated than that, he added. 'They've lost the picture of what they're going to be doing.' When he was growing up, he could see himself in his father's job. Not these young men.

### The generation gap

This generation gap was portrayed to me as being only a few years wide. A man from Birkenhead in his early thirties who had worked steadily from the time he left school until 1979, when he lost his job as an assembly-line worker, recalled how the humiliation and desperation to work remained even as his unemployment stretched from months into years. He – and the others in their thirties and forties and fifties – were the ones showing up at six in the morning when jobs were advertised. They were the ones who sought jobs even if they paid less than the benefit rate.

'The only income I wanted was enough to be free of the bloody benefit system,' he said. 'It was like a rope around my neck.' The phrase for being on benefit that some of them used, 'on the suck', says a great deal about how little they like their situation.

This attitude is no small asset to Britain. In some inner cities of the US, the slang for robbing someone is 'getting paid'. Compare that inversion of values with the values implied by 'on the suck'. Britain in 1989 has resources that make predicting the course of the underclass on the basis of the US experience very dicey.

But the same men who talk this way often have little in common with their sons and younger brothers. Talking to the boys in their late teens and early twenties about jobs, I heard nothing about the importance of work as a source of self-respect and no talk of just wanting enough income to be free of the benefit system. To make a decent living, a youth of 21 explained to me, you need £200 a week – after taxes. He would accept less if it was all he could get. But he conveyed clearly that he would feel exploited. As for the Government's employment training scheme, YTS, that's 'slave labour'. Why, another young man asked me indignantly, should he and his friends be deprived of their right to a full unemployment benefit just because they haven't reached 18 yet? It sounded strange to my ears – a 'right' to unemployment benefit for a school-age minor who's never held a job. But there is no question in any of their minds that that's exactly what the unemployment benefit is: a right, in every sense of the word. The boys did not mention what they considered to be their part of the bargain.

'I was brought up thinking work is something you are morally obliged to do,' as one older man put it. With the younger generation, he said, 'that culture isn't going to be there at all.' And there are anecdotes to go with these observations. For example, the contractors carrying out the extensive housing refurbishment now going on at Easterhouse are obliged to hire local youths for unskilled labour as part of a work-experience scheme. Thirty Easterhouse young men applied for a recent set of openings. Thirteen were accepted. Ten actually came to work the first day. By the end of the first week, only one was still showing up.

### A generation gap by class

My hypothesis – the evidence is too fragmentary to call it more than that – is that Britain is experiencing a generation gap by class. Well-educated young people from affluent homes are working in larger proportions and working longer hours than ever. The attitudes and behaviour of the middle-aged working class haven't changed much. The change in stance toward the labour force is concentrated among lower-class young men in their teens and twenties. It is not a huge change. I am not suggesting that a third or a quarter or even a fifth of lower-class young people are indifferent to work. An underclass doesn't have to be huge to become a problem.

That problem is remarkably difficult to fix. It seems simple – just make decent-paying jobs available. But it doesn't work that way. In the States, we've tried nearly everything – training programmes, guaranteed jobs, special 'socialization' programmes that taught not only job skills but also 'work-readiness skills' such as getting to work on time, 'buddy' systems whereby an experienced older man tried to ease the trainee into the world of work. The results of these strategies, carefully evaluated against control groups, have consistently showed little effect at best, no effect most commonly, and occasionally negative effects.

If this seems too pessimistic for British youth, the Government or some private foundation may easily try this experiment: go down to the Bull Ring near Waterloo Bridge where one of London's largest cardboard cities is located. Pass over the young men who are alcoholics or drug addicts or mentally disturbed, selecting only those who seem clear-headed (there are many). Then offer them jobs at a generous wage for unskilled labour and see what happens. Add in a training component if you wish. Or, if you sympathize with their lack of interest in unskilled jobs, offer them more extensive training that would qualify them for skilled jobs. Carry out your promises to them, spend as much as you wish, and measure the results after 2 years against the experience of similar youths who received no such help. I am betting that you, too, will find 'no effect'. It is an irretrievable disaster for young men to grow up without being socialized into the world of work.

*Work is at the centre of life*

The reason why it is a disaster is not that these young men cause upright taxpayers to spend too much money supporting them. That is a nuisance. The disaster is to the young men themselves and the communities in which they live. Looking around the inner cities of the United States, a view which has been eloquently voiced in the past by people as disparate as Thomas Carlyle and Karl Marx seems increasingly validated by events: work is at the centre of life. By remaining out of the work force during the crucial formative years, young men aren't just losing a few years of job experience. They are missing out on the time in which they need to have been acquiring the skills and the networks of friends and experiences that enable them to establish a place for themselves – not only in the workplace, but a vantage point from which they can make sense of themselves and their lives.

Furthermore, when large numbers of young men don't work, the communities around them break down, just as they break down when large numbers of young unmarried women have babies. The two phenomena are intimately related. Just as work is more important than merely making a living, getting married and raising a family are more than a way to pass the time. Supporting a family is a central means for a man to prove to himself that he is a *'mensch'*. Men who do not support families find other ways to prove that they are men, which tend to take various destructive forms. As many have commented through the centuries, young males are essentially barbarians for whom marriage – meaning not just the wedding vows, but the act of taking responsibility for a wife and children – is an indispensable civilizing force. Young men who don't work don't make good marriage material. Often they don't get married at all; when they do, they haven't the ability to fill their traditional role. In either case, too many of them remain barbarians.
[. . .]

## What can Britain learn from the American experience?

Britain is not the United States, and the most certain of predictions is that the British experience will play out differently from the US experience. At the close of this brief tour of several huge topics, I will be the first to acknowledge that I have skipped over complications and nuances and certainly missed all sorts of special British conditions of which I am ignorant. Still, so much has been the same so far. In both countries, the same humane impulses and the same intellectual fashions drove the reforms in social policy. The attempts to explain away the consequences have been similar, with British intellectuals in the 1980s saying the same things that American intellectuals were saying in the 1970s about how the problems aren't really as bad as they seem.

So if the United States has had so much more experience with a growing underclass, what can Britain learn from it? The sad answer is – not much. The central truth that the politicians in the United States are unwilling to face is our powerlessness to deal with an underclass once it exists. No matter how much money we spend on our cleverest social interventions, we don't know how to turn around the lives of teenagers who have grown up in an underclass culture. Providing educational opportunities or job opportunities doesn't do it. Training programmes don't reach the people who need them most. We don't know how to make up for the lack of good parents – day-care doesn't do it, foster homes don't work very well. Most of all, we don't know how to make up for the lack of a community that rewards responsibility and stigmatizes irresponsibility.

Let me emphasize the words: *we do not know how*. It's not money we lack, but the capability to social-engineer our way out of this situation. Unfortunately, the delusions persist that our social engineering simply hasn't been clever enough, and that we must strive to become more clever.

### Authentic self-government is the key

The alternative I advocate is to have the central government stop trying to be clever and instead get out of the way, giving poor communities (and affluent communities, too) a massive dose of self-government, with vastly greater responsibility for the operation of the institutions that affect their lives – including the criminal justice, educational, housing and benefit systems in their localities. My premise is that it is unnatural for a neighbourhood to tolerate high levels of crime or illegitimacy or voluntary idleness among its youth: that, given the chance, poor communities as well as rich ones will run affairs so that such things happen infrequently. And when communities with different values run their affairs differently, I want to make it as easy as possible for people who share values to live together. If people in one neighbourhood think marriage is an outmoded institution, fine; let them run their neighbourhood as they see fit. But make it easy for the couple who thinks otherwise to move into a neighbourhood where two-parent families are valued. There are many ways that current levels of expenditure for public systems could be sustained (if that is thought to be necessary) but control over them decentralized. Money isn't the key. Authentic self-government is.

But this is a radical solution, and the explanation of why it might work took me 300 pages the last time I tried. In any case, no one in either the United States or Britain is seriously contemplating such steps. That leaves both countries with similar arsenals of social programmes which don't work very well, and the prospect of an underclass in both countries that not only continues but grows.

Oddly, this does not necessarily mean that the pressure for major reforms will increase. It is fairly easy to propitiate the consciences of the well-off and pacify rebellion among the poor with a combination of benefits and social programmes that at least employ large numbers of social service professionals. Such is the strategy that the United States has willy-nilly adopted. Even if the underclass is out there and still growing, it needn't bother the rest of us too much as long as it stays in its own part of town. Everybody's happy – or at least not so unhappy that more action has to be taken.

### The bleak message

So, Britain, that's the bleak message. Not only do you have an underclass, not only is it growing, but, judging from the American experience, there's not much in either the Conservative or Labour agendas that has a chance of doing anything about it. A few years ago I wrote for an American audience that the real contest about social policy is not between people who want to cut budgets and people who want to help. Watching Britain replay our history, I can do no better than repeat the same conclusion. When meaningful reforms finally do occur, they will happen not because stingy people have won, but because generous people have stopped kidding themselves.

# 14

# Relative deprivation

## John Lea and Jock Young

[. . .]
Discontent is a product of *relative*, not *absolute*, deprivation. [. . .] Sheer poverty, for example, does not necessarily lead to a subculture of discontent; it may, just as easily, lead to quiescence and fatalism. Discontent occurs when comparisons between comparable groups are made which suggest that unnecessary injustices are occurring. If the distribution of wealth is seen as natural and just – however disparate it is – it will be accepted. An objective history of exploitation, or even a history of increased exploitation, does not explain disturbances. Exploitative cultures have existed for generations without friction: it is the perception of injustice – *relative deprivation* – which counts. [. . .]

### The causes of crime

For orthodox criminology crime occurs because of a lack of conditioning into values: the criminal, whether because of evil (in the conventional model) or lack of parental training (in the welfare model), lacks the virtues which keep us all honest and upright. In left idealism, crime occurs not because of lack of values but simply because of lack of material goods: economic deprivation drives people into crime. In the conventional viewpoint on crime, the criminal is flawed; he or she lacks human values and cognition. In the radical interpretation of this, the very opposite is true. The criminal, not the honest person, has the superior consciousness: he or she has seen through the foolishness of the straight world. To be well conditioned is to be well deceived. The criminal then enters into a new world of value – a subculture, relieved in part of the mystifications of the conventional world.

We reject both these positions. The radical version smacks of theories of absolute deprivation; we would rather put at the centre of our theory notions of relative deprivation. And a major source of one's making comparisons – or indeed the feeling that one should, in the first place, 'naturally' compete and compare oneself with others – is capitalism itself.

We are taught that life is like a racetrack: that merit will find its own reward. This is the central way our system legitimates itself and motivates people to compete. But what a strange racetrack! In reality some people seem to start half-way along the track (the rich), while others are forced to run with a millstone around their necks (for example, women with both domestic and

Abridged from *What is to be Done about Law and Order?*, pp. 81; 95–101; 218–25. (Harmondsworth: Penguin, 1984.)

non-domestic employment), while others are not even allowed on to the track at all (the unemployed, the members of the most deprived ethnic groups). The values of an equal or meritocratic society which capitalism inculcates into people are constantly at loggerheads with the actual material inequalities in the world. And, contrary to the conservatives, it is the well-socialized person who is the most liable to crime. Crime is endemic to capitalism because it produces both egalitarian ideals and material shortages. It provides precisely the values which engender criticism of the material shortages which the radicals pinpoint.

A high crime rate occurs in precise conditions: where a group has learnt through its past that it is being dealt with invidiously; where it is possible for it easily to pick up the contradictions just referred to and where there is no political channel for these feelings of discontent to be realized. There must be economic and political discontent and there must be an absence of economic and political opportunities.

## The nature of crime and criminal values

For conventional criminology, [. . .] crime is simply antisocial behaviour involving people who lack values. For left idealists it is the reverse: it is proto-revolutionary activity, primitive and individualistic, perhaps, but praiseworthy all the same. It involves, if it is a theft, a redistribution of income, or if it is part of youth culture, symbolic and stylistic awareness of, say, the loss of traditional working-class community or the repressive nature of the system. In either case it involves alternative values.

We would argue that both of these interpretations of crime are superficial. It is true that crime is antisocial – indeed the majority of working-class crime, far from being a prefigurative revolt, is directed against other members of the working class. But it is not antisocial because of lack of conventional values but precisely because of them. For the values of most working-class criminals are overwhelmingly conventional. They involve individualism, competition, desire for material goods and, often, machismo. Such crime could, without exaggeration, be characterized as the behaviour of those suitably motivated people who are too poor to have access to the Stock Exchange. Crime reflects the fact that our own worlds and our own lives are materially and ideo-logically riddled with the capitalist order within which we live. Street crime is an activity of marginals but its image is that of those right in the centre of convention and of concern. As Jeremy Seabrook puts it:

> What we cannot bear, rich and liberals alike, is to see our own image in actions that are ugly and more stark reflections of transactions in which we are all implicated in our social and economic relationships: the universal marketing, the superstitious faith in money, the instant profit, the rip-off, the easy money, the backhander, the quick fiddle, the comforting illusion that we can all get richer without hurting anyone, the way in which individual salvation through money has become a secularized and man-made substitute for divine grace. (1983: 64)

The radicals are correct when they see crime as a reaction to an unjust society. But they make a crucial mistake: they assume that the reaction to a just cause is necessarily a just one. On the contrary: it is often exactly the opposite. The reaction to poverty among poor whites, for example, may be to parade around waving Union Jacks: it may be the tawdry nationalism of the

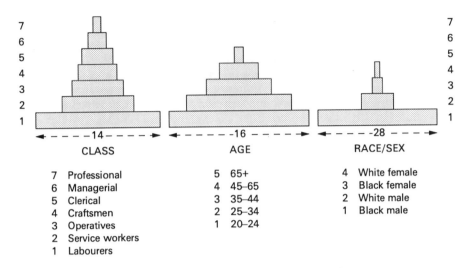

CLASS

| | |
|---|---|
| 7 | Professional |
| 6 | Managerial |
| 5 | Clerical |
| 4 | Craftsmen |
| 3 | Operatives |
| 2 | Service workers |
| 1 | Labourers |

AGE

| | |
|---|---|
| 5 | 65+ |
| 4 | 45–65 |
| 3 | 35–44 |
| 2 | 25–34 |
| 1 | 20–24 |

RACE/SEX

| | |
|---|---|
| 4 | White female |
| 3 | Black female |
| 2 | White male |
| 1 | Black male |

Figure 14.1 *Likelihood of going to prison*

National Front. The reaction to relative deprivation may, as Paul Willis (1977) has so ably shown, be sexism, racism and anti-intellectualism. Crime is one form of egoistic response to deprivation. Its roots are in justice but its growth often perpetuates injustice.

### The nature of the crime statistics

If we look at the official crime statistics in any Western capitalist country we see a remarkable similarity: the young are consistently seen to offend more than the old, the working class more than the middle class, black more than white, and men more than women. In Figure 14.1 we have constructed a series of Aztec pyramids each representing the likelihood of going to prison dependent on class, age, race and gender. We have used American statistics rather than British, as they are more complete. The British figures, particularly in terms of class and race, are kept much more closely guarded. The shape of these pyramids is, however, constant across cultures and there are close parallels; for example, one British study showed that the chances of going to prison by class were exactly the same as in America.

As can be seen, a labourer is 14 times more likely to go to prison than a professional; someone aged between 20 and 24 is 16 times more likely than a 65-year-old; a black male is 28 times more likely than a white female. If one compounds these figures, of course, one achieves much higher ratios, the most extreme being the contrast between the chances of going to prison of an elderly, white professional woman compared to a young, black, lower-working-class man. This has some very dramatic results; for example, on an average day in the United States one in 450 Americans is in prison, but one black man in 26 between the ages of 25 and 34. Offenders, like victims, are sharply focused in terms of social category; in fact, the same social attributes which tend towards high victimization rates tend also towards high offender rates. [. . .] Serious crime, according to the official statistics, is a minority phenomenon within which certain social categories most marginal to society are vastly over-represented. The prisoner is thus on the fringe of the economy (unemployed or a casual labourer), has missed out on the educational system, and belongs to a minority group.

Now, these pyramids illustrate the major empirical problem for understanding crime. For conventional criminology it is scarcely a problem: the lower orders are much more likely to be badly socialized than the middle and upper echelons of society – hence the pyramid. For left idealists, however, this fact poses a considerable quandary. For, on the one hand, gross economic deprivation will surely lead to crime; but on the other, is it not true that the police pick on the poor, ignoring the crimes of the rich? Our response to this contradiction is simply to ask why either/or is a realistic analysis. There is no doubt that different social categories of people behave differently both in their degree of orderliness and criminality and that this relates to their position in the world; but there is also no doubt that the police react differently to different categories of people. If both these points are true, then the official statistics are a product of differences in the 'real' rates of crime between groups and differences in the police predisposition to arrest them. Thus the crime rate of old ladies is no doubt actually very low, but it probably appears *even* lower in the official statistics because of the police disinclination to suspect or arrest elderly persons. And as far as lower-working-class youths are concerned, the exact opposite is true: they commit more crimes and they are excessively harassed, the result being an augmented crime statistic. Moreover, different types of people commit different types of crimes. This point is put particularly well by Reiman. He writes:

> There is evidence suggesting that the particular pressure of poverty leads poor people to commit a higher proportion of the crimes that people fear (such as homicide, burglary, and assault) than their number in the population. There is no contradiction between this and the recognition that those who are well off commit many more crimes than is generally acknowledged both of the widely feared and of the sort not widely feared (such as 'white-collar' crimes). There is no contradiction here, because, as will be shown, the poor are arrested far more frequently than those who are well off when they have committed the same crimes – and the well-to-do are almost never arrested for white-collar crimes. Thus, if arrest records were brought in line with the real incidence of crime, it is likely that those who are well off would appear in the records far more than they do at present, even though the poor would still probably figure disproportionately in arrests for the crimes people fear. In addition to this . . . those who are well off commit acts that are not defined as crimes and yet that are as harmful or more so than the crimes people fear. Thus, if we had an accurate picture of who is really dangerous to society, there is reason to believe that those who are well off would receive still greater representation. (1979: 7–8)

In other words, (a) the pyramids we have constructed with regards to class and crime (and the same is true of race, gender and age) are quantitatively too dramatic: if middle-class people were equally subject to arrest and conviction the contrasts between each level could not be as steep. (b) Qualitatively, given the above provision, they are reasonably correct if one does *not* include white-collar crime and focuses, as Reiman outlines, on the 'normal' crimes which people fear. If people were arrested and imprisoned for white-collar crimes, then the pyramid would remain in shape but its gradient would be lessened even more. (c) To admit to a pyramid of crime by class is not, of course, to believe in a pyramid of impact. That is, the fact that lower-working-class males commit more crime than their upper-class counterparts does not mean that the overall impact of such crimes is necessarily greater. [. . .] it is probably less, although none of this suggests that we should concentrate on either one or the other, as criminologists, both radical and conventional, have done in the past. Both types of crime create considerable problems for the population.

[. . .]

### Relative deprivation

Relative deprivation is the excess of expectations over opportunities. The importance of this concept is that it gets away from simplistic notions that try [to] relate discontent and collective violence to levels of absolute deprivation. The link between relative deprivation and political marginality is crucial for understanding riots and collective violence. Political marginality is unlikely to result in riot unless there is the added sense of frustration stemming from relative deprivation. A social group may be economically and politically marginalized, yet if it has no desire to participate in the structure of opportunities and social rights from which it is excluded, frustration need not occur. For the rioters of the eighteenth century the problem was not the failure to be included in a structure of opportunities stemming from industrial society, so much as the fact that an existing way of life was in the process of being destroyed by industrialization and its opportunity structure. In contemporary industrial societies social groups that have a high degree of economic and political marginality but a low sense of relative deprivation tend to be either deviant subcultures, particularly religious groups oriented to 'other-worldly pursuits', or first-generation immigrant communities. The latter, forced to take the worst jobs and the worst housing that industrial societies have to offer, may still, in the short term, be sheltered from a sense of relative deprivation by virtue of the fact that their standard of comparison is not so much the opportunity structure of the wider society from which they are excluded by racial discrimination or legal barriers, as the societies from which they recently emigrated by comparison with which living standards are higher.

Conversely, of course, a sense of relative deprivation can co-exist with the absence of economic or political marginality. This is the situation with regard to the majority of the organized working class in industrial societies faced with a marked inequality in the distribution of wealth and opportunities. Relative deprivation becomes the driving force of militant trade union and political struggles to increase living standards through the process of political negotiation and compromise. This distinction between relative deprivation combined with political integration and relative deprivation combined with political marginality enables us to understand some of the differences between the 1930s, with their relative absence of riots despite high levels of unemployment, and the present period. During the 1930s the experience of unemployment was not linked as closely as it is today with political marginality. Unemployment was concentrated in the older working-class communities centred in the basic industries of the north, iron and steel, shipbuilding, coal mining, etc. The experience of unemployment was often the collective experience of a whole community related to the slump of the industry around which the community lived and worked. This meant that the institutions of class politics – the trades councils, Labour Party and union branches – appeared to the unemployed as the natural weapons of struggle. The attempt to transfer these traditional methods of struggle *at* work into the arena of the struggle *for* work, such as in the construction of the National Unemployed Workers Movement, was an obvious course of action for the unemployed, most of whom had spent a period of their lives at work. Even the younger unemployed could be drawn into this through the general status and influence of labour-movement institutions in the cohesive working-class community.

The present period presents two contrasts to this. First, the working-class community, particularly in the inner-city areas throughout the country – not just in the older industrial areas – is far less cohesive. The fragmentation of employment between older, industrial employment in decline, newer state employment in the public services, and new small firms relying on cheap labour, combined with a greater cultural and ethnic diversity as older sections of the working class have moved out of the area or just ceased to exist and new immigrant communities have been established, has produced a much greater diversity of levels and types of labour-movement organization. It is not that organization has not emerged in the inner cities, but it no longer constitutes the cohesive and unifying force in the working-class community that it once did. Added to this is the massive growth in the number of young people who have never worked and therefore are not familiar with the organization and attitude of working-class politics. The isolation of youth from work and from class political organizations combines with the reduced hegemony of working-class institutions in the community, by comparison with the 1930s, to produce an acuteness of political marginality probably never previously experienced by any section of British society since industrialization.

But the burden of our argument here is that this acute political marginality is, for the young unemployed, combined with a greater sense of relative deprivation than in the 1930s. It is this volatile combination that underlies the rising street crime and collective violence that we see returning to our cities. This sharp growth of relative deprivation follows from quite fundamental changes, again by contrast with the 1930s, and even more with the nineteenth century, in the mechanisms determining the relationship between expectations and the opportunities for achieving them.

If we define relative deprivation as the excess of expectations over opportunities for fulfilling them, then it is easy to see a situation in which relative deprivation might be kept in check – one which undoubtedly corresponds to the vision of a stable society held by many belonging to what has come to be called the 'new right' in the Conservative Party, in which expectations and opportunities are generally determined by the same mechanism: the free competitive market. Where the competitive market exists not only as a mechanism for the allocation of society's resources but also as a 'moral force' in society, then expectations and opportunities will be brought into some sort of balance. People will not expect a higher income or standard of living than the sale of their particular skill or labour in the market brings, if it is generally considered that the standard of rewards obtaining from the competitive selling of labour or goods in the market is just. Also, in such a competitive society, if an individual does not achieve the same rewards as others from the sale of similar labour or goods, then that individual is likely to blame himself or herself on the grounds that this must be due to offering an inferior product for sale on the market.

Some politicians and academics would like to see this idealized world of *laissez-faire* present in society, in order to solve the problem of relative deprivation, but, to the extent that it actually functioned as a social force in industrial society, it did, and does, provide such a solution only for sections of the middle class. Under nineteenth and early twentieth century capitalism, the fact that the working-class community was insulated by both distance and communication from wealthier sections of society was a far more effective check on relative deprivation, especially coupled with the fact that remnants of pre-industrial religious and customary ways of thinking about society as an inevitable and justifiable hierarchy remained in the popular culture. As the working class became organized and the strength of trade unionism developed, the aims of working-class politics centred not so much around reaching the *same* standards of living as the employers and the ruling class as around the defence of existing working-class living standards, together with modest improvements.

What is even more important about the 1930s is that, despite the depths of the recession, militant discontent was never widespread. Wal Hannington, who led the National Unemployed Workers Movement, had to concede, despite the claims he made for the influence of his organization, that 'at no time has the standing membership approached even 10 per cent of the vast masses of the unemployed'. As Runciman notes:

> The Depression imposed severe and sometimes intolerable hardship on large sections of the working class and many non-manual workers also; but it did not heighten their feelings of relative deprivation in the way that both wars did. Particularly severe wage cuts were, as one would expect, resisted, notably in the textile industry. But the disposition to grin and bear it remained much more widespread than the disposition to storm the barricades. (1966: 64)

Particularly since the last war the growth of the Welfare State has combined with the mass media and mass secondary education to produce a steady growth in relative deprivation. The mass media have disseminated a standardized image of lifestyle particularly in the areas of popular culture and recreation which, for those unemployed and surviving through the dole queue, or only able to obtain employment at very low wages, has accentuated the sense of relative deprivation. The spread of mass state secondary education has had a similar effect, not so much by standardizing expectations of career patterns, living standards, etc., as by raising the minimum expectation. During the period of exceptional economic expansion of the 1950s and 1960s this posed no problems. But now the phenomenon of 'over-education' is beginning to appear. As Cloward and Ohlin (1960: 118–20) have pointed out, the excess of aspirations and opportunities can paradoxically lay the basis for social, racial and other forms of discrimination:

> The democratic ideology of Equality of Opportunity creates constant pressure for formal criteria of evaluation that are universalistic rather than particularistic, achieved rather than ascribed – that is, for a structure of opportunities that are available to all on an open and competitive basis . . . However, the democratic society, like other types of society, is characterized by a limited supply of rewards and opportunities. Although many are eligible for success on the basis of formal criteria, relatively few can succeed, even in a rapidly expanding economy. It is therefore necessary to make choices on some basis or other among candidates who are equally eligible on formal grounds . . . In this situation, criteria based on race, religion, or class, that have been publicly repudiated in favour of achievement

standards, are informally invoked to eliminate the surplus candidates. Thus the democratization of standards of evaluation tends to increase the competition for rewards and opportunities and hence the discrepancy between the formal and the actual criteria of selection for lower-class youngsters.

Finally, the Welfare State has had the same result. New concepts of need and minimum standards of living, coupled with a focus on the poorest sections of society have had the effect of raising the minimum expectation. The *Sunday Telegraph*, comparing the slump of the 1930s with that of today, grasped this well:

> Though unemployment is similar in scale, social security benefits today are not far short of average living standards then. Today's problem, though, is just as acute since expectations, fostered by television and advertising, are high and the frustrations generated by our own slump are vast and dangerous. (*Sunday Telegraph*, 21 February 1982)

The consequence is that expectations have become governed by a set of mechanisms much more loosely, if at all, related to opportunities. The latter are still to a large extent determined by the market mechanism coupled, of course, with the massive growth of state intervention and investment, which itself has had an effect on relative deprivation. As it has become perceived that the state has taken responsibility for major components of the opportunity structure through careers and employment in state services, as well as the general responsibility undertaken by post-war governments, until recently, for maintaining the level of employment, so the discrepancy between expectations and opportunities, now growing as a result of economic recession and cutbacks in state spending, becomes blamed on the 'system' rather than on the individual.

Meanwhile, another quite important change was taking place, the consequences of which are now much clearer. While the tendency, as far as expectations were concerned, was for greater standardization and raising the minimum, the nature of post-war economic expansion was to create a working-class opportunity structure which was increasingly differentiated in terms of wage levels and working conditions. The decline of manufacturing employment in general and the rise of new highly paid white-collar and technical occupations, combined with new sectors of low pay in services (often combining low pay and unsocial hours) and small firms, has produced a more diverse set of opportunities at the same time as expectations have been becoming more standardized. In the short run the solution to this problem in most Western industrial societies was immigrant labour. [. . .] The passivity of the early, post-war, immigrant communities was based on a combination of a cultural orientation towards the homeland and an expected short stay in Britain. This meant that immigrant workers were prepared to accept working conditions which would not be accepted by native workers, such as low pay and flexible shift systems involving long periods of night work. In addition, the legal barriers of alien status and racial prejudice of the native British population generally excluded immigrants from better paid forms of employment.

This situation has been brought to a conclusion during the 1970s by the growth of a second generation of Britons of immigrant parentage. Going through the same education system (despite various forms of discrimination operating there), the children of immigrant families have grown up with the same spectrum of aspirations and expectations derived from the mass media and the education system as young people in general. Expectations and opportunities, then, have been moving in opposite directions, relative deprivation has been increasing, and, as the state has increasingly been seen as the determinant of opportunities, the resentment of unfulfilled expectations increasingly takes the form of resentment against the state and its manifestations, particularly those, like the police, who are encountered on a day-to-day basis by the young unemployed.

[. . .]

## References

Cloward, R. and Ohlin, L. (1960) *Delinquency and Opportunity*. New York: The Free Press.

Reiman, J. (1979) *The Rich Get Richer and the Poor Get Prison*. New York: Wiley.

Runciman, W.G. (1966) *Relative Deprivation and Social Justice*. London: Routledge and Kegan Paul.

Seabrook, J. (1983) 'The crime of poverty', *New Society*, 14 (April).

Willis, P. (1977) *Learning to Labour*. London: Saxon House.

# 15

# Seductions and repulsions of crime

## Jack Katz

In 1835, in a small French village, Pierre Rivière killed half his family: his mother, a sister, and a brother. After his arrest, he wrote a lengthy explanation to the effect that he had killed his mother to protect his father from her ceaseless cruelties, which had frequently become public humiliations, and he had killed two siblings who were living with her because they had sided with her in the family quarrels, either actively or simply through sustained love. In addition, Rivière explained that by killing his young brother, whom he knew his father to love, he would turn his father against him, thus making less burdensome to his father Rivière's legally mandated death, which he expected would result from his crimes.[1] A team of scholars, led by Michel Foucault, traced the ensuing conflicts among the various 'discourses' engaged in by Rivière, the lawyers, doctors, the mayor, the priest, and the villagers, and they added their own.

Rivière wrote a carefully composed, emotionally compelling account of the background to his crime, recounting, as if reconstructing a contemporaneous journal, a long series of deceits and monetary exploitations by his mother against his father. But, although he entitled his account 'Particulars and Explanation of the Occurrence', in the sixty-seven pages his 'memoir' covers (in this translated reproduction), less than a sentence describes the 'particulars of the occurrence'. Rivière gave no specific significance to the aim or the force of the blows he struck with an axlike farm implement (he destroyed the vertebrae that had connected the head of his mother from her body, and he separated brain from skull, converting bone and muscle to mush); to the multiplicity of the blows, which extended far beyond what was necessary to accomplish death; to his mother's advanced state of pregnancy; or to details of the violence suffered by his brother and sister. Instead, he focused exclusively on the background of his family biography. Although Rivière's account was elaborately inculpating in substance, in style, it bespoke a sophisticated rationality, which in many eyes was exculpating. (Some even labeled it 'beautiful'.)

As an author, Pierre Rivière was primarily concerned with the moral power that the narrative could lend to his crime. By glossing over the homicidal event itself, he continued the attack on his mother before a new, larger audience. The state and lay professional interpreters of his crime followed his lead, relying largely on facts he had acknowledged and discounting the situational details in favor of biographical, historical, and social ecological factors. As Foucault suggested, the very barbarity of the attack made it an act of resistance against the forms of civility. But after the fact, Rivière and many

From *Seductions of Crime: Moral and Sensual Attractions in Doing Evil*, pp. 310–24. (New York: Basic Books, 1988.)

powerful groups in his society literally rationalized the event, locating it as the logical outcome of an ongoing family injustice, a form of madness or mental illness, or (in the comments offered later in the book by some of Foucault's colleagues) of the historical and class position of French peasants.[2]

In short, many of the interpreters sought to exploit too much from the murder to dwell on its gruesome lived reality. Rivière was motivated to construct an account that would make his viciously cruel, extremely messy act neatly reappear as a self-sacrificial, efficient blow for justice. The other commentators had general theoretical perspectives at stake: medical-psychological ideology, institutions of religious understanding, and politically significant interpretations (including the emergence of a school of thought around Foucault himself). On all sides, modern forms of civility would govern the posthumous experience of the crime.

Today, the contemporary incarnations of professional, legal-scientific, and civil interpretive spirits are both stronger and more petty than they were 150 years ago. The effective political spectrum for debate still features a Right and a Left, but most of the intellectual action is within a small and relatively tame segment on the left side of the scale. The length of the scale is much narrower than when the Church and tradition, and occasionally even anarchist voices, were powerful in the debate. Now various disciplines in the social sciences have a go at it, but they go at each other more than at 'lay' opinion, and what is at stake is less clearly the institutionalization of a field than the relative popularity of fads in research methodology.

[. . .] [T]he readily available, detailed meaning of common criminality has been systematically ruled out as ineligible for serious discussion in the conventions of modern sociological and political thought. Something important happened when it became obscenely sensational or damnably insensitive to track the lived experience of criminality in favor of imputing factors to the background of crime that are invisible in its situational manifestation. Somehow in the psychological and sociological disciplines, the lived mysticism and magic in the foreground of criminal experience became unseeable, while the abstractions hypothesized by 'empirical theory' as the determining background causes, especially those conveniently quantified by state agencies, became the stuff of 'scientific' thought and 'rigorous' method.

Whatever the historical causes for treating background factors as the theoretical core for the empirical study of crime, [. . .] it is not necessary to constitute the field back to front. We may begin with the foreground, attempting to discover common or homogeneous criminal projects and to test explanations of the necessary and sufficient steps through which people construct given forms of crime. If we take as our primary research commitment an exploration of the distinctive phenomena of crime, we may produce not just ad hoc bits of description or a collection of provocative anecdotes but a systematic empirical theory of crime – one that explains at the individual level the causal process of committing a crime and that accounts at the aggregate level for recurrently documented correlations with biographical and ecological background factors.

## Moral emotions and crime

The closer one looks at crime, at least at the varieties examined here, the more vividly relevant become the moral emotions. Follow vandals and amateur shoplifters as they duck into alleys and dressing rooms and you will be moved by their delight in deviance; observe them under arrest and you may be stunned by their shame. Watch their strutting street display and you will be struck by the awesome fascination that symbols of evil hold for the young men who are linked in the groups we often call gangs. If we specify the opening moves in muggings and stickups, we describe an array of 'games' or tricks that turn victims into fools before their pockets are turned out. The careers of persistent robbers show us, not the increasingly precise calculations and hedged risks of 'professionals', but men for whom gambling and other vices are a way of life, who are 'wise' in the cynical sense of the term, and who take pride in a defiant reputation as 'bad'. And if we examine the lived sensuality behind events of cold-blooded 'senseless' murder, we are compelled to acknowledge the power that may still be created in the modern world through the sensualities of defilement, spiritual chaos, and the apprehension of vengeance.

Running across these experiences of criminality is a process juxtaposed in one manner or another against humiliation. In committing a righteous slaughter, the impassioned assailant takes humiliation and turns it into rage; through laying claim to a moral status of transcendent significance, he tries to burn humiliation up. The badass, with searing purposiveness, tries to scare humiliation off; as one ex-punk explained to me, after years of adolescent anxiety about the ugliness of his complexion and the stupidity of his every word, he found a wonderful calm in making 'them' anxious about *his* perceptions and understandings. Young vandals and shoplifters innovate games with the risks of humiliation, running along the edge of shame for its exciting reverberations. Fashioned as street elites, young men square off against the increasingly humiliating social restrictions of childhood by mythologizing differences with other groups of young men who might be their mirror image. Against the historical background of a collective insistence on the moral non-existence of their people, 'bad niggers' exploit ethnically unique possibilities for celebrating assertive conduct as 'bad'.

What does the moral fascination in the foreground of criminal experience imply for background factors, particularly poverty and social class? Is crime only the most visible peak of a mountain of shame suffered at the bottom of the social order? Is the vulnerability to humiliation skewed in its distribution through the social structure? To address these questions, we should examine the incidence and motivational qualities of what is usually called 'white-collar' crime. Perhaps we would find a greater level of involvement in criminality, even more closely linked to shameful motivations. But the study of white-collar crime has been largely a muckraking operation from the outside; despite isolated exceptions, we have no general empirical understanding of the incidence or internal feel of white-collar crime. This absence of data makes all the more remarkable the influence, within both academic and lay political thought on crime, of the assumption of materialist causation.

### Sentimental materialism

But whatever the differential rates of deviant behavior in the several social strata, and we know from many sources that the official crime statistics uniformly showing higher rates in the lower strata are far from complete or reliable, it appears from our analysis that the greatest pressures toward deviation are exerted upon the lower strata.[3]

Just fifty years ago, Robert K. Merton published his 'Social Structure and Anomie', an article once counted as the single most frequently cited and reprinted paper in the history of American sociology.[4] Arguing against Freud and psychological analysis in general, Merton attributed deviance to a contradiction in the structure of modern society: 'Americans are bombarded on all sides' by the goal of monetary success, but the means or opportunities for achieving it are not as uniformly distributed. A generation later, Richard Cloward and Lloyd Ohlin, with a revised version of 'opportunity' theory, hit perhaps the pinnacle of academic and political success in the history of criminology, winning professional awards and finding their work adopted by the Kennedy administration as part of the intellectual foundations of what later became the War on Poverty.[5] After a hiatus during much of the Republican 1970s and 1980s, materialist theory – the Mertonian ideas now bolstered by rational-economic models of social action that had become academically attractive in the interim – is again promoting the lack of opportunity (unemployment, underemployment, and low 'opportunity cost') to explain crime.[6]

That this materialist perspective is twentieth century sentimentality about crime is indicated by its overwhelming inadequacy for grasping the experiential facts of crime. The 'model' or 'theory' is so persuasive that the observable facts really do not matter, as Merton put it: 'whatever the differential rates of deviant behavior in the several social strata . . . it appears from our analysis that the greatest pressures toward deviation are exerted upon the lower strata'.[7] Indeed, the Mertonian framework as originally presented, as elaborated in the 1960s, and as recently paralleled by the economist's perspective, should now be recognized as an institutionalized academic-political sensibility for systematically making literally unthinkable the contemporary horrors of deviance and for sustaining a quietist criminology.

Consider the many sensually explosive, diabolically creative, realities of crime that the materialist sentiment cannot appreciate. Where is the materialism in the experience of the *barrio* 'homeboy', the night before the first day of high school?

> Although I was not going to be alone, I still felt insecure . . . my mother, with an accentuated voice, ordered me to go to sleep. Nevertheless, my anxiety did not let my consciousness rest; instead, what I did was look in the mirror, and began practicing the traditional steps that would show my machismo. . . . Furthermore, I was nervously thinking about taking a weapon to the school grounds just to show Vatos from other barrios the answer of my holy clique. All kinds of evil thoughts were stirring in me.[8]

The problem for Merton and materialist theory is not simply with some youthful 'gang' activity. There is now strong evidence that a high proportion of those who go on to especially 'serious', 'heavy', 'career' involvements in criminality start in early adolescence, long before job opportunities could or, in a free social order, should become meaningful considerations.[9] Actually, when Albert Cohen pointed out, long ago, the '"versatility" and the "zest" with which some boys are observed to pursue their group-supported deviations', Merton was willing to concede that much of youth crime was beyond his theory of deviance.[10] It was enough if, as Cohen had offered in a conciliatory gesture, Merton's materialism applied to 'professional' or serious adult property criminals.

But if we look at persistent criminals, we see a life of action in which materialism is by no means the god. Instead, material goods are treated more like offerings to be burnt, quickly, lest retention become sacrilege. As suggested by 'dead presidents', a black street term for US cash, there is an aggressive attack on materialism as a potentially misleading, false deity. Robby Wideman seemed to have Merton in mind when he told his brother:

> Straight people don't understand. I mean, they think dudes is after the things straight people got. It ain't that at all. People in the life ain't looking for no home and grass in the yard and shit like that. We the show people. The glamour people. Come on the set with the finest car, the finest woman, the finest vines. Hear people talking about you. Hear the bar get quiet when you walk in the door. Throw down a yard and tell everybody drink up. . . . You make something out of nothing.[11]

The aspiration is not to what is advertised on television. Robby Wideman was not incapable of identifying what drove him; it was to be a star – something literally, distinctively transcendent. Street people are not inarticulate when they say that 'the endgame is to *get over*, to *get across*, to *make it*, to *step fast*'.[12] This language is only a 'poetic' indirect reference to aspirations for material status if we refuse to recognize that it directly captures the objective of transcendence.[13]

So, a lot of juvenile forms of violent crime and an important segment of serious adult crime do not fit the sentimentality of materialism. Neither does the central thrust that guides men and women to righteous slaughters, nor the project of primordial evil that makes 'senseless killings' compellingly sensible to their killers, nor the tactics and reverberations of sneaky thrills. None of these fits, in the Mertonian scheme, the actions of 'innovators' who accept the conventional aims but use deviant means. The aims are specifically unconventional: to go beyond the established moral definitions of the situation as it visibly obtains here and now. Nor can we categorize these deviants as 'retreatists' who reject conventional means and ends. For Merton, retreatists were a spiritually dead, socially isolated, lot of psychotics, drunkards, and vagrants; today's 'bag ladies' would fit that category. And, surely, these deviants are not 'rebels' with revolutionary ideas to implement new goals and means.

None of this argument denies the validity of the recurrent correlations between low socioeconomic status or relative lack of economic opportunity, on the one hand, and violent and personal property crime on the other. The issue is the causal significance of this background for deviance. A person's material background will not determine his intent to commit acquisitive crime, but a person, whether or not he is intent on acquisitive crime, is not likely to be unaware of his circumstances.

Instead of reading into ghetto poverty an unusually strong motivation to become deviant, we may understand the concentration of robbery among ghetto residents as being due to the fact that for people in economically more promising circumstances, it would literally make no sense – it would virtually be crazy – to commit robbery. Merton had no basis but the sentiments stirred by his theory to assume that crime, even materially acquisitive crime, was more common in the 'lower strata'. In part, the appeal of his theory was promoted by the obvious significance of material circumstance in the shaping of crime. We need fear only a few exceptions if we claim that lawyers will not stick up banks, 'frequent-flyer' executives will not kill their spouses in passionate rages, and physicians will not punch out their colleagues or that the unemployed will not embezzle, the indigent will not fix prices, and the politically powerless will not commit perjury in congressional testimony. But this is a different matter from claiming that crime or deviance is distributed in the social structure according to the relative lack of opportunity for material gain.

It is not inconsequential that major forms of contemporary criminality cannot simply be fit within the dominant sentimentality for understanding deviance. If it were recognized that changes in material circumstance affect the form more than the drive toward deviance, it would be more difficult to promote publicly financed programs to increase benefits or opportunities where they are most lacking. A revision of the theory of materialism that would limit it to the explanation of the quality, rather than the quantity, of deviance, would be much less palatable across the political spectrum. Such an analytic framework would not serve those on the Right who point to the social distribution of common crime, along with other pathologies, to discount the moral claims of lower-class minorities for governmental outlays. But neither would a comparative theory of the qualities of crime serve well the social-class sympathies that have often been promoted by the study of white-collar crime. For muckrakers, it has been important to depict the prevalence of elite deviance to weaken the moral basis of corporate political power; often they have argued that white-collar crime is every bit as 'real' and destructive a form of deviance as is street crime. But unless one agrees to reduce nonviolent crimes of deception to a less heinous status than violent personal crime, the comparative perspective will undercut traditional policies of social reform to aid the underprivileged. One has to promise more than a trade-off between street crime and administrative fraud to work up moral enthusiasm for job training programs.

More generally, from Marx through Durkheim and Freud to the contemporary sociological materialists, the hallmark of rhetorically successful theory has been its specification of the source of social evil.[14] Without the claim that background conditions breed the motivation to deviance, criminological theory would not serve the high priestly function of transforming diffuse anxiety about chaos into discrete problems that are confined to marginal segments of social life. Indeed, the research agenda implied by a theory that relates material conditions to the form or quality of deviance but not to its incidence or prevalence is profoundly disquieting.

### Repulsions of deviance

Whether their policy implications point toward increasing penalties to decrease crime or toward increasing legitimate opportunities or 'opportunity costs' to decrease crime, modern causal theories have obliterated a natural fascination to follow in detail the lived contours of crime. Perhaps the indecisive battle among competing determinist theories of crime is itself an important aspect of their persistent popularity, inside academia, in columnists' opinions, and in political speech. Methodological innovations, policy experiments, and the latest wave of governmental statistics continually stimulate the ongoing dialogue, with no side ever gaining a decisive advantage but all sharing in an ideological structure that blocks unsettling encounters with the human experience of crime.

What would follow if we stuck with the research tactic of defining the form of deviance to be explained from the inside and searching for explanations by examining how people construct the experience at issue and then, only as a secondary matter, turned to trace connections from the phenomenal foreground to the generational and social ecological background? We would have to acknowledge that just because blacks have been denied fair opportunity for so long, and so often,[15] the criminality of ghetto blacks can no longer be explained by a lack of opportunity. Just because the critique of American racial injustice has been right for so long, as criminological explanation it now is wrong. Even accepting the Mertonian analysis as initially valid, for how many generations can a community maintain a moral independence of means and ends, innovating deviance only to reach conventional goals? How does a people restrict its economic participation only to the stunted spiritual engagement permitted over centuries of racism? By what anthropological theory can one hold his real self somehow outside the cynical hustles he devises day by day, his soul, untouched by a constant pursuit of illicit action, waiting with confident innocence in some purgatory to emerge when a fair opportunity materializes? The realities of ghetto crime are literally too 'bad' to be confined to the role of 'innovative means' for conventional ends. This is not to deny that the history of racial injustice makes a morally convincing case for increasing opportunities for the ghetto poor. It is to say that materialist theories refuse to confront the spiritual challenge represented by contemporary crime.

The profundity of the embrace of deviance in the black ghetto and the tensions that will emerge among us if we discuss the lived details of these phenomena form one set of the contemporary horrors our positivist theories help us avoid facing. Another blindness they sustain is to the lack of any intellectual or political leadership to confront the massive bloodletting of mate against mate and brother against brother that continues to be a daily reality in the inner city. Each time the sentimentality of materialism is trotted out to cover the void of empirically grounded ideas, it seems more transparent and less inspiring; each time the exhortation to positivism carries a more desperate sentiment that it *has* to be right. And, finally, there is the incalculable chaos that would break out if the institutions of social science were to apply the methods of investigation used here to deviance all across the social order.

Theories of background causes lead naturally to a reliance on the state's definition of deviance, especially as assembled in official crime statistics, and they make case studies virtually irrelevant. But the state will never supply data describing white-collar crime that are comparable to the data describing street or common crime. Politically, morally, and logically, it can't.

The problem is due not to political bias in the narrow sense, but to the dialectical character of white-collar crime as a form of deviance that necessarily exists in a moral metaphysical suspense. To assess the incidence and consequences of common crimes like robbery, one can survey victims and count arrests in a research operation that may be conducted independently of the conviction of the offenders. But individual victims generally cannot authoritatively assert the existence of tax cheating, consumer fraud, insider trading, price fixing, and political corruption; when prosecutions of such crimes fail, not only can the defendants protest their personal innocence, but they can deny that *any* crime occurred. We are on especially shaky grounds for asserting with methodological confidence that white-collar crimes exist before the state fully certifies the allegation through a conviction.

On the one hand, then, white-collar crime can exist as a researchable social problem only if the state officially warrants the problem; on the other hand, white-collar crimes will *not* exist if the state gets too serious about them. The existence of prohibitions against white-collar crimes distinctively depends on the prohibitions not being enforced. The strength of public and political support for robbery and murder prosecutions is not weakened with increased enforcement. But if the official system for prosecuting tax cheating, pollution violations, and even immigration fraud becomes too vigorous, pressure will build to reduce the prohibitory reach of the underlying laws.[16] At the extreme, any group that becomes subject to massive state treatment as criminally deviant is either not an elite or is a class engaged in civil war.

Explanatory social research relies on the state's definition of deviance when it statistically manipulates the demographic and ecological variables quantified by the state, rather than documents in detail the experience and circumstances of the actual doings of deviance. So long as this reliance continues, we will be unable intellectually to constitute a field for the study of white-collar crime. Disparate, occasional studies of white-collar crime will continue to emerge from the margins of organization theory, from interests in equal justice that are sustained by the sociology of law, from studies of criminal justice agencies and of the professions, and from the atheoretical moral force generated by recurrent waves of scandal. But a reliance for explanation on background determinism has made twentieth century social theory fundamentally incapable of comprehending the causation of white-collar crime.

Consider how the traditional boundaries of the field of criminology would break down if we were to extend to white-collar crime the strategy taken in this work to explain common crime. [. . .] [I]n approaching criminal homicide, adolescent theft, gang delinquency and other forms of violent or personal property crime, we would begin, not with the state's official accounting of crime but by looking for lines of action, distinctive to occupants of high social position, that are homogeneously understood by the offenders themselves to enact a variety of deviance. We would quickly arrive at a broad field with vague boundaries between forms of conduct regarded by the offenders as criminal, civilly liable, professionally unethical, and publicly unseemly. Simultaneously, we would follow the logic of analytic induction and search for negative cases, which means that evidence would take the form of qualitative case studies.

Now, where would we get the data? With white-collar crime, we have a special problem in locating facts to demonstrate the lived experience of deviance. Despite their presumably superior capacity to write books and the healthy markets that await their publication efforts, we have virtually no 'how-I-did-it-and-how it-felt-doing-it' autobiographies by corrupted politicians, convicted tax frauds, and chief executive officers who have been deposed by scandals over insider trading. This absence of naturalistic, autobiographical, participant-observational data is itself an important clue to the distinctive emotional quality of white-collar crime. Stickup men, safecrackers, fences, and drug dealers often wear the criminal label with pride, apparently relishing the opportunity to tell their criminal histories in colorful, intimate detail. But white-collar criminals, perhaps from shame or because the ties to those whom they would have to incriminate are so intimate a part of their own identities that they can *never* be broken, rarely publicly confess; when they do confess, they virtually *never* confess with the sustained attention to detail that characterizes, for example, almost any mugging related by an ordinary, semiliterate hustler like Henry Williamson.[17]

As a result, to obtain data, etiological theorists of white-collar crime would have to join forces with public and private investigators and with enemy constituencies of the elites under focus – hardly a promising tack for winning academic, much less governmental-institutional, support for developing a broad data base. Even more absurd is the suggestion that the researcher take up the data-generating task directly by working from readily accessible gossip and looking around one or another local corner. Depending on time and place, that might mean studying the chancellor's project to remodel his home; the law professor's marijuana smoking; the medical researcher's practice of putting his name on research papers, the data for which he has never seen; the alumni's means of supporting the football team; the professor's management of expenditures and accounting in research grants; the administrator's exploitation through real estate profiteering of inside information about the expansion of the university; the process of defaulting on student loans; and so on. By maintaining background determinism as the dominant framework for the study of crime, the social sciences leave the serious academic investigation of elite deviance to those proper intellectual folk, the ethical philosophers, who exploit qualitative case materials in the innocuous forms of delightful illustrations from literature, lively hypotheticals, and colorful histories documented by others. All who already have them retain their jobs and their sanity.

But is it so absurd to imagine a democratic society that would treat the arrogance, the public frauds, and the self-deceptions of its elites as a field that would be amenable to theoretically guided, empirical investigation? Is it obvious that institutionally supported social research on the etiology of deviance should seek causal drives more in the shame and impotence of poverty than in the hubris of affluence and power?

And we can go one step further. The fear of chaos that blocks a truly empirical study of crime is not just a repulsion for a disquieting process of investigation. There is also a substantive chaos – a crisis of meaning in collective identity – lurking more deeply behind the dogged appeal of traditions that intimidate the contemporary intellectual confrontation with the lived experience of deviance.

If we were to develop a comparative analysis of the crimes committed by ghetto residents and by occupants of high social positions, we would surely not be examining the identical qualities of experience. Where the ghetto resident may be proud of his reputation as a 'bad nigger' at home and on the streets, the governmental leader is likely to be ashamed, at least in some family and community settings, of a breach in his pristine image. Although the stickup man focuses on the simple requirements for instantly and unambiguously conveying to victims the criminal intentions of his actions, organization men will tacitly work out a concerted ignorance that provides each with 'deniability' while they arrange the most complex frauds.[18]

But considering the third causal condition that we have been tracing in the paths toward common crime – emotional processes that seduce people to deviance – it is much less clear that the quality of the dynamic differs by social position. Putting aside differences in the practical means that social position makes available and the different degrees and forms of moral stereotype and prejudice that are attached to social position, there may be a

fundamental similarity in the dynamics that people create to seduce themselves toward deviance. Although the means differ, white middle-class youths
may as self-destructively pursue spatial mobility, through reckless driving, as
do ghetto youths in gang wars. The attractions of sneaky thrills may not
disappear with age, but instead may migrate from shoplifting to adultery and
embezzlement. And even the bump that the egocentric badass, strutting
arrogantly outside his own neighborhood, arranges as an 'accident' compelling
him to battle, is not without its analogies to the incidents that have been
arranged by ethnocentric nations, provocatively sailing in foreign waters, to
escalate wars.[19]

It would appear that, with respect to the moral-emotional dynamics of
deviance, we have grounds to pursue a parallel across the social hierarchy.
Consider two strong candidates for the status of most awful street and white-
collar crimes: the killing of defenseless victims to sustain a career of robberies
and the deception of democratic publics to support government-sponsored
killings of defenseless foreigners. In both the street and the high-government
cases, both the Left and the Right have their favored materialist-background
explanations and accusations: poverty and lack of economic opportunity
versus a liberal judiciary, 'handcuffed' police, and inadequate deterrents; the
value to capitalists of maintaining power in foreign economic spheres versus
the need to use military force against non-Russians to maintain a deterrent
strength *vis-à-vis* the ever-menacing Soviet Union. For the most part, public
discussion of both these lowly and exalted social problems proceeds as a
ritualized exchange between two politically opposed materialist interpretations.

But in both forms of deviance the actors are engaged in a transcendent
project to exploit the ultimate symbolic value of force to show that one 'means
it'. Those who persist in stickups use violence when it is not justified on cost-
benefit grounds because *not* to use violence would be to raise chaotic
questions about their purpose in life. They understand that to limit their
violence by materialist concerns would weaken them in conflicts with other
hardmen and would raise a series of questions about their commitment to
their careers that is more intimidating than is the prospect of prison. Just
because materialist motivations do not control the drive toward doing
stickups, the events are rife with foolish risks and fatal bungles.

It is a fair question whether the foreign exercises of Western governments
in legally undeclared, surreptitiously instigated, and secretly aided military
conflicts less often bungle into pathetic results – the shooting of innocent
fishermen, the kidnapping of CIA chiefs, the mechanical surprises from heli-
copters and explosive devices, the failures to make 'operational' defenses
against sea mines and air attacks, the lapses in security that allow massive
military casualties from terrorist tactics, and the like. What is more
remarkable still, is that utilitarian evaluations of success and failure do not
dominate the public discussions of such interventions, any more than they
dominate the career considerations of persistent robbers. In public debates,
symbolic displays of national will, like the cultural style of the hardman, give
cost-benefit analysis a cowardly overtone.

This is not to suggest that some collective machismo is behind the
conspiratorial deceptions of domestic publics undertaken to support state
killings of foreigners. (At the time of writing, the fresh examples are 'Contra-
gate', the secret, illegal American government program for generating lies to

promote the killing of Nicaraguans, and the French government's deceit over homicidal attacks on environmental activists.)[20] Postulated as a determining background factor, personality traits are no more convincing on the state level than on the individual street level. But in both arenas, the use of violence beyond its clear materialist justification is a powerful strategy for *constructing* purposiveness.

The case of Bernhard ('Bernie') Goetz provides us with a bridge between the street experience of the bad nigger and the collective moral perspective that state leaders may rely on in arranging their homicidal deceits. In 1984, Goetz, a white electrical engineer, shot four young 'bad' blacks in a New York City subway train. Acquitted (of all but the weapons charges) in 1987, Goetz became a hero for large segments of the public,[21] essentially because he manipulated to his advantage a detailed understanding of the doings of stickups.

First, Goetz identified a typical opening stratagem in street robberies – the use of civility to move into a position of moral dominance. One of his victims approached him and said,

> 'How are you?' just, you know, 'How are you?' . . . that's a meaningless thing, but in certain circumstances that can be, that can be a real threat. You see, there's an implication there. . . .[22]

Next followed a 'request' for money, which Goetz (and one of the victims) recalled as, 'Give me five dollars', Goetz recalled:

> I looked at his eyes and I looked at his face . . . his eyes were shiny. He was enjoying himself . . . had this big smile on his face. You know at that point, you're in a bad situation. . . . I know in my mind they wanted to play with me . . . like a cat plays with a mouse. . . . I know my situation. I knew my situation.[23]

Next Goetz seized on this opening ambiguity, which he understood the blacks had created not simply to further their robbery or assault but to ridicule him, as a pause in which he could draw out his gun unopposed.[24] Goetz likewise turned the tightly enclosed space of the subway car to his advantage; now the impossibility of escape was a problem for them, not for him. Goetz was aware of the fantastic moral reversal he had effected: 'It was so crazy . . . because they had set a trap for me and only they were trapped. . . . I know this is disgusting to say – but it was so easy. I can't believe it'.

As in many stickups, Goetz's violence was, to a significant degree if not completely, gratuitous within the situational context of his shooting. Since his victims did not have guns, just showing his gun probably would have been enough. Instead, his five shots continued after the end of any personal threat that may have been present; before the last shot, which was aimed at the fourth, as yet uninjured victim, he announced, 'You seem to be all right; here's another.' After the fact, he recalled, 'My intention was to do anything I could to hurt them . . . to murder them, to hurt them, to make them suffer as much as possible.'[25]

Overall, Goetz demonstrated the rational irrationality of violence that characterizes hardened stickup men. Earlier, and independent of this scene, he had arranged to have hollowed-out ('dum-dum') bullets in his gun to enhance destructive consequence should he fire his weapon. Having been victimized in muggings twice before, he found that a readiness to instigate violence had become especially relevant to him for making sense of continuing to travel the streets and subways of New York City. Like the stickup man who routinely keeps a weapon close at hand so he might exploit a fortuitous circumstance, Goetz would not have carried a gun to the scene had he not had this larger, transsituational project.

Beyond practical danger, Goetz was intent on not suffering further humiliation – not simply the humiliations that muggers could inflict, but the humiliation of his own fear, of continuing in the world with the common, cowardly wish to believe that such things would not happen to him. A similar project guides the career of the criminal hardman, whose violence may go beyond what the resistance of a victim may require because he must not only get out of *this* situation but stay 'out there' and be ready to get into *the next*. An inquiry that is limited to the situational reasonableness of violence, which social scientists have often asked in relation to data on robberies in which the offenders harm the victims and that courts must ask of a defendant like Goetz, is, to a great degree, absurd. In both cases, the moral inquiry ignores the transcendent purpose of violent men. Put another way, whether violence was reasonably necessary to escape harm or capture in the situated interaction, the decision to *enter* the situation prepared for violence is not, in itself, a matter for reasonable calculations.

The celebrity that Goetz received was, in significant measure, a celebration by 'good people' of his transcendent meanness. This same spirit more often wreaks devastation through the instrumentality of national foreign policy. Indeed, if youth 'gangs' rely on military metaphors to organize their conflicts, the mobilization of military action in Western democracies also depends, through the chief executive's histrionics and the jingoism of the press, on fashioning international conflicts into dramaturgic lines of street-fighting tactics (showdowns and callings of bluff, ambushes and quick-draw contests, 'bumps' and the issuance of dares to cross lines that have been artificially drawn over international waters).[26] Surely, there are fundamental differences between the processes of using violence to manifest meanness on city streets and to dramatize resolute purposiveness in relations with foreign states. But we will not know just what the spiritual-emotional-moral differences are until we use a comprehensive theoretical approach to analyze and compare the varieties of criminal experience across the social order, including the uses of deceit by elites for conduct they experience as morally significant.

So it is appropriate to begin a study of the seductions of crime with cases of the use of torture by the American military to interrogate Vietnamese peasants and to close this phase of the study by suggesting that, in the late twentieth century, the great powers of the West find themselves in one dubious foreign, militarized situation after another – promoting wars they cannot win, achieving victories that bring them only the prize of emotional domestic support, and entering battles they would lose for winning – all because, at least in the immediate calculations, not to use violence would signal a loss of meaning in national history. Like the bad nigger who, refusing to be a 'chump' like others of his humbled class and ethnicity, draws innocent blood to construct a more self-respecting career that leads predictably to prison confinement, the Western democracies, still seduced by the colonial myth of omnipotence, must again and again strike down thousands so that when the inevitable retreat comes, it will lead over masses of corpses toward 'peace with honor'. Perhaps in the end, what we find so repulsive about studying the reality of crime – the reason we so insistently refuse to look closely at how street criminals destroy others and bungle their way into confinement to save their sense of purposive control over their lives – is the piercing reflection we catch when we steady our glance at those evil men.

## Notes

1 Michel Foucault (ed.), *I, Pierre Rivière, having slaughtered my mother, my sister, and my brother . . .* (New York, Pantheon Books, 1975), p. 106.

2 In the short essay he included in the volume, Foucault continued his pioneering emphasis on the unique phenomenon of power/knowledge. Some of his colleagues and students, however, were quick to impute causal force to class formations, the hypocrisies of the Enlightenment, the market economy, the contractual form, and so on. We learn of the situational facts essentially through the initial, brief reports of doctors who performed what we would today recognize as a coroner's investigation.

3 Robert K. Merton, 'Social structure and anomie', in his *Social Theory and Social Structure* (New York, Free Press, 1968), p. 198.

4 Stephen Cole, 'The growth of scientific knowledge', in Lewis A. Coser (ed.), *The Idea of Social Structure,* (New York, Harcourt Brace Jovanovich, 1975), p. 175.

5 Richard A. Cloward and Lloyd E. Ohlin, *Delinquency and Opportunity* (New York, Free Press, 1960).

6 Robert J. Sampson, 'Urban black violence: the effect of male joblessness and family disruption', *American Journal of Sociology* 93 (September, 1987) pp. 348–82; William Julius Wilson, *The Truly Disadvantaged: the Inner City, the Underclass, and Public Policy* (Chicago, University of Chicago Press, 1987); David Rauma and Richard A. Berk, 'Remuneration and recidivism: the long-term impact of unemployment compensation on ex-offenders', *Journal of Quantitative Criminology* 3 (March, 1987), pp. 3–27.

7 Merton, 'Social structure and anomie', p. 198.

8 Gus Frias, *Barrio Warriors: Homeboys of Peace* (n.p., Diaz Publications, 1982), p. 19.

9 Alfred Blumstein et al., *Criminal Careers and 'Career Criminals'* (Washington, DC, National Academy Press, 1986), 1, pp. 46–7; and Christy A. Visher, 'The Rand Inmate Survey: a reanalysis', in ibid., 2, 168. A recent theory sees adolescents as a social class defined – through legal requirements of school attendance, legal restrictions on employing youths, and laws excepting youths from minimum-wage rates – as having a common position in relation to the means of production. Attractive for their historical and theoretical color, these ideas account no more convincingly than do Merton's for vandalism, the use of dope, intergroup fighting, and the character of initial experiences in property theft as sneaky thrills. David F. Greenberg 'Delinquency and the Age Structure of Society', *Contemporary Crises*, 1 (April 1977), pp. 189–224.

10 Cohen, as quoted in Merton, 'Social structure and anomie', p. 232.

11 John Edgar Wideman, *Brothers and Keepers* (New York, Penguin Books, 1985), p. 131. Recently, the revelations of insider trading in securities markets have produced strikingly similar statements from high-level miscreants. When the take runs into millions of dollars and comes in faster than the criminals can spend it, it is difficult to explain crime with ideas of overly socialized materialistic aspirations. As the offenders themselves put it, at this level, money quickly becomes a way of keeping score.

12 Edith A. Folb, *Running Down Some Lines: the Language and Culture of Black Teenagers* (Cambridge, MA, Harvard University Press, 1980), p. 128 (emphasis in original).

13 Indeed, if we look at what is used to make materialism seductive in advertising, it is not clear that we find the American dream of shiny material success more than a version of 'street culture': soul-wrenching intonations of black music, whorish styles, fleeting images of men shooting craps in alleys and hustling in pool halls, torn shirts and motorcycles, and all the provocatively sensual evils of 'the night'. Judging from Madison Avenue, materialism may be less essential to the motivation to become deviant than an association with deviance is essential to the motivation to be acquisitive.

14 As Davis noted, 'Each classical social theorist shows how their fundamental factor not only undermines the individual's integrity but also saps the society's vitality', See Murray Davis, '"That's Classic!" The Phenomenology and Rhetoric of Successful Social Theories', *Philosophy of Social Science* 16 (1986), p. 290.

15 And here the evidence continues to mount through increasingly sophisticated historical research that demonstrates the many episodes in which more-qualified Northern blacks were pushed aside when jobs were offered to less-qualified white immigrants. See Stanley Lieberson, *A Piece of the Pie* (Berkeley, CA, University of California Press, 1980). Roger Lane, *Roots of Violence in Black Philadelphia, 1860–1900* (Cambridge, MA, Harvard University Press, 1986), is a provocative argument that European ethnic groups who were new to the city in the nineteenth century (the Irish, then the Italians) initially had high rates of violent crime, sometimes higher than the rates for blacks, but the rates for white ethnics declined as these groups were incorporated into the industrial economy, while the rates for blacks, who were excluded from all but servile and dirty-work jobs by discriminatory preferences for less-qualified whites and by public segregation enforced by violence, continually rose.

16 Or when repeal would be too raw politically, the available alternative is to add constraints on the investigative-prosecutorial process. An obvious example from the 1980s is the move to abolish the office of special prosecutor. A less obvious example from the 1970s was built into the Tax Reform Act of 1976. For this and other examples that marked the closing of the Watergate era, see Jack Katz, 'The social movement against white-collar crime', in Egon Bittner and Sheldon Messinger (eds), *Criminology Review Yearbook* (Beverly Hills, CA, Sage, 1980), 2, pp. 161–84. An important appreciation of the distinctively negotiable character of enforcement efforts against white-collar crime in class-related partisan politics is found in Vilhelm Aubert, 'White collar crime and social structure', *American Journal of Sociology*, 58 (November, 1952), pp. 263–71.

17 See Henry Williamson, *Hustler! The Autobiography of a Thief*, ed. R. Lincoln Keiser (New York, Doubleday, 1965). In his encyclopedic study of bribery, Noonan found an admitted awareness of participating in bribery only in the diaries of Samuel Pepys. See John T. Noonan, Jr, *Bribes* (New York, Macmillan, 1984), p. xiv. In relation to differences in the quality of moral autobiographies written by authors of different social classes, we should consider the differential demands on writing talent. Much more interpersonal insight and attention to subtle interactional detail are required to trace the inside experience of white-collar crimes, given their elaborate diffusion of deceit over long careers and in complex social relations. The extraordinary biographies of Robert Moses and Lyndon Johnson by Robert Caro indicate the dimensions of the task. See Robert A. Caro, *The Power Broker: Robert Moses and the Fall of New York* (New York, Alfred A. Knopf, 1974); and *The Path to Power: the Years of Lyndon Johnson* (New York, Alfred A. Knopf, 1982). Talent aside, we should also consider that, for our deceitful elites, to bare all that was involved might entail unbearable self-disgust. It is notable that our social order is so constructed that it is virtually impossible emotionally for our elites truly to confess.

18 Jack Katz, 'Concerted ignorance: the social construction of cover-up', *Urban Life*, 8 (October, 1979), pp. 295–316; and Jack Katz, 'Cover-up and collective integrity', *Social Problems*, 25 (Fall, 1977), pp. 1–25.

19 See J.C. Goulden, *Truth Is the First Casualty: the Gulf of Tonkin Affair – Illusion and Reality* (Chicago, Rand McNally, 1969); and Anthony Austin, *The President's War* (Philadelphia, J.B. Lippincott, 1971).

20 John Dyson, *Sink the Rainbow! An Inquiry into the 'Greenpeace' Affair* (London, Gollancz, 1986); Leslie Cockburn, *Out of Control* (New York, Atlantic Monthly Press, 1987).

21 Ray Innis of the Congress on Racial Equality stated with regard to Goetz's attack, 'Some black men ought to have done it long before. . . . I wish it had been me'. And Geoffrey Alpert, director of the University of Miami's Center for the Study of Law and Society, noted, 'It's something we'd all like to do. We'd all like to think we'd react the way he did'. And Patrick Buchanan, soon to be President Ronald Reagan's press chief, commented, 'The universal rejoicing in New York over the gunman's success is a sign of moral health'. See Lillian Rubin, *Quiet Rage: Bernie Goetz in a Time of Madness* (New York, Farrar, Straus and Giroux, 1986), pp. 10, 11, and 15, respectively.

22 Kirk Johnson, 'Goetz's account of shooting 4 men is given on tape to New York City jury', *New York Times*, April 30, 1987, p. 14, quotes a tape of Goetz's initial interview with the police.

23 Ibid.

24 There was some indecisive evidence that Goetz responded in kind, with an inverted morally aggressive, ambiguity. According to one victim, who recalled saying to Goetz, 'Mister, give me five dollars', Goetz responded with 'You all can have it'. Kirk Johnson,

'Goetz shooting victims say youths weren't threatening', *New York Times*, May 2, 1987, p. 31. Another version by the same victim, reported in Rubin, *Quiet Rage*, p. 7, had Goetz approached with, 'Hey man, you got five dollars for me and my friends to play video games?' and Goetz responding: 'Yeah, sure . . . I've got five dollars for each of you'. According to a paramedic, shortly after the shooting another victim commented that Goetz had preceded his attack with a threat: 'The guys I were with were hassling this guy for some money. He threatened us, then he shot us'. Kirk Johnson, 'A reporter's notebook', *New York Times*, June 15, 1987, p. B1.

25 Johnson, 'Goetz's account of shooting'.

26 And on blocking the public's encounter with the resulting corpses, injuries, and sorrows of relatives, even in popularly supported military conflicts. See Susan Greenberg, *Rejoice! Media Freedom and the Falklands* (London, Campaign for Press and Broadcasting Freedom, 1983), pp. 9–12; and Arthur Gavshon and Desmond Rice, *The Sinking of the Belgrano* (London, Secker and Warburg, 1984).

# 16

# The etiology of female crime

## Dorie Klein

### Introduction

The criminality of women has long been a neglected subject area of criminology. Many explanations have been advanced for this, such as women's low official rate of crime and delinquency and the preponderance of male theorists in the field. Female criminality has often ended up as a footnote to works on men that purport to be works on criminality in general.

There has been, however, a small group of writings specifically concerned with women and crime. This paper will explore those works concerned with the etiology of female crime and delinquency, beginning with the turn-of-the-century writing of Lombroso and extending to the present. Writers selected to be included have been chosen either for their influence on the field, such as Lombroso, Thomas, Freud, Davis and Pollak, or because they are representative of the kinds of work being published, such as Konopka, Vedder and Somerville, and Cowie, Cowie and Slater. The emphasis is on the continuity between these works, because it is clear that, despite recognizable differences in analytical approaches and specific theories, the authors represent a tradition to a great extent. It is important to understand, therefore, the shared assumptions made by the writers that are used in laying the groundwork for their theories.

The writers see criminality as the result of *individual* characteristics that are only peripherally affected by economic, social and political forces. These characteristics are of a *physiological* or *psychological* nature and are uniformly based on implicit or explicit assumptions about the *inherent nature of women*. This nature is *universal*, rather than existing within a specific historical framework.

Since criminality is seen as an individual activity, rather than as a condition built into existing structures, the focus is on biological, psychological and social factors that would turn a woman toward criminal activity. To do this, the writers create two distinct classes of women: good women who are 'normal' non-criminals, and bad women who are criminals, thus taking a moral position that often masquerades as a scientific distinction. The writers, although they may be biological or social determinists to varying degrees, assume that individuals have *choices* between criminal and non-criminal activity. They see persons as atomistically moving about in a social and political vacuum; many writers use marketplace models for human interaction.

Although the theorists may differ on specific remedies for individual criminality, ranging from sterilization to psychoanalysis (but always stopping

From 'The etiology of female crime: a review of the literature', *Issues in Criminology*, 1973, 8(2): 3–30.

far short of social change), the basic thrust is toward *individual adjustment*, whether it be physical or mental, and the frequent model is rehabilitative therapy. Widespread environmental alterations are usually included as casual footnotes to specific plans for individual therapy. Most of the writers are concerned with *social harmony* and the welfare of the existing social structure rather than with the women involved or with women's position in general. None of the writers come from anything near a 'feminist' or 'radical' perspective.

In *The Female Offender*, originally published in 1903, Lombroso described female criminality as an inherent tendency produced in individuals that could be regarded as biological atavisms, similar to cranial and facial features, and one could expect a withering away of crime if the atavistic people were prohibited from breeding. At this time criminality was widely regarded as a physical ailment, like epilepsy. Today, Cowie, Cowie and Slater (1968) have identified physical traits in girls who have been classified as delinquent, and have concluded that certain traits, such as bigness, may lead to aggressiveness. This theme of physiological characteristics has been developed by a good number of writers in the last seventy years, such as the Gluecks (Glueck and Glueck, 1934). One sees at the present time a new surge of 'biological' theories of criminality; for example, a study involving 'violence-prone' women and menstrual cycles has recently been proposed at UCLA.[1]

Thomas, to a certain degree, and Freud extend the physiological explanation of criminality to propose a psychological theory. However, it is critical to understand that these psychological notions are based on assumptions of universal *physiological* traits of women, such as their reproductive instinct and passivity, that are seen as invariably producing certain psychological reactions. Women may be viewed as turning to crime as a *perversion of* or *rebellion against* their *natural feminine roles*. Whether their problems are biological, psychological or social-environmental, the point is always to return them to their roles. Thomas (1907, 1923), for example, points out that poverty might prevent a woman from marrying, whereby she would turn to prostitution as an alternative to carry on her feminine service role. In fact, Davis (1961) discusses prostitution as a parallel illegal institution to marriage. Pollak (1950) discusses how women extend their service roles into criminal activity due to inherent tendencies such as deceitfulness. Freud (1933, Jones, 1961) sees any kind of rebellion as the result of a failure to develop healthy feminine attitudes, such as narcissism, and Konopka (1966) and Vedder and Somerville (1970) apply Freudian thought to the problem of female delinquency.

The specific characteristics ascribed to women's nature and those critical to theories of female criminality are uniformly *sexual* in their nature. Sexuality is seen as the root of female behavior and the problem of crime. Women are defined as sexual beings, as sexual capital in many cases, physiologically, psychologically and socially. This definition *reflects* and *reinforces* the economic position of women as reproductive and domestic workers. It is mirrored in the laws themselves and in their enforcement, which penalize sexual deviations for women and may be more lenient with economic offenses committed by them, in contrast to the treatment given men. The theorists accept the sexual double standard inherent in the law, often noting that 'chivalry' protects women, and many of them build notions of the universality of *sex repression* into their explanations of women's position. Women are thus the sexual backbone of civilization.

In setting hegemonic standards of conduct for all women, the theorists define *femininity*, which they equate with healthy femaleness, in classist, racist and sexist terms, using their assumptions of women's nature, specifically their sexuality, to justify what is often in reality merely a defense of the existing order. Lombroso, Thomas and Freud consider the upper-class white woman to be the highest expression of femininity, although she is inferior to the upper-class white man. These standards are adopted by later writers in discussing femininity. To most theorists, women are inherently inferior to men at masculine tasks such as thought and production, and therefore it is logical that their sphere should be reproductive.

Specific characteristics are proposed to bolster this sexual ideology, expressed for example by Freud, such as passivity, emotionalism, narcissism and deceitfulness. In the discussions of criminality, certain theorists, such as Pollak, link female criminality to these traits. Others see criminality as an attempt away from femininity into masculinity, such as Lombroso, although the specifics are often confused. Contradictions can be clearly seen, which are explained by the dual nature of 'good' and 'bad' women and by the fact that this is a mythology attempting to explain real behavior. Many explanations of what are obviously economically motivated offenses, such as prostitution and shoplifting, are explained in sexual terms, such as prostitution being promiscuity, and shoplifting being 'kleptomania' caused by women's inexplicable mental cycles tied to menstruation. Different explanations have to be made for 'masculine' crimes, e.g., burglary, and for 'feminine' crimes, e.g., shoplifting. Although this distinction crops up consistently, the specifics differ wildly.

The problem is complicated by the lack of knowledge of the epidemiology of female crime, which allows such ideas as 'hidden crime', first expressed by Pollak (1950), to take root. The problem must be considered on two levels: women, having been confined to certain tasks and socialized in certain ways, are *in fact* more likely to commit crime related to their lives which are sexually oriented; yet even non-sexual offenses are *explained* in sexual terms by the theorists. The writers ignore the problems of poor and Third World women, concentrating on affluent white standards of femininity. The experiences of these overlooked women, who *in fact* constitute a good percentage of women caught up in the criminal justice system, negate the notions of sexually motivated crime. These women have real economic needs which are not being met, and in many cases engage in illegal activities as a viable economic alternative. Furthermore, chivalry has never been extended to them.

The writers largely ignore the problems of sexism, racism and class, thus their work is sexist, racist and classist in its implications. Their concern is adjustment of the woman to society, not social change. Hence, they represent a tradition in criminology and carry along a host of assumptions about women and humanity in general. It is important to explore these assumptions and traditions in depth in order to understand what kinds of myths have been propagated around women and crime. The discussions of each writer or writers will focus on these assumptions and their relevance to criminological theories. These assumptions of universal, biological/psychological characteristics, of individual responsibility for crime, of the necessity for maintaining social harmony, and of the benevolence of the state link different theories along a continuum, transcending political labels and minor divergences. The road from Lombroso to the present is surprisingly straight.

## Lombroso: 'There must be some anomaly . . .'

Lombroso's work on female criminality (1920) is important to consider today despite the fact that his methodology and conclusions have long been successfully discredited. Later writings on female crime by Thomas, Davis, Pollak and others use more sophisticated methodologies and may proffer more palatable liberal theories. However, to varying degrees they rely on those sexual ideologies based on *implicit* assumptions about the physiological and psychological nature of women that are *explicit* in Lombroso's work. Reading the work helps to achieve a better understanding of what kinds of myths have been developed for women in general and for female crime and deviance in particular.

One specific notion of women offered by Lombroso is women's physiological immobility and psychological passivity, later elaborated by Thomas, Freud and other writers. Another ascribed characteristic is the Lombrosian notion of women's adaptability to surroundings and their capacity for survival as being superior to that of men. A third idea discussed by Lombroso is women's amorality: they are cold and calculating. This is developed by Thomas (1923), who describes women's manipulation of the male sex urge for ulterior purposes; by Freud (1933), who sees women as avenging their lack of penis on men; and by Pollak (1950), who depicts women as inherently deceitful.

When one looks at these specific traits, one sees contradictions. The myth of compassionate women clashes with their reputed coldness; their frailness belies their capacity to survive. One possible explanation for these contradictions is the duality of sexual ideology with regard to 'good' and 'bad' women.[2] Bad women are whores,driven by lust for money or for men, often essentially *'masculine'* in their orientation, and perhaps afflicted with a touch of penis envy. Good women are chaste, 'feminine', and usually not prone to criminal activity. But when they are, they commit crime in a most *ladylike* way such as poisoning. In more sophisticated theory, all women are seen as having a bit of both tendencies in them. Therefore, women can be compassionate *and* cold, frail *and* sturdy, pious *and* amoral, depending on which path they choose to follow. They are seen as rational (although they are irrational, too!), atomistic individuals making choices in a vacuum, prompted only by personal, physiological/psychological factors. These choices relate only to the *sexual* sphere. Women have no place in any other sphere. Men, on the other hand, are not held sexually accountable, although, as Thomas notes (1907), they are held responsible in *economic* matters. Men's sexual freedom is justified by the myth of masculine, irresistible sex urges. This myth, still worshipped today, is frequently offered as a rationalization for the existence of prostitution and the double standard. As Davis maintains, this necessitates the parallel existence of classes of 'good' and 'bad' women.

These dual moralities for the sexes are outgrowths of the economic, political and social *realities* for men and women. Women are primarily workers within the family, a critical institution of reproduction and socialization that services such basic needs as food and shelter. Laws and codes of behavior for women thus attempt to maintain the smooth functioning of women in that role, which requires that women act as a conservative force in the continuation of the nuclear family. Women's main tasks are sexual, and the law embodies sexual limitations for women, which do not exist for men, such as the prohibition of promiscuity for girls. This explains why theorists of female criminality are not only concerned with sexual violations by female offenders, but attempt to account for even *non-sexual* offenses, such as prostitution, in sexual terms, e.g., women enter prostitution for sex rather than for money. Such women are not only economic offenders but are sexual deviants, falling neatly into the category of 'bad' women.

The works of Lombroso, particularly *The Female Offender* (1920), are a foremost example of the biological explanation of crime. Lombroso deals with crime as an atavism, or survival of 'primitive' traits in individuals, particularly those of the female and non-white races. He theorizes that individuals develop differentially within sexual and racial limitations which differ hierarchically from the most highly developed, the white men, to the most primitive, the non-white women. Beginning with the assumption that criminals must be atavistic, he spends a good deal of time comparing the crania, moles, heights etc. of convicted criminals and prostitutes with those of normal women. Any trait that he finds to be more common in the 'criminal' group is pronounced an atavistic trait, such as moles, dark hair, etc., and women with a number of these telltale traits could be regarded as potentially criminal, since they are of the atavistic type. He specifically rejects the idea that some of these traits, for example obesity in prostitutes, could be the *result* of their activities rather than an indicator of their propensity to them. Many of the traits depicted as 'anomalies', such as darkness and shortness, are characteristic of certain racial groups, such as the Sicilians, who undoubtedly comprise an oppressed group within Italy and form a large part of the imprisoned population.

Lombroso traces an overall pattern of evolution in the human species that accounts for the uneven development of groups: the white and non-white races, males and females, adults and children. Women, children and non-whites share many traits in common. There are fewer variations in their mental capacities: 'even the female criminal is monotonous and uniform compared with her male companion, just as in general woman is inferior to man' (1920: 122), due to her being 'atavistically nearer to her origin than the male' (1920: 107). The notion of women's mediocrity, or limited range of mental possibilities, is a recurrent one in the writings of the twentieth century. Thomas and others note that women comprise 'fewer geniuses, fewer lunatics and fewer morons' (Thomas, 1907: 45); lacking the imagination to be at either end of the spectrum, they are conformist and dull . . . not due to social, political or economic constraints on their activities, but because of their innate physiological limitations as a sex. Lombroso attributes the lower female rate of criminality to their having fewer anomalies, which is one aspect of their closeness to the lower forms of less differentiated life.

Related characteristics of women are their passivity and conservatism. Lombroso admits that women's traditional sex roles in the family bind them to a more sedentary life. However, he insists that women's passivity can be directly traced to the 'immobility of the ovule compared with the zoosperm' (1920: 109), falling back on the sexual act in an interesting anticipation of Freud.

Women, like the lower races, have greater powers of endurance and resistance to mental and physical pain than men. Lombroso states: 'denizens of female prisons . . . have reached the age of 90, having lived within those walls since they were 29 without any grave injury to health' (1920: 125). Denying the humanity of women by denying their capability for suffering justifies exploitation of women's energies by arguing for their suitability to hardship. Lombroso remarks that 'a duchess can adapt herself to new surroundings and become a washerwoman much more easily than a man can transform himself under analogous conditions' (1920: 272). The theme of women's adaptability to physical and social surroundings, which are male initiated, male controlled, and often expressed by saying that women are actually the 'stronger' sex, is a persistent thread in writings on women.

Lombroso explains that because women are unable to feel pain, they are insensitive to the pain of others and lack moral refinement. His blunt denial of the age-old myth of women's compassion and sensitivity is modified, however, to take into account women's low crime rate:

> Women have many traits in common with children; that their moral sense is deficient; that they are revengeful, jealous . . . In ordinary cases these defects are neutralized by piety, maternity, want of passion, sexual coldness, weakness and an undeveloped intelligence. (1920: 151)

Although women lack the higher sensibilities of men, they are thus restrained from criminal activity in most cases by lack of intelligence and passion, qualities which *criminal* women possess as well as all *men*. Within this framework of biological limits of women's nature, the female offender is characterized as *masculine* whereas the normal woman is *feminine*. The anomalies of skull, physiognomy and brain capacity of female criminals, according to Lombroso, more closely approximate that of the man, normal or criminal, than they do those of the normal woman; the female offender often has a 'virile cranium' and considerable body hair. Masculinity in women is an anomaly itself, rather than a sign of development, however. A related notion is developed by Thomas, who notes that in 'civilized' nations the sexes are more physically different.

> What we look for most in the female is femininity, and when we find the opposite in her, we must conclude as a rule that there must be some anomaly . . . Virility was one of the special features of the savage woman . . . In the portraits of Red Indian and Negro beauties, whom it is difficult to recognize for women, so huge are their jaws and cheek-bones, so hard and coarse their features, and the same is often the case in their crania and brains. (1907: 112)

The more highly developed races would therefore have the most feminized women with the requisite passivity, lack of passion, etc. This is a *racist* and *classist* definition of femininity – just as are almost all theories of *femininity* and as, indeed, is the thing itself. The ideal of the lady can only exist in a society built on the exploitation of labor to maintain the woman of leisure who can *be* that ideal lady.

Finally, Lombroso notes women's lack of *property sense*, which contributes to their criminality.

> In their eyes theft is . . . an audacity for which account compensation is due to the owner . . . as an individual rather than a social crime, just as it was regarded in the primitive periods of human evolution and is still regarded by many uncivilized nations. (1920: 217)

One may question this statement on several levels. Can it be assumed to have any validity at all, or is it false that women have a different sense of property than men? If it is valid to a degree, is it related to women's lack of property ownership and non-participation in the accumulation of capitalist wealth?

Indeed, as Thomas (1907) points out, women are considered property themselves. At any rate, it is an interesting point in Lombroso's book that has only been touched on by later writers, and always in a manner supportive of the institution of private property.

### Thomas: 'The stimulation she craves'

The works of W.I. Thomas are critical in that they mark a transition from purely physiological explanations such as Lombroso's to more sophisticated theories that embrace physiological, psychological and social-structural factors. However, even the most sophisticated explanations of female crime rely on implicit assumptions about the *biological* nature of women. In Thomas's *Sex and Society* (1907) and *The Unadjusted Girl* (1923), there are important contradictions in the two approaches that are representative of the movements during that period between publication dates: a departure from biological Social-Darwinian theories to complex analyses of the interaction between society and the individual, i.e., societal repression and manipulation of the 'natural' wishes of persons.

In *Sex and Society* (1907), Thomas poses basic biological differences between the sexes as his starting point. Maleness is 'katabolic', the animal force which is destructive of energy and allows men the possibility of creative work through this outward flow. Femaleness is 'anabolic', analogous to a plant which stores energy, and is motionless and conservative. Here Thomas is offering his own version of the age-old male/female dichotomy expressed by Lombroso and elaborated on in Freud's paradigm, in the structural-functionalist 'instrumental-expressive' duality, and in other analyses of the status quo. According to Thomas, the dichotomy is most highly developed in the more civilized races, due to the greater differentiation of sex roles. This statement ignores the hard physical work done by poor *white* women at home and in the factories and offices in 'civilized' countries, and accepts a *ruling-class* definition of femininity.

The cause of women's relative decline in stature in more 'civilized' countries is a subject on which Thomas is ambivalent. At one point he attributes it to the lack of 'a superior fitness on the motor side' in women (1907: 94); at another point, he regards her loss of *sexual freedom* as critical, with the coming of monogamy and her confinement to sexual tasks such as wifehood and motherhood. He perceptively notes:

> Women were still further degraded by the development of property and its control by man, together with the habit of treating her as a piece of property, whose value was enhanced if its purity was assured. (1907: 297)

However, Thomas's underlying assumptions in his explanations of the inferior status of women are *physiological* ones. He attributes to men high amounts of sexual energy, which lead them to pursue women for their sex, and he attributes to women maternal feelings devoid of sexuality, which lead *them* to exchange sex for domesticity. Thus monogamy, with chastity for women, is the *accommodation* of these basic urges, and women are domesticated while men assume leadership, in a true market exchange.

Why, then, does Thomas see problems in the position of women? It is because modern women are plagued by 'irregularity, pettiness, ill health and inserviceableness' (1907: 245). Change is required to maintain *social harmony*, apart from considerations of women's needs, and women must be educated to make them better wives, a theme reiterated throughout this century by 'liberals' on the subject. Correctly anticipating a threat, Thomas urges that change be made to stabilize the family, and warns that 'no civilization can remain the highest if another civilization adds to the intelligence of its men the intelligence of its women' (1907: 314). Thomas is motivated by considerations of social integration. Of course, one might question how women are to be able to contribute much if they are indeed anabolic. However, due to the transitional nature of Thomas's work, there are immense contradictions in his writing.

Many of Thomas's specific assertions about the nature of women are indistinguishable from Lombroso's; they both delineate a biological hierarchy along race and sex lines.

> Man has, in short, become more somatically specialized an animal than woman, and feels more keenly any disturbance of normal conditions with which he has not the same physiological surplus as woman with which to meet the disturbance . . . It is a logical fact, however, that the lower human races, the lower classes of society, women and children show something of the same quality in their superior tolerance of surgical disease. (1907: 36)

Like Lombroso, Thomas is crediting women with superior capabilities of survival because they are further down the scale in terms of evolution. It is significant that Thomas includes the lower classes in his observation; is he implying that the lower classes are in their position *because* of their natural unfitness, or perhaps that their *situation* renders them less sensitive to pain? At different times, Thomas implies both. Furthermore, he agrees with Lombroso that women are more nearly uniform than men, and says that they have a smaller percentage of 'genius, insanity and idiocy' (1907: 45) than men, as well as fewer creative outbursts of energy.

Dealing with female criminality in *Sex and Society* (1907), Thomas begins to address the issue of morality, which he closely links to legality from a standpoint of maintaining social order. He discriminates between male and female morality:

> Morality as applied to men has a larger element of the contractual, representing the adjustment of his activities to those of society at large, or more particularly to the activities of the male members of society; while the morality which we think of in connection with women shows less of the contractual and more of the personal, representing her adjustment to men, more particularly the adjustment of her person to men. (1907: 172)

Whereas Lombroso barely observes women's lack of participation in the institution of private property, Thomas's perception is more profound. He points out that women *are* property of men and that their conduct is subject to different codes.

> Morality, in the most general sense, represents the code under which activities are best carried on and is worked out in the school of experience. It is preeminently an adult and male system, and men are intelligent enough to realize that neither women nor children have passed through this school. It is on this account that man is merciless to woman from the standpoint of personal behavior, yet he exempts her from anything in the way of contractual morality, or views her defections in this regard with allowance and even with amusement. (1907: 234)

Disregarding his remarks about intelligence, one confronts the critical point about women with respect to the law: because they occupy a *marginal* position in the productive sphere of exchange commodities outside the home, they in turn occupy a marginal position in regard to 'contractual' law which regulates relations of property and production. The argument of differential treatment of men and women by the law is developed in later works by Pollak and others, who attribute it to the 'chivalry' of the system which is lenient to women committing offenses. As Thomas notes, however, women are simply not a serious *threat* to property, and are treated more 'leniently' because of this. Certain women do become threats by transcending (or by being denied) their traditional role, particularly many Third World women and political rebels, and they are *not* afforded chivalrous treatment! In fact, chivalry is reserved for the women who are least likely to ever come in contact with the criminal justice system: the ladies, or white middle-class women. In matters of *sexual* conduct, however, which embody the double standard, women are rigorously prosecuted by the law. As Thomas understands, this is the sphere in which women's functions *are* critical. Thus it is not a matter of 'chivalry' how one is handled, but of different forms and thrusts of social control applied to men and women. Men are engaged in productive tasks and their activities in this area *are* strictly curtailed.

In *The Unadjusted Girl* (1923), Thomas deals with female delinquency as a 'normal' response under certain social conditions, using assumptions about the nature of women which he leaves unarticulated in this work. Driven by basic 'wishes', an individual is controlled by society in her activities through institutional transmission of codes and mores. Depending on how they are manipulated, wishes can be made to serve social or antisocial ends. Thomas stresses the institutions that socialize, such as the family, giving people certain 'definitions of the situation'. He confidently – and defiantly – asserts:

> There is no individual energy, no unrest, no type of wish, which cannot be sublimated and made socially useful. From this standpoint, the problem is not the right of society to protect itself from the disorderly and antisocial person, but the right of the disorderly and antisocial person to be made orderly and socially valuable . . . The problem of society is to produce the right attitudes in its members. (1923: 232–3)

This is an important shift in perspective, from the traditional libertarian view of protecting society by punishing transgressors, to the *rehabilitative* and *preventive* perspective of crime control that seeks to control *minds* through socialization rather than to merely control behavior through punishment. The autonomy of the individual to choose is seen as the product of his environment which the state can alter. This is an important refutation of the Lombrosian biological perspective, which maintains that there are crime-prone individuals who must be locked up, sterilized or otherwise incapacitated. Today, one can see an amalgamation of the two perspectives in new theories of 'behavior control' that use tactics such as conditioning and brain surgery, combining biological and environmental viewpoints.[3]

Thomas proposes the manipulation of individuals through institutions to prevent antisocial attitudes, and maintains that there is no such person as the 'crime prone' individual. A hegemonic system of belief can be imposed by sublimating natural urges and by correcting the poor socialization of slum families. In this perspective, the *definition* of the situation rather than the situation *itself* is what should be changed; a situation is what someone *thinks* it is. The response to a criminal woman who is dissatisfied with her conventional sexual roles is to change not the roles, which would mean widespread social transformations, but to change her attitudes. This concept of civilization as repressive and the need to adjust is later refined by Freud.

Middle-class women, according to Thomas, commit little crime because they are socialized to sublimate their natural desires and to behave well, treasuring their chastity as an investment. The poor woman, however, 'is not immoral, because this implies a loss of morality, but amoral' (1923: 98). Poor women are not objectively driven to crime; they long for it. Delinquent girls are motivated by the desire for excitement or 'new experience', and forget the repressive urge of 'security'. However, these desires are well within Thomas's conception of *femininity*: delinquents are not rebelling against womanhood, as Lombroso suggests, but merely acting it out illegally. Davis and Pollak agree with this notion that delinquent women are not 'different' from non-delinquent women.

Thomas maintains that it is not sexual desire that motivates delinquent girls, for they are no more passionate than other women, but they are *manipulating* male desires for sex to achieve their own ulterior ends.

> The beginning of delinquency in girls is usually an impulse to get amusement, adventure, pretty clothes, favorable notice, distinction, freedom in the larger world . . . The girls have usually become 'wild' before the development of sexual desire, and their casual sex relations do not usually awaken sex feeling. Their sex is used as a condition of the realization of other wishes. It is their capital. (1923: 109)

Here Thomas is expanding on the myth of the manipulative woman, who is cold and scheming and vain. To him, good female sexual behavior is a protective measure – 'instinctive, of course' (1907: 241), whereas male behavior is uncontrollable as men are caught by helpless desires. This is the common Victorian notion of the woman as seductress which in turn perpetuates the myth of a lack of real sexuality to justify her responsibility for upholding sexual mores. Thomas uses a market analogy to female virtue: good women *keep* their bodies as capital to sell in matrimony for marriage and security, whereas bad women *trade* their bodies for excitement. One notes, of course, the familiar dichotomy. It is difficult, in this framework, to see how Thomas can make *any* moral distinctions, since morality seems to be merely good business sense. In fact, Thomas's yardstick is social harmony, necessitating *control*.

Thomas shows an insensitivity to real human relationships and needs. He also shows ignorance of economic hardships in his denial of economic factors in delinquency.

> An unattached woman has a tendency to become an adventuress not so much on economic as on psychological grounds. Life is rarely so hard that a young woman cannot earn her bread; but she cannot always live and have the stimulation she craves. (1907: 241)

This is an amazing statement in an era of mass starvation and illness! He rejects economic causes as a possibility at all, denying their importance in criminal activity with as much certainty as Lombroso, Freud, Davis, Pollak and most other writers.

### Freud: 'Beauty, charm and sweetness'

The Freudian theory of the position of women is grounded in explicit bio-logical assumptions about their nature, expressed by the famous 'Anatomy is Destiny'. Built upon this foundation is a construction incorporating psycho-logical and social-structural factors.

Freud himself sees women as anatomically inferior; they are destined to be wives and mothers, and this is admittedly an inferior destiny as befits the inferior sex. The root of this inferiority is that women's *sex organs* are inferior to those of men, a fact *universally* recognized by children in the Freudian scheme. The girl assumes that she has lost a penis as punishment, is traumatized, and grows up envious and revengeful. The boy also sees the girl as having lost a penis, fears a similar punishment himself, and dreads the girl's envy and vengeance. Feminine traits can be traced to the inferior genitals themselves, or to women's inferiority complex arising from their response to them: women are exhibitionistic, narcissistic, and attempt to compensate for their lack of a penis by being well dressed and physically beautiful. Women become mothers trying to replace the lost penis with a baby. Women are also masochistic, as Lombroso and Thomas have noted, because their *sexual* role is one of receptor, and their sexual pleasure consists of pain. This woman, Freud notes, is the *healthy* woman. In the familiar dichotomy, the men are aggressive and pain inflicting. Freud comments:

> The male pursues the female for the purposes of sexual union, seizes hold of her, and penetrates into her . . . by this you have precisely reduced the characteristic of masculinity to the factor of aggressiveness. (Millett, 1970: 189)

Freud, like Lombroso and Thomas, takes the notion of men's activity and women's inactivity and *reduces* it to the sexual level, seeing the sexual union itself through Victorian eyes: ladies don't move.

Women are also inferior in the sense that they are concerned with personal matters and have little social sense. Freud sees civilization as based on repression of the sex drive, where it is the duty of men to repress their strong instincts in order to get on with the worldly business of civilization. Women, on the other hand,

> have little sense of justice, and this is no doubt connected with the preponderance of envy in their mental life; for the demands of justice are a modification of envy; they lay down the conditions under which one is willing to part with it. We also say of women that their social interests are weaker than those of men and that their capacity for the sublimation of their instincts is less. (1933: 183)

Men are capable of sublimating their individual needs because they rationally perceive the Hobbesian conflict between those urges and social needs. Women are emotional and incapable of such an adjustment because of their innate inability to make such rational judgements. It is only fair then that they should have a marginal relation to production and property.

In this framework, the deviant woman is one who is attempting to be a *man*. She is aggressively rebellious, and her drive to accomplishment is the expression of her longing for a penis; this is a hopeless pursuit, of course, and she will only end up 'neurotic'. Thus the deviant woman should be treated and helped to *adjust* to her sex role. Here again, as in Thomas's writing, is the notion of individual accommodation that repudiates the possibility of social change.

In a Victorian fashion, Freud rationalizes women's oppression by glorifying their duties as wives and mothers:

> It is really a stillborn thought to send women into the struggle for existence exactly the same as men. If, for instance, I imagined my sweet gentle girl as a competitor, it would only end in my telling her, as I did seventeen months ago, that I am fond of her, and I implore her to withdraw from the strife into the calm, uncompetitive activity of my home . . . Nature has determined woman's destiny through beauty, charm and sweetness . . . in youth an adored darling, in mature years a loved wife. (Jones, 1961: 117–18)

In speaking of femininity, Freud, like his forebears, is speaking along racist and classist lines. Only upper- and middle-class women could possibly enjoy lives as sheltered darlings. Freud sets hegemonic standards of femininity for poor and Third World women.

It is important to understand Freudianism because it reduces categories of sexual ideology to explicit sexuality and makes these categories *scientific*. For the last fifty years, Freudianism has been a mainstay of sexist social theory. Kate Millett notes that Freud himself saw his work as stemming the tide of feminist revolution, which he constantly ridiculed:

> Coming as it did, at the peak of the sexual revolution, Freud's doctrine of penis envy is in fact a superbly timed accusation, enabling masculine sentiment to take the offensive again as it had not since the disappearance of overt misogyny when the pose of chivalry became fashionable. (Millett, 1970: 189)

Freudian notions of the repression of sexual instincts, the sexual passivity of women, and the sanctity of the nuclear family are conservative not only in their contemporary context, but in the context of their own time. Hitler writes:

> For her [woman's] world is her husband, her family, her children and her home . . . The man upholds the nation as the woman upholds the family. The equal rights of women consist in the fact that in the realm of life determined for her by nature, she experience the high esteem that is her due. Woman and man represent quite different types of being. Reason is dominant in man . . . Feeling, in contrast, is much more stable than reason, and woman is the feeling, and therefore the stable, element. (Millett, 1970: 170)

One can mark the decline in the position of women after the 1920s through the use of various indices: by noting the progressively earlier age of marriage of women in the United States and the steady rise in the number of children born to them, culminating in the birth explosion of the late 1940s and 1950s; by looking at the relative decline in the number of women scholars; and by seeing the failure to liberate women in the Soviet Union and the rise of fascist sexual ideology. Freudianism has had an unparalleled influence in the United States (and came at a key point to help swing the tide against the women's movement) to facilitate the return of women during the depression and postwar years to the home, out of an economy which had no room for them. Freud affected such writers on female deviance as Davis, Pollak and Konopka, who turn to concepts of sexual maladjustment and neurosis to explain women's criminality. Healthy women would now be seen as masochistic, passive and sexually indifferent. Criminal women would be seen as *sexual* misfits. Most importantly, *psychological* factors would be used to explain criminal activity, and social, economic and political factors would be ignored. Explanations would seek to be *universal*, and historical possibilities of change would be refuted.

### Davis: 'The most convenient sexual outlet for armies . . .'

Kingsley Davis's work on prostitution (1961) is still considered a classical analysis on the subject with a structural-functionalist perspective. It employs assumptions about 'the organic nature of man' and woman, many of which can be traced to ideas proffered by Thomas and Freud.

Davis sees prostitution as a structural necessity whose roots lie in the *sexual* nature of men and women; for example, female humans, unlike primates, are sexually available year-round. He asserts that prostitution is *universal* in time and place, eliminating the possibilities of historical change and ignoring critical differences in the quality and quantity of prostitution in different societies. He maintains that there will always be a class of women who will be prostitutes, the familiar class of 'bad' women. The reason for the universality of prostitution is that sexual *repression*, a concept stressed by Thomas and Freud, is essential to the functioning of society. Once again there is the notion of sublimating 'natural' sex urges to the overall needs of society, namely social order. Davis notes that in our society sexuality is permitted only within the structure of the nuclear family, which is an institution of stability. He does not, however, analyse in depth the economic and social functions of the family, other than to say it is a bulwark of morality.

> The norms of every society tend to harness and control the sexual appetite, and one of the ways of doing this is to link the sexual act to some stable or potentially stable social relationship . . . Men dominate women in economic, sexual and familial relationships and consider them to some extent as sexual property, to be prohibited to other males. They therefore find promiscuity on the part of women repugnant. (1961: 264)

Davis is linking the concept of prostitution to promiscuity, defining it as a *sexual* crime, and calling prostitutes sexual transgressors. Its origins, he claims, lie not in economic hardship, but in the marital restraints on sexuality. As long as men seek women, prostitutes will be in demand. One wonders why sex-seeking women have not created a class of male prostitutes.

Davis sees the only possibility of eliminating prostitution in the liberalization of sexual mores, although he is pessimistic about the likelihood of total elimination. In light of the contemporary American 'sexual revolution' of commercial sex, which has surely created more prostitutes and semi-prostitutes rather than eliminating the phenomenon, and in considering the revolution in China where, despite a 'puritanical' outlook on sexuality, prostitution has largely been eliminated through major economic and social change, the superficiality of Davis's approach becomes evident. Without dealing with root economic, social and political factors, one cannot analyse prostitution.

Davis shows Freudian pessimism about the nature of sexual repression:

> We can imagine a social system in which the motive for prostitution would be completely absent, but we cannot imagine that the system will ever come to pass. It would be a regime of absolute sexual freedom with intercourse practiced solely for pleasure by both parties. There would be no institutional control of sexual expression . . . All sexual desire would have to be mutually complementary . . . Since the basic causes of prostitution – the institutional control of sex, the unequal scale of attractiveness, and the presence of economic and social inequalities between classes and between males and females – are not likely to disappear, prostitution is not likely to disappear either. (1961: 286)

By talking about 'complementary desire', Davis is using a marketplace notion of sex: two attractive or unattractive people are drawn to each other and exchange sexual favors; people are placed on a scale of attractiveness and may be rejected by people above them on the scale; hence they (men) become frustrated and demand prostitutes. Women who become prostitutes do so for good pay *and* sexual pleasure. Thus one has a neat little system in which everyone benefits.

> Enabling a small number of women to take care of the needs of a large number of men, it is the most convenient sexual outlet for armies, for the legions of strangers, perverts and physically repulsive in our midst. (1961: 288)

Prostitution 'functions', therefore it must be good. Davis, like Thomas, is motivated by concerns of social order rather than by concerns of what the needs and desires of the women involved might be. He denies that the women involved are economically oppressed; they are on the streets through autonomous, *individual* choice.

> Some women physically enjoy the intercourse they sell. From a purely economic point of view, prostitution comes near the situation of getting something for nothing . . . Women's wages could scarcely be raised significantly without also raising men's. Men would then have more to spend on prostitution. (1961: 277)

It is important to understand that, given a *sexual* interpretation of what is an *economic* crime, and given a refusal to consider widespread change (even equalization of wages, hardly a revolutionary act), Davis's conclusion is the logical technocratic solution.

In this framework, the deviant women are merely adjusting to their feminine role in an illegitimate fashion, as Thomas has theorized. They are *not* attempting to be rebels or to be 'men', as Lombroso's and Freud's positions suggest. Although Davis sees the main difference between wives and prostitutes in a macrosocial sense as the difference merely between legal and illegal roles, in a personal sense he sees the women who *choose* prostitution as maladjusted and neurotic. However, given the universal necessity for prostitution, this analysis implies the necessity of having a perpetually ill and maladjusted class of women. Thus oppression is *built into* the system, and a healthy *system* makes for a sick *individual*. Here Davis is integrating Thomas's notions of social integration with Freudian perspectives on neurosis and maladjustment.

### Pollak: 'A different attitude toward veracity'

Otto Pollak's *The Criminality of Women* (1950) has had an outstanding influence on the field of women and crime, being the major work on the subject in the postwar years. Pollak advances the theory of 'hidden' female crime to account for what he considers unreasonably low official rates for women.

A major reason for the existence of hidden crime, as he sees it, lies in the *nature* of women themselves. They are instigators rather than perpetrators of criminal activity. While Pollak admits that this role is partly a socially enforced one, he insists that women are inherently deceitful for *physiological* reasons.

Man must achieve an erection in order to perform the sex act and will not be able to hide his failure. His lack of positive emotion in the sexual sphere must become overt to the partner, and pretense of sexual response is impossible for him, if it is lacking. Woman's body, however, permits such pretense to a certain degree and lack of orgasm does not prevent her ability to participate in the sex act. (1950: 10)

Pollak *reduces* women's nature to the *sex act*, as Freud has done, and finds women inherently more capable of manipulation, accustomed to being sly, passive and passionless. As Thomas suggests, women can use sex for ulterior purposes. Furthermore, Pollak suggests that women are innately deceitful on yet another level:

Our sex mores force women to conceal every four weeks the period of menstruation . . . They thus make concealment and misrepresentation in the eyes of women socially required and must condition them to a different attitude toward veracity than men. (1950: 11)

Women's abilities at concealment thus allow them to successfully commit crimes in stealth.

Women are also vengeful. Menstruation, in the classic Freudian sense, seals their doomed hopes to become men and arouses women's desire for vengeance, especially during that time of the month. Thus Pollak offers new rationalizations to bolster old myths.

A second factor in hidden crime is the roles played by women which furnish them with opportunities as domestics, nurses, teachers and house-wives to commit undetectable crimes. The *kinds* of crimes women commit reflect their nature: false accusation, for example, is an outgrowth of women's treachery, spite or fear and is a sign of neurosis; shoplifting can be traced in many cases to a special mental disease – kleptomania. Economic factors play a minor role; *sexual-psychological* factors account for female criminality. Crime in women is *personalized* and often accounted for by mental illness.

Pollak notes:

Robbery and burglary . . . are considered specifically male offenses since they represent the pursuit of monetary gain by overt action . . . Those cases of female robbery which seem to express a tendency toward masculinization come from . . . [areas] where social conditions have favored the assumptions of male pursuits by women . . . The female offenders usually retain some trace of femininity, however, and even so glaring an example of masculinization as the 'Michigan Babes,' an all woman gang of robbers in Chicago, shows a typically feminine trait in the modus operandi. (1950: 29)

Pollak is defining crimes with economic motives that employ overt action as *masculine*, and defining as *feminine* those crimes for *sexual* activity, such as luring men as baits. Thus he is using circular reasoning by saying that feminine crime is feminine. To fit women into the scheme and justify the statistics, he must invent the notion of hidden crime.

It is important to recognize that, to some extent, women *do* adapt to their enforced sexual roles and may be more likely to instigate, to use sexual traps, and to conform to all the other feminine role expectations. However, it is not accidental that theorists label women as conforming even when they are *not*; for example, by inventing sexual motives for what are clearly crimes of economic necessity, or by invoking 'mental illness' such as kleptomania for shoplifting. It is difficult to separate the *theory* from the *reality*, since the reality of female crime is largely unknown. But it is not difficult to see that

Pollak is using sexist terms and making sexist assumptions to advance theories of hidden female crime.

Pollak, then, sees criminal women as extending their sexual role, like Davis and Thomas, by using sexuality for ulterior purposes. He suggests that the condemnation of extramarital sex has 'delivered men who engage in such conduct as practically helpless victims' (1950: 152) into the hands of women blackmailers, overlooking completely the possibility of men blackmailing women, which would seem more likely, given the greater taboo on sex for women and their greater risks of being punished.

The final factor that Pollak advances as a root cause of hidden crime is that of 'chivalry' in the criminal justice system. Pollak uses Thomas's observation that women are differentially treated by the law, and carries it to a sweeping conclusion based on *cultural* analyses of men's feelings toward women.

> One of the outstanding concomitants of the existing inequality . . . is chivalry, and the general protective attitude of man toward woman . . . Men hate to accuse women and thus indirectly to send them to their punishment, police officers dislike to arrest them, district attorneys to prosecute them, judges and juries to find them guilty, and so on. (1950: 151)

Pollak rejects the possibility of an actual discrepancy between crime rates for men and women; therefore, he must look for factors to expand the scope of female crime. He assumes that there is chivalry in the criminal justice system that is extended to the women who come in contact with it. Yet the women involved are likely to be poor and Third World women or white middle-class women who have stepped *outside* the definitions of femininity to become hippies or political rebels, and chivalry is *not* likely to be extended to them. Chivalry is a racist and classist concept founded on the notion of women as 'ladies' which applies only to wealthy white women and ignores the double sexual standard. These 'ladies', however, are the least likely women to ever come in contact with the criminal justice system in the first place.[4]

## The legacy of sexism

A major purpose in tracing the development and interaction of ideas pertaining to sexual ideology based on implicit assumptions of the inherent nature of women throughout the works of Lombroso, Thomas, Freud, Davis and Pollak, is to clarify their positions in relation to writers in the field today. One can see the influence their ideas still have by looking at a number of contemporary theorists on female criminality. Illuminating examples can be found in Gisela Konopka's *Adolescent Girl in Conflict* (1966), Vedder and Somerville's *The Delinquent Girl* (1970) and Cowie, Cowie and Slater's *Delinquency in Girls* (1968). The ideas in these minor works have direct roots in those already traced in this paper.

Konopka justifies her decision to study delinquency in girls rather than in boys by noting girls' *influence* on boys in gang fights and on future generations as mothers. This is the notion of women as instigators of men and influencers on children.

Konopka's main point is that delinquency in girls can be traced to a specific emotional response: loneliness.

> What I found in the girl in conflict was . . . loneliness accompanied by despair. Adolescent boys too often feel lonely and search for understanding and friends. Yet

> in general this does not seem to be the central core of their problems, not their most outspoken ache. While these girls also strive for independence, their need for dependence is unusually great. (1966: 40)

In this perspective, girls are driven to delinquency by an emotional problem – loneliness and dependency. There are *inherent* emotional differences between the sexes.

> Almost invariably her [the girl's] problems are deeply personalized. Whatever her offense – whether shoplifting, truancy or running away from home –it is usually accompanied by some disturbance or unfavorable behavior in the sexual area. (1966: 4)

Here is the familiar resurrection of female personalism, emotionalism, and above all, *sexuality* – characteristics already described by Lombroso, Thomas and Freud. Konopka maintains:

> The delinquent girl suffers, like many boys, from lack of success, lack of opportunity. But her drive to success is never separated from her need for people, for interpersonal involvement. (1966: 41)

Boys are 'instrumental' and become delinquent if they are deprived of the chance for creative success. However, girls are 'expressive' and happiest dealing with people as wives, mothers, teachers, nurses or psychologists. This perspective is drawn from the theory of delinquency as a result of blocked opportunity and from the instrumental/expressive sexual dualism developed by structural-functionalists. Thus female delinquency must be dealt with on this *psychological* level, using therapy geared to their needs as future wives and mothers. They should be *adjusted* and given *opportunities* to be pretty, sociable women.

The important point is to understand how Konopka analyses the roots of girls' feelings. It is very possible that, given women's position, girls may be in fact more concerned with dependence and sociability. One's understanding of this, however, is based on an understanding of the historical position of women and the nature of their oppression. Konopka says:

> What are the reasons for this essential loneliness in girls? Some will be found in the nature of being an adolescent girl, in her biological make-up and her particular position in her culture and time. (1966: 41)

Coming from a Freudian perspective, Konopka's emphasis on female emotions as cause for delinquency, which ignores economic and social factors, is questionable. She employs assumptions about the *physiological* and *psychological* nature of women that very well may have led her to see only those feelings in the first place. For example, she cites menstruation as a significant event in a girl's development. Thus Konopka is rooted firmly in the tradition of Freud and, apart from sympathy, contributes little that is new to the field.[5]

Vedder and Somerville (1970) account for female delinquency in a manner similar to that of Konopka. They also feel the need to justify their attention to girls by remarking that (while female delinquency may not pose as much of a problem as that of boys) because women raise families and are critical agents of socialization, it is worth taking the time to study and control them. Vedder and Somerville also stress the dependence of girls on boys and the instigatory role girls play in boys' activities.

Like Freud and Konopka, the authors view delinquency as blocked access or maladjustment to the normal feminine role. In a blatant statement that ignores the economic and social factors that result from racism and poverty, they attribute the high rates of delinquency among black girls to their lack of 'healthy' feminine narcissism, *reducing* racism to a psychological problem in totally sexist and racist terms.

> The black girl is, in fact, the antithesis of the American beauty. However loved she may be by her mother, family and community, she has no real basis of female attractiveness on which to build a sound feminine narcissism . . . Perhaps the 'black is beautiful' movement will help the Negro girl to increase her femininity and personal satisfaction as a black woman. (1970: 159–60)

Again the focus is on a lack of *sexual* opportunities for women, i.e., the Black woman is not Miss America. *Economic* offenses such as shoplifting are explained as outlets for *sexual* frustration. Since healthy women conform, the individual delinquents should be helped to adjust; the emphasis is on the 'definition of the situation' rather than on the situation.

The answer lies in *therapy*, and racism and sexism become merely psychological problems.

> Special attention should be given to girls, taking into consideration their constitutional biological and psychological differences, and their social position in our male dominated culture. The female offender's goal, as any woman's, is a happy and successful marriage; therefore her self-image is dependent on the establishment of satisfactory relationships with the opposite sex. The double standard for sexual behavior on the part of the male and female must be recognized. (1970: 153)

Like Konopka, and to some extent drawing on Thomas, the authors see female delinquents as extending femininity in an illegitimate fashion rather than rebelling against it. The assumptions made about women's goals and needs, including *biological* assumptions, lock women into a system from which there is no escape, whereby any behavior will be sexually interpreted and dealt with.

The resurgence of biological or physiological explanations of criminality in general has been noteworthy in the last several years, exemplified by the XYY chromosome controversy and the interest in brain waves in 'violent' individuals.[6] In the case of women, biological explanations have *always* been prevalent; every writer has made assumptions about anatomy as destiny. Women are prey, in the literature, to cycles of reproduction, including menstruation, pregnancy, maternity and menopause; they experience emotional responses to these cycles that make them inclined to irrationality and potentially violent activity.

Cowie, Cowie and Slater (1968) propose a *chromosomal* explanation of female delinquency that hearkens back to the works of Lombroso and others such as Healy (Healy and Bronner, 1926), Edith Spaulding (1923) and the Gluecks (Glueck and Glueck, 1934). They write:

> The chromosomal difference between the sexes starts the individual on a divergent path, leading either in a masculine or feminine direction . . . It is possible that the methods of upbringing, differing somewhat for the two sexes, may play some part in increasing the angle of this divergence. (Cowie et al., 1968: 171)

This is the healthy, normal divergence for the sexes. The authors equate *masculinity* and *femininity* with *maleness* and *femaleness*, although contemporary feminists point out that the first categories are *social* and the latter ones *physical*.[7] What relationship exists between the two – how femaleness determines femininity – is dependent on the larger social structure. There is no question that a wide range of possibilities exist historically, and in a non-sexist society it is possible that 'masculinity' and 'femininity' would disappear, and that the sexes would differ only biologically, specifically by their sex organs. The authors, however, lack this understanding and assume an ahistorical sexist view of women, stressing the *universality* of femininity in the Freudian tradition, and of women's inferior role in the nuclear family.[8]

In this perspective, the female offender is *different* physiologically and psychologically from the 'normal' girl.

The authors conclude, in the tradition of Lombroso, that female delinquents are *masculine*. Examining girls for physical characteristics, they note:

> Markedly masculine traits in girl delinquents have been commented on . . . [as well as] the frequency of homosexual tendencies . . . Energy, aggressiveness, enterprise and the rebelliousness that drives the individual to break through conformist habits are thought of as being masculine . . . We can be sure that they have some physical basis. (1968: 172)

The authors see crime as a *rebellion* against sex roles rather than as a maladjusted expression of them. By defining rebellion as *masculine*, they are ascribing characteristics of masculinity to any female rebel. Like Lombroso, they spend time measuring heights, weights, and other *biological* features of female delinquents with other girls.

Crime defined as masculine seems to mean violent, overt crime, whereas 'ladylike' crime usually refers to sexual violations and shoplifting. Women are neatly categorized no matter *which* kind of crime they commit: if they are violent, they are 'masculine' and suffering from chromosomal deficiencies, penis envy, or atavisms. If they conform, they are manipulative, sexually maladjusted and promiscuous. The *economic* and *social* realities of crime – the fact that poor women commit crimes, and that most crimes for women are property offenses – are overlooked. Women's behavior must be *sexually* defined before it will be considered, for women count only in the sexual sphere. The theme of sexuality is a unifying thread in the various, often contradictory theories.

### Conclusion

A good deal of the writing on women and crime being done at the present time is squarely in the tradition of the writers that have been discussed. The basic assumptions and technocratic concerns of these writers have produced work that is sexist, racist and classist; assumptions that have served to maintain a repressive ideology with its extensive apparatus of control. To do a new kind of research on women and crime – one that has feminist roots and a radical orientation – it is necessary to understand the assumptions made by the traditional writers and to break away from them. Work that focuses on human needs, rather than those of the state, will require new definitions of criminality, women, the individual and her/his relation to the state. It is beyond the scope of this paper to develop possible areas of study, but it is none the less imperative that this work be made a priority by women *and* men in the future.

## Notes

1 Quoted from the 1973 proposal for the Center for the Study and Reduction of Violence prepared by Dr Louis J. West, Director, Neuropsychiatric Institute, UCLA: 'The question of violence in females will be examined from the point of view that females are more likely to commit acts of violence during the pre-menstrual and menstrual periods' (1973: 43).

2 I am indebted to Marion Goldman for introducing me to the notion of the dual morality based on assumptions of different sexuality for men and women.

3 For a discussion of the possibilities of psychosurgery in behavior modification for 'violence-prone' individuals, see Frank Ervin and Vernon Mark, *Violence and the Brain* (1970). For an eclectic view of this perspective on crime, see the proposal for the Center for the Study and Reduction of Violence (note 1).

4 The concept of hidden crime is reiterated in Reckless and Kay's report to the President's Commission on Law Enforcement and the Administration of Justice. They note:

> A large part of the infrequent officially acted upon involvement of women in crime can be traced to the masking effect of women's roles, effective practice on the part of women of deceit and indirection, their instigation of men to commit their crimes (the Lady Macbeth factor), and the unwillingness on the part of the public and law enforcement officials to hold women accountable for their deeds (the chivalry factor). (1967: 13)

5 Bertha Payak in 'Understanding the Female Offender' (1963) stresses that women offenders have poor self-concepts, feelings of insecurity and dependency, are emotionally selfish, and prey to irrationality during menstruation, pregnancy, and menopause (a good deal of their life!).

6 See Theodore R. Sarbin and Jeffrey E. Miller, 'Demonism revisited: the XYY chromosomal anomaly', *Issues in Criminology* 5(2), (1970).

7 Kate Millett notes that 'sex is biological, gender psychological and therefore cultural . . . if proper terms for sex are male and female, the corresponding terms for gender are masculine and feminine; these latter may be quite independent of biological sex' (1970: 30).

8 Zelditch (1960), a structural-functionalist, writes that the nuclear family is an inevitability and that within it, women, the 'expressive' sex, will inevitably be the domestics.

## References

Bishop, C. (1931) *Women and Crime*. London: Chatto and Windus.

Cowie, J., Cowie V. and Slater, E. (1968) *Delinquency in Girls*. London: Heinemann.

Davis, K. (1961) 'Prostitution', in R.K. Merton and R.A. Nisbet (eds), *Contemporary Social Problems*. New York: Harcourt Brace and Jovanovich. Originally published as 'The sociology of prostitution', *American Sociological Review*, 1937, 2(5).

Ervin, F. and Mark, V. (1970) *Violence and the Brain*. New York: Harper and Row.

Freud, S. (1933) *New Introductory Lectures on Psychoanalysis*. New York: W.W. Norton.

Glueck, E. and Glueck, S. (1934) *Four Hundred Delinquent Women*. New York: Alfred A. Knopf.

Healy, W. and Bronner, A. (1926) *Delinquents and Criminals: their Making and Unmaking*. New York: Macmillan and Company.

Jones, E. (1961) *The Life and Works of Sigmund Freud*. New York: Basic Books.

Konopka, G. (1966) *The Adolescent Girl in Conflict*. Englewood Cliffs, NJ: Prentice-Hall.

Lombroso, C. (1920) *The Female Offender* (trans.). New York: Appleton. Originally published in 1903.

Millett, K. (1970) *Sexual Politics*. New York: Doubleday.

Monahan, F. (1941) *Women in Crime*. New York: I. Washburn.

Payak, B. (1963) 'Understanding the female offender', *Federal Probation*, XXVII.

Pollak, O. (1950) *The Criminality of Women*. Philadelphia: University of Pennsylvania Press.

Reckless, W. and Kay, B. (1967) *The Female Offender*. Report to the President's Commission on Law Enforcement and the Administration of Justice. Washington, DC: U.S. Government Printing Office.

Sarbin, T.R. and Miller, J.E. (1970) 'Demonism revisited: the XYY chromosomal anomaly', *Issues in Criminology*, 5(2) (Summer).

Spaulding, E. (1923) *An Experimental Study of Psychopathic Delinquent Women*. New York: Rand McNally.

Thomas, W.I. (1907) *Sex and Society*. Boston: Little, Brown.

Thomas, W.I. (1923) *The Unadjusted Girl*. New York: Harper and Row.

Vedder, C. and Somerville, D. (1970) *The Delinquent Girl*. Springfield, Ill.: Charles C. Thomas.

West, J. (1973) *Proposal for the Center for the Study and Reduction of Violence*. Neuropsychiatric Institute, UCLA (10 April).

Zelditch, M. Jr (1960) 'Role Differentiation in the nuclear family: a comparative study', in N. Bell and E. Vogel (eds), *The Family*. Glencoe, Ill.: The Free Press.

## Afterword: Twenty years ago . . . today*

'The Etiology of Female Crime: a Review of the Literature', written two decades ago, ended in a call for 'a new kind of research on women and crime – one that has feminist roots and a radical orientation . . . that focuses on human needs, rather than those of the state, [and that] will require new definitions of criminality, women, the individual and her/his relation to the state.' At that time, in 1973, there was a new women's movement, paralleling other international and domestic liberation movements. It consisted of thousands of women forming groups, reading the few books or articles available, demonstrating, writing, and swapping pamphlets. At the School of Criminology at the University of California, Berkeley, where I was studying, there flourished a radical, oppositional criminology, determined to remake the field in the image of the movements of the time: prisoners' rights, community control of the police, and decriminalization of victimless offenses.

The presence of a critical mass of politically active women graduate students, at a time when few criminologists were female, allowed us to share and build on what little knowledge we had.[1] At that time there were no professional ethnographies of women law-breakers, no recent theoretical readings in criminology that centered on women or gender, no studies of female prisoners that did not focus on their homosexuality or 'affective' needs.

For a term paper, I decided to take what had been written on the causes of women's offenses and scrutinize it for its unexamined assumptions about women offenders.[2] Writing up what I found, I wondered naively, angrily, how, in our era and given the women's movement, such stereotypes about women could be taken seriously. The paper appeared in the special issue devoted to women by the School's journal (*Issues in Criminology*, 1973).

In the years since, the feminist critique of mainstream academic disciplines has exploded in volume and advanced light-years in depth, and interest in the issues of women, crime, victimization and justice has also grown. Today 'Etiology' may strike one as a long-ago first step, the passionate reaction of a beginner armed with the rhetoric of a young movement.

But have the concerns and hopes voiced in 'Etiology' been met, or vanished with time? I would suggest neither; rather, they have been expressed in numerous ways and in the process gone through sea-changes. In this Afterword, I will pose the challenge for feminist criminology in three areas which trace a common history to 'Etiology' and hold importance for the

---

* From *The Criminal Justice System and Women* (eds B.R. Price and N.J. Sokoloff), pp. 47–53. (New York: McGraw-Hill, Inc., 1995.)

future: the scientific basis of theories, the gender and racial bias in science, and the definition of crime. The common thread of my discussion is a simple premise: It is time to move away from considering 'the feminist question in criminology' and toward exploring 'the criminology question in feminism' (see Bertrand, 1991, paraphrasing Harding). Specifically, how can feminist insights into gender, power and knowledge help us critically examine our understanding of crime, criminality, and victimization?

**1.** The debates over the scientific basis of theories of women's and men's behaviors have continued fiercely over two decades, although with new twists and turns around questions of biology and psychology.

Most recently, feminist philosophical and scientific critiques have argued that for many traditional European-identified thinkers, including Lombroso and his followers, femaleness was associated with biology or nature (e.g., primitive, irrational, nurturing), in contrast to male civilization. What is especially radical about these recent critiques is that they do not merely challenge the gender assignment of certain constructs, as earlier feminist work did (e.g., femaleness as a Lombrosian primitive). Rather, they question the very validity of these dichotomies: nature *versus* civilization, emotion *versus* reason, developed *versus* undeveloped world, female *versus* male (see Benhabib and Cornell, 1987; Nicholson, 1990; Sunstein, 1990).

The contemporary feminist argument is this: a quality that appears natural or biological must not be exclusively assigned to a gender; this very quality may be a historical ideological construction rather than an eternal objective truth. Woman herself is a constructed 'Other', in Simone de Beauvoir's classic phrase, who by definition exists only in contrast to man. This is much like the criminal, who cannot exist without the contrast of the law-abiding citizen. Women, like minority-group members, criminals, and other relatively less powerful 'Others', tend to be perceived in the dominant culture more one-dimensionally, more restrictively, than their opposites. Hence one finds the origins of the stereotyping of female offenders in traditional criminology, as discussed in 'Etiology'.

In contemporary criminology, on the other hand, there is now agreement that differences in women's and men's behaviors are social rather than natural, just as there is agreement that the sources of criminality are social rather than natural. Very few criminologists today argue that prostitution or shoplifting emerges out of women's nature or that violence is hormonal. More generally, few theories of criminality are based on nature. To this extent, criminology has moved away from overt biologism.[3] However, criminological work on women continues to focus on their experiences or qualities as they exist in comparison with those of men: in other words, the differences between the genders. Moreover, much work on women focuses uncritically on sexuality: first, as a natural, as opposed to a social, force, and second, as a female, rather than male, concern. Furthermore, in nearly all criminology, maleness remains the universal, femaleness the special case.

During the years, feminists have also wrestled with theoretical psychological perspectives on gender and sexuality, reexamining Freudianism with a far more sophisticated eye (certainly more so than mine in 1973!). One objective, among others, has been to understand how and why women and men are in fact made, as opposed to being born. The spotlight has been on such 'gender factories' as families, although much of the psychoanalytic theorization is limited in its relevance to affluent populations in modern Western societies.

Within feminist and critical criminology, there is much distrust of psychology as the discourse used in 'blaming the victim' and in the practices of social control. Within radical and critical feminism in general, there is similar distrust of psychological approaches to gender domination, such as those that put primacy on sex roles. Structurally oriented and Marxist-influenced feminisms have instead focused on large-scale institutional and cultural aspects of life, such as the division of paid and unpaid labor.

Yet today there is interest in exploring people's personal choices as well as their structural constraints: in other words, in deepening our understanding of the subjective relations between an individual and society. For example, there has been the intriguing and much-debated work of Carol Gilligan (1982) on differences in women's and men's views of morality. One question now being asked of any psychological theory of gender is not so much what is its specific content, but upon what scientific basis is it making psychological claims about gender differences? Is a psychological theory, for example, implicitly biological (e.g., resting on women's childbearing capacity), psycho-analytic, culturally bound (e.g., based on women's childrearing role), or structural?

Much mainstream criminology today, like the positivist correctionalism of the past, is psychological in orientation, focusing on the personal charac-teristics of known offenders and victims. Only recently has this criminology shown any likelihood of drawing upon feminist work, with recent attention paid to the possibilities of investigating why certain forms of criminality are disproportionately male behaviors.

In the 1970s and early 1980s, many feminist scholars in different fields, abandoning biology and psychology, searched for the social roots of women's oppression, which cuts across many eras and cultures. Most argued that whatever the causes of patriarchy, they were due to the structuring of gender rather than either to the biological fact of sexual difference or to differential psychological development alone.[4]

Some feminist scholars have recently called for abandoning the search for the primary universal social cause of sexism, not because the search has failed but because, they argue, there is no such thing. Rather, they argue, there are diverse, geographically specific, historically varying causes and fragmented standpoints inclusive of gender and other (ethnic, class, sexual) forces (Nicholson, 1990).

This brings us to the contemporary feminist argument I noted at the outset, which states, at its most extreme, that it is not just the dualism of femininity/masculinity that is socially constructed but femaleness/maleness itself. It is not the existence of two genders that generates sexism but the other way around; in other words, women and men are not just made, but made up. Not only is there no essential woman's nature, as traditionalists (and some feminists) have believed. And not only is there no universal female experience, as most feminists have heretofore argued, in their advocacy of sisterhood. That we divide humans into two genders is a social artifact, according to this radical new argument, and the way this division happens differs enormously across eras and societies.

This approach to the study of gender, and hence of sexism with all its institutional and ideological facets, parallels schools of thought that view many taken-for-granted concepts and problems as socially constructed rather than as naturally occurring or arising spontaneously in society. One particular example is race, and another is crime. What this approach suggests is not that real experiences around gender, race, or crime do not exist. It means that how we label and explain these experiences involves fluid choices rather than inevitabilities. There are no essences to such concepts as woman or man, black or white, criminal or victim, other than what we attach to them. What it means to be a woman or man, black or white, a criminal or victim changes dramatically with time and varies tremendously across cultures.

After acknowledging that something is socially constructed, there is still much to be done. Sexism, no more than racism or crime, cannot be 'deconstructed' away by academic analysis such as the aforementioned. We want to know how and, if possible, who and why, and, above all, what to do about it. This practical urgency will require the continuous generation of 'feminist roots and a radical orientation' for criminology as it considers specific victimizations and injustices.

**2.** A second, related aspect of the feminist critique concerns the question of whether science and expertise are fundamentally gendered and racially based.

Within criminology, the necessary first steps of this critique, including those begun in 'Etiology', were to challenge traditional assumptions about women, redirect the search for the causes of women's behaviors to their circumstances and experiences, and implicitly hold out the desirability of a fuller range of experiences and behaviors open to all, regardless of gender.

But the next steps were to explore whether science and philosophy are masculine in an even more profound sense than merely male-dominated and male-oriented. Only recently has feminism undertaken critiques of both science and law as gendered in method and philosophical base as well as in overt content (Benhabib and Cornell, 1987; Nicholson, 1990; Sunstein, 1990). In other words, the argument is that the fundamental premises of science and law are not neutral with respect to gender or with respect to cultural ethnicity. It has been difficult to see these biases because they are hidden in taken-for-granted ways of conceptualization, often nearly invisible.

One task, along with making visible and depathologizing femaleness in science and law, is to make visible and denormalize maleness. Unfortunately, criminology and criminal law have not yet been subjected to this level of critique, although recent efforts have been made (Daly and Chesney-Lind, 1988; Smart, 1989). As was true 20 years ago, criminology is implicitly about men, unless it is feminist – in which case it is only about women! And much of the latter is restricted to querying which traditional (masculinist) theories may pertain to women's behaviors!

An example of how criminology might conduct this critique of criminology as fundamentally gendered would be to use the problem of women not being taken seriously as victims and witnesses. Alongside the challenges to common negative images of women victims/witnesses (untrustworthy, provocative, complicit), we would analyse for its gendered content the normal or idealized positive image of the victim/witness (uninvolved with the victimizer, randomly chosen, harmed in public). One question would be, Is this an implicitly male victim/witness?

Another undone task is to constitute a feminist epistemology and methodology, and there has been much debate over what these might look like, if grounded in women's experiences. There has been little development of an explicitly feminist criminological methodology, although some recent studies of women offenders and victims attempt to involve them as subjects rather than examine them as objects. There is only a glimmer of understanding of exactly how women are made the objects of knowledge and power, of the unconscious male identification of the omniscient gaze of experts in criminology (see Benhabib and Cornell, 1987; Diamond and Quinby, 1988). To see the nexus of policing and correctional power, one must first transgress the traditional framework of criminology (Cain, 1989).

For those attempting to reorient their gaze from that of the controller to the standpoint of the dominated, the question changes from What should the discipline do with these people? to How can certain groups of people use the discipline?

One aspect of this shift must be the denormalizing and stepping outside of the dominant ethnic perspective. Race, unlike gender, has never been ignored in criminology, but this is not to say that mainstream criminology has sensitively or accurately addressed the deep and complex associations between criminalization and racism, or between violence and inequality.[5]

Critical criminology, from the days of 'Etiology' onward, certainly has perceived the enormous effects of race and class on criminal justice. A basic premise has been that correctionalism serves to shape and control the lives of the lower classes and people of color, incorporating different strategies: sometimes universalizing standards of the affluent, other times applying differential standards for the poor.

None the less, there has been little development of these issues within either the critical or feminist paradigms during the past 20 years. There has been scant in-depth examination of criminal justice in minority communities. Among feminists, there has been infrequent intellectual exchange between those concerned with criminalized women offenders, who emphasize the repressive and racist character of criminal justice, and those supporting victims of violence, who emphasize the protective and potentially reconciliatory aspects (Klein, 1988). Yet feminist criminology has the greatest potential of any discipline to make these connections (Bertrand, Daly and Klein, 1992). Women in minority communities often directly perceive criminal justice as neither simple protector nor mere oppressor but as the hydra-headed hybrid it is (Gordon, 1988; Klein, 1990). Feminist criminology would benefit from a reexamination of criminal justice from these women's view-point, thus addressing 'human needs, rather than those of the state'.

**3.** A third issue that feminist criminology must tackle is that of the definition of crime. As an applied field, criminology has tended to take its scope of study from government and policy rather than chart its own course. But to say merely that crime is anything that breaks the law, while self-evident, is tautological. Crime certainly has no natural or universal status. In fact, formerly criminalized activities are continually being legalized, such as abortion or (in Nevada) prostitution; and new crimes are continually being politically constructed, as in the case of recent laws on domestic violence (Klein, 1981). To take for granted the official definition of crime is to forgo both an analysis of the roots of law and the penal system and the possibility of developing alternative visions of justice.

Early radical criminologists of the 1970s, while not always explicitly challenging the official definition of crime in every discussion such as 'Etiology', rarely accepted it as given, arguing that it is steeped in racial and class and gender domination. Which activities are legal and which illegal and which laws are enforced are connected to the relative degrees of power of those involved. Many of us were very much aware of the necessity for disaggregating and transforming the suspect category crime (Schwendinger and Schwendinger, 1970). Yet even now this enterprise remains in the formative stages.

The feminist critique has the specific potential to contribute to what could be called the deconstruction of the taken-for-granted concept we call crime, through the prism of gender. Both law and order, on the one hand, and its opposite, criminality, on the other, are very much linked to complex constructions of power, including masculinity. But these possible connections are concealed by layers of rarely debated official morality.

In more practical terms, feminists have wrestled with whether to advocate the enhancement or the abolition of the criminal justice 'apparatus of control'. An example of the dilemma is the feminist debate over criminalizing violent or harmful pornography. Recently there have emerged tentative discussions about what feminist justice might look like (Gilligan, 1982; Daly, 1989; Sunstein, 1990; Bertrand et al., 1992). Despite many disagreements over the potential role of criminal justice, there is consensus that it should not resemble the existing cycles of partial punishment that characterize contemporary US criminal justice, 'partial' referring to the deeply rooted systemic biases (Rafter, 1985).

In conclusion, the current feminist debates relevant to criminology are those concerning defining crime and justice for women and men, gender and racial bias in science, and the validity of fundamental scientific concepts based on nature and dualism. Few of these debates have been concluded, few dilemmas resolved. Yet they have advanced our understanding to the point that today a proposed article titled 'Etiology of Female Crime' would probably be challenged. One would very likely be informed that the scientific concept of etiology is suspect, that the term 'female' must be deconstructed, and that the definition of crime itself should be reexamined.

## Notes

1 One important thing to note in assessing our accomplishments and limits is that most of us were European-American (as distinct from African-, Asian-, or Latino-American), although we did focus on racism as a fundamental issue for feminist criminology.

2 I was inspired to do this by the work then being engaged in by one of my professors, Herman Schwendinger (Schwendinger and Schwendinger, 1974).

3 Ironically, biologism is more influential in feminist theory than in contemporary criminology. Within the movement to end violence against women, influential works have drawn upon implicit assumptions about male biology (e.g., physical strength, sexual aggression) as explaining rape and other victimizations (Brownmiller, 1975; MacKinnon, 1989). Furthermore, feminist legal defenses for accused women have evolved around such controversial conceptualizations as the premenstrual syndrome.

4 Within mainstream criminology, and its ongoing search for the causes of crime, there has been little interest in this search for the roots of patriarchy. Unfortunately, gender issues have largely remained ignored, as in the days of 'Etiology'.

5 Instead, criminologists debate the accuracy and meaning of African-American, Latino, and Anglo/European rates of criminality in an exercise even longer and less productive than the debate over women's and men's rates.

# References

Benhabib, S. and Cornell, D. (eds) (1987) *Feminism as Critique: On the Politics of Gender.* Minneapolis: University of Minnesota.

Bertrand, M.-A. (1991) 'Advances in feminist epistemology of the social control of women'. Presented at the American Society of Criminology, San Francisco, November.

Bertrand, M.-A., Daly, K. and Klein, D. (eds) (1992) *Proceedings of the International Feminist Conference on Women, Law and Social Control.* Vancouver: International Centre for the Reform of Criminal Law and Criminal Justice Policy.

Brownmiller, S. (1975) *Against Our Will: Men, Women and Rape.* New York: Simon and Schuster.

Cain, M. (ed.) (1989) *Growing Up Good: Policing the Behaviour of Girls in Europe.* Newbury Park, CA: Sage.

Daly, K. (1989) 'New feminist definitions of justice', *Proceedings of the First Annual Women's Policy Research Conference.* Washington, DC: Institute for Women's Policy Research.

Daly, K. and Chesney-Lind, M. (1988) 'Feminism and criminology', *Justice Quarterly*, 5: 4.

Diamond, I. and Quinby, L. (eds) (1988) *Feminism and Foucault: Reflections on Resistance.* Boston, MA: Northeastern University Press.

Gilligan, C. (1982) *In a Different Voice: Psychological Theory and Women's Development.* Cambridge, MA: Harvard University Press.

Gordon, L. (1988) *Heroes of Their Own Lives: the Politics and History of Family Violence.* New York: Viking.

Klein, D. (1981) 'Violence against women: some considerations regarding its causes and its elimination', *Crime and Delinquency*, 27: 1.

Klein, D. (1988) 'Women and criminal justice in the Reagan era'. Presented at the Academy of Criminal Justice Sciences, San Francisco, April.

Klein, D. (1990) 'Losing (the war on) the war on crime', *Critical Criminologist*, 2: 4.

MacKinnon, C. (1989) *Towards a Feminist Theory of the State.* Cambridge, MA: Harvard University Press.

Nicholson, L. (ed.) (1990) *Feminism/Postmodernism.* New York: Routledge.

Rafter, N. (1985) *Partial Justice: Women in State Prisons, 1800–1935.* Boston, MA: Northeastern University Press.

Schwendinger, H. and Schwendinger, J. (1970) 'Defenders of order or guardians of human rights?' *Issues in Criminology*, 5: 2.

Schwendinger, H. and Schwendinger, J. (1974) *The Sociologists of the Chair.* New York: Basic Books.

Smart, C. (1989) *Feminism and the Power of Law.* New York: Routledge.

Sunstein, C. (ed.) (1990) *Feminism and Political Theory.* Chicago: University of Chicago Press.

# 17

# Explaining male violence

*Lynne Segal*

'I have never been free of the fear of rape,' Susan Griffin declared in a memorable article in the radical Californian magazine *Ramparts* back in 1971, adding: 'I never asked why men raped; I simply thought it one of the many mysteries of human nature.'[1] Nearly two decades later – decades in which feminists have repeatedly asked the question, devoting books and articles to finding the answer – the puzzle of men's cruelty to women remains only just a little less mysterious. Griffin herself had an answer. In patriarchal culture, she argued, the basic elements of rape are present in all heterosexual relationships: 'If the professional rapist is to be separated from the average dominant heterosexual, it may be mainly a quantitative difference.'[2] Men in our culture are taught and encouraged to rape women as the symbolic expression of male power. Rape serves as 'a kind of terrorism' enabling men to control women and make them dependent: 'Rape is the quintessential act of our civilization.'[3]

Other feminists in those early days of women's liberation, including Kate Millett and Shulamith Firestone in the US, did not share Griffin's analysis that rape and male violence play such a central role in establishing and perpetuating male power.[4] Germaine Greer's popular feminism, urging women to become tough, hedonistic and autonomous, dismissed outright the significance of men's use of violence against women.[5] And in Britain, the early feminist texts (the classic books of Juliet Mitchell and Sheila Rowbotham, for example) assigned male violence little weight in their analysis of the way in which the sexual division of labour and its concordant ideologies produce men's power and women's subordination.[6] It was the publication of Susan Brownmiller's international bestseller *Against Our Will* in 1975 which was to prove a landmark in feminist thinking, in providing an analysis of male power which placed rape and male violence at the centre of the feminist problematic.[7]

Retrospectively, it is startling to realize that rape and men's violence towards women became a serious social and political issue only through feminist attention to them. There is no woman over 40 who cannot recall men's jokes trivializing rape as a violation which women secretly desire. This was true whatever the grouping of men, and however terrifying and violent the sexual assaults in the headline a mere twenty or so years ago. There was much merriment, at that time, among male staff in the psychology department of Sydney University when I was a student over a rapist known as 'The Slasher', who climbed into women's bedrooms at dead of night raping and knifing women. The day the joking died was the day the headlines replaced

Abridged from *Slow Motion: Changing Masculinities, Changing Men*, pp. 233–71. (London: Virago, 1990.)

'the Slasher' stories with accounts of 'the Mutilator' – the deadly deeds of a man attacking *men's* genitals late at night in the Sydney parks.

There are still men today, pronouncing legal judgments, treating wounded women, writing psychological tracts, laughing with their peers, who downgrade women's suffering at the hands of men. The same cultural misogyny fuels their sentiments, but not the same casual ignorance, the same 'innocent' complicity with men's expressions of hatred and contempt for women. Today, they know they are doing it despite, and perhaps because of, the passionate protests and organized resistance of so many women against the many acts of male violence towards their sex. The first job of feminist analysis – and one which was performed with considerable success – was to expose the myths surrounding rape and male violence.

### Myths of rape: sexist and anti-sexist

The first rape myth, swiftly exposed in feminist writing, was the idea that rape was a rare event in modern society, the product of some pathological sex-crazed maniac. Rape is a common event, often planned by the rapist, who usually has a wife or girlfriend, and attacks a woman he knows. The second rape myth concerns the assumption of men's desire to protect women from violence. Police, hospital and judicial treatment of rape victims were rapidly revealed to be frequently hostile to the assaulted woman, more protective of the 'rights' of the rapist (of his self-proclaimed 'misreading' of a woman's rejection as assent) than the rights of a woman – at any time, in any place – to say 'no' to sex. To take just one example from what is now a multitude of studies, Elizabeth Stanko's *Intimate Intrusions* (1985), based upon her research in Britain and the United States, describes the police and the courts as 'the second assailant' in so far as they have in practice so often made it hard for women to press charges against attackers or get convictions: 'Above all, the process of inquiry – from police to prosecutors to judges – is assaultive to women.'[8] Feminists emphasized that the prevalence of rape as a social practice exists precisely because of the myths surrounding it: because of the belief that women 'invite' or provoke attack, that men can be 'victims' of their own overpowering sex drive. Rape is a product, they argued, not of male libido, but rather of a culture which encourages men to see sexual activity as a way of 'conquering' women, and of a society which allows men to indulge in the sexual exploitation and physical abuse of women without, in many cases, fear of punishment.[9]

There are other rape myths, however, which dominant strands of feminist thinking have not demolished. Indeed, they have underwritten them. Susan Griffin, for example, states bluntly (and falsely): 'Men are not raped.'[10] And Brownmiller's popular elaboration of Griffin's analysis begins from certain basic definitions and premises about 'rape' which endorse at least some of the prevailing beliefs and myths surrounding it. She sees it as an 'accident of biology' that men can rape, and women cannot:

> When men discovered that they could rape, they proceeded to do it . . . Indeed one of the earliest forms of male bonding must have been the gang rape of one woman by a band of marauding men. This accomplished, rape became not only a male prerogative, but man's basic weapon of force against woman, the principal agent of his will and her fear.[11]

But what, apart from lack of inclination and possibly access to weapons, is to prevent a woman (or marauding gang of women) from buggering a man with bottle, fist or tongue, or from demanding orgasm through oral sex? These are, after all, among the most common forms of male sexual assault on women, and well within women's capacities should we so choose. (Feminists long ago rejected the misleading definition of 'rape' exclusively as forced penile penetration of the vagina.) I have little doubt that just a few women have precisely so chosen, as I seem to remember one or two men have alleged in courts in the US. After all – any woman could argue in her own defence should prosecution attend such rape – do men not fantasize about sexual assault by women? Against Brownmiller it seems clear to me that men's capacity to rape has very little to do with some men's *proclivity* to rape, and other men's tendency to condone it – any more than women's capacity to cook can explain why a few wives drop poison in their husband's supper, and other women have celebrated such deeds in song.[12] So why do men rape?

To men's biological capacity to rape, Brownmiller adds her conviction that men rape women as part of a conscious and collective, transhistorical and transcultural, political strategy to ensure women's subjection to them. Rapists are the 'shock troops' of patriarchy, necessary for male domination.[13] Some men may not rape, but only because their power over women is already secured by the rapists who have done their work for them: rape 'is nothing more or less than a conscious process of intimidation by which *all men* keep *all women* in a state of fear'.[14]

The force of Brownmiller's argument derives from her exposure of men's long-standing silence about violence against women, which in itself enables her to clarify many aspects of the history of rape. Although this very silence means we have little evidence of the historical incidence of rape, it seems unlikely that it was unknown in, say, late nineteenth-century Vienna. Yet Sigmund Freud, who not only developed the most complex and sophisticated psychology of human behaviour we possess, but based his life's work on theories of human sexuality and human aggression, failed to give even passing mention to rape – except in a philosophical aside illustrating differences between conscious and unconscious motivation.[15] Alfred Kinsey and the sex researchers at the Kinsey Institute, although interviewing tens of thousands of men and women in the late 1940s and early 1950s, dismissed the significance and horror of rape in women's lives, suggesting most 'rape' cases, as they referred to them, were the result of women attempting to conceal their sexual activity. They further claimed that only a small proportion of sexual advances made to young girls involved physical assault, and that when they did any consequent psychological damage could be attributed to 'cultural conditioning' rather than to anything intrinsic to the experience itself.[16] Like so many feminists in the years just before and since the publication of her book, Brownmiller exposed the routine and chilling under-reporting of rape, its extremely high incidence, the tendency of authorities and professionals (mostly male) to blame women who are raped for 'victim-precipitation' – that is, causing men's violence against them. The explanation of rape, Brownmiller – and all feminists – would now agree, cannot be sought in terms of isolated acts by individual rapists. It can only be seriously approached in terms of the wider social context of the power of men, and a general cultural contempt for women.

The weakness of Brownmiller's argument, however, is its sweeping generalization in the face of evidence that the prevalence of rape in modern

Western societies is neither historically nor cross-culturally universal. Peggy Reeves Sanday in her oft-cited anthropological work shows that the extent of rape in different societies varies considerably. She contrasts societies which are relatively 'rape-free', like West Sumatra, with those which are most 'rape-prone', like the United States. The former, in her description, are societies in which women are respected and influential members of their community, participating in public decision making, and where 'the relationship between the sexes tends to be symmetrical and equal'.[17] They are also societies with far lower levels of overall violence. Other anthropological studies of pre-industrial societies have reported little or no sexual violence. Margaret Mead's well-known study of the Arapesh American Indians, although now surrounded by controversy, reported a gentle, non-aggressive society and culture, free from sexual violence.[18] The accounts we possess of some African hunter–gatherer societies, like that of the Mbuti, report the same low incidence of violence, and no evidence of rape or sexual violence. Notwithstanding the method-ological problems associated with such studies, they do seem to indicate that sexual violence against women (or men) corresponds closely to the general level of violence in a society.[19]

Somewhat less controversially, historical studies of Western societies also suggest wide variation in the incidence of rape. Roy Porter has carefully sifted historical data on British society. The writings of women in diaries and elsewhere provide no evidence of female fears of the menace of rape in pre-industrial England – despite the expression of a multitude of other fears.[20] Early feminists – from Mary Astell to Mary Wollstonecraft – decried the wrongs of women, yet did not mention rape. Those nineteenth-century feminists who wrote and campaigned against sexual abuses (child prostitution and the forcible medical examination of prostitutes) likewise fail to mention anxiety about rape. Porter concludes that rape, and women's fears of it, probably did not loom so large then as they do today. Contrary to Brown-miller's history of rape, it does not seem that rape was the principal agent used to subordinate women in this period. The historical reality of men's oppression and exploitation of women in British society is not in doubt. But what Porter suggests is that men had little need to employ the threat of rape to maintain their dominance: 'Men no more cherished the threat of the rapist in the wings to maintain their authority over women than property owners encouraged thieves to justify the apparatus of law and order.'[21]

A study of eighteenth-century Massachusetts by Barbara Lindemann comes to similar conclusions.[22] Only one rape per decade reached the high court before 1729, and the *recorded* rape level remained consistently low throughout the century, averaging one every two years. Neither wars, the presence of high concentrations of bored and lonely American and British troops, nor economic crises and rootless destitution affected recorded rape levels. Lindemann considers, more fully than Porter, the possibilities of unreported rape and, more significantly still, the narrow definition of rape – defined by law and custom to refer exclusively to a woman who resisted a man who had no rights of sexual access to her. One reason so few rape cases occurred, she suggests, was because sexual assaults committed by upper- and middle-class men on servants would not be perceived as rapes, even by the women victims. They were a form of men's sexual assertion of authority for which neither wives nor servants would have legal redress. Notwithstanding these factors, however, Lindemann nevertheless argues that 'The conclusion is inescapable that the number of rape prosecutions was so much smaller in eighteenth-century Massachusetts than it is today because many fewer rapes were committed in proportion to the population.'[23] She attributes this to the cultural condemnation and frequent punishment of extra-marital sexual activity by men and women alike, and to the belief that women were as interested in sex as men: 'The rape prototype of female enticement, coy female resistance, and ultimate male conquest was not built into the pattern of normal sexual relations.'[24] This was a culture which, while securely patriarchal, discouraged rape, and a community which offered fewer opportunities for its perpetration.

Other studies highlight historical contrasts in men's expression of sexual violence. Writing of the high incidence of husband–wife violence in working-class lives in London between 1870 and 1914, when many wives 'did not hesitate to beat up their husbands' (though it was the former who would more likely be injured in violent rows), Ellen Ross links such violence to the upheavals of domestic life and men's power in the home caused, in particular, by male unemployment and chronic family poverty.[25] This overt physical antagonism between men and women was usually over money; men's failure or inability to provide for wife and children inducing women to challenge their domestic authority. And yet despite this violence, and despite men's belief in the 'right' of husbands to beat up wives, Ross suggests that London's pub culture in the generations before the First World War was 'less poisonously misogynous' than it would later become: 'Sexuality was not yet the domestic and social battleground it had become by the mid-twentieth century or the locus of the belligerent assertion of male power.'[26]

Even in contemporary Western societies the prevalence of rape, and its threat, seem to vary greatly: the United States, for example, has not twice, but over seventeen times the rate of reported rapes as Britain, (34.5 forcible rapes per 100,000 of population in 1979 compared to 2 per 100,000 in the United Kingdom in 1981).[27] Rather than being the indispensable weapon used by men to ensure the subordination of women, might not rape be the deformed behaviour of men accompanying the destabilization of gender relations, and the consequent contradictions and insecurities of male gender identities, now at their peak in modern America? It may be, as Porter wryly observes, an anachronism 'to assume that all the world has been America'.[28] Although it may be a possibility, of course, and a disastrous one – not only for women – that all the world could become North America!

In terms of developing a sexual politics against rape and male violence, it hardly seems helpful to refuse to distinguish, in the manner of Brownmiller and so many subsequent Western feminists, between men who rape and men who don't. Although not without its justifications, it is a politics of the profoundest pessimism. Feminists' increasing despair at the ever-mounting evidence of men's sexual violence against women is captured by Brownmiller when she says: 'Never one to acknowledge my vulnerability, I found myself forced by my sisters in feminism to look it squarely in the eye.'[29] It was the new visibility of the extent and the horror of rape, especially for feminists engaged in aiding its victims to cope with the trauma, which created the rising levels of feminist fear and anger. 'All men are potential rapists', became the disturbing slogan of many a feminist activist in the late 1970s and 1980s. The rapist is 'the man next door', whoever he might be; he is the man in our beds, the father of our children, the man who 'pays the rent'.[30] 'It was almost as if,'

Ann Snitow comments, 'by naming the sexual crimes, by ending female denial, we frightened ourselves more than anyone else.'[31]

Is any man a potential rapist? The simple answer, I believe, is 'no' – in so far as the word 'potential' has any practical significance. Is any woman a potential victim? In theory, yes; in practice, the risk we face is far greater for some women than for others. Both these statements, however, are not just controversial but explosive in feminist discourse. They need the most careful study.

They are explosive because what feminist analysis has so far been unwilling to explore is why *some* men become rapists and use violence against women, and *some* men do not. The reasons feminists have been unwilling to make such distinctions are important. First, it is seen as a reversion to an individual, rather than a social, treatment of the problem of rape. (Although it seems to me that no human problems, however apparently 'individual', from cancer to catatonic schizophrenia, can ever be adequately understood isolated from their social context.) Secondly, it is seen as facilitating victim-blaming – if we can differentiate between men, then it can be suggested that some women are more likely to choose violent rather than non-violent men – a form of explanation insidiously popular amongst male (and a few female) professionals and social scientists. Finally, it is seen as letting men off the hook, for all men are certainly a part of the climate and culture of misogyny which permits violence against women to occur with so very little protest or protection from men, (though a handful of men, now growing in number, have always protested – from John Stuart Mill to pro-feminist men today).

[. . .] [F]eminists are right to proclaim that the cause of violent crimes against women cannot be located *simply* in pathological individuals, brutal families, or the stresses and humiliations of poverty and racism (alongside the violent sub-cultures) of many rapists, batterers and murderers. But, contrary to many feminist claims currently being made, these factors are also crucial in understanding *which* men are most likely to resort to sexual violence or violence against women and children, what *type* of violence they are most likely to display, and which women are most likely to be its targets. The wider causes of men's violence must be located in societies which construct 'masculinity' in terms of the assertion of heterosexual power (in its polarized difference from 'femininity'), and which continue to see sex as sinful, while locating the object of sexuality in women, and the subject of sexual desire in men. But this does not mean that any man could be Peter Sutcliffe, even when, like his younger peers on the Leeds football grounds, they may delight in taunting police with chants of 'You'll never catch the Ripper' and '11–0' (referring to what was then the number of Sutcliffe's victims).[32]

Peter Sutcliffe was nicknamed 'the Yorkshire Ripper'. In her analysis of the hundred years of 'Ripper' stories and iconography since the original Jack the Ripper murdered and mutilated five prostitute women in London in 1888, Judith Walkowitz points to the crucial role of the popular press in establishing the Ripper as a media hero, and amplifying the threat of male violence to women. The message of the Ripper mythology, as Walkowitz sees it, was to establish the cities as a dangerous place for women, and to sanction the covert expression of male antagonism toward women, as well as to buttress male authority over them. But feminists, Walkowitz agues, need to probe behind Ripper mythology to uncover the complex reality it masks:

By flattening history into myth, the Ripper story has rendered all men suspect, vastly increasing female anxieties, and obscuring the distinct material conditions that generate sexual antagonism and male violence . . . In the 'real' world, neither male violence nor female victimization has single-root causes or effects. Only our cultural nightmares and media fantasies construct life this way.[33]

Women are right to see our society as riddled with the cultural expression of contempt for them as the subordinate sex – a contempt by no means confined to pornography. The continuum of men's violence is real in the very particular sense that it is experienced by women as such, in a world where we are everywhere threatened by petty acts of violence or at least of sexual intrusiveness. Overall, women are less at risk from men's violence in public than are other men. But women feel more vulnerable. They feel more vulnerable because, as Elizabeth Stanko illustrates from her research, and women know from everyday experience, if we include all the forms of intimidation women suffer at men's hands – the smacking of lips, muttering of obscenities, kerb crawling, grabbing of breasts and so on – women are subject to a kind of constant intimidation.[34] When a flasher jumps out at a woman, or a voyeur lurks at our window, he is usually not a rapist or killer. But he just might be. His actions certainly serve to make the world feel unsafe for women, particularly when we are likely to have read fairly recently of some serious sex attack – always given greater media prominence than men's attacks on men.

There is a continuum of men's violence in so far as the effects of the variety of men's intrusive acts all contribute to women's experience of lack of safety. What is not convincing, however, is some feminists' insistence that all men really are similar in terms of the individual threat they pose for women. We need to get to grips with the paradox that while women are mainly afraid of men whom they do not know, those women who are physically attacked are generally assaulted by men they do know.

As feminists, however, we can agree that a society which equates masculinity with assertiveness, sexual and otherwise, is one which encourages and condones men's violence against women. People with power have usually been allowed to express anger at, and often use force against, the less powerful with relative impunity. It is surely true that a central aspect of men's use of violence against women lies in social assumptions of men's right to dominate women and expect servicing from them. This has allowed men to express anger and use physical force to get what they want, and get away with it – at least in the domestic sphere.
[. . .]

## Is violence masculine?

One reason it has been so easy to ignore women's relationship to violence is that terms like 'power', 'force', 'aggression' – so seemingly direct and obvious – are not the simplest to define. Feminism begins from an awareness that relations between men and women have, in all known places and times, occurred in a context in which there has been an apparently inextricable connection between gender and power – though it has assumed different forms and obtained to differing degrees. Feminists writing on men and violence have always tended to see this power as an exclusively unidirectional, top-down process. Viewed in this way, women's participation in maintaining or undermining men's ability to control them according to their own needs, is obscured. But this is not how power has been theorized in more traditional sociological literature or, indeed, more sophisticated feminist analysis. Power relations imply a process whereby those with power can organize those who are less powerful according to their own ends. Yet this, according to sociologists like Anthony Giddens, does not necessarily – indeed, does not 'normally' – take the form of any straightforward process of control through threat, force or violence. Rather, the exercise of power involves the deployment of resources and skills to which some people have easier access, the use of force being exceptional.[35] And despite this differential access to resources, power relations, as Kathy Davis argues, are always reciprocal, involving some degree of autonomy and dependence in each direction:

> Power is never a simple matter of 'have's' and 'have-not's'. Such a conception can only lead to an over-estimation of the power of the powerful, closing our eyes to the chinks in the armour of the powerful as well as the myriad ways that the less powerful have to exercise control over their lives, even in situations where stable, institutionalised power relations are in operation.[36]

[. . .] [I]n the area of personal life it has been women's traditional lack of any access to independent economic resources within the institution of marriage which has been pivotal to the normal functioning of domestic arrangements to suit men's needs. That institution is now changing, and the most significant common characteristic of women who are battered today is not their gender as such, but their lack of resources to escape marriages which are violent.[37] That domestic violence is not some fatality inscribed in male–female relationship is apparent if we look at the different types of family forms which have generated violence. In *Naming the Violence: Speaking Out About Lesbian Battery*, various women in the United States write of their experience of violence from other women. 'We were so clear about violence as a feature of heterosexual relationships', Barbara Hart announces with dismay, that it was hard to accept that 'women were beating and terrorizing other women'.[38] These women report daily episodes of violence which had become almost a ritual in some lesbian bars in the US. Moreover, as with heterosexual violence, other lesbians 'shunned the victim', and the battered lesbian tended to blame herself.[39] In addition to psychological and emotional abuse, these battered lesbians reported physical assault with guns, knives and other weapons, experiences of rape, sex on demand, forced sex with others and involuntary prostitution – as well as economic dependence through their partners' control over income and assets.

Most of the dynamics of lesbian battering seem similar to heterosexual abuse – in particular, the tendency of women to remain in an abusive relationship because they feel sorry for the abuser: 'I still feel sorry for her . . . She came from a home situation where she was the victim of what ranged from severe neglect to severe violence,' writes Donna Cecere of her experience of lesbian battering;[40] 'I had returned once again because . . . she said she had changed . . . when she held me I felt loved . . . In those years love was a scarcity and myself hardly lovable,' explains Cedar Gentlewind;[41] 'On a subconscious level I felt I got what I deserved . . . Our social life was limited to gay bars where physical violence was also the norm,' writes Breeze.[42] The majority of the lesbian abusers and victims in these accounts are working-class lesbians, many from ethnic minorities, often already victims of family violence, as well as of the violence and racism which surrounded them.

That women, like men, are affected by the general levels of violence in their immediate social world is illustrated by the dramatic increase in young women's involvement in crimes of violence over the last fifteen years – an increase which, comparatively, exceeds that of men. As Anne Campbell[43] argues in criticism of much feminist rhetoric, virtually all our ideas of 'femininity' are derived from the middle-class 'lady': 'To be pampered, egotistical, passive, nurturant, care-taking requires a certain level of economic security.'[44] Surveying a sample of 251 16-year-old schoolgirls from working-class areas of London, Liverpool and Oxford, Campbell found that 89 per cent of them had engaged in at least one physical fight. These girls were mostly negative in their attitudes towards fighting, but did not see it as 'unfeminine'. The Borstal girls whom Campbell interviewed, on the other hand, mostly felt positive about fighting, regarding it as a good way of releasing anger and perhaps settling disputes.[45] As with young male delinquents, most of them had been systematically encouraged to fight by their parents: 'In the subcultures from which these girls come . . . interpersonal violence emerges as the vicious expression of hatred and resentment and is bound up more with establishing and maintaining a tough reputation than with settling disputes.'[46] Campbell is critical of a feminism which can see women only as the victims of men, rather than of a whole economic system: 'Without more radical change in the *status quo*, we shall succeed only in liberating women into poverty, alienation, despair and crime – along with the men who are there already.'[47]

Somewhat analogously, in his study of soccer hooliganism David Robins asks, 'What were the girls doing while the boys were putting the boot in on the terraces?' Many, he says, were up there with them. There are more boys than girls, but the girls do join in the fighting and encourage the boys to fight. Where girls' gangs do exist, they not only emulate but may try to outdo the boys: 'We go to fight,' the 'Leeds Angels' told Robins. 'At Norwich and Ipswich, there's sometimes more lasses than boys . . . When Man. United played Norwich . . . there were forty arrests and must have been thirty lasses got arrested.'[48] It is obvious that in our society physical violence and aggression are still predominantly seen as masculine, and acted out by men. Working-class images of masculinity in terms of physical hardness have been analysed, by Tolson and others, as bound up with the requirements of manual labour and earning a wage.[49] This image persists. But with nearly 50 per cent of young people in Britain leaving school for the dole, enjoying little hope and not much self-esteem, Robins argues, 'working-class youth is being forced into a position of wildness and irresponsibility'.[50] And while they may lack the symbolic trappings of power which unite the boys in their sexist jibes, and rarely be afforded the same freedom of action and choice as men, young women, Robins believes, are learning that they can give as good as they get.[51]

Nevertheless, even if aggressiveness is not exclusively masculine, there is no doubt that the media and the public at large display their greatest anxiety in connection with violence from men – mostly from young, working-class men in the form of vandalism, gang fighting and football hooliganism. Football hooliganism is now a prominent cause of social concern, feeding the appeal of the law-and-order politics of the right. Some researchers, like Peter Marsh, Elizabeth Rosser and Rom Harre, have stressed that the degree of serious violence, as distinct from ritual violence, on and around the football terraces is exaggerated by the media.[52] But the extent of young men's violence is not merely a media creation; nor is its association with lower working-class men merely middle-class phobia. Sociological studies of football hooliganism like that of Eric Dunning and his co-workers conclusively demonstrate men in football gangs are overwhelmingly from the lower levels of the working class.[53]

We need to ask why a type of working-class aggressive masculinity seems such a perennial feature of the social environment, a feature which feeds today's feminist imagination in its equation of violence as male. Dunning stresses the inevitable homogeneity, circumscribed horizons and narrow neighbourhood loyalty of men who, at best, will find work in low-paid, insecure and monotonous jobs at the bottom of all authority and status hierarchies. Moreover, in jobs sex-typed as male, and with home lives which remain strongly male-dominated (the equivalent jobs for women of this class, if any, being even less well-paid, lower in status and more insecure) the lower working class tends to produce sharper sex-role distinctions than other classes. Just as there is a Black underclass, so too a white underclass exists, in which the men are the most likely of all men to adopt aggressive masculine styles and values whereby status is imparted to males who display loyalty and bravery in confrontation with 'outsiders':

> Apart from the 'street smartness' and the ability and willingness to fight of [these] adolescent and adult males, they have few power resources. This combination of narrowness of experience and relative lack of power tends to lead them to experience unfamiliar territories and people as potentially threatening. Usually it is only in the company of people with whom they are familiar and who are like themselves that it is possible for them to feel a relatively high degree of social assurance . . . Being part of a group augments their sense of power. It also provides an opportunity to hit back at the established order and a context in which they can 'get their own back' by taking the lid off . . . For a short illusory moment, the outsiders are the masters; the downtrodden come out on top.[54]

The aggressive masculine style which lower working-class men are more likely to value and adopt is not exclusive to them, of course. It is part of the fantasy life, if not the lived reality, of the majority of men enthralled by images of masculinity which equate it with power and violence (where would Clint Eastwood be without his gun?). However, [. . .] there is no simple, direct transmission from men's shared collective fantasies to individual action. Many social mediators – from school, jobs, friends, family, religion and politics – affect the way fantasies may, or may not, be channelled into any active expression, and determine what form, if any, they take. It is the sharp and frustrating conflict between the lives of lower working-class men and the image of masculinity as power, which informs the adoption and, for some, the enactment, of a more aggressive masculinity. There was a time, it seems to me, when feminists would not so readily have lost sight of the significance of class oppression for the sake of identifying a universal male beastliness. But that was in the early 1970s, when they were more actively a part of a left politics and culture which was itself more aware than it has since become of the alienation and exploitation of class relations.

It is true that women can be, and some women are, as aggressive and violent in their behaviour as men. It is equally true, however, that from an early age most women are made aware of obstacles to, and restrictions upon, the expression of their own desires – if only in terms of the expectations of those around them. More importantly, they are sensitized to greater social condemnation of female aggressiveness – shouting, fighting, swearing, and so on. Men, by contrast, in sport and elsewhere, are more likely to engage in at least the rituals of aggressive display, and to enjoy greater social tolerance for many forms of aggressiveness.[55] But I think we should be aware that women's greater suppression of their own aggressiveness is not necessarily healthy. Women's attempts to disown and repress their feelings of frustration and aggression almost certainly result in them turning such aggressive feelings against themselves, or their children. This would account for women's greater vulnerability to depression (twice as high as that for men), or expression of their own pain in emotional abuse of children.[56] It can also lead, as Janet Sayers, Jean Temperley and other clinicians have commented, to women projecting their aggressiveness and violence onto others, or onto the world in general, as in paranoia and agoraphobia.[57] [. . .] Jane Temperley suggests from her work with women patients that we need to consider whether women's perception of, preoccupation with, and (as she sees it), attempts to provoke, men's violence towards them may not be overlaid by women's projection onto men of their own frustration and aggression; thereby permitting women to retain for themselves a monopoly of moral righteousness and virtue.[58]

Some feminists, as well as therapists like Temperley, have seen in women's image of the all-pervasive, all-threatening nature of male sexuality a projection of women's own aggression and frustrated power. The political journalist and feminist Sarah Benton, for example, suggests that because it is less legitimate for women to be aggressive and powerful, and because women are so much less accustomed to taking responsibility for the state of the world, 'We project all power, all aggression onto men.'[59] Moreover, she detects in this projection, women's denial of sexuality itself. It is a denial bound up with women's difficulties, in sexist culture, in accepting and expressing their own sexuality; in particular, acknowledging that female sexuality can be violent, cruel and 'perverse', as well as masochistic, yielding and submissive. 'The barrier to that acceptance and expression,' she concludes, 'is more to do with our difficulty in getting, exercising and accepting power in the world at large than any specific sexual threat from men.'[60] The fact that women are the main readers of true-crime magazines, which provide salacious case histories of the most violent, often sexual, murders,[61] and that it is women who appear in large numbers at the trials of sex-murderers, where they feel entitled to display extremes of punitive moral aggression, verbal and even physical violence, would seem to lend credence to such interpretations.

However, the extent of some men's violence (and many men's viciousness) towards women, the tendency of those with power either to ignore, or to blame women for, its occurrence, and the general context of men's greater power and control over women, all dictate that we must proceed very carefully – more carefully, at any rate, than Temperley and most psycho-analytic commentators have done – in assigning weight to arguments which suggest that women may have an investment in feeling victimized. There is no doubt that many women's entrapment in dependency and powerlessness makes it hard for them to envisage any positive alternative to suppressing their own anger and aggression, while suffering, however resentfully, aggression from men. At the same time, it is equally necessary for us to be aware of the need to understand what happens to women's aggression, and for us to abandon the dominant conservative and, more recently, popular feminist attachment to idealized views of women as inherently less aggressive than men (the former regarding the connection as biological, the latter, more often as cultural).

Some of our perception of the social and cultural linkages between 'masculinity' and violence derives from the fact that most of the socially approved uses of force and violence are the jobs of men – the police, army, prison officers and other agencies of 'defence' or correction. It is men, rarely women, who are officially trained to use violence in our society. Yet, as David Morgan has suggested, it is possible in this context to reverse the assumed causal links between 'masculinity' and 'violence'. It could be that it is men's socially determined, systematic involvement in various forms of violence which constructs our notions of 'masculinity' as indissolubly linked with 'violence'.[62] The idea that what is at stake here is state violence in the hands of men (rather than, as many feminists believe, male violence in the hands of the state) is supported by reports of women's use of force and violence when they are placed in jobs analogous to men's. For example, women prison officers were found in the late nineteenth century to enforce especially severe physical and corporal punishments on their female charges for any infraction of rules, by comparison with those meted out to male prisoners and, to this day, women prisoners are more consistently punished and put on report by their female warders than are men.[63] Similar tales of women's zealous use of force, including conventionally defined acts of violence, appear in many accounts of women's behaviour when in positions of power. I have written elsewhere of the importance, often repressed or denied, of women's relationship to war and military enterprises – both as passionate supporters of war or in active military engagement themselves.[64] Nevertheless, it is apparent that some men's far more formal training in the use of violence is something which can, and from the evidence of women who are battered, frequently does, spill over into these men's greater resort to violence in their personal relations with women. It also provides opportunities for men to be particularly vicious to women (and men) in the performance of their public 'duties'.

Black feminists have been especially clear on the importance of distinguishing state violence from male violence. Kum-Kum Bhavnani, for example, rejects the idea that violence is 'essentially masculine'.[65] Such a belief denies Black people's knowledge of white women's past-and-present involvement in violence against them – both directly and indirectly, in the support and maintenance of racism. And it denies the reality of the violent resistance from women and men which state violence brings forth, not only in the streets of South Africa, but in the street-uprisings in Britain. The idea prevalent in white feminism that women 'have a peaceful past', Bhavnani argues, is offensive to Black women. (It is also, she points out, offensive to white working-class women, who have resisted, sometimes violently, attacks on their class; and to the many other women who have fought against violent and oppressive conditions; not to mention its erasure from the history of the British Suffragettes.) 'Non-violence' and 'peace', she suggests, 'end up being meaningless terms unless given tactical accuracy and political definition.'[66] Bell Hooks also writes of learning to oppose war from the persistent anti-war stance of her grandfather, and of so many other southern Black males who despised militarism: 'Their attitudes showed us that all men do not glory in war, that all men who fight in wars do not necessarily believe that wars are just, that men are not inherently capable of killing.'[67] The sex-role division of labour, she adds, does not necessarily mean that women think differently from men about violence and about war, or, if empowered to do so, would behave differently from men.

'Violence', it seems clear, cannot simply be equated with 'masculinity'. Neither are unitary phenomena.[68] There are many different types of violence, some legitimated (from sport and beating children to policing and warfare), and some not (from corporal punishment in state schools to rape and murder). It is easier to understand and attempt to change men's engagement in these practices if we see them as operating relatively autonomously from each other. Fear of violent attack from men is the number one fear of women in both the United States and Britain today. But if we want to get to the heart of this fear, and the escalating rates of violence in modern society, we shall have to include, but also progress beyond, an analysis simply in terms of gender.

There are links between the prevalence of violence in our society and men's endeavours to affirm 'masculinity'. And these links may even be reinforced, as the assumption of men's dominance over women – part of the traditional definition of 'masculinity' – continues to crumble. Some men, increasingly less sure of such dominance, may resort more to violence in their attempt to shore up a sense of masculine identity. Others, however, may not. Some, indeed, may turn towards new ways of being men, even to support for the struggle to put an end to men's use of violence against women. For it should be remembered that some men have always worked in organizations committed to non-violence – even when this has provoked the harshest ridicule and punishment, including loss of life. At the same time, there are links between the prevalence of violence in our society and forces which are not those of gender: forces, indeed, which have impacted as strongly on certain groups of men as on certain groups of women. There are close and frightening links between sexual assaults on women and the steep rise in crimes of violence generally – the primary targets of which remain other men.

These links derive from the creation of a permanent underclass in many Western societies – an underclass built around dependency, self-destruction, crimes against property and crimes against people. Twenty years ago Martin Luther King was shot dead for his vision of a more equal society in the United States. Today, that society is less equal than it was then: the number of Black men leaving college is dropping, the life expectancy of Black men is decreasing, and economic segregation of Blacks and other ethnic minorities into the worst schools, worst neighbourhoods, worst housing (if they are lucky), is increasing.[69] Drugs, crime and violence are the desperate and bitter legacy of the withdrawal of federal funds for welfare provision at local and national levels throughout the United States, in combination with the smashing of the trade union movement and the restructuring of labour which has destroyed many traditional working-class jobs and communities. With welfare all but eliminated, homelessness, joblessness, and hopelessness are now escalating in the US. Comparing the contrasting appeals of Martin Luther King for peaceful Black protest thirty years ago, with Malcolm X's justification of violent protest a decade later, Black film-maker Spike Lee announces today:

> Things are leaning more towards Malcolm than King. I think black people are getting tired of being on the receiving end of police shotguns and nightsticks.[70]

Who or what, then, do we identify as the epitome of 'violence', 'abuse' and 'aggression' in that society? Those who are brutalized within an underworld of fear and exploitation? Or those who may never directly engage in acts of violence or physical force, but orchestrate the degradation and brutalization of others? The entrenchment of poverty and inequality in the world's richest nation has occurred precisely to enable the US to spend ever-greater sums on 'defence', and to conduct aggressive interventions in Central America, the Caribbean and the Middle East.

The USA shows the way, and through the International Monetary Fund (IMF) and other such agencies attempts to force the American Way on the rest of the world. If feminists are seriously to confront the problem of sexual violence, we shall have to realize that what we are up against is something far worse, something far more destructive, than the power of any man, or group of men – something worse even than the mythic qualities of Dworkin's atomic phallus. However old-fashioned it may sound in these 'post-political' days, what we are confronting here is the barbarism of private life reflecting back the increased barbarism of public life, as contemporary capitalism continues to chisel out its hierarchies along the familiar grooves of class, race and gender.

## Notes

1 Susan Griffin, Reprint from 'Rape: the All-American Crime', *Ramparts*, September (1971), pp. 26–35.

2 Ibid.

3 Ibid., p. 35.

4 Shulamith Firestone, *The Dialectic of Sex* (London, Paladin; 1971); Kate Millett, *Sexual Politics* (London, Abacus, 1972).

5 Germaine Greer, *The Female Eunuch*, (London, MacGibbon and Kee, 1970).

6 Sheila Rowbotham, *Women's Consciousness, Man's World* (Harmondsworth, Penguin, 1973); Juliet Mitchell, *Woman's Estate* (Harmondsworth, Penguin, 1971).

7 Susan Brownmiller, *Against Our Will: Men, Women and Rape* (Harmondsworth, Penguin, 1976).

8 Elizabeth Stanko, *Intimate Intrusions: Women's Experience of Male Violence*, (London, Routledge and Kegan Paul, 1985).

9 For example, see Rape Crisis Centre, *First Annual Report* (London, Rape Counselling and Research Project, 1977).

10 Griffin, 'Rape', p. 22.

11 Brownmiller, *Against Our Will*, p. 14.

12 For example, as portrayed in the British film, *Distant Voices, Still Lives*, Terrence Davies, 1988.

13 Brownmiller, *Against Our Will*, p. 209.

14 Ibid., p. 15.

15 See John Forrester, 'Rape, seduction and psychoanalysis' in Tomaselli, S. and Porter, R. (eds), *Rape* (Oxford, Basil Blackwell, 1985), p. 62.

16 See Alfred Kinsey et al., *Sexual Behaviour in the Human Female*, (Philadelphia, W.B. Saunders, 1953), p. 410, pp. 116–22.

17 Peggy Reeves Sanday, 'Rape and the silencing of the feminine', in Tomaselli and Porter, *Rape*, p. 85.

18 Margaret Mead, *Sex and Temperament in Three Primitive Societies* (London, Routledge and Kegan Paul, 1985).

19 For these and other examples see Julia Schwendinger and Herman Schwendinger, *Rape and Inequality* (London, Sage, 1983).

20 Roy Porter, 'Rape – does it have a historical meaning?', in Tomaselli and Porter, *Rape*.

21 Ibid., p. 223.

22 Barbara Lindemann, '"To ravish and carnally know": rape in eighteenth-century Massachusetts', *Signs*, Autumn, vol. 10 (1984), 1.

23 Ibid., p. 72.

24 Ibid., p. 81.

25 Ellen Ross, '"Fierce questions and taunts": married life in working-class London, 1870–1914', *Feminist Studies*, 8, 2 (Fall) (1982).

26 Ibid., p. 596.

27 Figures quoted in Donald West, 'The victim's contribution to sexual offences' in June Hopkins (ed.), *Perspectives on Rape and Sexual Assault* (London, Harper and Row, 1984), p. 2. See also Jennifer Temkin, *Rape and the Legal Process* (London, Sweet and Maxwell, 1987), p. 9.

28 Porter, 'Rape', p. 223.

29 Brownmiller, *Against Our Will*, p. 9.

30 Ruth Hall et al., *The Rapist Who Pays the Rent: Evidence Submitted by Women Against Rape, Britain to the Criminal Law Revision Committee* (Bristol, Falling Wall Press, 1981); Ruth Hall, *Ask Any Woman: a London Inquiry into Rape and Sexual Assault* (Bristol, Falling Wall Press, 1985).

31 Ann Snitow, 'Retrenchment vs transformation: the politics of the anti-pornography movement', in Kate Ellis et al., *Caught Looking* (New York, Caught Looking Inc., 1985).

32 Quoted in David Robins, *We Hate Humans* (Harmondsworth, Penguin, 1984).

33 Judith Walkovitz, 'Jack the Ripper and the myth of male violence', in *Feminist Studies*, 8, 3 (Fall) (1982), p. 570.

34 A recent survey by Granada Television found that nearly 70 per cent of women said they either would not go out alone after dark or would go out only if absolutely necessary: 34 per cent of these women had been sworn at in the street, 18 per cent had experienced unwelcome physical contact and 17 per cent had been flashed at. (World In Action, Granada TV 9.1.89.)

35 Anthony Giddens, *The Constitution of Society* (Cambridge, Polity, 1984), p. 175.

36 Kathy Davis, 'The Janus-Face of power: some theoretical considerations involved in the study of gender and power'. Paper presented at the symposium, *The Gender of Power* (Leiden, 1987).

37 J. Pahl, *Private Violence and Public Policy* (London, Routledge and Kegan Paul, 1985).

38 Barbara Hart, in Kerry Lobel (ed.), *Naming the Violence: Speaking Out About Lesbian Battery* (Washington: Seal Press, 1986), p. 9.

39 Ibid., p. 11.

40 In ibid., p. 24.

41 Ibid., p. 46.

42 Ibid., p. 52.

43 Anne Campbell, *Girl Delinquents* (Oxford, Basil Blackwell, 1981), p. 133.

44 Ibid., p. 150.

45 Ibid., p. 181.

46 Ibid., p. 196.

47 Ibid., p. 237.

48 Robins, *We Hate Humans*, p. 95.

49 Andrew Tolson, *The Limits of Masculinity* (London, Tavistock, 1977).

50 Robins, *We Hate Humans*, p. 153.

51 Ibid., p. 152.

52 Peter Marsh, Elizabeth Rosser and Rom Harre, *The Rules of Disorder* (London, Routledge and Kegan Paul, 1978).

53 Eric Dunning, Patrick Murphy and John Williams, *The Roots of Football Hooliganism: an Historical and Sociological Study* (London, Routledge, 1988), p. 187.

54 Ibid., p. 206.

55 Marsh et al., *Rules of Disorder*.

56 See Janet Sayers, *Sexual Contradictions: Psychology, Psychoanalysis, and Feminism* (London, Tavistock, 1986), p. 142.

57 Ibid., p. 157; Jane Temperley, 'Our Own Worst Enemies: Unconscious Factors in Female Disadvantage', *Free Associations*, Pilot Issue (1984).

58 Temperley, ibid.

59 Sarah Benton, (unpub.), 'Notes on sex and violence'.

60 Ibid.

61 D. Cameron and E. Frazer, *The Lust to Kill* (Cambridge, Polity, 1987).

62 David Morgan (unpub.), Research Proposals for a Study of Masculinity and Violence.

63 Russell Dobash, R. Emerson Dobash, Sue Gutteridge, *The Imprisonment of Women* (Oxford, Basil Blackwell, 1986), p. 86, p. 147.

64 Lynn Segal, *Is the Future Female?* (London, Virago, 1987), ch. 5.

65 Kum-Kum Bhavnani, 'Turning the World Upside Down' in *Charting the Journey* (London, Sheba, 1987), p. 264.

66 Ibid., p. 268.

67 Bell Hooks, 'Feminism and militarism: a comment', in Hooks, *Talking Back: Thinking Feminist - Thinking Black* (London, Sage, 1989).

68 Morgan, Masculinity and Violence.

69 Martin Walker, *The Guardian*, 16 January 1989.

70 Spike Lee talks to Steve Goldman, 'Heat of the Moment', *Weekend Guardian*, 24–5 June, 1989, p. 15.

# PART THREE
# THE PROBLEM OF CRIME II: CRIMINALIZATION

## Introduction

This selection of readings has been chosen to reflect the parameters of a *radical criminology* which first emerged in the 1960s in Britain and the USA. Although the readings reveal the disparate nature of such an enterprise, they all mark a reappraisal of the purpose and function of criminology, in particular by taking to task positivism's obsession with scientifically establishing the causes of crime. Here the key concern is with definitional questions – why have certain behaviours and situations come to be defined as criminal? – rather than with questions of individual motivation. Collectively, they illustrate how the central problematic of criminology is not simply one of crime causation, but of accounting for particular processes of criminalization.

The publication of Taylor, Walton and Young's *The New Criminology* in 1973 has long been taken as the starting-point of a radical criminology in Britain. The text remains influential because it provides a sweeping critique of the hitherto unchallenged sovereignty of traditional criminology in which psychologists, psychiatrists and forensic scientists dominated. Rather than focusing on the elusive search for the individual causes of crime, Taylor, Walton and Young sought to illustrate how 'crime' was socially constructed through the power and capacity of state institutions to define and confer criminality on others. This intellectual shift set out to reject notions of 'crime as behaviour' and to promote a more critical conception of 'crime as a political process'. In tandem, the aim was to transform criminology from a science of social control and into a struggle for social justice.

*The New Criminology* did not, however, emerge from some social and intellectual vacuum. Its impact lay as much in its attempt to synthesize several different existing theoretical traditions, as it did in the desire to establish a new criminological agenda. In particular it maintained links with interactionism (and questions of meaning and authenticity), labelling (and questions of power and social control) and Marxism (and questions of class relations and political economy).

This part thus opens with readings from the American criminologists Matza and Sykes, Becker and Chambliss who have provided classic expressions of these three important theoretical precursors. Matza and Sykes's contribution not only provides a critique of positivism and its tendency to dehumanize delinquent behaviours, but also contends that most delinquent values are not particularly different from those held by the mainstream. Their work forces us to appreciate the ways in which young people themselves view and justify their actions. Becker's work also adopts a position of anti-positivism by arguing that definitions of crime and deviance will remain forever problematic because deviance only arises through the imposition of social judgements on the behaviour of others. Deviance can never be an absolutely known fact, because it is constructed through a series of transactions between rule makers and rule violators. Deviance only occurs when a particular social group is able to make its own rules and enforce their application onto others. The proposition that the causes of deviance lie in processes of law creation and social control effectively stood the premises of mainstream criminology on their head. Whilst labelling opened the way for analyses of how deviance was defined and processed, a Marxist-based analysis furthered that the relations between definer and defined are not simply subjective encounters. Control agencies have an institutional location and function within particular structures of power. Chambliss contends that processes of criminalization depend not simply on relations of power, but on power derived from particular class and economic positions: thus the propositions that acts are defined as criminal because it is in the interests of a ruling class to define them as such and that criminal law, in the main, is designed to protect ruling class interests.

In these ways the study of crime was effectively politicized as part of a more comprehensive sociology of the state and political economy, in which questions of political and social control took precedence over behavioural and correctional issues. Criminology's horizons were expanded, whereby the key problematic was no longer to simply account for individual criminal acts, but to reach a critical understanding of the social order and the power to criminalize.

The radical agenda established by Taylor, Walton and Young subsequently burgeoned in a number of directions. The reading from Box illustrates how 'common sense' assumptions about crime can be effectively challenged once we acknowledge the widespread nature of personal and property crime engaged in by corporate officials, manufacturers, governments and governmental control agencies. The prevalence of a restricted image of 'the crime problem' in public and political discourse, he argues, is but another way in which the social control of the underprivileged and the powerless is maintained.

Hall's contribution is to account for the origins and impact of an increasingly authoritarian – law and order – society in Britain in the 1970s. Here he finds the signifier of 'crime' to play a crucial role not only in legitimating greater powers for law enforcement agencies, but in justifying the diminution of civil, welfare and labour rights and the development of disciplinary forms of regulation in all walks of life. The end result, he envisages, will be the further criminalization of protest movements and deviant lifestyles.

Keith applies such an argument to the particular position of black people in Britain. The construction of crimes, such as mugging, as racial crimes, he argues, serves to reinforce images of black externality and alienness. The black = crime equation is particularly powerful in its coalescence with a number of other referents of crime – the inner-city, 'outsiders', alien cultures, threats to legality and the nation state. As a result, representations of 'race' come to play a key part in dominant perceptions of the 'crime problem'. 'Crime' is also a predominantly racialized discourse.

Scraton and Chadwick set out the parameters for a critical criminology in the 1990s. Acknowledging earlier tendencies to reduce all crime to the materialism of capitalist economies, they argue that the true complexity of processes of power, the marginalization of particular groups and criminalization can only be grasped by remaining alive to the impact of, and interplay between, the three primary determining contexts of production, reproduction and neo-colonialism. As such, a critical analysis of crime and criminal justice must be grounded in analyses of patriarchy and racism as well as class and economic production.

The final selection from Hulsman takes critical criminology in yet another direction. Again noting that notions of crime depend crucially on formulations of criminal law, he argues that the concept of crime should be abandoned once and for all. The development of a radical and critical understanding of crime, criminalization and criminal justice is continually hampered by the continual return to a state-constructed category as its key empirical referent. Rather he suggests the development of alternative conceptual tools – troubles, problems – which can be recognized and responded to without recourse to the formal, narrow and inflexible processes of criminal justice.

# 18

# Techniques of neutralization

## Gresham M. Sykes and David Matza

In attempting to uncover the roots of juvenile delinquency, the social scientist has long since ceased to search for devils in the mind or stigma of the body. It is now largely agreed that delinquent behavior, like most social behavior, is learned and that it is learned in the process of social interaction.

The classic statement of this position is found in Sutherland's theory of differential association, which asserts that criminal or delinquent behavior involves the learning of (a) techniques of committing crimes and (b) motives, drives, rationalizations, and attitudes favorable to the violation of law.[1] Unfortunately, the specific content of what is learned – as opposed to the process by which it is learned – has received relatively little attention in either theory or research. Perhaps the single strongest school of thought on the nature of this content has centered on the idea of a delinquent subculture. The basic characteristic of the delinquent subculture, it is argued, is a system of values that represents an inversion of the values held by respectable, law-abiding society. The world of the delinquent is the world of the law-abiding turned upside down and its norms constitute a countervailing force directed against the conforming social order. Cohen[2] sees the process of developing a delinquent subculture as a matter of building, maintaining, and reinforcing a code for behavior which exists by opposition, which stands in point by point contradiction to dominant values, particularly those of the middle class. Cohen's portrayal of delinquency is executed with a good deal of sophistication, and he carefully avoids overly simple explanations such as those based on the principle of 'follow the leader' or easy generalizations about 'emotional disturbances'. Furthermore, he does not accept the delinquent sub-culture as something given, but instead systematically examines the function of delinquent values as a viable solution to the lower-class, male child's problems in the area of social status. Yet in spite of its virtues, this image of juvenile delinquency as a form of behavior based on competing or countervailing values and norms appears to suffer from a number of serious defects. It is the nature of these defects and a possible alternative or modified explanation for a large portion of juvenile delinquency with which this paper is concerned.

The difficulties in viewing delinquent behavior as springing from a set of deviant values and norms – as arising, that is to say, from a situation in which the delinquent defines his delinquency as 'right' – are both empirical and theoretical. In the first place, if there existed in fact a delinquent subculture such that the delinquent viewed his illegal behavior as morally correct, we could reasonably suppose that he would exhibit no feelings of guilt or shame

From 'Techniques of neutralization: a theory of delinquency', *American Sociological Review*, 1957, 22: 664–70.

at detection or confinement. Instead, the major reaction would tend in the direction of indignation or a sense of martyrdom.[3] It is true that some delinquents do react in the latter fashion, although the sense of martyrdom often seems to be based on the fact that others 'get away with it' and indignation appears to be directed against the chance events or lack of skill that led to apprehension. More important, however, is the fact that there is a good deal of evidence suggesting that many delinquents *do* experience a sense of guilt or shame, and its outward expression is not to be dismissed as a purely manipulative gesture to appease those in authority. Much of this evidence is, to be sure, of a clinical nature or in the form of impressionistic judgements of those who must deal first hand with the youthful offender. Assigning a weight to such evidence calls for caution, but it cannot be ignored if we are to avoid the gross stereotype of the juvenile delinquent as a hardened gangster in miniature.

In the second place, observers have noted that the juvenile delinquent frequently accords admiration and respect to law-abiding persons. The 'really honest' person is often revered, and if the delinquent is sometimes overly keen to detect hypocrisy in those who conform, unquestioned probity is likely to win his approval. A fierce attachment to a humble, pious mother or a forgiving, upright priest (the former, according to many observers, is often encountered in both juvenile delinquents and adult criminals) might be dismissed as rank sentimentality, but at least it is clear that the delinquent does not necessarily regard those who abide by the legal rules as immoral. In a similar vein, it can be noted that the juvenile delinquent may exhibit great resentment if illegal behavior is imputed to 'significant others' in his immediate social environment or to heroes in the world of sport and entertainment. In other words, if the delinquent does hold to a set of values and norms that stand in complete opposition to those of respectable society, his norm-holding is of a peculiar sort. While supposedly thoroughly committed to the deviant system of the delinquent subculture, he would appear to recognize the moral validity of the dominant normative system in many instances.[4]

In the third place, there is much evidence that juvenile delinquents often draw a sharp line between those who can be victimized and those who cannot. Certain social groups are not to be viewed as 'fair game' in the performance of supposedly approved delinquent acts while others warrant a variety of attacks. In general, the potentiality for victimization would seem to be a function of the social distance between the juvenile delinquent and others and thus we find implicit maxims in the world of the delinquent such as 'don't steal from friends' or 'don't commit vandalism against a church of your own faith'.[5] This is all rather obvious, but the implications have not received sufficient attention. The fact that supposedly valued behavior tends to be directed against disvalued social groups hints that the 'wrongfulness' of such delinquent behavior is more widely recognized by delinquents than the literature has indicated. When the pool of victims is limited by consideration of kinship, friendship, ethnic group, social class, age, sex, etc., we have reason to suspect that the virtue of delinquency is far from unquestioned.

In the fourth place, it is doubtful if many juvenile delinquents are totally immune from the demands for conformity made by the dominant social order. There is a strong likelihood that the family of the delinquent will agree with respectable society that delinquency is wrong, even though the family may be engaged in a variety of illegal activities. That is, the parental posture conducive to delinquency is not apt to be a positive prodding. Whatever may be the influence of parental example, what might be called the 'Fagin' pattern of socialization into delinquency is probably rare. Furthermore, as Redl has indicated, the idea that certain neighborhoods are completely delinquent, offering the child a model for delinquent behavior without reservations, is simply not supported by the data.[6]

The fact that a child is punished by parents, school officials, and agencies of the legal system for his delinquency may, as a number of observers have cynically noted, suggest to the child that he should be more careful not to get caught. There is an equal or greater probability, however, that the child will internalize the demands for conformity. This is not to say that demands for conformity cannot be counteracted. In fact, as we shall see shortly, an understanding of how internal and external demands for conformity are neutralized may be crucial for understanding delinquent behavior. But it is to say that a complete denial of the validity of demands for conformity and the substitution of a new normative system is improbable, in light of the child's or adolescent's dependency on adults and encirclement by adults inherent in his status in the social structure. No matter how deeply enmeshed in patterns of delinquency he may be and no matter how much this involvement may outweigh his associations with the law-abiding, he cannot escape the condemnation of his deviance. Somehow the demands for conformity must be met and answered; they cannot be ignored as part of an alien system of values and norms.

In short, the theoretical viewpoint that sees juvenile delinquency as a form of behavior based on the values and norms of a deviant subculture in precisely the same way as law-abiding behavior is based on the values and norms of the larger society is open to serious doubt. The fact that the world of the delinquent is embedded in the larger world of those who conform cannot be overlooked nor can the delinquent be equated with an adult thoroughly socialized into an alternative way of life. Instead, the juvenile delinquent would appear to be at least partially committed to the dominant social order in that he frequently exhibits guilt or shame when he violates its proscriptions, accords approval to certain conforming figures, and distinguishes between appropriate and inappropriate targets for his deviance. It is to an explanation for the apparently paradoxical fact of his delinquency that we now turn.

As Morris Cohen once said, one of the most fascinating problems about human behavior is why men violate the laws which they believe. This is the problem that confronts us when we attempt to explain why delinquency occurs despite a greater or lesser commitment to the usages of conformity. A basic clue is offered by the fact that social rules or norms calling for valued behavior seldom if ever take the form of categorical imperatives. Rather, values or norms appear as *qualified* guides for action, limited in their applicability in terms of time, place, persons, and social circumstances. The moral injunction against killing, for example, does not apply to the enemy during combat in time of war, although a captured enemy comes once again under the prohibition. Similarly, the taking and distributing of scarce goods in a time of acute social need is felt by many to be right, although under other circumstances private property is held inviolable. The normative system of a society, then, is marked by what Williams has termed *flexibility*; it does not consist of a body of rules held to be binding under all conditions.[7]

This flexibility is, in fact, an integral part of the criminal law in that measures for 'defenses to crimes' are provided in pleas such as nonage, necessity, insanity, drunkenness, compulsion, self-defense, and so on. The individual can avoid moral culpability for his criminal action – and thus avoid the negative sanctions of society – if he can prove that criminal intent was lacking. *It is our argument that much delinquency is based on what is essentially an unrecognized extension of defenses to crimes, in the form of justifications for deviance that are seen as valid by the delinquent but not by the legal system or society at large.*

These justifications are commonly described as rationalizations. They are viewed as following deviant behavior and as protecting the individual from self-blame and the blame of others after the act. But there is also reason to believe that they precede deviant behavior and make deviant behavior possible. It is this possibility that Sutherland mentioned only in passing and that other writers have failed to exploit from the viewpoint of sociological theory. Disapproval flowing from internalized norms and conforming others in the social environment is neutralized, turned back, or deflected in advance. Social controls that serve to check or inhibit deviant motivational patterns are rendered inoperative, and the individual is freed to engage in delinquency without serious damage to his self image. In this sense, the delinquent both has his cake and eats it too, for he remains committed to the dominant normative system and yet so qualifies its imperatives that violations are 'acceptable' if not 'right'. Thus the delinquent represents not a radical opposition to law-abiding society but something more like an apologetic failure, often more sinned against than sinning in his own eyes. We call these justifications of deviant behavior techniques of neutralization; and we believe these techniques make up a crucial component of Sutherland's 'definitions favorable to the violation of law'. It is by learning these techniques that the juvenile becomes delinquent, rather than by learning moral imperatives, values or attitudes standing in direct contradiction to those of the dominant society. In analyzing these techniques, we have found it convenient to divide them into five major types.

*The denial of responsibility* In so far as the delinquent can define himself as lacking responsibility for his deviant actions, the disapproval of self or others is sharply reduced in effectiveness as a restraining influence. As Justice Holmes has said, even a dog distinguishes between being stumbled over and being kicked, and modern society is no less careful to draw a line between injuries that are unintentional, i.e., where responsibility is lacking, and those that are intentional. As a technique of neutralization, however, the denial of responsibility extends much further than the claim that deviant acts are an 'accident' or some similar negation of personal accountability. It may also be asserted that delinquent acts are due to forces outside of the individual and beyond his control such as unloving parents, bad companions, or a slum neighborhood. In effect, the delinquent approaches a 'billiard ball' conception of himself in which he sees himself as helplessly propelled into new situations. From a psychodynamic viewpoint, this orientation toward one's own actions may represent a profound alienation from self, but it is important to stress the fact that interpretations of responsibility are cultural constructs and not merely idiosyncratic beliefs. The similarity between this mode of justifying illegal behavior assumed by the delinquent and the implications of a 'sociological' frame of reference or a 'humane' jurisprudence is readily apparent.[8] It is not the validity of this orientation that concerns us here, but its function of deflecting blame attached to violations of social norms and its relative independence of a particular personality structure.[9] By learning to view himself as more acted upon than acting, the delinquent prepares the way for deviance from the dominant normative system without the necessity of a frontal assault on the norms themselves.

*The denial of injury*   A second major technique of neutralization centers on the injury or harm involved in the delinquent act. The criminal law has long made a distinction between crimes which are *mala in se* and *mala prohibita* – that is between acts that are wrong in themselves and acts that are illegal but not immoral – and the delinquent can make the same kind of distinction in evaluating the wrongfulness of his behavior. For the delinquent, however, wrongfulness may turn on the question of whether or not anyone has clearly been hurt by his deviance, and this matter is open to a variety of interpretations. Vandalism, for example, may be defined by the delinquent simply as 'mischief' – after all, it may be claimed, the persons whose property has been destroyed can well afford it. Similarly, auto theft may be viewed as 'borrowing', and gang fighting may be seen as a private quarrel, an agreed upon duel between two willing parties, and thus of no concern to the community at large. We are not suggesting that this technique of neutralization, labelled the denial of injury, involves an explicit dialectic. Rather, we are arguing that the delinquent frequently, and in a hazy fashion, feels that his behavior does not really cause any great harm despite the fact that it runs counter to law. Just as the link between the individual and his acts may be broken by the denial of responsibility, so may the link between acts and their consequences be broken by the denial of injury. Since society sometimes agrees with the delinquent, e.g., in matters such as truancy, 'pranks', and so on, it merely reaffirms the idea that the delinquent's neutralization of social controls by means of qualifying the norms is an extension of common practice rather than a gesture of complete opposition.

*The denial of the victim*   Even if the delinquent accepts the responsibility for his deviant actions and is willing to admit that his deviant actions involve an injury or hurt, the moral indignation of self and others may be neutralized by an insistence that the injury is not wrong in light of the circumstances. The injury, it may be claimed, is not really an injury; rather, it is a form of rightful retaliation or punishment. By a subtle alchemy the delinquent moves himself into the position of an avenger and the victim is transformed into a wrongdoer. Assaults on homosexuals or suspected homosexuals, attacks on members of minority groups who are said to have gotten 'out of place', vandalism as revenge on an unfair teacher or school official, thefts from a 'crooked' store owner – all may be hurts inflicted on a transgressor, in the eyes of the delinquent. As Orwell has pointed out, the type of criminal admired by the general public has probably changed over the course of years and Raffles no longer serves as a hero;[10] but Robin Hood, and his latter day derivatives such as the tough detective seeking justice outside the law, still capture the popular imagination, and the delinquent may view his acts as part of a similar role.

To deny the existence of the victim, then, by transforming him into a person deserving injury is an extreme form of a phenomenon we have mentioned before, namely, the delinquent's recognition of appropriate and inappropriate targets for his delinquent acts. In addition, however, the existence of the victim may be denied for the delinquent, in a somewhat different sense, by the circumstances of the delinquent act itself. In so far as the victim is physically absent, unknown or a vague abstraction (as is often the case in delinquent acts committed against property), the awareness of the victim's existence is weakened. Internalized norms and anticipations of the reactions of others must somehow be activated, if they are to serve as guides for behavior; and it is possible that a diminished awareness of the victim plays an important part in determining whether or not this process is set in motion.

*The condemnation of the condemners*  A fourth technique of neutralization would appear to involve a condemnation of the condemners or, as McCorkle and Korn have phrased it, a rejection of the rejectors.[11] The delinquent shifts the focus of attention from his own deviant acts to the motives of his violations. His condemners, he may claim, are hypocrites, deviants in disguise, or impelled by personal spite. This orientation toward the conforming world may be of particular importance when it hardens into a bitter cynicism directed against those assigned the task of enforcing or expressing the norms of the dominant society. Police, it may be said, are corrupt, stupid and brutal. Teachers always show favoritism and parents always 'take it out' on their children. By a slight extension, the rewards of conformity – such as material success – become a matter of pull or luck, thus decreasing still further the stature of those who stand on the side of the law-abiding. The validity of this jaundiced viewpoint is not so important as its function in turning back or deflecting the negative sanctions attached to violations of the norms. The delinquent, in effect, has changed the subject of the conversation in the dialogue between his own deviant impulses and the reactions of others; and by attacking others, the wrongfulness of his own behavior is more easily repressed or lost to view.

*The appeal to higher loyalties*  Fifth, and last, internal and external social controls may be neutralized by sacrificing the demands of the larger society for the demands of the smaller social groups to which the delinquent belongs such as the sibling pair, the gang, or the friendship clique. It is important to note that the delinquent does not necessarily repudiate the imperatives of the dominant normative system, despite his failure to follow them. Rather, the delinquent may see himself as caught up in a dilemma that must be resolved, unfortunately, at the cost of violating the law. One aspect of this situation has been studied by Stouffer and Toby in their research on the conflict between particularistic and universalistic demands, between the claims of friendship and general social obligations, and their results suggest that 'it is possible to classify people according to a predisposition to select one or the other horn of a dilemma in role conflict'.[12] For our purposes, however, the most important point is that deviation from certain norms may occur not because the norms are rejected but because other norms, held to be more pressing or involving a higher loyalty, are accorded precedence. Indeed, it is the fact that both sets of norms are believed in that gives meaning to our concepts of dilemma and role conflict.

The conflict between the claims of friendship and the claims of law, or a similar dilemma, has of course long been recognized by the social scientist (and the novelist) as a common human problem. If the juvenile delinquent frequently resolves his dilemma by insisting that he must 'always help a buddy' or 'never squeal on a friend', even when it throws him into serious difficulties with the dominant social order, his choice remains familiar to the supposedly law-abiding. The delinquent is unusual, perhaps, in the extent to which he is able to see the fact that he acts in behalf of the smaller social groups to which he belongs as a justification for violations of society's norms, but it is a matter of degree rather than of kind.

'I didn't mean it.' 'I didn't really hurt anybody.' 'They had it coming to them.' 'Everybody's picking on me.' 'I didn't do it for myself.' These slogans or their variants, we hypothesize, prepare the juvenile for delinquent acts. These 'definitions of the situation' represent tangential or glancing blows at the dominant normative system rather than the creation of an opposing ideology; and they are extensions of patterns of thought prevalent in society rather than something created *de novo*.

Techniques of neutralization may not be powerful enough to fully shield the individual from the force of his own internalized values and the reactions of conforming others, for as we have pointed out, juvenile delinquents often appear to suffer from feelings of guilt and shame when called into account for their deviant behavior. And some delinquents may be so isolated from the world of conformity that techniques of neutralization need not be called into play. None the less, we would argue that techniques of neutralization are critical in lessening the effectiveness of social controls and that they lie behind a large share of delinquent behavior. Empirical research in this area is scattered and fragmentary at the present time, but the work of Redl,[13] Cressey,[14] and others has supplied a body of significant data that has done much to clarify the theoretical issues and enlarge the fund of supporting evidence. Two lines of investigation seem to be critical at this stage. First, there is need for more knowledge concerning the differential distribution of techniques of neutralization, as operative patterns of thought, by age, sex, social class, ethnic groups, etc. On a priori grounds it might be assumed that these justifications for deviance will be more readily seized by segments of society for whom a discrepancy between common social ideals and social practice is most apparent. It is also possible however, that the habit of 'bending' the dominant normative system – if not 'breaking' it – cuts across our cruder social categories and is to be traced primarily to patterns of social interaction within the familial circle. Secondly, there is a need for a greater understanding of the internal structure of techniques of neutralization, as a system of beliefs and attitudes, and its relationship to various types of delinquent behavior. Certain techniques of neutralization would appear to be better adapted to particular deviant acts than to others, as we have suggested, for example, in the case of offenses against property and the denial of the victim. But the issue remains far from clear and stands in need of more information.

In any case, techniques of neutralization appear to offer a promising line of research in enlarging and systematizing the theoretical grasp of juvenile delinquency. As more information is uncovered concerning techniques of neutralization, their origins, and their consequences, both juvenile delinquency in particular, and deviation from normative systems in general may be illuminated.

## Notes

1 E.H. Sutherland, *Principles of Criminology*, revised by D.R. Cressey (Chicago, Lippincott, 1955), pp. 77–80.

2 Albert, K. Cohen, *Delinquent Boys* (Glencoe, Ill., The Free Press, 1955).

3 This form of reaction among the adherents of a deviant subculture who fully believe in the 'rightfulness' of their behavior and who are captured and punished by the agencies of the dominant social order can be illustrated, perhaps, by groups such as Jehovah's Witnesses, early Christian sects, nationalist movements in colonial areas, and conscientious objectors during World Wars I and II.

4 As Weber has pointed out, a thief may recognize the legitimacy of legal rules without accepting their moral validity. Cf. Max Weber, *The Theory of Social and Economic Organization* (translated by A.M. Henderson and Talcott Parsons) (New York, Oxford University Press, 1947), p. 125. We are arguing here, however, that the juvenile delinquent frequently recognizes *both* the legitimacy of the dominant social order and its moral 'rightness'.

5 Thrasher's account of the 'Itschkies' – a juvenile gang composed of Jewish boys – and the immunity from 'rolling' enjoyed by Jewish drunkards is a good illustration. Cf. F. Thrasher, *The Gang* (Chicago, The University of Chicago Press, 1947), p. 315.

6 Cf. Solomon Kobrin, 'The conflict of values in delinquency areas', *American Sociological Review*, 16 (October, 1951), pp. 653–61.

7 Cf. Robin Williams Jr, *American Society* (New York, Knopf, 1951), p. 28.

8 A number of observers have wryly noted that many delinquents seem to show a surprising awareness of sociological and psychological explanations for their behavior and are quick to point out the causal role of their poor environment.

9 It is possible, of course, that certain personality structures can accept some techniques of neutralization more readily than others, but this question remains largely unexplored.

10 George Orwell, *Dickens, Dali, and Others* (New York, Revnal, 1946).

11 Lloyd W. McCorkle and Richard Korn, 'Resocialization within walls', *Annals of the American Academy of Political and Social Science, 293* (May, 1954), pp. 88–98.

12 See Samuel A. Stouffer and Jackson Toby, 'Role conflict and personality', in T. Parsons and E.A. Shils (eds), *Toward a General Theory of Action* (Cambridge, MA, Harvard University Press, 1951), p. 494.

13 See Fritz Redl and David Wineman, *Children Who Hate* (Glencoe, Ill., The Free Press, 1956).

14 See D.R. Cressey, *Other People's Money* (Glencoe, Ill., The Free Press, 1953).

# 19

# Outsiders

## *Howard Becker*

All social groups make rules and attempt, at some times and under some circumstances, to enforce them. Social rules define situations and the kinds of behavior appropriate to them, specifying some actions as 'right' and forbidding others as 'wrong'. When a rule is enforced, the person who is supposed to have broken it may be seen as a special kind of person, one who cannot be trusted to live by the rules agreed on by the group. He is regarded as an *outsider*.

But the person who is thus labeled an outsider may have a different view of the matter. He may not accept the rule by which he is being judged and may not regard those who judge him as either competent or legitimately entitled to do so. Hence, a second meaning of the term emerges: the rule-breaker may feel his judges are *outsiders*.

In what follows, I will try to clarify the situation and process pointed to by this double-barreled term: the situations of rule-breaking and rule-enforcement and the processes by which some people come to break rules and others to enforce them.

Some preliminary distinctions are in order. Rules may be of a great many kinds. They may be formally enacted into law, and in this case the police power of the state may be used in enforcing them. In other cases, they represent informal agreements, newly arrived at or encrusted with the sanction of age and tradition; rules of this kind are enforced by informal sanctions of various kinds.

Similarly, whether a rule has the force of law or tradition or is simply the result of consensus, it may be the task of some specialized body, such as the police or the committee on ethics of a professional association, to enforce it; enforcement, on the other hand, may be everyone's job or, at least, the job of everyone in the group to which the rule is meant to apply.

Many rules are not enforced and are not, in any except the most formal sense, the kind of rules with which I am concerned. Blue laws, which remain on the statute books though they have not been enforced for a hundred years, are examples. (It is important to remember, however, that an unenforced law may be reactivated for various reasons and regain all its original force, as recently occurred with respect to the laws governing the opening of commercial establishments on Sunday in Missouri.) Informal rules may similarly die from lack of enforcement. I shall mainly be concerned with what we can call the actual operating rules of groups, those kept alive through attempts at enforcement.

Abridged from *Outsiders: Studies in the Sociology of Deviance*, pp. 1–18. (New York: Free Press, 1963.)

Finally, just how far 'outside' one is, in either of the senses I have mentioned, varies from case to case. We think of the person who commits a traffic violation or gets a little too drunk at a party as being, after all, not very different from the rest of us and treat his infraction tolerantly. We regard the thief as less like us and punish him severely. Crimes such as murder, rape, or treason lead us to view the violator as a true outsider.

In the same way, some rule-breakers do not think they have been unjustly judged. The traffic violator usually subscribes to the very rules he has broken. Alcoholics are often ambivalent, sometimes feeling that those who judge them do not understand them and at other times agreeing that compulsive drinking is a bad thing. At the extreme, some deviants (homosexuals and drug addicts are good examples) develop full-blown ideologies explaining why they are right and why those who disapprove of and punish them are wrong.

### Definitions of deviance

The outsider – the deviant from group rules – has been the subject of much speculation, theorizing and scientific study. What laymen want to know about deviants is: why do they do it? How can we account for their rule-breaking? What is there about them that leads them to do forbidden things? Scientific research has tried to find answers to these questions. In doing so it has accepted the common-sense premise that there is something inherently deviant (qualitatively distinct) about acts that break (or seem to break) social rules. It has also accepted the common-sense assumption that the deviant act occurs because some characteristic of the person who commits it makes it necessary or inevitable that he should. Scientists do not ordinarily question the label 'deviant' when it is applied to particular acts or people but rather take it as given. In so doing, they accept the values of the group making the judgment.

It is easily observable that different groups judge different things to be deviant. This should alert us to the possibility that the person making the judgment of deviance, the process by which that judgment is arrived at, and the situation in which it is made may all be intimately involved in the phenomenon of deviance. To the degree that the common-sense view of deviance and the scientific theories that begin with its premises assume that acts that break rules are inherently deviant and thus take for granted the situations and processes of judgment, they may leave out an important variable. If scientists ignore the variable character of the process of judgment, they may by that omission limit the kinds of theories that can be developed and the kind of understanding that can be achieved.[1]

Our first problem, then, is to construct a definition of deviance. Before doing this, let us consider some of the definitions scientists now use, seeing what is left out if we take them as a point of departure for the study of outsiders.

The simplest view of deviance is essentially statistical, defining as deviant anything that varies too widely from the average. When a statistician analyses the results of an agricultural experiment, he describes the stalk of corn that is exceptionally tall and the stalk that is exceptionally short as deviations from the mean or average. Similarly, one can describe anything that differs from what is most common as a deviation. In this view, to be left-handed or redheaded is deviant, because most people are right-handed and brunette.

So stated, the statistical view seems simple-minded, even trivial. Yet it simplifies the problem by doing away with many questions of value that ordinarily arise in discussions of the nature of deviance. In assessing any particular case, all one need do is calculate the distance of the behavior involved from the average. But it is too simple a solution. Hunting with such a definition, we return with a mixed bag – people who are excessively fat or thin, murderers, redheads, homosexuals and traffic violators. The mixture contains some ordinarily thought of as deviants and others who have broken no rule at all. The statistical definition of deviance, in short, is too far removed from the concern with rule-breaking which prompts scientific study of outsiders.

A less simple but much more common view of deviance identifies it as something essentially pathological, revealing the presence of a 'disease'. This view rests, obviously, on a medical analogy. The human organism, when it is working efficiently and experiencing no discomfort, is said to be 'healthy'. When it does not work efficiently, a disease is present. The organ or function that has become deranged is said to be pathological. Of course, there is little disagreement about what constitutes a healthy state of the organism. But there is much less agreement when one uses the notion of pathology analogically, to describe kinds of behavior that are regarded as deviant. For people do not agree on what constitutes healthy behavior. It is difficult to find a definition that will satisfy even such a select and limited group as psychiatrists; it is impossible to find one that people generally accept as they accept criteria of health for the organism.[2]

Sometimes people mean the analogy more strictly, because they think of deviance as the product of mental disease. The behavior of a homosexual or drug addict is regarded as the symptom of a mental disease just as the diabetic's difficulty in getting bruises to heal is regarded as a symptom of his disease. But mental disease resembles physical disease only in metaphor:

> Starting with such things as syphilis, tuberculosis, typhoid fever, and carcinomas and fractures, we have created the class 'illness'. At first, this class was composed of only a few items, all of which shared the common feature of reference to a state of disordered structure or function of the human body as a physiochemical machine. As time went on, additional items were added to this class. They were not added, however, because they were newly discovered bodily disorders. The physician's attention had been deflected from this criterion and had become focused instead on disability and suffering as new criteria for selection. Thus, at first slowly, such things as hysteria, hypochondriasis, obsessive-compulsive neurosis, and depression were added to the category of illness. Then, with increasing zeal, physicians and especially psychiatrists began to call 'illness' (that is, of course, 'mental illness') anything and everything in which they could detect any sign of malfunctioning, based on no matter what norm. Hence, agoraphobia is illness because one should not be afraid of open spaces. Homosexuality is illness because heterosexuality is the social norm. Divorce is illness because it signals failure of marriage. Crime, art, undesired political leadership, participation in social affairs, or withdrawal from such participation – all these and many more have been said to be signs of mental illness.[3]

The medical metaphor limits what we can see much as the statistical view does. It accepts the lay judgment of something as deviant and, by use of analogy, locates its source within the individual, thus preventing us from seeing the judgment itself as a crucial part of the phenomenon.

Some sociologists also use a model of deviance based essentially on the medical notions of health and disease. They look at a society, or some part of a society, and ask whether there are any processes going on in it that tend to reduce its stability, thus lessening its chance of survival. They label such processes deviant or identify them as symptoms of social disorganization. They discriminate between those features of society which promote stability (and thus are 'functional') and those which disrupt stability (and thus are 'dysfunctional'). Such a view has the great virtue of pointing to areas of possible trouble in a society of which people may not be aware.[4]

But it is harder in practice than it appears to be in theory to specify what is functional and what dysfunctional for a society or social group. The question of what the purpose or goal (function) of a group is and, consequently, what things will help or hinder the achievement of that purpose, is very often a political question. Factions within the group disagree and maneuver to have their own definition of the group's function accepted. The function of the group or organization, then, is decided in political conflict, not given in the nature of the organization. If this is true, then it is likewise true that the questions of what rules are to be enforced, what behavior regarded as deviant, and which people labeled as outsiders must also be regarded as political.[5] The functional view of deviance, by ignoring the political aspects of the phenomenon, limits our understanding.

Another sociological view is more relativistic. It identifies deviance as the failure to obey group rules. Once we have described the rules a group enforces on its members, we can say with some precision whether or not a person has violated them and is thus, on this view, deviant.

This view is closest to my own, but it fails to give sufficient weight to the ambiguities that arise in deciding which rules are to be taken as the yardstick against which behavior is measured and judged deviant. A society has many groups, each with its own set of rules, and people belong to many groups simultaneously. A person may break the rules of one group by the very act of abiding by the rules of another group. Is he, then, deviant? Proponents of this definition may object that while ambiguity may arise with respect to the rules peculiar to one or another group in society, there are some rules that are very generally agreed to by everyone, in which case the difficulty does not arise. This, of course, is a question of fact, to be settled by empirical research. I doubt there are many such areas of consensus and think it wiser to use a definition that allows us to deal with both ambiguous and unambiguous situations.

## Deviance and the responses of others

The sociological view I have just discussed defines deviance as the infraction of some agreed-upon rule. It then goes on to ask who breaks rules, and to search for the factors in their personalities and life situations that might account for the infractions. This assumes that those who have broken a rule constitute a homogeneous category, because they have committed the same deviant act.

Such an assumption seems to me to ignore the central fact about deviance: it is created by society. I do not mean this in the way it is ordinarily understood, in which the causes of deviance are located in the social situation of the deviant or in 'social factors' which prompt his action. I mean, rather, that *social groups create deviance by making the rules whose infraction constitutes deviance*, and by applying those rules to particular people and labeling them as outsiders. From this point of view, deviance is *not* a quality of the act the person commits, but rather a consequence of the application by others of rules and sanctions to an 'offender'. The deviant is one to whom that label has successfully been applied; deviant behavior is behavior that people so label.[6]

Since deviance is, among other things, a consequence of the responses of others to a person's act, students of deviance cannot assume that they are dealing with a homogeneous category when they study people who have been labeled deviant. That is, they cannot assume that these people have actually committed a deviant act or broken some rule, because the process of labeling may not be infallible; some people may be labeled deviant who in fact have not broken a rule. Furthermore, they cannot assume that the category of those labeled deviant will contain all those who actually have broken a rule, for many offenders may escape apprehension and thus fail to be included in the population of 'deviants' they study. In so far as the category lacks homogeneity and fails to include all the cases that belong in it, one cannot reasonably expect to find common factors of personality or life situation that will account for the supposed deviance.

What, then, do people who have been labeled deviant have in common? At the least, they share the label and the experience of being labeled as outsiders. I will begin my analysis with this basic similarity and view deviance as the product of a transaction that takes place between some social group and one who is viewed by that group as a rule-breaker. I will be less concerned with the personal and social characteristics of deviants than with the process by which they come to be thought of as outsiders and their reactions to that judgment.

Malinowski discovered the usefulness of this view for understanding the nature of deviance many years ago, in his study of the Trobriand Islands:

> One day an outbreak of wailing and a great commotion told me that a death had occurred somewhere in the neighborhood. I was informed that Kima'i, a young lad of my acquaintance, of sixteen or so, had fallen from a coco-nut palm and killed himself. . . . I found that another youth had been severely wounded by some mysterious coincidence. And at the funeral there was obviously a general feeling of hostility between the village where the boy died and that into which his body was carried for burial.
>
> Only much later was I able to discover the real meaning of these events. The boy had committed suicide. The truth was that he had broken the rules of exogamy, the partner in his crime being his maternal cousin, the daughter of his mother's sister. This had been known and generally disapproved of but nothing was done until the girl's discarded lover, who had wanted to marry her and who felt personally injured, took the initiative. This rival threatened first to use black magic against the guilty youth, but this had not much effect. Then one evening he insulted the culprit in public – accusing him in the hearing of the whole community of incest and hurling at him certain expressions intolerable to a native.
>
> For this there was only one remedy; only one means of escape remained to the unfortunate youth. Next morning he put on festive attire and ornamentation, climbed a coco-nut palm and addressed the community, speaking from among the palm leaves and bidding them farewell. He explained the reasons for his desperate deed and also launched forth a veiled accusation against the man who had driven him to his death, upon which it became the duty of his clansmen to avenge him. Then he wailed aloud, as is the custom, jumped from a palm some sixty feet high

and was killed on the spot. There followed a fight within the village in which the rival was wounded; and the quarrel was repeated during the funeral. . . .

If you were to inquire into the matter among the Trobrianders, you would find . . . that the natives show horror at the idea of violating the rules of exogamy and that they believe that sores, disease and even death might follow clan incest. This is the ideal of native law, and in moral matters it is easy and pleasant strictly to adhere to the ideal – when judging the conduct of others or expressing an opinion about conduct in general.

When it comes to the application of morality and ideals to real life, however, things take on a different complexion. In the case described it was obvious that the facts would not tally with the ideal of conduct. Public opinion was neither outraged by the knowledge of the crime to any extent, nor did it react directly – it had to be mobilized by a public statement of the crime and by insults being hurled at the culprit by an interested party. Even then he had to carry out the punishment himself. . . . Probing further into the matter and collecting concrete information, I found that the breach of exogamy – as regards intercourse and not marriage – is by no means a rare occurrence, and public opinion is lenient, though decidedly hypocritical. If the affair is carried on *sub rosa* with a certain amount of decorum, and if no one in particular stirs up trouble – 'public opinion' will gossip, but not demand any harsh punishment. If, on the contrary, scandal breaks out – everyone turns against the guilty pair and by ostracism and insults one or the other may be driven to suicide.[7]

Whether an act is deviant, then, depends on how other people react to it. You can commit clan incest and suffer from no more than gossip as long as no one makes a public accusation; but you will be driven to your death if the accusation is made. The point is that the response of other people has to be regarded as problematic. Just because one has committed an infraction of a rule does not mean that others will respond as though this had happened. (Conversely, just because one has not violated a rule does not mean that he may not be treated, in some circumstances, as though he had.)

The degree to which other people will respond to a given act as deviant varies greatly. Several kinds of variation seem worth noting. First of all, there is variation over time. A person believed to have committed a given 'deviant' act may at one time be responded to much more leniently than he would be at some other time. The occurrence of 'drives' against various kinds of deviance illustrates this clearly. At various times, enforcement officials may decide to make an all-out attack on some particular kind of deviance, such as gambling, drug addiction, or homosexuality. It is obviously much more dangerous to engage in one of these activities when a drive is on than at any other time. (In a very interesting study of crime news in Colorado newspapers, Davis found that the amount of crime reported in Colorado newspapers showed very little association with actual changes in the amount of crime taking place in Colorado. And, further, that people's estimate of how much increase there had been in crime in Colorado was associated with the increase in the amount of crime news but not with any increase in the amount of crime.)[8]

The degree to which an act will be treated as deviant depends also on who commits the act and who feels he has been harmed by it. Rules tend to be applied more to some persons than others. Studies of juvenile delinquency make the point clearly. Boys from middle-class areas do not get as far in the legal process when they are apprehended as do boys from slum areas. The middle-class boy is less likely, when picked up by the police, to be taken to the station; less likely when taken to the station to be booked; and it is extremely unlikely that he will be convicted and sentenced.[9] This variation occurs even though the original infraction of the rule is the same in the two cases. Similarly, the law is differentially applied to Negroes and whites. It is well known that a Negro believed to have attacked a white woman is much more likely to be punished than a white man who commits the same offense; it is only slightly less well known that a Negro who murders another Negro is much less likely to be punished than a white man who commits murder.[10] This, of course, is one of the main points of Sutherland's analysis of white-collar crime: crimes committed by corporations are almost always prosecuted as civil cases, but the same crime committed by an individual is ordinarily treated as a criminal offense.[11]

Some rules are enforced only when they result in certain consequences. The unmarried mother furnishes a clear example. Vincent[12] points out that illicit sexual relations seldom result in severe punishment or social censure for the offenders. If, however, a girl becomes pregnant as a result of such activities the reaction of others is likely to be severe. (The illicit pregnancy is also an interesting example of the differential enforcement of rules on different categories of people. Vincent notes that unmarried fathers escape the severe censure visited on the mother.)

Why repeat these commonplace observations? Because, taken together, they support the proposition that deviance is not a simple quality, present in some kinds of behavior and absent in others. Rather, it is the product of a process which involves responses of other people to the behavior. The same behavior may be an infraction of the rules at one time and not at another; may be an infraction when committed by one person, but not when committed by another; some rules are broken with impunity, others are not. In short, whether a given act is deviant or not depends in part on the nature of the act (that is, whether or not it violates some rule) and in part on what other people do about it.

Some people may object that this is merely a terminological quibble, that one can, after all, define terms any way he wants to and that if some people want to speak of rule-breaking behavior as deviant without reference to the reactions of others they are free to do so. This, of course, is true. Yet it might be worthwhile to refer to such behavior as *rule-breaking behavior* and reserve the term *deviant* for those labeled as deviant by some segment of society. I do not insist that this usage be followed. But it should be clear that in so far as a scientist uses 'deviant' to refer to any rule-breaking behavior and takes as his subject of study only those who have been *labeled* deviant, he will be hampered by the disparities between the two categories.

If we take as the object of our attention behavior which comes to be labeled as deviant, we must recognize that we cannot know whether a given act will be categorized as deviant until the response of others has occurred. Deviance is not a quality that lies in behavior itself, but in the interaction between the person who commits an act and those who respond to it.

### Whose rules?

I have been using the term 'outsiders' to refer to those people who are judged by others to be deviant and thus to stand outside the circle of 'normal' members of the group. But the term contains a second meaning, whose analysis leads to another important set of sociological problems: 'outsiders', from the point of view of the person who is labeled deviant, may be the people who make the rules he had been found guilty of breaking.

Social rules are the creation of specific social groups. Modern societies are not simple organizations in which everyone agrees on what the rules are and how they are to be applied in specific situations. They are, instead, highly differentiated along social class lines, ethnic lines, occupational lines, and cultural lines. These groups need not and, in fact, often do not share the same rules. The problems they face in dealing with their environment, the history and traditions they carry with them, all lead to the evolution of different sets of rules. In so far as the rules of various groups conflict and contradict one another, there will be disagreement about the kind of behavior that is proper in any given situation.

Italian immigrants who went on making wine for themselves and their friends during Prohibition were acting properly by Italian immigrant standards, but were breaking the law of their new country (as, of course, were many of their Old American neighbors). Medical patients who shop around for a doctor may, from the perspective of their own group, be doing what is necessary to protect their health by making sure they get what seems to them the best possible doctor; but, from the perspective of the physician, what they do is wrong because it breaks down the trust the patient ought to put in his physician. The lower-class delinquent who fights for his 'turf' is only doing what he considers necessary and right, but teachers, social workers, and police see it differently.

While it may be argued that many or most rules are generally agreed to by all members of a society, empirical research on a given rule generally reveals variation in people's attitudes. Formal rules, enforced by some specially constituted group, may differ from those actually thought appropriate by most people.[13] Factions in a group may disagree on what I have called actual operating rules. Most important for the study of behavior ordinarily labeled deviant, the perspectives of the people who engage in the behavior are likely to be quite different from those of the people who condemn it. In this latter situation, a person may feel that he is being judged according to rules he has had no hand in making and does not accept, rules forced on him by outsiders.

To what extent and under what circumstances do people attempt to force their rules on others who do not subscribe to them? Let us distinguish two cases. In the first, only those who are actually members of the group have any interest in making and enforcing certain rules. If an orthodox Jew disobeys the laws of kashruth only other orthodox Jews will regard this as a transgression; Christians or non-orthodox Jews will not consider this deviance and would have no interest in interfering. In the second case, members of a group consider it important to their welfare that members of certain other groups obey certain rules. Thus, people consider it extremely important that those who practice the healing arts abide by certain rules; this is the reason the state licenses physicians, nurses, and others, and forbids anyone who is not licensed to engage in healing activities.

To the extent that a group tries to impose its rules on other groups in the society, we are presented with a second question: Who can, in fact, force others to accept their rules and what are the causes of their success? This is, of course, a question of political and economic power. [. . .] [P]eople are in fact always *forcing* their rules on others, applying them more or less against the will and without the consent of those others. By and large, for example, rules are made for young people by their elders. Though the youth of this country exert a powerful influence culturally – the mass media of communication are tailored to their interests, for instance – many important kinds of rules are made for our youth by adults. Rules regarding school attendance and sex behavior are not drawn up with regard to the problems of adolescence. Rather, adolescents find themselves surrounded by rules about these matters which have been made by older and more settled people. It is considered legitimate to do this, for youngsters are considered neither wise enough nor responsible enough to make proper rules for themselves.

In the same way, it is true in many respects that men make the rules for women in our society (though in America this is changing rapidly). Negroes find themselves subject to rules made for them by whites. The foreign-born and those otherwise ethnically peculiar often have their rules made for them by the Protestant Anglo-Saxon minority. The middle class makes rules the lower class must obey – in the schools, the courts, and elsewhere.

Differences in the ability to make rules and apply them to other people are essentially power differentials (either legal or extralegal). Those groups whose social position gives them weapons and power are best able to enforce their rules. Distinctions of age, sex, ethnicity, and class are all related to differences in power, which accounts for differences in the degree to which groups so distinguished can make rules for others.

In addition to recognizing that deviance is created by the responses of people to particular kinds of behavior, by the labeling of that behavior as deviant, we must also keep in mind that the rules created and maintained by such labeling are not universally agreed to. Instead, they are the object of conflict and disagreement, part of the political process of society.

## Notes

1 Cf. Donald R. Cressey, 'Criminological research and the definition of crimes', *American Journal of Sociology*, LVI (May, 1951), pp. 546–51.

2 See the discussion in C. Wright Mills, 'The professional ideology of social pathologists', *American Journal of Sociology*, XLIX (September, 1942), pp. 165–80.

3 Thomas Szasz, *The Myth of Mental Illness* (New York, Paul B. Hoeber, 1961), pp. 44–5; see also Erving Goffman, 'The medical model and mental hospitalization', in *Asylums: Essays on the Social Situation of Mental Patients and Other Inmates* (Garden City, NY, Anchor Books, 1961), pp. 321–86.

4 See Robert K. Merton, 'Social problems and sociological theory', in Robert K. Merton and Robert A. Nisbet (eds), *Contemporary Social Problems* (New York, Harcourt, Brace and World, 1961), pp. 697–737; and Talcott Parsons, *The Social System* (New York, The Free Press of Glencoe, 1951), pp. 249–325.

5 Howard Brotz similarly identifies the question of what phenomena are 'functional' or 'dysfunctional' as a political one in 'Functionalism and dynamic analysis', *European Journal of Sociology*, II (1961), pp. 170–9.

6 The most important earlier statements of this view can be found in Frank Tannenbaum, *Crime and the Community* (New York, McGraw-Hill, 1951), and E.M. Lemert, *Social Pathology* (New York, McGraw-Hill, 1951). A recent article stating a position very similar to mine is John Kitsuse, 'Societal reaction to deviance: problems of theory and method', *Social Problems*, 9 (Winter, 1962), pp. 247–56.

7 Bronislaw Malinowski, *Crime and Custom in Savage Society* (New York, Humanities Press, 1926), pp. 77–80. Reprinted by permission of Humanities Press and Routledge and Kegan Paul Ltd.

8 F. James Davis, 'Crime news in Colorado newspapers', *American Journal of Sociology,* LVII (January, 1952), pp. 325–30.

9 See Albert K. Cohen and James F. Short Jr, 'Juvenile delinquency', in Merton and Nisbet, *Contemporary Social Problems,* p. 87.

10 See Harold Garfinkel, 'Research notes on inter- and intra-racial homicides', *Social Forces,* 27 (May, 1949), pp. 369–81.

11 Edwin H. Sutherland, 'White Collar Criminality', *American Sociological Review,* V (February, 1940), pp. 1–12.

12 Clark Vincent, *Unmarried Mothers* (New York: The Free Press of Glencoe, 1961), pp. 3–5.

13 Arnold M. Rose and Arthur E. Prell, 'Does the punishment fit the crime? – a study in social valuation', *American Journal of Sociology,* LXI (November, 1955), pp. 247–59.

# 20

# Toward a political economy of crime

## William J. Chambliss

In attempting to develop a Marxist theory of crime and criminal law we are handicapped by the fact that Marx did not devote himself very systematically to such a task. There are none the less several places in his analysis of capitalism where Marx did direct his attention to criminality and law.[1] Furthermore, the logic of the Marxian theory makes it possible to extrapolate from the theory to an analysis of crime and criminal law in ways that are extremely useful. Thus, in what follows I will be focusing on the implications of the Marxist paradigm as well as relying heavily on those Marxist writings that directly addressed these issues.

As with the general Marxist theory, the starting-point for the understanding of society is the realization that the most fundamental feature of people's lives is their relationship to the mode of production. The mode of production consists of both the means of production (the technological processes) and the relationship of different classes to the means of production – whether they own them or work for those who do. Since ultimately, the only source of an economic surplus is that amount of goods which is produced beyond what the worker consumes, then the distinction between those who own and those who work for others is crucial to understanding the control of the surplus in the society.

All of this is of course elementary Marxism and was only briefly summarized here to get us started.

We must then speak of historical periods according to the mode of production which characterizes them. The most fundamental distinction would be between those societies where the means of production are owned privately, and societies where the means of production are not. Obviously there are many possible variations on these two ideal types: societies where the means of production are owned by the state (for example, the Soviet Union) as contrasted with societies where the means of production are controlled by small groups of workers (for example, Yugoslavia), or where the means of production are owned by collective units of workers, farmers, peasants and other strata (China, for example). Each of these different modes of production would of course lead to quite different social relations and therefore to different forms of crime and criminal law.

Capitalist societies, where the means of production are in private hands and where there inevitably develops a division between the class that rules (the owners of the means of production) and the class that is ruled (those who work for the ruling class), create substantial amounts of crime, often of the

---

Abridged from *Theory and Society*, 1975, 2: 149–70.

most violent sort, as a result of the contradictions that are inherent in the structure of social relations that emanate from the capitalist system.

The first contradiction is that the capitalist enterprise depends upon creating in the mass of the workers a desire for the consumption of products produced by the system. These products need not contribute to the well-being of the people, nor do they have to represent commodities of any intrinsic value; none the less, for the system to expand and be viable, it is essential that the bulk of the population be oriented to consuming what is produced. However, in order to produce the commodities that are the basis for the accumulation of capital and the maintenance of the ruling class, it is also necessary to get people to work at tedious, alienating and unrewarding tasks. One way to achieve this, of course, is to make the accumulation of commodities dependent on work. Moreover, since the system depends as it does on the desire to possess and consume commodities far beyond what is necessary for survival, there must be an added incentive to perform the dull meaningless tasks that are required to keep the productive process expanding. This is accomplished by keeping a proportion of the labor force impoverished or nearly so.[2] If those who are employed become obstreperous and refuse to perform the tasks required by the productive system, then there is a reserve labor force waiting to take their job. And hanging over the heads of the workers is always the possibility of becoming impoverished should they refuse to do their job.

Thus, at the outset the structure of capitalism creates both the desire to consume and – for a large mass of people – an inability to earn the money necessary to purchase the items they have been taught to want.

A second fundamental contradiction derives from the fact that the division of a society into a ruling class that owns the means of production and a subservient class that works for wages *inevitably* leads to conflict between the two classes. As those conflicts are manifest in rebellions and riots among the proletariat, the state, acting in the interests of the owners of the means of production will pass laws designed to control, through the application of state sanctioned force, those acts of the proletariat which threaten the interests of the bourgeoisie. In this way, then, acts come to be defined as criminal.

It follows that as capitalism develops and conflicts between social classes continue or become more frequent or more violent (as a result, for example, of increasing proletarianization), more and more acts will be defined as criminal.

The criminal law is thus *not* a reflection of custom (as other theorists have argued), but is a set of rules laid down by the state in the interests of the ruling class, and resulting from the conflicts that inhere in class structured societies; criminal behavior is, then, the inevitable expression of class conflict resulting from the inherently exploitative nature of the economic relations. What makes the behavior of some criminal is the coercive power of the state to enforce the will of the ruling class; criminal behavior results from the struggle between classes whereby those who are the subservient classes individually express their alienation from established social relations. Criminal behavior is a product of the economic and political system, and in a capitalist society has as one of its principal consequences the advancement of technology, use of surplus labor and generally the maintenance of the established relationship between the social classes. Marx says, somewhat facetiously, in response to the functionalism of bourgeois sociologists:

crime takes a part of the superfluous population off the labor market and thus reduces competition among the laborers – up to a certain point preventing wages from falling below the minimum – the struggle against crime absorbs another part of this population. Thus the criminal comes in as one of those natural 'counterweights' which bring about a correct balance and open up a whole perspective of 'useful' occupation . . . the criminal . . . produces the whole of the police and of criminal justice, constables, judges, hangmen, juries, etc.; and all these different lines of business, which form equally many categories of the social division of labor, develop different capacities of the human spirit, create new needs and new ways of satisfying them. Torture alone has given rise to the most ingenious mechanical inventions, and employed many honorable craftsmen in the production of its instruments.[3]

Paradigms, as we are all well aware, do much more than supply us with specific causal explanations. They provide us with a whole set of glasses through which we view the world. Most importantly, they lead us to emphasize certain features of the world and to ignore or at least de-emphasize others.

The following propositions highlight the most important implications of a Marxian paradigm of crime and criminal law.[4]

### A  On the content and operation of criminal law

1  Acts are defined as criminal because it is in the interests of the ruling class to so define them.
2  Members of the ruling class will be able to violate the laws with impunity while members of the subject classes will be punished.
3  As capitalist societies industrialize and the gap between the bourgeoisie and the proletariat widens, penal law will expand in an effort to coerce the proletariat into submission.

### B  On the consequences of crime for society

1  Crime reduces surplus labor by creating employment not only for the criminals but for law enforcers, locksmiths, welfare workers, professors of criminology and a horde of people who live off the fact that crime exists.
2  Crime diverts the lower classes' attention from the exploitation they experience, and directs it toward other members of their own class rather than towards the capitalist class or the economic system.
3  Crime is a reality which exists only as it is created by those in the society whose interests are served by its presence.

### C  On the etiology of criminal behavior

1  Criminal and non-criminal behavior stem from people acting rationally in ways that are compatible with their class position. Crime is a reaction to the life conditions of a person's social class.
2  Crime varies from society to society depending on the political and economic structures of society.
3  Socialist societies should have much lower rates of crime because the less intense class struggle should reduce the forces leading to and the functions of crime.

[. . .]

## On the content and operation of the criminal law

The conventional, non-Marxian interpretation of how criminal law comes into being sees the criminal law as a reflection of widely held beliefs which permeate all 'healthy consciences' in the society. This view has been clearly articulated by Jerome Hall:

> The moral judgements represented in the criminal law can be defended on the basis of their derivation from a long historical experience, through open discussion . . . the process of legislation, viewed broadly to include participation and discussion by the electorate as well as that of the legislature proper, provides additional assurance that the legal valuations are soundly established . . . .[5]

## The Marxian theory of criminal law

There is little evidence to support the view that the criminal law is a body of rules which reflect strongly held moral dictates of the society.[6] Occasionally we find a study on the creation of criminal law which traces legal innovations to the 'moral indignation' of a particular social class.[7] It is significant, however, that the circumstances described are quite different from the situation where laws emerge from community consensus. Rather, the research points up the rule by a small minority which occupies a particular class position and shares a viewpoint and a set of social experiences which brings them together as an active and effective force of social change. For example, Joseph Gusfield's astute analysis of the emergence of prohibition in the United States illustrates how these laws were brought about through the political efforts of a downwardly mobile segment of America's middle class. By effort and some good luck this class was able to impose its will on the majority of the population through rather dramatic changes in the law.[8] Svend Ranulf's more general study of *Moral Indignation and Middle Class Psychology* shows similar results, especially when it is remembered that the lower middle class, whose emergence Ranulf sees as the social force behind legal efforts to legislate morality, was a decided *minority* of the population. In no reasonable way can these inquiries be taken as support for the idea that criminal laws represent *community* sentiments.

By contrast, there is considerable evidence showing the critically important role played by the interests of the ruling class as a major force in the creation of criminal laws. Jerome Hall's analysis of the emergence of the laws of theft and Chambliss's study of vagrancy laws both point up the salience of the economic interests of the ruling class as the fountainhead of legal changes.[9] A more recent analysis of the legislative process behind the creation of laws attempting to control the distribution of amphetamine drugs has also shown how the owners of the means of production (in this case, the large pharmaceutical companies) are involved in writing and lobbying for laws which affect their profits.[10]

The surface appearance of legal innovations often hides the real forces behind legislation. Gabriel Kolko's studies of the creation of laws controlling the meat packing and railroad industries in the United States have shown how the largest corporations in these industries were actively involved in a campaign for federal control of the industries, as this control would mean increased profits for the large manufacturers and industrialists.[11]

Research on criminal law legislation has also shown the substantial role played by state bureaucracies in the legislative process.[12] In some areas of criminal law it seems that the law enforcement agencies are almost solely responsible for the shape and content of the laws. As a matter of fact, drug laws are best understood as laws passed as a result of efforts of law enforcement agencies which managed to create whatever consensus there is. Other inquiries point up the role of conflicting interests between organized groups of moral entrepreneurs, bureaucrats and businessmen.[13]

In all of these studies there is substantial support for the Marxian theory. The single most important force behind criminal law creation is doubtless the economic interest and political power of those social classes which either (1) own or control the resources of the society, or (2) occupy positions of authority in the state bureaucracies. It is also the case that conflicts generated by the class structure of a society act as an important force for legal innovation. These conflicts may manifest themselves in an incensed group of moral entrepreneurs (such as Gusfield's lower middle class, or the efforts of groups such as the ACLU, NAACP or Policemen's Benevolent Society) who manage to persuade courts or legislatures to create new laws.[14] Or the conflict may manifest itself in open riots, rebellions or revolutions which force new criminal law legislation.

There is, then, evidence that the Marxian theory with its emphasis on the role of the ruling classes in creating criminal laws and social class conflict and as the moving force behind legal changes is quite compatible with research findings on this subject.

[. . .]

### The etiology of criminal behavior

It is obviously fruitless to join the debate over whether or not contemporary theories of criminal etiology are adequate to the task. The advocates of 'family background', 'differential association', 'cultural deprivation', 'opportunity theory', and a host of other 'theories' have debated the relative merits of their explanations *ad infinitum* (one might even say *ad nauseam*).

[. . .] Everyone commits crime. And many, many people whether they are poor, rich or middling are involved in a way of life that is criminal; and furthermore, no one, not even the professional thief or racketeer or corrupt politician commits *crime all the time*. To be sure, it may be politically useful to say that people become criminal through association with 'criminal behavior patterns', and thereby remove the tendency to look at criminals as pathological. But such a view has little scientific value, since it asks the wrong questions. It asks for a psychological cause of what is by its very nature a socio-political event. Criminality is simply *not* something that people have or don't have; crime is not something some people do and others don't. Crime is a matter of who can pin the label on whom, and underlying this socio-political process is the structure of social relations determined by the political economy.

[. . .]

The argument that criminal acts, that is, acts which are a violation of criminal law, are more often committed by members of the lower classes is not tenable. Criminal acts are widely distributed throughout the social classes in capitalist societies. The rich, the ruling, the poor, the powerless and the working classes *all* engage in criminal activities on a regular basis. It is in the enforcement of the law that the lower classes are subject to the effects of ruling class domination over the legal system, and which results in the appearance of a concentration of criminal acts among the lower classes in the official records. In actual practice, however, class differences in rates of criminal activity are probably negligible. What difference there is would be a difference in the type of criminal act, not in the prevalence of criminality.

The argument that the control of the state by the ruling class would lead to a lower propensity for crime among the ruling classes fails to recognize two fundamental facts. First is the fact that many acts committed by lower classes and which it is in the interests of the ruling class to control (e.g., crimes of violence, bribery of public officials, and crimes of personal choice, such as drug use, alcoholism, driving while intoxicated, homosexuality, etc.) are just as likely – or at least very likely – to be as widespread among the upper classes as the lower classes. Thus, it is crucial that the ruling class be able to control the discretion of the law enforcement agencies in ways that provide them with immunity; for example, having a legal system encumbered with procedural rules which only the wealthy can afford to implement and which, if implemented, nearly guarantees immunity from prosecution, not to mention more direct control through bribes, coercion and the use of political influence.

The Marxian paradigm must also account for the fact that the law will also reflect conflict between members of the ruling class (or between members of the ruling class and the upper class 'power elites' who manage the bureaucracies). So, for example, laws restricting the formation of trusts, misrepresentation in advertising, the necessity for obtaining licenses to engage in business practices are all laws which generally serve to reduce competition among the ruling classes and to concentrate capital in a few hands. However, the laws also apply universally, and therefore apply to the ruling class as well. Thus, when they break these laws they are committing criminal acts. Again, the enforcement practices obviate the effectiveness of the laws, and guarantee that the ruling class will rarely feel the sting of the laws, but their violation remains a fact with which we must reckon.

[. . .]

## Summary and conclusion

As Gouldner and Fredrichs have recently pointed out, social science generally, and sociology in particular is in the throes of a 'paradigm revolution'.[15] Predictably, criminology is both a reflection of and a force behind this revolution.

The emerging paradigm in criminology is one which emphasizes social conflict – particularly conflicts of social class interests and values. The paradigm which is being replaced is one where the primary emphasis was on consensus, and within which 'deviance' or 'crime' was viewed as an aberration shared by some minority. This group had failed to be properly socialized or adequately integrated into society or, more generally, had suffered from 'social disorganization'.

The shift in paradigm means more than simply a shift from explaining the same facts with new causal models. It means that we stretch our conceptual framework and look to different facets of social experience. Specifically, instead of resorting inevitably to the 'normative system', to 'culture' or to socio-psychological experiences of individuals, we look instead to the social relations created by the political and economic structure. Rather than treating 'society' as a full-blown reality (reifying it into an entity with its own life), we seek to understand the present as a reflection of the economic and political history that has created the social relations which dominate the moment we have selected to study.

The shift means that crime becomes a rational response of some social classes to the realities of their lives. The state becomes an instrument of the ruling class enforcing laws here but not there, according to the realities of political power and economic conditions.

There is much to be gained from this re-focusing of criminological and sociological inquiry. However, if the paradigmatic revolution is to be more than a mere fad, we must be able to show that the new paradigm is in fact superior to its predecessor. In this paper I have tried to develop the theoretical implications of a Marxian model of crime and criminal law [. . .] The general conclusion is that the Marxian paradigm provides a long neglected but fruitful approach to the study of crime and criminal law.

## Notes

1 Primary source materials for Marx's analysis of crime and criminal law are: *Capital, v.1* (London, Lawrence and Wishart, 1970), pp. 231–98, 450–503, 556–7, 574, 674–8, 718–25, 734–41; *The Cologne Communist Trial* (London, Lawrence and Wishart, 1971); *The German Ideology (1845–6)* (London, Lawrence and Wishart, 1965), pp. 342–79; *Theories of Surplus Value, v. 1*, pp. 375–6; 'The state and the law', in T.B. Bottomore and Maximilien Rubel (eds), *Karl Marx: Selected Writings in Sociology and Social Philosophy* (New York, McGraw-Hill, 1965), pp. 215–31.

2 In the United Sates the proportion of the population living in poverty is between 15 and 30 per cent of the labor force.

3 Marx, *Theories of Surplus Value*, pp. 375–6.

4 For an excellent statement of differences in 'order and conflict' theories, see John Horton, 'Order and conflict approaches to the study of social problems', *American Journal of Sociology*, May (1966); see also Gerhard Lenski, *Power and Privilege* (New York, McGraw-Hill, 1966); William J. Chambliss, *Sociological Readings in the Conflict Perspective* (Reading, MA, Addison-Wesley, 1973).

5 Jerome Hall, *General Principles of Criminal Law* (Indianapolis, Bobbs-Merrill, 1947), pp. 356–7.

6 For a more thorough analysis of this issue, see William J. Chambliss 'The state, the law and the definition of behavior as criminal or delinquent, in Daniel Glaser (ed.), *Handbook of Criminology* (Chicago, Rand McNally, 1974), ch. 1, pp. 7–43.

7 Svend Ranulf, *The Jealousy of the Gods*, vols 1 and 2 (London, Williams and Northgate, 1932) and *Moral Indignation and Middle Class Psychology* (Copenhagen, Levin and Monkagord, 1938); Joseph Gusfield, *Symbolic Crusade: Status Politics and the American Temperance Movement* (Urbana, Ill., University of Illinois Press, 1963).

8 Gusfield, *Symbolic Crusade*; see also Andrew Sinclair *Era of Excess: A Social History of the Prohibition Movement* (New York, Harper and Row, 1964).

9 Jerome Hall, *Theft, Law and Society* (Indianapolis: Bobbs-Merill and Co., 1952); William J. Chambliss, 'A sociological analysis of the law of vagrancy', *Social Problems*, Summer (1964), pp. 67–77.

10 James M. Graham, 'Profits at all costs: amphetamine profits on Capitol Hill', *Transaction*, January (1972), pp. 14–23.

11 Gabriel Kolko, *Railroads and Regulations* (Princeton, NJ, Princeton University Press, 1965) and *The Triumph of Conservatism* (New York, The Free Press of Glencoe, 1963).

12 Alfred R. Lindesmith, *The Addict and the Law* (Bloomington, Ind., Indiana University Press, 1965); Edwin M. Lemert, *Social Action and Legal Change: Revolution Within the Juvenile Court* (Chicago, Aldine, 1964); Troy Duster, *The Legislation of Morality: Law, Drugs and Moral Judgement* (New York, The Free Press, 1970).

13 Pamela A. Roby, 'Politics and criminal law: revision of the New York State Penal Law on Prostitution', *Social Problems*, Summer (1969), pp. 83–109.

14 William J. Chambliss and Robert B. Seidman, *Law, Order and Power* (Reading, MA, Addison-Wesley, 1971).

15 Alvin W. Gouldner, *The Coming Crisis in Western Sociology* (New York, Basic Books, 1970); Robert W. Frederichs, *A Sociology of Sociology* (New York, The Free Press, 1970). For a more general discussion of paradigm revolution in science, see Thomas S. Kuhn, *The Structure of Scientific Revolutions*, 2nd edn (Chicago, University of Chicago Press, 1970).

21

# The new criminology

## Ian Taylor, Paul Walton and Jock Young

[. . .]

The *formal* requirements of [a fully social theory of deviance] are concerned with the scope of the theory. It must be able to cover, and sustain, the connections between:

### 1 The wider origins of the deviant act

The theory must be able, in other words, to place the act in terms of its wider structural origins. These 'structural' considerations will involve recognition of the intermediate structural questions that have traditionally been the domain of sociological criminology (e.g. ecological areas,[1] subcultural location,[2] distribution of opportunities for theft) (cf. Armstrong and Wilson, 1973) but it would place these against the overall social context of inequalities of power, wealth and authority in the developed industrial society. Similarly, there would be consideration of the questions traditionally dealt with by psychologists concerned with the structures conducive to individual breakdown, that is with an individual's exclusion from 'normal' interaction (Hepworth, 1971, 1972). But, again, there would be an attempt, as in the later work of the anti-psychiatry school, to place these psychological concerns (e.g. with the schizophrenic nature of the bourgeois nuclear family) in the context of a society in which families are just one part of an interrelating but contradictory structural whole. The move would be away from the view of man as an atomistic individual, cut off within families or other specific subcultural situations, insulated from the pressures of existence under the prevailing social conditions.

The wider origins of the deviant act could only be understood, we would argue, in terms of the rapidly changing economic and political contingencies of advanced industrial society. At this level, the formal requirement is really for what might be called *a political economy of crime*.

### 2 Immediate origins of the deviant act

It is, of course, the case, however, that men do not experience the constraints of a society in an undifferentiated fashion. Just as subcultural theorists, operating in the anthropological tradition, have argued that the subcultural notion is useful to explain the different kinds of ways in which men resolve

Abridged from *The New Criminology*, pp. 268–82. (London: Routledge, 1973.)

the problems posed by the demands of a dominant culture (Downes, 1966: ch. 1), so we would argue that an adequately social theory of deviance must be able to explain the different events, experiences or structural developments that precipitate the deviant act. The theory must explain the different ways in which structural demands are interpreted, reacted against, or used by men at different levels in the social structure, in such a way that an essentially deviant choice is made. The formal requirement, at this level, that is, is for a *social psychology of crime*: a social psychology which, unlike that which is implicit in the work of the social reaction theorists, recognizes that men may *consciously* choose the deviant road, as the one solution to the problems posed by existence in a contradictory society (cf. Hepworth, 1971, 1972; L. Taylor, 1972).

## 3 The actual act

Men may choose to engage in particular solutions to their problems, without being able to carry them out. An adequate social theory of deviance would need to be able to explain the relationship between beliefs and action, between the optimum 'rationality' that men have chosen and the behaviours they actually carry through. A working-class adolescent, for example, confronted with blockage of opportunity, with problems of status frustration, alienated from the kind of existence offered out to him in contemporary society, may want to engage in hedonistic activities (e.g. finding immediate pleasure through the use of alcohol, drugs, or in extensive sexual activities) or he may choose to kick back at a rejecting society (e.g. through acts of vandalism). He may also attempt to assert some degree of control over, for example, the pace at which he is asked to work (cf. L. Taylor and Walton, 1971) or the ways in which his leisure time interests are controlled (cf. S. Cohen, 1972a; I. Taylor, 1971a, 1971b). But he may find that these options themselves are not easily achieved. Cloward and Ohlin have argued that adolescent 'drop-outs' in the United States, failures in the legitimate society, can also experience 'double-failure' in being rejected in delinquent sub-cultures themselves. Deviant individuals can find that they are rejected by other deviants (as 'uncool', physically inadequate or unattractive, or generally undesirable). Whilst we would argue that there is always a relationship between individual choice (a set of beliefs) and action it is not necessarily a simple one: an adolescent boy could choose the hedonistic, the rejective or the assertive options without there being any chance of sustaining them. Adjustments of some kind would then be necessitated. The formal requirement at this level then is for an explanation of the ways in which the actual acts of men are explicable in terms of the rationality of choice or the constraints on choice at the point of precipitation into action. The formal requirement, here, is for an account of real *social dynamics* surrounding the actual acts.

## 4 Immediate origins of social reaction

Just as the deviant act itself may be precipitated by the reactions of others (e.g. as a result of an adolescent's attempt to win acceptance as 'cool' or 'tough' in a subculture of delinquency, or from a businessman's attempt to show ability as a sharp practitioner) so the subsequent definition of the act is the product of close personal relationships. A certain behaviour may encourage a member of the actor's family or peer group to refer that actor to a doctor, to a child guidance clinic, or to a psychiatrist (because that behaviour is seen to be odd). Or another behaviour may result in the individual being reported to the police by people outside the individual's immediate family circle or friendship group (because he has been acting suspiciously, or actually been seen committing an illegal act). In both instances, there is a degree of choice on the part of the social audience: it may be thought that the behaviour *is* odd, but that it is preferable to keep it in the family; or it may be thought that although the individual *has* been acting suspiciously or has been behaving illegally, it would be too troublesome to involve the police.

Even when the formal agencies of social control themselves – in particular, the police, but also the various agencies of the 'Welfare State' – directly apprehend the individual in the course of his law-breaking (which is relatively rare), a degree of choice is exercised by the agent in his reaction to the deviant. The complex mix of classical liberalism (emphasizing, for example, 'police discretion' and the role of the local constable as a part-time social worker) and the lay theories of criminality (emphasizing what a real criminal, hooligan, junkie, or 'villain' actually looks like)[3] contributes to the moral climate and lays down the boundaries within which informal social reaction to deviance is likely to occur.

The requirement at this level is for an explanation of the immediate reaction of the social audience in terms of the range of choices available to that audience. The requirement, in other words, is for a *social psychology of social reaction*: an account of the contingencies and the conditions which are crucial to the decision to act against the deviant.

## 5 Wider origins of deviant reaction

In the same way that the choices available to the deviant himself are a product of his structural location, primarily, and, secondarily, his *individual* attributes (his acceptability to significant others – both those involved in legitimate activity and those who are engaged in rule-breaking activity of one kind or another), so the social psychology of social reaction (and the lay theories of deviance behind it) is explicable only in terms of the position and the attributes of those who instigate the reaction against the deviant. It is obviously the case that members of a law-breaker's immediate family group are far less likely to react against his activity than those who are strangers to him.[4] But it is also the case that the 'lay' theories of criminality and deviance adhered to by strangers will vary enormously: social work ideology (with its positivistic stress on reform) is continually at odds with the more classically punitive ideologies of correctional institutions and their controllers; police ideology is sometimes at odds with the philosophies of courtroom practice (in particular, the adjudicatory powers of the non-professional jury);[5] and even amongst those without formal positions in the structure of social control (the 'public') the lay theories found to be acceptable will vary across the contours of social class, ethnic group and age (Simmons and Chambers, 1965).

The predominant tendencies in criminological treatments of the wider origins of deviant reaction, so far as they have been dealt with at all, have been to see these as located in occupational groups and their particular needs

(Box, Dickson), in a rather ambiguously defined set of pluralistic interests (Quinney, Lemert), in authority–subject relationships within 'imperatively-coordinated associations' (Turk), or in simple superordinate–subordinate political relationships (Becker). All of these treatments of the sources of reactions against the deviant are, of course, implicit political sociologies of the state; and [. . .] few criminologists have really grappled in an effective way with the debates about social structure in the traditions of grand social theory. In particular, few criminologists have been able to deal with the ways in which the political initiatives that give rise to (or abolish) legislation, that define sanctionable behaviour in society or ensure the enforcement of that legislation, are intimately bound up with the structure of the *political economy* of the state. Sutherland's treatment of white-collar crime, for example, was informed hardly at all by an examination of the ways in which white-collar infractions were (and are) functional to industrial-capitalist societies at points in their development: rather it was concerned with illuminating what he saw to be the inequitable use of law in controlling behaviour in defiance of formally defined rules of conduct (cf. Pearce, 1973). The fact that the political sociologies of crime in criminology remain implicit and ambiguous is some indication of the extent to which criminology has moved away from the concerns of the classical social thinkers. [. . .] [I]t was impossible for Durkheim to conceive of crime and deviance without his conceiving also of a certain set of productive social arrangements overarched by a certain collective conscience (a forced division of labour being associated with 'functional rebellion' as well as with the 'skewed deviant' adaptation). [. . .] [F]or him it was impossible to talk of the dimunition of crime without talking politically of the abolition of the forced division of labour, the abolition of inherited wealth, and the setting up of occupational associations in tune with (politically enforceable) social arrangements based on a biological meritocracy. [. . .] Marx's political sociology of crime was also inextricably bound up with a political critique and a clear-headed analysis of existing social arrangements. For him, crime was expression of men's situation of constraint within alienating social arrangements – and in part an indication of a struggle to overcome them. The fact that criminal action was no political answer in itself to those situations was explained in terms of the political and social possibilities of the *Lumpenproletariat* as a parasitical agency on the organized working class itself. [. . .] [F]or the time being, it is sufficient to mention them not only as evidence of the *dilution of theory* in twentieth century investigations of crime but also as an indictment of the *depoliticization* of the issues involved in the classical discussions in social theory on crime, accomplished and applauded by those who carry out work in the field of contemporary 'applied' criminology.

For the moment it is sufficient to assert that one of the important formal requirements of a fully social theory of deviance, that is almost totally absent in existing literature, is an effective model of the political and economic imperatives that underpin on the one hand the 'lay ideologies' and on the other the 'crusades' and initiatives that emerge periodically either to control the amount and level of deviance (cf. Manson and Palmer, 1973) or else (as in the cases of prohibition, certain homosexual activity, and, most recently, certain 'crimes without victims') to remove certain behaviours from the category of 'illegal' behaviours. We are lacking a *political economy of social reaction*.

## 6 The outcome of the social reaction on deviants' further action

One of the most telling contributions of the social reaction theorists to an understanding of deviance was their emphasis on the need to understand deviant action as being, in part, an attempt to come to terms by the rule-breaker with the reaction against his initial infraction. [. . .] [O]ne of the superficial strengths of the social reaction perspective was its ability to see the actor as using the reaction against him in a variety of ways (that is, in exercising choice). This [was] an advance on the deterministic view of the impact of sanctions on further behaviour in positivistic views of 'reform', 'rehabilitation', and, most particularly, 'conditioning'. We argue, however, that the notion of secondary deviation was undialectical; that is, that it could have the same status as an explanation of what the social reaction theorists separate out as primary deviation, and that, in reality, it might be impossible to distinguish between the causes of primary and secondary deviation.

A fully social theory of deviance – premised on the notion of man as consciously involved (however inarticulately) in deviant choices – would require us to see the reaction he evolves to rejection or stigmatization (or, for that matter, sanction in the form of institutionalization) as being bound up with the conscious choices that precipitated the initial infraction. It would require us to reject the view which is paramount in Lemert's discussion of secondary deviation (1967: 51), namely that 'most people drift into deviance by specific actions rather than by formed choices of social roles and statuses' and that, because of this, they unintentionally, unwittingly and (implicitly) rather tragically enter what Lemert terms a 'staging area set up for an ideological struggle between the deviant seeking to normalize his actions and thoughts, and agencies seeking the opposite (1967: 44). Actually, Lemert [. . .] is not able to show that the problems faced by the deviant are always the result of his being apprehended and reacted against (either formally or informally) in this rather straightforward sense. He writes at one point (1967: 48) that:

> Becoming an admitted homosexual ('coming out') may endanger one's livelihood or professional career, but it also absolves the individual from failure to assume the heavy responsibilities of marriage and parenthood, and it is a ready way of fending off painful involvements in heterosexual affairs.

In other words, the act of breaking through what Gouldner has termed the normalized repression of everyday routine expectations, consciously and wittingly, does not always require precipitation in the form of social reaction. It only requires one to know one's enemy and to know how to deal with the stigmatization and exclusion that may then result. Just as a homosexual preparing to 'come out' may take a long time to prepare his revelation (and thus be consciously prepared for the reaction against him), so any deviant can be understood as having some degree of consciousness of what to expect in the event of apprehension and reaction. A fully social explanation of the outcome of social reaction to the further actions of the apprehended deviant, therefore, would be one in which the deviant actor is always endowed with some degree of consciousness about the likelihood and consequences of reaction against him, and in which his subsequent decisions are developed from that initial degree of consciousness.[6] All those writers who see deviants as 'naive' must now realize that they are dealing with a minority of deviants, even in situations where the degree or extent of social reaction is unexpected (because, for example, of a moral panic amongst the powerful about a particular kind of offence, or because a campaign of control has been instigated against it – as in the case of the white adolescents who received unexpectedly heavy sentences for their role during the Notting Hill race riots in 1959), it would still be important to have a social explanation of the ways in which the deviants responded to their sentences with a degree of consciousness about 'the law' which they had developed before they had had a formal contact with it.

In a fully social theory, then, the consciousness conventionally allowed deviants in the secondary deviation situation would be seen as explicable – at least in part – in terms of the actors' consciousness of the world in general.

## 7 The nature of the deviant process as a whole

The formal requirements of a fully social theory are formal in the sense that they refer to the *scope* of the theoretical analysis. In the real world of social action, these analytical distinctions merge, connect and often appear to be indistinguishable. We have already indicted social reaction theory, which is in many ways the most sophisticated rejection of the simpler forms of positivism (concentrating as they do on the pathologies of the individual actor), as onesidedly deterministic: in seeing the deviant's problems and consciousness simply as a response to apprehension and the application of social control. Positivistic explanations stand accused of being unable to approach an explanation not only of the *political economy* of crime (the background to criminal action) but also of what we have called the *political economy*, the *social psychology* and the *social dynamics* of social reaction to deviance. And most of the classical and earlier biological psychological positivists [. . .] are unable to offer out even a satisfactorily social explanation of the relationship between the individual and society: the individual in these accounts appears by and large as an isolated atom unaffected by the ebb and flow of social arrangements, social change, and contradictions in what is, after all, a society of social arrangements built around the capitalist mode of production.

The central requirement of a fully social theory of deviance, however, is that these formal requirements must not be treated simply as essential factors all of which need to be present (in invariant fashion) if the theory is to be social. Rather it is that these formal requirements must all appear in the theory, as they do in the real world, in a complex, dialectical relationship to one another. Georg Lukács's criticism of Solzhenitsyn's early work is instructive here, if only because it is so well applicable to the work of Goffman, Garfinkel, Becker, Lemert and other thinkers who have been concerned with the impact that 'social control' (whether institutional or otherwise) has on its victims. Writing of Solzhenitsyn's early work on the prison camp (which Lukács correctly takes as a metaphor intended to apply to the whole society), Lukács (1971) observed that:

Solzhenitsyn's development . . . of [his] technique from his first story not only, of necessity, increases the number of prisoners whose life is shown . . . it also demands that the initiators and organisers of this internment of large masses of people must also be depicted on a wider basis and more concretely. . . . Only thus does the 'place of action' receive its concrete socially determined significance. . . . In the last resort it is a social fact that the internment camp confronts both its victims and its organisers spontaneously and irresistibly with its provocative basic questions . . .

[. . .]

The great merit of Solzhenitsyn, using the skills and the techniques of the novelist, is that he is able, in a way that many formal models in existing social theory are not, to encompass the substance of man in his many manifestations. Man is both determined by the fact of his imprisonment, and also determining, in the sense that he creates (and is able to struggle against) his own imprisonment. Some men (the guards) have interests (up to a point) in the maintenance of imprisonment; others (the inmates, their relatives and sympathizers) do not. There is, in Solzhenitsyn's 'prison', a sense of the contingencies and sequences that may lead some men to imprison others: a view of the social and political origins of repression and the segregation of deviants. There is some conception too of the real political, material and symbolic imperatives that lie at the back of such sequences and processes. And, finally, there is an implicit prescription in Solzhenitsyn, a *politics* for which he is now experiencing exclusion and segregation himself, a politics which implies that man is able consciously to abolish the imprisonment that he consciously created.

It may well be, as Lukács's criticism implies, that these substantive features of Solzhenitsyn's writings are not held together and continuously, in an ongoing dialectic of resistance and control. Nevertheless, Solzhenitsyn's attempts to achieve this fare well by comparison with many sociological excursions into the area. The substantive history of twentieth century criminology is, by and large, the history of the empirical emasculation of theories (like those of Marx and Durkheim) which attempted to deal with the whole society, and a history therefore of the depoliticization of criminological issues.

## The new criminology

The conditions of our time are forcing a reappraisal of this compartmentalization of issues and problems. It is not just that the traditional focus of applied criminology on the socially deprived working-class adolescent is being thrown into doubt by the criminalization of vast numbers of middle-class youth (for 'offences' of a hedonistic or specifically oppositional nature) (S. Cohen, 1971c; I. Taylor, 1971d). Neither is it only that the crisis of our institutions has deepened to the point where the 'master institutions' of the state, and of the political economy, are unable to disguise their own inability to adhere to their own rules and regulations (cf. Kennedy, 1970; Pearce, 1973). It is largely that the total interconnectedness of these problems and others is being revealed.

A criminology which is to be adequate to an understanding of these developments, and which will be able to bring politics back into the discussion of what were previously technical issues, will need to deal with the society as a totality. This 'new' criminology will in fact be an *old* criminology, in that it will face the same problems that were faced by the classical social theorists. Marx saw the problem with his usual clarity when he began to develop his critique of the origins of German idealism:

The first work which I undertook for a solution to the doubts which assailed me was a critical review of the Hegelian philosophy of right, a work the introduction to which appeared in 1844 in the *Deutsch-Französische Jahrbücher* published in Paris. My investigations led to the result that legal relations as well as forms of state are to be grasped neither from themselves nor from the so-called general development of the human mind, but rather have their roots in the material conditions of life, the sum total of which Hegel, following the example of Englishmen and Frenchmen of the eighteenth century, combines under the name 'civil society', that however the anatomy of civil society is to be sought in political economy. (1951: 328–9)

We have argued here for a political economy of criminal action, and of the reaction it excites, and for a politically informed social psychology of these ongoing social dynamics. We have, in other words, laid claim to have constructed the formal elements of a theory that would be adequate to move criminology out of its own imprisonment in artificially segregated specifics. We have attempted to bring the parts together again in order to form the whole.

Implicitly, we have rejected that contemporary trend which may claim for itself the mantle of a new criminology, or a new deviance theory, and which presumably claims to find a solution to our present discontents largely in the search for the sources of individual meaning. Ethnomethodology, however, is a historical creature too: its pedigree goes back to the phenomenological contemplations that were so prominent in an earlier period of uncertainty and doubt: the collapse of European social democracy and the rise of fascism. Phenomenology looks at the prison camp and searches for the *meaning* of the 'prison' rather than for its alternative; and it searches for the meaning in terms of individual definitions rather than in terms of a political explanation of the necessity to imprison.

Indeed, one of the recurring criticisms we have [. . .] of many theorists [. . .] is the way in which they place men apart from society. The view of man in society is sometimes *additive* (in the sense that environmental 'factors' are seen as having a more or less significant impact on some fundamental fact of human nature – as in Eysenck); sometimes it is *discontinuous* (in that there is a recognition of interplay between man and social influences, but an interplay which is curtailed by men's differential ability to be socialized – as in Durkheim – or in the appropriateness of certain social patterns for different men in different periods – as in Durkheim and in Merton), and when there is a fusion of man and society, it is only in terms of man's given biological or psychological pathologies (which, for example, force him to gravitate into delinquent areas, as in Shaw and Mackay and the early ecologists). Phenomenology and ethnomethodology make the break between man and society by reifying experience and meaning, as specifics in their own right, which we cannot take (for granted) to be socially determined in any currently identifiable manner.

Increasingly, it is becoming clear that the contemplation and suspension involved in these (and other) traditions are not enough. There is a crisis not just in social theory and social thought (Gouldner, 1971) but in the society itself. The new criminology must therefore be a normative theory: it must hold out the possibilities of a resolution to the fundamental questions, and a social resolution.

It is this normative imperative that separates out the European schools of criminology from the eclecticism and reformism in professional American sociology (cf. Nicolaus, 1969)[7]. The domination of orthodox positivism over European criminology has been most clearly challenged recently by the emergence of a social welfare-oriented criminology in Scandinavia, centring particularly around the Institute of Criminology and Criminal Law at the University of Oslo, and by the beginnings of a politically informed 'structuralism' in the formation of the National Deviancy Conference in Britain.

The new Scandinavian criminology, which has been several years in the making (N. Christie, 1965, 1968, 1971; Mathiesen, 1965, 1972) has been fundamentally concerned with the description and explanation of the forms assumed, as the titles of their publications imply, by the 'aspects of social control in welfare states'. Working in relatively underpopulated societies, and in the urban centres where the major bureaucracies of the city and the university were constantly meeting up and interpenetrating, the Scandinavian criminologist originally took on a role and an ideology not unlike that of the early Chicago ecologists – or indeed the role of the cautious rebel as advocated by Merton. That is, they acted as agitators of public opinion *and* advisers to governments on questions of prison administration, the reform of juvenile training schools, preventive programmes and the like. The result of this interpenetration was not so much the alleviation of social problems or of social control as it was the co-optation of the new criminologists. The new criminology has now split, on friendly terms, into two distinct tendencies: on the one hand, the poetic social democratic, and the other, the direct action revolutionary.

The first tendency is described by Nils Christie (1971):

> We have not made clear that our role as criminologists is not first and foremost to be received as useful problem-solvers, *but as problem-raisers*. Let us turn our weakness into strength by admitting – and enjoying – that our situation has a great resemblance to that of artists and men of letters. We are working on a culture of deviance and social control. . . . Changing times create new situations and bring us to new crossroads. Together with other cultural workers – because these fields are central to all observers of society – but equipped with our special training in scientific method and theory, it is our obligation as well as pleasure to penetrate these problems. Together with other cultural workers, we will probably have to keep a constant fight going against being absorbed, tamed, and made responsible, and thereby completely socialized into society – as it is.

For Thomas Mathiesen and others, however, the limitations of the original social welfare approach to social control did not dissolve simply into the problem of avoiding personal co-option. For him, the problem, even in the relatively benign atmosphere of Scandinavia, was action; to change society 'as it is': not simply to describe 'The Defences of the Weak' but to organize them. The normative prescription of the new Scandinavian criminology led to the formation of the KRUM, a trade union for inmates of Scandinavian prisons, and a union which was able [in 1971] to co-ordinate a prison strike across three national boundaries and across several prison walls (Mathiesen, 1972).

Something of the same dilemma faces the normative criminology of the kind being developed in Britain (cf. S. Cohen, 1971a; Rock, 1973; Rock and McIntosh, 1973; I. Taylor, 1971d) and advocated via an immanent critique of other explanations of crime, deviance and dissent. [. . .] The retreat from theory is over, and the politicization of crime and criminology is imminent. Close reading of the classical social theorists reveals a basic agreement; the abolition of crime *is* possible under certain social arrangements. Even

Durkheim, with his notion of human nature as a fixed biological given, was able to allow for the substantial diminution of crime under conditions of a free division of labour, untramelled by the inequalities of inherited wealth and the entrenchment of interests of power and authority (by those who were not deserving of it).

It should be clear that a criminology which is not normatively committed to the abolition of inequalities of wealth and power, and in particular of inequalities in property and life-chances, is inevitably bound to fall into correctionalism. And all correctionalism is irreducibly bound up with the identification of deviance with pathology. A fully social theory of deviance must, by its nature, break entirely with correctionalism (even with social reform of the kind advocated by the Chicagoans, the Mertonians and the romantic wing of Scandinavian criminology) precisely because [. . .] the causes of crime must be intimately bound up with the form assumed by the social arrangements of the time. Crime is ever and always that behaviour seen to be problematic within the framework of those social arrangements: for crime to be abolished, then, those social arrangements themselves must also be subject to fundamental social change.

It has often been argued, rather misleadingly, that for Durkheim *crime* was a normal social fact (that it was thus a fundamental feature of human ontology). For us, as for Marx and for other new criminologists, *deviance* is normal – in the sense that men are now consciously involved (in the prisons that are contemporary society and in the real prisons) in asserting their human diversity. The task is not merely to 'penetrate' these problems, not merely to question the stereotypes, or to act as carriers of 'alternative phenomenological realities'. The task is to create a society in which the facts of human diversity, whether personal, organic or social, are not subject to the power to criminalize.

## Notes

1 A highly suggestive attempt to wed the concerns of ecological analysis with the wider context of power, authority and political domination is made by Gail Armstrong and Mary Wilson (1973).

2 The largely uncharted history of youth subcultures in Britain since the war is at last being attempted against the background of some kind of structural analysis. (Cf. P. Cohen, 1972; S. Cohen, 1971a, 1972a 1972b; Rock and Cohen, 1970; Willis, 1972.)

3 The notion of 'lay theories of criminality' is taken up by Box (1971: 180–1) in a discussion of the particular 'theories' informing the everyday exercise of police discretion. He writes:

> In order to cope with the chaos of an infinite number of suspects, the police develop theories on the causes of crime and the nature of the criminal. These theories are refractions of professional theories, past and present, which have been transmitted, like rumours, from the writings of 'experts' through the mass media and into the heads of the lay public, including policemen, who then mould and slightly recast them to fit in with their occupational experiences, and to facilitate occupational performances.

One of the central features of lay theories, as adopted by the police and the magistracy in particular, is what one of the present authors has termed their 'absolutist' view of society. In this version of 'theory', deviants are divided into the real – committed, pathological – types (e.g. the drug-pusher, or, as in Yablonsky, the disturbed sociopath who wins positions of authority in working-class fighting gangs and in the middle-class communes of hippies) on the one hand, and the misled innocents on the other (the immature and stupid youth who buys –

under pressure – from the ruthless pusher; or the ordinary street-kid who follows a gang leader because he has no healthy youth club leader as an alternative focus of identification). Cf. the discussion of the ways in which policemen encourage the drug-user to accept this distinction in exchange for sympathetic treatment in court, in Young (1971a: 188–9).

4 This is evidenced, most significantly, in the low rate of reportability of certain kinds of sexual offences (e.g. forcible rape) – a large proportion of which (contrary to media representation) occur within family groups or amongst relatively close acquaintances (cf. for example, Menachem Amir, 1967, 1971).

5 From time to time, of course, attempts are made by one interest group to win other groups to its own version of lay theory. At the time of writing, for example, proposals are being mooted by the Criminal Law Revision Committee (under pressure from the Police Federation, the press and others) to the Home Secretary in the United Kingdom, to withdraw certain safeguards traditionally accorded defendants. The net effect of these proposals (centring around the withdrawal of the right to remain silent, the placing of the accused in the witness-box and the admissibility of forcibly obtained confessions) would be that the lay theory of the non-professional juries would be replaced as the decisive courtroom reality by the lay theory adhered to by the police (cf. Michael Zander, *Guardian*, 7 April 1972).

6 It is worth noting that studies of prison subcultures are moving precisely in this direction. Where many writers have adopted a view of inmates as relatively passive and malleable creatures of institutional regime, capable at most of what Goffman terms 'secondary adjustment' in the face of the mortification of imprisonment, there has been a tendency in recent literature towards an examination of 'what the inmates bring with them'. This tendency has been most noticeable in studies of adult prisons, and in a sense is an inevitable consequence of the rise of the prison movement in the United States (especially amongst blacks and especially in California), the inmate unions in Scandinavia, some acts of resistance in British maximum security prisons and the formation of the Preservation of Rights of Prisoners. Cf. L. Taylor and S. Cohen (1972); and also, in a less detailed and empirical fashion, John Irwin and Donald Cressey (1962). Less dramatic evidence of the connections between the consciousness of *juvenile* delinquents prior to apprehension and their 'adjustments' in juvenile institutions is presented in an unpublished paper 'Theories of action in juvenile correctional institutions', by Ian Taylor (1971c).

7 The eclecticism of American criminology and deviancy theory is probably explicable partly in terms of a critique of American social thought in general, of the kind that Gouldner is currently engaged in. For the time being we can characterize the two central themes in American criminology as reformism and millenarianism, both of which have in common a theoretical naïveté and a normative incongruity. Criminal lawyers like Sanford Kadish and 'radical' sociologists like Howard Becker can both identify the 'care-taking institutions' as 'overcriminalizing' American youth and American deviants in general, and argue for change at the attitude level amongst the guardians of public order (Becker, 1967, 1972; Kadish, 1968). The more radical wing can respond to the politicization of deviance and the rise of a prison movement amongst the black *Lumpenproletariat* by polemics which pass for theory, calling for the removal of a legal system which is unjust in its choice of victims (Quinney, 1972). The continuing crisis of American institutions, and the continuing polarization of social forces within the society, may result in a clarification of criminological politics, and a revival of theory to accompany it. As yet, these possibilities exemplify themselves only in an embryonic sociology of law (Chambliss and Siedman, 1971) and in a return to social history (Quinney, 1970; Weis, 1971) – both of these tendencies basing themselves on an ambiguous middle-range 'theory' of interest group conflict. They are open to all the limitations of the new conflict theorists in general.

## References

Amir, M. (1967) 'Patterns of forcible rape', in M.B. Clinard and R. Quinney (eds), *Criminal Behavior Systems*.New York: Holt, Rinehart and Winston.

Amir, M. (1971) *Patterns in Forcible Rape*. Chicago: University of Chicago Press.

Armstrong, G. and Wilson, M. (1973) 'City politics and deviancy amplification', in L. Taylor and I. Taylor (eds), *Politics and Deviance*. Harmondsworth: Penguin (for the National Deviancy Conference).

Becker, H.S. (1967) 'Whose side are we on?', *Social Problems*, 14(3): 239–47.

Becker, H.S. (1971) *Sociological Work*. London: Allen Lane.

Becker, H.S. (1972) 'Labelling theory revisited', in P. Rock and M. McIntosh, (eds) *Deviance and Social Control*. London: Tavistock.

Box, S. (1971) *Deviance, Reality and Society*. London: Holt, Rienhart and Winston.

Chambliss, W.J. and Siedman, R.B. (1971) *Law, Order and Power*. Reading, MA: Addison-Wesley.

Christie, N. et al. (1965, 1968, 1971) *Scandinavian Studies in Criminology*. London: Tavistock; Oslo: Universitetsforlaget (3 vols).

Christie, N. (1971) 'Scandinavian criminology facing the 1970's', in N. Christie et al. (1971), pp. 121–49.

Cohen, P. (1972) 'Subcultural conflict and working class community', in *Working Papers in Cultural Studies* (2) (Centre for Contemporary Cultural Studies, University of Birmingham). pp. 5–52.

Cohen, S. (ed.) (1971a) *Images of Deviance*. Harmondsworth: Penguin (for the National Deviancy Conference).

Cohen, S. (1971b) 'Directions for research on adolescent group violence and vandalism', *British Journal of Criminology*, 11(4): 319–40.

Cohen, S. (1971c) 'Protest, unrest and delinquency: convergences in labels or behaviour?'. Paper given to the International Symposium on Youth Unrest, Tel-Aviv, 25–27 October.

Cohen, S. (1972a) *Moral Panics and Folk Devils*. London: MacGibbon and Kee.

Cohen, S. (1972b) 'Breaking out, smashing up, and the social context of aspiration', in B. Riven (ed.), *Youth at the Beginning of the Seventies*. London: Martin Robertson.

Downes, D. (1966) *The Delinquent Solution*. London: Routledge and Kegan Paul.

Gouldner, A.W. (1971) *The Coming Crisis of Western Sociology*. London: Heinemann Educational (New York: Basic Books, 1970).

Hepworth, M. (1971) 'Deviants in disguise: blackmail and social acceptance', in S. Cohen (ed.), *Images of Deviance*. Harmondsworth: Penguin. pp. 192–218.

Hepworth, M. (1972) 'Missing persons', in P. Rock and M. McIntosh (eds), *Deviance and Social Control*. London: Tavistock.

Irwin, J. and Cressey, D. (1962) 'Thieves, convicts and the inmate culture', *Social Problems*, 10(2): 142–55.

Jackson, G. (1970) *Soledad Brother*. Harmondsworth: Penguin.

Kadish, S. (1968) 'The crisis of overcriminalization', *American Criminal Law Quarterly*, 7: 17.

Kennedy, M. (1970) 'Beyond incrimination: some neglected facets in the theory of punishment', *Catalyst*, 5 (Summer): 1–37.

Lemert, E.M. (1967) *Human Deviance, Social Problems and Social Control*. New York: Prentice-Hall.

Lukács, G. (1971) *Solzhenitsyn*. London: Merlin Press.

Manson, I. and Palmer, J. (1973) *The Dirty Old Man on the Last Tube: the Social Response to Pornography*. London: Davis-Poynter.

Marx, K. (1951) Preface to *A Contribution to the Critique of Political Economy*, in *Marx–Engels Selected Works*, vol. 1. Moscow: Foreign Languages Publishing House.

Mathiesen, T. (1965) *The Defences of the Weak: a Study of a Norwegian Correctional Institution*. London: Tavistock.

Mathiesen, T. (1972) *Beyond the Boundaries of Organizations*. California: Glendessary Press.

Nicolaus, M. (1969) 'The professional organization of sociology: a view from below', *Antioch Review*, Fall, pp. 375–87.

Pearce, F. (1973) 'Crime, corporations and the American social order', in L. Taylor and I. Taylor, (eds) *Politics and Deviance*. Harmondsworth: Penguin (for the National Deviancy Conference).

Quinney, R. (1970) *The Social Reality of Crime*. Boston: Little Brown and Co.

Quinney, R. (1972) 'The ideology of law: notes for a radical alternative to legal oppression', *Issues in Criminology*, 7(1): 1–36.

Rock, P. (1973) *A Sociology of Deviance*. London: Hutchinson.

Rock, P. and Cohen, S. (1970) 'The Teddy Boys', in V. Bogdanor and R. Skidelsky (eds), *The Age of Affluence 1951–1964*. London, Macmillan. pp. 288–320.

Rock, P. and McIntosh, M. (eds) (1973) *Deviance and Social Control.* London: Tavistock (for the British Sociological Association).

Simmons, J.L. and Chambers, H. (1965) 'Public stereotypes of deviants', *Social Problems*, 13: 223–32.

Taylor, I. (1971a) 'Soccer consciousness and soccer hooliganism', in S. Cohen (ed.), *Images of Deviance.* Harmondsworth: Penguin. pp. 134–64.

Taylor, I. (1971b) '"Football mad" – a speculative sociology of soccer hooliganism' in Eric Dunning (ed.), *The Sociology of Sport: a Selection of Readings.* London: Cass.

Taylor, I. (1971c) 'Theories of action in juvenile correctional institutions'. Unpublished paper given to the First Anglo-Scandinavian Seminar in Criminology, Norway, September 1971.

Taylor, I. (1971d) 'The new criminology in an age of doubt', *New Edinburgh Review*, 15 (November): 14–17.

Taylor, L. (1972) 'The significance and interpretation of replies to motivational questions: the case of sex offenders', *Sociology*, 6(1): 23–40.

Taylor, L. and Cohen, S. (1972) *Psychological Survival: the Experience of Long-Term Imprisonment.* Harmondsworth: Penguin.

Taylor, L. and Walton, P. (1971) 'Industrial sabotage: motives and meanings', in S. Cohen (ed.), *Images of Deviance.* Harmondsworth: Penguin.

Weis, J.G. (1971) 'Dialogue with David Matza', *Issues in Criminology*, 6(1): 33–53.

Willis, P. (1972) 'The motorbike within a subcultural group', *Working Papers in Cultural Studies*, 2 (Centre for Contemporary Cultural Studies, University of Birmingham).

Young, J. (1971a) *The Drugtakers: the Social Meaning of Drug Use.* London: MacGibbon and Kee/Paladin.

Young, J. (1971b) 'The role of the police as amplifiers of deviancy, negotiators of reality and translators of fantasy: some consequences of our present system of drug control as seen in Notting Hill', in S. Cohen (ed.), *Images of Deviance.* Harmondsworth: Penguin. pp. 27–61.

# 22

# Crime, power and ideological mystification

## Steven Box

Murder! Rape! Robbery! Assault! Wounding! Theft! Burglary! Arson! Vandalism! These form the substance of the annual official criminal statistics on indictable offences (or the Crime Index offences in America). Aggregated, they constitute the major part of 'our' crime problem. Or at least, we are told so daily by politicians, police, judges and journalists who speak to us through the media of newspapers and television. And most of us listen. We don't want to be murdered, raped, robbed, assaulted, or criminally victimized in any other way. Reassured that our political leaders are both aware of the problem's growing dimensions and receptive to our rising anxieties, we wait in optimistic but realistic anticipation for crime to be at least effectively reduced. But apart from the number of police rapidly increasing, their technological and quasi-military capacities shamelessly strengthened, their discretionary powers of apprehension, interrogation, detention and arrest liberally extended, and new prisons built or old ones extensively refurbished (all with money the government claims the country has not got to maintain existing standards of education, health, unemployment welfare, and social services), nothing much justifies the optimism.

The number of recorded serious crimes marches forever upward. During the decade 1970–80, serious crimes recorded by the police increased for nearly every category: violence against the person rose by 136 per cent, burglary by 44 per cent, robbery by 138 per cent, theft and handling by 54 per cent and fraud and forgery by 18 per cent. These increases were not merely artefacts of an increased population available to commit serious crimes. For even when the changing population size is controlled statistically, crimes continue to rise. Thus in 1950, there were 1,094 per 100,000 population. This rose to 1,742 by 1960, then to 3,221 by 1970, and reached 5,119 by 1980. From 1980 to 1981 they rose a further 10 per cent, to reach an all-time record. Ironically, as 'our' crime problem gets worse, the demand for even more 'law and order' policies increases, even though these are blatantly having no effect on the level of serious crimes. At least not on the level recorded by the police.

The result, so we are told, is that the 'fear of crime' has now been elevated into a national problem. Techniques for avoiding victimization have become a serious preoccupation: more locks on doors and windows, fewer visits after dark to family, friends, and places of entertainment, avoidance of underground and empty train carriages, mace sprays or personal alarm sirens held nervously in coat pockets, a growing unwillingness to be neighbourly or engage in local collective enterprises, furtive suspicious glances at any

From *Power, Crime and Mystification*, pp. 1–15. (London: Tavistock, 1983.)

stranger, and attempts to avoid any encounter except with the most trusted and close friends.

Who are these 'villains' driving us into a state of national agoraphobia? We are told a fairly accurate and terrifying glimpse can be obtained of 'our' Public Enemies by examining the convicted and imprisoned population. For every 100 persons convicted of these serious crimes, 85 are male. Amongst this convicted male population, those aged less than 30 years, and particularly those aged between 15 and 21 years are over-represented. Similarly, the educational non-achievers are over-represented – at the other end of the educational achievement ladder there appear to be hardly any criminals, since only 0.05 per cent of people received into prison have obtained a university degree. The unemployed are currently only (sic) 14 per cent of the available labour force, but they constitute approximately 40 per cent of those convicted. Only 4 per cent of the general population are black, but nearly one-third of the convicted and imprisoned population are black. Urban dwellers, particularly inner-city residents, are over-represented. Thus the typical people criminally victimizing and forcing us to fear each other and fracture our sense of 'community' are young uneducated males, who are often unemployed, live in a working-class impoverished neighbourhood, and frequently belong to an ethnic minority. These villains deserve, so 'law and order' campaigners tell us ceaselessly in their strident moral rhetoric, either short, sharp, shock treatment, including death by hanging or castration by chemotherapy – 'off with their goolies' – or long, endless, self-destroying stretches as non-paying guests in crumbling, insanitary, overcrowded prisons constructed for the redemption of lost Christian souls by our Victorian ancestors. If only these ideas were pursued vigorously and with a vengeance morally justified by the offender's wickedness, then 'our' society would be relatively crime-free and tranquil. So 'law and order' campaigners tell us.

It is tempting to call all this hype – but that would be extreme! 'Conventional' crimes do have victims whose suffering is real; steps should be taken to understand and control these crimes so that fewer and fewer people are victimized. A radical criminology which appears to deny this will be seen as callous and rightly rejected. Furthermore, those crimes so carefully recorded and graphed in official criminal statistics *are* more likely to be committed by young males, living in poor neighbourhoods and so on. A radical criminology which appears to deny this will be seen as naive and rightly rejected. Finally, there are very good grounds for believing that the rising crime wave is real – material conditions for large sections of the community have deteriorated markedly. A radical criminology which remained insensitive of this would be guilty of forgetting its theoretical roots and rightly rejected. So the official portrait of crime and criminals is not entirely without merit or truth.

None the less, before galloping off down the 'law and order' campaign trail, it might be prudent to consider whether murder, rape, robbery, assault, and other crimes focused on by state officials, politicians, the media, and the criminal justice system do constitute the major part of our real crime problem. Maybe they are only *a* crime problem and not *the* crime problem. Maybe what is stuffed into our consciousness as *the* crime problem is in fact an illusion, a trick to deflect our attention away from other, even more serious crimes and victimizing behaviours, which objectively cause the vast bulk of avoidable death, injury and deprivation.

At the same time, it might be prudent to compare persons who commit other serious but under-emphasized crimes and victimizing behaviours with those who are officially portrayed as 'our' criminal enemies. For if the former, compared to the latter, are indeed quite different types of people, then maybe we should stop looking to our political authorities and criminal justice system for protection from those beneath us in impoverished urban neighbourhoods. Instead maybe we should look up accusingly at our political and judicial 'superiors' for being or for protecting the 'real' culprits.

If we do this, we might also cast a jaundiced eye at the view that serious criminals are 'pathological'. This has been the favourite explanatory imagery of mainstream positivistic criminology. It was, however, an explanation that only remained plausible if crimes were indeed committed by a minority of individuals living in conditions of relative deprivation. For whilst this was true it was obvious, at least to the conservative mind, that 'something must be wrong with them'. However, if we look up rather than down the stratification hierarchy and see serious crimes being committed by the people who are respectable, well-educated, wealthy and socially privileged then the imagery of pathology seems harder to accept. If these upper- and middle-class criminals are also pathological, then what hope is there for any of us! Wanting to avoid this pessimistic conclusion, we might instead entertain the idea that these powerful persons commit crimes for 'rational' – albeit disreputable – motives which emerge under conditions that render conformity a relatively unrewarding activity. Having rescued the powerful from 'abnormality' we might do the same for the powerless. Maybe they too are rational rather than irrational, morally disreputable rather than organically abnormal, over-whelmed by adversity rather than by wickedness.

If these are the lessons of prudence, then standing back from the official portrait of crime and criminals and looking at it critically might be a very beneficial move towards getting our heads straight.

However, there is an agonizing choice to make between at least two pairs of spectacles we might wear to take this critical look. We could wear the liberal 'scientific' pair, as did many young trendy academics during the 1960s and early 1970s when the stars of interactionism and phenomenology were in the ascendant. Or we might wear the radical 'reflexive' pair, whose lenses have been recently polished to a fine smoothness by those same trendy academics who have now entered a middle-age period of intellectual enlightenment! These spectacles do provide quite different views on the official portrait of crime and criminals.

## Liberal 'scientism': partially blind justice

One way of getting a clear perspective on those crimes and criminals causing us most harm, injury and deprivation is to excavate unreported, unrecorded and non-prosecuted crimes. This can be achieved by sifting evidence from numerous self-reported crime studies and criminal victimization surveys. This is undoubtedly an important exercise for it leads us to reconsider the *validity* of official criminal statistics and the more extreme pronouncements made directly and uncritically from them.

What lessons are there to be learnt from the results of these surveys? First, there is much more serious crime being committed than the official police records indicate. The emerging consensus is that one serious crime in three (excluding burglary and car theft) is reported to the police. This knowledge can and does add fuel to the alarmist 'law and order' fire: 'it's even worse than we imagined!' Second, although the official portrait of criminals is not untrue, it is inaccurate. It is more like a distorting mirror; you immediately recognize yourself, but not quite in a flattering shape and form familiar to you. Thus self-report data indicate that serious crimes are disproportionately committed by the young uneducated males amongst whom the unemployed and ethnically oppressed are over-represented, but the contribution they make is less than the official data implies. There are, it appears, more serious crimes being committed by white, respectable, well-educated, slightly older males and females than we are led to believe (Box, 1981a: 56–93).

To the liberal 'scientific' mind, there are two problems here of 'slippage', one more slight than the other. Too many people fail to report crimes because they consider the police inefficient; we need to restore police efficiency in order to increase the reportage rate and hence obtain a better, more reliable gauge of crime. The second, more important slippage, is that the administration of criminal justice is fine in principle, but is failing slightly in practice. The police pursue policies of *differential deployment* (for example, swamping certain parts of London where the West Indian population is prominent) and *'methodological suspicion'* (that is, routinely suspecting only a limited proportion of the population, particularly those with criminal records or known criminal associates). Coupled with these practices are *plea-bargaining* (negotiating a guilty plea in return for being charged with a less serious offence) and *'judicious' judicial decisions* (which take as much notice of who you are as they do of what you have apparently done). In other words, the police, magistrates, judges, and other court officials have too much discretion. The result is too much 'street-justice', 'charge-dealing', 'plea-bargaining' and 'disparate sentencing'. In these judicial negotiations and compromises, the wealthy, privileged and powerful are better able to secure favourable outcomes than their less powerful counterparts (Box, 1981a: 157–207). This slippage between ideal and practice reveals a slightly disturbing picture. The process of law enforcement, in its broadest possible interpretation, operates in such a way as to *conceal* crimes of the powerful against the powerless, but to *reveal* and *exaggerate* crimes of the powerless against 'everyone'.

Furthermore, because a substantial section of this criminalized population is stigmatized and discriminated against, particularly in the field of employment, its reproduction is secured; many of them, out of resentment, injustice, or desperation, turn to more persistent and even more serious forms of crime. This vicious circle increases the over-representation of the powerless in the highly publicized 'hardened' criminal prisoner population.

The outcome of these processes is that the official portrait of crime and criminals is highly selective, serving to conceal crimes of the powerful and hence shore up their interests, particularly the need to be legitimated through maintaining the appearance of respectability. At the same time, crimes of the powerless are revealed and exaggerated, and this serves the interests of the powerful because it legitimizes their control agencies, such as the police and prison service, being strengthened materially, technologically and legally, so that their ability to survey, harass, deter, both specifically and generally, actual and potential resisters to political authority is enhanced.

To the liberal 'scientific' mind, a solution of this second and more important slippage would involve a strict limitation on police and judicial discretion and less stigmatization either by decriminalizing some behaviours, or imposing less incarceration (Schur, 1973). The adoption of these policies would narrow the 'official' differential in criminal behaviour between the disreputable poor and the respectable middle class so that it approximated more closely the actual differences in criminal behaviour – at least criminal behaviour as defined by the state.

*[handwritten: ... identification of crime is ideologically & politically motivated]*

## Radical 'reflexiveness': artful criminal definitions

Although an enormous amount of carefully buried crime can be unearthed by this liberal 'scientific' excavation work, we will still be denied an adequate view of those whose crimes and victimizing behaviours cause us most harm, injury and deprivation.

Through radical 'reflexive' spectacles, all this excavation work occurs so late in the process of constructing crime and criminals that it never gets to the foundations. Those committed to self-report and victimization surveys do not start off asking the most important question of all: 'what is serious crime?' Instead they take serious crime as a pre- and state-defined phenomenon. But by the time crime categories or definitions have been established, the most important foundation stone of 'our crime problem' has been well and truly buried in cement, beyond the reach of any liberal 'scientific' shovel.

Aware that liberal 'scientists' arrive too late on the scene, radicals resolve to get up earlier in the morning. Instead of merely examining how the law enforcement process in its broadest sense constructs a false image of serious crime and its perpetrators, they suggest we should consider the *social construction of criminal law categories*. This involves not only reflecting on why certain types of behaviours are defined as criminal in some historical periods and not others, but also why a particular criminal law comes to incorporate from relatively homogeneous behaviour patterns only a portion and excludes the remainder, even though each and every instance of this behaviour causes avoidable harm, injury, or deprivation.

Some sociologists have pondered these issues and come to the conclusion that *criminal law categories are ideological constructs* (Sumner, 1976). Rather than being a fair reflection of those behaviours objectively causing us collectively the most avoidable suffering, criminal law categories are artful, creative constructs designed to criminalize only some victimizing behaviours, usually those more frequently committed by the relatively powerless, and to exclude others, usually those frequently committed by the powerful against subordinates.

Numerous researchers (Chambliss 1964; Duster 1970; Graham 1972; Gunningham 1974; Hall 1952; Haskins 1960; Hay 1975; Hopkins 1978; McCaghy and Denisoff 1973; Platt 1969; Thompson 1975) have produced evidence consistent with the view that criminal law categories are ideological reflections of the interests of particular powerful groups. As such, criminal law categories are resources, tools, instruments, designed and then used to criminalize, demoralize, incapacitate, fracture and sometimes eliminate those problem populations perceived by the powerful to be potentially or actually threatening the existing distribution of power, wealth and privilege. They constitute one, and only one way by which social control over subordinate, but 'resisting', populations is exercised. For once behaviour more typically engaged in by subordinate populations has been incorporated into criminal law, then legally sanctioned punishments can be 'justifiably' imposed.

In a society such as ours, populations more likely to be controlled in part through criminalization,

> tend to share a number of social characteristics but most important among these is the fact that their behaviour, personal qualities, and/or position threaten the social relationships of production. . . . In other words, populations become generally eligible for management as deviant when they disturb, hinder, or call into question . . . capitalist modes of appropriating the product of human labour . . . the social conditions under which capitalist production takes place . . . patterns of distribution and consumption . . . the process of socialization for productive and non-productive roles . . . and . . . the ideology which supports the functioning of capitalist society. (Spitzer, 1975: 642)

However, this argument needs qualification. It does not maintain that all criminal laws directly express the interests of one particular group, such as the ruling class. Clearly some legislation reflects temporary victories of one interest or allied interest groups over others, and none of these may necessarily be identical or coincide with the interests of the ruling class. Yet the above argument does not demand or predict that every criminal law directly represents the interests of the ruling class. It recognizes that some laws are passed purely as symbolic victories which the dominant class grants to inferior interest groups, basically to keep them quiet; once passed, they need never be efficiently or systematically enforced. It also recognizes that occasionally the ruling class is forced into a tactical retreat by organized subordinate groups, and the resulting shifts in criminal law enshrine a broader spectrum of interests. But these victories are short lived. Powerful groups have ways and means of clawing back the spoils of tactical defeats. In the last instance, definitions of crime reflect the interests of those groups who comprise the ruling class. This is not to assume that these interests are homogeneous and without serious contradictions (Chambliss, 1981). Indeed, it is just the space between these contradictions that subordinate groups fill with their demands for legal change.

It might be objected that even though *some* criminal laws are in the interests of the dominant class and that others which are obviously not in these interests are ineffectively enforced, thus making them dead-letter laws, it still remains true that laws proscribing those types of victimizing behaviours of which we are all too aware and which set the nerve-ends of neo-classical/ conservative criminologists, such as Wilson (1975) and Morgan (1978) tingling with fear and loathing, *are in all our interests*. None of us wants to be murdered, raped, or robbed; none of us wants our property stolen, smashed, or destroyed, none of us wants our bodies punched, kicked, bitten, or tortured. In that sense, criminal laws against murder, rape, arson, robbery, theft and assault are in all our interests, since in principle we all benefit equally from and are protected by their existence. Without them life would be 'nasty, poor, solitary, brutish, and short'.

This is all true, but it is not all the truth. For some groups of people benefit more than others from these laws. It is not that they are less likely to be murdered, raped, robbed or assaulted – although the best scientific evidence based on victimization surveys shows this to be true (Hindelang et al., 1978) – but that in the criminal law, definitions of murder, rape, robbery, assault, theft and other serious crimes are so constructed as to exclude many similar, and in important respects, identical acts, and these are just the acts likely to be committed more frequently by powerful individuals.

Thus the criminal law defines only some types of avoidable killing as murder: it excludes, for example, deaths resulting from acts of negligence, such as employers' failure to maintain safe working conditions in factories and mines (Swartz, 1975); or deaths resulting from an organization's reluctance to maintain appropriate safety standards (Erickson, 1976); or deaths that result from governmental agencies' giving environmental health risks a low priority (Liazos, 1972); or deaths resulting from drug manufacturers' failure to conduct adequate research on new chemical compounds before embarking on aggressive marketing campaigns (Silverman and Lee, 1974); or deaths from a dangerous drug that was approved by health authorities on the strength of a bribe from a pharmaceutical company (Braithwaite and Geis, 1981); or deaths resulting from car manufacturers refusing to recall and repair thousands of known defective vehicles because they calculate that the costs of meeting civil damages will be less (Swigert and Farrell, 1981); and in most jurisdictions deaths resulting from drunken or reckless people driving cars with total indifference to the potential cost in terms of human lives are also excluded.

The list of avoidable killings not legally construed as murder even in principle could go on and on. But the point should be clear. We are encouraged to see murder as a particular act involving a very limited range of stereotypical actors, instruments, situations and motives. Other types of avoidable killing are either defined as a less serious crime than murder, or as matters more appropriate for administrative or civil proceedings, or as events beyond the justifiable boundaries of state interference. In all instances, the perpetrators of these avoidable 'killings' deserve, so we are told, less harsh community responses than would be made to those committing legally defined murder. The majority of people accept this because the state, by excluding these killings from the murder category, has signified its intention that we should not treat them as capital offenders. As the state can muster a galaxy of skilled machiavellian orators to defend its definitions, and has, beyond these velvet tongues, the iron fist of police and military physical violence, it is able to persuade most people easily and convincingly.

It may be just a strange coincidence, as Vonnegut often suggests, that the social characteristics of those persons more likely to commit these types of avoidable killings differ considerably from those possessed by individuals more likely to commit killings legally construed in principle as murder. That the former are more likely to be relatively more powerful, wealthy and privileged than the latter could be one of nature's accidents. But is it likely?

The criminal law sees only some types of property deprivation as robbery or theft; it excludes, for example, the separation of consumers and part of their money that follows manufacturers' malpractices or advertisers' misrepresentations; it excludes shareholders losing their money because managers behaved in ways which they thought would be to the advantage of shareholders even though the only tangible benefits accrued to the managers (Hopkins, 1980b); it excludes the *extra* tax citizens, in this or other countries, have to pay because: (i) corporations and the very wealthy are able to employ financial experts at discovering legal loopholes through which money can be safely transported to tax havens; (ii) Defence Department officials have been bribed to order more expensive weaponry systems or missiles in 'excess' of those 'needed'; (iii) multinational drug companies charge our National Health Services prices which are estimated to be at least £50 millions in excess of alternative supplies. If an employee's hand slips into the governor's pocket and removes any spare cash, that is theft; if the governor puts his hand into employees' pockets and takes their spare cash, i.e. reduces wages, even below the legal minimum, that is the labour market operating reasonably. To end the list prematurely and clarify the point, the law of theft includes, in the words of that anonymous poet particularly loved by teachers of 'A' level economic history, 'the man or woman who steals the goose from off the common, but leaves the greater villain loose who steals the common from the goose'.

The criminal law includes only one type of non-consensual sexual act as rape, namely the insertion of penis in vagina by force or threatened force; it excludes sexual intercourse between husband and wife, no matter how much the latter is beaten by the former to exercise his 'conjugal right'; it excludes most sexual acts achieved by fraud, deceit, or misrepresentation – thus a man may pose as a psychiatrist and prescribe sexual intercourse as therapy to a 'gullible female', because he knows the law will regard this as acceptable seduction rather than rape; it excludes men who use economic, organizational, or social power rather than actual or threatened force to overcome an unwilling but subordinate, and therefore vulnerable female; it excludes the forced insertion of any other instrument, no matter how sharp or dangerous. Thus out of a whole range of 'sexual' acts where the balance of consent versus coercion is at least ambiguous, the criminal law draws a line demarcating those where physical force is used or threatened from those where any other kind of power is utilized to overcome a female's resistance. The outcome is that men who have few resources other than physical ones are more likely to commit legally defined rape, whilst those men who possess a whole range of resources from economic patronage to cultural charm are likely to be viewed by the law as 'real men' practising their primeval arts – and that is something the majesty of the law should leave alone!

The criminal law defines only some types of violence as criminal assault; it excludes verbal assaults that can, and sometimes do, break a person's spirit; it excludes forms of assault whose injuries become apparent years later, such as those resulting from working in a polluted factory environment where the health risk was known to the employer but concealed from the employee (Swartz, 1975); it excludes 'compulsory' drug-therapy or electric-shock treatment given to 'mentally disturbed' patients or prisoners who are denied the civilized rights to refuse such beneficial medical help (Mitford, 1977; Szasz, 1970, 1977a, 1977b); it excludes chemotherapy prescribed to control 'naughty' schoolboys, but includes physically hitting teachers (Box, 1981b; Schrag and Divoky, 1981).

The criminal law includes and reflects our proper stance against 'murderous' acts of terrorism conducted by people who are usually exploited or oppressed by forces of occupation. But it had no relevance, and its guardians remained mute ten years ago, when bombs, with the United States' and allied governments' blessing, fell like rain on women and children in Cambodia (Shawcross, 1979), or when the same governments aid and support other political/military regimes exercising mass terror and partial genocide against a subjugated people (Chomsky and Herman, 1979a, 1979b). The criminal law, in other words, condemns the importation of murderous terrorist acts usually against powerful individuals or strategic institutions, but goes all quiet when governments export or support avoidable acts of killing usually against the underdeveloped countries' poor. Of course there are exceptions – the Russian 'invasion' of Afghanistan was a violation of international law and a crime against humanity. It may well have been, but what about Western governments' involvement in Vietnam, Laos, Cambodia, Chile, El Salvador, Nicaragua, Suez, and Northern Ireland? Shouldn't they at least be discussed within the same context of international law and crimes against humanity? And if not, why not?

Thus criminal laws against murder, rape, robbery and assault do protect us all, but they do not protect us all equally. They do not protect the less powerful from being killed, sexually exploited, deprived of what little property they possess, or physically and psychologically damaged through the greed, apathy, negligence, indifference and the unaccountability of the relatively more powerful.

Of course, what constitutes murder, rape, robbery, assault and other forms of serious crime varies over historical periods and between cultural groups, as the changes and contradictions *within* and *between* powerful interest groups, and the shifting alliances of the less powerful bring about slight and not-so-slight tilts of society's power axis (Chambliss, 1981). But it is not justifiable to conclude from this that criminal law reflects a value-consensus or even results from the state's neutral refereeing among competing interest groups. It is, however, plausible to view criminal laws as the outcomes of clashes between groups with structurally generated conflicting interests, and to argue that the legislators' intention, or if that is too conspiratorial, then the law's latent function, is to provide the powerful with a resource to reduce further the ability of some groups to resist domination. Needless to stress the point, it is a resource eagerly used to punish and deter actual and potential resisters and thereby help protect the established social order.

## Nothing but mystification

Unfortunately for those committed to the radical 'reflexive' view, there is nothing but mystification. Most people accept the 'official' view. They are very aware and sensitized to muggers, football hooligans, street vandals, housebreakers, thieves, terrorists and scroungers. But few are aware and sensitized to crimes committed by *corporate top and middle management* against stockholders, employees, consumers and the general public. Similarly there is only a fog, when it comes to crimes committed by *governments* (Douglas and Johnson, 1977), particularly when these victimize Third World countries (Shawcross, 1979) or become genocidal (Brown, 1971; Horowitz, 1977), or by *governmental control agencies* such as the police when they assault or use deadly force unwarrantedly against the public or suspected persons, or prison officers (Coggan and Walker, 1982; Thomas and Pooley, 1980), or special prison hospital staff when they brutalize and torture persons in their protective custody.

Few people are aware how men, who on the whole are more socially, economically, politically and physically powerful than women, use these resources frequently to *batter* wives and cohabitees (Dobash and Dobash, 1981), *sexually harass* their female (usually subordinate) co-workers, or *assault/ rape* any woman who happens to be in the way. But we are very aware of female shoplifters and prostitutes, and those poor female adolescents who are 'beyond parental control' and in 'need of care and protection', even though this is a gross misrepresentation of female crime and though the relative absence of serious female crime contradicts the orthodox view that crime and powerlessness go hand in hand.

Few people become aware of crimes of the powerful or how serious these are, because their attention is glued to the highly publicized social characteristics of the convicted and imprisoned population. It is not directed to the records, files and occasional publications of those quasi-judicial organizations (such as the Factory Inspectorate in the UK or the Federal Drug Administration in the US) monitoring and regulating corporate and governmental crimes. Because of this, people make the attractive and easy deduction that those behind bars constitute our most serious criminals. As this captive audience is primarily young males amongst whom the unemployed and ethnic minorities are over-represented, it is believed that they, and those like them, constitute our 'public enemies'. Had the results of self-report/victimization surveys and the investigations of quasi-judicial agencies been publicized as much as 'official criminal statistics', and had the radical jaundiced and cynical view of criminal definitions been widely publicized, then the mystification produced by focusing exclusively on the characteristics of the prison population would not be so easily achieved. Instead, there would be a greater awareness of how the social construction of criminal definitions and the criminal justice system operate to bring about this misleading image of serious criminals.

Definitions of serious crime are essentially ideological constructs. They do not refer to those behaviours which objectively and *avoidably* cause us the most harm, injury and suffering. Instead they refer to only a sub-section of these behaviours, a sub-section which is more likely to be committed by young, poorly educated males who are often unemployed, live in working-class impoverished neighbourhoods, and frequently belong to an ethnic minority. Crime and criminalization are therefore *social control strategies.* They:

1  render underprivileged and powerless people more likely to be arrested, convicted and sentenced to prison, even though the amount of personal damage and injury they cause may be less than the more powerful and privileged cause;
2  create the illusion that the 'dangerous' class is primarily located at the bottom of various hierarchies by which we 'measure' each other, such as occupational prestige, income level, housing market location, educational achievement, racial attributes – in this illusion it fuses relative poverty and criminal propensities and sees them both as effects of moral inferiority, thus rendering the 'dangerous' class deserving of both poverty and punishment;
3  render invisible the vast amount of avoidable harm, injury and deprivation imposed on the ordinary population by the state, transnational and other corporations, and thereby remove the effects of these 'crimes' from the causal nexus for explaining 'conventional crimes' committed by ordinary people. The conditions of life for the powerless created by the powerful are simply ignored by those who explain crime as a manifestation of individual pathology or local neighbourhood friendship and cultural

patterns – yet in many respects the unrecognized victimization of the powerless by the powerful constitutes a part of those conditions under which the powerless choose to commit crimes;

4   elevate the criminal justice into a 'community service' – it is presented as being above politics and dispensing 'justice for all' irrespective of class, race, sex, or religion – this further legitimates the state and those whose interests it wittingly, or otherwise, furthers;

5   make ordinary people even more dependent upon the state for protection against 'lawlessness' and the rising tidal wave of crime, even though it is the state and its agents who are often directly and indirectly victimizing ordinary people.

Not only does the state with the help and reinforcement of its control agencies, criminologists and the media conceptualize a particular and partial ideological version of serious crime and who commits it, but it does so by concealing and hence mystifying its own propensity for violence and serious crimes on a much larger scale. Matza captured this sad ironic 'truth' when he wrote:

in its avid concern for public order and safety, implemented through police force and penal policy, the state is vindicated. By pursuing evil and producing the *appearance* of good, the state reveals its abiding method – the perpetuation of its good name in the face of its own propensity for violence, conquest, and destruction. Guarded by a collective representation in which theft and violence reside in a dangerous class, morally elevated by its correctional quest, the state achieves the legitimacy of its pacific intention and the acceptance of legality – even when it goes to war and massively perpetuates activities it has allegedly banned from the world. But that, the reader may say, is a different matter altogether. So says the state – and that is the final point of the collective representation [i.e. ideological construction – author]. (Matza, 1969: 196)

For too long too many people have been socialized to see crime and criminals through the eyes of the state. There is nothing left, as Matza points out, but mystification. This is clearly revealed in the brick wall of indignation which flattens any suggestion that the crime problem defined by the state is not the only crime problem, or that criminals are not only those processed by the state. There is more to crime and criminals than the state reveals. But most people cannot see it.

## References

Box, S. (1981a) *Deviance, Reality and Society*, 2nd edn. London: Holt, Rinehart and Winston.
Box, S. (1981b) 'Where have all the naughty children gone?', in National Deviancy Symposium, *Permissiveness and Control*, London: Macmillan.
Braithwaite, J. and Geis, G. (1981) 'On theory and action for corporate crime control'. Unpublished paper.
Brown, D. (1971) *Bury My Heart at Wounded Knee*. New York: Holt, Rinehart and Winston.
Chambliss, W.J. (1964) 'A sociological analysis of the law of vagrancy', *Social Problems*, 12: 46–67.
Chambliss, W.J. (1978) *On The Take: From Petty Crooks to Presidents*. Indiana: Indiana University Press.
Chambliss, W.J. (1981) 'The criminalization of conduct', in H.L. Ross (ed.), *Law and Deviance*. London: Sage.

Chomsky, N. and Herman, E.S. (1979a) *The Washington Connection and Third World Fascism*. Nottingham: Spokesman.

Chomsky, N. and Herman, E.S. (1979b) *After the Cataclysm*. Nottingham: Spokesman.

Coggan, G. and Walker, M. (1982) *Frightened For My Life: An Account of Deaths in British Prisons*. London: Fontana.

Dobash, R.E. and Dobash, R. (1981) *Violence Against Wives*. London: Open Books.

Douglas, J.D. and Johnson, J.M. (eds) (1977) *Official Deviance*. New York: Lippincott.

Duster, T. (1970) *The Legislation of Morality*. New York: Free Press.

Erickson, K.T. (1976) *Everything in its Path*. New York: Simon and Schuster.

Graham, J.M. (1972) 'Amphetamine politics on Capitol Hill', *Society*, 9: 14–23.

Gunningham, N. (1974) *Pollution, Social Interest and the Law*. London: Martin Robertson.

Hall, J. (1952) *Theft, Law and Society*, rev. edn. Indianapolis: Bobbs–Merrill.

Haskins, G. (1960) *Law and Authority in Early Massachusetts*. New York: Macmillan.

Hay, D. (1975) 'Property, authority and criminal law', in D. Hay et al., *Albion's Fatal Tree*. London: Allen Lane.

Hindelang, M.J., Gottfredson, M. and Garofalo, L. (1978) *Victims of Personal Crimes*. Cambridge, MA: Ballinger.

Hopkins, A. (1978) *Crime, Law and Business*. Canberra: Australian Institute of Criminology.

Hopkins, A. (1980a) 'Controlling corporate deviance', *Criminology*, 18: 198–214.

Hopkins, A. (1980b) 'Crimes against capitalism – an Australian case', *Contemporary Crises*, 4: 421–32.

Horowitz, I.L. (1977) *Genocide: State-Power and Mass Murder*, end edn. New Jersey: Transaction Books.

Liazos, A. (1972) 'The poverty of the sociology of deviance: nuts, sluts and perverts', *Social Problems*, 20: 103–20.

Matza, D. (1969) *Becoming Deviant*, Englewood Cliffs, NJ: Prentice-Hall.

Mitford, J. (1977) *The American Prison Business*. London: Penguin.

Morgan, P. (1978) *Delinquent Fantasies*. London: Temple Smith.

McCaghy, C.H. and Denisoff, R.S. (1973) 'Pirates and politics', in R.S. Denisoff and C.H. McCaghy (eds), *Deviance, Conflict and Criminality*. Chicago: Rand-McNally.

Platt, A. (1969) *The Child Savers*. Chicago: Chicago University Press.

Schrag, P. and Divoky, D. (1981) *The Myth of the Hyperactive Child*. Harmondsworth: Penguin.

Schur, E.M. (1973) *Radical Non-Intervention*. Englewood Cliffs, NJ: Spectrum.

Shawcross, W. (1979) *Side Show: Kissinger, Nixon and the Destruction of Cambodia*. London: Andre Deutsch.

Silverman, M. and Lee, P.R. (1974) *Pills, Profits and Politics*. Berkeley, CA: University of California Press.

Smith, D.C. (1974) *'We're Not Mad, We're Angry'*. Vancouver: Women's Press.

Spitzer, S. (1975) 'Towards a Marxian theory of crime', *Social Problems*, 22: 368–401.

Sumner, C. (1976) Marxism and deviance theory, in P. Wiles (ed.), *Crime and Delinquency in Britain*, vol. 2. London: Martin Robertson.

Swartz, J. (1975) 'Silent killers at work', *Crime and Social Justice*, 3: 15–20.

Swigert, V. and Farrell, R. (1976) *Murder, Inequality and the Law*. Lexington, MA: Heath.

Swigert, V. and Farrell, R. (1981) 'Corporate homicide: definitional processes in the creation of deviance', *Law and Society Review*, 15: 161–82.

Szasz, T. (1970) *Ideology and Insanity*. New York: Anchor.

Szasz, T. (1977a) *Psychiatric Slavery*. New York: Free Press.

Szasz, T. (1977b) *The Theology of Medicine*. Oxford: Oxford University Press.

Thomas, J.E. and Pooley, R. (1980) *The Exploding Prison*. London: Junction Books.

Thompson, E.P. (1975) *Whigs and Hunters*. London: Allen Lane.

Wilson, J.Q. (1975) *Thinking About Crime*. New York: Basic Books.

# 23

# Drifting into a law and order society

## Stuart Hall

We are now in the middle of a deep and decisive movement towards a more disciplinary, authoritarian kind of society. This shift has been in progress since the 1960s; but it has gathered pace through the 1970s and is heading, given the spate of disciplinary legislation now on the parliamentary agenda, towards some sort of interim climax.

This drift into a 'Law and Order' society is no temporary affair. No doubt it is, in part, a response to the deepening economic recession, as well as to the political polarization, social tensions and accumulating class antagonisms which are inevitably accompanying it. In difficult times, it is tempting to avert the gaze from problems whose remedy will require a profound reorganization of social and economic life and to fasten one's eyes, instead, on the promise that the continuity of things as they are can be somehow enforced by the imposition of social order and discipline 'from above'. Nevertheless, in my view, the drive for 'more Law and Order' is no short-term affair; nor is it a mere backlash against the 'permissive excesses' of the 1960s. It has its roots in the structural backwardness of the British economy, a fact which has been with us since the closing decades of the last century, only temporarily obscured by a brief period of 'affluence' resulting from post-war reconstruction.

It also has its roots in the much augmented power and presence of the state, something which also, and not coincidentally, dates from the imperialist crisis of the 1880s and 1890s, but which has assumed a qualitatively new dimension in post-war British society. At the popular level, it feeds on the social anxieties and tensions generated by the great sea-change in Britain's position in the world. And it has been tutored and educated by a new philosophical rationale: that which seeks a restoration of social harmony through the return to a traditionalist morality and the unqualified respect for authority as such.

This regression to a stone-age morality is a theme to which some of the most articulate public spokesmen and women have turned their minds in recent months. Its counterpart, at the popular level, is what can only be defined as a blind spasm of control: the feeling that the *only* remedy for a society which is declared to be 'ungovernable' is the imposition of order, through a disciplinary use of the law by the state.

Governments in trouble, it might be said, always have a strong temptation to reach for discipline and regulation in times of social crisis. These are not times when human freedoms and civil liberties flourish. But the new aspect to this ancient habit is the capacity of those in power to use the augmented

---

Abridged from *Drifting into a Law and Order Society*, pp. 3–17. (London: Cobden Trust, 1980.)

means of communication now available to them, in order to *shape* public opinion, constructing a definition of 'the crisis' which has, as its inevitable corresponding echo, a popular demand for 'more Law and Order'.

The construction of this 'Law and Order' consensus, the forging of a disciplinary common sense, is one of the most troubling features of the drift. For it draws attention to the ways in which the disciplinarians of the state, and their populist supporters, can couple to them the mass media of communication; those ventriloquists of the popular press, for example, who give voice to the 'silent majority', representing it in its most virulently traditionalist and authoritarian disguise, without a single memorandum passing from Whitehall to Fleet Street.

By this means, first, forming public opinion; then, disingenuously, consulting it, the tendency to 'reach for the law', above, is complemented by a popular demand to be governed more strictly, from below. Thereby, the drift to Law and Order, above, secures a degree of popular support and legitimacy amongst the powerless, who see no other alternative. And this leads to a sharp closure in the whole movement.

### Free economy, strong state

Against this background, we must speak not only of the tendency towards an authoritarian state, but rather of the production of an *authoritarian populism*. In such a climate of closure, to raise the question of rights and civil liberties is tantamount to declaring oneself a 'subversive'. We have come to a dangerous pass when the reaction of the Chairman of the Police Federation to the news that the report of the death of a Merseyside man while in the hands of the police has been passed to the DPP is to tell local policemen that critics of the police, who brought this worrying case to public attention, are either 'mischievous or misguided'. Or when as experienced a senior police officer as the last Metropolitan Police Commissioner. Sir Robert Mark, feels free to put in print his considered opinion that the National Council of Civil Liberties is 'a self-appointed political pressure group with a misleading title . . . usually trying to usurp the function of the democratically appointed agencies for the achievement of political change' (*In the Office of Constable* (1978) London: Collins, p. 133).

All this may seem paradoxical in the context of the recent return to power of a populist government of the 'radical right', with a militant hostility to what it describes as the creeping collectivism of an overweening state, and committed to the policy of 'rolling the state back'. But this is only a seeming paradox. The new *laissez-faire* doctrine, in which social market values are to predominate, many would say, like the old *laissez-faire*, is not at all inconsistent with a strong, disciplinary state. Indeed, if the state is to stop meddling in the fine-tuning of the economy, in order to let 'social market values' rip, while containing the inevitable fall-out, in terms of social conflict and class polarization, then a strong, disciplinary regime is a necessary corollary.

In 'social market doctrine', the state should intervene less in some areas, but more in others. Its preferred slogan is 'Free economy: Strong state'. There is much talk, within this doctrine, of 'Liberty'. But here, too, the definition is highly selective. It is the 'liberty' of property and contract, of the free movement of capital, of unbridled market forces and of competitive man and 'possessive individualism' to which this slogan refers. It is not the 'liberty' of those who have nothing to sell but their labour to withdraw it. Make no mistake about it: under this regime, the market is to be Free; the people are to be Disciplined.

## Undermining welfare rights

We can see how this profound shift in public sentiment has been engineered by looking at an area where the language of 'Rights' has gained, at best, little more than a temporary toe-hold: that of the Welfare State and of 'Welfare Rights'.

The Welfare State was one of the founding principles of the post-war political settlement. It marked the boundaries of a consensus within whose limits both major political parties agreed to contend. True, as the economic storm clouds have gathered, both the consensus about, and the materiality of, the Welfare State have been steadily eroded, by governments of both political stripes. Yet the principle remained, until recently, tattered but intact.

Now, the fact is that the Welfare State entailed a major, substantive re-definition and expansion of social rights. Without this expansion, it is doubtful whether the achievement of universal rights of political representation, accomplished only as the result of a protracted, bitter and deeply divisive political struggle by the unenfranchised, and not concluded until the achievement of women's suffrage in the early years of this century, would have been enough to give the state a substantive basis of popular legitimacy, especially amongst the poor, the powerless and the dominated classes.

'Welfare rights' are *not* a new form of public charity. They are at the core of the 'social contract' which has made it possible for the popular classes and the poor to consent to be governed as they are within a class-divided society. They cannot be withdrawn, any more than the franchise can be limited, without eroding that pact of social association which makes democratic class society a viable proposition. The foundation of 'welfare rights' gave a new definition and content to the concept of 'the citizen'.

Nevertheless, we have witnessed in recent months, not merely the savaging of welfare provision, but a steady undermining of the philosophy of 'welfare rights', and of the Welfare State itself. It is not difficult to see where this concerted assault on the principle of welfare is primarily coming from. In social market philosophies, 'welfare' is one of those so-called 'rigidities' from which free-market men and women seek to be 'liberated'. In the context of such doctrines, it has become acceptable for a paper like the *Daily Telegraph* to describe Britain in the 1970s as a 'Land Fit For Scroungers'; to comment not only on the 'waste' which welfare represents but on its 'damage to the natural character', and to recommend that 'supplementary benefit should be what it used to be known as in a less euphemistic era: assistance. It should be a safety net, strictly for emergencies, not a featherbed for every hard luck case around'.

Here we see how a popular base is laid for that substantial destruction of the Welfare State which is now on the cards. And nothing has been more effective, in coupling this regressive social doctrine with popular anxieties and discontents than the massive investment which the mass media have made in recent months in stories about 'Scroungers'. Hardly a week passes without another cluster of stories about the Scrounger and Welfare State rip-offs. These stories have been heavily embroidered with epithets drawn from the stock of populist demonology: the workshy, the feckless poor, the surly rudeness, the feigned infirmities, the mendacity, lack of gratitude, scheming idleness, endless hedonism and 'something-for-nothing' qualities of 'Britain's army of dole-queue swindlers'. So the Welfare State has been constructed in the media as a populist folk-devil: Britain's undeserving poor, the great majority of whom, if the *Mail* and the *Sun* are to be believed, spend most of their days, between signing on, lolling about on the Costa Brava.

The fact is, of course, that proven welfare frauds represent a tiny proportion of those claiming benefits and a very small percentage of the sums expended. Of the 662,000 odd claims for Family Allowance and Child Benefits, proven frauds account for only 0.42 per cent of the total; of the 5,548,000 claims for Supplementary Benefit, fraud accounts for only 0.59 per cent of the total. By contrast, of the two million people estimated as eligible for Supplementary Benefits, only 60–65 per cent take them up. In short, the really worrying problem about the Welfare State is not the number of proven fraudulent claims, but the vast numbers who need to exercise welfare rights in order to survive, and the significant number whom the Welfare State, for one reason or another, is not reaching. This is the 'problem' which needs public discussion and official action: it is, in fact, the normal problem in democratic class societies, of making the formal rights of the powerless practically and materially effective.

### Scroungers as folk-devils

But this is not how the media have constructed the 'problem of Welfare'. They have exploited the Scrounger as a popular folk-devil. They have trawled their lines in the rich and murky pool of popular myth, dredging up the man who wants something for nothing, the scrounger who lives at the expense of others, who has abandoned the puritan ethic of reward-for-hard-graft and disappeared down the hole of endless protracted pleasure – abroad. What could be more undermining of the national character, the moral fibre of the nation? And, if the Welfare State and welfare rights are principally represented through this composite hate-figure, you can see how the people themselves can be won to consent to, if not actively mobilized behind, the government, when the cutting and the savaging and the dismantling begins.

Here, a critical area of social rights has become progressively vulnerable, not only to economic erosion and regressive social doctrines, but to what can only be described as ideological subversion. Of course, ordinary people are not simple dupes of the media. They don't believe everything they are told. In an era of racing inflation, a pretty large proportion of the two million people eligible for Supplementary Benefit know how much they need it. But we must not underestimate the critical role of the media in holding the pass between the governing classes and the governed. They provide the inside knowledge, the privileged opinion, the 'larger view' on which the definitions of social problems depend. By representing a problem, systematically, in a certain way, for example, by representing the Welfare State in the personification of 'The Scrounger', the media can, and do, *construct* public opinion, which they then re-present, in militantly populist and traditionalist accents.

It is not surprising that, when popular opinion is then 'consulted', it tends spontaneously to coincide with regressive opinion. It can then be declared to be 'what the people want'. Thus 'the people' also come to be represented, as consenting to the erosion of their own hard-won and barely secured 'rights', in a society where massive inequalities of power, property and wealth continue to be secured. This is how a consensus *against* social rights is ideologically constructed. This is one of the mechanisms of 'authoritarian populism' at work.

### Rights – outcome of struggle

I have deliberately used the language of 'social rights' in an area somewhat outside that of the litany of more traditional 'liberties' so frequently invoked. But the question of terminology deserves a little deeper consideration.

There are at least two problems, as I see it, with the language of 'rights'. First, it is clear that 'rights' can be advanced as enclaves of defined liberties within, or as exceptions to, the dominant and determinate tendencies of a society without necessarily altering the structures, or the basic disposition of wealth, property and power within which those rights have to be exercised.

Social rights to 'welfare' intruded the language of 'needs' into a system whose dynamic still dominantly depends on the discourses and practices of property, competitive exchange and profit maximization. They were a check against the savage distribution of wealth which the market and private accumulation accomplishes when left to their own devices. It made significant inroads. Its effective establishment represented the countervailing power of the propertyless, the poor and the dependent once, but not until, they had gained, through extended struggle, the right of political representation. They have thus profoundly modified, but not so far transformed, the system within and against which they operate. Certainly, they have helped to humanize and democratize modern capitalism. They have also, as I argued earlier, come to constitute that minimal basis through which the dominated classes secure a measure of economic representation in a society based on private property and thus form a critical element in making democratic class society viable.

The question of whether this counter-vailing principle and power can profoundly modify, or merely marginally deflect, the driving tendencies of the social system is not, of course, written into their status as newly won 'rights'. It depends on the level and character of continuing struggle by which they are defended, maintained and expanded. Society may recuperate these rights to its dominant tendencies and the 'welfare state', failing on the whole to transform the private corporate property system, had indeed come to institute, as well as a limit, one of its principal legitimating supports. But that recuperation is *always* a point of contention, conflict and struggle to define.

The state, in that sense, is not a monolithic thing; nor is it a neutral engine, representing the interests of all, equally. It is constantly conformed and conforming relations to the economic system on whose viability the social order ultimately depends. But it is also a space of contending forces. And it is the outcomes of those struggles which define and limit the degree to which 'rights' can be expanded into the basis for a new kind of society, a different form of the state, or effectively neutralized.

However, as we shall see in a moment, the 'language of rights' is frequently deployed to obscure and mystify this fundamental basis which rights have in the struggle between contending social forces. It constantly *abstracts* rights from their real historical and social context, ascribes them a timeless universality, speaks of them as if they were 'given' rather than *won* and as if they were given once-and-for-all, rather than having to be constantly secured.

The second problem is, then, just this sleight-of-hand, this *legerdemain*, by which the historical process through which rights are defined, won or lost is commonly misinterpreted. Of course, they are prized as what makes our society a half-way decent place to live in. They differentiate democratic class societies from more authoritarian and arbitrary regimes. But they do appear in this discourse as if descended from Heaven; bestowed on their grateful recipients through the goodwill and beneficence of their rulers as if this 'granting' was unproblematic. But this is to collapse a protracted and bloody series of historical engagements into a Whig myth of inevitable progress.

### Rights – formal and substantive

This naturalization of the historical process may have something to do with the belief that those rights which we now enjoy are the direct legacy of the doctrine of 'natural right'. Now 'natural rights' were generated in the struggle of the rising commercial classes against arbitrary and absolutist power. They constitute one of the great historic achievements of a rising bourgeoisie. But they were, of course, predicated on a particular form of society – market societies, societies of private property, of 'contract' and free exchange and rooted in a 'possessive individualist' image of human nature. Not only were the poor, the property-less, the unenfranchised and women not thought fit and proper subjects of this naturalistic universe; the very form in which 'liberty' was conceived was *intrinsically hostile* to democracy. Professor Macpherson has shown, definitively, that this main liberal tradition was either 'undemocratic or anti-democratic'.

These natural rights had to be profoundly transformed and others which were utterly foreign to the universe of natural rights had to be defined and fought for in order that in the form of the liberal democratic society we have today, a scheme of democratic government could be fitted on to a class-divided society with some minimal expectation not that antagonisms would disappear but that they could be largely contained within a framework of legal regulation, on the basis of a measure of popular consent. The so-called right to express opinions and to publish cannot be understood outside of the struggle of the radical and working-class press against the actions of a succession of profoundly illiberal governments; and its 'progress' has to be trailed through the prisons and the courts, through charges of sedition and imprisonment, as well as through the legislature.

And then, today, this formal freedom to publish, vital as it is, has to be seen in the context of the vast, substantive unfreedom constituted by the size and scale of corporate capital, at the disposal of a very few 'citizens', on which the 'right' to publish *effectively* substantively depends. Still, more than half a century after the winning of a universal franchise, we have several national newspapers which claim to speak *to* working people, as well as *at* them; none which is *by* them or *for* them. I don't discard this formal right lightly. But it must also be insisted that, here as elsewhere, freedoms precious to our form of society were wrested from vested power and property, not given by them. And they continue to operate within a system of real and substantive power, to which, in the end, every formal right must be referred.

## Conquest of violence?

The paradox is that nowadays this real history is not defined as the basis for taking such further measures as would make our formal freedoms practically and substantively more effective, or for the deepening and expansion of their democratic content. Instead, the same history has been rewritten as the legitimating excuse for an increased exercise of regulation and control. The argument runs that, in previous times, when the state was an instrument of government largely at the disposal of the powerful and propertied classes, social conflict and class antagonisms were often legitimately expressed in the form of militant collective action: and the forces of public order, which so frequently appeared on the scene, were, it can now be acknowledged, with convenient hindsight, largely functioning as an extended arm of propertied interests. But, so the argument runs, now that these rights have been 'universalized' and 'institutionalized', the state has become 'fully representative', a state of popular sovereignty; and, for that reason, it not only has the sole, legitimate monopoly of the means of violence, but has itself the right to limit and discipline any further conflict over rights which might arise.

This is the famous thesis of the 'conquest of violence' which is supposed to have occurred magically some time between 1880 and 1920, a period, incidentally, of deep and extensive class conflict in which the so-called rights to combine and to strike were constantly at issue; and where the critical struggle to contain and educate the challenge of organized labour within the framework of representative democracy was conducted with a considerable measure of practical success. The 'conquest of violence' is an updated Whig fiction much loved by historians of public order and the police, and a historical thesis to which senior police spokesmen are particularly addicted.

We are arguing, then, that the civil rights and freedoms which make our society what it is are rights which were defined and won in struggle against the dominant interests in society, not bestowed on society by them. These rights, crucial as they are in securing for the powerless and unpropertied classes a measure of representation within the state, are constantly subject, in practice, to the real and substantive dispositions of power, wealth and property, the systems of real relations within which they have to be exercised. In so far as they can or have been given a substantive *democratic* content, they have run counter to society's main dynamic and therefore have to be constantly secured and defended. And, since the society is both a representative democracy and a class society, such 'rights' may be used as a defence against the exercise of arbitrary power: but they *cannot* provide the basis, in themselves, of the dissolution of class antagonisms and social conflict. They hold out no promise of a 'harmony of social interests'. To abrogate them is tantamount to dismantling the fragile basis on which what can only be the legal regulation of conflict depends.

### The freedom of organized labour

One critical test case is the 'freedom' of those who have only their labour, mental or manual, to sell, to withdraw that labour under the conditions of a breakdown in the legal regulation of class conflict. Lord Denning, Master of the Rolls, will immediately enter the lists, as he did [. . .] at Birmingham University, to remind us that 'there is no such right known to the law'. And in the literal sense, of course, he is correct. The French and Italian constitutions define a positive 'right to strike'. There is no such freedom proclaimed in Britain. Nevertheless, as is so often the case, that freedom *is* positively expressed, as a series of exceptions from the common law; and, as is again so frequently the case, it was established by a protracted struggle, whose progress is staked out by a series of fateful legal decisions (and some remarkable reversals).

The freedom to combine and organize dates back to the repeal of the Combination Acts in 1824: but for another fifty years, until the *Conspiracy and Protection of Property Act* of 1875, strikers were frequently brought before the law on charges of criminal conspiracy. The Act of 1875 was it says the direct result of the enfranchisement of the urban working class following the agitations of the 1860s. It was almost immediately replaced by a switch to attack under the charge of civil conspiracy, within the law of tort. This in turn was bitterly contested, through the labour unrest of the 1880s and 1890s, in the period of the unionization of the unskilled, right up to the infamous Taff Vale judgment; and only brought to an end with the *Trade Disputes Act* of 1906. Those who have followed its subsequent career through Rookes *vs* Barnard, the Trade Union and Labour relations legislation of the 1970s, including the attempts of the Heath government to recruit the law, again, directly into the management of the economic struggle; the intense campaign against the 'overweening power of the unions' of recent years; bringing us to the threshold of yet another attempt to deploy the law to limit and contain the power of organized labour, will, no doubt, have some difficulty in recognizing in this sordid progress the clear lines of the 'conquest of violence' or the growth to social harmony.

And yet, as Sir Otto Kahn-Freund has argued, 'There can be no equilibrium in industrial relations without a freedom to strike. In protecting that freedom, the law protects the legitimate expectation of workers that they can make use of their collective power: it corresponds to the protection of the legitimate expectation of management that it can use the right of property for the same purpose on its side'. This lucid statement has the considerable advantage of not being bemused by the religion of a 'social harmony of interests' or the myths of the 'conquest of conflict'. It has not allowed itself to fall into the pit of false illusions that, in a capitalist system, the economic class struggle will disappear if only one systematically renames it instead, 'industrial relations'. 'Any approach to the relations between management and labour is fruitless unless the diversity of their interests is plainly recognized and articulated', Sir Otto has also argued. 'The conflict between capital and labour is inherent in an industrial society and therefore in the labour relationships. Conflicts of interest are inevitable in all societies. There are rules for their adjustment, there can be no rules for their elimination.'

The rights to organize, to combine, to withdraw labour and to picket are rights, established only by means of a brutal and extended struggle, which set some minimal exceptions to the rights of property against labour. The 'bargain' to contain and regulate the conflicts of interest by negotiation rests, ultimately, on this ultimate freedom to contest the rules of the game themselves. But this inevitable structural conflict continues in and through the rights which organized labour have won. Against this background, the postulation of a 'pre-established harmony of management and labour', now the received doctrinal wisdom of Ministers of the Crown, newspaper and television editors, judges and public spokespersons is, as Sir Otto put it, 'sheer utopia' – and dangerous nonsense besides.

The attempts, by Labour and Conservative governments alike, in their efforts to secure particular economic policies, to tamper with and whittle away this freedom, progressively employing the law and the police as the principal instruments of disciplinary regulation, must be seen as nothing more or less than an attempt to intervene in the economic struggle between the classes, and to do so in a way which settles that inevitable conflict of interest at the expense of working people and to the profit of the dominant classes and their interests.

## The police, Law and Order front line

We come, finally, to the most contentious area of all: the role of the Law itself and the police as the hard front, the pioneer corps, the disciplinary arm, the shock troops of the 'Law and Order society'. This is a tough charge to make and sustain and I am aware of the imminent danger of falling into either Mr Jardine's 'mischievous' or his 'misguided' category and, most probably, into both at once. The effort, nevertheless, must be undertaken, for the matter is exceedingly serious.

The problems of exercising the 'policing function' in a period of growing social conflict must certainly not be overlooked. Wherever the Law draws the line, the police are required to hold it. Conflicts with the state, with employers, with specific laws and regulations, with policies and conditions, are inevitably displaced on to the police in any serious confrontation. As a society, we lay on them the responsibility for discharging what may be mutually irreconcilable responsibilities: they must enforce the Law impartially, defend the liberties of the citizen, while maintaining public order and the Queen's Peace. These tasks have become more pressing in a period of declining recruitment, when manpower is stretched to the limit. Increasingly, it is the 'public order' role which comes to the fore and this brings the police into the public eye in the role which most clearly aligns them with the interests of the state, the powers that be and the *status quo*.

It may be this which, for example, led Sir Robert Mark to itemize the pressures on the Metropolitan police force in 1973 as consisting of '72,750 burglaries, 2,680 robberies and 450 demonstrations'. All the same, it is a worrying elision where public demonstrations can be associated so easily, and without qualification, with crime. Demonstrations are not yet, so far as we know, a criminal offence. Indeed, from the perspective we have been trying to elaborate, the right of political manifestation is one of those freedoms on which the viability of class democracies fundamentally depends. It is therefore a worrying, tell-tale slide.

The fact is that, increasingly, the police are not only to be seen policing industrial conflict in a tough manner, but actively involved in formulating official views which are publicly hostile to the rights of workers to strike and to picket. Sir Robert did not hesitate to make public his view that the Shrewsbury pickets had 'committed the worst of all crimes, worse even than murder, the attempt to achieve an industrial or political objective by criminal violence'. Mr George Ward, of Grunwick fame, however, he regarded as someone who 'courageously and successfully stood firm against politically motivated violence'. He is not alone in this tendency for the police to intervene publicly in a highly contentious area, where the government intention to legislate is certain to provoke divisive contention within the society. The Chief Constable of Greater Manchester is also on record as holding the view that mass picketing is necessarily intimidatory. 'I can't understand the reluctance to make this area of the law precise', he said. The government has since abandoned any such reluctance.

Sir Robert gave, in his autobiography, *In the Office of Constable*, the political independence of the police as one of his three conditions for the British tradition of successful 'policing with consent'. But there has clearly emerged in recent months what one can only call a 'police view' in the sensitive matter of policing industrial conflict and picketing: and this viewpoint is not a whit less 'political' in its effect because it appears to have been adopted on grounds of technical efficiency. The rights of workers to withdraw their labour, and to make that withdrawal effective through peaceful picketing, is too serious a matter to be discarded as a consequence of convenience to the police.

The second area in which the police have come to play a highly visible and prominent role is in the policing of racial conflict. This is not a matter which requires, at this point, detailed elaboration. Since the late 1960s, a sort of war of attrition has been going on between the police and black people in areas of high urban concentration; and, despite the consistent adverse publicity which this has attracted, those who know these communities at first hand will attest that it shows little sign of abating. The sordid history of these relations runs from the singling out of the Mangrove for special treatment, through the campaigns against black muggers (the two consistently identified as indistinguishable by the police and the media) the saturation tactics of the Special Patrol Group in Lewisham and other parts of London, in Birmingham and Manchester and other cities; all the way through to the revelations, to which both the Runnymede Trust study and Home Office research have given substantiation, of the clear bias against black youth in the pervasive application of 'arrest on suspicion', 'sus', to give it its familiar name, under the ancient statutes of the Vagrancy Act of 1824.

I have no wish to repeat here this terrifying tale of the use of police powers to contain and constrain, and in effect to help to criminalize, parts of the black population in our urban colonies. Not all the stories and rumours are, of course, true. Not all of them are traceable to racism within the local police forces. But when all the reasonable allowances have been made, this series of episodes leaves us with no other conclusion than that the police have undertaken, whether willingly or no, to constrain by means which would not long stand up to inspection within the rule of law, an alienated black population and thereby, to police the social crisis of the cities.

What defies explanation, in a police force which prides itself on the practice of policing by consent, is why they seem unable to remedy this situation to any significant degree; if not for the sake of justice to black people then for the more limited reason of securing their own legitimacy. It is now sometimes argued, apparently in mitigation that, since the police inevitably reflect society, and British society is undeniably racist, the police are bound to have their proportion of racists too. This is an utterly cynical and quite unacceptable proposition. The same thing could be said of the criminal population. And, indeed, the last ten years have revealed the quite appalling degree to which the criminal penetration and corruption of the police has advanced. But no Chief Constable could afford to be so cavalier about the criminalization of his own force. Indeed, Sir Robert Mark's tenure of the office of Chief Constable was distinguished by the lengthy, arduous and by no means as yet completed cleaning up of the Augean stables within major sections of the force and at worryingly senior levels. This was undertaken to 'put our own house in order'. I know of no evidence that the equally clear evidence of racism within the police forces in sensitive black urban areas is a matter to which similar attention has been given.

The third area which must now be the source of serious concern is the manner in which the technical factors associated with the problems of policing an increasingly restless society have become the legitimate basis for a far-reaching administrative restructuring of the policing function, virtually without reference to the public and certainly without that legislative debate which alone would give substance to Sir Robert's claim to be 'the most accountable and therefore the most acceptable police in the world'.

Both the Home Office Working Party in 1973 and, more recently, the National Security Committee (a title to give most civil libertarians pause), resisted the idea of the creation of a so-called 'third force' in the para-military style so infamous on the Continent. And yet, it is now clear that, after the substantial revision of riot and public order training and reorganization undertaken in 1972, the Special Patrol Groups have substantially changed their role and function from that of a support anti-crime squad to an advanced and highly equipped 'responsive or reactive' force of a distinctly public order kind. Its functions are conceived, as the Chief Constable of Devon and Cornwall himself has said, within the framework of a 'quasi-military reactive concept'.

The swamping role of the SPGs in the black areas, their notorious (and exceedingly low-yield) 'stop and search' activities, and their highly questionable presence and role at the flash points of a whole series of public demonstrations, Red Lion Square, Southhall, etc., are well beyond the framework of traditional policing as practised in Britain. Activities, as the 1972 Metropolitan Police Commissioner's Report noted, at demonstrations 'at which militant elements were thought likely to cause disorder . . . and in protracted industrial disputes involving dockers and building workers'; and without so much as a public by-your-leave.

Since the reformation and equipping of the SPGs and the Spaghetti House disaster, it has become increasingly clear that the claim that the British police remains substantially an unarmed force, the only one in the world, is largely a semantic quibble. The fact that the accessibility to arms and similar equipment is still limited does not undermine the substantive fact that, for good or ill, in all those cases where it matters, the British police are now in effect an armed and fully equipped technical force. I have searched the pages of Hansard in vain for the days when this momentous move was debated by those to whom senior policemen insist they are ultimately accountable. I may have missed it. Otherwise, I feel bound to say that this profound change in the character and exercise of the policing function has been accomplished, as so much else in this society these days, under the apparently neutral sign of technical rationalization and modernization.

Administrative rationale has become one of the principal means by which even formal representative democracy is being short-circuited. The extensive and unchecked amassing and computerization of information, much of which, to judge from the tit-bits which have become available, of a hearsay or otherwise dubious and unreliable character, is another field in which the rights of the public, of democratic accountability and the fundamental exercise of the police function under the civil power, have been subject to techno-logical 'up-dating'.

The encroachments on the liberties of the citizen, on civil rights and on democratic control and accountability which stem from these and related developments, hardly need to be more extensively spelled out. It may well be, as we were assured in a recent radio discussion of the Chief Constable of Devon and Cornwall's book, *Policing Freedom*, that law-abiding citizens have nothing to fear from these developments. The evidence does not, unfor-tunately, support this optimistic view. And it is no longer possible and, so far as democratic rights are concerned, no longer advisable, to take these matters on trust. The massive campaign which the police waged against any increase in the independent element in its own complaints investigation procedure is not calculated to inspire confidence.

The plain fact is that these worries and concerns about the arbitrary extension of police powers, and the exercise of police discretionary justice in private have been escalating in recent months; much of it on the basis of hard and disturbing evidence, which would never have come to light but for the persistence of some journalists, 'crackpot' civil libertarians and the sense of outrage of victims and their relatives and friends. When members of the public come forward with evidence which has to be taken seriously of having received physical injury while in the hands or custody of the police, we have gone beyond the moment when civil assurances will do. Frankly, *one* such case is one too many.

These, then, are only some of the ways in which the police forces themselves are being progressively transformed for a wider disciplinary and 'Law and Order' role at the present time. But I want to end by drawing to your attention an equally important, but in some ways even more disquieting change, the emergence of the police as what can only be described as an organized ideological force. Sir Robert himself pioneered a substantive shift in the attitude of senior policemen to public opinion, the media and entering directly into public debate. He became, indeed, a relentless and effective publicist. Sir David McNee is less effective at it and has chosen a lower profile. But this has been more than compensated for by the Chief Constable of Greater Manchester, Mr James Anderton, whom a *Sunday Telegraph* (and favourable) profile describes as 'Britain's Toughest Policeman', with, 'the gift of feeling the pulse of the public and then making it beat quicker', and 'an uncannily successful populist'.

As the issues of policing become big news and attract the publicists, so we have come to know more and more about the highly conservative and traditionalist views and values of our most senior policemen: Mr Anderton's view of his job as 'an extension of his Christian mission to raise the moral quality of life', his preoccupation with moral standards, his clean-up pornography crusade, his sombre views of the 'over-influence of the libertarian lobby', his commitment to tough sentencing, his militant evangelicalism; Sir David McNee's fundamentalism; or Sir Robert's common gauge traditionalism.

Policemen, too, are entitled to their views. We, in turn, are entitled to ask whether it is just by chance that those who get the lion's share of the publicity are *all* committed to such deep social conservatism and whether it is altogether right that there should be so blurred a line between their personal viewpoints and their professional roles. Such publicity has undoubtedly helped to stamp the police indelibly with the inscription of a force of social traditionalism. But that, as they say, is their right.

What cannot be treated so lightly is the constitution of the police as an active 'Law and Order' lobby, an ideological force, mobilizing public opinion behind a very special and particular set of 'Law and Order' policies. The extensive evidence which the police have submitted to the Royal Commission on Criminal Procedure is, in its sober way, little short of a disciplinary manifesto. The campaigns which Sir Robert initiated when in office, against suspects' rights and the Judges Rules, for majority verdicts and extensive police discretion, have found their way into the philosophy which inspires the evidence.

The same philosophy is to be found in the widely publicized views of the Association of Chief Police Officers; and, with an accession of pungent imagery which was only to be expected from that quarter, from the Police Federation: 'If someone had drawn up these rules', their Chairman, Mr Jardine, told a recent conference, 'and sent the idea to the makers of "Monopoly" as a new board game, Waddingtons would have turned it down because one player, the criminal, was bound to win every time'.

These, and similar sentiments now constitute a well-formed and actively publicized 'police view'. But this is only one throw in what has been, in fact, a substantial public campaign on 'Law and Order', launched by the Police Federation in 1975, and culminating in the provocative 'Law and Order' advertisement – 'an open letter to all General Election candidates from the Police Federation' – which appeared during the General Election of [1979]. The Police Superintendents Association has, in fact, expressed its fears that only the police and a small minority of the legal profession will 'speak for law and order'.

Of course, the police are entitled to form views about the best way to carry out the duties with which they are saddled. And certainly, they are, and are bound to be, constantly consulted by senior Ministers of Government on public order questions. But there is a long tradition that, in this area, it is critical that the *making* of law and its *enforcement* be strictly separated. With the ideological mobilization of the police as the best informed, more knowledgeable and now most organized voice, campaigning in a consistently 'Law and Order' direction, forming a core element in the law and order bloc, that strict separation of powers and functions is becoming seriously blurred. The police themselves are beginning to shape the identity of public opinion on these crucial questions. They are beginning to wield a deep ideological influence and they are consistently exerting that influence in the disciplinary direction.

The Police Federation, to take only one case, now functions in the public domain as a professional association representing the 'men in blue' (the body which was constructed out of the debris of the police strikes for the right to unionize, which were routed). But it also functions as an expert, neutral witness on 'policing problems' *and* as an active, militant, 'Law and Order' campaigning force. These are, to put it mildly, two functions too many. And the third is the most dubious of all. It blurs a distinction which, if the role of the police under the civil power is to be maintained (and our liberties could come, one day, to depend on its being so maintained), cannot be permitted to be confused. The police cannot both constitute a powerful crusading part of the 'Law and Order' lobby and maintain for long the semblance of social and political impartiality. They cannot both claim to 'police by consent' and be so actively and publicly involved in constructing public opinion, in shaping consent and producing it, in its most traditionalist and disciplinary form.

It the police now form a sort of vanguard in the drift towards the disciplinary society, they are by no means the only social or political force propelling us along this road. I have singled them out for comment because, in its widest sense, the question of who polices the police is a matter which has been, historically, at the very heart and centre of our civil liberties. But also because they have so successfully cast anyone who raises questions about the police, the law, civil liberties and democratic rights in the role of the 'subversive element', the 'mischievous and the misguided'. And the fears of being so labelled and pricked, marked and damned, has undoubtedly had the effect of rendering the liberal and libertarian public conscience quiescent on these important but controversial matters.

[. . .]

# 24

# Criminalization and racialization

## Michael Keith

[. . .]

### Racialization

Social divisions which appear self-evident or neutral are frequently inseparable from normative judgements. Demographic divisions of sex and age are
commonly value-loaded with tacit assumptions about gender roles and rites of
passage. Similarly, with the notion of 'race' little is quite as it appears on the
surface. The concept of 'race' assumes different meanings in different
contexts. It is imperative to question how debates about civil order and crime
produce and draw on particular coinages of this concept before accepting a
straightforward correspondence between the term itself and some taken for
granted empirical reality.

'Race' is not an essential characteristic. The pervasive practices of racism,
however, and the evolution of racial formations over time and space (Omi and
Winant, 1986), guarantee some correspondence in the harsh reality of the day-
to-day world between the ideological fictions of racial divisions between
people and the empirical circumscription of specific groups in society. The
generation of racial divisions in society is most easily grasped by use of the
notion of racialization, which stresses both the reality of the group formation
process as well as the social construction of the differences between the racial
collective identities so formed. The process of racialization is also of particular
significance because it is one of the principal means through which subordination is produced and reproduced in an unjust society.

### Action and reaction: criminalization, racial formations and racial mobilization

The sheer scale of criminalization of Afro-Caribbean people in Britain is hard
to exaggerate (Herbert and Omambala, 1990). A Home Office report in 1989
highlighted the stark figure that, between 1984 and 1985, there were 521
prosecutions for indictable offences per 1,000 of the young (aged 17–20) Afro-
Caribbean male population in the Metropolitan Police District – that is, over
half of the age cohort.

If it were not for the proportion of those involved, this pattern, although an
indictment of British *justice*, might not be surprising, After all, there is a long

Abridged from *Race, Riots and Policing*, pp. 238–52. (London: UCL Press, 1993.)

tradition in Britain of certain communities being scapegoated by the criminal justice system. But with British Black communities this scale is now without precedent, so much so that it is suggested here that whereas the Criminal justice system was once an arena in which migrant communities came face to face with British injustice, it now provides one of the racializing institutions by which 'racial difference' is reproduced.

[T]his chapter attempts to put this case by advancing four connected propositions. The first is to suggest that the history of relations between British Black people and the police must be set against a theoretical analysis of criminalization. The second is to suggest that this process of criminalization must in turn be placed in the context of the racializing discourses that circumscribe British Black communities. The third is to suggest that the process of criminalization itself now constitutes a significant racializing discourse. Through racist constructions of criminality the criminal justice system has become a locus of racialization, manufacturing a criminalized classification of 'race' which co-exists with alternative, often contradictory, invocations of 'race' that derive from other racializing discourses. Finally, I want to propose that it is possible for so many contradictory constructions of 'race' to co-exist because of the deployment of social relations as products in time and space.

The term 'Black' [. . .] does not, in any straightforward sense refer to a specific demographic fraction of society. Although it [is] used here principally, but not exclusively, to refer to the experiences of people of Afro-Caribbean ethnicity, it is a term that draws its meaning instead from the context in which it is used. In short it is a category that is discursively constructed.

The discursive field with which this chapter is concerned links together the themes of criminality, policing and race. This discursive field thus connotes its own construction of race. It is a construction which is racist in the most invidious sense of the term and cannot be equated with any natural social divisions of society or rendered equivalent to any single (old or new) articulation of ethnicity. It can and does connote a racist and sexist *definition* of the meaning of Blackness. It is for this reason that it is important to differentiate between the notion of criminalization advanced here and standard labelling theory. In standard labelling theory a demographic fraction of society is picked out and victimized. Here it is not so straightforward. A construction of criminality which draws on the glossary of racial difference is applied to define the varying subject positions of Black communities at particular times and places.

*Racialization . . . multiple processes of racialization*

Within a framework that broadly accepts his critique of 'race relations sociology' (1982, 1984a), I want to take as a starting point Miles's axiom that the

> process of social (i.e. ideological) construction, of attributing meaning to particular patterns of phenotypical variation, must always be explained rather than assumed to be unproblematic. (Miles, 1984b)

In short, 'race' cannot be taken for granted. Yet, at times, this fundamental can lead analysis to the point at which it is the ontological status of 'race' which, explicitly or implicitly, becomes 'a problem'. Even within various currents of modern Marxian analysis of 'race' (Hall, 1980a; Miles, 1982,

1984a, 1989; Solomos, 1988) the analytical problem has generally been that some empirical phenomenon exists, whether as natural social grouping, racialized class fraction or outcome of racist constructions of social identity. Consequently, with the theoretical imperative to explain this phenomenon, there is a theoretical prerequisite to classify the ontological status of the phenomenon. In this sense, within a broadly critical perspective, it is now considered normal to trace patterns of racialization in history (e.g. Carter et al., 1987; Miles, 1984b; Sherwood, 1984).

I want to suggest here that to periodize processes of racialization is not always enough. To understand how it is possible for several, often contradictory, constructions of 'race' to permeate society simultaneously, it is necessary to tie the evolution of racial formations to particular places as well as particular times. The advantage of such an approach is that the ontological status of the concept of 'race', which has so bedevilled critical analysis, is resolved by acknowledging that 'race' exists, has causal powers, and epistemological validity, but is not necessarily reified.

Throughout this chapter it is stressed that constructions of race are the outcome of this array of different processes of racialization. At any one time a plurality of processes of racialization may co-exist. In part, the multiplicity of racisms cited by Hall (1980a) can be equated with an array of connected but distinct processes of racialization. The racism which mediated the insertion of migrant labour into the political economy of post-war Western Europe differs from the racism associated with the racial divisions of labour of post-Fordism, which is not quite the same as the racism of the authoritarian state, which is not quite the same as the racist politics of nationalism. Yet all are empirically realized as processes of racialization.

Several of these processes relate to the shared experiences of migrant minorities –expressions of ethnicity, collective struggles around community and processes of collective consumption, mobilizations of racial solidarity – common experiences of British racism. As has been suggested, race effectively gains ontological status by its positioning at the intersection of all these discursive fields. Abstracted, race assumes a reality that is the sum of these racializing discourses. The different but inseparable processes of racialization which relate to the common cause and common Black experience in Britain are consciously not addressed here. All social groups, or collective social identities, including the British Black community, have flexible parameters defined by various forces external and internal to the collective. In this sense the boundaries of a racial formation are stalked both by racism and solidarity. Hence, the emphasis on the production and reproduction of racism in this chapter is not intended in any way to diminish the significance of the forces of mobilization in racial formation (Gilroy, 1987), or the salience of new ethnicities (Hall, 1988) and identity politics in the overall determination of race in economy and society, only to acknowledge that this chapter is centrally concerned with only one discursive field of racialization, that of the criminal justice system.

A plurality of identities is the logical result of the creation of subjects set in discursive formations. This is the power of Laclau and Mouffe's statement that

all identity is relational. . . . It is not the poverty of signifieds but, on the contrary, polysemy that disarticulates a discursive structure. That is what establishes the overdetermined, symbolic dimension of every social identity. (Laclau and Mouffe, 1985: 113)

What is crucial to an understanding of a decentred conceptualization of race is that a multiplicity of end products of racialization may be simultaneously present. The term 'race' takes a specific meaning when multiple, frequently contradictory, discursive attempts to define a racial identity are stopped in a moment of closure.

The process of racialization is of particular significance because it is one of the principal media through which subordination is produced and reproduced in an unjust society. Criminalization of Black people in Britain is only one of several processes of racialization.

### Punishment . . .

There is little purpose here in once again specifying in detail the obscene treatment of migrant minorities by the British criminal justice system throughout history, or the overt and wholesale racist nature of this same experience for British Black communities over the past 30 years. In every single part of the system there is well documented evidence of the racism of British society incorporated into the arenas of some of its most powerful institutions.

The broad contours of the historical processes of criminalization of migrant minorities are now relatively uncontroversial, whether the group concerned is the Irish at the turn of the century, Maltese and Cypriots in the 1930s and 1940s, or the British Black community over the past thirty and more years. Racist stereotypes of racial difference feed into public knowledge and policing practice. A conflict with the reality of 'unjust' policing echoes through the 'due process of the law' into courts and penal institutions, and reinforces the portrayal of migrant groups as involved in particular forms of criminal activity and legitimates particular repressive policing strategies targeted on these communities. The potential for the perpetuation of this pattern is exacerbated by the institutionalization of stereotypes in the fabric of the agencies of social reproduction.

Therefore, criminalization is a process that is tied to production relations as well as to consumption relations; empirically tied to the institutional racism of housing, education and social services as well as to the major institutions of the criminal justice system such as the police, the courts, the prison service and the probation service. Constructions of criminality are linked to racially circumscribed processes of criminalization.

Yet at the heart of most analyses of criminalization a group is picked out of society and victimized, an analytical tradition which consciously echoes and expands the theories of labelling and social deviancy (e.g. Becker, 1971; Goffman, 1963). In the seminal work on the social construction of Black criminality in Britain, Stuart Hall and his associates (1978), when deconstructing the ghetto, regularly resort to the metaphor of the 'Black colony' as both victim of these racist practices of criminalization and (apparently) social reality (1978: ch. 10). Yet there is an imaginative uncertainty at the heart of their work. The ghetto is sometimes a stage, sometimes a metaphor for the Black experience, and sometimes a metonym for racist practice. The authors point out the way in which racist classification of mugging can be connoted by place, by highlighting Black areas of settlement. A case in which a White youth assaults a Black bus conductor can still reproduce the racialized imagery of mugging because, 'The specification of certain venues reactivates earlier and subsequent associations: Brixton and Clapham (Hall et al., 1978: 329). Crime, race and the ghetto could be conflated as social problems after incidents such as the Brockwell Park clashes because they 'located and situated Black crime, geographically and ethnically, as peculiar to Black youth in the inner-city ghettos' (Hall et al., 1978: 329).

The slippage between race and crime is here seen to work both ways; each may connote the other. It was in taking up many of the themes of *Policing the Crisis* that Hall developed the notion of authoritarian populism in his landmark Cobden Lecture of 1979, which outlines a political project that uses the 'forging of a disciplinary common sense' (1980b: 3) to undermine welfare rights, notions of citizenship, and the freedoms of organized labour. At its formative stages Hall's analysis takes as its driving force the realization of urban crisis (1980b: 13) with 'the use of police powers to contain and constrain, and in effect to help to criminalize, parts of the Black population in our urban colonies' (1980b: 3) defining the Black community again as the victim of these changes.

There is obviously a danger that a perception of Margaret Thatcher as the personification of injustice will obscure the continuities of racial injustice in British society. Paul Gilroy (Gilroy, 1987; Gilroy and Sim, 1985) has questioned the notion of 'a drift' into a law-and-order society, preferring to explain criminalization more in terms of continuities within the construction of nationalism. In broad terms, if not in detail, this approach squares more with a general historical invention of tradition within the imagined community of the nation state (cf. Anderson, 1983; Hobsbawm, 1983) and which ties in with Benedict Anderson's concept of *imagined communities* (Anderson, 1983) which, contrary to Anderson's own argument, manipulates racist ideology as an exclusionary mechanism.

> The ability of law and the ideology of legality to express and represent the nation state and national unity precedes the identification of racially distinct crimes and criminals. (Gilroy, 1987: 74)

> Black law breaking supplies the historic proof that Blacks are incompatible with the standards of decency and civilization which the nation requires of its citizenry. (Gilroy, 1982: 215)

> It is precisely this unified national culture articulated around the theme of legality and constitution which Black criminality is alleged to violate, thus jeopardizing both state and civilization. (Gilroy, 1987: 76)

At this stage it is not necessary to arbitrate between the different emphases of Hall and Gilroy here. The point is more simple. Both analyses contain a tension which is not clearly resolved between the empirical reality of racial groupings who are victimized by racist processes of marginalization/ criminalization and the invention of cultural significations of race as criminality. The tension is not so much a flaw of the analyses as the point at which the processes of criminalization and racialization become one.

Random developments occur which lend themselves to particular forms of manipulation. The crises of legitimacy and economic restructuring lent themselves to a form of new authoritarianism, whether rhetorical or real, in 1970s Britain. New Commonwealth migrants and their children provided an important medium through which this logic was extended into an invidious process of systematic criminalization. The historical groundwork of racist (criminal) stereotyping coincided with a shift away from liberal consensus nationally and a need to explain, or at least rationalize, the early 1970s crisis in police/Black relations. A specific conjunction of issues provided the raw material for a more general drift of history.

*Discipline . . .*

It is not easy to specify a particular historical watershed in the encounters between Black people and the British criminal justice system but I want to suggest that a change in the nature of these encounters has become increasingly distinguishable over time. Heuristically, if not literally, it might be possible to conceptualize this change in the following terms. Whereas once migrant communities were the object of racism in the criminal justice system, today's Black communities are in part a subject created by the racializing discourse of criminalization. There is, of course, no suggestion that this subject exhausts the empirical description of a British Black community.

A criminalized subject category, 'Blackness', is one racist construction of the British criminal justice system. Yet this subject position, an imagined racial identity, does not refer exclusively and immutably to any empirically defined section of the population. It is an invidiously powerful categorization that connotes an imagery of 'Black criminality', which achieves empirical realization in particular times and at specific places.

Certainly, the folk devils of the mugging panic in *Policing the Crisis* were the creations of racist discourses. Yet the initiation of the Urban Programme in 1968 can be traced further back, at least to folk images of civil disorder linked not only to Powell's 'Rivers of Blood' speech but also to particular common-sense understandings of the American urban crisis in the 1960s.

The relationship, never one way, is rarely predetermined. At a micro-level such constructions are the outcome of day-to-day interactions and mobilization, exemplified both by the sorts of real social movements of resistance witnessed on 'Front Lines' in the 1980s and by the manner in which these movements are reconstructed and represented as conventional rhetoric in [. . .] discourses of common sense [. . .].

Through time and over space the dominant themes in racializing discourses fluctuate and contradict each other. The precise nature of 'Blackness' that is connoted evolves. In Britain, at a crude level, the succession of racist images of (gender-specific) Afro-Caribbean criminality have followed on from the pimp of the 1950s, to the Black power activist of the 1960s, to the mugger of the 1970s, to the rioter of the 1980s and, quite possibly, to the ultimate folk devil, the underworld 'Yardie' of the 1990s.

At another level, the existence of a degree of gang violence in all youth cultures across Britain is indisputable. But a phenomenon of more recent times has been deployment of the tropes of Black criminality in the simplistic portrayals of the violent subcultures of both Punjabi youth in Southall, West London and Bengalis in the East End. In spite of the more dominant racialized imagery of reputed 'Asian' entrepreneurial skills, a medium of localized criminalization opens up the potential for particular localized forms of (racial) criminalization, drawing on the structures of sensibility established by the discursive field of lore and disorder.

The central point about this process of criminalization is that it may run concurrently with more sophisticated political projects which relate to the ostensibly contradictory nature of policies of 'economic regeneration', accompanied by the ideological construction of 'ethnic' entrepreneurial skills. In the eyes of the White majority it is now, and may continue to be, quite acceptable for crudely racist constructions of Black criminality to co-exist alongside a social reality of young upwardly mobile Black professionals, a Buppefied minority; indeed the existence of the latter lends a legitimation to the former.

'Race' is constructed as a facet of criminality through the institutionally racist channels of White society. Criminalization must be conceptualized with reference to *both* social practices and the accounts given publicly and privately to make sense of these practices, with reference to both the more obvious roles of police and other elements of the criminal justice system, and to a whole series of normalizing institutions from educational provision to welfare service delivery. And of course the restructuring of British society in the 1980s has radically altered the social context in which such organizations operate. It is now unexceptionable to acknowledge the routine nature of regulation of populations that is embossed on all of these institutions from the discipline of the classroom to the surveillance of the welfare state. But significantly, in an era rhetorically committed to deregulation in all spheres, a contradictory outcome of social policy has been the ever increasing demands placed on explicit and implicit institutions of social control (Gamble, 1988).

It is against this context that common-sense understandings of criminality, civil disorder and race are inextricably interconnected. *Analysis* of any single element of this trinity commonly conjures up overt or latent images of these connections. [. . .] Consequently, with social constructions and representations of violent uprisings, there are at least two processes of racialization going on at the same time, which appear complementary but may be nothing of the sort. The signification of *riot* in terms of a racist construction of the social problem group 'Black Youth' may come to permeate common sense through the combined influences of political, media and academic discourse. The configuration of White dominated institutions, particularly the criminal justice system, may appropriate this common sense as a central organizing theme in their imaginative representations of multi-racial Britain, setting up one process of racialization. Indeed it is suggested here that the role of the criminal justice system, in particular, over the past thirty years has been so profoundly significant that a class of subject positions has been created by its influence. A *de facto* racist partitioning of legal rights in the courts, the prisons, the offices of lawyers and barristers and the probation service reflects this.

Yet simultaneously another process operates which derives from the forms of mobilization that emerge from the crucible of violent conflict, derived from the manner in which uprisings are signified positively as acts of popular resistance. It is these movements that set up the counter-memories which claim rebellion as part of an alternative history of resistance, which place scenes of uprising on municipal murals and personal recollections. Signified positively, the 1980s riots are claimed as part of British Black experience. So, when the early 1990s witnessed disorder in predominantly White estates, it was not insignificant that the cultural forms of expression adopted by the young on the estates of Meadowell in the North-East drew on Afro-Caribbean musical forms to celebrate insurrection. This chapter is not about such movements, but this does not imply that they are not at least as significant an outcome of the events of the 1980s as the various responses of the White establishment.

The potential racial formations emerging from disorder are complex. It is not just that, as the misleading notion of 'the average rioter' [. . .] suggests, civil disorder was not the historical property of, even an empirically defined notion of, Black Youth, although this is important. In the 1970s the *articulating principle* through which dominant society understood the rich diversity of British Afro-Caribbean communities was through the tainted debates around this imaginary Black Youth (Solomos, 1988), and in the 1980s this principle became increasingly focused around rioting. More significantly, the manner in which disorders are taken as expressions of Black solidarity in the face of oppression sets up multiple agendas of political and social strategy and mobilization. Violent conflict is again the medium through which racialization occurs, but the racial formations which emerge are more than likely to contradict notions of 'race' established in other arenas, not least in the discursive construction of 'Black Youth' itself.

At a simple symbolic level British Black communities are, for White society, associated with racist stereotypical notions of law and disorder, powerfully connoted by the images of burning buildings and angry crowds so frequently seen on the screens of British television sets in the 1980s.

Yet just as the invidious stereotypical force of such imagery is manifest, the painful reality of those clashes is undeniable.

Similarly, it is impossible to conceive of an objective empirical reality of 'Black crime' which can be investigated by social research. This is because criminality, a chameleon concept defined by the histories of legal whim and political fashion, is at once both social reality and emotive myth. Clearly, demographically concentrated both in social areas and economic classes structured by material deprivation, it is no surprise to find individuals from migrant minority backgrounds committing individual crimes. But this does not mean that 'Black crime' can be reified, subjected to scrutiny as a subject category in its own right, without reference to the broader social, political and moral context in which such scrutiny occurs.

It is precisely this disingenuous divorce of the statistical from the empirical that periodically emerges under occasional calls for hard evidence of the extent of Black involvement in crime. So it was unsurprising to see the *Evening Standard* on 4 June 1990 touting a story on 'How 60 muggers hold us to ransom', reporting that some police research had suggested that violent theft was caused in the main by a very small minority. In spite of the police deliberately refraining from playing the race card, the *Standard* comments that 'Commander Stevens was at pains to play down *the fact* that the majority of muggers in the area were Black' (my emphasis) following this up with a comment that barely hides its racialized agenda: 'the typical mugger is not a poor youth. He wears £100 tracksuits, the latest trainers and is streetwise and style conscious'. The identikit rioter, the alienated criminal, the designer mugger; there is no need to say *they* are Black because *we* already know it.

As the Home Office statistics on the relations between young Black people and the criminal justice system already alluded to demonstrate, there is something much more significant going on than putative disproportionate involvement in criminal activity. Lives are structured by a notion of Black criminality.

In short, the role of the criminal justice system in the reproduction of a racialized society has changed. Where once the criminal justice system was an arena in which migrant minorities came face to face with the racist injustices of White society, the system itself has now assumed a determining role in constructing particular racial groups. These processes must also be set against the dramatic material and social restructuring of British cities that has accompanied the Thatcher years.

*Space mediating racialization*

As several authors have suggested (CCCS, 1982a; Gilroy, 1987; Hall et al., 1978) there is nothing particularly new in linking the construction of racist notions of Black criminality with the massive restructuring of society that followed the economic crisis of the 1970s. In broad terms the creation of a criminalized racial formation accentuated the ideological scope of authoritarian populism (Hall, 1980b), lent a spurious legitimacy to social control innovations (Bridges and Gilroy, 1982; CCCS, 1982a), and provided raw material for the racist projects of the New Right (Gilroy, 1987).

But this restructuring demanded the spatialization of such changes, a new city radically transformed from the economic contours of the era of post-war settlement and labour shortage. And it was a city that also demanded more than the control of labour surplus in the era of 3–4 million unemployed (Cross and Keith, 1993; Keith, 1993).

The urban crisis of the 1960s and 1970s rapidly acquired the status of political reality, even if the concept often masked more about social change than it revealed. A great many issues were subsumed in and connoted by the evolution of the inner city as a social problem in the 1970s and not all of them can be addressed here. However, rooted among the images of the decaying metropolis was a series of debates that drew on a picture of late twentieth century urbanism which recalled the Hobbesian nightmare of life as 'solitary, poor, nasty, brutish and short'. Obviously this provided the raw material for the political rhetoric of the law and order lobby. Implicitly, what was needed was the 'safe city'; Oscar Newman was to provide everyone's salvation by designing 'defensible space'. In the UK by the end of the decade the then minister of state at the Home Office, John Patten, decided to play heir to Baron Haussmann, who so dramatically reshaped the urban fabric of Paris, backed by the full resources of Home Office Crime Prevention and the newly created 'Safer Cities' programme.

There were both obvious and less obvious ramifications for such political projects. Race could be used systematically to conjure up the urban crisis. Neighbourhood watch and active citizens, along with fear of crime based on the public knowledge generated by the ever reliable tabloid press, all quite clearly invoked arenas in which the reproduction and legitimation of racist images of Black criminality could flourish (Christian, 1983).

Less apparent, but equally significant, were the overarching trends which are still influential in shaping the overall form of the city. The call for safe streets, which has surfaced on both sides of the Atlantic in the movement for Crime Protection through Environmental Design, involves a conception of social control which is complete in embracing both formal and informal structures of surveillance. The focus on 'defensible space' and secure 'urban fortresses' invokes the one just as the stress on the informal structures of socialization and the alleged breakdown of community responsibility and involvement invoke the other (Cohen, 1985: 214). The community itself has become the site of models of social control, most crudely witnessed in the UK in the liberal prose of high-profile police officers such as John Alderson and Kenneth Newman.

Of course this ties in with many of Foucault's examinations of the nature of what he describes as carceral cities. As Cohen puts it:

> For Foucault, the city was not a place for other metaphors, but was to provide a powerful spatial metaphor itself. Here could be observed the new dispersed discourse of power actually spreading itself out, passing though finer and finer channels. He continually uses the spatial metaphors of 'geopolitics' to describe the dispersal of discipline: city, archipelago, maps, streets, topology, vectors, landscapes. (Cohen, 1985: 210)

This project of reshaping the city for the postmodern relations of social control also needed legitimation. The manipulation of 'fear of crime' as a legitimate social problem throughout the 1980s has obviously provided one source for such projects. But there is also the demand for the ready made folk-devil and here there was already a dreadful metaphoric continuity. In a work that barely touches on issues of race and racism Cohen inadvertently goes on to sum up the appeal of demands for a safer city as emotively tied to:

> the dreadful realization that while the medieval fortress town has been a place of safe retreat against the external enemy, the enemy was now within the gates. (1985: 211)

Full circle. The enemy within. In multi-racial, multi-racist British cities the connotations of race too readily transferred the notion of Black youth as this self same 'enemy within'.

There is no space here to detail the sort of analysis that is required in understanding the racialized landscape of the contemporary city. It is now a commonplace to periodize the manner in which race becomes significant, to trace the way in which the articulating principle of racialization has changed from the naked colonialism of the 'coloured migrant' of the post-war years to a much more subtle set of racisms with associated racial formations. Likewise, whereas the popular mobilizations once emphasized the strength of a Black unity that corresponded to the monolith of the colonial legacy, the distinctive experiences of different migrant minorities [have] more recently prompted a stress on the *new ethnicities* so developed, united by difference within a post-colonial context of such a plurality of racisms.

All these developments have their spatial referents. There is space here only to point to the sort of analysis that is required. I can only suggest that such mapping is a direct equivalent of the periodizing of processes of racialization which is now considered so essential (Carter et al., 1987; Harris, 1987). The street, the tower block and the council estate are just three examples of how the socially constructed sites of social relations are loaded with barely hidden racial codes.

In part such spatialization represents the differential focus of the process of racialization, what Gilroy (1987: 230) suggested was the displacing of 'race' and 'class' by the language of 'community'. But it is also about the manner in which space provides one of the principal means by which competing constructions of 'racialized identities' can co-exist simultaneously. Although the two can never be completely separated, such racialized identities are created both by collective action and by the inventions of racist discourse. The discursive field of lore and disorder is just one example of the latter;

racialization and criminalization are conflated in a set of rationalizations and practices that are articulated at specific times and particular places.

Criminalization may create subject positions but it does not create real people. The struggles of community provide only one very important set of sites of racialization. For there are other forces shaping the social form of the contemporary city. As Cooke has remarked, current labour process changes suggest high levels of labour market segmentation:

> the sociological profile of the postmodern era, the development of an hourglass shape to the social structure with a burgeoning service class, an attenuating working class and a burgeoning underclass of unemployed, subemployed and the 'waged poor' of part time and/or casualized labour, classically found in fast food outlets and service stations. (Cooke, 1988: 485)

The highly contingent fault lines along which urban society divides to provide this sort of division of labour in the postmodern city are precisely the places at which a sophisticated theorization of racial formation is required in an urban political economy.

The liberal common-sense image is one of the ghetto and the underclass, the privileged and the dispossessed, the free riders of postmodern capitalism controlling the total exclusion of the truly disadvantaged. Such notions frequently contain a straightforward understanding of ethnicity as a defensive cultural reaction to the forces of change (Keith, 1993). Here I am trying to work towards something slightly more subtle; such naked exclusions are mobilized on some occasions but not on others.

The logic of racial exclusion in liberal texts is consonant with certain dystopian visions of the future which invoke a social control rhetoric of suppression. Cohen, in a work generally more subtle, evokes a vision in which

> we arrive at a vision not too far from Orwell's. Middle class thought crime is subject to inclusionary controls; when these fail and the party members present a political threat, then 'down the chute'. Working-class deviant behaviour is segregated away and contained; if the proles become threatening, they can be 'subjected' like animals by a few simple rules. (Cohen, 1985: 234)

It is here that the realms of social control become so relevant to a conceptualization of racism. For the architecture of models of punitive cities expresses quite clearly the possibilities of forces of exclusion operating *simultaneously* with forces of inclusion, not in opposition to each other but both towards the end of social control in the widest sense of the term.

In the past the insertion of migrant labour at strategic points in the British political economy was facilitated by the creation of a racialized fraction of labour mediated by the force of racism. The apparent long-term economic irrationality of such divisions prompted Sivanandan to predict in the mid-1970s that 'racism dies that capital may survive' (1976: 367) and today underscores the optimism of some liberal analysis of racial formations (Banham, 1988)

But workplace identities and the racial divisions of labour they promote tell only half the story and it is perhaps here that the notion of change implicit in conceptions of the postmodern city [is] analytically most powerful. This is the era of flexible accumulation and highly demarcated market segmentation. The identities of the workplace are not necessarily those of the community, which are not necessarily those of the family. The new racial divisions can be tied functionally to the related notions of disciplined communities and flexible workplaces. The racism expressed in the imagery of a criminalized underclass co-exists alongside a form of racism, different in form if not in kind, which constructs racial divisions of labour. This is at the root of why a leitmotif of notions of Asian entrepreneurial skills can co-exist alongside a contemporary criminalization of Bengali youth in the East End and young Punjabis in Southall which draws on notions of Blackness constructed by the discourse of *lore and disorder*.

The partial nature of the process of racialization as criminalization may simultaneously allow the evolution of a symbolically more successful racialized fraction which serves publicly to rebuke the immiserated majority, and divest White society of any responsibility for such immiseration.
[. . .]

## References

Anderson, B. (1983) *Imagined Communities*. London: Verso.

Banham, J. (1988) 'Urban renewal and ethnic minorities; the challenge to the private sector', *New Community*, 15(1): 15–30.

Becker, H. (1971) *Outsiders*. New York: Free Press.

Bridges, L. and Gilroy, P. (1982) 'Striking back: race and crime', *Marxism Today*, June.

Carter, B.C. Harris, C. and Joshi, S. (1987) 'The 1951–55 Conservative Government and the racialisation of Black immigration', *Immigrants and Minorities*, 6: 335–47.

CCCS (Centre for Contemporary Cultural Studies) (1982a) *The Empire Strikes Back*. London: Hutchinson.

CCCS (Centre for Contemporary Cultural Studies) (1982b) *Making Histories: Studies in History-writing and Politics*. London: Hutchinson.

Christian, L. (1983) *Policing by Coercion*. London: Greater London Council.

Cohen, S. (1985) *Visions of Social Control*. Cambridge: Polity.

Cooke, P. (1988) 'Modernity, postmodernity and the city', *Theory, Culture and Society*, 5: 475–92.

Cross, M. and Keith, M. (eds) (1993) *Racism, the City and the State*. London: Routledge.

Gamble, A. (1988) *The Free Economy and the Strong State: the Politics of Thatcherism*. London: Macmillan.

Gilroy, P. (1982) 'The myth of Black criminality', *Socialist Register*, pp. 47–56.

Gilroy, P. (1987) *There Ain't no Black in the Union Jack*. London: Hutchinson.

Gilroy, P. and Sim, J. (1985) 'Law, order and the state of the left', *Capital and Class*, 25: 15–21.

Goffman, E. (1963) *Stigma*. Harmondsworth: Penguin.

Hall, S. (1980a) 'Race, articulation and societies structured in dominance', in UNESCO (ed.), *Sociological Theories: Race and Colonialism*. Paris: UNESCO.

Hall, S. (1980b) Popular democratic versus authoritarian populism, in A. Hunt (ed.), *Marxism and Democracy*. London: Lawrence & Wishart.

Hall, S. (1988) *A Hard Road to Renewal*. London: Verso.

Hall, S., Critcher, C., Jefferson, T., Clarke, J. and Roberts, B. (1978) *Policing the Crisis*. London: Macmillan.

Harris, C. (1987) 'British capitalism, migration and relative surplus population', *Migration*, 1: 47–90.

Herbert, P. and Omambala, I. (1990) *Policing in the 1990s: a Black Perspective*. London: Society of Black Lawyers.

Hobsbawm, E.J. (1983) 'Mass-producing traditions: Europe, 1870–1914', in E.J. Hobsbawm and T. Ranger (eds), *The Invention of Tradition*. Cambridge: Cambridge University Press.

Keith, M. (1993) 'From punishment to discipline? Racism, racialisation and social control', in M. Cross and M. Keith (eds), *Racism, the City and the State*. London: Routledge.

Laclau, E. and Mouffe, C. (1985) *Hegemony and Socialist Strategy*. London: Verso.

Miles, R. (1982) *Racism and Migrant Labour*. London: Routledge & Kegan Paul.

Miles, R. (1984a) 'Marxism versus the sociology of race relations', *Ethnic and Racial Studies*, 7: 217–37.

Miles, R. (1984b) 'The riots of 1958', *Immigrants and Minorities*, 3: 252–75.

Miles, R. (1989) *Racism*. London: Routledge.

Omi, M. and Winant, H. (1986) *Racial Formation in the United States*, London: Routledge.

Sherwood, M. (1984) *Many Struggles: West Indian Workers and Service Personnel in Britain 1939–45*. London: Karia Press.

Sivanandan, A. (1976) 'Race, class and the state', in A. Sivanandan, *A Different Hunger*. London: Pluto (1982).

Solomos, J. (1988) *Black Youth, Racism and the State: the Politics of Ideology and Policy*. Cambridge: Cambridge University Press.

# 25

# The theoretical and political priorities of critical criminology

*Phil Scraton and Kathryn Chadwick*

[. . .]

### Establishing a framework for critical analysis

> We should admit that power produces knowledge (and not *simply* by encouraging it because it serves power or applying it because it is useful); that power and knowledge *directly* imply one another; that there is no power relation without the correlative constitution of a field of knowledge, or any knowledge that does not presuppose and constitute at the same time power relations. (Foucault, 1977: 27–8, emphases added)

Gouldner's (1969, 1973) devastating indictment of Western sociology established that the 'domain assumptions' of academic disciplines and their preeminent theoretical perspectives had been influenced massively by those powerful vested interests who commissioned research. Academic research was identified as essential to the management of advanced capitalism's inherent contradictions and conflicts. For Foucault, however, power is not unidimensional nor is it restricted to those formal relations of dominance in the economic or political spheres. As Sim (1990: 9) remarks, power is 'dispersed through the body of society' and exercised through the processes of 'discipline, surveillance, individualization and normalization'. Crucially the power–knowledge axis permeates all formal or official discourses, their language, logic, forms of definition and classification, measurement techniques and empiricism as essential elements in the technology of discipline and the process of normalization. 'Professionals', as key interventionists in societal relations and in the political management of social arrangements, pursue a 'logic and language of control' revealing a daunting 'power to classify' with clear consequences for the reproduction of 'bodies' of knowledge and for the maintenance of dominant power relations (Cohen, 1985: 196).

Foucault's work demonstrates that the challenges to mainstream theoretical traditions have adopted the agendas of those traditions, taking their premises as legitimate points of departure. While starting with 'knowledge-as-it-stands', that which is 'known', a radical alternative must also contextualize knowledge – its derivation, consolidation and recognition – within dominant structural relations. Undoubtedly professionals, be they employed in the caring agencies,

Abridged from *The Politics of Crime Control* (eds K. Stenson and D. Cowell), pp. 166–85. (London: Sage, 1991.)

the military, the criminal justice system or private industry, operate on the basis of professional training and work experience enjoying discretionary powers in accord with their rank and status. Yet whatever the quality and implications of decisions formulated and administered at the interpersonal level of 'agency', their recognition and legitimacy are rooted in the determining contexts of 'structure' and their manifestation in the professional ideologies of control and political management (Giddens, 1979, 1984).

The dynamics and visibility of power, however, are not always so obvious. For, 'power may be at its most alarming, and quite often at its most horrifying, when applied as a sanction of force' but it is 'typically at its most intense and durable when running through the repetition of institutionalized practices' (Giddens, 1987: 9). As power is mediated through the operational practices of institutions their daily routines become regularized, even predictable. It is important to establish that the routine world of 'agency', of interpersonal relations, is neither spontaneous nor random. Personal reputations and collective identities are ascribed and become managed via official discourses, themselves derived within the dominant social relations of production, reproduction and neocolonialism. For these represent the primary determining contexts which require and reproduce appropriate relations of power and knowledge.

The structural contradictions of advanced capitalist patriarchies require political management. While grassroots resistance has remained a persistent feature in Western social democracies their great achievement has been to contain opposition through relying on 'consensus' rather than 'coercion'. Relations of domination and exploitation, both material and physical, have become redefined and broadly accepted as the justifiable pursuit of competing interests. The smooth and successful operation of power in this context is dependent on social arrangements, forms of political management and cultural traditions which together contribute towards hegemony (Gramsci, 1971). Dissent and disorder are regulated by social forces and cultural transmission rather than by physical coercion. To challenge orthodoxy, to question the established order or to raise doubts concerning formal authority are not perceived as acts of progression towards worthwhile change but are presented in official discourses as acts of subversion which undermine shared identities and common interests.

While 'power', 'regulation' or 'control' can be identified in personal action and social reaction as part and parcel of the daily routine of *agency*, critical analysis seeks to bring to the fore *structural* relations, involving the economy, the state and ideology, in explaining the significance of the power–knowledge axis and relating it to the processes by which dominant ideas gain political legitimacy. Discrimination on the basis of class, gender, sexuality and perceived ethnicity clearly operates at the level of attitude, on the street, in the home, at the workplace or at social venues. Once institutionalized, however, classism, sexism, heterosexism and racism become systematic and structured. They become the taken-for-granted social histories and contemporary priorities which constitute state institutions, informing policies and underwriting practices, and which provide legitimacy to interpersonal discrimination. Through the process of institutionalization, relations of dominance and subjugation achieve structural significance. Critical analysis of crime and the criminal justice process must be grounded in these theoretical imperatives.

### Class analysis and the determining context of production

Much of the post-war optimism over capital reconstruction and economic growth was derived in the 'Butskellite' compromises which married Keynesian principles concerning state management of the economy to a protected programme of capital investment and development in the private sector (Gamble, 1981; Taylor-Gooby, 1982). This programme was made possible through the initiation of effective, albeit often illusory, programmes of state welfare and social justice. Through initiatives in public housing, access to health care and medicine, new educational priorities and state benefits the popular assumption, also embodied in academic accounts of welfarism, was that benevolent reformism and its commitment to social justice had broken the hold of the free enterprise economy and its market forces over the social well-being of the nation. The era of 'welfare capitalism' had arrived, led by entrepreneurs of conscience who claimed 'people before profit'.

A cursory glance, however, at the relationship between the public and private sectors which emerged during this period reveals the grand illusion through a series of ambiguities and contradictions. In all sections of public service and ownership – schooling, housing, health and medicine – a strong and privileged private sector, bolstered by the inheritance of wealth, was maintained. Property ownership continued to become more centralized and concentrated within fewer hands. The expansion of state interventionism, local and central, ensured that the state became the largest employer and also the primary customer of private capital. Those industries which came under 'state ownership' were those essential to the reconstruction and consolidation of private manufacturing capital yet those deemed to be the least profitable or in need of the most reinvestment: coal, roads, railways, steel, communications, etc. The optimistic portrayal of this new pluralist society – based on equality of opportunity and access, on cradle-to-grave welfarism – disguised the structural contradictions inherent within the social arrangements and relations of the new dawn of economic expansionism.

Friend and Metcalfe (1981) graphically illustrate the divisions, well-established and noted during the depression of the 1920s and 1930s, of regional decline. Although unemployment in the 1950s remained relatively low so too did wages, job security, working conditions and living standards (Nightingale, 1980). The growth in immigration during the 1950s provided further evidence of this apparent expansionism. What was never made clear, however, was that throughout this period emigration exceeded immigration and that many immigrants, particularly from black Commonwealth countries and from Ireland, were fed directly into the worst jobs with the lowest pay and the fewest prospects (Cashmore, 1989; Hall et al., 1978; Miles, 1982; Sivanandan, 1983).

The 'attack on poverty' meant the virtual end of widespread destitution and starvation and there were major advances in housing, health care, schooling and the general 'quality of life' – but the divisions remained. Capital reconstruction, despite the veneer of state interventionism in the management of the economy, meant capital accumulation and this, in turn, delivered the further centralization and concentration of capital. National monopolies became multinational conglomerates and, despite the institution of tiers of executive management as the 'controllers' of industry, ownership – and *effective* control – of industry became even more focused.

Parsons (1951) proclaimed the success of 'integration' of diverse elements within the social system, and Lipset (1960) announced that the fundamental conflicts of early capitalism had been resolved. The argument was that through the decomposition of capital and labour and the 'end of ideology' (Bell, 1960) more affluent and secure workers had taken on the characteristics, lifestyle and ambitions of the middle-class white-collar workers – the consolidation of contemporary industrial societies as essentially classless (Dahrendorf, 1959). This gave academic legitimacy to the dubious claim that the period of economic reconstruction was also one of significant political reconstruction. Class conflict represented a politics of the past matched by class analysis as a theoretical endeavour of the past. In its rush to bury Marxism and to proclaim the arrival of a new, meritocratic form of industrialism, structural functionalism replaced class analysis with stratification theory. Effectively this work failed to recognize that the post-war reconstruction of capital brought with it the reconstruction of class relations including the consolidation of the new professional and managerial class forms, in both the private and public domain, and their internal hierarchies. It also produced new hierarchies of labour within the transitional working class. These were complex developments, particularly as the dynamics of intra-class location encompassed divisions around gender, ethnicity and region as new contexts of class fragmentation.

The broadsides fired by stratification theorists and 'grand theorists' such as Parsons led to the reappraisal of Marxist analysis. Ten years after Dahrendorf's requiem for Marxism, Miliband (1969) and Quinney (1970) published their influential analyses of the advanced capitalist state. There followed a decade of important commentary on the state which picked up and developed the complexities of Miliband's central thesis that those who have occupied the key positions of state power for generations have been drawn from a different class position than those to whom the state administers, and that the legitimacy for that power is found within the dominant political–economic relations and not in the body politic. It proposed that in its mediation of existing class relations and conflict the state, through the rule of law, intervenes to protect, maintain and reproduce the very contradictions which it sets out to mediate (Thompson, 1975). Class rule, claimed Therborn (1978: 132), 'is exercised through state power . . . through the interventions or policies of the state'.

Braverman (1974: 110) noted that the complexity of the class structure of advanced capitalism lay in the fact that 'almost all of the population has been transformed into employees of capital' through 'the purchase and sale of labor power'. For Braverman, as with Thompson, the historical relations of production have given rise to class formations within modes of production, each set of relations bearing the birthmarks of the previous mode. Given that productive relations create shared positions within the process of production it is logical to conclude that the social relations of production are structurally determined. Thus, while class represents a social process reflected in the concrete world of 'human relationships', it represents also a *structural location* within capitalist modes of production. It is precisely because class relations are in process, historically determined yet *responsive* to human relationships, that specific class locations shift as capitalism develops, refines and reconstructs through its stages of accumulation. Any interpretation of the political economy demands the theorization of class relations, for these relations are part of the essential foundations of contemporary social policy, of welfare programmes, of family relations, of culture and subculture of 'community' and of government.

The reaffirmation of class analysis produced important work on class location (Carchedi, 1977; Hunt, 1977; Miliband, 1977; Poulantzas, 1973, 1975; Wright, 1976, 1978) in which the process by which classes were conceptualized and class location established was explored. Braverman and Wright each indicated that class boundaries are located in terms of the economic demands of capital while emphasizing the structural significance of ideological and political criteria. As Poulantzas argued, the divisions which arise out of supervisory or managerial functions occur at the political level. Functionaries of capital, be they in the factory, the state or the police, occupy ambiguous and contradictory class locations. Classes, however, remain 'in motion', they organize and disorganize, they extend and retract their capacities and they are fixed permanently in struggle. The fundamental criteria for the location of classes are economic, however, and this has been clearly evident in the 1980s as the free market economy has expanded but not required a comparable expansion of labour, and substantial numbers of workers have been forced into the relative surplus population.

Marginality, and the process of marginalization, is an important concept in the structural analysis of contemporary class location, class fragmentation and Wright's discussion of contradictory class locations. Implicit in this analysis is the premise that during periods of economic recession part of the total workforce is used as the disposable surplus of wage-labour essential to the reconstruction of capital. During the 1980s while international companies enjoyed unprecedented profits and those with secure incomes took part in a decade of unchecked consumerism, approximately one-third of the population sat, marginalized, on or below the poverty line (Walker and Walker, 1987). While the private sector in housing, education, health care and transport flourished, the National Health Service, state schools, council housing and public transport offered a reduced service staffed by disillusioned workers.

Set within the context of the structural location of class the concept of marginality is both rigorous and significant. Marginality is manifested not only in terms of economic relations but also in terms of the subsequent political and ideological responses to those relations. Just as certain groups occupy 'contradictory class locations' so groups are pushed beyond the marginal locations of the relative surplus population. A range of identifiable groups and individuals, while relying on the capitalist mode of production and social democracy to provide them with an economic opportunity structure, live outside the 'legitimate' social relations of production. Marx (1961: 644) identified those condemned to 'pauperism', 'the hospital of the active labour army . . .' as the 'demoralized and ragged'. They constituted the 'dangerous classes' because their conditions were seen as the breeding ground of dissension and a real threat to civil order and social stability.

The link – unemployment, destitution, crime – has provided an important starting-point for research which has developed the 'surplus population' thesis and its relevance in explaining not only certain categories of crime but also the process of criminalization of certain groups of people. While the 'immiseration thesis' cannot explain fully 'all' crimes it has demonstrated that the broader structural contexts of production and distribution, of poverty and unemployment, are significant in the involvement of people in 'crime' but also in the processes which define, adjust, enforce and administer the criminal law. The policy of targeting identifiable and vulnerable groups through heavy or saturation policing, for example, often precipitates a quasi-political resistance from marginal groups. While street crime might arise out of social, political and economic conditions it is not a progressive 'political' expression. Not only is it unlikely to stimulate long-term solutions to structural problems but inevitably it carries negative consequences. It divides the working class, nourishes racism, popularizes 'law and order' campaigns, victimizes the poor, consolidates the threat of violence towards women and increases the vulnerability of poor neighbourhoods. Consequently street crime, burglary and assault are often intra-class, and exacerbate problems and sharpen contradictions. Clearly poverty and long-term unemployment increase the propensity of the poor to commit 'survival' crime (Box, 1987; Franey, 1983) but this process of immiseration has divisive and threatening consequences as well as the potential for sharpening political consciousness and action.

Criminalization, the application of the criminal label to an identifiable social category, is dependent on *how* certain acts are labelled and on *who* has the power to label, and is directly limited to the political economy of marginalization. The power to criminalize is not derived necessarily in consensus politics but it carries with it the ideologies associated with marginalization and it is within these portrayals that certain actions are named, contained and regulated. This is a powerful process because it mobilizes popular approval and legitimacy in support of powerful interests within the state. As Hillyard's (1987) discussion of Northern Ireland illustrates clearly, public support is more likely to be achieved for state intervention against 'criminal' acts than for the repression or suppression of a 'political' cause. Further, even where no purposeful political intention is involved, the process of criminalization can divert attention from the social or political dynamics of a movement and specify its 'criminal' potential. If black youth is portrayed exclusively as 'muggers' (Hall et al., 1978) there will be less tolerance of organized campaigns which emphasize that they have legitimate political and economic grievances (Gilroy, 1987a). The marginalization of women who campaign for rights or for peace and the questioning of their sexuality is a further example of the process by which meaningful and informed political action can be undermined, de-legitimized and criminalized (Chadwick and Little, 1987; Young, 1990). Fundamental to the criminalization thesis is the proposition that while political motives are downplayed, the degree of *violence* involved is emphasized. In industrial relations, for example, it is the violence of the pickets which is pinpointed (Beynon, 1985; Fine and Millar, 1985; Scraton and Thomas, 1985), rather than the importance, for the success of a strike, of preventing supplies getting through to a factory. The preoccupation with the 'violence' of political opposition makes it easier to mobilize popular support for measures of containment.

In many of these examples, 'criminalization' is a process which has been employed to underpin the repressive or control functions of the state. This compounds further the difficult distinction between 'normal' and 'social' crime, since criminalization fuses the categories. The problem remains that even when violence is only used tactically it is double-edged. It breaks the assumed agreement to pursue conflicts by 'democratic', 'parliamentary' means which is the basis of the social contract and the legitimacy of the liberal-democratic state. The state is then certain to react, by fair means or foul

(Poulantzas, 1975). Consequently it becomes difficult to disentangle those instances in which criminalization is part of the maintenance of social order, and where it is not. Theoretically, however, it highlights a significant function of the law in the ideological containment of class conflict. Married to the process of marginalization, through which identifiable groups systematically and structurally become peripheral to the core relations of the political economy, criminalization offers a strong analytical construct. Taken together these theses provide the foundations to critical analyses of the state, the rule of law and social conflict in advanced capitalist society.

### Racism, crime and the politics of neo-colonialism

> . . . if you were to ask a taxi driver, hotel clerk or news vendor in London they would explain the increase in violent crime, especially robbery, by the presence of West Indians. (Wilson, 1977: 69)

This statement, made by one of the leading New Right criminologists in the USA, directly attributes the escalation of street crime – and other 'predatory' crime – to the behaviour of a clearly identifiable group. It consolidated the media-hyped imagery of the 1970s which first named 'mugging' and then located it within the actions of black Afro-Caribbean youth. What this confirmed, according to Gilroy (1987b: 108), was a generally held assumption that 'undesired immigrants' are infected by a 'culture of criminality and inbred inability to cope with that highest achievement of civilization – the rule of law'. That these views are prevalent in popular culture, the media coverage of 'hard news' and political commentaries is sufficient evidence of the breadth and depth of racism in Britain, but it is their institutionalization as all-pervasive (Gordon, 1983) which transforms imagery into ideology. The ideological construction of the race–crime–black criminality debate has been an essential condition upon which the differential policing and discriminatory punishment afforded to specific neighbourhoods has been based.

Following the serious disturbances in Toxteth, Liverpool, during the summer of 1981 the then Chief Constable of Merseyside Kenneth Oxford justified the well-established principle of heavy policing of Liverpool's black population by direct references to immigration. Immigrants, from as early as 1335, had contributed to the 'turbulent character of the Liverpool populace': 'Each of these new communities brought with them associated problems, disputes and tensions, which on occasion spilled over into outbreaks of violence' (Oxford, 1981: 4). On this basis Oxford defended differential policing and discriminatory practices and discounted allegations of racial harassment or violence. These views, combining traditional criminological theories of individual pathology with those of social pathology, create a 'neat dovetail of genetic characteristics and environmentalism' (Scraton, 1982: 35). They are commonly held throughout the criminal justice process (Gordon, 1983), and inform the decisions and actions of powerful definers throughout all institutions of the British state. While evidence of this was overwhelming in the police-commissioned Policy Studies Institute study of police–community relations in London (PSI, 1983), Scarman (1981) denied the existence of 'institutionalized racism' either in the police or in other state agencies.

Essential to understanding the process of institutionalized racism, however, is the proposition that:

marginalization is not a 'condition' suddenly inflicted on the Afro-Caribbean or Asian community simply by a downturn in the economy. It is written into the statutory definitions of immigration law and reflected in the political management of identities throughout state practices. (Sim et al., 1987: 44)

In constructing an analysis of the social relations of neocolonialism as a determining context, clearly the connection has to be made with class and the relations of production. Advanced capitalism persistently has required relations based on national domination as well as the provision of a ready supply of cheap materials, fuel and labour power. Central to this is the historical development of class fragmentation, particularly the use and abuse of immigrant or migrant labour as 'reserve armies'. Ironically named 'guest workers', the exploitation of cheap labour from the colonies has been a key feature in the construction of European and US labour forces throughout the twentieth century. Sivanandan's (1982) work, as with the excellent Institute of Race Relations' journal *Race and Class*, has done much to remind critical theorists that the connection between 'race' and labour power has formed an essential basis for the consolidation of multinational capitalism. Certainly the relationship between immigrant/ migrant labour and the 'core' working class has created a complex dynamic in the interpretation of class locations. With the political and ideological criteria referred to earlier clearly evident in the politics of racism, black workers, like their late nineteenth century Irish equivalents, have been allocated the least desirable, most insecure and poorest paid work. Their marginalization (some authors argue that they constitute an underclass) is primarily economic and the political and ideological struggles around this process have certainly contributed to the fractionalizing of the working class (Miles, 1982). As Sivanandan suggests, the process of economic marginalization, manifest at all material levels, has brought with it organized resistance and spontaneous rebellion. In his 'reversal' of the orthodoxy Gilroy (1987a) is not as far away from this position as it first seems when he emphasizes the reciprocity of race and class as determining contexts. His concern is to free racism of its subservience to classism, that racism is simply reduced to its function for capital. Racism *can be* and often is implicated in intra-class struggle but it has become central in establishing rational explanations, in the minds as well as the hearts of working class white communities, for diminishing circumstances. Racism, in that sense, is part of British hegemonic consciousness – it carries convincing explanations, it offers plausible accounts and its *logic* must not be underestimated (Cashmore, 1987). What has become clear during the 1980s, however, is the simple proposition that the differential policing and targeting of particular communities has not only led to rebellion (Scraton, 1987) but has also completed the process of marginalization. While it is incorrect to homogenize groups under the ascribed labels of 'black', 'brown', 'people of colour', this is precisely what racism does and organized resistance has emerged. Yet these are the very groups that remain targeted and, as with the earlier discussion on class, the process of criminalization has been hand-in-glove with that of marginalization. Even if identifiable groups have a greater propensity to commit crimes than other comparable groups, and there is no evidence to suggest that 'black crime' is any more prevalent than 'crime' in other communities, that does not explain the ferocity with which the criminal justice process has reacted to the black people with which it deals.

A House of Lords debate in March 1989 on violent crime brought claims by

Conservative peers that 61 per cent of all street robbery was committed by black people. It was alleged that in London boroughs where only 14 per cent of the population were black 72 per cent of rapes were committed by black men. This brought renewed calls to identify the racial background of offenders. Given that further crime surveys in Britain have found that 49 per cent of people 'feared' personal attack on the streets it is clear that the renewed campaign directed towards connecting race and crime has encouraged people to fear young blacks on the streets.

Black defendants are more likely to go to prison earlier, for longer periods and their social workers' reports are more likely to be ignored by the courts, than in the case of comparable offences committed by whites. Afro-Caribbean youths are given custodial sentences more readily and are remanded in custody, despite fewer convictions, than whites. In 1987 83.8 per cent of the male and 72.7 per cent of the women's prison population was classified as 'white'. The increase in black and 'ethnic' imprisonment has been rising by 1 per cent per year since the mid-1980s. In all offence categories black people are sentenced for longer periods, have fewer previous convictions and less serious charges. While the number of young people in black/ethnic groups is approximately 4.3 per cent of the population in most detention or remand centres they number 20–30 per cent of those incarcerated.

The main conclusion to be drawn from the above material is that the reassurances given by the Home Office, by government inquiries and by the liberal commentaries of academics – that racism in the criminal justice process is an issue of the attitudinal approach of individuals and not an institutional problem – are false. It is clear that in terms of access, recruitment, training and development the criminal justice institutions and their professions have failed to deal with their well-established traditions of discrimination. Further, it is clear that racism is endemic in the policies, priorities and practices of the criminal justice institutions.

The shift from labour-intensive production and the uneven distribution of the effects of economic crisis in Britain have contributed significantly to the imposition of long-term, structural unemployment. The inevitable consequences of the economic, political and ideological location of black communities is that they are overrepresented in this surplus population.

> As with the late nineteenth century constructions of moral degeneracy and social contagion, black people have found themselves on the wrong end of the rough–respectable and nondeserving–deserving continua. This series of factors have created the preconditions in which black communities can be identified as the new 'dangerous classes'. (Sim et al., 1987)

## The feminist critiques and the determining context of patriarchy

> Women appear in a sociology predicated on the universe occupied by men . . . its methods, conceptual schemes and theories [have] been based on and built up within the male social universe. (Smith, 1973: 7)

Patriarchy, as the systematic domination of women by men both in the public and private spheres, embodies more than material and physical processes of power. It legitimates its rule, its politics, its universalism through knowledge forms based on 'themes, assumptions, metaphors and images' (Smith, 1975: 354) which underpin academic discourse, as self-evident truths. One such truth is fundamental, that is the defining and differentiating of women with reference to men: 'He is the Subject, He is the Absolute . . . She is the Other' (de Beauvoir, 1972: 16). What academic discourse has assumed is the 'fixed and inevitable destiny' of women as daughters, wives, mothers, mistresses and servicers to their menfolk whose consolidation of power rests on the cultural–legal regulation of paternity (O'Brien, 1981).

Undoubtedly patriarchies develop distinctive and unique characteristics which produce complex institutional forms and social arrangements (Segal, 1987) but the subordination of women is both universal and structural (Connell, 1987; Morgan, 1986). The marginalization of women within patriarchies takes a variety of political and economic forms: the unwaged and unrecognized domestic mode of production (Delphy, 1984); the 'control of women's labour power' (Hartmann, 1979: 14) and the all-pervasiveness of masculine values and processes in paid work (Cockburn, 1986; Walby, 1986); the threat and reality of physical violence (Kelly, 1988; Stanko, 1985). While the caveat of 'false universalism' (Eisenstein, 1984: 141) has recognized the diversity of women's experiences, needs and desires, the project of the feminist critiques of patriarchy has been the deconstruction of the power–knowledge axis within advanced capitalist societies.

While the standpoints and priorities of feminist analyses remain distinctive, particularly in the debates around the relationship between advanced capitalist relations and patriarchal relations, the critiques have been successful and progressive in challenging 'the assumptions which historically have normalized and subordinated political relations based on perceived natural constructs of gender and sexuality . . . assumptions etched deep in the institutional fabric of the political economy which form part of the national consciousness and which become central to the professionalisation of knowledge' (Scraton, 1990: 15). In terms of the earlier discussion of power these assumptions not only underwrite, even encourage, the institutionalized sexism and heterosexism of state institutions but also form part of the daily, hourly round of interpersonal relations which deny women access to social space, silence their voices, violate their bodies and denigrate their resistance.

While state institutions 'coercively and authoritatively constitute the social order in the interest of men as a gender' (Mackinnon, 1983: 44) and advanced capitalism has been eminently successful in its assimilation of quite diverse forms of patriarchies, academic knowledge has provided both the legitimacy and justification for the determining contexts of gender and sexuality (Harding, 1986; Smith, 1988; Sydie, 1987). Within criminology, as Carol Smart first noted in 1976, the 'wider moral, political economic and sexual spheres which influence women's status and position in society' [have] been neglected or seen as irrelevant to the priority of studying men and crime (Smart, 1976: 185). More recent feminist research and publication has posed 'fundamental questions about the adequacy' of criminological analyses which [have] taken for granted the 'exclusion of women' (Gelsthorpe and Morris, 1990: 7). The substantive debates have prioritized: the relationship between patriarchy, the rule of law and the underpinnings of theoretical criminology (Smart, 1989); the universality of violence against women and the persistent reluctance of the state to intervene (Kelly and Radford, 1987); women's incarceration in prisons (Carlen, 1983) and in mental institutions (Showalter, 1987); family law and its 'role in enforcing women's position in society' (Bottomley, 1985: 184).

In addition to this work there has been further critical research into women and crime (Carlen, 1988; Carlen and Worrall, 1987; Heidensohn, 1985). Hilary Allen's (1987: 1) work, for example, confirmed previous research in showing that women are 'twice as likely as a man to be dealt with by psychiatric rather than penal means'. Further, the trend – first reported in 1988 – of a sharp increase in the imprisonment of women, more readily and for longer sentences, has consolidated as courts have become more severe on women offenders. This trend applies also to women with dependent children. In June 1988, 58 per cent of women taken into custody had committed offences involving theft, handling stolen property or fraud. Twenty-five per cent of women prisoners admitted were black. The average sentence increased by 36 per cent on 1987. Of the 1,765 women in prison over half had dependent children and most were convicted of non-violent crimes.

What this range of work has achieved has been to locate these issues within the material base of patriarchy demonstrating the diversity of women's oppression and the dynamics of male dominance. This includes 'women's access to production' and 'control over biological reproduction' but also through 'control of women's sexuality through a particular form of hetero-sexuality' (Mahony, 1985: 70). For 'male identity' and 'male sexuality' are 'crucial to the maintenance of male power' (Mahony, 1985). The determining context of patriarchal relations is based on the material and physical power appropriated by – but also ascribed to – men, and this is supported by a 'hegemonic form of masculinity in the society as a whole' with women 'oriented to accommodating the interests and desires of men' (Connell, 1987: 183). While women fight back individually and collectively, 'emphasized femininity' internalizes the ideology of servicing and use-value, and feeds the politics of dependency. It is within this process that gender divisions and ascribed sexualities become legitimated as 'natural' and, therefore, inevitable.

As with Connell's work, Brittan (1989) and Segal (1990) have explored the importance of hegemonic masculinity or masculinism in its subordination not only of women's sexuality, but also other male sexualities. As Mort (1987) observes, it is the historical processing of medico-legal discourses concerning 'dangerous sexualities' which has rendered alternative expressions of sexuality unacceptable, abnormal and unnatural. The broad consensus around what Rich (1977) labelled 'compulsory heterosexuality' has had a major impact on legislation but also has lessened significantly official responses to crimes against lesbians and gay men. Once again, the duality of marginaliz-ation is clear: the criminalization of the 'outcrop' (prostitutes not clients, homosexuals not harassers etc.), and the reluctance to regulate or act against the oppressors.

Clearly all women are controlled by the public and private realities and fears inherent within male power relations but when they assert their rights, contest their oppression or organize against the discriminatory practices of the law, they become the threat. These are the women, already economically marginalized by the dependency relations of advanced capitalist patriarchy, who are further marginalized by their politics of opposition. Ultimately, as Chadwick and Little (1987) show, they are criminalized. The feminist critiques of criminology, both old and new, have demonstrated that critical criminology must have at its core the marginalization and criminalization of women, women's experiences of the criminal justice process and relationship of women to crime. They provide not only an essential contribution to critical analysis but also to the realization of a critical methodology which interprets the interpersonal experiences of women within the broader structural relations of advanced capitalist patriarchy.

## Conclusion

What this discussion has pursued is the central argument that critical criminology recognizes the reciprocity inherent in the relationship between *structure* and *agency* but also that structural relations embody the primary determining contexts of production, reproduction and neocolonialism. In order to understand the dynamics of life in advanced capitalist societies and the institutionalization of ideological relations within the state and other key agencies it is important to take account of the historical, political and economic contexts of classism, sexism, heterosexism and racism. These categories do not form hierarchies of oppression, they are neither absolute nor are they totally determining, but they do carry with them the weight and legitimacy of official discourse. They reflect and succour the power-knowledge axis both in popular culture and in academic endeavour.

While the state, as a series of often contradictory relations, negotiates with oppositional forces and develops administrative and professional strategies/alliances to deal with political struggle, its essential objective is the maintenance of the established order. The politics of liberal democracy demands room for manoeuvre, some discretionary possibilities and occasional progressive reform but the state's legacy is essentially conservative. It is that of containment, caution and political management. As Sim et al. (1987: 62) state:

> Advanced capitalism, with the added complexity of managerial relations and class fractions, is served and serviced but rarely confronted by the state's institutions whose members share its ends, if not always its means, in a common ideology. It is at this level that the function of institutions, exemplified by the rule of law, tutors and guides the broad membership of society.

The above discussion demonstrates the basis upon which class fragmentation occurs and how those economically marginalized are exposed to the processes of criminalization. Additionally the post-colonial exploitation of migrant and immigrant labour has served capitalism and has led to a form of immiseration connected directly to racism. Finally, patriarchy has been functional for capital both in the public and private spheres. The interpretation and analysis of these primary determining contexts, however, cannot be limited to economic imperatives. Patriarchy and neo-colonialism are also political forms which give rise to opposition and challenge. Yet, at the ideological level, their construction as oppressive social and political orders is justified and reinforced. The criminal justice process and the rule of law assist in the management of structural contradictions and the process of criminalization is central to such management. While maintaining the face of consent, via negotiation, the tacit understanding is that coercion remains the legitimate and sole prerogative of the liberal democratic state. Liberalism and authoritarianism do not form distinctive regimes or administrations within the context of democracy, they constitute a well-established spectrum of legitimate state rule and its use of legal censures.

## References

Allen, H. (1987) *Justice Unbalanced: Gender, Psychiatry and Judicial Decisions*. Milton Keynes: Open University Press.

Bell, D. (1960) *The End of Ideology*. New York: Free Press.

Beynon, H. (1985) *Digging Deeper: Issues in the Miners' Strike*. London: Verso.

Bottomley, A. (1985) 'What is happening to family law? A feminist critique of conciliation', in J. Brophy and C. Smart (eds), *Women in Law*. London: Routledge and Kegan Paul.

Box, S. (1987) *Recession, Crime and Punishment*. London: Macmillan.

Braverman, H. (1974) *Labor and Monopoly Capital*. New York: Monthly Review Press.

Brittan, A. (1989) *Masculinity and Power*. Cambridge: Polity.

Carchedi, G. (1977) *On the Economic Identification of Social Classes*. London: Routledge and Kegan Paul.

Carlen, P. (1983) *Women's Imprisonment*. London: Routledge and Kegan Paul.

Carlen, P. (1988) *Women, Crime and Poverty*. Milton Keynes: Open University Press.

Carlen, P. and Worrall, A. (1987) *Gender, Crime and Justice*. Milton Keynes: Open University Press.

Cashmore, E.E. (1987) *The Logic of Racism*. London: Allen and Unwin.

Cashmore, E.E. (1989) *United Kingdom? Class, Race and Gender since the War*. London: Unwin Hyman.

Chadwick, K. and Little, C. (1987) 'The criminalisation of women', in P. Scraton (ed.), *Law, Order and the Authoritarian State*. Milton Keynes: Open University Press.

Cockburn, C. (1986) *Machineries of Dominance*. London: Pluto.

Cohen, S. (1985) *Visions of Social Control*. Cambridge: Polity.

Connell, R.W. (1987) *Gender and Power*. Cambridge: Polity.

Dahrendorf, R. (1959) *Class and Class Conflict in Industrial Society*. Stanford, CA: Stanford University Press.

de Beauvoir, S. (1972) *The Second Sex*. Harmondsworth: Penguin.

Delphy, C. (1984) *Close to Home: a Materialist Analysis of Women's Oppression*. London: Hutchinson.

Eisenstein, H. (1984) *Contemporary Feminist Thought*. London: Counterpoint.

Fine, B. and Millar, R. (eds) (1985) *Policing the Miners' Strike*. London: Lawrence and Wishart.

Foucault, M. (1977) *Discipline and Punish: the Birth of the Prison*. London: Allen Lane.

Franey, R. (1983) *Poor Law*. London: CHAR/NCCL.

Friend, A. and Metcalfe, A. (1981) *Slump City: the Politics of Mass Unemployment*. London: Pluto Press.

Gamble, A. (1981) *Britain in Decline*. London: Papermac.

Gelsthorpe, L. and Morris, A. (eds) (1990) *Feminist Perspectives in Criminology*. Milton Keynes: Open University Press.

Giddens, A. (1979) *Central Problems in Social Theory*. London: Macmillan.

Giddens, A. (1984) *The Constitution of Society*. Cambridge: Polity.

Giddens, A. (1987) *The Nation-State and Violence*. Cambridge: Polity.

Gilroy, P. (1987a) *There Ain't No Black in the Union Jack*. London: Hutchinson.

Gilroy, P. (1987b) 'The myth of black criminality', in P. Scraton (ed.), *Law, Order and the Authoritarian State*. Milton Keynes: Open University Press.

Gordon, P. (1983) *White Law*. London: Pluto Press.

Gouldner, A.W. (1969) *The Coming Crisis in Western Sociology*. London: Heinemann.

Gouldner, A.W. (1973) 'Foreword' in I. Taylor, P. Walton and J. Young, *The New Criminology*. London: Routledge and Kegan Paul.

Gramsci, A. (1971) *Selections from the Prison Notebooks*. London: Lawrence and Wishart.

Hall, S., Critcher, C., Jefferson, T., Clarke, J. and Roberts, B. (1978) *Policing the Crisis*. London: Macmillan.

Harding, S. (1986) *The Science Question in Feminism*. Milton Keynes: Open University Press.

Hartmann, H. (1979) 'The unhappy marriage of Marxism and feminism: towards a progressive union', *Capital and Class*, 8.

Heidensohn, F. (1985) *Women and Crime*. London: Macmillan.

Hillyard, P. (1987) 'The normalization of special powers: from Northern Ireland to Britain', in

P. Scraton (ed.), *Law, Order and the Authoritarian State*. Milton Keynes: Open University Press.

Hunt, A. (ed.) (1977) *Class and Class Structure*. London: Lawrence and Wishart.

Kelly, L. (1988) *Surviving Sexual Violence*. Cambridge: Polity.

Kelly, L. and Radford, J. (1987) 'The problem of men: feminist perspectives on sexual violence', in P. Scraton (ed.), *Law, Order and the Authoritarian State*. Milton Keynes: Open University Press.

Lipset, S. (1960) *Political Man*. New York: Doubleday.

Mackinnon, C.A. (1983) 'Feminism, Marxism, method and the state: toward feminist jurisprudence', *Signs*, 8(4): 635–58.

Mahony, P. (1985) *Schools for the Boys? Co-education Reassessed*. London: Hutchinson.

Marx, K. (1961) *Capital*, vols I–III. London: Lawrence and Wishart.

Miles, R. (1982) *Racism and Migrant Labour*. London: Routledge and Kegan Paul.

Miliband, R. (1969) *The State in Capitalist Society*. London: Weidenfeld and Nicolson.

Miliband, R. (1977) *Class and Politics*. London: Macmillan.

Morgan, R. (ed.) (1986) *Sisterhood is Global*. Harmondsworth: Penguin.

Mort, F. (1987) *Dangerous Sexualities*. London: Routledge and Kegan Paul.

Nightingale, M. (1980) *Merseyside in Crisis*. Liverpool: Merseyside Socialist Research Group.

O'Brien, M. (1981) *The Politics of Reproduction*. London: Routledge and Kegan Paul.

Oxford, K. (1981) *Report of the Police Committee on Merseyside Disorders* (Evidence to the Scarman Inquiry) [K. Oxford, Chief Constable]. Liverpool: Merseyside Police.

Parsons, T. (1951) *The Social System*. London: Routledge and Kegan Paul.

Poulantzas, N. (1973) 'On social classes', *New Left Review*, 78: 27–55.

Poulantzas, N. (1975) *Political Power and Social Classes*. London: New Left Books.

PSI Report (1983) *Police and People in London*, vols I–IV. London: Policy Studies Institute.

Quinney, R. (1970) *The Social Reality of Crime*. Boston: Little Brown.

Rich, A. (1977) *Of Woman Born: Motherhood as Experience and Institution*. London: Virago.

Scarman, Lord (1981) *The Scarman Report: the Brixton Disorders 10–12 April 1981*. Cmnd 8427. London: HMSO.

Scraton, P. (1982) 'Policing and institutionalised racism on Merseyside', in D. Cowell, T.Jones and J. Young (eds), *Policing the Riots*. London: Junction Books.

Scraton, P. (1987) 'Unreasonable force: policing, punishment and marginalisation', in P. Scraton (ed.), *Law, Order and the Authoritarian State*. Milton Keynes: Open University Press.

Scraton, P. (1990) 'Scientific knowledge or masculine discourses? Challenging patriarchy in criminology', in L. Gelsthorpe and A. Morris (eds), *Feminist Perspectives in Criminology*. Milton Keynes: Open University Press.

Scraton, P. and Thomas, P. (1985) *The State v. The People: Lessons from the Coal Dispute* (*Journal of Law and Society*, special issue). Oxford: Basil Blackwell.

Segal, L. (1987) *Is the Future Female? Troubled Thoughts on Contemporary Feminism*. London: Virago.

Segal, L. (1990) *Slow Motion: Changing Masculinities, Changing Men*. London: Virago.

Showalter, E. (1987) *The Female Malady. Women, Madness and English Culture, 1830–1980*. London: Virago.

Sim, J. (1990) *Medical Power in Prisons: the Prison Medical Service in England 1774–1989*. Milton Keynes: Open University Press.

Sim, J., Scraton, P. and Gordon, P. (1987) 'Crime, the state and critical analysis: an introduction', in P. Scraton (ed.), *Law, Order and the Authoritarian State*. Milton Keynes: Open University Press.

Sivanandan, A. (1982) 'From resistance to rebellion', *Race and Class*, special issue, XXIII.

Sivanandan, A. (1983) *A Different Hunger*. London: Pluto Press.

Smart, C. (1976) *Women, Crime and Criminology*. London: Routledge and Kegan Paul.

Smart, C. (1989) *Feminism and the Power of Law*. London: Routledge.

Smith, D. (1973) 'Women's perspective as a radical critique of sociology', *Sociological Inquiry*, 44.

Smith, (1975) 'An analysis of the ideological structures and how women are excluded', *Canadian Journal of Sociology and Anthropology*, 12(4).

Smith, D. (1988) *The Everyday World as Problematic: a Feminist Sociology*. Milton Keynes: Open University Press.

Stanko, E. (1985) *Intimate Intrusions*. London: Routledge and Kegan Paul.

Sydie, R. (1987) *Natural Women, Cultured Men: a Feminist Perspective on Sociological Theory*. Milton Keynes: Open University Press.

Taylor-Gooby, P. (1982) *The Welfare State from the Second World War to the 1980s*. D355 Social Policy and Social Welfare. Milton Keynes: Open University Press.

Therborn, G. (1978) *What Does the Ruling Class Do When It Rules?* London: New Left Books.

Thompson, E.P. (1975) *Whigs and Hunters: the Origin of the Black Act*. London: Allen Lane.

Walby, S. (1986) *Patriarchy at Work*. Cambridge: Polity.

Walker, A. and Walker, C. (eds) (1987) *The Growing Divide: a Social Audit 1979–1987*. London: CPAG.

Wilson, J.Q. (1977) 'Crime and punishment in England', in R.E. Tyrrell Jr (ed.), *The Future that Doesn't Work: Social Democracy's Failures in Britain*. New York: Doubleday.

Wright, E.O. (1976) 'Class boundaries in advanced capitalist societies;, *New Left Review*, 98: 3–41.

Wright, E.O. (1978) *Class, Crisis and the State*. London: New Left Books.

Young, A. (1990) *Femininity in Dissent*. London: Routledge.

# 26

# Critical criminology and the concept of crime

## *Louk H.C. Hulsman*

### Are criminal events exceptional? Problematizing the normal outlook on crime

[. . .]

People who are involved in 'criminal' events do not appear in themselves to form a special category of people. Those who are officially recorded as 'criminal' constitute only a small part of those involved in events that legally are considered to require criminalization. Among them young men from the most disadvantaged sections of the population are heavily over-represented.

Within the concept of criminality a broad range of situations are linked together. Most of these, however, have separate properties and no common denominator: violence within the family, violence in an anonymous context in the streets, breaking into private dwellings, completely divergent ways of illegal receiving of goods, different types of conduct in traffic, pollution of the environment, some forms of political activities. Neither in the motivation of those who are involved in such events, nor in the nature of the consequences or in the possibilities of dealing with them (be it in a preventive sense, or in the sense of the control of the conflict) is there any common structure to be discovered. All [that] these events have in common is that the CJS [criminal justice system] is authorized to take action against them. Some of these events cause considerable suffering to those involved, quite often affecting both perpetrator and victim. Consider for example traffic accidents and violence within the family. The vast majority of the events which are dealt with within the CJS in the sphere of crime, however, would not score particularly high on an imaginary scale of personal hardship. Matrimonial difficulties, difficulties between parents and children, serious difficulties at work and housing problems will, as a rule, be experienced as more serious both as to degree and duration. If we compare 'criminal events' with other events, there is – on the level of those directly involved – nothing which distinguishes those 'criminal' events intrinsically from other difficult or unpleasant situations. Nor are they singled out as a rule by those directly involved themselves to be dealt with in a way differing radically from the way other events are dealt with. Last, not least, some of these events are considered by those directly involved (and sometimes also by 'observers') as positive and harmless.

It is therefore not surprising that a considerable proportion of the events

---

Abridged from *Contemporary Crises*, 1986, 10(1): 63–80.

which would be defined as serious crime within the context of the CJS remain completely outside that system. They are settled within the social context in which they take place (the family, the trade union, the professional association, the circle of friends, the workplace, the neighbourhood) in a similar way as other non-criminal trouble.

All this means that there is no 'ontological reality' of crime.

## Critical criminology and the concept of crime: what has been problematized and what not?

Critical criminology has naturally problematized and criticized many of the 'normal' notions about crime [. . .]. The contribution to this form of 'debunking' varies according to the different perspectives of the stream of critical criminology involved. In a certain period, Marxist criminology predominantly took the stand that 'crime' was a product of the capitalistic system, and that crime would disappear if a new society took birth. In this perspective the disappearance of 'crime' was seen as a disappearance of the 'problematic situations' which are supposed to trigger the criminalization processes. Disappearance of crime was not seen as 'the disappearance of criminalization processes *as an answer* to problematic situations'. In a later stage, critical criminology problematized the class-biased and 'irrational' aspects of the processes of primary and secondary criminalization. In those endeavours the 'functionality' as well as the 'legal equality principle', which are so often invoked as legitimation of processes of primary criminalization, were demystified. On the basis of such a de-mystification, critical criminology has argued for partial decriminalization, a more restrictive policy with respect to recourse to criminal law, radical non-intervention with respect to certain crimes and certain criminals. It has pointed to the far more weighty crimes of the powerful and asked for a change in criminal justice activities from the weak and the working class towards 'white-collar crime'. It has pictured the war against crime as a sidetrack from the class struggle, at best an illusion invented to sell news, at worst an attempt to make the poor scapegoats. With very few exceptions, however, the concept of crime as such, the ontological reality of crime, has not been challenged.
[. . .]

## What does it mean when we do not problematize (and reject) the concept of crime?

When we do not problematize (and reject) the concept of crime it means that we are stuck in a catascopic view on society in which our informational base (as well the 'facts' as their 'interpretational frame') depends mainly on the institutional framework of criminal justice. It means therefore that we do not take effectively into account the critical analyses of this institutional framework by 'critical criminology'. [. . .] [C]ritical criminology has to abandon a catascopic view on social reality, based on the definitional activities of the system which is the subject of its study, and has instead to take an anascopic stance towards social reality. This makes it necessary to abandon as a tool in the conceptual frame of criminology the notion of 'crime'. Crime has no ontological reality. Crime is not the *object* but the *product* of criminal policy. Criminalization is one of the many ways to construct social reality. In other words, when someone (person or organization) wants to criminalize, this implies that he:

1  deems a certain 'occurrence' or 'situation' as undesirable;
2  attributes that undesirable occurrence to an individual;
3  approaches this particular kind of individual behaviour with a specific style of social control: the style of punishment; ·
4  applies a very particular style of punishment which is developed in a particular (legal) professional context and which is based on a 'scholastic' (last-judgement) perspective on the world. In this sense the style of punishment used in criminal justice differs profoundly from the styles of punishment in other social contexts;
5  wants to work in a special organizational setting – criminal justice. This organizational setting is characterized by a very developed division of labour, a lack of accountability for the process as a whole and a lack of influence of those directly involved in the 'criminalized' event on the outcome of the process.

[. . .]


## Developing an anascopic view

*Defining and dealing with trouble outside a formal context*

[. . .]

The meanings which those directly involved (and observers) bestow upon situations influence how they will deal with them. Laura Nader (1980) distinguishes the following procedures people use in dealing with trouble:

- *Lumping it.* The issue or problem that gave rise to a disagreement is simply ignored and the relationship with the person who is part of the disagreement is continued.
- *Avoidance or exit.* This option entails withdrawing from a situation or curtailing or terminating a relationship by leaving.
- *Coercion.* This involves unilateral action.
- *Negotiation.* The two principal parties are the decision makers, and the settlement of the matter is one to which both parties agree, without the aid of a third party. They do not seek a solution in terms of rules, but try to create the rules by which they can organize their relationship with one another.
- *Mediation.* Mediation, in contrast, involves a third party who intervenes in a dispute to aid the principals in reaching an agreement.
- Other procedural modes that are used in attempts to handle trouble are *arbitration* and *adjudication*. In *arbitration* both principals consent to the intervention of a third party whose judgement they must agree to accept beforehand. When we speak about *adjudication* we refer to the presence of a third party who has the authority to intervene in a dispute whether or not the principals wish it.

The list of ways of dealing with trouble which Nader gives is by no means exhaustive. People can address themselves for help to different professional or non-professional settings. They may engage in a 'ritual of reordering' which does not involve the other person earlier implied in the problematic situation (Pfohl, 1981).

People may also engage in collective action to bring about a structural change in the situations which cause them trouble (Abel, 1982).

Which of these many courses of action will an involved person choose?

The meaning which a directly involved person bestows upon a situation will influence [. . .] his course of action. That course of action will also be influenced by the degree to which different strategies to deal with trouble are available and accessible for him; in other words, the degree to which he has a real possibility of choice. This degree of choice is largely influenced by his place in the network of power which shapes his environment and by his practical possibilities to change the 'tribes' of which he is a part for other ones.

*Formal and informal ways of defining trouble and dealing with it compared*

The process of bestowing meaning on what is going on in life is flexible in face to face relations in so far as those involved in this process feel relatively 'free' towards each other as equal human beings. In other words, if they feel not constrained by the requirements of organizational or professional roles, and [if] they are not caught in a power relation which prevents some of the parties [from fully taking part] in this process. This flexibility has many advantages. It increases the possibilities to reach by negotiation a common meaning of problematic situations. It provides also possibilities for learning. Experience can teach people that the application of a certain frame of interpretation and a certain focus does not lead very far in certain sectors of life.

This flexibility is often lacking when situations are defined and dealt with in a highly formalized context. The more such a context is specialized, the more the freedom of definition – and thus of reaction – is limited by a high degree of division of labour or by a high degree of professionalization. In such a case it depends on the type of institution which has – fortuitously – taken the case up which definition and which answer will be given. It is improbable that a definition and a reaction provided for in such a context [will correspond] with the definition and reactions of [those directly] involved.

There are, however, important differences in the degree of flexibility which formal institutions involved in a problematic situation show. In many countries we find a high degree of flexibility in parts of the police organization, e.g. the neighbourhood police. The same may be true of the first echelons of the health and social work system. Of all formalized control systems the criminal justice system seems the most inflexible. The organizational context (high division of labour) and the internal logic of its specific frame of interpretation (peculiar style of punishment in which a gravity scale modelled according to the 'last judgement' plays an overriding role) both contribute to this inflexibility. Another factor in the particularly alienating effect of criminal justice involvement in problematic situations is its extremely narrow focus: only very specific events modelled in accordance with a legal incrimination may be taken into account and these may only be considered as they were supposed to be [at] a certain moment in time. The dynamic side of constructing reality [is lacking] completely in this particular system. Thus the construction of reality as it is pursued in criminal justice will practically never coincide with the dynamics of the construction of reality of [those directly] involved. In criminal justice one is generally deciding on a reality which exists only within the system and seldom finds a counterpart in the outside world.

[. . .]

## Conclusion

What would be the task of a critical criminology which has abandoned, according to the view developed above, 'crime' as a conceptual tool? The main tasks of such a critical criminology can be summarized as follows:

1   Continue to describe, explain and demystify the activities of criminal justice and its adverse social effects. This activity should, however, be more directed than up till now to the defining activities of this system. To do that, it would be necessary to compare in concrete fields of human life the activities of criminal justice (and their social effects) with those of other formal control systems (legal ones, like the civil justice system, and non-legal ones, like the medical and social work systems). The activities of those formal control systems with respect to a certain area of life should be at the same time compared with informal ways of dealing with such an area of life. In such a task, critical criminology can be stimulated by the developments in (legal) anthropology and in a more general way by sociology in an interpretative paradigm. This implies abandoning 'behaviour' and deviance as a starting-point for analysis and adopting instead a situation-oriented approach, micro and macro.

2   Illustrate – but only as a way of example without pretending to be a 'science of problematic situations' – how in a specific field problematic situations could be addressed at different levels of the societal organization without having recourse to criminal justice.

3   Study strategies [on] how to abolish criminal justice; in other words, how to liberate organizations like the police and the courts [from] a system of reference which turns them away [from] the variety of life and the needs of those directly involved.

4   One of these strategies ought to be to contribute to the development of another overall language in which questions related to criminal justice and to public problems which generate claims to criminalization can be discussed without the bias (Cohen, 1985) of the present 'control babble'.

## References

Abel, R. (ed.) (1982) *The Politics of Informal Justice*. New York: Academic Press.

Cohen, S. (1985) *Visions of Social Control*. Cambridge: Polity.

Nader, L. (ed.) (1980) *No Access to Law: Alternatives to the American Judicial System*. New York: Academic Press.

Pfohl, S.J. (1981) 'Labelling criminals', in H.L. Ross (ed.), *Law and Deviance*, Beverly Hills, CA: Sage.

# PART FOUR
# CRIME CONTROL I: CRIMINAL JUSTICE AND SOCIAL POLICY

## Introduction

In 1974 Robert Martinson declared that '[w]ith few and isolated exceptions, the rehabilitative efforts that have been reported so far have had no appreciable effect on recidivism' ('What works? Questions and answers about penal reform', *The Public Interest*, no. 35, p. 25). This 'nothing works' statement heralded the final death knell for those who believed that modern post-war Western societies had the capacity to rehabilitate and/or treat offenders and reduce recidivism. As the readings in this section indicate, it also sparked off a wide-ranging, high profile post-rehabilitation debate about whether and how crime could be controlled effectively.

James Q. Wilson argues that we need to forget theorizing about the causes of crime and concentrate on the realities and pragmatics of crime and criminality. He stresses that a significant and meaningful reduction could be achieved by recognizing that crime was a quasi-economic endeavour whose occurrence could be made to vary with the costs imposed upon it. By imposing prison sentences swiftly and without exception, society could remove from circulation the most frequently convicted and most active criminals for a significant portion of their criminal careers. The knowledge of swift processing and near certain incarceration, he argues, could, in addition to incapacitating convicted criminals, also intimidate potential offenders. Thus society could, if it chose to, control crime to some degree by recognizing that punishment is a worthy objective of the criminal justice system and by raising the stakes considerably.

Andrew von Hirsch proposes what he and the members of the Committee for the Study of Incarceration view as a politically feasible alternative to the populist 'lock 'em up' approach of Wilson. 'Just and commensurate deserts' or retributivism stressed that punishment rather than rehabilitation or treatment is important because it implies blame and the severity of the punishment symbolizes the degree of blame. Once we have acknowledged that certain forms of action and behaviour are wrong and ought to be punished, we can set reasonable limits on the extent of the punishment and retribution. The severity of the punishment should be proportionate to the gravity of the offence. Stringent punishments should be limited to crimes that inflict serious harm and indicate considerable culpability on the part of the offender. As the magnitude of the crime diminishes so should the nature of the punishment. This theory attempts to centre the question 'What is fair and just?' rather than 'What works?'. In doing so, it is not interested in speculating on the motives of offenders or in attempting to socially engineer lower crime rates.

In the next reading, Francis T. Cullen and K.E. Gilbert mount a spirited defence of the rehabilitative ideal against both Wilson and 'just deserts'. They argue that liberals and those on the Left should not abandon rehabilitation because it: imposes positive obligations on the state to have regard for the welfare of offenders; can act as a bulwark against the punitive law and order demands of the Right; has considerable support within the criminal justice system; and is essentially humanitarian, compassionate and optimistic in orientation.

Ron Clarke offers another highly pragmatic vision of what effective crime control would entail. If we view crime as being the consequence of immediate choices and decisions by offenders then a whole series of possibilities for preventing crime situationally present themselves. He argues that it is perfectly possible to reduce substantially the physical opportunities for offending and to increase the chances of a given offender being caught in the act. Despite being initially berated for its 'crude' suppositions about human nature and anti-theoretical stance, this approach enjoyed a remarkable political popularity in the 1980s and 1990s. It carried the positive message that a multitude of crimes could be effectively designed out and eradicated and that all of us could take active collective and individual steps to protect ourselves and our property from the criminal.

By contrast Elliot Currie presents us with a left realist social crime prevention programme. For him the transition to a market-based society has had a devastating impact on key areas of social, economic and cultural life. The result is spiralling crime rates, social fragmentation and individual alienation. Currie stresses that effective crime control requires confronting the roots of the problem. To tackle economic and social inequalities we need pro-active state coordinated labour market policies and comprehensive welfare strategies which are based on the notion of inclusive citizenship. We also need as a matter of urgency to develop a package of very specific child and family interventions, youth-oriented policies and imaginative drug regulation programmes.

Willem De Haan argues beyond the other approaches by stating that responding positively and constructively requires abandoning the notion of 'crime'. We need to talk and think about diverse troubles, conflicts, harms, damage, conflicting interests, unfortunate events and accidents. We also need to break with the crime control = punishment = imprisonment nexus. It is only then that we will be in a position to construct rational, innovative and constructive redress-based mechanisms for resolving conflicts, settling disputes and preventing social negativity. De Haan does not under-estimate the problems that such a radical imaginary will encounter but he argues forcefully that the other proposals have manifestly failed to deliver long-term crime control and should be in fact viewed as part of the problem rather than as part of the solution.

The final reading brings us back to the 'real' world with Malcolm Feeley and Jonathan Simon relating the emergence of a new late twentieth century penological discourse. This in essence is the managerialist approach to the problem of crime. It is not interested in philosophizing about or assessing the respective merits of deterrence, just deserts, individual rehabilitation or recidivism. It is committed to the effective management of the criminal justice system and its component parts. Cost-effectiveness, efficient forms of custody and control, the identification and classification of risk, performance indicators, quasi-competition and organizational targets are the concerns of the new managerial regime. The system is not concerned about what is happening in the outside world – it has its own specific set of internal goals to meet. However, Feeley and Simon also suggest that this new systems approach overlaps with more general authoritarian discourses on how to manage problem populations and communities.

# 27

# On deterrence

## James Q. Wilson

The average citizen hardly needs to be persuaded of the view that crime will be more frequently committed if, other things being equal, crime becomes more profitable compared to other ways of spending one's time. Accordingly, the average citizen thinks it obvious that one major reason why crime has gone up is that people have discovered it is easier to get away with it; by the same token, the average citizen thinks a good way to reduce crime is to make the consequences of crime to the would-be offender more costly (by making penalties swifter, more certain, or more severe), or to make the value of alternatives to crime more attractive (by increasing the availability and pay of legitimate jobs), or both. Such opinions spring naturally to mind among persons who notice, as a fact of everyday life, that people take their hands off hot stoves, shop around to find the best buy, smack their children to teach them not to run out into a busy street, and change jobs when the opportunity arises to earn more money for the same amount of effort.

These citizens may be surprised to learn that social scientists who study crime are deeply divided over the correctness of such views. To some scholars, especially economists, the popular view is also the scientifically correct one – becoming a criminal can be explained in much the same way we explain becoming a carpenter or buying a car. To other scholars, especially sociologists, the popular view is wrong – crime rates do not go up because people discover they can get away with it and will not come down just because society decides to get tough on criminals.

The debate over the effect on crime rates of changing the costs and benefits of crime is usually referred to as a debate over deterrence – a debate, that is, over the efficacy (and perhaps even the propriety) of trying to prevent crime by making would-be offenders more fearful of committing crime. But that is something of a misnomer, because the theory of human nature on which is erected the idea of deterrence (the theory that people respond to the penalties associated with crime) is also the theory of human nature that supports the idea that people will take jobs in preference to crime if the jobs are more attractive. In both cases, we are saying that would-be offenders are reasonably rational and respond to their perception of the costs and benefits attached to alternative courses of action. When we use the word 'deterrence', we are calling attention only to the cost side of the equation. There is no word in common scientific usage to call attention to the benefit side of the equation; perhaps 'inducement' might serve. To a psychologist, deterring persons from

Abridged from *Thinking About Crime*, pp. 117–23; 142–4. (New York: Basic Books, 1983. Second Revised Edition. First published 1975.)

committing crimes or inducing persons to engage in non-criminal activities are but special cases of using 'reinforcements' (or rewards) to alter behavior.

The reason there is a debate among scholars about deterrence is that the socially imposed consequences of committing a crime, unlike the market consequences of shopping around for the best price, are characterized by delay, uncertainty, and ignorance. In addition, some scholars contend that a large fraction of crime is committed by persons who are so impulsive, irrational, or abnormal that even if there were no delay, uncertainty, or ignorance attached to the consequences of criminality, we would still have a lot of crime.

Imagine a young man walking down the street at night with nothing on his mind but a desire for good times and high living. Suddenly he sees a little old lady standing alone on a dark corner stuffing the proceeds of her recently cashed social security check into her purse. There is nobody else in view. If the boy steals the purse, he gets the money immediately. That is a powerful incentive, and it is available immediately and without doubt. The costs of taking it are uncertain; the odds are at least fourteen to one that the police will not catch a given robber, and even if he is caught the odds are very good that he will not go to prison, unless he has a long record. On the average, no more than three felonies out of 100 result in the imprisonment of the offender. In addition to this uncertainty, whatever penalty may come his way will come only after a long delay; in some jurisdictions, it might take a year or more to complete the court disposition of the offender, assuming he is caught in the first place. Moreover, this young man may, in his ignorance of how the world works, think the odds in his favor are even greater and that the delay will be even longer.

Compounding the problems of delay and uncertainty is the fact that society cannot feasibly reduce the uncertainty attached to the chances of being arrested by more than a modest amount and though it can to some degree increase the probability and severity of a prison sentence for those who are caught, it cannot do so drastically by, for example, summarily executing all convicted robbers or even by sending all robbers to 20-year prison terms. Some scholars add a further complication: the young man may be incapable of assessing the risks of crime. How, they ask, is he to know his chances of being caught and punished? And even if he does know, is he perhaps 'driven' by uncontrollable impulses to snatch purses whatever the risks?

As if all this were not bad enough, the principal method by which scholars have attempted to measure the effect on crime of differences in the probability and severity of punishment has involved using data about aggregates of people (entire cities, counties, states, and even nations) rather than about individuals. In a typical study, of which there have been several dozen, the rate at which, say, robbery is committed in each state is 'explained' by means of a statistical procedure in which the analyst takes into account both the socioeconomic features of each state that might affect the supply of robbers (for example, the percentage of persons with low incomes, the unemployment rate, or the population density of the big cities) and the operation of the criminal justice system of each state as it attempts to cope with robbery (for example, the probability of being caught and imprisoned for a given robbery and the length of the average prison term for robbery). Most such studies find, after controlling for socioeconomic differences among the states, that the higher the probability of being imprisoned, the lower the robbery rate. Isaac Ehrlich, an economist, produced the best known of such analyses using data on crime in the United States in 1940, 1950, and 1960. To simplify a complex analysis, he found, after controlling for such factors as the income level and age distribution of the population, that the higher the probability of imprisonment for those convicted of robbery, the lower the robbery rate. Thus, differences in the certainty of punishment seem to make a difference in the level of crime. At the same time, Ehrlich did not find that the severity of punishment (the average time served in prison for robbery) had, independently of certainty, an effect on robbery rates in two of the three time periods (1940 and 1960).[1]

But there are some problems associated with studying the effect of sanctions on crime rates using aggregate data of this sort. One is that many of the most important factors are not known with any accuracy. For example, we are dependent on police reports for our measure of the robbery rate, and these undoubtedly vary in accuracy from place to place. If all police departments were inaccurate to the same degree, this would not be important; unfortunately, some departments are probably much less accurate than others, and this variable error can introduce a serious bias into the statistical estimates of the effect of the criminal justice system.

Moreover, if one omits from the equation some factor that affects the crime rate, then the estimated effect of the factors that are in the equation may be in error because some of the causal power belonging to the omitted factor will be falsely attributed to the included factors. For example, suppose we want to find out whether differences in the number of policemen on patrol among American cities are associated with differences in the rate at which robberies take place in those cities. If we fail to include in our equation a measure of the population density of the city, we may wrongly conclude that the more police there are on the streets, the *higher* the robbery rate and thus give support to the absurd policy proposition that the way to reduce robberies is to fire police officers. Since robberies are more likely to occur in larger, densely settled cities (which also tend to have a higher proportion of police), it would be a grave error to omit such measures of population from the equation. Since we are not certain what causes crime, we always run the risk of inadvertently omitting a key factor from our efforts to see if deterrence works.

Even if we manage to overcome these problems, a final difficulty lies in wait. The observed fact (and it has been observed many times) that states in which the probability of going to prison for robbery is low are also states which have high rates of robbery can be interpreted in one of two ways. It can mean *either* that the higher robbery rates are the results of the lower imprisonment rates (and thus evidence that deterrence works) *or* that the lower imprisonment rates are caused by the higher robbery rates. To see how the latter might be true, imagine a state that is experiencing, for some reason, a rapidly rising robbery rate. It arrests, convicts, and imprisons more and more robbers as more and more robberies are committed, but it cannot quite keep up. The robberies are increasing so fast that they 'swamp' the criminal justice system; prosecutors and judges respond by letting more robbers off without a prison sentence, or perhaps without even a trial, in order to keep the system from becoming hopelessly clogged. As a result, the proportion of arrested robbers who go to prison goes down while the robbery rate goes up. In this case, we ought to conclude, not that prison deters robbers, but that high robbery rates 'deter' prosecutors and judges.

The best analysis of these problems in statistical studies of deterrence is to be found in a report of the Panel on Research on Deterrent and Incapacitative Effects, set up by the National Research Council (an arm of the National Academy of Sciences). That panel, chaired by Alfred Blumstein of Carnegie-Mellon University, concluded that the available statistical evidence (as of 1978) did not warrant reaching any strong conclusions about the deterrent effect of existing differences among states or cities in the probability of punishment. The panel (of which I was a member) noted that 'the evidence certainly favors a proposition supporting deterrence more than it favors one asserting that deterrence is absent' but urged 'scientific caution' in interpreting this evidence.[2]

Subsequently, other criticisms of deterrence research, generally along the same lines as those of the panel, were published by Colin Loftin[3] and by Stephen S. Brier and Stephen E. Feinberg.[4]

Some commentators believe that these criticisms have proved that 'deterrence doesn't work' and thus the decks have now been cleared to get on with the task of investing in those programs, such as job creation and income maintenance, that *will* have an effect on crime. Such a conclusion is, to put it mildly, a bit premature.

### Rehabilitating deterrence

People are governed in their daily lives by rewards and penalties of every sort. We shop for bargain prices, praise our children for good behavior and scold them for bad, expect lower interest rates to stimulate home building and fear that higher ones will depress it, and conduct ourselves in public in ways that lead our friends and neighbors to form good opinions of us. To assert that 'deterrence doesn't work' is tantamount to either denying the plainest facts of everyday life or claiming that would-be criminals are utterly different from the rest of us. They may well be different to some degree – they most likely have a weaker conscience, worry less about their reputation in polite society, and find it harder to postpone gratifying their urges – but these differences of degree do not make them indifferent to the risks and gains of crime. If they were truly indifferent, they would scarcely be able to function at all, for their willingness to take risks would be offset by their indifference to loot. Their lives would consist of little more than the erratic display of animal instincts and fleeting impulses.

The question before us is whether feasible changes in the deferred and uncertain penalties of crime [. . .] will affect crime rates in ways that can be detected by the data and statistical methods at our disposal. Though the unreliability of crime data and the limitations of statistical analysis are real enough and are accurately portrayed by the Panel of the National Research Council, there are remedies and rejoinders that, on balance, strengthen the case for the claim that not only does deterrence work (the panel never denied that), it probably works in ways that can be measured, even in the aggregate.

The errors in official statistics about crime rates have been addressed by employing other measures of crime, in particular reports gathered by Census Bureau interviewers from citizens who have been victims of crime. While these victim surveys have problems of their own (such as the forgetfulness of citizens), they are not the same problems as those that affect police reports of crime. Thus, if we obtain essentially the same findings about the effect of sanctions on crime from studies that use victim data as we do from studies using police data, our confidence in these findings is strengthened. Studies of this sort have been done by Itzhak Goldberg at Stanford and by Barbara Boland and myself, and the results are quite consistent with those from research based on police reports.[5] As sanctions become more likely, crime becomes less common.

There is a danger that important factors will be omitted from any statistical study of crime in ways that bias the results, but this problem is no greater in studies of penalties than it is in studies of unemployment rates, voting behavior, or any of a hundred other socially significant topics. Since we can never know with certainty everything that may affect crime (or unemployment, or voting), we must base our conclusions not on any single piece of research, but on the general thrust of a variety of studies analyzing many different causal factors. The Panel of the National Research Council took exactly this position. While noting that 'there is the possibility that as yet unknown and so untested' factors may be affecting crime, 'this is not a sufficient basis for dismissing' the common finding that crime goes up as sanctions become less certain because 'many of the analyses have included some of the more obvious possible third causes and they still find negative associations between sanctions and crimes.'[6]

It is possible that rising crime rates 'swamp' the criminal justice system so that a negative statistical association between, say, rates of theft and the chances of going to prison for theft may mean not that a decline in imprisonment is causing theft to increase, but rather that a rise in theft is causing imprisonment to become less likely. This might occur particularly with respect to less serious crimes, such as shoplifting or petty larceny; indeed, the proportion of prisoners who are shoplifters or petty thieves has gone down over the last two decades. But it is hard to imagine that the criminal justice system would respond to an increase in murder or armed robbery by letting some murderers or armed robbers off with no punishment. There is no evidence that convicted murderers are any less likely to go to prison today than they were 20 years ago. Moreover, the apparent deterrent effect of prison on serious crimes, such as murder and robbery, was apparently as great in 1940 or 1950, when these crimes were much less common, as it is today, suggesting that swamping has not occurred.[7]

The best studies of deterrence that manage to overcome many of these problems provide evidence that deterrence works. Alfred Blumstein and Daniel Nagin studied the relationship between draft evasion and the penalties imposed for evading the draft. After controlling for the socioeconomic characteristics of the states, they found that the higher the probability of conviction for draft evasion, the lower the evasion rates. This is an especially strong finding because it is largely immune to some of the problems of other research. Draft evasion is more accurately measured than street crime, hence errors arising from poor data are not a problem. And draft evasion cases did not swamp the federal courts in which they were tried, in part because such cases (like murder in state courts) make up only a small fraction of the courts' workload (7 per cent in the case of draft evasion) and in part because the attorney general had instructed federal prosecutors to give high priority to these cases. Blumstein and Nagin concluded that draft evasion is deterrable.[8]

Another way of testing whether deterrence works is to look, not at differences among states at one point in time, but at changes in the nation as a whole over a long period of time. Historical data on the criminal justice system in America is so spotty that such research is difficult to do here, but it is not at all difficult in England where the data are excellent. Kenneth I. Wolpin analyzed changes in crime rates and in various parts of the criminal justice system (the chances of being arrested, convicted, and punished) for the period 1894 to 1967, and concluded that changes in the probability of being punished seemed to cause changes in the crime rate. He offers reasons for believing that this causal connection cannot be explained away by the argument that the criminal justice system was being swamped.[9]

Given what we are trying to measure – changes in the behavior of a small number of hard-to-observe persons who are responding to delayed and uncertain penalties – we will never be entirely sure that our statistical manipulations have proved that deterrence works. What is impressive is that so many (but not all) studies using such different methods come to similar conclusions. [. . .]

The relationship between crime on the one hand and the rewards and penalties at the disposal of society on the other is complicated. It is not complicated, however, in the way some people imagine. It is not the case (except for a tiny handful of pathological personalities) that criminals are so unlike the rest of us as to be indifferent to the costs and benefits of the opportunities open to them. Nor is it the case that criminals have no opportunities. [. . .]

It is better to think of both people and social controls as arrayed on a continuum. People differ by degrees in the extent to which they are governed by internal restraints on criminal behavior and in the stake they have in conformity;[10] they also differ by degrees in the extent to which they can find, hold, and benefit from a job. Similarly, sanctions and opportunities are changeable only within modest limits. We want to find out to what extent feasible changes in the certainty, swiftness, or severity of penalties will make a difference in the behavior of those 'at the margin' – those, that is, who are neither so innocent nor so depraved as to be prepared to ignore small changes (which are, in fact, the only feasible changes) in the prospects of punishment. By the same token, we want to know what feasible (and again, inevitably small) changes in the availability of jobs will affect those at the margin of the labor market – those, that is, who are neither so eager for a good job or so contemptuous of 'jerks' who take 'straight jobs' as to ignore modest changes in job opportunities. I am aware of no evidence supporting the conventional liberal view that while the number of persons who will be affected by changing penalties is very small, the number who will be affected by increasing jobs is very large; nor am I aware of any evidence supporting the conventional conservative view, which is the opposite of this.

I believe that the weight of the evidence – aggregate statistical analyses, evaluations of experiments and quasi-experiments, and studies of individual behavior – supports the view that the rate of crime is influenced by its costs. This influence is greater – or easier to observe – for some crimes and persons than for others. It is possible to lower the crime rate by increasing the certainty of sanctions, but inducing the criminal justice system to make those changes is difficult, especially if committing the offense confers substantial benefits on the perpetrator, if apprehending and punishing the offender does not provide substantial rewards to members of the criminal justice system, or if the crime itself lacks the strong moral condemnation of society. In theory, the rate of crime should also be sensitive to the benefits of non-crime – for example, the value and availability of jobs – but thus far efforts to show that relationship have led to inconclusive results.[11] Moreover, the nature of the connection between crime and legitimate opportunities is complex: unemployment (and prosperity!) can cause crime, crime can cause unemployment (but probably not prosperity), and both crime and unemployment may be caused by common third factors. Economic factors probably have the greatest influence on the behavior of low-rate, novice offenders and the least on high-rate, experienced ones. Despite the uncertainty that attaches to the connection between the economy and crime, I believe the wisest course of action for society is to try simultaneously to increase both the benefits of non-crime and the costs of crime, all the while bearing in mind that no feasible changes in either part of the equation are likely to produce big changes in crime rates.

Some may grant my argument that it makes sense to continue to try to make those marginal gains that are possible by simultaneously changing in desirable directions both the costs of crime and benefits of non-crime, but they may still feel that it is better to spend more heavily on one side or the other of the cost-benefit equation. I have attended numerous scholarly gatherings where I have heard learned persons subject to the most searching scrutiny any evidence purporting to show the deterrent effect of sanctions but accept with scarcely a blink the theory that crime is caused by a 'lack of opportunities.'[12] Perhaps what they mean is that since the evidence on both propositions is equivocal, then it does less harm to believe in – and invest in – the 'benign' (that is, job-creation) program. If so, they are surely wrong. If we try to make the penalties for crime swifter and more certain, and it should turn out that deterrence does not work, then all we have done is increase the risks facing persons who commit a crime. If we fail to increase the certainty and swiftness of penalties, and it should turn out that deterrence *does* work, then we have needlessly increased the risk of innocent persons being victimized.

[. . .]

## Notes

1 Isaac Ehrlich, 'Participation in illegitimate activities: a theoretical and empirical investigation', *Journal of Political Economy*, 81 (1973), pp. 521–65.

2 Alfred Blumstein, Jacqueline Cohen and Daniel Nagin (eds.), *Deterrence and Incapacitation: Estimating the Effects of Criminal Sanctions on Crime Rates* (National Academy of Sciences, Washington, DC, 1978). Isaac Ehrlich responds to this report and its criticisms of his work in Ehrlich and Mark Randall, 'Fear of deterrence', *Journal of Legal Studies*, 6 (1977), pp. 293–316.

3 Colin Loftin, 'Alternative estimates of the impact of certainty and severity of punishment on levels of homicide in American states', in Stephen E. Feinberg and Albert J. Reiss (eds), *Indicators of Crime and Criminal Justice: Quantitative Studies*, report number NCJ-62349 of the Bureau of Justice Statistics (US Department of Justice, Washington, DC, 1980), pp. 75–81.

4 Stephen S. Brier and Stephen E. Feinberg, 'Recent econometric modeling of crime and punishment: support for the deterrence hypothesis?' in Feinberg and Reiss, *Indicators of Crime and Criminal Justice*, pp. 82–97.

5 Itzhak Goldberg, 'A note on using victimization rates to test deterrence', Technical

Report CERDCR-5-78, Center for Econometric Studies of the Justice System, Stanford University (December 1978); James Q. Wilson and Barbara Boland, 'Crime', in William Gorham and Nathan Glazer (eds), *The Urban Predicament* (Urban Institute, Washington, DC, 1976).

6 Blumstein et al., *Deterrence and Incapacitation*, p. 23.

7 Isaac Ehrlich and Mark Randall, 'Fear of deterrence', *Journal of Legal Studies*, 6 (1977), pp. 304–7.

8 Alfred Blumstein and Daniel Nagin, 'The deterrent effect of legal sanctions on draft evasion', *Stanford Law Review*, 28 (1977), pp. 241–75.

9 Kenneth I. Wolpin, 'An economic analysis of crime and punishment in England and Wales, 1894–1967', *Journal of Political Economy*, 86 (1978), pp. 815–40.

10 The concept of a 'stake in the conformity' is from Jackson Toby, 'Social disorganization and stake in conformity', *Journal of Criminal Law and Criminology*, 48 (1957), pp. 12–17.

11 Cf. Richard B. Freeman, 'Crime and unemployment' in James Q. Wilson (ed.), *Crime and Public Policy* (Institute for Contemporary Studies, San Francisco, 1983), ch. 6.

12 An egregious example of the double standard at work is Charles Silberman, *Criminal Violence, Criminal Justice* (Random House, New York, 1978), wherein the studies on deterrence are closely criticized (pp. 182–95) in a way that leads the author to conclude that 'more punishment is not the answer' (p. 197) but 'community development programs' are found (on the basis of virtually no data whatsoever) to lead to 'community regeneration' and a virtual absence of criminal violence (pp. 430–66).

# 28

# Giving criminals their just deserts

## *Andrew von Hirsch*

The limits on state power over the individual have yet to be charted in the field of criminal sentencing. The state now has virtually untrammeled authority to sentence a convicted criminal for any purpose and with any degree of severity. It is incumbent upon civil libertarians to suggest, in the interest of fairness to those being sentenced, what the constraints on the state's sentencing power should be.

Attitudes about the criminal sentence have changed. Until recently the ideal of treatment dominated: The sentence was supposed to rehabilitate, and sentencing judges and parole boards were supposed to have wide discretion so they could tailor the sentence to the offender's needs. This notion still had sufficient vitality to prompt David J. Rothman to warn of its dangers in his thoughtful article, 'De-carcerating Prisoners and Patients', in the Fall 1973 issue of *Civil Liberties Review*. Is it rational or fair, he asked, to sentence for treatment without good reason to expect that the therapy will work? Might not the rehabilitative ideology give a misleading aura of beneficence to the harsh realities of punishing people – and thus legitimize more intervention in offenders' lives with fewer constraints on official behavior? Since that article was published, there has been a marked decline of faith in rehabilitation.

Although penal reformers have urged the treatment of offenders for over a century, it was not until the 1940s and 1950s that experimental programs were widely tried and evaluated. The results were disappointing: Offenders placed in correctional treatment programs usually returned to crime about as often as those who did not participate. Thus, for example, a survey by Robert Martinson and his collaborators of most of the major experimental programs between 1945 and 1967 concludes that 'with few and isolated exceptions, the rehabilitative efforts that have been reported so far have had no appreciable effect on recidivism'.

Since spring 1974, when Martinson published the conclusions of his survey, the thesis that treatment seldom works has become familiar in professional circles, has been mentioned in newspaper articles, and has been noted in several presidential speeches. Now it is the advocates of treatment who are on the defensive – who insist, almost plaintively, that the failure of many treatment programs in the past does not necessarily mean that all treatments are doomed to fail. As doubts about the effectiveness of treatment grow, traditional faith in the rehabilitative sentence – the sentence especially designed to meet the offender's need for correctional therapy – is declining, and may already be moribund.

Abridged from *Civil Liberties Review*, 1976, No. 3, pp. 23–35.

What has persisted, however, is the idea that the sentence should primarily be a crime control technique. This assumption underlay the rehabilitative sentence: the offender would be less likely to offend again if consigned to the proper treatment. Now, when rehabilitation seemingly has failed, interest has shifted to other sentencing approaches that supposedly will do the crime control job more effectively.

A renewed faith in incapacitation is symptomatic of this continuing search for the sentence that best prevents crime. If offenders cannot be cured of their criminal tendencies, it is argued, they can at least be isolated – placed behind bars where they cannot prey on those outside. Simple restraint replaces therapy, and restraint works: prisons may have few other merits, but they surely can protect the community against offense-prone persons – at least during the period of confinement. As former Attorney General William B. Saxbe put it in a 1974 speech to a convention of police chiefs: 'Too many dangerous convicted offenders are placed back in society . . . and that simply must stop.'

Those less conservative than Saxbe have also been attracted to this approach. The National Council on Crime and Delinquency, a vocal critic of American prisons, issued a policy statement that 'prisons are destructive to prisoners and to those charged with holding them', and that the only offenders who should be sentenced to prison are those 'who, if not confined, would be a serious danger to the public'. The prison sanction, in other words, should be a means of restraining those who would harm others if released. The recent National Advisory Commission on crime likewise urged that the prison sentence be used chiefly to isolate the dangerous recidivist. The theory has been embraced even by those who see themselves as radical critics of today's criminal justice system.

[. . .]

Gary Wills, in an article in the *New York Review of Books*, denounced prisons as 'human sewers' and declared that their supposed justifications – rehabilitation, deterrence, or retribution – have no merit whatever. Conclusion: abolish the prison, right? Wrong. A letter from a prisoner in a subsequent issue of the *New York Review* asked Wills what he proposed to do with 'people who go about chronically molesting children, or continually stealing and burglarizing'. Wills replied: 'once we properly identify the chronic molester he should be removed from society. . . . There is an irreducible minimum of people who present an active danger to society whenever they are released into it. They should be sequestered, in places which have no other aim *except* sequestration.' In plain English, dangerous offenders should be locked up.

Confining the 'dangerous' has its undeniable attractions: low-risk offenders can be decarcerated, and use of the prison can be limited to those who present high risks of returning to crime. But there are hazards. One is the difficulty of distinguishing the dangerous individuals from the non-dangerous. As Leonard Orland pointed out in 'Can we establish the rule of law in prisons?' (*Civil Liberties Review*, Fall 1975), 'our ability to predict *future* criminal behavior is very limited; it may be nonexistent'. When forecasting serious crimes, there is a strong tendency to over-predict; most of those identified as risks will be 'false positives' – persons mistakenly predicted to offend.

Class bias is another problem. If the sole aim of the sentence is to prevent recurrences, its severity will depend on the offender's status. When a public official or corporation executive commits a heinous crime in office, he can be prevented from doing it again simply by depriving him of his position of power. By contrast, the poor person who commits a grave offense has no position of power to lose, and he is sent to prison to keep him from offending again. Finally, there is the potential for escalation. When the sentence is viewed as a means for isolating dangerous convicts, sentencers will be criticized every time they release someone who subsequently commits a crime, and will respond by steadily widening the net – by opting for confinement whenever there is any doubt whether the individual will stay within the law. They will, in other words, adopt the maxim of California's Attorney General Evelle Younger: 'I'd rather run the risk of keeping the wrong man [in prison] a little longer than let the wrong man out too soon.'

Harvard's James Q. Wilson suggests a more sophisticated approach to incapacitating criminals in his thoughtful and widely read book *Thinking About Crime* (whose influence, incidentally, is manifest in President Ford's and Senator Edward Kennedy's proposals for mandatory minimum sentences). Wilson starts with the hypothesis that most serious crimes are committed by a relatively small number of repeaters who, because of the large number of crimes they perpetrate, sooner or later are caught and convicted. Current sentencing policy imposes long prison terms on a few of these individuals, but allows most of them to be released on probation and thus to return to crime if they so choose. (In Los Angeles County, Wilson notes, the proportion of convicted robbers with major prior records who were sent to prison in 1970 was only 27 per cent.)

If prison sentences – even of modest length – were invariably imposed in such cases, the incapacitative payoff would be substantial, Wilson suggests. One would be taking out of circulation most of those responsible for serious crimes, at least for a portion of their criminal careers. (There would be no need to try to predict which individual convicts are dangerous; instead, there would simply be a rule that conviction for certain crimes results in a stated period of imprisonment.) The crime control benefits from such a strategy, he claims, would be very large. 'Were we to devote [our] resources to a strategy [that is] well within our abilities – namely, to incapacitating a larger fraction of the convicted serious robbers,' he says, 'then not only is a 20 per cent reduction [in robbery] possible, but even larger ones are conceivable.'

Wilson's proposals certainly sound appealing: moderate sentences, less disparity (because judges would have less discretion), and huge payoffs in community protection – with 20 per cent fewer robberies. But Wilson does not ask the uncomfortable question: What if the promised crime-control benefits do not materialize? The history of sentencing reform has been characterized by high hopes for reducing crime followed by disappointment. In the 1820s, long sentences to penitentiaries offering inmates 'moral therapy' were supposed to cut the crime rate. They did not. In the 1900s, probation for treatable offenders and lengthy sentences for dangerous ones were supposed to do the job. They did not. In the 1960s, fewer prison sentences and more sentences to treatment in the community were supposed to succeed. They did not. Now Wilson claims that imprisoning a larger proportion of those convicted will do the crime control job where previous strategies failed. But can one really be so sure?

To sustain his claim, Wilson has to assume that relatively few 'habitual criminals' are responsible not only for the crimes for which they are convicted, but also for the bulk of the unsolved crimes as well. While this is a plausible assumption, it is no more than that: the evidence on who is responsible for crimes committed with impunity is, for obvious reasons, sketchy at best. (Wilson cites calculations by Reuel Shinnar of the CCNY School of Engineering that purport to show a large reduction in the crime rate if every person convicted of a serious crime is imprisoned for a stated period. Shinnar's calculations, however, are no more accurate than the postulates he makes about who commits the unsolved crimes. He himself admits that his estimates would be seriously awry if much of unsolved crime were committed either by occasional criminals or by skilled professionals who never are convicted for a serious crime. The estimates would also be in error if such crimes as robbery were economically attractive enough so that the removal of some robbers from circulation would result in newly recruited robbers taking their places.) Were these assumptions mistaken, the incapacitative payoff from Wilson's sentencing strategy could be much smaller than he expects.

One must therefore be prepared for the possibility of disappointing results. As David Rothman has wisely counselled, strategies for sentencing reform should be based on a failure model – of what is minimally acceptable even if the hoped-for crime control benefits do not materialize. Wilson's plan is the archetypal success model, and that is its weakness. Despite the formidable record of past failures and the speculative nature of his own estimates, Wilson does not seriously ask: 'and what if the scheme led to only 1 per cent fewer robberies, or none fewer?'

That question leads to others that are worrisome. For example, how much extra suffering is inflicted in the interest of a crime control strategy that may fail? Wilson's proposals, if implemented, could mean imprisoning many more people than are confined today. Such persons will lose their liberty on the supposition that their loss will protect the rights of others, the potential victims of crime. But to the extent that Wilson's plan fails, that supposition will have been wrong. We will have added to offenders' suffering without gaining the promised protection of the rights of others, scarcely a morally satisfactory outcome. Granted, we are speaking of persons who have already been convicted of crimes. But if such persons are sent to prison when – but for Wilson's incapacitative theories – they would have received lighter punishments, the moral difficulty persists. (Wilson might reply that his program is experimental, that it should be tried and if it does not work we can still go back to incarcerating fewer people. But the question remains: how much added suffering would there be while this experiment was being carried out? An experiment can be ethically unacceptable if it exacts too great a human toll.)

This problem of inflicting unnecessary suffering is highlighted by Wilson's comments about new prison construction. Disagreeing with many reformers who have urged a moratorium on new prisons, Wilson calls for building more facilities to house those whom he would incapacitate. Imagine, then, the following scenario. To accommodate Wilson's sentencing scheme, new prisons go up. Then, contrary to expectation, the promised reduction in the crime rate does not occur. What are we left with? The same old high crime rate, but more prisons with more beds to fill. Experience suggests that once the facilities are built, the pressures to keep them full of inmates are hard to resist. Wilson's experiment, in short, is apt to be irreversible, whether or not it succeeds in reducing crime.

Another danger is the possibility of escalation of sentences. Wilson assumes that prison terms of moderate length, if invariably imposed on those who have been convicted, will interfere sufficiently with most offenders' criminal careers to diminish crime rates. But suppose his 'modest' sentences do not work? Does not his incapacitative rationale point, then, to much longer sentences? After all, the only sure way to prevent criminally inclined persons from offending again is to hold them until they 'burn out' – until aging has depleted their criminal propensities. Wilson argues that the longer sentences are, the more reluctant sentencers will be to impose them. But if those in charge of the sentencing system take his incapacitative aims seriously, and if experience convinces them that shorter sentences are not enough to do the job, that reluctance may disappear. The possibility of escalation raises the issue [of what] *moral* limits [there should] be on the use of very long prison terms to incapacitate, even if such sentences were effective in reducing crime.

Where Wilson goes wrong, I think, is in his underlying assumption: his preoccupation with crime control to the near exclusion of considerations of justice. It has commonly been supposed – and Wilson continues in this tradition – that justice has largely been satisfied once an offender has been tried and convicted with due process. Thereafter, the focus has been almost exclusively on crime prevention – on which sentencing strategies (rehabilitation or incapacitation? long sentences or short?) serve public safety best. Seldom is the word justice found in the sentencing literature.

The emphasis, I am convinced, should be precisely the reverse: primacy should be given to considerations of justice in sentencing. A system of criminal justice can be tolerable in a free society only if we are determined to make it what its name implies: a system of justice, not a social engineering project. In punishing the convicted, the consequences to the individual are too harsh to permit us to act as if we were merely totting up costs and benefits, seeking the maximum efficiency in preventing crime. Concededly, no sentencing system operating in a society as fraught with inequalities as ours can come close to being truly just. But after conviction as before, justice should not be merely a euphemism for law enforcement; it should be an ideal which we should at least try to approximate.

In the [early 1970s] I was involved in an effort to think through a sentencing scheme grounded mainly on ideas about justice. It was undertaken by the Committee for the Study of Incarceration,[1] an interdisciplinary group which included law professors, sociologists, a psychoanalyst, a criminologist, and (atypically for an inquiry about sentencing) a historian and a philosopher. Instead of continuing the debate about what 'works', we decided at the outset to focus on the question: What is the just sentence?

Suppose one begins with a general definition of justice – (Aristotle's) – that like cases should be treated alike and unlike cases should be treated proportionate to their differences. One must then ask what kind of likeness is relevant for purposes of justice. (Is it, for example, the equally deserving or the equally needy who should be treated alike?) That is a hard question when there are no clues: there is nothing about wealth, for example, that suggests on its face whether it should be distributed according to merit or need. In the case of punishments, rewards and grades, however, the answer should be more obvious. Justice requires that they be distributed according to their recipients' deserts, because they *purport* to be deserved.

Academic grades illustrate this point. Suppose a student writes a poor exam paper. Suppose he needs an A to get into law school. Why not give him the grade he needs? The answer is, of course, that an A symbolizes a superior performance; that the student's performance, in fact, was poor; and hence that he simply does not deserve the A, whatever his needs. Desert is the only fair criterion, because that is precisely what a grade connotes. The same is true of punishment. It treats the person as though he deserves the pain inflicted – and does so because of its symbolism, its implicit moral condemnation of the offender. Punishment is not merely disagreeable (so are taxes and conscription); it implies that the person acted wrongfully and is blameworthy for having done so. Where standards of what constitutes criminal behavior are concerned, this point is a familiar one. It was made two decades ago by the late Henry M. Hart of Harvard Law School in his defense of the criminal law's requirements of culpable intent. Since punishment characteristically ascribes blame, he argued, violations should not be punished unless the offender was at fault (i.e., acted intentionally, or negligently). Accidental violations should not be punished because they are not blameworthy.

What is usually overlooked, however, is that the same argument holds after conviction, when sentence is imposed. By then, it has been decided that the offender deserves punishment, but the question of how much he deserves remains. The severity of the punishment connotes the degree of blame: the sterner the penalty, the greater the implicit reproof. Sending someone away to prison for years implies that he is more to be condemned than does jailing him for a few months or putting him on probation. In deciding severity, therefore, the crime must be sufficiently serious to merit the blame.

This means that sentences should, as a matter of justice, be decided according to a principle of *commensurate deserts*. The severity of punishment should comport with the seriousness of the crime. Stringent punishments should be limited to crimes that are serious; as the gravity of the crime diminishes, so should the severity of the punishment. When this principle is not observed, the degree of blame becomes inappropriate. If an offender convicted of a lesser crime is punished severely, the moral obloquy which so drastic a penalty carries will attach to him – and unjustly so, given the not-so-very-wrongful character of his offense. Conversely, giving a mild punishment to someone convicted of a serious crime understates the blame – and thus depreciates the importance of the values at stake. [. . .]

Once it is accepted as a requirement of justice, the commensurate-deserts principle should determine the sentencing structure. The seriousness of the offender's crime – not his need for treatment, his dangerousness, or the deterrence of others – ought to be decisive. Penalties must be scaled in accordance with the gravity of the offense, and departures from the deserved sentence should be impermissible – even if they had some crime-control usefulness.

A sentencing system based on this conception of justice would have the following principal features.

- The degree of likelihood that the offender might return to crime would be irrelevant to the choice of sentence. Even if crime forecasting techniques could be improved, an offender simply doesn't deserve to have his punishment increased on the basis of what he may do rather than on the basis of what he has done.

- Indeterminacy of sentence would be abolished. Since the seriousness of the crime (the only proper basis for the sentence, in our theory) is known at the time of verdict, there would be no need to delay the decision on sentence length to see how well the offender is adjusting. Prisoners would no longer be kept in agonizing suspense for years, waiting for the parole board to make up its mind about discharge.

- Sentencing discretion would be sharply reduced (and hence today's problem of vast disparities among sentences alleviated). The wide leeway which sentencers now enjoy was sustained by the traditional assumption that the sentence was a means for altering the offender's behavior and had to be especially fashioned to his needs. When this assumption is given up, the basis for such broad discretion crumbles. In order for the sentence to be deserved, there must be standards governing how severely offenders should be punished for different crimes. (Otherwise, sentences will not be consistent; one judge could treat an offense as serious and punish accordingly, while another judge, having a different set of values, could treat the same infraction as minor.) The Incarceration Committee's report thus proposes a system of standardized penalties. For each gradation in seriousness of criminal behavior, a definite penalty – the 'presumptive sentence' – would be set. Offenders convicted of crimes of that degree of gravity would normally receive that specific sentence – except when there were unusual circumstances of mitigation or aggravation.

- Imprisonment would be limited to serious offenses. The commensurate-deserts principle allows severe punishments only for serious crimes. Imprisonment is necessarily a severe penalty. (Even if prison conditions are improved, the loss of liberty itself is a great deprivation.) Prison thus should be the sanction only for crimes, which cause or risk grievous harm – such as assault, armed robbery, and rape – and not for most non-violent larcenies of personal belongings. Even for serious crimes, moreover, the length of imprisonment ought to be stringently rationed, given the painfulness of the prison sanction. The Incarceration Committee's report recommends that most prison sentences be kept below three years. (Bear in mind that we are speaking of actual time in prison, not of a purported sentence that can later by cut back by a parole board.)

- Penalties less severe than imprisonment would be for the non-serious offences which constitute the bulk of the criminal justice system's caseload. These milder penalties would not be rehabilitative measures but, simply and explicitly, less severe punishments. Warnings, limited deprivations of leisure time (and perhaps fines) would be used in lieu of imprisonment. Probation would be phased out because of its discretionary and treatment-oriented features.

There is potential for disagreement, of course, about which crimes are serious. Yet assessments of seriousness – of how harmful the conduct is, and how culpable the offender – at least are moral judgments akin to those we make in everyday life. It should be easier (or certainly no harder) to make such judgments than to surmise on slight evidence how a given sentencing policy will affect crime rates. Moreover, the extent of disagreement on questions of seriousness should not be exaggerated. Beginning [. . .] with the work of the criminologists Thorsten Sellin and Marvin Wolfgang at the University of Pennsylvania, several studies have measured popular perceptions of the gravity of crimes and found a surprising degree of consensus. When asked to rank common acts of theft, fraud and violence on a scale according to their degree of heinousness, people from widely different walks of life tend to make similar ratings.

In this highly compressed description, I have skipped several of the harder (and more interesting) issues. Why should punishment exist at all? (Why shouldn't we, instead, adopt a wholly different kind of social control mechanism?) How can a just deserts model for sentencing be defended in a society that is not itself just? Is one permitted, in a desert-based system, to take an offender's earlier crimes into account? We try to wrestle with these questions in the Incarceration Committee's report.

In sketching this sentencing scheme, I have considered only the requirements of justice. But the system could have some collateral usefulness in controlling crime, even if it is not fashioned with crime control specifically in mind. While sentences would be much shorter, they would be more certain: Anyone convicted of a sufficiently serious crime would face some time in prison – and increasing the certainty of a substantial punishment may be useful as a deterrent. There also could be some incapacitative benefit. Since all offenders convicted of serious crimes would be imprisoned, those who were inclined to offend again would be restrained, at least temporarily. But we would always bear in mind that these benefits might fail to materialize. Perhaps there will not be a sufficiently large increase in certainty of punishment – because too many of those who commit serious crimes do not get caught, or too many of those caught avoid conviction or succeed in bargaining the charges down. But even with such disappointed hopes (even, in fact, if the scheme proves to have no greater efficiency than today's system), it is still defensible because it is a fairer system. Offenders' punishments would more closely approximate what they deserve, and equally blameworthy individuals would receive more nearly similar sentences. Because the scheme is grounded chiefly on equity, a failure in its crime control effectiveness (always a risk to any criminal justice strategy) would not be so devastating as it would be to a scheme such as Wilson's, which relies almost exclusively on the promise that it will work.

A desert-based scheme can serve, moreover, as a baseline – a norm for judging sentencing systems that have been devised with crime control more immediately in mind. Let us suppose that a penologist wants to build an 'efficient' sentencing system and, for the sake of crime-control efficacy, proposes sentences which diverge from those that are deserved. Is it enough for him to show that his system is likely to work? Certainly not, for our desert-based system may work also. Perhaps his system is capable of reducing serious crime by, say, 5 per cent – but our system of deserved sentences might, conceivably, also affect the crime rate by a similar percentage. In that event, his system should be rejected out of hand, for it sacrifices justice while having little or no greater impact on crime than a more just system would. The burden thus falls on him to show not merely how his system will discourage crime, but how it will do so more effectively than a desert-based system would – and that would be no easy matter to establish. Even if this burden were met, a moral decision would have to be made: whether the added crime-control benefits warranted the sacrifice of equity involved. The greater the departure from just (that is, deserved) sentences, the stronger the moral argument for rejecting the proposal, notwithstanding its expected usefulness in curbing crime.

To illustrate this point, let us look once more at Wilson's proposals. Where serious offenses are concerned, his recommended sentences are not dissimilar to the ones we suggest, despite his different rationale. Wilson proposes that anyone convicted of a major offense such as armed robbery (especially when it is a second or third conviction) be sentenced to prison, but that long sentences be avoided. He promises a dramatic (20 per cent or more) reduction in robberies as the result of such a policy. As we have seen, one well might be skeptical that this result will occur. But even if there were no measurable reduction in the robbery rate, Wilson's recommendation could still be defended – but on our grounds of desert: armed robbery is serious, and serious crimes deserve severe punishments.

The conclusion differs, however, with less serious offenses. Wilson proposes that these more venial infractions (unless 'manifestly trivial') be punished by a 'deprivation of liberty' for a few days, weeks, or months. He allows that the deprivation might be something less than full-time imprisonment (confinement only at night, for example, leaving the offender free to go to work during the day), but states that the choice between full and partial restraint should depend on the need to 'protect society'. This leaves open the possibility that lesser offenders could suffer full-time imprisonment if (as is often the case) they seemed likely to return to crime if released. Here, the moral objection is evident: crimes such as shoplifting, passing bad checks, and the like are not serious enough to deserve the harsh sanction of imprisonment.

As this aspect of Wilson's scheme departs from the requirements of justice, one would have to ask, what reason is there to believe that such stiff penalties for lesser offenses would be appreciably more effective than the more modest sanctions of a desert-based system? And even if they were more effective, is the crime-control payoff really worth the sacrifice of fairness? To the second question, my answer would clearly be no, given my philosophical assumption that primacy ought to be accorded the ends of justice. But the answer might still be no, even were one a little readier to compromise ideals of fairness for the sake of crime control – since the suggested severer than just penalties are for crimes which, being less serious, pose no terrible threat to the community's safety.

It may seem strange that the Incarceration Committee's liberal professors and activists, when faced with the choice between rehabilitation and desert, chose desert. Why go back to so ancient a notion? Why not continue to focus on what works best, and leave what is deserved to casuists and theologians? Unfashionable as the idea of desert has been, we found it essential to justice in sentencing. It is crucial to the question that civil libertarians ought to be asking: What are the ethical limits on making convicted individuals suffer for the sake of preventing crime? The point was aptly stated ninety years ago by F.H. Wines, one of the few prison reformers of that age to question the then dominant ideal of rehabilitation, when he said: 'Of the retribution theory, it may at least be said that if it is an assertion of the right to inflict all the pain which a particular criminal act may merit, it is the denial of the right to inflict on any human being any needless and unmerited pain'.

## Notes

1 See A. von Hirsch, *Doing Justice: the Choice of Punishments*. Report of the Committee for the Study of Incarceration (New York, Hill and Wang, 1976).

# 29

# The value of rehabilitation

## Francis T. Cullen and Karen E. Gilbert

[. . .] [P]reoccupation with the misuses and limitations of treatment programs has perhaps blinded many current-day liberals to the important benefits that have been or can be derived from popular belief in the notion that offenders should be saved and not simply punished. In this respect, the persistence of a strong rehabilitative ideology can be seen to function as a valuable resource for those seeking to move toward the liberal goal of introducing greater benevolence into the criminal justice system. Alternatively, we can begin to question whether the reform movement sponsored by the Left will not be undermined should liberal faith in rehabilitation reach a complete demise. In this context, four major reasons are offered below for why we believe that liberals should reaffirm and not reject the correctional ideology of rehabilitation.

*1 Rehabilitation is the only justification of criminal sanctioning that obligates the state to care for an offender's needs or welfare.* Admittedly, rehabilitation promises a payoff to society in the form of offenders transformed into law-abiding, productive citizens who no longer desire to victimize the public. Yet treatment ideology also conveys the strong message that this utilitarian outcome can only be achieved if society is willing to punish its captives humanely and to compensate offenders for the social disadvantages that have constrained them to undertake a life in crime. In contrast, the three competing justifications of criminal sanctioning - deterrence, incapacitation and retribution (or just deserts) - contain not even the pretence that the state has an obligation to do good for its charges. The only responsibility of the state is to inflict the pains that accompany the deprivation of liberty or of material resources (e.g., fines); whatever utility such practices engender flows only to society and not to its captives. Thus, deterrence aims to protect the social order by making offenders suffer sufficiently to dissuade them as well as onlookers entertaining similar criminal notions from venturing outside the law on future occasions. Incapacitation also seeks to preserve the social order but through a surer means; by caging criminals - 'locking 'em up and throwing away the keys' - inmates will no longer be at liberty to prey on law-abiding members of society. The philosophy of retribution, on the other hand, manifests a disinterest in questions of crime control, instead justifying punishment on the grounds that it presumably provides society and crime victims with the psychic satisfaction that justice has been accomplished by harming offenders in doses commensurate with the harms their transgressions have caused. [. . .]

These considerations lead us to ask whether it is strategically wise for

---

Abridged from *Reaffirming Rehabilitation*, pp. 247–63. (Cincinnati, OH: Anderson, 1982.)

liberals wishing to mitigate existing inhumanities in the criminal justice system to forsake the only prevailing correctional ideology that is expressly benevolent toward offenders. It is difficult to imagine that reform efforts will be more humanizing if liberals willingly accept the premise that the state has no responsibility to do good, only to inflict pain. Notably, Gaylin and Rothman, proponents of the justice model, recognized the dangers of such a choice when they remarked that 'in giving up the rehabilitative model, we abandon not just our innocence but perhaps more. The concept of deserts is intellectual and moralistic; in its devotion to principle, it turns back on such compromising considerations as generosity and charity, compassion and love'.[1] They may have shown even greater hesitation in rejecting rehabilitation and affirming just deserts had they had an opportunity to dwell on the more recent insights of radical thinkers Herman and Julia Schwendinger:

> Nevertheless, whatever the expressed qualifications, the justice model now also justifies objectively retrogressive outcomes because of its insistence that social policies give priority to punishment rather than rehabilitation. Punishment, as we have seen, is classically associated with deprivation of living standards. Rehabilitation, on the other hand, has served as the master symbol in bourgeois ideology that legitimated innumerable reformist struggles against this deprivation. By discrediting rehabilitation as a basic principle of penal practice, the justice modelers have undermined their own support for better standards of living in penal institutions.[2]

Now it might be objected by liberal critics of rehabilitation that favoring desert as the rationale for criminal sanctioning does not mean adopting an uncaring orientation toward the welfare of offenders. The reform agenda of the justice model not only suggests that punishment be fitted to the crime and not the criminal, but also that those sent to prison be accorded an array of rights that will humanize their existence. The rehabilitative ideal, it is countered, justifies the benevolent treatment of the incarcerated but only as a means to achieving another end – the transformation of the criminal into the conforming. In contrast, the justice perspective argues for humanity as an end in and of itself, something that should not in any way be made to seem conditional on accomplishing the difficult task of changing the deep-seated criminogenic inclinations of offenders. As such, liberals should not rely on state enforced rehabilitation to somehow lessen the rigors of imprisonment, but instead should campaign to win legal rights for convicts that directly bind the state to provide its captives with decent living conditions. [. . .]

It is not with ease that those of us on the political Left can stop short of completely and publically embracing the concept that 'humanity for humanity's sake' is sufficient reason for combating the brutalizing effects of prison life. This value-stance is, after all, fundamental to the logic that informs liberal policies on criminal justice issues. In this light, it should be clear that we applaud attempts to earn inmates human rights [. . .] and urge their continuance. However, we must stand firm against efforts to promote the position that the justice model with its emphasis on rights should replace the rehabilitative ideal with its emphasis on caring as the major avenue of liberal reform. [. . .] [S]upport for the principles of just deserts and determinacy has only exacerbated the plight of offenders both before and after their incarceration. But there are additional dangers to undertaking a reform program that abandons rehabilitation and seeks *exclusively* to broaden prisoner rights. Most importantly, the realities of the day furnish little optimism that such a campaign would enjoy success. [. . .]

Further, the promise of the rights perspective is based on the shaky assumption that more benevolence will occur if the relationship of the state to its deviants is fully adversarial and purged of its paternalistic dimensions. Instead of the government being entrusted to reform its charges through care, now offenders will have the comfort of being equipped with a new weapon – 'rights' – that will serve them well in their battle against the state for a humane and justly administered correctional system. Yet this imagery contains only surface appeal. As David Rothman has warned, 'an adversarial model, setting interest off against interest, does seem to run the clear risk of creating a kind of ultimate shoot-out in which, by definition, the powerless lose and the powerful win. How absurd to push for confrontation when all the advantages are on the other side'.[3]

[. . .]

Moreover, the rights perspective is a two-edged sword. While rights ideally bind the state to abide by standards insuring a certain level of due process protection and acceptable penal living conditions, rights also establish the limits of the good that the state can be expected or obligated to provide. A rehabilitative ideology, in contrast, constantly pricks the conscience of the state with its assertion that the useful and moral goal of offender reformation can only be effected in a truly humane environment. Should treatment ideology be stripped away by liberal activists and the ascendancy of the rights model secured, it would thus create a situation in which criminal justice officials would remain largely immune from criticism as long as they 'gave inmates their rights' – however few they may be at the time. [. . .]

Even more perversely, the very extension of new rights can also be utilized to legitimate the profound neglect of the welfare of those under state control. The tragic handling of mental patients [. . .] is instructive in this regard. As it became apparent that many in our asylums were being either unlawfully abused or deprived of their liberty, the 'mentally ill' won the right to be released to or remain in the community if it could be proven that they were of no danger to themselves or others. [. . .] Yet, what has been the actual result of this 'right' to avoid state enforced therapy? It brought forth not a new era in the humane treatment of the troubled but a new era of state neglect. Instead of brutalizing people within institutional structures, the state now permits the personally disturbed to be brutalized on the streets of our cities. [. . .]

*2 The ideology of rehabilitation provides an important rationale for opposing the conservatives' assumption that increased repression will reduce crime.* Those embracing the conservatives' call for 'law and order' place immense faith in the premise that tough rather than humane justice is the answer to society's crime problem. In the political Right's view, unlawful acts occur only when individuals have calculated that they are advantageous, and thus the public's victimization will only subside if criminal choices are made more costly. This can be best accomplished by sending more offenders away to prison for more extended and uncomfortable stays. Indeed, the very existence of high crime rates is *prima facie* evidence that greater repression is required to insure that lawlessness in our nation no longer pays.

Liberals have traditionally attacked this logic on the grounds that repressive tactics do not touch upon the real social roots of crime and hence rarely succeed in even marginally reducing criminal involvement. Campaigns to heighten the harshness of existing criminal penalties – already notable for their severity – will only serve to fuel the problem of burgeoning prison populations and result in a further deterioration of penal living standards. The strategy of 'getting tough' thus promises to have substantial costs, both in terms of the money wasted on the excessive use of incarceration and in terms of the inhumanity it shamefully introduces.

It is clear that proponents of the justice model share these intense liberal concerns over the appealing but illusory claims of those preaching law and order. However, their opposition to repressive crime control policies encounters difficulties because core assumptions of the justice model converge closely with those found in the paradigm for crime control espoused by conservatives. Both perspectives, for instance, argue that (1) offenders are responsible beings who freely choose to engage in crime; (2) regardless of the social injustices that may have prompted an individual to breach the law, the nature of the crime and not the nature of the circumstances surrounding a crime should regulate the severity of the sanction meted out; and (3) the punishment of offenders is deserved – that is, the state's infliction of pain for pain's sake is a positive good to be encouraged and not a likely evil to be discouraged. Admittedly, those wishing to 'do justice' would contend that current sanctions are too harsh and that prison conditions should be made less rigorous. But having already agreed with conservatives that punishing criminals is the fully legitimate purpose of the criminal justice system, they are left with little basis on which to challenge the logic or moral justification of proposals to get tough. Instead, their opposition to such measures is reduced to a debate with conservatives over the exact amount of deprivation of liberty and of living conditions during incarceration that each criminal act 'justly deserves'. [. . .]

In contrast, the ideology of rehabilitation disputes every facet of the conclusion that the constant escalation of punishment will mitigate the spectre of crime. To say that offenders are in need of rehabilitation is to reject the conservatives' notion that individuals, regardless of their position in the social order – whether black or white, rich or poor – exercise equal freedom in deciding whether to commit a crime. Instead, it is to reason that social and personal circumstances often constrain, if not compel, people to violate the law; and unless efforts are made to enable offenders to escape these criminogenic constraints, little relief in the crime rate can be anticipated. Policies that insist on ignoring these realities by assuming a vengeful posture toward offenders promise to succeed only in fostering hardships that will, if anything, deepen the resentment that many inmates find difficult to suppress upon their release back into society [. . .]

A rehabilitative stance thus allows us to begin to speak about, in Karl Menninger's words, not the 'punishment of crime' but the 'crime of punishment'.[4] The conservatives' plea for repression is exposed as a 'crime' because it both needlessly dehumanizes society's captives and falsely deceives the public that strict crime control measures will afford citizens greater safety. Drawing on the logic of the Positivist School of criminology while casting aside the classical image of the law-breaker, the concept of rehabilitation reveals that fundamental changes in offenders will not be realized as long as inflicting deprivation remains the legitimate goal of our system of criminal 'injustice'. [. . .] [A] treatment ideology prompts us first to appreciate the troubles and disadvantages that drive many into crime and then to reach out and assist offenders to deal with the conditions and needs that have moved them to break the law. The demand is made, in short, that caring rather than hurting be the guiding principle of the correctional process. Moreover, in sensitizing us to the fact that much of the illegality that plagues society is intimately linked to existing social inequalities and injustices, rehabilitative ideology makes clear that a true solution to the crime problem ultimately rests in the support of reform programs that will bring about a more equitable distribution of resources through a broad structural transformation of the social order. This is in notable contrast to the philosophy of just deserts that assumes full individual responsibility, focuses on the culpability of the single perpetrator, and therefore 'acquits the existing social order of any charge of injustice'.[5]

It is apparent, then, that the ideology of rehabilitation is fully oppositional to the conservatives' agenda for the repression of crime. Importantly, it thus furnishes liberals seeking to effect criminal justice reform with a coherent framework with which to argue that benevolence and not brutality should inform society's attempts to control crime. Sharing no assumptions with the Right's paradigm of law and order, it does not, as in the case of the justice model, easily give legitimacy to either repressive punishment policies or the neglect of offender well-being. Instead, it remains a distinctly liberal ideology that can be utilized as a resource in the Left's quest to illustrate the futility of policies that increase pain but accomplish little else.

*3 Rehabilitation still receives considerable support as a major goal of the correctional system.* With prison populations exploding and punitive legislation being passed across the nation, it is of little surprise to find opinion polls indicating a hardening of public attitudes toward crime control [. . .] In this light, it can be imagined that public opinion would constitute a serious and perhaps insurmountable obstacle to any proposals advocating the treatment rather than the mere punishment of offenders. The viability of liberal reform strategies aimed at reaffirming rehabilitation would thus seem questionable at best.

But this is not the case. While the average citizen clearly wants criminals to be severely sanctioned – in particular, sent to prison for longer stays – survey research consistently reveals that the American public also believes that offenders should be rehabilitated. [. . .]

[E]xisting survey data suggest that rehabilitation persists as a prevailing ideology within the arena of criminal justice. This does not mean that treatment programs in our prisons are flourishing and remain unthreatened by the pragmatics and punitiveness of our day. But it is to assert that the rehabilitative ideal and the benevolent potential it holds are deeply anchored within our correctional and broader cultural heritage. That is, rehabilitation constitutes an ongoing rationale that is accepted by or 'makes sense to' the electorate as well as to criminal justice interest groups and policy-makers. Consequently, it provides reformers with a valuable vocabulary with which to justify changes in policy and practice aimed at mitigating the harshness of criminal sanctions – such as the diversion of offenders into the community for 'treatment' or the humanization of the prison to develop a more effective 'therapeutic environment'. Unlike direct appeals for inmate rights to humane and just living conditions that can be quickly dismissed as the mere coddling of the dangerous ('Why should we care about their rights when they certainly didn't care about the rights of their innocent victims?'), liberal reforms undertaken in the name of rehabilitation have the advantage of resonating with accepted ideology and hence of retaining an air of legitimacy. [. . .] If the public is not willing to pay now to facilitate the betterment of those held in captivity, it can be made clear to them that they will be forced to pay in more bothersome, if not tragic, ways at a later date.

Our message here is simple but, in light of the advent of the justice model, telling in its implications: for liberals to argue vehemently against the ideology of rehabilitation – to say that treatment cannot work because the rehabilitative ideal is inherently flawed – is to undermine the potency of one of the few resources that can be mobilized in the Left's pursuit of less repression in the administration of criminal punishments.

*4 Rehabilitation has historically been an important motive underlying reform efforts that have increased the humanity of the correctional system.* Liberal critics have supplied ample evidence to confirm their suspicions that state enforced therapy has too frequently encouraged the unconscionable exploitation of society's captives. Their chilling accounts of the inhumanities completed under the guise of 'treatment' call forth the compelling conclusion that far greater benevolence would grace the criminal justice system had notions of rehabilitation never taken hold.

However, while the damages permitted by the corruption of the rehabilitative ideal should neither be denied nor casually swept aside, it would be misleading to idealize the 'curious' but brutal punishments of 'bygone days' and to ignore that reforms undertaken in the name of rehabilitation have been a crucial humanizing influence in the darker regions of the sanctioning process. [. . .] It is instructive as well to contemplate fully the thoughtful observations of Graeme Newman:

> Yet it would seem that to throw out the whole idea of good intentions, because most of the time they do not reach the lofty heights they were supposed to achieve, may be to throw out many other values that have often accompanied them: human values, the wish, at least, to treat people humanely. Some argue that we do not need the medical [rehabilitative model] as an 'excuse' to treat offenders humanely, that we ought to do it for the sake of being humane in and of itself. But this argument, although admirably principled, does not recognize the great cultural difficulties (largely unconscious) that we have had, and continue to have, in acting humanely to those who are society's outcasts. Surely this is the lesson of history. It is only a couple of hundred years since we gave up mutilating, disemboweling, and chopping up criminals, and we still cannot make up our minds whether to stop killing them. It would seem to me, therefore, that while the medical [rehabilitative] model has its own drawbacks, it has brought along with it a useful baggage of humane values that might never have entered the darkness of criminal justice otherwise.[6]

Those who have traditionally sought to treat offenders have also sought to lessen the discomforts convicts are made to suffer. In part, this occurs, as Allen has remarked, because 'the objectives both of fundamental decency in the prisons and the rehabilitation of prisoners . . . appears to require the same measures'.[7] Yet the studies of Torsten Eriksson suggest that it is the case as well that those endeavoring to pioneer 'the more effective treatment of criminals' have commonly been united in their 'indomitable will to help their erring brother'. They stand out as 'beacons in the history of mankind, the part that deals with compassion with one's fellow man'.[8] In this context, we can again question the wisdom of liberal attempts to unmask the rehabilitative ideal as at best a 'noble lie' and at worst an inevitably coercive fraud. For in discrediting rehabilitation, liberal critics may succeed in deterring a generation of potential reformers from attempting to do good in the correctional system by teaching that it is a futile enterprise to show care for offenders by offering to help these people lead less destructive lives. And should rehabilitation be forfeited as the prevailing liberal ideology, what will remain as the medium through which benevolent sentiments will be expressed and instituted into meaningful policy? Will the medium be a justice model that is rooted in despair and not optimism, that embraces punishment and not betterment, that disdains inmate needs and disadvantages in favor of a concern for sterile and limited legal rights, and whose guiding principle of reform is to have the state do less for its captives rather than more? Or will, as we fear, this vacuum remain unfilled and the liberal camp be left without an ideology that possesses the vitality – as has rehabilitation over the past 150 years – to serve as a rallying cry for or motive force behind reforms that will engender lasting humanizing changes?

## Notes

1 Willard Gaylin and David J. Rothman, 'Introduction' in Andrew von Hirsch, *Doing Justice: the Choice of Punishments* (New York, Hill and Wang, 1976), p. xxxix.

2 Herman and Julia Schwendinger, 'The new idealism and penal living standards', in Tony Platt and Paul Takagi (eds), *Punishment and Penal Discipline: Essays on the Prison and the Prisoners' Movement* (Berkeley, CA., Crime and Social Justice Associates, 1980), p. 187.

3 David J. Rothman, 'The state as parent: social policy in the Progressive era', in Willard Gaylin, Ira Glasser, Steven Marcus, and David Rothman (eds), *Doing Good: the Limits of Benevolence* (New York, Pantheon, 1978), p. 94.

4 Karl Menninger, *The Crime of Punishment* (New York, Penguin Books, 1966).

5 Jeffrey H. Reiman, *The Rich Get Richer and the Poor Get Prison: Ideology, Class and Criminal Justice* (New York, John Wiley, 1979), p. 144.

6 Graeme Newman, 'Book Review of *Conscience and Convenience: the Asylum and its Alternatives in Progressive America, David J. Rothman'*, *Crime and Delinquency*, 27 (July 1981), p. 426.

7 Francis A. Allen, *The Decline of the Rehabilitative Ideal: Penal Policy and Social Purpose* (New Haven, CT, Yale University Press, 1981), p. 81.

8 Torsten Eriksson, *The Reformers: an Historical Survey of Pioneer Experiments in the Treatment of Criminals* (New York, Elsevier, 1976), p. 252.

# 30

# 'Situational' crime prevention: theory and practice

## Ronald V.G. Clarke

Conventional wisdom holds that crime prevention needs to be based on a thorough understanding of the causes of crime. Though it may be conceded that preventive measures (such as humps in the road to stop speeding) can sometimes be found without invoking sophisticated causal theory, 'physical' measures which reduce opportunities for crime are often thought to be of limited value. They are said merely to suppress the impulse to offend which will then manifest itself on some other occasion and perhaps in even more harmful form. Much more effective are seen to be 'social' measures (such as the revitalization of communities, the creation of job opportunities for unemployed youth, and the provision of sports and leisure facilities), since these attempt to remove the root motivational causes of offending. These ideas about prevention are not necessarily shared by the man-in-the-street or even by policemen and magistrates, but they have prevailed among academics, administrators and others who contribute to the formulation of criminal policy. They are also consistent with a preoccupation of criminological theory with criminal 'dispositions' (cf. Gibbons, 1971; Jeffery, 1971; Ohlin, 1970) and the purpose of this paper is to argue that an alternative theoretical emphasis on choices and decisions made by the offender leads to a broader and perhaps more realistic approach to crime prevention.

### 'Dispositional' theories and their preventive implications

With some exceptions noted below, criminological theories have been little concerned with the situational determinants of crime. Instead, the main object of these theories (whether biological, psychological, or sociological in orientation) has been to show how some people are born with, or come to acquire, a 'disposition' to behave in a consistently criminal manner. This 'dispositional' bias of theory has been identified as a defining characteristic of 'positivist' criminology, but it is also to be found in 'interactionist' or deviancy theories of crime developed in response to the perceived inadequacies of positivism. Perhaps the best-known tenet of at least the early interactionist theories, which arises out of a concern with the social definition of deviance and the role of law enforcement agencies, is that people who are 'labelled' as criminal are thereby prone to continue in delinquent conduct (see especially

From *British Journal of Criminology*, 1980, 20(2): 136–47.

Becker, 1962). In fact, as Tizard (1976) and Ross (1977) have pointed out, a dispositional bias is prevalent throughout the social sciences.

The more extreme forms of dispositional theory have moulded thought about crime prevention in two unfortunate ways. First, they have paid little attention to the phenomenological differences between crimes of different kinds, which has meant that preventive measures have been insufficiently tailored to different kinds of offence and of offender; secondly they have tended to reinforce the view of crime as being largely the work of a small number of criminally disposed individuals. But many criminologists are now increasingly agreed that a 'theory of crime' would be almost as crude as a general 'theory of disease'. Many now also believe, on the evidence of self-report studies (see Hood and Sparks, 1970), that the bulk of crime – vandalism, auto-crime, shoplifting, theft by employees – is committed by people who would not ordinarily be thought of as criminal at all.

Nevertheless, the dispositional bias remains and renders criminological theory unproductive in terms of the preventive measures which it generates. People are led to propose methods of preventive intervention precisely where it is most difficult to achieve any effects, i.e. in relation to the psychological events or the social and economic conditions that are supposed to generate criminal dispositions. As James Q. Wilson (1975) has argued, there seem to be no acceptable ways of modifying temperament and other biological variables, and it is difficult to know what can be done to make parents more inclined to love their children or exercise consistent discipline. Eradicating poverty may be no real solution either, in that crime rates have continued to rise since the war despite great improvements in economic conditions. And even if it were possible to provide people with the kinds of jobs and leisure facilities they might want, there is still no guarantee that crime would drop; few crimes require much time or effort, and work and leisure in themselves provide a whole range of criminal opportunities. As for violent crime, there would have to be a much clearer link between this and media portrayals of violence before those who cater to popular taste would be persuaded to change their material. Finally, given public attitudes to offending, which, judging by some opinion surveys, can be quite punitive, there may not be a great deal of additional scope for policies of diversion and decriminalization which are favoured by those who fear the consequences of 'labelling'.

These difficulties are primarily practical, but they also reflect the uncertainties and inconsistencies of treating distant psychological events and social processes as the 'causes' of crime. Given that each event is in turn caused by others, at what point in the infinitely regressive chain should one stop in the search for effective points of intervention? This is an especially pertinent question in that it is invariably found that the majority of individuals exposed to this or that criminogenic influence do not develop into persistent criminals. Moreover, 'dispositions' change so that most 'official' delinquents cease to come to the attention of the police in their late 'teens or early twenties (presumably because their lives change in ways incompatible with their earlier pursuits, cf. Trasler, 1979). Finally, it is worth pointing out that even the most persistently criminal people are probably law-abiding for most of their potentially available time, and this behaviour, too, must equally have been 'caused' by the events and experiences of their past. Some of the above theoretical difficulties could be avoided by conceiving of crime not in dispositional terms, but as being the outcome of immediate choices and decisions made by the offender. This would also have the effect of throwing a different light on preventive options.

An obvious problem is that some impulsive offences, and those committed under the influence of alcohol or strong emotion, may not easily be seen as the result of choices or decisions. Another difficulty is that the notion of 'choice' seems to fit uncomfortably with the fact that criminal behaviour is to some extent predictable from knowledge of a person's history. This difficulty is not properly resolved by the 'soft' determinism of Matza (1964) under which people retain some freedom of action albeit within a range of options constrained by their history and environment. A better formulation would seem to be that recently expounded by Glaser (1977): 'both free will and determinism are socially derived linguistic representations of reality' brought into play for different explanatory purposes at different levels of analysis and they may usefully co-exist in the scientific enterprise.

Whatever the resolution of these difficulties – and this is not the place to discuss them more fully – commonsense as well as the evidence of ethnographic studies of delinquency (e.g. Parker, 1974) strongly suggest that people are usually aware of consciously choosing to commit offences. This does not mean that they are fully aware of all the reasons for their behaviour nor that their own account would necessarily satisfy a criminologically sophisticated observer, who might require information at least about: (i) the offender's motives; (ii) his mood; (iii) his moral judgements concerning the act in question and the 'techniques of moral neutralization' open to him (cf. Matza, 1964); (iv) the extent of his criminal knowledge and his perception of criminal opportunities; (v) his assessment of the risks of being caught as well as the likely consequences; and finally, as well as of a different order, (vi) whether he has been drinking. These separate components of subjective state and thought processes which play a part in the decision to commit a crime will be influenced by immediate situational variables and by highly specific features of the individual's history and present life circumstances in ways that are so varied and countervailing as to render unproductive the notion of a generalized behavioural disposition to offend. Moreover, as will be argued below, the specificity of the influences upon different criminal behaviours gives much less credence to the 'displacement' hypothesis; the idea that reducing opportunities merely results in crime being displaced to some other time or place has been the major argument against situational crime prevention.

In so far as an individual's social and physical environments remain relatively constant and his decisions are much influenced by past experience, this scheme gives ample scope to account not only for occasional offending but also for recidivism; people acquire a repertoire of different responses to meet particular situations and if the circumstances are right they are likely to repeat those responses that have previously been rewarding. The scheme also provides a much richer source of hypotheses than 'dispositional' views of crime for the sex differences in rates of offending: for example, shoplifting may be a 'female' crime simply because women are greater users of shops (Mayhew, 1977). In view of the complexity of the behaviours in question, a further advantage (Atkinson, 1974) is that the scheme gives some accommodation to the variables thought to be important in most existing theories of crime, including those centred on dispositions. It is perhaps closest to a social learning theory of behaviour (Bandura, 1973; Mischel, 1968) though it owes something to the sociological model of crime proposed by the 'new criminologists' (Taylor et al., 1973). There are three features, however, which are particularly worth drawing out for the sake of the ensuing discussion about crime prevention: first, explanation is focused more directly on the criminal event; second, the need to develop explanations for separate categories of crime is made explicit; and, third, the individual's current circumstances and the immediate features of the setting are given considerably more explanatory significance than in 'dispositional' theories.

## Preventive implications of a 'choice' model

In fact, just as an understanding of past influences on behaviour may have little preventive pay-off, so too there may be limited benefits in according greater explanatory importance to the individual's current life circumstances. For example, the instrumental attractions of delinquency may always be greater for certain groups of individuals such as young males living in inner-city areas. And nothing can be done about a vast range of misfortunes which continually befall people and which may raise the probability of their behaving criminally while depressed or angry.

Some practicable options for prevention do arise, however, from the greater emphasis upon situational features, especially from the direct and immediate relationship between these and criminal behaviour. By studying the spatial and temporal distribution of specific offences and relating these to measurable aspects of the situation, criminologists have recently begun to concern themselves much more closely with the possibilities of manipulating criminogenic situations in the interests of prevention. To date studies have been undertaken of residential burglary (Brantingham and Brantingham, 1975; Reppetto, 1974; Scarr, 1973; Waller and Okihiro, 1978) shoplifting (Walsh, 1978) and some forms of vandalism (Clarke, 1978; Ley and Cybrinwsky, 1974) and it is easy to foresee an expansion of research along these lines. Since offenders' perceptions of the risks and rewards attaching to different forms of crime cannot safely be inferred from studies of the distribution of offences, there might be additional preventive benefits if research of this kind were more frequently complemented by interviews with offenders (cf. Tuck, 1979; Walker, 1979).

The suggestions for prevention arising out of the 'situational' research that has been done can be conveniently divided into measures which (i) reduce the physical opportunities for offending or (ii) increase the chances of an offender being caught. These categories are discussed separately below though there is some overlap between them; for example, better locks which take longer to overcome also increase the risks of being caught. The division also leaves out some other 'situational' crime prevention measures such as housing allocation policies which avoid high concentrations of children in certain estates or which place families in accommodation that makes it easier for parents to supervise their children's play and leisure activities. Both these measures make it less likely that children will become involved in vandalism and other offences (cf. Wilson, 1978).

### Reducing physical opportunities for crime and the problem of displacement

Variations in physical opportunities for crime have sometimes been invoked to explain differences in crime rates within particular cities (e.g. Boggs, 1965; Baldwin and Bottoms, 1975) or temporal variations in crime; for example, Wilkins (1964) and Gould and his associates (Gould, 1969; Mansfield et al., 1974) have related levels of car theft to variations in the number of vehicles on the road. But these studies have not generally provided practicable preventive ideas – for example, the number of cars on the road cannot be reduced simply to prevent their theft – and it is only recently that there has been a concerted effort on the part of criminologists to find viable ways of blocking the opportunities for particular crimes.

The potential for controlling behaviour by manipulating opportunities is illustrated vividly by a study of suicide in Birmingham (Hassal and Trethowan, 1972). This showed that a marked drop in the rates of suicide between 1962 and 1970 was the result of a reduction in the poisonous content of the gas supplied to householders for cooking and heating, so that it became much more difficult for people to kill themselves by turning on the gas taps. Like many kinds of crime, suicide is generally regarded as being dictated by strong internal motivation and the fact that its incidence was greatly reduced by a simple (though unintentional) reduction in the opportunities to commit it suggests that it may be possible to achieve similar reductions in crime by 'physical' means. Though suicide by other methods did not increase in Birmingham, the study also leads to direct consideration of the fundamental theoretical problem of 'displacement' which, as Reppetto (1976) has pointed out, can occur in four different ways: time, place, method and type of offence. In other words, does reducing opportunities or increasing the risks result merely in the offender choosing his moment more carefully or in seeking some other, perhaps more harmful method of gaining his ends? Or, alternatively, will he shift his attention to a similar but unprotected target, for example, another house, car or shop? Or, finally, will he turn instead to some other form of crime?

For those who see crime as the outcome of criminal disposition, the answers to these questions would tend to be in the affirmative ('bad will out') but under the alternative view of crime represented above matters are less straightforward. Answers would depend on the nature of the crime, the offender's strength of motivation, knowledge of alternatives, willingness to entertain them, and so forth. In the case of opportunistic crimes (i.e. ones apparently elicited by their very ease of accomplishment such as some forms of shoplifting or vandalism) it would seem that the probability of offending could be reduced markedly by making it more difficult to act. For crimes such as bank robbery, however, which often seem to be the province of those who make a living from crime, reducing opportunities may be less effective. (This may be less true of increasing the risks of being caught except that for many offences the risks may be so low at present that any increase would have to be very marked.) Providing effective protection for a particular bank would almost certainly displace the attention of potential robbers to others, and if all banks were given increased protection many robbers would no doubt consider alternative means of gaining their ends. It is by no means implausible, however, that others – for example, those who do not have the ability to develop more sophisticated methods or who may not be willing to use more violence – may accept their reduced circumstances and may even take legitimate employment.

It is the bulk of offences, however, which are neither 'opportunistic' nor 'professional' that pose the greatest theoretical dilemmas. These offences include many burglaries and instances of auto-crime where the offender, who may merely supplement his normal income through the proceeds of crime, has gone out with the deliberate intention of committing the offence and has sought out the opportunity to do so. The difficulty posed for measures which reduce opportunity is one of the vast number of potential targets combined with the generally low overall level of security. Within easy reach of every house with a burglar alarm, or car with an anti-theft device, are many others without such protection.

In some cases, however, it may be possible to protect a whole class of property, as the Post Office did when they virtually eliminated theft from telephone kiosks by replacing the vulnerable aluminium coin-boxes with much stronger steel ones (cf. Mayhew et al., 1976). A further example is provided by the [UK] law which requires all motor-cyclists to wear crash helmets. This measure was introduced to save lives, but it has also had the unintended effect of reducing thefts of motor-cycles (Mayhew et al., 1976). This is because people are unlikely to take someone else's motorbike on the spur of the moment unless they happen to have a crash helmet with them – otherwise they could easily be spotted by the police. But perhaps the best example comes from West Germany where, in 1963, steering column locks were made compulsory on *all* cars, old and new, with a consequent reduction of more than 60 per cent in levels of taking and driving away (Mayhew et al., 1976). (When steering column locks were introduced in this country in 1971 it was only to new cars and, although these are now at much less risk of being taken, overall levels of car-taking have not yet diminished because the risk to older cars had increased as a result of displacement.)

Instances where criminal opportunities can be reduced for a whole class of property are comparatively few, but this need not always be a fatal difficulty. There must be geographical and temporal limits to displacement so that a town or city may be able to protect itself from some crime without displacing it elsewhere. The less determined the offender, the easier this will be; a simple example is provided by Decker's (1972) evidence that the use of 'slugs' in parking-meters in a New York district was greatly reduced by replacing the meters with ones which incorporated a slug-rejector device and in which the last coin inserted was visible in a plastic window. For most drivers there would be little advantage in parking their cars in some other district just because they could continue to use slugs there.

The question of whether, when stopped from committing a particular offence, people would turn instead to some other quite different form of crime is much more difficult to settle empirically, but many of the same points about motivation, knowledge of alternatives and so forth still apply. Common-sense also suggests, for example, that few of those Germans prevented by steering column locks from taking cars to get home at night are likely to have turned instead to hijacking taxis or to mugging passers-by for the money to get home. More likely, they may have decided that next time they would make sure of catching the last bus home or that it was time to save up for their own car.

## Increasing the risks of being caught

In practice, increasing the chances of being caught usually means attempting to raise the chances of an offender being seen by someone who is likely to take action.The police are the most obvious group likely to intervene effectively, but studies of the effectiveness of this aspect of their deterrent role are not especially encouraging (Clarke and Hough, 1980; Kelling et al., 1974; Manning, 1977). The reason seems to be that, when set against the vast number of opportunities for offending represented by the activities of a huge population of citizens for the 24 hours of the day, crime is a relatively rare event. The police cannot be everywhere at once and, moreover, much crime takes place in private. Nor is much to be expected from the general public (Mayhew et al., 1979). People in their daily round rarely see crime in progress; if they do they are likely to place some innocent interpretation on what they see; they may be afraid to intervene or they may feel the victims would resent interference; and they may encounter practical difficulties in summoning the police or other help in time. They are much more likely to take effective action to protect their own homes or immediate neighbourhood, but they are often away from these for substantial periods of the day and, moreover, the risks of crime in residential settings, at least in many areas of this country, are not so great as to encourage much vigilance. For instance, assuming that about 50 per cent of burglaries are reported to the police (cf. Home Office, 1979), a house in this country will on average be burgled once every 30 years. Even so, there is evidence (Department of the Environment, 1977; Wilson, 1978) that 'defensible space' designs on housing estates confer some protection from vandalism, if not as much as might have been expected from the results of Newman's (1973) research into crime on public housing projects in the United States (cf. Clarke,1979; Mayhew, 1979).

A recent Home Office Research report (Mayhew et al., 1979) has argued, however, that there is probably a good deal of unrealized potential for making more deliberate use of the surveillance role of employees who come into regular and frequent contact with the public in a semi-official capacity. Research in the United States (Newman, 1973; Reppetto, 1974) and Canada (Waller and Okihiro, 1978) has shown that apartment blocks with doormen are less vulnerable to burglary, while research in [the UK] has shown that vandalism is much less of a problem on buses with conductors (Mayhew et al., 1976) and on estates with resident caretakers (Department of the Environment, 1977). There is also evidence (in Post Office Records) that public telephones in places such as pubs or launderettes, which are given some supervision by staff, suffer almost no vandalism in comparison with those in kiosks; that car parks with attendants in control have lower rates of auto-crime (*The Sunday Times*, 9 April 1978); that football hooliganism on trains has been reduced by a variety of measures including permission for club stewards to travel free of charge; and that shoplifting is discouraged by the presence of assistants who are there to serve the customers (Walsh, 1978). Not everybody employed in a service capacity would be suited or willing to take on additional security duties, but much of their deterrent role may result simply from their being around. Employing more of them, for greater parts of the day, may therefore be all that is needed in most cases. In other cases, it may be necessary to employ people more suited to a surveillance role, train them better to carry it out, or even provide them with surveillance aids. Providing the staff at four London Underground stations with closed circuit television has been shown in a recent Home Office Research Unit study (Mayhew et al., 1979) to have substantially reduced theft and robbery offences at those stations.

## Some objections

Apart from the theoretical and practical difficulties of the approach advocated in this paper, it is in apparent conflict with the 'nothing works' school of criminological thought as given recent expression by Wolfgang (1977): 'the weight of empirical evidence indicates that no current preventative, deterrent, or rehabilitative intervention scheme has the desired effect of reducing crime'. But perhaps a panacea is being sought when all it may be possible to achieve is a reduction in particular forms of crime as a result of specific and sometimes localized measures. Examples of such reductions are given above and, while most of these relate to rather commonplace offences of theft and vandalism, there is no reason why similar measures cannot be successfully applied to other quite different forms of crime. It has been argued by many people (Rhodes, 1977, provides an example) that reducing the availability of hand-guns through gun-control legislation would reduce crimes of violence in the United States and elsewhere. Speeding and drunken driving could probably be reduced by fitting motor vehicles with devices which are now at an experimental stage (Ekblom, 1979). And there is no doubt (Wilkinson, 1977) that the rigorous passenger and baggage screening measures introduced at airports, particularly in the United States, have greatly reduced the incidence of airline hijackings. There are many crimes, however, when the offender is either so determined or so emotionally aroused that they seem to be beyond the scope of this approach. A further constraint will be costs: many shops, for example, which could reduce shoplifting by giving up self-service methods and employing more assistants or even store detectives, have calculated that this would not be worth the expense either in direct costs or in a reduction of turnover. Morally dubious as this policy might at first sight appear, these shops may simply have learned a lesson of more general application, i.e. a certain level of crime may be the inevitable consequence of practices and institutions which we cherish or find convenient and the 'cost' of reducing crime below this level may be unacceptable.

The gradualist approach to crime prevention advocated here might also attract criticism from some social reformers, as well as some deviancy theorists, for being unduly conservative. The former group, imbued with dispositional theory, would see the only effective way of dealing with crime as being to attack its roots through the reduction of inequalities of wealth, class and education – a solution which, as indicated above, has numerous practical and theoretical difficulties. The latter group would criticize the approach, not for its lack of effectiveness but – on the grounds that there is insufficient consensus in society about what behaviour should be treated as crime – for helping to preserve an undesirable status quo. Incremental change, however, may be the most realistic way of achieving consensus as well as a more equitable society. Most criminologists would probably also agree that it would be better for the burden of crime reduction to be gradually shifted away from the criminal justice system, which may be inherently selective and punitive in its operation, to preventive measures whose social costs may be more equitably distributed among all members of society. The danger to be guarded against would be that the attention of offenders might be displaced away from those who can afford to purchase protection to those who cannot. This probably happens already to some extent and perhaps the best way of dealing with the problem would be through codes of security which would be binding on car manufacturers, builders, local transport operators and so forth. Another danger is that those who have purchased protection might become less willing to see additional public expenditure on the law enforcement and criminal justice services – and this is a problem that might only be dealt with through political leadership and public education.

Many members of the general public might also find it objectionable that crime was being stopped, not by punishing wrong-doers, but by inconveniencing the law-abiding. The fact that opportunity-reducing and risk-increasing measures are too readily identified with their more unattractive aspects (barbed wire, heavy padlocks, guard-dogs and private security forces) adds fuel to the fire. And in some of their more sophisticated forms (closed circuit television surveillance and electronic intruder alarms) they provoke fears, on the one hand, of 'big brother' forms of state control and, on the other, of a 'fortress society' in which citizens in perpetual fear of their fellows scuttle from one fortified environment to another.

Expressing these anxieties has a value in checking potential abuses of power, and questioning the means of dealing with crime can also help to keep the problem of crime in perspective. But it should also be said that the kind of measures discussed above need not always be obtrusive (except where it is important to maximize their deterrent effects) and need not in any material way infringe individual liberties or the quality of life. Steel cash compartments in telephone kiosks are indistinguishable from aluminium ones, and vandal-resistant polycarbonate looks just like glass. Steering column locks are automatically brought into operation on removing the ignition key, and many people are quite unaware that their cars are fitted with them. 'Defensible space' designs in housing estates have the additional advantage of promoting feelings of neighbourliness and safety, though perhaps too little attention has been paid to some of their less desirable effects such as possible encroachments on privacy as a result of overlooking. And having more bus conductors, housing estate caretakers, swimming bath attendants and shop assistants means that people benefit from improved services – even if they have to pay for them either directly or through the rates.

Finally, the idea that crime might be most effectively prevented by reducing opportunities and increasing the risks is seen by many as, at best, representing an over-simplified mechanistic view of human behaviour and, at worst, a 'slur on human nature' (cf. Radzinowicz and King, 1977). (When the contents of *Crime as Opportunity* (Mayhew et al., 1976) were reported in the press in advance of publication an irate psychiatrist wrote to the Home Secretary demanding that he should suppress the publication of such manifest nonsense.) As shown above, however, it is entirely compatible with a view of criminal behaviour as predominantly rational and autonomous and as being capable of adjusting and responding to adverse consequences, anticipated or experienced. And as for being a pessimistic view of human behaviour, it might indeed be better if greater compliance with the law could come about simply as a result of people's free moral choice. But apart from being perilously close to the rather unhelpful dispositional view of crime, it is difficult to see this happening. We may therefore be left for the present with the approach advocated [here], time-consuming, laborious and limited as it may be.

## Summary

It is argued that the 'dispositional' bias of most current criminological theory has resulted in 'social' crime prevention measures being given undue prominence and 'situational' measures being devalued. An alternative theoretical emphasis on decisions and choices made by the offender (which in turn allows more weight to the circumstances of offending) results in more support for a situational approach to prevention. Examples of the effectiveness of such an approach are provided and some of the criticisms that have been made of it on social and ethical grounds are discussed.

## References

Atkinson, M. (1974) 'Versions of deviance', Extended review in *Sociological Review*, 22: 616–24.

Baldwin, J. and Bottoms, A.E. (1975) *The Urban Criminal*. London: Tavistock.

Bandura, A. (1973) *Aggression: a Social Learning Analysis*. London: Prentice Hall.

Becker, H.S. (1962) *Outsiders: Studies in the Sociology of Deviance*. Glencoe, Ill.: The Free Press.

Boggs, S.L. (1965) 'Urban crime patterns', *American Sociological Review*, 30: 899–908.

Brantingham, P.J. and Brantingham, P.L. (1975) 'The spatial patterning of burglary', *Howard Journal of Penology and Crime Prevention*, 14: 11–24.

Clarke, R.V.G. (ed.) (1978) *Tackling Vandalism*. Home Office Research Study No. 47. London: HMSO.

Clarke, R.V.G. (1979) 'Defensible space and vandalism: the lessons from some recent British research', *Stadtebau und Kriminalamt (Urban planning and Crime)*. Papers of an international symposium, Bundeskriminalamt, Federal Republic of Germany, December, 1978.

Clarke, R.V.G. and Hough, J.M. (eds) (1980) *The Effectiveness of Policing*. Farnborough, Hants: Gower.

Decker, J.F. (1972) 'Curbside deterrence: an analysis of the effect of a slug-rejector device, coin view window and warning labels on slug usage in New York City parking meters', *Criminology*, August, pp. 127–42.

Department of the Environment (1977) *Housing Management and Design*. (Lambeth Inner Area Study). IAS/IA/18. London: Department of the Environment.

Ekblom, P. (1979) 'A crime-free car?', *Research Bulletin No. 7*. Home Office Research Unit. London: Home Office.

Gibbons, D.C. (1971) 'Observations on the study of crime causation', *American Journal of Sociology*, 77: 262–78.

Glaser, D. (1977) 'The compatibility of free will and determinism in criminology: comments on an alleged problem', *Journal of Criminal Law and Criminology* 67: 486–90.

Gould, L.C. (1969) 'The changing structure of property crime in an affluent society', *Social Forces*, 48: 50–9.

Hassal, C. and Trethowan, W.H. (1972) 'Suicide in Birmingham', *British Medical Journal*, 1: 717–18.

Home Office (1979) *Criminal Statistics: England and Wales 1978*. London: HMSO.

Hood, R. and Sparks, R. (1970) *Key Issues in Criminology*. London: Weidenfeld and Nicolson.

Jeffery, C.R. (1971) *Crime Prevention Through Environmental Design*. Beverly Hills, CA: Sage.

Kelling, G.L., Pate, T., Dieckman, D. and Brown C.E. (1974) *The Kansas City Preventive Patrol Experiment*. Washington, DC: Police Foundation.

Ley, D. and Cybrinwsky, R. (1974) 'The spatial ecology of stripped cars', *Environment and Behaviour*, 6: 53–67.

Manning, P. (1977) *Police Work: the Social Organisation of Policing*. London: Massachusetts Institute of Technology Press.

Mansfield, R., Gould, L.C. and Namenwirth, J.Z. (1974) 'A socioeconomic model for the prediction of societal rates of property theft'. *Social Forces*, 52: 462–72.

Matza, D. (1964) *Delinquency and Drift*. New York: John Wiley and Sons.

Mayhew, P. (1977) 'Crime in a man's world', *New Society*, 16 June.

Mayhew, P. (1979) 'Defensible space: the current status of a crime prevention theory', *The Howard Journal of Penology and Crime Prevention*, 18: 150–9.

Mayhew, P., Clarke, R.V.G., Sturman, A. and Hough, J.M. (1976) *Crime as Opportunity*. Home Office Research Study No. 34. London: HMSO.

Mayhew, P., Clarke, R.V.G., Burrows, J.N., Hough, J.M. and Winchester, S.W.C. (1979) *Crime in Public View*. Home Office Research Study No. 49. London: HMSO.

Mischel, W. (1968) *Personality and Assessment*. New York: John Wiley and Sons.

Newman, O. (1973) *Defensible Space: People and Design in the Violent City*. London: Architectural Press.

Ohlin, L.E. (1970) *A Situational Approach to Delinquency Prevention*. Youth Development and Delinquency Prevention Administration. US Department of Health, Education and Welfare.

Parker, H. (1974) *View from the Boys*. Newton Abbot: David and Charles.

Radzinowicz, L. and King, J. (1977) *The Growth of Crime*. London: Hamish Hamilton.

Reppetto, T.A. (1974) *Residential Crime*. Cambridge, MA: Ballinger.

Reppetto, T.A. (1976) 'Crime prevention and the displacement phenomenon', *Crime and Delinquency*, April, 166–77.

Rhodes, R.P. (1977) *The Insoluble Problems of Crime*. New York: John Wiley and Sons.

Ross, L. (1977) 'The intuitive psychologist and his shortcomings: distortions in the attribution process', in L. Berkowitz (ed.), *Advances in Experimental Social Psychology*, Vol. 10. New York: Academic Press.

Scarr, H.A. (1973) *Patterns of Burglary*. US Department of Justice, Washington DC: Government Printing Office.

Taylor, I., Walton, P. and Young, J. (1973) *The New Criminology*. London: Routledge and Kegan Paul.

Tizard, J. (1976) 'Psychology and social policy', *Bulletin of the British Psychological Society*, 29: 225–33.

Trasler, G.B. (1979) 'Delinquency, recidivism, and desistance', *British Journal of Criminology*, 19: 314–22.

Tuck, M. (1979) 'Consumer behaviour theory and the criminal justice system: towards a new strategy of research', *Journal of the Market Research Society*, 21: 44–58.

Walker, N.D. (1979) 'The efficacy and morality of deterrents', *Criminal Law Review*, March, 129–44.

Waller, I. and Okihiro, N. (1978) *Burglary: the Victim and the Public*. Toronto: University of Toronto Press.

Walsh, D.P. (1978) *Shoplifting: Controlling a Major Crime*. London: Macmillan.

Wilkins, L.T. (1964) *Social Deviance*. London: Tavistock.

Wilkinson, P. (1977) *Terrorism and the Liberal State*. London: Macmillan.

Wilson, J.Q. (1975) *Thinking About Crime*. New York: Basic Books.

Wilson, S. (1978) 'Vandalism and "defensible space" on London housing estates', in R.V.G. Clarke, (ed.), *Tackling Vandalism*. Home Office Research Study No. 47. London: HMSO.

Wolfgang, M.E. (1977) 'Real and perceived changes in crime', in S.F. Landau and L. Sebba, (eds), *Criminology in Perspective*. Lexington, MA: Lexington Books.

# 31

# Social crime prevention strategies in a market society

## *Elliott Currie*

[. . .]

All societies make some use of market mechanisms to allocate goods and services. And most of us would acknowledge that the exact determination of what the market does better in this regard and what is best accomplished by other means is often an empirical question. The best balance of private and public is not easy to weigh, and it shifts over time as social needs and technological capacities change. But 'market society', as I will use the term, is a different animal altogether. By market society I mean a society in which the pursuit of private gain increasingly becomes the organizing principle for all areas of social life, not simply a mechanism which we use to accomplish certain circumscribed economic ends. The balance between private and public shifts dramatically, so that the public retreats to a minuscule and disempowered part of social and economic life and the idea of common purposes and common responsibility steadily withers as an important social value.

In market society all other principles of social organization become subordinated to the over-reaching one of private gain. Alternative sources of livelihood, of social support and of cultural value, even of personal identity, become increasingly eroded or obliterated. As a result, individuals, families and communities are more and more dependent on what we somewhat misleadingly call the 'free' market to provide for their human needs, not only material needs but also cultural, symbolic and psychic needs. I say 'somewhat misleadingly' because, as critics have often pointed out, this sort of society – as it is increasingly found in the US, for example – isn't really adequately characterized by the notion of the 'free' market. Economic and social power and the expanded life-chances and opportunities that go with them are not 'free' in the classical Adam Smithian sense of being equally accessible to all who demonstrate sufficient merit, skill and enterprise. Instead, some groups have increasingly been able to protect themselves against the judgement of the economic market and from the need to perform efficiently at all, while others are subjected to the market's mercies at an ever-accelerating pace.

Now, as I'm using the term, 'market society' is an abstraction, an 'ideal type', and it doesn't, yet, exist anywhere in a pure form. But it has approximations in the real world, both developed and developing, and the United States again has proceeded farther down the road towards market society than any other advanced industrial nation. The UK has, of course,

Abridged from *International Developments in Crime and Social Policy*, NACRO Crime and Social Policy, pp. 107–20. (London: NACRO, 1991.)

made very considerable efforts in that direction over the past 12 years, but there's still a long way to go before arriving at the evolution of market society we've 'attained'. But something like a broad drift towards market society is increasingly apparent in many other countries across the world. And that's troubling for a variety of reasons but, for our purposes here, specifically because market societies are extraordinarily fertile ground for the growth of crime. I stress again that market society is not the same as the mere existence of a market *economy*. The idea that a serious crime problem is an inevitable accompaniment of a vibrant economy or a free political order is both wrong and pernicious. It is, however, a predictable accompaniment of the growth of market *society*. Why?

Well, let me offer you five propositions about market society's impact on several overlapping areas of social, economic and cultural life which in turn strongly influence the shape and dimensions of the crime problem. (That close overlap is, in fact, what makes the concept of market society helpful in understanding the nature of crime in the industrial societies today. It helps, among other things, to explain why some factors taken individually – say, the unemployment rate, or levels of poverty – may not always fit so well as explanations of crime, an issue much seized upon by some of our conservative colleagues. Looking at the role of these factors through the more holistic perspective offered by the idea of 'market society' helps us understand why poverty, for example, is much more salient for understanding crime in some kinds of societies, at some points in their development, than in others.)

[. . .]

## Links between market society and crime

### First mechanism

**Market society promotes crime by increasing inequality and concentrated economic deprivation.** In the US the rise in violent crime has – not at all unexpectedly from the standpoint of several different lines of criminological theory – gone hand-in-hand with the sharpest rise of economic inequality in our postwar history, the attainment of the widest gap in incomes since we began gathering statistics after the Second World War. In turn, that rising economic inequality in the US can be traced to several related trends.

One is the deterioration of the labour market, both private and public. Throughout the economy, vast numbers of 'middle-level' jobs, especially but not exclusively in blue-collar industry, have disappeared to be replaced by a significant rise in extremely well-rewarded jobs at the top, and a much larger increase in poor jobs, including unstable and part-time ones, at the bottom. This downward shift has been especially destructive to the prospects of younger people. According to data from the US Senate Budget Committee, more than four-fifths of the net new jobs available to young men under 35 during the 1980s paid poverty-level wages or below. In the course of that decade there was a net loss of 1.6 million middle-level jobs available to men of that age group.

This shift in the labour market is not, of course, a matter of the mysterious workings of fate or even of politically neutral changes in technology or demography. It has been driven by deliberate social policy in several ways:

- through the continuing flight of capital and jobs to low-wage havens both in parts of the US itself and, increasingly, overseas, especially to Asia and the Caribbean;
- through the lowering of the real value of the minimum wage, which ensures that new job creation has been overwhelmingly concentrated in poverty-level, low productivity jobs;
- and relatedly, by a more or less conscious policy of achieving profits and staying afloat in the face of international economic competition primarily by lowering wages rather than by increasing the productivity of the workforce and the efficiency of management, what some writers in the US call the deliberate 'dumbing-down' of the labour force.

All of this has resulted in a growing tendency toward what has been called an 'hourglass' income distribution. This tendency is compounded by two other important thrusts of the market-driven social policy of the past fifteen years: the erosion of income support benefits for low-income people and the unemployed, and a pattern of systematically regressive taxation [. . .]

The result of these compounded distributional policies has been to raise the top to unprecedented pinnacles of wealth and of personal consumption, while dropping the poor into a far deeper and more abysmal hole than they were in before, which was already the deepest among advanced industrial societies.

Today we not only have about six million more poor Americans than we did in 1979, but they are much poorer both relative to the affluent and, often, in absolute terms. As the job structure has narrowed and income support shrivelled, it is now far more difficult, as surveys have discovered, for them to get *out*, at least through legitimate means, a fact which is not lost on the urban poor, especially the young.

We are now in real danger of creating something like an economic apartheid and it is by no means just a problem of the so-called, hard-core urban 'underclass', but of an increasingly threatened and declining bottom third of the American population.

Nor are these general trends confined to the US. [. . .] The trend towards growing inequality is increasingly international in scope and international in its consequences. And it is deeply implicated in the pattern of crime.

*Second mechanism*

**Market society promotes crime by weakening the capacity of local communities for 'informal' support, mutual provision and socialization and supervision of the young.** This is closely related to the first link: it is, in part, a function of the declining economic security and rising deprivation in low income communities, as well as the rapid movement of capital and accordingly of opportunities for stable work which are hallmarks of the advance of market society.

Under the sustained impact of market forces, communities suffer not only from the long-term loss of stable livelihoods, but also from the excessive geographic mobility that results from that loss. The process is by no means confined to the US; it is central to the experience of many countries and especially many in the developing world and those on the periphery of European prosperity. It is compounded, in the US, by the crisis in housing for low-income people as market forces drive up the cost of shelter at the same time that they drive down wages. The loss of stability of shelter, in turn, helps destroy the basis of local social cohesion.

Communities suffering these compounded stresses begin to exhibit the phenomenon some researchers call 'drain': as the ability of families to support themselves and care for their children drops below a certain critical point, they can no longer sustain those informal networks of social support and help that can otherwise be a buffer against the impact of the economic grinding of the market. If you're having tough times you can't lean on your neighbours or your cousins, even if they still live in the same community, because they're having tough times too; and there are therefore decreasing resources, both emotional and material, to offer to anyone else.

### Third mechanism

**Market society promotes crime by stressing and fragmenting the family.** Again, this is deeply enmeshed with the first and second mechanisms. The growing economic deprivation and community fragmentation characteristic of market society put enormous pressures on family life, and it is partly through these pressures that the growth of market society generates crime.

These connections are many and complex: let me just mention two of them for now, again using the American experience as an example.

First, the long-term economic marginalization of entire communities which characterizes market society tends to inhibit the formation of stable families in the first place – as the sociologist William J. Wilson has powerfully argued for the US case – by diminishing the 'pool' of marriageable men who are seen as capable of achieving a legitimate livelihood that can support a family. The result is to encourage single parenthood and its associated poverty.

But unemployment itself is only one way in which the deterioration of the labour market has affected families. The flip side is overwork in inadequate jobs. Because so much of the employment recently created pays poverty-level wages, great numbers of families, especially young families, can only stay afloat by drastically increasing their hours of work, often taking on two or even three jobs. This is an increasingly common phenomenon in low-income communities in the US and one I've encountered over and over again in working with delinquent kids. [. . .] This has given us a generation of parents, especially young parents and single parents, who have virtually no leisure time and who are (a) constantly stressed to breaking point and (b) absent from the home and the community for most of the time.

It is important not to only blame parents for this. But the results are very real and very troubling. The socializing and nurturing capacities of many families have been seriously compromised and children in America are too often thrown back on their own resources and their own peer groups for guidance, support and supervision.

Again, these mechanisms overlap. The pressure of market forces on community stability aggravates the strains on families. Once upon a time, families facing adverse economic conditions could look to other families in the community for help; parents burdened by overwork could look to informal networks of relatives and friends to help care for children. As market society advances, families are increasingly severed from these informal connections and forced to struggle against the uncertainties and deprivations of the market economy alone. The resulting 'social impoverishment' fuses with economic deprivation and insecurity to produce overwhelming stresses, domestic violence and child abuse. [. . .]

These adverse impacts on families are all the more severe because of the *fourth* link between market society and crime.

### Fourth mechanism

**Market society promotes crime by withdrawing public provision of basic services for those it has already stripped of livelihoods, economic security and 'informal' communal support.** Once again, this process has been most advanced in the US among industrial societies. But we are not alone. Before the advent of the Reagan Administration, the US already stood lowest among several industrial countries in the rate at which public benefits brought families and children out of poverty. We became much more miserly during the 1980s when, for example, our income benefits lifted one in five families out of poverty in 1979; the figure is less than one in nine today, and falling.

Beyond public income support there have been substantial cuts in those public services which could prevent or repair some of the damages inflicted by the compound impacts of economic deprivation, family stress and community breakdown. That process has accelerated enormously in the current fiscal crisis of the 1990s, leading to huge cuts in the kind of preventative health and mental health care that might help intervene with some of the children most 'at risk' of delinquency and drug abuse; a tragic shortfall of effective intervention for families at high risk of child abuse; and a continuing inability to develop nurturing and accessible child care for low-income families whipsawed by low wages and overwork.

All these impacts also must be understood in the light of the fifth link between market society and crime.

### Fifth mechanism

**Market society promotes crime by magnifying a culture of Darwinian competition for status and dwindling resources and by urging a level of consumption that it cannot fulfil for everyone through legitimate channels.** I won't dwell on this now: it's been a recurrent theme in criminological theory. My own favourite exposition of this point is that of the great Dutch criminologist Willem Bonger.

Bonger believed that, 'To make prosperity and culture as general as possible' was the 'best preventive against crime'. But he stressed that he meant 'prosperity, not luxury': for 'There is not a weaker spot to be found in the social development of our times than the ever-growing and ever-intensifying covetousness, which, in its turn, is the result of powerful social forces.' Bonger wrote in the early 1930s; . . . what he would see today in the US and in many parts of the world would surely blow his mind.

A full-blown market culture promotes crime in several ways: by holding out standards of economic status and consumption which increasing numbers of people cannot legitimately meet, and more subtly, by weakening other values more supportive of the intrinsic worth of human life and well-being and of the value of what we might call 'craft', the value of creative work, of productive contribution, of a job well done.

One of the most chilling features of much violent street crime in America today, and also in some developing countries, is how directly it expresses the logic of immediate gratification in the pursuit of consumer goods, or of instant status and recognition. Some of our delinquents will cheerfully acknowledge that they blew someone away for their running shoes or because they made the mistake of looking at them disrespectfully on the street. People who study crime, perhaps especially from a 'progressive' perspective, sometimes shy away from looking hard at these less tangible 'moral' aspects. In the US we are certainly witnessing a kind of demoralization that must be acknowledged and confronted if we wish to understand crime today. [. . .] The point is not simply to bemoan the ascendancy of those values among some of the urban young, but to recognize that they are, as Bonger said, the 'result of powerful social forces', a direct and unmediated reflection of the inner logic of market society, part of the total package that we must be prepared to accept if we accept that package at all.

There are other links as well between the growth of market society, market culture and crime. A full analysis of those connections would need to consider, for example, the impact on crime of the specifically psychological distortions of market society, its tendency to produce personalities less and less capable of relating to others except as consumer items or as trophies in a quest for recognition among one's peers. And we need also to consider the long-term political impacts of market society that are related to crime, in particular its tendency to weaken and erode the alternative political means by which those who are victimized by destructive social and economic policies might express their frustration and their desperation in transformative rather than predatory ways. And, finally, the ways of market society also magnify the opportunities for white-collar crime and may simultaneously minimize the seriousness of the governmental response to it.

It is not, then, simply by increasing one or another specific social ill that market policies stimulate crime: it's when you put them together that the effects emerge in full force. But that is precisely what market society does. The growth of market society is a multifaceted process which is at its core destructive of the economic, social and cultural requisites of social peace and personal security.

## Key strategies

To me these developments point directly to some key strategies that ought to be essential parts of our approach to social crime prevention in the 1990s and in the next century. I will only point to three 'macro' and, briefly, three 'micro' strategies which I believe are especially critical in the face of these global transformations.

The three 'macro' policies are central because they directly attack the growing inequality in the emerging market society. There is much we can do by way of crime prevention without them but we will most certainly be swimming upstream.

First, and I believe central to much else, genuinely social crime prevention strategy requires a supportive labour market policy – what in Scandinavia is called an 'active' labour market policy which seeks to provide all citizens with both the competence and skills to participate in the necessary work of the larger society *and* concrete opportunities to put those skills to work. This necessarily involves a substantial role for the public sector – a deliberate and unapologetic use of public resources not merely to train the labour force for hoped-for jobs in the private sector, but also to create dignified public and non-profit jobs in areas of pressing social need.

One of the most wistfully myopic economic ideas of our time is the belief that an adequate supply of such good, stable jobs, of the kind that can provide a sense of membership in a productive community and the livelihood to support a family in dignity and security, will flow automatically from the normal operation of the private market if we just leave that market alone. Our American pundits, in particular, are much given to expressing confidence that the massive levels of unemployment and subemployment in the US, in the Third World and, increasingly, in some countries of Eastern Europe are simply 'transitional', and they will go away once the market has been left alone long enough to work its magic. The trouble is, of course, that we've already been waiting for generations for that transition to be over in Harlem and Appalachia and Detroit, not to mention San Paulo and San Juan.

Now don't get me wrong. The idea that the private market unaided will provide dignified and meaningful employment for all is a delightful and soothing idea. I too would like to believe it because it would make life, and social policy, a great deal easier. The hard reality is that the long-term tendency of the unaided market is to sharply divide societies into those who have and those who do not have access to stable and rewarding work. The lesson of both historical experience and careful research is abundantly clear. Those countries that have managed to maintain full and dignified human resources are those that have taken on a deliberate, active national commitment to full employment and comprehensive training, usually including the strategic use of public sector employment. The countries that have recently done the worst in this regard, including the US and the UK, have on the contrary worked to dismantle much of the public employment and training system they once had. That strategy flies in the face of everything we know about human resources and economic productivity: it is foolish, self-defeating, counterproductive, and expensive.

Exactly what such an active labour market policy should look like will vary in different countries. Some, of course, including Sweden and, in its' own way, Japan, have already committed themselves to remarkably effective full employment strategies. In the US, it translates into the crying need for a national commitment to publicly supported, community-oriented job creation, especially in the provision of those critical needs of the social and physical infrastructure that have been sorely neglected or systematically attacked for many years. With that kind of strategy we will kill several birds with one stone. We rebuild that eroded social and material infrastructure in health care, housing, community amenities and we also create an economic base that can serve as the catalyst for overall economic development in communities that the private market has essentially abandoned. And we also provide a whole spectrum of new and genuinely challenging opportunities for respected work and community contribution for young people now lured by the very genuine challenges of high-risk delinquency and the drug culture.

Secondly, a long-term approach to social crime prevention also requires a concerted, unapologetic strategy to reduce extremes of social and economic inequality by upgrading earnings and public benefits and services for low-

income people both in and out of the paid labour force. This is complementary to an active labour market policy and is precisely the opposite of
what many governments have lately been doing in the name of freeing the
'free market'.

I've suggested that one of the links between market society and crime lies
in the stripping away of public services and supports which is today routinely
justified in the name of a supposedly beneficial privatization of public
functions. But the long-term result, which we see increasingly in the US, is
that we are now perilously close to creating two distinct classes of citizenship.
On one side are those who by virtue of their connection with the stable part of
the labour force can afford what are increasingly private, and increasingly
expensive, fundamentals of social life, from health care to housing to education. Those essentials are today more often tied to high-wage employment
and are frequently part of the fruits of the 'semi-private welfare state' that has
grown up to serve the well-employed. But on the other side are those who are
condemned to scramble after the shrinking and increasingly inadequate
vestiges of public provision for these needs.

In place of that trend toward two classes of citizenship, we need to
counterpose what might be thought of as a post-industrial version of the 'basic
needs' strategy often advocated for developing countries. We need to insist
that it is society's *first* responsibility, not its last and most expendable, to
ensure equal access to those institutions which allow for competent, healthy
and respected citizenship: and that means an unshakeable national-level
commitment to public health care for all, quality public education and the
guarantee of dignified shelter as well as adequate and non-demeaning income
benefits for those out of the paid labour force. This, of course, requires the
existence of an active labour market policy, because without a productive and
an employed labour force you cannot support universally accessible, high-
quality public services or generous social benefits.

Meanwhile, for those in that paid labour force, we need likewise to reverse
the dramatic present trend toward earnings inequality, especially the growth
of what the Senate Budget Committee study in the US calls 'wage
impoverishment' at the lower end of the scale. This means a commitment to
steadily rising minimum wages. But beyond establishing a minimum floor
on earnings, we also need to move in the long run toward what the
Scandinavians call a 'solidaristic' wage policy, one that is explicitly aimed at
reducing earnings inequality throughout the workforce.

This strategy should explicitly include an effort to reduce the gaps in the
earnings of men and women. We have not yet talked much about gender
issues, but we should. The low earnings of women are deeply implicated in
crime in a variety of complex ways of which only the most obvious is the way
they encourage violence against women in the home. As long as women's
capacity for self-support is compromised by poor wages – and meagre benefits
– then they are especially vulnerable to being trapped in abusive and violent
relationships with men, as are their children. Increasing women's economic
independence would go a very long way toward reducing the massive tragedy
of family violence especially in countries like the US and many in the
developing world where violence against women and children is very high
and women's overall economic condition is very low. Not to mention the
benefits of making greater resources available for poor children, great
numbers of whom are growing up in families maintained by women.

Measures like these, designed to reduce inequality and promote competent citizenship, have been systematically attacked by conservative governments around the world on the grounds that they interfere with the market and thereby hinder economic efficiency. Yet nothing could be farther from reality. Again, the lessons of both research and experience are crystal clear. Healthy, well-educated, competent and self-confident citizens are what makes an economy work. The state of the United States economy, today, I'm afraid, is a tragic demonstration of what happens when that lesson is ignored.

Thirdly, we should work internationally toward an active, supportive child and family policy, one that firmly and unapologetically puts the needs of families and children for adequate furtherance, time and income above the private pursuit of material gain.

The two strategies I've already suggested – an active labour market policy and a concerted attack on the widening inequalities of wages and benefits – are in themselves two of the most important elements of that kind of supportive family policy.

But more is needed as well. In particular, we need strategies to reduce the sharp and in many countries growing conflicts between family and work. That means (1) freeing up time from work for parents to be with their children through generous family and parental leave policies and (2) putting in place a high-quality accessible child care system for working families.

In the US, both of these have been fought tooth and nail by the private business community. Here we are far behind some European countries like Sweden or France. In the US, our stunningly timid legislative effort to provide six weeks of unpaid parental leave at the birth of a child has been successfully resisted for years by the business community and its political allies. Once again, that resistance has been justified, fantastically, in the name of economic efficiency. But the reality is that our failure to develop policies to reduce the intolerable work-related stresses of families amounts to a massive, covert subsidy to private business in that it requires the rest of us to pay in the long run for the consequences of the resulting economic strains on families; consequences including child abuse, delinquency, mental illness and a mush-rooming expenditure for the remedial programmes to contain them.

The long-range vision behind all three proposals and others is to progressively replace what I've called 'market society' with what I'll call a 'sustaining' society.

That kind of vision calls for creative programmes on the 'micro' level as well, on the close-in level of working directly with individuals and families who've been made most vulnerable by the massive changes now reshaping our societies. For now, I'll only mention briefly three kinds of interventions that I think, on the evidence, must be among the most urgent in a truly effective strategy of social crime prevention: (a) comprehensive child and family support programmes; (b) a youth intervention strategy that focuses on the expansion of tangible opportunities; and (c) a 'user-friendly' approach to drug abuse prevention and treatment.

First, [we need] a comprehensive 'package' of child and family inter-ventions that emphasizes (1) the prevention of child abuse, (2) the provision of early childhood education and (3) of a wide range of supports for parents in coping with the real-world stresses in their communities. [. . .] Let me focus on child abuse and neglect prevention for a moment. In the US, and I think in many other countries as well, there's been a tendency for the people who deal with child abuse and neglect to be different from, and unconnected with, those who deal with crime policy. Child abuse thus becomes somebody else's problem, and it is not, at least where I come from, taken very seriously, certainly not as an integral part of a strategy of social crime prevention. But that's a mistake. Where serious violent crime is concerned, I'm increasingly convinced of the critical role of abusive, neglectful, harshly punitive childhood experiences. Our experience in the US does not suggest a simple programmatic response that can be replicated in cookie-cutter fashion, but it does point to successful programmes that show promise. One is hands-on work with high-risk parents from pre-natal period, following them up from birth with counselling on child-rearing methods, home visits, and help with day care, health care and transportation. Another is comprehensive family support programmes of a kind now springing up across the US, that offer high-risk families the tangible help they need to take better care of their children: better knowledge about child-rearing, support groups of other parents in similar conditions, and help in securing the necessities – health care for themselves and their children, housing, income support. These are best delivered in a comprehensive setting that is community-based and culturally sensitive.

Secondly, we need a comprehensive youth intervention strategy. Again, many of the disruptive changes now affecting societies across the world are having their most profound and alienating effect on young people. I'm convinced that the single most important part of a youth strategy is the active labour market policy I spoke of already, for without it we are frankly condemning vast numbers of young men and women around the world to a bleak and uncertain life on the periphery of purposive society. But we also need more specific interventions to work with the young at highest risk. But here, perhaps even more than in other areas of social policy, it is terribly important to separate wheat from chaff and there is a great deal of chaff in the world of youth policy, certainly in the US. There is some tendency to see any youth programme that isn't prison as a worthy endeavour and to tout programmes that are poorly evaluated and theoretically weak as saviours of inner-city youth or, at best, to over-promise on the capacity of very minor interventions to make a big difference in the lives of kids who face very real and profound deprivations.

I believe the accumulating evidence strongly suggests that the youth-oriented strategies that work best are those which actually provide changed lives, that offer new and expanded possibilities for young people where few existed before. I think that what our programme experience in the US shows most clearly is that if you simply try to offer social services of various kinds to youth without changing their probable futures, without genuinely altering their realistic trajectory in life, then you are probably not going to make much of a difference. You are not going to wean many kids away from drug and alcohol abuse, away from the distinct and very powerful appeal of some kinds of delinquency, away from the comradeship and satisfaction that they can find in gangs.

But much of our debate on youth policy, such as it is, in the US today is stuck on the level at best of what I'd call a 'service' strategy of the kind we have recurrently tried, without much success, at various periods since the nineteenth century. In turn, this strategy is typically based on what I've called a 'deficiency' model of delinquency. In a nutshell, the deficiency model assumes that the problem is some lack or deficit within the young person which needs fixing, or filling; we then design some service to patch it. But two years of intensive interviewing of delinquent kids has convinced me that for most American delinquents, extreme cases aside, far more critical than any such internal deficits is the rapidly shrinking opportunity for them to make legitimate use of the strengths and capacities they already have – a problem greatly exacerbated by the 'dumbing-down' of the economy I spoke of earlier. Quite simply, the kids often have far more skill than the increasingly constricted labour markets allow them to use in legitimate ways; delinquency allows them to *be* more than the straight world can.

To me, this suggests the usefulness of what I'd call an 'opportunity model' of intervention in place of the 'deficiency model' and that is supported by my reading of what works best in the youth programmes we've tried in the US – serious and intensive skills training programmes, such as the Job Corps, which actually provide usable formal skills; or the equally tangible opportunities by a programme like Eugene Lang's 'I Have a Dream', which guarantees college tuition for disadvantaged kids who stay in school. These have among the most consistently encouraging evaluations, and I think that's no accident.

Thirdly, similar considerations apply to a third area of priority, what I'd call 'user-friendly' drug and alcohol assistance. Today in the US, where of course the drug-crime problem is worst, the debate about drugs is now mainly between those who continue to push for more incarceration and harsher penalties for drug users and dealers, versus those who push for more conventional 'treatment'. But I don't think *either* path is the right one.

Like our approach to delinquency, our drug intervention strategies are often rooted in a model which is almost schizophrenically divorced from what the evidence tells us about the causes of the problem. In the US, the model typically underlying drug treatment efforts is some version of an individual medical or psychiatric model. Yet the accumulating research tells us over and over again that mass drug abuse of the kind that is now endemic in many American (and some British) communities is driven less by any identifiable pharmacological or psychological needs than by the systematic, long-term blockage of opportunities and the often overwhelmingly stressful and depriving conditions of life in communities suffering from multiple economic and social deprivation. This is a syndrome that is deepening with the advance of market society, here in Britain as in the US. [. . .]

We need to rethink treatment as well as expand it. Our current models of treatment tend to assume that addiction is a medical condition, rather like a broken leg or a kidney infection; it is not. People don't catch it and then want to come in and fix it. We're learning that addiction has less to do with the physical properties of the drugs themselves than with the barriers to alternative ways of achieving gratification, status, structure and esteem. The lesson too little heeded is that interventions should be tailored accordingly; they should be oriented more closely to the social context of addiction; should help abusers move away successfully from the drug cultures in which they're enmeshed; open realistic opportunities for stable employment, and offer help with starting and maintaining strong relationships and family ties which the research increasingly tells us is key to successfully moving away from drugs.

In turn, this means making drug programmes more 'user-friendly', in particular addressing the specific needs of groups who are now, at least in the US, largely left out or alienated by conventional treatment including teenagers, women and some minority groups. Much of our conventional treatment in the US is actually user-hostile to those critically important potential clients. It is shaped by what are essentially middle-class, male, adult and psychological models and assumptions, often relying on invasive group therapies based on a kind of 'encounter' model that appeals at best to a sliver of the drug-abusing population, which is why the great majority of that population is not in treatment. We especially need youth-supportive drug programmes that are capable of attracting the young rather than alienating them. Ideally, these ought to be part of a broader commitment to community-based, comprehensive adolescent health-care services that also engage problems of risk-taking behaviour, violence and sexually transmitted disease. Similarly, many treatment programmes for women will not even take pregnant women, much less address the crucial real-world issues many addicted women present; issues of child care, housing, poor employment and relationships with abusive men. These are just three specific directions but there are many more.

[. . .]

What all this means is that real social crime prevention, like the prevention of other social ills, is now more than ever dependent on our capacity to build more effective movements for social action and social change. These movements should challenge effectively those forces dimming the life chances of vast numbers of people in the developed and developing worlds. Building organisations should be committed to the long-range effort to replace a society based increasingly on the least inspiring of human values with one based on the principles of social solidarity and contributive justice.

[. . .]

# 32

# Abolitionism and crime control

## Willem De Haan

An abolitionist perspective on crime control might seem like a contradiction in terms not unlike a peace research approach to waging a war. Abolitionism is based on the moral conviction that social life should not and, in fact, cannot be regulated effectively by criminal law and that, therefore, the role of the criminal justice system should be drastically reduced while other ways of dealing with problematic situations, behaviours and events are being developed and put into practice. Abolitionists regard crime primarily as the result of the social order and are convinced that punishment is not the appropriate reaction. Instead a minimum of coercion and interference with the personal lives of those involved and a maximum amount of care and service for all members of society is advocated.

The term 'abolitionism' stands for a social movement, a theoretical perspective and a political strategy. As a social movement committed to the abolition of the prison or even the entire penal system, abolitionism originated in campaigns for prisoners' rights and penal reform. Subsequently, it developed into a critical theory and praxis concerning crime, punishment and penal reform. As a theoretical perspective, abolitionism takes on the two-fold task of providing a radical critique of the criminal justice system while showing that there are other, more rational ways of dealing with crime. As a political strategy, abolitionism is based on an analysis of penal reform and restricted to negative reforms, such as abolishing parts of the prison system, rather than providing concrete alternatives.

[. . .] [T]he abolitionist perspective will be discussed along the lines of this distinction. First, we will deal with abolitionism as a penal reform movement, then as a theoretical perspective on crime and punishment and, more specifically, the prison. Next, a conceptualization of the notions of crime and punishment will be offered in the form of the concept of redress. At the same time, strategies for penal reform will be examined. Finally, the implications of the abolitionist perspective for crime control will be discussed. In conclusion, it will be argued that what is needed is a wide variety of social responses rather than a uniform state reaction to the problem of crime. In policy terms it is claimed that social policy instead of crime policy is needed in dealing with the social problems and conflicts that are currently singled out as the problem of crime.

Abridged from 'Abolitionism and crime control: a contradiction in terms', in *The Politics of Crime Control* (eds K. Stenson and D. Cowell), pp. 203–17. (London: Sage, 1991.)

### Abolitionism as a social movement

Abolitionism emerged as an anti-prison movement when, at the end of the 1960s, a destructuring impulse took hold of thinking about the social control of deviance and crime among other areas (Cohen, 1985). In Western Europe, anti-prison groups aiming at prison abolition were founded in Sweden and Denmark (1967) Finland and Norway (1968), Great Britain (1970), France (1970), and the Netherlands (1971). Their main objective was to soften the suffering which society inflicts on its prisoners. This implied a change in general thinking concerning punishment, humanization of the various forms of imprisonment in the short run and, in the long run, the replacement of the prison system by more adequate and up-to-date measures of crime control.

It has been suggested that abolitionism typically emerged in small countries or countries with little crime and 'would never have been "invented" in a country like the United States of America with its enormous crime rate, violence, and criminal justice apparatus' (Scheerer, 1986: 18). However, in Canada and the United States family members of (ex-)convicts, church groups and individuals were also engaged in prisoners' support work and actively struggling for prison reform. More specifically, these prison abolitionists in the United States considered their struggle for abolition of prisons to be a historical mission, a continuation and fulfilment of the struggle against slavery waged by their forebears. Imprisonment is seen as a form of blasphemy, as morally objectionable and indefensible and, therefore, to be abolished (Morris, 1976: 11). To this aim, a long-term strategy in the form of a three-step 'attrition model' is proposed, consisting of a total freeze on the planning and building of prisons, excarceration of certain categories of lawbreakers by diverting them from the prison system and decarceration, or the release of as many inmates as possible.

Originating in prison reform movements in the 1960s and 1970s in both Western Europe and North America, abolitionism developed as a new paradigm in (critical) criminology and as an alternative approach to crime control. As academic involvement increased and abolitionism became a theoretical perspective, its focus widened from the prison system to the penal system, thereby engaging in critical analyses of penal discourse and, in particular, the concepts of crime and punishment, penal practices, and the penal or criminal justice system.

### Abolitionism as a theoretical perspective

As a theoretical perspective abolitionism has a negative and a positive side. Negatively, abolitionism is deeply rooted in a criticism of the criminal justice system and its 'prison solution' to the problem of crime. Positively, on the basis of this criticism an alternative approach to crime and punishment is offered both in theory and in practice. Thus, the abolitionist approach is essentially reflexive and (de)constructivist. We will first take a look at the negative side of abolitionism which will be followed by a brief exposé of its positive side.

From the abolitionist point of view, the criminal justice system's claim to protect people from being victimized by preventing and controlling crime, seems grossly exaggerated. Moreover, the notion of controlling crime by penal intervention is ethically problematic as people are used for the purpose of 'deterrence', by demonstrating power and domination. Punishment is seen as a self-reproducing form of violence. The penal practice of blaming people for their supposed intentions (for being bad and then punishing and degrading them accordingly) is dangerous because the social conditions for recidivism are thus reproduced. Morally degrading and segregating people is especially risky when the logic of exclusion is reinforced along the lines of differences in sex, race, class, culture or religion.

For the abolitionist, current crime policies are irrational in their assumptions that: crime is caused by individuals who for some reason go wrong; that crime is a problem for the state and its criminal justice system to control; and that criminal law and punishment or treatment of individual wrongdoers are appropriate means of crime control (Steinert, 1986). Crime control is based on the fallacy of taking *pars pro toto* or, as Wilkins (1984) has put it, crime control policy is typically made by reference to the dramatic incident, thereby assuming that all that is necessary is to get the micro-model right in order for the macro-model to follow without further ado. According to Wilkins, we must consider not only the specific criminal act but also the environment in which it is embedded. It could be added that the same argument holds for punishment and, more specifically, for imprisonment as an alleged solution to the problem of crime.

### Abolitionism about prison

For abolitionists, the United States is a prime example of a country suffering from the consequences of a punitive obsession. In the course of a 'get tough' policy of crime control, increasing numbers of people are being sent to prison for longer periods of time. As a result, the prison population in the United States has increased dramatically from roughly 350,000 in the 1970s to 850,000 at the end of the 1980s. Almost 80 per cent of the recent increase in prison admissions is accounted for by drugs offenders. By September 1988 about 44 per cent of all federal prisoners were incarcerated for drug law violations. According to the 1989 National Council of Crime and Delinquency Prison Population Forecast the impact of the 'war on drugs' will be yet another increase of the prison population 1989–1994 by over 68 per cent to a total of 1,133,000 prisoners among whom people of colour will remain strongly over-represented. With an incarceration rate of 440 prisoners per 100,000 population, the United States will more than consolidate its top rank position in the world. Even with its incarceration rate increasing from about 30 in 1980 to about 50 in the mid-1990s, the Netherlands will remain at the bottom end of the scale. At the same time, the crime problem in the Netherlands can hardly be considered worse than in the United States.

As in the United States, 'street crime' is also considered a major social problem in the Netherlands. In fact, the first International Crime Survey (van Dijk et al., 1990) showed that overall victimization rates 1983–1988 in the United States and the Netherlands were higher than in any other country in the survey. However, there were considerable differences both in the seriousness of the crime problem and the effectiveness of its control. Whereas overall victimization rates in the Netherlands and the United States were similarly high, in the Dutch case this was strongly influenced by the extraordinarily high prevalence of bicycle theft, whereas victimization rates for homicide, robbery and (sexual) assault were particularly high in the United States.

If anything, this proves that the relationship between crime and crime control by imprisonment is much more complex than proponents of the prison solution seem to assume. In terms of protection the 'get tough' approach to crime control has little to offer, and the 'war on drugs' can never be won but has serious repercussions.

Taken together, the prison system is counter-productive, difficult to control, and itself a major social problem. Therefore, abolitionists have given up entirely on the idea that the criminal justice system has anything to offer in terms of protection. They are also pessimistic about the criminal law's potential for conflict resolution. It is felt that the present penal system is making things worse, not better.

In the course of the 'war against drugs' which is currently being waged in the United States and many other countries around the world, the use of ethically problematic techniques for apprehending suspects is being condoned if not required. As a result various forms of organizational complicity undermine the already waning legitimacy of the criminal justice system even further. According to Roshier (1989), the 'war against drugs' must be seen as a forced attempt to reach efficiency in the field of law enforcement or, at least, the appearance of it by using purely technical or even military means of surveillance and policing. It is the criminal justice system that defines, selects, documents and disposes of crime. As a result, legal definitions of suspicion, criminal offence etc., are being stretched. Thus, the criminal justice system itself increasingly specifies both the nature of the crime problem and what is to be done about it (Roshier, 1989: 128).

Thus, the criminal justice system is part of the crime problem rather than its solution. Not only does it fail to work in terms of its own stated goals and not only are the negative consequences of the infliction of suffering by the state threatening to get out of hand but, more importantly, it is based on a fundamentally flawed way of understanding. Therefore, there is no point in trying to make the criminal justice system more effective or more just. The abolitionist critique of the criminal justice system and its approach to crime control may be summarized by saying that if this is the solution, what is the problem? Or, put differently, crime as a social problem and object of social analysis needs to be rethought.

## Abolitionism about 'crime'

The current approach to crime control, the definition of crime and the justification of punishment is 'systemic', that is, based on an instrumentalist point of view and confined within the limits of the criminal justice system. From an abolitionist point of view, these issues require a fundamental reconceptualization in a broader social context. This is where the alternative, positive side of abolitionism starts from. Abolitionists argue that there is no such thing as 'crime'. In fact, 'the very form of criminal law, with its conception of "crime" (not just the contents of what is at a given time and place defined into that category, but the category itself) and the ideas on what is to be done about it, are historical "inventions"' (Steinert, 1986: 26). 'Crime' is a social construction, to be analysed as a myth of everyday life (Hess, 1986).

As a myth, crime serves to maintain political power relations and lends legitimacy to the expansion of the crime control apparatus and the intensification of surveillance and control. It justifies inequality and relative deprivation. Public attention is distracted from more serious problems and injustices. Thus, the bigger the social problems are, the greater the need for the crime myth (Hess, 1986: 24–5).

However, not only should the concept of crime be discarded (Hulsman, 1986), but we need to get rid of the theories of crime as well. As Quensel (1987) has pointed out, theories about 'crime' acquire their plausibility largely by virtue of their building on and, at the same time, reinforcing an already-present 'deep structure'. One element of this 'deep structure' is the notion that 'crime' is inherently dangerous and wicked; another is that crime control is a 'value-inspired' call for action against that evil (p. 129).

Abolitionists argue that the crucial problem is not explaining but rather understanding crime as a social event. Thus, what we need is not a better theory of crime, but a more powerful critique of crime. This is not to deny that there are all sorts of unfortunate events, more or less serious troubles or conflicts which can result in suffering, harm, or damage to a greater or lesser degree. These troubles are to be taken seriously, of course, but not as 'crimes' and, in any case, they should not be dealt with by means of criminal law. When we fully appreciate the complexity of a 'crime' as a socially constructed phenomenon any simplified reaction to crime in the form of punishment becomes problematic.

Spector (1981) has argued that when a person offends, disturbs, or injures other people, various forms of social disapproval exist to remedy the situation. The matter may be treated as a disease, a sin, or, indeed, as a crime. However, other responses are also feasible, like considering the case as a private conflict between the offender and the victim or defining the situation in an administrative way and responding, for example by denial of a licence, permit, benefit or compensation. Our images, language, categories, knowledge, beliefs and fears of troublemakers are subject to constant changes. Nevertheless, crime continues to occupy a central place in our thinking about troublesome people (1981: 154). Spector suggests that, perhaps, 'we pay too much attention to crime because the disciplines that study trouble and disapprove – sociology and criminology – were born precisely in the era when crime was at its zenith' (Quensel, 1987; Spector, 1981).

The concept of 'crime' figures prominently in common sense and has definite effects on it. By focusing public attention on a definite class of events, these 'crimes' can then be almost automatically seen as meriting punitive control. 'Punishment' is thereby regarded as the obvious and proper reaction to 'crime'.

## Abolitionism about punishment

Abolitionists do not share the current belief in the criminal law's capacity for crime control. They radically deny the utility of punishment and claim that there can be no valid justification for it, particularly since other options are available for law enforcement. They discard criminal justice as an absurd idea. It is ridiculous to claim that one pain can or, indeed, ought to be compensated by another state-inflicted one. According to them, the 'prison solution' affects the moral quality of life in society at large. Therefore, the criminal justice perspective needs to be replaced by an orientation towards all avoidance of harm and pain (Steinert, 1986: 25). Christie (1982), particularly, has attacked the traditional justifications for punishment. He criticizes deterrence theory for its sloppy definitions of concepts, its immunity to challenge, and for the fact that it gives the routine process of punishment a false legitimacy in an epoch where the infliction of pain might otherwise have appeared problematic. The neo-classicism of the justice model is also criticized: punishment is justified and objectified, the criminal is blamed, the victim is ignored, a broad conception of justice is lacking, and a 'hidden message' is transmitted which denies legitimacy to a whole series of alternatives which should, in fact, be taken into consideration. However, Christie not only criticizes the 'supposed justifications' for punishment, but also claims a decidedly moral position with regard to punishment, which is the intentional infliction of pain which he calls 'moral rigorism'. He deliberately co-opts the terms 'moralism' and 'rigorism' associated primarily with protagonists of 'law and order' and more severe penal sanctions. His 'rigorist' position, however, is that there is no reason to believe that the recent level of pain infliction is the right or natural one and that there is no other defensible position than to strive for a reduction of man-inflicted pain on earth. Since punishment is defined as pain, limiting pain means an automatic reduction of punishment.

More recently, Christie and Mathiesen have both suggested that the expansion of the prison system involves general ethical and political questions such as what could be the effects of all the punishments taken together? What would constitute an acceptable level of punishment in society? What would be the right prison population within a country? How should we treat fellow human beings? And, last but not least, how do we want to meet the crime problem (Christie, 1986; Mathiesen, 1986)?

However, in common-sense and legal discourse alike, 'crime' and 'punishment' continue to be seen 'as independent species – without reference to their sameness or how continuity of both depends on the character of dominating institutions' (Kennedy, 1974: 107). It should be kept in mind, however, that crime comprises but one of several kinds of all norm violations, that punishment is but one of many kinds of reprisals against such violations, that criteria for separating them refer to phenomena external to actual behaviours classed by legal procedure as crime versus punishment, and that even within the criminal law itself, the criteria by which crime is identified procedurally apply with equal validity to punishment (Kennedy, 1974: 108).

Criminology needs to rid itself of those theories of punishment which assume there are universal qualities in forms of punishment or assume a straightforward connection between crime and punishment. Given the perseverance of this conventional notion of 'punishment' as essentially a 'good' against an 'evil', any effort at changing common-sense notions of 'crime' and 'crime control' requires a reconceptualization of both concepts: 'crime' and 'punishment'.

**Redress**

We need to concern ourselves with the interrelationship and combined effects of crime and punishment. Crime and punishment are closely related with 'social negativity' (Baratta, 1986), destructive developments within contemporary society, in particular, as they affect its already most vulnerable members. In order to formulate a convincing politics of penal reform, crime and punishment should not be seen as action and reaction, but as spiralling cycles of harm (Pepinsky, 1986).

Elsewhere, I have introduced the concept of 'redress' as an alternative to both the concepts of 'punishment' and 'crime' (de Haan, 1990). This seemingly 'obsolete' concept carries an elaborate set of different meanings. The *Concise Oxford Dictionary* offers a wide variety of meanings for 'redress': for instance, to put right or in good order again, to remedy or remove trouble of any kind, to set right, repair, rectify something suffered or complained of like a wrong, to correct, amend, reform or do away with a bad or faulty state of things, to repair an action, to atone a misdeed or offence, to save, deliver from misery, to restore or bring back a person to a proper state, to happiness or prosperity, to the right course, to set a person right by obtaining or (more rarely) giving satisfaction or compensation for the wrong or loss sustained, teaching, instructing and redressing the erroneous by reason (Sixth Edition, 1976: 937).

To claim redress is merely to assert that an undesirable event has taken place and that something needs to be done about it. It carries no implications concerning what sort of reaction would be appropriate; nor does it define reflexively the nature of the initial event. Since claiming redress invites an open discussion about how an unfortunate event should be viewed and what the appropriate response ought to be, it can be viewed as a rational response par excellence. It puts forth the claim for a procedure rather than for a specific result. Punitive claims already implied in defining an event as a 'crime' are opened up to rational debate. Thus, to advocate 'redress' is to call for 'real dialogue' (Christie, 1982). Christie has suggested that social systems be constructed in ways that 'crimes' are more easily seen as expressions of conflicting interests, thereby becoming a starting-point for a 'real dialogue' (1982: 11).

The conceptual innovation suggested here offers a perspective for a politics of redress, aimed at the construction and implementation of procedures along the lines of an ethic of practical discourse. As we have seen, the handling of normative conflicts by rational discourse presupposes other procedures than the present criminal ones. In order to increase chances for participation for those involved, procedures based on the rules and preconditions of rational discourse would, therefore, need to be established outside the realm of criminal law; that is in civil law or even in the life world itself. Instead of the panacea which the criminal justice system pretends to provide for problems of crime control, abolitionism seeks to remedy social problems, conflicts, or troubles within the context of the real world, taking seriously the experiences of those directly involved and taking into account too the diversity which is inherent [in] the social world. The aim of a politics of redress would be to 'arrange it so that the conflict settling mechanisms themselves, through their organization reflect the type of society we should like to see reflected and help this type of society come into being' (Christie, 1982: 113). Social problems or conflicts might be absorbed in order to use them as valuable aids to the social integration of real life and the prevention of social harm.

Abolitionism assumes that social problems or conflicts are unavoidable as they are inherent to social life as such. Therefore, they will have to be dealt with in one way or another. Rather than delegating them to professional specialists, however, they should be dealt with under conditions of mutuality and solidarity. These very conditions will have to be created by social and political action.

The urgent question that remains, of course, is how this might be done. To begin with, no single solution to the problem should be expected. Taking into account the diversity of relevant social phenomena requires the development of a wide variety of forms of social regulation which are not located in or defined by the state but operate (semi-)autonomously as alternative, progressive and emancipatory forms of dispute settlement and conflict resolution.

In reaction to the deeply felt dissatisfaction with the present penal system and, more generally, with the legal system, we see an increasing interest in 'autonomous' forms of conflict resolution and dispute settlement. Other 'styles of social control' (Black, 1976: 4–5) are seen as attractive, promising to provide the parties involved with more chances for participation in settling a dispute or problem. The aim is compensation rather than retaliation; reconciliation rather than blame allocation. To this end, the criminal justice system needs to be decentralized and neighbourhood courts established as a complement or substitute.

The development of alternative procedures for conflict resolution and dispute settlement faces some rather ticklish questions which have proved intractable in current debates, questions concerning voluntarism versus determinism, 'accountability', 'responsibility' and 'guilt', that is, the moral evaluation of behaviour, the fair allocation of blame and the proper dissemination of consequences. Emphasis on participatory processes of definition or the contextuality of conflicts may be welcome, but it can also lead to problematic outcomes. Among the wide variety of reactions the notion of redress entails there might be sanctions which need to be subjected to legal principles and restraints. For these reasons, legal form is still required to ensure fairness. Just as we need sociological imagination to ensure an open discussion, we need legal imagination to be able to put an end to potentially endless debates as well as allow for the possibility of appeal.

However, by allowing for more complexity in the interpretation of social behaviour, social situations and events, the simplistic image of human beings and their activities currently employed in criminal law and reproduced in criminal justice could be avoided. Through contextualization, the dichotomized character of criminal justice (Christie, 1986: 96) could be replaced with a continuum. Participants would be urged to confront and grapple with complexities around notions of human 'agency', 'intentionality', 'responsibility' and 'guilt' rather than reducing them to manageable proportions by applying the binary logic of criminal law. By dropping the simplistic dichotomies of the criminal law and allowing for differential meanings, justice might finally be done to the complexity of human actions and social events. Such a discourse would feature a concept of 'social responsibility' allowing for interpretations which primarily blame social systems rather than individuals (Christie, 1986: 97).

## Abolitionism as a political strategy

Initially, a political strategy had been developed on the bases of the experiences of prison reform groups in their political struggle for penal and social reform. This 'politics of abolition' (Mathiesen, 1974, 1986) consistently refuses to offer 'positive' alternatives or solutions. It restricts itself to advancing open-ended, 'unfinished', 'negative' reforms, such as abolishing parts of the prison system. This requires that they be conceptualized in terms alien to current criminal justice discourse.

More recently, positive alternatives to punishment are also being considered. Various proposals have been made by abolitionists and others to decentralize or even completely dismantle the present penal system in order to create forms of 'informal justice' as an addition to or replacement of the present criminal justice system.

Their implementation also raises many questions, however, concerning allegations about widening the net of social control and, at the same time, thinning the mesh, extending and blurring the boundaries between formal penal intervention and other, informal forms of social control, thereby masking the coercive character of alternative interventions (Abel, 1982: Cohen, 1985).

Fundamental reform of the penal system requires not only imaginative alternatives but, at the same time, a radical change in the power structure. Thus a 'politics of abolition' aims at a negative strategy for changing the politics of punishment by abolishing not only the criminal justice system but also the repressive capitalist system part by part or step by step (Mathiesen, 1986).

A fundamental reform of the penal system presupposes not only a radical change of the existing power structure but also of the dominant culture. However, currently there is no appropriate social agency for any radical reform of the politics of punishment. There seems no immediate social basis upon which a progressive, let alone an abolitionist, strategy of crime control might be spontaneously constructed (Matthews, 1987: 389). Abolitionists tend to refer to the re-emergence of the subcultures of the new social movements with their own infrastructure of interaction and communication and their new ethics of solidarity, social responsibility, and care (Steinert, 1986: 28–9; see also Christie, 1982: 75–80). As Harris argues, the inadequacy of virtually all existing reform proposals lies in the failure to step outside the traditional and dominant ways of framing the issues. To explore alternative visions of justice we need to consider 'philosophies, paradigms, or models that transcend not only conventional criminological and political lines, but also natural and cultural boundaries and other limiting habits of the mind' (Harris, 1987: 11). According to Harris a wide range of visions of a better world and a better future offer a rich resource for a fundamental rethinking of our approach to crime and justice. The new social movements, in particular the women's movement, have pointed out fundamental weaknesses or biases in criminology's background assumptions, conceptual frameworks, methodology and tacit morality (Gelsthorpe and Morris, 1990). However, the relationship between abolitionism and, for example, feminism is not without stress (van Swaaningen, 1989).

## Abolitionism on crime control

Abolitionism argues for a structural approach to the prevention of 'social negativity', or redressing problematic situations by taking social problems, conflicts and troubles seriously but not as 'crime'. Therefore, abolitionism argues for social policy rather than crime control policy. Examples of this structural approach would be dealing with drug problems in terms of mental health, with violence in terms of social pathology, and with property crime in terms of economy.

Abolitionism calls for decriminalization, depenalization, destigmatization, decentralization and deprofessionalization, as well as the establishment of other, informal, participatory, (semi-)autonomous ways of dealing with social problems. Problematic events may just as well be defined as social troubles, problems or conflicts due to negligence or caused by 'accident' rather than by purpose or criminal intent. What is needed is a wide variety of possible responses without a priori assuming criminal intent and responsibility.

As we have seen, prison abolition, let alone penal abolition, requires an imaginative rethinking of possible ways of handling problematic situations as social problems, conflicts, troubles, accidents etc., as well as reconceptualizing punishment and developing new ways of managing 'deviance' on the basis of, at least partial, suspension of the logic of guilt and punishment. Without fixation on individual guilt, responsibility and punishment, 'crimes' would appear as 'conflicts', 'accidents' or 'problematic events' to be dealt with in a more reasonable and caring way by using forms of conflict management which are not exclusively geared towards individuals and confined to the limitations of criminal law in the books as well as in action (Steinert, 1986: 30). Therefore, abolitionists focus instead on extra-legal, autonomous ways for dealing with social problems and conflicts involving offences. The abolitionist challenge to abolish the present prison system now is to construct more participatory, popular or socialist forms of penality (Garland and Young, 1983).

This way of looking at crime and crime control is, of course, controversial. The abolitionist perspective is sometimes criticized for being naive and idealistic. In practice, however, the abolitionist approach turns out to be realistic in that social problems and conflicts are seen as inherent to social life. Since it is illusory that the criminal justice system can protect us effectively against such unfortunate events, it seems more reasonable to deal with troubles pragmatically rather than by approaching them in terms of guilt and punishment. Effectively to prevent and control unacceptable situations and behaviours requires a variety of social responses, one and only one of which is the criminal justice system. Its interventions are more of symbolic importance than of practical value. With some social, technical and organizational imagination 'crime' could be coped with in ways much more caring for those immediately involved. A variety of procedures could be established and institutionalized where social problems or conflicts, problematic events or behaviours could be dealt with through negotiation, mediation, arbitration, at intermediate levels. For dealing with the most common or garden varieties of crime, which is in any case the vast bulk of all recorded criminality, criminal prosecutions are simply redundant.

Certainly for those who are most directly concerned there is little or no benefit. Also in such cases as state or corporate crime where a full abolitionist agenda of dispute settlement – like the criminal justice approach – has profound limitations, it does make sense to look for more workable alternatives to the criminal justice system's mechanisms of apprehension, judgment and punishment. Most of these problems could be dealt with by means of economic, administrative, environmental, health or labour law, rather than by criminal law. Even in cases where a person has become an unacceptable burden to his or her relatives or community, imprisonment could be avoided.

Agreements might be reached or orders might be given about temporary or permanent limitations in access to certain people, places or situations. The problems of the really bad and the really mad remain. In these relatively few cases and by way of last resort it might be unavoidable to deprive someone of their liberty, at least for the time being. This exceptional decision should be simply in order to incapacitate and be carried out in a humane way, that is as a morally problematic decision in a dilemma. However, even in these cases it would make sense to look for more just and humane alternatives based on mutual aid, good neighbourliness and real community rather than continue to rely on the solutions of bureaucracies, professionals and the centralized state. Criticism of the inhumanity and irrationality of the prison solution is as valid today as it was twenty or seventy years ago. Therefore, Cohen suggests that three interrelated strategies be followed: first, cultivating an experimental and inductive attitude to the actual historical record of alternatives, innovations and experiments; secondly, being sensitive, not just to failures, co-options and con-tricks, but to success stories – the criterion for success should be, and can be nothing other than, an approximation to preferred values; and thirdly, escaping the clutches of criminology (radical or realistic) by expanding the subject of social control way beyond the scope of the criminal justice system (for example, to systems of informal justice, utopian communes and experiments in self-help) (Cohen, 1988: 131).

In countries with an elaborate welfare system like the Scandinavian countries or the Netherlands, these strategies may seem more reasonable given that their crime problem is less dramatic and, traditionally, their crime control policy is already more cautious. In the context of a relatively mild penal climate with a pragmatic and reductionist penal policy already being implemented, even penal abolition may seem realistic as a long-term goal. However, in those countries where prison populations are enormous and penal institutions are simply 'warehousing' people in order to incapacitate them from reoffending, prison abolition is more acute. When in the early 1970s several commissions and task forces concluded that the American prison system is beyond reform and, therefore, other ways of dealing with criminal offenders need to be developed, the prison population was about one-third of the current one. These criticisms hold true even more under the present conditions of overcrowding in the prisons. Prisons are places where a lot more harm is done than is necessary or legitimate. Moreover, these institutions contribute to a further brutalization of social conditions. Even in the United States where average prison sentences are much longer than for example in the Netherlands, 99 per cent of the prison population will sooner or later hit the streets again. Therefore, there is a definite need not only for prison reform but also for penal reform. Current crime control policy boils down to doing more of the same. In the long run, however, the resulting spiral of harm needs to be reversed in a downward direction. This can only be achieved by doing more rather than less, albeit not more of the same but more of what generally might be called care.

## References

Abel, R. (ed.) (1982) *The Politics of Informal Justice*, vols 1 and 2. New York: Academic Press.
Baratta, A. (1986) 'Soziale Probleme und Konstruktion der Kriminalität', *Kriminologisches Journal*, 1: 200–18.

Black, D. (1976) *The Behavior of Law*. New York: Academic Press.

Christie, N. (1982) *Limits to Pain*. Oxford: Martin Robertson.

Christie, N. (1986) 'Images of man in modern penal law', *Contemporary Crises*, 10: 95–106.

Cohen, S. (1985) *Visions of Social Control. Crime, Punishment and Classification*. Cambridge: Polity Press.

Cohen, S. (1988) *Against Criminology*. New York: Transaction Books.

Dijk, J. van, Mayhew, P. and Killias, M. (1990) *Experiences of Crime across the World. Key Findings from the 1989 International Crime Survey*. Boston: Kluwer.

Garland, D. and Young, P. (1983) 'Towards a social analysis of penality', in D. Garland and P. Young (eds), *The Power to Punish. Contemporary Penality and Social Analysis*. London: Heinemann, pp. 1–36.

Gelsthorpe, L. and Morris, A. (eds) (1990) *Feminist Perspectives in Criminology*. Milton Keynes: Open University Press.

Haan, W. de (1990) *The Politics of Redress. Crime, Punishment and Penal Abolition*. London: Unwin Hyman.

Harris, K. (1987) 'Moving into the new millennium: toward a feminist vision of justice', *The Prison Journal*, 67: 27–38.

Hess, H. (1986) 'Kriminalität als Alltagsmythos. Ein Plädoyer dafür, Kriminologie als Ideologiekritik zu betreiben', *Kriminologisches Journal*, 18(1): 22–44.

Hulsman, L. (1986) 'Critical criminology and the concept of crime', *Contemporary Crises*, 10: 63–80.

Kennedy, M. (1974) 'Beyond incrimination', in C. Reasons (ed.), *The Criminologist and the Criminal*. Pacific Palisades: Goodyear. pp. 106–35.

Mathiesen, T. (1974) 'The politics of abolition. Essays', in *Political Action Theory*. London: Martin Robertson.

Mathiesen, T. (1986) 'The politics of abolition', *Contemporary Crises*, 10: 81–94.

Matthews, R. (1987) 'Taking realist criminology seriously', *Contemporary Crises*, 11: 371–401.

Morris, M. (ed.) (1976) *Instead of Prisons: a Handbook for Abolitionists*. Syracuse, NY: Prison Research Action Project.

Pepinsky, H. (1986) 'A sociology of justice', *Annual Review for Sociology*, 12: 93–108.

Quensel, S. (1987) 'Let's abolish theories of crime', in J. Blad, H. van Mastrigt and N. Uitdriks (eds), *The Criminal Justice System as a Social Problem: an Abolitionist Perspective*. Rotterdam: Mededelingen can het Juridisch Instituut van de Erasmus Universiteit. pp. 123–32.

Roshier, B. (1989) *Controlling Crime. The Classical Perspective in Criminology*. Milton Keynes: Open University Press.

Scheerer, S. (1986) 'Towards abolitionism', *Contemporary Crises*, 10: 5–20.

Spector, M. (1981) 'Beyond crime: seven methods to control troublesome rascals', in H. Ross (ed.), *Law and Deviance*. Beverly Hills, CA: Sage, pp. 127–57.

Steinert, H. (1986) 'Beyond crime and punishment', *Contemporary Crises*, 10: 21–39.

Swaaningen, R. van (1989) 'Feminism and abolitionism as critiques of criminology', *International Journal of the Sociology of Law*, 17: 287–306.

Wilkins, L. (1984) *Consumerist Criminology*. London: Heinemann.

# 33

# The new penology

## Malcolm M. Feeley and Jonathan Simon

### Distinguishing features of the new penology

What we call the new penology is not a theory of crime or criminology. Its uniqueness lies less in conceptual integration than in a common focus on certain problems and a shared way of framing issues. This strategic formation of knowledge and power offers managers of the system a more or less coherent picture of the challenges they face and the kinds of solutions that are most likely to work. While we cannot reduce it to a set of principles, we can point to some of its most salient features.

### The new discourse

A central feature of the new discourse is the replacement of a moral or clinical description of the individual with an actuarial language of probabilistic calculations and statistical distributions applied to populations. Although social utility analysis or actuarial thinking is commonplace enough in modern life – it frames policy considerations of all sorts – in recent years this mode of thinking has gained ascendancy in legal discourse, a system of reasoning that traditionally has employed the language of morality and been focused on individuals (Simon, 1988). For instance, this new mode of reasoning is found increasingly in tort law, where traditional fault and negligence standards – which require a focus on the individual and are based upon notions of individual responsibility – have given way to strict liability and no-fault. These new doctrines rest upon actuarial ways of thinking about how to 'manage' accidents and public safety. They employ the language of social utility and management, not individual responsibility (Simon, 1987; Steiner, 1987). [. . .]

Although crime policy, criminal procedure and criminal sanctioning have been influenced by such social utility analysis, there is no body of commentary on the criminal law that is equivalent to the body of social utility analysis for tort law doctrine. Nor has strict liability in the criminal law achieved anything like the acceptance of related no-fault principles in tort law. Perhaps because the criminal law is so firmly rooted in a focus on the individual, these developments have come late to criminal law and penology.

Scholars of both European and North American penal strategies have noted the recent and rising trend of the penal system to target categories and subpopulations rather than individuals (Bottoms, 1983; Cohen, 1985;

Abridged from 'The new penology: notes on the emerging strategy of corrections and its implications', *Criminology*, 1992, 30(4): 452–74.

Mathiesen, 1983; Reichman, 1986). This reflects, at least in part, the fact that actuarial forms of representation promote quantification as a way of visualizing populations.

Crime statistics have been a part of the discourse of the state for over 200 years, but the advance of statistical methods permits the formation of concepts and strategies that allow direct relations between penal strategy and the population. Earlier generations used statistics to map the responses of normatively defined groups to punishment; today one talks of 'high-rate offenders', 'career criminals', and other categories defined by the distribution itself. Rather than simply extending the capacity of the system to rehabilitate or control crime, actuarial classification has come increasingly to define the correctional enterprise itself.

The importance of actuarial language in the system will come as no surprise to anyone who has spent time observing it. Its significance, however, is often lost in the more spectacular shift in emphasis from rehabilitation to crime control. No doubt, a new and more punitive attitude toward the proper role of punishment has emerged in recent years, and it is manifest in a shift in the language of statutes, internal procedures and academic scholarship. Yet looking across the past several decades, it appears that the pendulum-like swings of penal attitude moved independently of the actuarial language that has steadily crept into the discourse.

The discourse of the new penology is not simply one of greater quantification; it is also characterized by an emphasis on the systemic and on formal rationality. While the history of systems theory and operations research has yet to be written, their progression from business administration to the military and, in the 1960s, to domestic public policy must be counted as among the most significant of current intellectual trends. [. . .]

Some of the most astute observers identified this change near the outset and understood that it was distinct from the concurrent rightward shift in penal thinking. Jacobs (1977) noted the rise at Stateville Penitentiary of what he called a 'managerial' perspective during the mid-1970s. The regime of Warden Brierton was characterized, according to Jacobs, by a focus on tighter administrative control through the gathering and distribution of statistical information about the functioning of the prison. Throughout the 1980s this perspective grew considerably within the correctional system. Jacobs presciently noted that the managerial perspective might succeed where traditional and reform administrations had failed because it was capable of handling the greatly increased demands for rationality and accountability coming from the courts and the political system.

### The new objectives

The new penology is neither about punishing nor about rehabilitating individuals. It is about identifying and managing unruly groups. It is concerned with the rationality not of individual behavior or even community organization, but of managerial processes. Its goal is not to eliminate crime but to make it tolerable through systemic coordination.

One measure of the shift away from trying to normalize offenders and toward trying to manage them is seen in the declining significance of recidivism. Under the old penology, recidivism was a nearly universal criterion for assessing success or failure of penal programs. Under the new penology, recidivism rates continue to be important, but their significance has changed. The word itself seems to be used less often precisely because it carries a normative connotation that reintegrating offenders into the community is the major objective. High rates of parolees being returned to prison once indicated program failure; now they are offered as evidence of efficiency and effectiveness of parole as a control apparatus.

It is possible that recidivism is dropping out of the vocabulary as an adjustment to harsh realities and is a way of avoiding charges of institutional failure. [. . .] However, in shifting to emphasize the virtues of return as an indication of *effective* control, the new penology reshapes one's understanding of the functions of the penal sanction. By emphasizing correctional programs in terms of aggregate control and system management rather than individual success and failure, the new penology lowers one's expectations about the criminal sanction. These redefined objectives are reinforced by the new discourses discussed above which take deviance as a given, mute aspirations for individual reformation, and seek to classify, sort and manage dangerous groups efficiently.

The waning of concern over recidivism reveals fundamental changes in the very penal processes that recidivism once was used to evaluate. For example, although parole and probation have long been justified as means of reintegrating offenders into the community [. . .] increasingly they are being perceived as cost-effective ways of imposing long-term management on the dangerous. Instead of treating revocation of parole and probation as a mechanism to short-circuit the supervision process when the risks to public safety become unacceptable, the system now treats revocation as a cost-effective way to police and sanction a chronically troublesome population. In such an operation, recidivism is either irrelevant or, as suggested above, is stood on its head and transformed into an indicator of success in a new form of law enforcement.

The importance that recidivism once had in evaluating the performance of corrections is now being taken up by measures of system functioning. Heydebrand and Seron (1990) have noted a tendency in courts and other social agencies toward decoupling performance evaluation from external social objectives. Instead of social norms like the elimination of crime, reintegration into the community, or public safety, institutions begin to measure their own outputs as indicators of performance. Thus, courts may look at docket flow. Similarly, parole agencies may shift evaluations of performance to, say the time elapsed between arrests and due process hearings. In much the same way, many schools have come to focus on standardized test performance rather than on reading or mathematics, and some have begun to see teaching itself as the process of teaching students how to take such tests (Heydebrand and Seron, 1990: 190–4; Lipsky, 1980: 4–53).

Such technocratic rationalization tends to insulate institutions from the messy, hard-to-control demands of the social world. By limiting their exposure to indicators that they can control, managers ensure that their problems will have solutions. No doubt this tendency in the new penology is, in part, a response to the acceleration of demands for rationality and accountability in punishment coming from the courts and legislatures during the 1970s (Jacobs, 1977). It also reflects the lowered expectations for the penal system that result from failures to accomplish more ambitious promises of the past. Yet in the end, the inclination of the system to measure its success against its own production processes helps lock the system into a mode of operation that has only an attenuated connection with the *social* purposes of punishment. In the long term it becomes more difficult to evaluate an institution critically if there are no references to substantive social ends.

The new objectives also inevitably permeate through the courts into thinking about rights. The new penology replaces consideration of fault with predictions of dangerousness and safety management and, in so doing, modifies traditional individual-oriented doctrines of criminal procedure. [. . .]

### New techniques

These altered, lowered expectations manifest themselves in the development of more cost-effective forms of custody and control and in new technologies to identify and classify risk. Among them are low frills, no-service custodial centers; various forms of electronic monitoring systems that impose a form of custody without walls; and new statistical techniques for assessing risk and predicting dangerousness. These new forms of control are not anchored in aspirations to rehabilitate, reintegrate, retrain, provide employment, or the like. They are justified in more blunt terms: variable detention depending upon risk assessment.

Perhaps the clearest example of the new penology's method is the theory of incapacitation, which has become the predominant utilitarian model of punishment (Greenwood, 1982; Moore et al., 1984). Incapacitation promises to reduce the effects of crime in society not by altering either offender or social context, but by rearranging the distribution of offenders in society. If the prison can do nothing else, incapacitation theory holds, it can detain offenders for a time and thus delay their resumption of criminal activity. According to the theory, if such delays are sustained for enough time and for enough offenders, significant aggregate effects in crime can take place although individual destinies are only marginally altered.

These aggregate effects can be further intensified, in some accounts, by a strategy of selective incapacitation. This approach proposes a sentencing scheme in which lengths of sentence depend not upon the nature of the criminal offense or upon an assessment of the character of the offender, but upon risk profiles. Its objectives are to identify high-risk offenders and to maintain long-term control over them while investing in shorter terms and less intrusive control over lower risk offenders.

[. . .]

### The new penology in perspective

The correctional practices emerging from the shifts we identified above present a kind of 'custodial continuum'. But unlike the 'correctional con-tinuum' discussed in the 1960s, this new custodial continuum does not design penal measures for the particular needs of the individual or the community. Rather, it sorts individuals into groups according to the degree of control warranted by their risk profiles.

At one extreme the prison provides maximum security at a high cost for those who pose the greatest risks, and at the other probation provides low-cost surveillance for low-risk offenders. In between stretches a growing range of intermediate supervisory and surveillance techniques. The management concerns of the new penology – in contrast to the transformative concerns of the old – are displayed especially clearly in justifications for various new intermediate sanctions.

What we call the new penology is only beginning to take coherent shape. Although most of what we have stressed as its central elements – statistical prediction, concern with groups, strategies of management – have a long history in penology, in recent years they have come to the fore, and their functions have coalesced and expanded to form a new strategic approach. Discussing the new penology in terms of discourse, objective and technique risks a certain repetitiveness. Indeed, all three are closely linked, and while none can be assigned priority as the cause of the others, each entails and facilitates the others.

Thus, one can speak of normalizing individuals, but when the emphasis is on separating people into distinct and independent categories the idea of the 'normal' itself becomes obscured if not irrelevant. If the 'norm' can no longer function as a relevant criterion of success for the organizations of criminal justice, it is not surprising that evaluation turns to indicators of internal system performance. The focus of the system on the efficiency of its own outputs, in turn,places a premium on those methods (e.g., risk screening, sorting and monitoring) that fit wholly within the bureaucratic capacities of the apparatus.

But the same story can be told in a different order. The steady bureaucratization of the correctional apparatus during the 1950s and 1960s shifted the target from individuals, who did not fit easily into centralized administration, to categories or classes,which do. But once the focus is on categories of offenders rather than individuals, methods naturally shift toward mechanisms of appraising and arranging groups rather than intervening in the lives of individuals. In the end the search for causal order is at least premature.

In the section below we explore the contours of some of the new patterns represented by these developments, and in so doing suggest that the enterprise is by now relatively well established.

## New functions and traditional forms

Someday, perhaps, the new penology will have its own Jeremy Bentham or Zebulon Brockway [. . .], some gigantic figure who can stamp his or her own sense of order on the messy results of incremental change. For now it is better not to think of it so much as a theory or program conceived in full by any particular actors in the system, but as an interpretative net that can help reveal in the present some of the directions the future may take. The test of such a net, to which we now turn, is not its elegance as a model but whether it enables one to grasp a wide set of developments in an enlightening way (in short, does it catch fish?). Below we re-examine three of the major features of the contemporary penal landscape in light of our argument – the expansion of the penal sanction, the rise of drug testing and innovation within the criminal process – and relate them to our thesis.

### *The expansion of penal sanctions*

During the past decade the number of people covered by penal sanctions has expanded significantly. Because of its high costs, the growth of prison populations has drawn the greatest attention, but probation and parole have increased at a proportionate or faster rate. The importance of these other sanctions goes beyond their ability to stretch penal resources; they expand and redistribute the use of imprisonment. Probation and parole violations now constitute a major source of prison inmates, and negotiations over probation revocation are replacing plea bargaining as modes of disposition (Greenspan, 1988; Messinger and Berecochea, 1990).

Many probation and parole revocations are triggered by events, like failing a drug test, that are driven by parole procedures themselves (Simon, 1990; Zimring and Hawkins, 1991). The increased flow of probationers and parolees into prisons is expanding the prison population and changing the nature of the prison. Increasingly, prisons are short-term holding pens for violators deemed too dangerous to remain on the streets. To the extent the prison is organized to receive such people, its correctional mission is replaced by a management function, a warehouse for the highest risk classes of offenders.

From the perspective of the new penology, the growth of community corrections in the shadow of imprisonment is not surprising. The new penology does not regard prison as a special institution capable of making a difference in the individuals who pass through it. Rather, it functions as but one of several custodial options. The actuarial logic of the new penology dictates an expansion of the continuum of control for more efficient risk management. [. . .]

Thus, community-based sanctions can be understood in terms of risk management rather than rehabilitative or correctional aspirations. Rather than instruments of reintegrating offenders into the community, they function as mechanisms to maintain control, often through frequent drug testing, over low-risk offenders for whom the more secure forms of custody are judged too expensive or unnecessary.

[. . .]

## Drugs and punishment

Drug use and its detection and control have become central concerns of the penal system. No one observing the system today can fail to be struck by the increasingly tough laws directed against users and traffickers, well-publicized data that suggest that a majority of arrestees are drug users, and the increasing proportion of drug offenders sent to prison.

In one sense, of course, the emphasis on drugs marks a continuity with the past thirty years of correctional history. Drug treatment and drug testing were hallmarks of the rehabilitative model in the 1950s and 1960s. The recent upsurge of concern with drugs may be attributed to the hardening of social attitudes toward drug use (especially in marked contrast to the tolerant 1970s), the introduction of virulent new drug products, like crack cocaine, and the disintegrating social conditions of the urban poor.

Without dismissing the relevance of these continuities and explanations for change, it is important to note that there are distinctive changes in the role of drugs in the current system that reflect the logic of the new penology. In place of the traditional emphasis on treatment and eradication, today's practices track drug use as a kind of risk indicator. The widespread evidence of drug use in the offending population leads not to new theories of crime causation but to more efficient ways of identifying those at highest risk of offending. With drug use so prevalent that it is found in a majority of arrestees in some large cities [. . .], it can hardly mark a special type of individual deviance.

From the perspective of the new penology, drug use is not so much a measure of individual acts of deviance as it is a mechanism for classifying the offender within a risk group.

Thus, one finds in the correctional system today a much greater emphasis on drug testing than on drug treatment. This may reflect the normal kinds of gaps in policy as well as difficulty in treating relatively new forms of drug abuse. Yet, testing serves functions in the new penology even in the absence of a treatment option. By marking the distribution of risk within the offender population under surveillance, testing makes possible greater coordination of scarce penal resources.

Testing also fills the gap left by the decline of traditional intervention strategies. [. . .] If nothing else, testing provide[s] parole (and probably probation) agents [with] a means to document compliance with their own internal performance requirements. [. . .] Testing provides both an occasion for requiring the parolee to show up in the parole office and a purpose for meeting. The results of tests have become a network of fact and explanation for use in a decision-making process that requires accountability but provides little substantive basis for distinguishing among offenders.

### Innovation

Our description may seem to imply the onset of a reactive age in which penal managers strive to manage populations of marginal citizens with no concomitant effort toward integration into mainstream society. This may seem hard to square with the myriad new and innovative technologies introduced over the past decade. Indeed the media, which for years have portrayed the correctional system as a failure, have recently enthusiastically reported on these innovations: boot camps, electronic surveillance, high security 'campuses' for drug users, house arrest, intensive parole and probation, and drug treatment programs.

Although some of the new proposals are presented in terms of the 'old penology' and emphasize individuals, normalization and rehabilitation, it is risky to come to any firm conviction about how these innovations will turn out. If historians of punishment have provided any clear lessons, it is that reforms evolve in ways quite different from the aims of their proponents (Foucault, 1977; Rothman, 1971). Thus, we wonder if these most recent innovations won't be recast in the terms outlined in this paper. Many of these innovations are compatible with the imperatives of the new penology, that is, managing a permanently dangerous population while maintaining the system at a minimum cost.

One of the current innovations most in vogue with the press and politicians is correctional 'boot camps'. These are minimum security custodial facilities, usually for youthful first offenders, designed on the model of a training center for military personnel, complete with barracks, physical exercise and tough drill sergeants. Boot camps are portrayed as providing discipline and pride to young offenders brought up in the unrestrained culture of poverty (as though physical fitness could fill the gap left by the weakening of families, schools, neighborhoods, and other social organizations in the inner city).

The camps borrow explicitly from a military model of discipline, which has influenced penality from at least the eighteenth century. No doubt the image of inmates smartly dressed in uniforms performing drills and calisthenics appeals to long-standing ideals of order in post-Enlightenment culture. But in its proposed application to correction, the military model is even less appropriate now than when it was rejected in the nineteenth century; indeed, today's boot camps are more a simulation of discipline than the real thing.

In the nineteenth century the military model was superseded by another model of discipline, the factory. Inmates were controlled by making them work at hard industrial labor (Ignatieff, 1978; Rothman, 1971). It was assumed that forced labor would inculcate in offenders the discipline required of factory laborers, so that they might earn their keep while in custody and join the ranks of the usefully employed when released. One can argue that this model did not work very well, but at least it was coherent. The model of discipline through labor suited our capitalist democracy in a way the model of a militarized citizenry did not.

The recent decline of employment opportunities among the populations of urban poor most at risk for conventional crime involvement has left the applicability of industrial discipline in doubt. But the substitution of the boot camp for vocational training is even less plausible. Even if the typical 90-day regime of training envisioned by proponents of boot camps is effective in reorienting its subjects, at best it can only produce soldiers without a company to join. Indeed, the grim vision of the effect of boot camp is that it will be effective for those who will subsequently put their lessons of discipline and organization to use in the street gangs and drug distribution networks. However, despite the earnestness with which the boot camp metaphor is touted, we suspect that the camps will be little more than holding pens for managing a short-term, mid-range risk population.

Drug testing and electronic monitors being tried in experimental 'intensive supervision' and 'house arrest' programs are justified in rehabilitative terms, but both sorts of programs lack a foundation in today's social and economic realities. The drug treatment programs in the 1960s encompassed a regime of coercive treatment: 'inpatient' custody in secured settings followed by community supervision and reintegration [. . .]. The record suggests that these programs had enduring effects for at least some of those who participated in them (Anglin et al., 1990). Today's proposals are similar, but it remains to be seen whether they can be effective in the absence of long-term treatment facilities, community-based follow-up, and prospects for viable conventional lifestyles and employment opportunities. In the meantime it is obvious that they can also serve the imperative of reducing the costs of correctional jurisdiction while maintaining some check on the offender population.

Our point is not to belittle the stated aspirations of current proposals or to argue that drug treatment programs cannot work. Indeed, we anticipate that drug treatment and rehabilitation will become increasingly attractive as the cost of long-term custody increases. However, given the emergence of the management concerns of the new penology, we question whether these innovations will embrace the long-term perspective of earlier successful treatment programs, and we suspect that they will emerge as control processes for managing and recycling selected risk populations. If so, these new programs will extend still further the capacity of the new penology. The undeniable attractiveness of boot camps, house arrest, secure drug 'centers', and the like, is that they promise to provide secure custody in a more flexible format and at less cost than traditional correctional facilities. Indeed, some of them are envisioned as private contract facilities that can be expanded or reduced with relative ease. Further, they hold out the promise of expanding the range of low- and mid-level custodial alternatives, thereby facilitating the transfer of offenders now held in more expensive, higher security facilities that have been so favored in recent years. Tougher eligibility requirements, including job offers, stable residency and promises of sponsorship in the community, can be used to screen out 'higher risk' categories for non-custodial release programs (Petersilia, 1987). Thus, despite the lingering language of rehabilitation and reintegration, the programs generated under the new penology can best be understood in terms of managing costs and controlling dangerous populations rather than social or personal transformation.

## Social bases of the new penology

The point of these reinterpretations is not to show that shifts in the way the penal enterprise is understood and discussed inexorably determine how the system will take shape. What actually emerges in corrections over the near and distant future will depend on how this understanding itself is shaped by the pressures of demographic, economic and political factors. Still, such factors rarely operate as pure forces. They are filtered through and expressed in terms in which the problems are understood. Thus, the strategic field we call the new penology itself will help shape the future.

### The new discourse of crime

Like the old penology, traditional 'sociological' criminology has focused on the relationship between individuals and communities. Its central concerns have been the causes and correlates of delinquent and criminal behavior, and it has sought to develop intervention strategies designed to correct delinquents and decrease the likelihood of deviant behavior. Thus, it has focused on the family and the workplace as important influences of socialization and control.

The new penology has an affinity with a new 'actuarial' criminology, which eschews these traditional concerns of criminology. Instead of training in sociology or social work, increasingly the new criminologists are trained in operations research and systems analysis. This new approach is not a criminology at all, but an applied branch of systems theory. This shift in training and orientation has been accompanied by a shift in interest. A concern with successful intervention strategies, the province of the former, is replaced by models designed to optimize public safety through the management of aggregates, which is the province of the latter.

In one important sense this new criminology is simply a consequence of steady improvements in the quantitative rigor with which crime is studied. No doubt the amassing of a statistical picture of crime and the criminal justice system has improved researchers' ability to speak realistically about the distribution of crimes and the fairness of procedures. But, we submit, it has also contributed to a shift, a reconceptualization, in the way crime is understood as a social problem. The new techniques and the new language have facilitated reconceptualization of the way issues are framed and policies pursued. Sociological criminology tended to emphasize crime as a relationship between the individual and the normative expectations of his or her community (Bennett, 1981). Policies premised on this perspective addressed problems of reintegration, including the mismatch among individual motivation, normative orientation and social opportunity structures. In contrast, actuarial criminology highlights the interaction of criminal justice institutions and specific segments of the population. Policy discussions framed in its terms emphasize the management of high-risk groups and make less salient the qualities of individual delinquents and their communities.

Indeed, even the use of predictive statistics by pioneers like Ernest Burgess (1936) reflected sociological criminology's emphasis on normalization. Burgess's statistics (and those of most other quantitative criminologists before the 1960s) measured the activity of subjects defined by a specifiable set of individual or social factors (e.g., alcoholism, unemployment etc.). In the actuarial criminology of today, by contrast, the numbers generate the subject itself (e.g., the high-rate offender of incapacitation research). In short, criminals are no longer the organizing referent (or logos) of criminology. Instead, criminology has become a subfield of a generalized public policy analysis discourse. This new criminal knowledge aims at rationalizing the operation of the systems that manage criminals, not dealing with criminality. The same techniques that can be used to improve the circulation of baggage in airports or delivery of food to troops can be used to improve the penal system's efficiency.

## The discourse of poverty and the underclass

The new penology may also be seen as responsive to the emergence of a new understanding of poverty in America. The term *underclass* is used [. . .] to characterize a segment of society that is viewed as permanently excluded from social mobility and economic integration. The term is used to refer to a largely black and Hispanic population living in concentrated zones of poverty in central cities, separated physically and institutionally from the suburban locus of mainstream social and economic life in America.

In contrast to groups whose members are deemed employable, even if they may be temporarily out of work, the underclass is understood as a permanently marginal population, without literacy, without skills and without hope; a self-perpetuating and pathological segment of society that is not integratable into the larger whole, even as a reserve labor pool (Wilson, 1987). Conceived of this way, the underclass is also a dangerous class, not only for what any particular member may or may not do, but more generally for collective potential misbehavior. It is treated as a high-risk group that must be managed for the protection of the rest of society. Indeed, it is this managerial task that provides one of the most powerful sources for the imperative of preventative management in the new penology. The concept of 'underclass' makes clear why correctional officials increasingly regard as a bad joke the claim that their goal is to reintegrate offenders back into their communities.

Reintegration and rehabilitation inevitably imply a norm against which deviant subjects are evaluated. As Allen (1981) perceived [. . .], rehabilitation as a project can only survive if public confidence in the viability and appropriateness of such norms endures. Allen viewed the decline of the rehabilitative ideal as a result of the cultural revolts of the 1960s, which undermined the capacity of the American middle classes to justify their norms and the imposition of those norms on others. It is this decline in social will, rather than empirical evidence of the failure of penal programs to rehabilitate, that, in Allen's analysis, doomed the rehabilitative ideal.

Whatever significance cultural radicalism may have had in initiating the break-up of the old penology in the mid-1970s, the emergence of the new penology in the 1980s reflects the influence of a more despairing view of poverty and the prospects for achieving equality (views that can hardly be blamed on the Left). Rehabilitating offenders, or any kind of reintegration strategy, can only make sense if the larger community from which offenders come is viewed as sharing a common normative universe with the communities of the middle classes – especially those values and expectations derived from the labor market. The concept of an underclass, with its connotation of a permanent marginality for whole portions of the population, has rendered the old penology incoherent and laid the groundwork for a strategic field that emphasizes low-cost management of a permanent offender population.

The connection between the new penality and the (re)emergent term *underclass* also is illustrated by studies of American jails. For instance, [. . .] Irwin's 1985 book *The Jail*, is subtitled *Managing the Underclass in American Society*. His thesis is that 'prisoners in jails share two essential characteristics: detachment and disrepute' (p. 2). For Irwin, the function of jail is to manage the underclass, which he reports is also referred to as 'rabble', 'disorganized', 'disorderly', and the 'lowest class of people'.

In one rough version of Irwin's analysis, the jail can be viewed as a means of controlling the most disruptive and unsightly members of the underclass. But in another version, it can be conceived of as an emergency service net for those who are in the most desperate straits. As other social services have shrunk, increasingly this task falls on the jail.

Whichever version one selects, few of those familiar with the jails in America's urban centers find it meaningful to characterize them only as facilities for 'pre-trial detention' or for serving 'short-term sentences'. Although not literally false, this characterization misses the broader function of the jail. The high rates of those released without charges filed, the turnstile-like frequency with which some people reappear, and the pathological characteristics of a high proportion of the inmates lead many to agree with Irwin that the jail is best understood as a social management instrument rather than an institution for effecting the purported aims of the criminal process.

Social management, not individualized justice, is also emphasized in other discussions of the criminal process. Long-time public defender James M. Doyle (1992) offers the metaphors 'colonial', 'White Man's burden', and 'Third World', in an essay drawing parallels between the careers of criminal justice officials and colonial administrators. Both, he argues,

are convinced that they are menaced by both inscrutable, malign natives and ignorant, distant, policy-makers. They believe they are hamstrung by crazy legalities. Young Assistant District Attorneys, like young Assistant District Commissioners, hurriedly seize, then vehemently defend, a conventional wisdom as a protection against these threats. They pledge themselves to a professional code that sees the world in which people are divided into various collectives. Where they might have seen individuals, they see races, types and colors instead. Like the colonialists before them, they embrace a 'rigidly binomial opposition of "ours" and "theirs"'. In the criminal justice system as on the frontiers of empire 'the impersonal communal idea of being a White Man' rules; it becomes 'a very concrete way of being-in-the-world, a way of taking hold of reality, language and thought'. (1992: 74)

Sustaining his metaphor, Doyle parallels the corrupting influence of the White Man's effort to 'manage' Third World natives with those of the criminal justice professionals' effort to handle cases. He concludes, 'we have paid too much attention to the superficial exotic charms by which the reports of the colonial and criminal justice White Man entertain us, too little to the darker strains they also share' (1992: 126).

Whether one prefers Irwin's notion of underclass or Doyle's 'colonial' and 'Third World' metaphors, both resonate with our notion of the new penology. They vividly explain who is being managed and why. But in providing an explanation of these relationships, there is a danger that the terms will reify the problem, that they will suggest the problem is inevitable and permanent. Indeed, it is this belief, we maintain, that has contributed to the lowered expectations of the new penology – away from an aspiration to affect individual lives through rehabilitative and transformative efforts and toward the more 'realistic' task of monitoring and managing intractable groups.

The hardening of poverty in contemporary America reinforces this view. When combined with a pessimistic analysis implied by the term *underclass*, the structural barriers that maintain the large islands of Third World misery in America's major cities can lead to the conclusion that such conditions are inevitable and impervious to social policy intervention. This, in turn, can push corrections ever further toward a self-understanding based on the imperative of herding a specific population that cannot be disaggregated and transformed but only maintained – a kind of waste management function.

[. . .]

## References

Allen, F. (1981) *The Decline of the Rehabilitative Idea*. New Haven, CT: Yale University Press.
Anglin, D., Speckhart, G. and Piper Deschenes, E. (1990) *Examining the Effects of Narcotics Addiction*. Los Angeles: UCLA Neuropsychiatric Institute, Drug Abuse Research Group.
Bennett, J. (1981) *Oral History and Delinquency: the Rhetoric of Criminology*. Chicago: University of Chicago Press.
Bottoms, A. (1983) 'Neglected features of contemporary penal systems', in D. Garland and P. Young (eds), *The Power to Punish*. London: Heinemann.
Burgess, E.W. (1936) 'Protecting the public by parole and parole prediction', *Journal of Criminal Law and Criminology*, 27: 491–502.
Cohen, S. (1985) *Visions of Social Control: Crime, Punishment and Classification*. Cambridge: Polity.
Doyle, J.M. (1992) '"It's the Third World down there": The colonialist vocation and American criminal justice', *Harvard Civil Rights – Civil Liberties Law Review*, 27: 71–126.
Foucault, M. (1977) *Discipline and Punish*. New York: Pantheon.
Greenspan, R. (1988) 'The transformation of criminal due process in the administrative state', Paper prepared for delivery at the annual meeting of the Law and Society Association, Vail, Colorado, June 1988.
Greenwood, P. (1982) *Selective Incapacitation*. Santa Monica, CA: Rand.
Heydebrand, W. and Seron, C. (1990) *Rationalizing Justice: the Political Economy and Federal District Courts*. New York: State University of New York Press.
Ignatieff, M. (1978) *A Just Measure of Pain: the Penitentiary in the Industrial Revolution, 1750–1850*. London: Macmillan.
Irwin, J. (1985) *The Jail: Managing the Underclass in American Society*. Berkeley, CA: University of California Press.
Jacobs, J.B. (1977) *Stateville: the Penitentiary in Mass Society*. Chicago: University of Chicago Press.
Lipsky, M. (1980) *Street Level Bureaucrats*. New York: Russell Sage Foundation.

Mathiesen, T. (1983) 'The future of control systems – the case of Norway', in D. Garland and P. Young (eds), *The Power to Punish*. London: Heinemann.

Messinger, S. and Berecochea, J. (1990) 'Don't stay too long but do come back soon'. Proceedings, Conference on Growth and Its Influence on Correctional Policy, Center for the Study of Law and Society, University of California at Berkeley.

Moore, M.H., Estrich, S.R., McGillis, D. and Spelman, W. (1984) *Dangerous Offenders: the Elusive Target of Justice*. Cambridge, MA: Harvard University Press.

Petersilia, J. (1987) *Expanding Options for Criminal Sentencing*. Santa Monica, CA: Rand.

Reichman, N. (1986) 'Managing crime risks: toward an insurance-based model of social control', *Research in Law, Deviance and Social Control*, 8: 151–72.

Rothman, D. (1971) *The Discovery of the Asylum: Social Order and Disorder in the New Republic*. Boston, MA: Little, Brown.

Simon, J. (1987) 'The emergence of a risk society: insurance law and the state', *Socialist Review*, 95: 61–89.

Simon, J. (1988) 'The ideological effect of actuarial practices', *Law and Society Review*, 22: 771–800.

Simon, J. (1990) 'From discipline to management: strategies of control in parole supervision, 1890–1900'. PhD dissertation, Jurisprudence and Social Policy Program, University of California at Berkeley.

Steiner, H.J. (1987) *Moral Vision and Social Vision in the Court: a Study of Tort Accident Law*. Madison, WI: University of Wisconsin Press.

Wilson, W.J. (1987) *The Truly Disadvantaged: the Inner City, the Underclass, and Public Policy*. Chicago: University of Chicago Press.

Zimring, F. and Hawkins, G. (1991) *The Scale of Imprisonment*. Chicago: University of Chicago Press.

# PART FIVE
# CRIME CONTROL II: SOCIAL CONTROL, DISCIPLINE AND REGULATION

## Introduction

In the prevailing popular discourse about 'the crime problem' everything is straightforward: a crime is a crime and a criminal deserves to be caught and punished. In other words, crime is self-evident, its meaning inherent in the actions of a particular individual, from which the consequences follow according to the due process of law. In fact, as will have emerged from the readings so far, things are rather more complicated. What is defined as a criminal act varies widely in different societies and at different times. Far from having an absolute character, crime is a socially constructed and historically contingent phenomenon.

Furthermore, the institutions and procedures which provide any society with its mechanism for 'crime control' cannot merely be taken at face value as methods of dealing with particular behaviours of particular individuals. Such measures reflect wider concerns about the existing social order and, as the readings in this section indicate, they are a key part of the framework for exerting control, discipline and regulation over society.

V.A.C. Gatrell's survey of the social history of crime in Britain provides a useful historical introduction to the discussion of crime control. He suggests that the modern understanding of the concept 'crime' is quite different from that of the eighteenth century and that the extensive measures of state intervention now accepted in the name of crime control would at that time have been regarded as repressive and intolerable. Insisting that the history of crime is not so much about crime as about power, he traces the evolution of the concept of 'crime' in response to changing power relations over the past two centuries.

In particular he emphasizes the emergence of 'crime' as a symbol of 'moral deterioration' in the early nineteenth century, a time of hectic social changes associated with industrialization and the emergence of the working class. The concept of crime developed further in response to growing anxieties about the threat to the established order resulting from the weakening of respect for hierarchy. Once the law-breaker was identified as a threat to society as well as to the victim of his offence, the way was clear for the state to assume its now-familiar role as 'policeman'.

One of the most influential students of the 'disciplinary society' that emerged in Western Europe in the early nineteenth century was the French philosopher Michel Foucault, whose major works were published in the 1970s. In his detailed study of the prison system established in France (and elsewhere) in this period, he emphasized that the methods of dealing with criminals in the modern penitentiaries were part of a wider process of regimentation in society. The criminal was no longer regarded merely as somebody who had broken the law and had to be punished. Now he was an individual in the grip of a pathological process. He required close surveillance and expert intervention with a view to returning him to normality.

For Foucault, the prison was one island in a 'carceral archipelago' of disciplinary institutions, including schools, hospitals and asylums, and extending through a 'carceral continuum' to the workplace and home. In this process the traditional disciplinary mechanisms of the law were powerfully supplemented by new fields of knowledge (medicine, psychiatry, pedagogy, criminology) and new cadres of professionals. As Foucault argues in the reading included here, the crucial role of the modern prison was to pioneer and legitimize a method of dealing with deviants from prescribed norms which could then be generalized to 'the entire social body'. This theme is taken further in the next three readings which are explicitly influenced by Foucault's work.

Foucault may be accused of rhetorical exaggeration in his notion of a carceral continuum, which appears to efface the distinction between institutions in which individuals are confined against their will and those in which they participate voluntarily. Yet as Stanley Cohen showed in his 1979 discussion of 'community control', modern trends in the treatment of offenders suggested that this distinction was being blurred in practice, providing a striking vindication of Foucault's thesis.

Under the banner of the 'anti-institutional' consensus that emerged in the 1960s, advocates of 'community treatment' claimed that it offered an *alternative* to prison, and that through preventative or pre-trial programmes, it could *divert* potential offenders from embarking on a career of incarceration. Cohen showed that the blurring of boundaries between 'inside' and 'outside' also blurred the distinctions between convicted delinquents and potential delinquents or 'high-risk populations'. He drew attention to the tendency of community control programmes to embody an *increased* level of state intervention in a *larger* population than would be affected by the conventional criminal justice system. He also questioned whether the proliferation of such programmes was accompanied by a commensurate decline in the use of traditional prisons.

In many respects, community control appears more coercive than prison (particularly in the imposition of behaviourist psychological techniques). But, perhaps more importantly, it indicates a deeper penetration of new techniques of social control into society as a whole – a step closer to the 'punitive city' anticipated by Foucault.

Shearing and Stenning are interested in the mechanisms through which the disciplinary society achieves social control. They contrast the essentially *moral* basis of the traditional criminal justice system (including the prison system) with the more *instrumental* character of control methods which operate in the burgeoning private sector. Here the aim is not to reform individuals but to restrict the opportunities for crime; surveillance shifts from morally culpable individuals to groups which might create openings for offenders. Using Disney World as an example, they show how such 'non-carceral' but unmistakably 'disciplinary' control measures are 'embedded' in the structures of modern social practice.

From a feminist perspective, Carol Smart insists that, while the 'new' mechanisms of social discipline (especially through the discourses of medicine and the 'psy' professions) may have become more important, we should not neglect the influence of the 'old contrivances of power'. Whereas Foucault emphasized the declining role of the juridical sphere, she draws attention to the growing legalization of everyday life, extending from the regulation of embryo research to controversies over brain death. Through a discussion of two important legal cases in the late 1980s, she shows that in conflicts over women's rights, the legal sphere remains central – despite the proliferation of extra-legal methods of social control.

In the final reading in Part Five the Australian criminologist John Braithwaite puts the case for a genuine alternative to carceral and coercive methods of social control: 'reintegrative shaming'. By this he means dealing with offenders in ways which embody an expression of community disapproval, but also incorporate gestures of re-acceptance. Rather than stigmatizing deviants and excluding them from society, this approach aims to bring them back into society and thus to enhance social solidarity. While Braithwaite has elsewhere advocated this method for dealing with corporate crime, in the reading included here he insists that it is also relevant to 'ordinary' crime. Braithwaite is impressed by the success of such methods in deterring much crime in Japan. Could it work for us too?

# 34

# Crime, authority and the policeman-state

## *V.A.C. Gatrell*

### Introduction

For centuries in Britain, stealing from and hurting other people have been pursuits as common and traditional as drinking and fornicating. All social classes have participated in them. Poorer and younger people have stolen to procure food or clothing, to demonstrate daring, or to relieve tedium. Affluent, older or upwardly mobile people have embezzled, evaded taxes, excise and currency regulations, defrauded each other and their clients under the guise of commercial or professional practice, and lifted from shops. They have done these things far more frequently than the courts have ever recognized, as self-report studies nowadays show. And in times past, for good measure, the rich no less than the poor used violence to assert prowess, relieve tension and settle disputes. 'Crime' in these many senses has been as much a part of our national heritage as has a taste for beer, politics and sex.

This makes the history of crime an unimaginably large subject. Commentators usually therefore take a short cut. They address themselves not to the ubiquity of law-breaking at all social levels, but to those actions, merely, which come to be labelled as crimes by the reactions of the law enforcement and judicial systems. This in turn, however, puts them at the mercy of the prejudices and constraints which determine how the law selects some targets and ignores others. That is why no discussion of 'crime' can sensibly proceed which does not first discuss how, by whom and why attitudes and policies towards crime are formed, and what often covert purposes those policies serve.

[. . .] [I]n and after the later eighteenth century anxiety about the lawlessness of poorer people was greatly intensified. This was part of a mounting disciplinary assault on those mainly proletarian classes who were assumed to threaten dominant and newly articulated definitions of order: those reluctant to enter a disciplined labour force, for example, or those who were excluded from, or who dissented from, the consensual society which the political nation was beginning to try to construct. In these years, also, 'crime' became (as it remains) the repository of fears which had little to do with its relatively trivial cost to the society and economy at large. It came to be invested with large significance because it provided a convenient vehicle for the expression of fears about social change itself. For a century and a half it has been next to

---

Abridged from *Cambridge Social History of Britain, 1750–1950* (ed. F.M.L. Thompson), vol. 3, pp. 243–57. (Cambridge: Cambridge University Press, 1990.)

impossible to perceive the meanings of crime except through these ideological filters. How and why those filters were constructed may be of greater interest even than the ubiquity of lawlessness itself.

One agency behind this reshaping of attitudes (as well as one effect of it) was what is here termed the 'policeman-state' [. . .] In the nineteenth century, the state assumed increasing control of the criminal justice system, as it did of the police who were put in the vanguard of the disciplinary enterprise. This process was not unchallenged, unqualified, or unresponsive to its critics. But it generated its own momentum, none the less, as 'experts' accumulated evidence that more and yet more bureaucratic control was needed to solve 'problems'. Politicians and public connived in this growth in the interests of reinforcing social discipline in an increasingly fissiparous society. Law was the means and order the primary objective of this enterprise, and the state became its necessary agent. In the rhetoric of the powerful, the direct Whiggish appeal to 'English liberties' became ever more qualified and muted. [. . .]

Major themes in the history of policing must be omitted from this discussion. These include the policing of industrial relations; of the nation's drunks, vagrants, paupers, prostitutes, homosexuals and aliens; of those who might service allegedly deviant cultures, like publicans and pawnbroker-receivers and sellers of pistols or of obscene publications; or of those whose practices subverted an increasingly rigid ideal of urban order, whether they be street-traders, traffic offenders, or those who merely beat carpets in the highway. The statutes, bye-laws and policing practices which were to enmesh all these groups were largely in place as early as 1914. They exemplify the developing range and potency of the policeman-state even in the nineteenth century, and they should not be forgotten. But there is one justification for their omission here. It would be vain to seek a public acknowledgement on the part of politicians or of policemen in 1900 or in 1950 (or today) that the major functions of policing – absorbing most man-hours and resources – were expressed in its attention to these non-criminal constituencies. To win their consent, the public has instead been enticed into the belief that the primary rationale of the policeman-state has been to contain and detect crimes against property and the person. This was and is a self-serving and convenient obfuscation; but it is such a large and pervasive obfuscation that this chapter is content to see how it came to pass and with what justifications and effects.

[. . .] Over the past couple of centuries, the policeman-state protected and still protects an unequal and fissiparous society; and it did so supported by the convenient and enduring belief that most criminals were likely to be found among poorer people. The history of crime, accordingly, is largely the history of how better-off people disciplined their inferiors; of how elites used selected law-breakers to sanction their own authority; or of how in modern times bureaucrats, experts and policemen used them to justify their own expanding functions and influences. The history of crime is also always about how public fears about change and disorder were displaced on to 'criminals', even when criminals were inappropriate objects of those fears. It can never be about the real extent of law-breaking which goes on at all social levels. In these senses, the history of crime is not always about legality – or about liberty, either. Certainly, the rhetoric of liberty, justice and impartiality has always been usefully turned against the pretensions of the great; but those values have been more frequently compromised before the more expediential, discretionary and prejudicial devices of law as they were wielded in practice by policemen, judges and politicians. Historians might profitably remind themselves that the history of crime is a grim subject, not because it is about crime, but because it is about power.

## Changing responses to crime, 1750–1850

Is there any meaningful watershed in the history of crime? Did it acquire new meanings and invite new responses in the early nineteenth century unprecedented in the eighteenth century?

Watersheds in history are always debatable: continuities have to be acknowledged. All elites have worried about lawlessness, and eighteenth century elites were no exception. They deplored the thieving instincts of the poor, their unruly pastimes and secret economies, their vagrancy and fecklessness, and their turbulence at times of dearth and political excitement. These things subverted deference. They also caused inconvenience. 'One is forced to travel, even at noon', Horace Walpole lamented of the London streets, 'as if one were going to battle.'

Reactions were always harsh, too. The crimes which touched elite interest provoked spectacular displays of legal force. Even if eighteenth century judges and hangmen enmeshed only a few offenders in their grisly rituals, they enmeshed enough to testify to the majesty of the law and the power of those who wielded it. Middling sorts of people used the law as well. Artisans, shopkeepers and farmers were fond of prosecuting their equals and fonder still of prosecuting their inferiors. Even labourers prosecuted each other (though rarely their betters) with surprising frequency. By European standards the British were a litigious people; they used their law as seriously as any later generation did.[1]

[. . .]

And yet when all is said and done, people who looked back on eighteenth century law enforcement a century later would have believed that they were contemplating an *ancien régime*. They would have been struck, for example, by the fact that eighteenth century law remained for most people an expensive discipline of last resort; cheaper disciplines often did as well. Eighteenth century society was cemented less by law than by the informal sanctions neighbour wielded against neighbour, landlords against tenants, employers against labourers. Control was exercised face-to-face, not bureaucratically. Few, moreover, wished law enforcement to be better coordinated for fear of the centralized despotism which had been so bitterly resisted in the seventeenth century. Local autonomy was a bastion of liberty. Cheapness was a consideration too. Popular lawlessness cost eighteenth century gentlemen little: it was farmers and tradesmen who bore the brunt of its costs – or the poor themselves. When it cost them so little, gentlemen were sensibly concerned that the business of curtailing it should cost less. And so (by later standards) the state kept a low profile. Detection and prosecution remained at the discretion and mainly at the expense of victims or of associations of local farmers and businessmen. Sentencing was discretionary also, and character testimony deeply influenced an offender's fate. Judges might process up to thirty felonies a day with a low regard for rules of evidence and without restraint of appeal.

Above all, Victorian observers would have been struck by their forefathers' relative indifference to crime as a 'problem', and by their relative satisfaction with the apparently arbitrary and capricious mechanisms which contained it. This was not because crime was infrequent then: it is not at all clear that there was less thieving and violence *per capita* in eighteenth century cities than in nineteenth. But crime did not as yet appear to threaten hierarchy, and the terms in which crime might be debated as a 'problem' were not yet formed. Historians of early modern crime must realize not only that 'their subject was not known then by that name'[2] but that as a subject it did not exist. The word 'crime' when used at all before the 1780s, usually referred to a personal depravity. It lacked the problematic and aggregative resonance it was soon to acquire. Despite occasional panics about the ubiquity of thieving, crime in aggregate was not yet thought to be increasing as a necessary and potentially uncontrollable effect of social change. Similarly, the 'criminal' was not yet discerned as a social archetype, symbolic of the nation's collective ill-health.

It was in and after the 1780s that these attitudes began to alter. Sensibilities became softer, and pragmatic pressures for change came into play as well. Prosecutors, juries and even judges got queasier about visiting the full penalty of death on lesser offenders. The abolition of transportation to the American colonies after their revolution necessitated some hard thinking about alternative forms of punishment. Large intellectual currents, too, were making it difficult to regard crime in the old way as a simple function of individual depravity. Materialist psychology led Bentham and others to argue that criminals were driven not by original sin but by their ignorance of how best to calculate the costs of their wrongdoing. And a few reformers were beginning to think about 'crime' aggregatively, as a social issue bred in the squalor of the back streets. Thus Paley and then Colquhoun denounced the growth of great cities for the 'refuge they afford to villainy, in means of concealment, and of subsisting in secrecy'. Colquhoun attributed the 'depraved habits and loose conduct of a great proportion of the lower classes' to 'the enlarged state of Society, the vast extent of moving property, and the unexampled growth of the Metropolis'. It was Colquhoun, too, who, in the light of French events and to justify his call for stronger policing, first equated the dangerous classes with the excesses of revolution. This intruded a new resonance into the debates on the increasing insubordination and presumed politicization of the poor which was not to be lost for half a century.[3]

Responses to these pressures were hesitant because events in France dampened English zeal for reform. But slowly elites' relative tolerance of and indifference to the criminal poor (as of the riotous poor) were eroded. By the time Peel took up the challenge of penal, police and law reform in the 1820s, the political and cultural climate was quite transformed. Crime was fast becoming 'important'. In the postwar world, and on into the 1840s, the subject came to be cemented into an ideology about the Condition of England. Crime was becoming a vehicle for articulating mounting anxieties about issues which really had nothing to do with crime at all: social change and the stability of social hierarchy. These issues invested crime with new meanings, justified vastly accelerated action against it, and have determined attitudes to it ever since. These are the issues which determine that the history of crime from the early nineteenth century onwards is indeed a 'modern' history.

## Crime and its modern meanings: 'change'

If, from the early nineteenth century onwards, crime has assumed a looming importance for modern sensibilities, it is not because of its real cost to society, which even today is relatively trivial. It is because it has come to bear an emblematic relationship to other, larger anxieties – first about 'change' and secondly about 'order'.

'Change' was not commonly, before the second quarter of the nineteenth century, identified as an independent force. By 1831, however, J.S. Mill was not alone in identifying it as 'the first of the leading peculiarities of the present age'. This, he wrote, is 'an age of transition', a fact 'obvious a few years ago only to the more discerning: at present it forces itself upon the most unobservant'.[4] For Mill the problem was that popular clamour for political rights exceeded the readiness of the populace to appreciate the obligations attached to those rights: 'the world of opinions' had become 'mere chaos'. For many others contemplating the costs of the economic, urban and demographic growth which later generations were to call the industrial revolution, what was at issue in urban and industrial society was 'the natural progress of barbarian habits', the 'explosive violence' of the poor, the decay of deference, the collapse of family life, the diffusion of pauperism. The criminal – always the working-class criminal – fast assumed a privileged position in this constellation of bogeys. Onto him were displaced fears about these other changes which were otherwise difficult to express, and must otherwise remain diffuse and without focus.

Why the criminal should be specially targeted in early nineteenth-century debates is no mystery. The judicial system since 1805 had been generating spurious evidence, through statistics, that crime was increasing alarmingly. There could be no more eloquent support for the notion that the moral condition of England was deteriorating and that crime was the emblem of that deterioration.

We know now that what was increasing in the first half of the nineteenth century was not crime but the prosecution rate, a very different matter. In the half-century after 1780, disciplinary responses to the poor and the workshy accelerated markedly. Partly this was because business activity was expanding. In pursuit of an economical and comprehensive way of disciplining recalcitrant workmen, manufacturers were among the loudest in their demand for less random and capricious law-enforcement. In many districts they added most to the mounting volume of summary prosecutions as they clamped down on the often custom-sanctioned and petty embezzlements of their workforces.[5] Partly these responses reflected anxieties about the Malthusian threat and, after 1815, the escalation of poor rates to support the idle able-bodied who should properly be harnessed to work. It was now being affirmed that both the pauper and the criminal shared cognate moral failing: both wilfully refused to enter the respectable community at work. Laziness, not hunger or environment, explained theft and pauperism alike, and why both were apparently increasing. In 1818 a select committee had already referred without irony to 'that class of persons who ordinarily commit crime, meaning the poor and indigent'. By 1839, the Royal Commission on the County Constabulary could insist that 'In scarcely any cases is [crime] attributable to the pressure of unavoidable want or destitution; . . . it arises from the temptation of obtaining property with a less degree of labour than by regular industry'.[6] The association of criminality with the indigent underclasses was now axiomatic.

[. . .]

When they analysed prosecution figures, early Victorians were no more critical of their meaning than many of us are today. From that day to this, questionable crime rates have always been used to inflame unreal fears and to give shape to imagined problems. Moreover, on to crime were projected anxieties about social changes which had nothing directly to do with crime itself. A critical displacement occurred when 'change' became part of an *explanation* of crime, and embedded in a broad thesis of social deterioration. By the 1840s this motif was firmly in place. The growth of towns; working-class politicization; the employment of women and the alleged erosion of the family resulting from it; industrial employment and the false values it induced in those who lived by it – fear of all these things was transferred to their emblem.

[. . .]

In the long term the displacements of meaning and anxiety which suffused all these explanations and judgements carried with them their own linguistic effects. 'Crime', as a word, acquired the aggregative and problematic meaning it had only dimly possessed in the eighteenth century and which it will never now discard. And as the nineteenth century progressed, the term became enshrouded in the metaphors of disease, cancer, contamination, contagion, the associations with which it also retains. Attention shifted from the iniquity of the individual act, which eighteenth century law had sought to penalize, to the symbolic meaning of the act and the pathological nature of the actor. So the 'criminal' was transformed by Victorian and subsequent policy and cate-gorization into a special and an afflicted type, even a dehumanized object. By the end of the century 'experts' like the chairman of the prison commission (Du Cane) had no doubt that men turned to crime because of physical and mental as well as moral defectiveness. The psychiatrist Dr Bevan Lewis agreed that habitual criminals were 'simply a degenerate offspring of a very degenerate stock; and if I may be allowed to express my opinion more freely, I would say that both insanity and crime are simply morbid branches of the same stock'.[7]

To be sure, the perceived problem in criminality, even if not the meanings ascribed to it or its social location, shifted many times in the nineteenth and twentieth centuries. The march of 'social science', and the increasing expertise of prison governors, doctors, civil servants, social investigators and 'criminologists' subjected those who broke the law and were foolish enough to be caught to ever sharper categorization, the better to shape policy for their management. The collectivized image of the dangerous classes gave way after mid-century, in Mayhew and in the 1863 Royal Commission on Penal Servitude, for example, to an ever sharper discrimination between the opportunistic and the professional criminal; in debates on reformatories distinctions between the young offender and the hardened habitual were clarified; or in later nineteenth-century penology the necessitous thief was to be distinguished from the irremediable 'moral defective'. The image has been fragmented further ever since. The twentieth century introduced new archetypes: the motor car bandit, the cat burglar, the black-marketeer, the gang leader, down to the mugger, armed robber and drug dealer today. These all had plausible and more or less unpleasant real-life representations. Most of them were worth catching and penalizing. What was in question was the ideological burden these scapegoats continued to carry, and the cost in clear-sightedness paid by those who imposed it.

For the old core images in terms of which these archetypes were explained remained intact. Even in the interwar years, when eugenist theories of crime (though still current) yielded supremacy to new forms of criminological positivism, pundits were still identifying the criminal as an emblem of assumed social changes for the worse, as writers had a century before. H.Mannheim, for example, in his influential study of *Crime Between the Wars* (1940), was still presenting crime as an effect on the working classes of deplored changes in communal and work relations, consumer expectations and affluence, the extension of welfarism to the undeserving, the economic and sexual freedoms of women and the young, and of urban alienation – in short, as an effect of 'the decay of moral values'. Thus 'crime' was still a metaphor for 'change'. It was still, as by axiom, located among the under-classes. Old issues still worried people. Only the language got fancier.

## Crime and its modern meanings: 'order'

Early nineteenth century thinking about crime became entangled in a second set of associations, clustering around the ever more insistent social value of 'order'.[8] Established hierarchical relationships were perceived to be under chronic threat. The populace was expanding, increasingly insubordinate, unshackled from rural controls, and politically opinionated. Accordingly, in political and journalistic rhetoric, and in common usage too, the old Whig notion that the proper end of civil society was the defence of natural liberty against the despot was slowly eclipsed by the assumption that order was a sufficient social value in terms of which the legitimacy of policy might be assessed. It became less thinkable that the law-breaker should be pursued largely for the offence he delivered to his victim. However trivial in real terms his depredations might be, the law-breaker was now also to be pursued for the offence he delivered to 'society', as one of the 'enemies within' whom the mass society engendered, a threat to social order itself. This shift gave the nineteenth century state the ideological sanction to take unambiguous charge of the law-breaker's containment.

Law-enforced order had been a component of the eighteenth century moral universe. When has it not been? In the 1760s, the Whig jurist William Blackstone had quoted Locke axiomatically: 'where there is no law, there is no freedom'. Nonetheless, liberty remained the primary value in mid-eighteenth-century Whig ideology, even if property was both its guarantor and justification. For Blackstone, liberty was rooted in natural rights: 'the principal aim of society is to protect individuals in the enjoyment of those absolute rights, which were vested in them by the immutable laws of nature. . . . The first and primary end of human law is to maintain and regulate these absolute rights of individuals.' Every man, on entering society, necessarily surrendered part of his natural liberty; but he retained political or civil liberty, which was 'coeval with our form of government'. It was, moreover, only to ensure the 'grand ends of civil society, the peace and security of individuals' that the legislature ensured that 'to everything capable of ownership a legal and determinate owner' was assigned.[9]

To lament the progressive dilution of this ideology would be to lament the passing of a bucolic idyll which never existed. In the eighteenth century, 'liberty' was not meant to accrue to those who lacked property. All that the language of liberty entailed was a defence against the threat to elite interests delivered by the despotic, central state; property was always the reference point. Property remained the reference point in the nineteenth century ('order', indeed, was only a Victorian euphemism for it). But in the nineteenth century there was a change: a greater threat to elites came to be discerned not in the state, as hitherto, but in the urban working classes. Against that plebeian threat, the state could now plausibly be represented as property's bastion and ally. The result was assured. The old language of liberty and natural rights had been anti-statist in its rationale. As that rationale became less self-evident, executive authority could be massively extended. The state itself gradually became the implicit source of rights, for it could fairly claim that rights were conditional on the order which it alone had the resources to protect.

One early indication of the shift – even in Whig discourse – was the lament of the Royal Commission on the Criminal Law in 1839 that rights were susceptible of wide and expediential definition; their 'natural' basis was, in short, no longer self-evident. The commissioners resorted instead to Beccarian and Benthamite certainties. 'A scale of crimes may be found, of which the first degree should consist of those which immediately tend to the dissolution of society, and the last, of the smallest possible injustice done to a private member of society.' As its fifth report put it in 1840: 'It is manifest that all specific laws for the security of persons or property would be unavailing, unless the due operation of such laws were protected by imposing efficient restraints upon forcible violations of public order.' The protection not of natural rights but of social and political order – equated with the state itself – was elevated into law's primary objective.[10]

Police campaigners were also saying that the principle of liberty was a mere derivative of the principle of order: liberty was what was left over when order was guaranteed. In this spirit, Edwin Chadwick campaigned for a national and centralized police force by offering the public a fair exchange: liberty diminished, but security gained. After marshalling a highly alarmist case to establish the extent of contemporary disorders and criminality, the 1839 Royal Commission on the County Constabulary put it as follows. It admitted that centralized policing might diminish the liberty of the subject. It insisted none the less that 'the [criminal] evils we have found in existence in some districts, and the abject subjection of the population to fears [of crime] which might be termed a state of slavery . . . form a condition much worse in all respects than any condition that could be imposed by any government that could exist in the present state of society in this country'.[11] Fears that the state might erode liberty were supernumerary when the greatest threat to liberty could now be defined as the criminal disorder of the plebeian mass.

In modern times the appeal of this formulation was and has remained a compelling one, for citizens and governments alike. By the later nineteenth century, indeed, 'new' liberal politicians and a managerial civil service were even beginning to make clear what in Chadwick's day could only be put circumspectly: that the primary source of rights was in fact the state itself. As Haldane put it in 1896, Liberals' must be willing and desirous to assign *a new meaning to liberty*; it must no longer signify the absence of restraint, but the presence of opportunity'. The state, in short, should ever more actively intervene, extending rights (or opportunities) to the deserving or withholding them from the undeserving in the interests of stabilizing society.[12] Mill's fear that 'a tendency towards over-government' would be at the cost of liberty was coming closer to fulfilment. And the ideological structures in which debate about crime had to be located were now irretrievably established.

## Notes

1 D. Hay, 'Property, authority and the criminal law', in D. Hay, P. Linebaugh and E.P. Thompson (eds), *Albion's Fatal Tree: Crime and Society in Eighteenth-Century England*. (London, Allen Lane, 1975); P. King, 'Decision-making and decision-makers in the English criminal law, 1750–1800', *Historical Journal*, 27 (1984), pp. 25–58. See J.A. Sharpe *Crime in Early Modern England, 1550–1750* (London, Edward Arnold, 1984), and J.M. Beattie, *Crime and the Courts in England, 1660–1800* (Oxford, Clarendon Press, 1986), for a general guide.

2 G.R. Elton, 'Introduction', in J.S. Cockburn (ed.), *Crime in England, 1550–1800* (London, Methuen, 1977).

3 M. Ignatieff, *A Just Measure of Pain: the Penitentiary in the Industrial Revolution, 1750–1850* (London, Macmillan, 1979); D. Philips, '"A New Engine of Power and Authority": the Institutionalization of law-enforcement in England, 1780–1830', in V.A.C. Gatrell, B. Lenman and G. Parker, (eds), *Crime and the Law: the Social History of Crime in Western Europe since 1500* (London, Europa, 1980).

4 J.S. Mill, 'The spirit of the age' (1831), in G.L. Williams (ed.), *Mill on Politics and Society* (Brighton, Harvester, 1976), p. 171.

5 D. Hay, 'Manufacturers and the criminal law in the later eighteenth century: crime and "police" in South Staffordshire'. (Unpublished paper, *Past & Present* colloquium (Oxford, 1983); J. Styles, 'Embezzlement, industry and law in England, 1550–1980', in M. Berg et al. (eds), *Manufacture in Town and Country before the Factory* (Cambridge, Cambridge University Press, 1984).

6 *SC on the State of the Police of the Metropolis*, 3rd Report, PP 1818, VIII, p. 34; *RC on the County Constabulary*, PP 1839, XIX, p. 181.

7 *Report from the Department Committee on Prisons*, PP 1895, LVI, 99.10,968–72.9083. For a general introduction to Victorian ideologies of crime, see Sir L. Radzinowicz and R. Hood, *A History of English Criminal Law*, vol. 5: *The Emergence of Penal Policy* (London, Stevens, 1986), Part 1.

8 A. Silver, 'The demand for order in civil society: a review of some themes in the history of urban crime, police and riot', in D. Bordua (ed.), *The Police: Six Sociological Essays* (New York, Wiley, 1967).

9 William Blackstone, *Commentaries on the Laws of England* (Oxford, Clarendon Press, 1765–9), Book I, ch. 4.

10 *RC on the Criminal Law*, 4th Report, PP 1839, XIX, p. vii; 5th Report, PP 1840, XX, p. 90.

11 *RC County Constabulary*, 1839, pp. 184–5.

12 *Progressive Review*, 1 (1896), p. 4, cited in R. Kamm, 'The Home Office, public order and civil liberties, 1880–1914'. Unpublished PhD dissertation (Cambridge University, 1986), in which there is a full discussion of this general theme.

# 35

# The carceral

## Michel Foucault

[. . .] [I]n penal justice, the prison transformed the punitive procedure into a penitentiary technique; the carceral archipelago transported this technique from the penal institution to the entire social body. With several important results.

1   This vast mechanism established a slow, continuous, imperceptible gradation that made it possible to pass naturally from disorder to offence and back from a transgression of the law to a slight departure from a rule, an average, a demand, a norm. In the classical period, despite a certain common reference to offence in general, the order of the crime, the order of sin and the order of bad conduct remained separate in so far as they related to separate criteria and authorities (court, penitence, confinement). Incarceration with its mechanisms of surveillance and punishment functioned, on the contrary, according to a principle of relative continuity. The continuity of the institutions themselves, which were linked to one another (public assistance with the orphanage, the reformatory, the penitentiary, the disciplinary battalion, the prison; the school with the charitable society, the workshop, the almshouse, the penitentiary convent; the workers' estate with the hospital and the prison). A continuity of the punitive criteria and mechanisms, which on the basis of a mere deviation gradually strengthened the rules and increased the punishment. A continuous gradation of the established, specialized and competent authorities (in the order of knowledge and in the order of power) which, without resort to arbitrariness, but strictly according to the regulations, by means of observation and assessment hierarchized, differentiated, judged, punished and moved gradually from the correction of irregularities to the punishment of crime. The 'carceral' with its many diffuse or compact forms, its institutions of supervision or constraint, of discreet surveillance and insistent coercion, assured the communication of punishments according to quality and quantity; it connected in series or disposed according to subtle divisions the minor and the serious penalties, the mild and the strict forms of treatment, bad marks and light sentences. You will end up in the convict-ship, the slightest indiscipline seems to say; and the harshest of prisons says to the prisoners condemned to life: I shall note the slightest irregularity in your conduct. The generality of the punitive function that the eighteenth century sought in the 'ideological' technique of representations and signs now had as its support the extension, the material framework, complex, dispersed,but coherent, of the various carceral mechanisms. As a result, a certain significant generality moved between the least irregularity and the greatest crime; it was

Abridged from *Discipline and Punish* (trans. Alan Sheridan), pp. 298–308. (London: Allen Lane, 1977.)

no longer the offence, the attack on the common interest, it was the departure from the norm, the anomaly; it was this that haunted the school, the court, the asylum or the prison. It generalized in the sphere of meaning the function that the carceral generalized in the sphere of tactics. Replacing the adversary of the sovereign, the social enemy was transformed into a deviant, who brought with him the multiple danger of disorder, crime and madness. The carceral network linked, through innumerable relations, the two long, multiple series of the punitive and the abnormal.

2   The carceral, with its far-reaching networks, allows the recruitment of major 'delinquents'. It organizes what might be called 'disciplinary careers' in which, through various exclusions and rejections, a whole process is set in motion. In the classical period, there opened up in the confines or interstices of society the confused, tolerant and dangerous domain of the 'outlaw' or at least of that which eluded the direct hold of power: an uncertain space that was for criminality a training ground and a region of refuge; there poverty, unemployment, pursued innocence, cunning, the struggle against the powerful, the refusal of obligations and laws, and organized crime all came together as chance and fortune would dictate; it was the domain of adventure that Gil Blas, Sheppard or Mandrin, each in his own way, inhabited. Through the play of disciplinary differentiations and divisions, the nineteenth century constructed rigorous channels which, within the system, inculcated docility and produced delinquency by the same mechanisms. There was a sort of disciplinary 'training', continuous and compelling, that had something of the pedagogical curriculum and something of the professional network. Careers emerged from it, as secure, as predictable, as those of public life: assistance associations, residential apprenticeships, penal colonies, disciplinary battalions, prisons, hospitals, almshouses. These networks were already well mapped out at the beginning of the nineteenth century:

> Our benevolent establishments present an admirably coordinated whole by means of which the indigent does not remain a moment without help from the cradle to the grave. Follow the course of the unfortunate man: you will see him born among foundlings; from there he passes to the nursery, then to an orphanage; at the age of six he goes off to primary school and later to adult schools. If he cannot work, he is placed on the list of the charity offices of his district, and if he falls ill he may choose between twelve hospitals . . . Lastly, when the poor Parisian reaches the end of his career, seven almshouses await his age and often their salubrious régime has prolonged his useless days well beyond those of the rich man. (Moreau de Jonnès, quoted in Touquet)

The carceral network does not cast the unassimilable into a confused hell; there is no outside. It takes back with one hand what it seems to exclude with the other. It saves everything, including what it punishes. It is unwilling to waste even what it has decided to disqualify. In this panoptic society of which incarceration is the omnipresent armature, the delinquent is not outside the law; he is, from the very outset, in the law, at the very heart of the law, or at least in the midst of those mechanisms that transfer the individual imperceptibly from discipline to the law, from deviation to offence. Although it is true that prison punishes delinquency, delinquency is for the most part produced in and by an incarceration which, ultimately, prison perpetuates in its turn. The prison is merely the natural consequence, no more than a higher degree, of that hierarchy laid down step by step. The delinquent is an institutional product. It is no use being surprised, therefore, that in a considerable proportion of cases the biography of convicts passes through all these mechanisms and establishments, whose purpose, it is widely believed, is to lead away from prison. That one should find in them what one might call the index of an irrepressibly delinquent 'character': the prisoner condemned to hard labour was meticulously produced by a childhood spent in a reformatory, according to the lines of force of the generalized carceral system. Conversely, the lyricism of marginality may find inspiration in the image of the 'outlaw', the great social nomad, who prowls on the confines of a docile, frightened order. But it is not on the fringes of society and through successive exiles that criminality is born, but by means of ever more closely placed insertions, under ever more insistent surveillance, by an accumulation of disciplinary coercion. In short, the carceral archipelago assures, in the depths of the social body, the formation of delinquency on the basis of subtle illegalities, the overlapping of the latter by the former and the establishment of a specified criminality.

3   But perhaps the most important effect of the carceral system and of its extension well beyond legal imprisonment is that it succeeds in making the power to punish natural and legitimate, in lowering at least the threshold of tolerance to penality. It tends to efface what may be exorbitant in the exercise of punishment. It does this by playing the two registers in which it is deployed – the legal register of justice and the extra-legal register of discipline – against one another. In effect, the great continuity of the carceral system throughout the law and its sentences gives a sort of legal sanction to the disciplinary mechanisms, to the decisions and judgements that they enforce. Throughout this network, which comprises so many 'regional' institutions, relatively autonomous and independent, is transmitted, with the 'prison-form', the model of justice itself. The regulations of the disciplinary establishments may reproduce the law, the punishments imitate the verdicts and penalties, the surveillance repeat the police model; and, above all these multiple establishments, the prison, which in relation to them is a pure form, unadulterated and unmitigated, gives them a sort of official sanction. The carceral, with its long gradation stretching from the convictship or imprisonment with hard labour to diffuse, slight limitations, communicates a type of power that the law validates and that justice uses as its favourite weapon. How could the disciplines and the power that functions in them appear arbitrary, when they merely operate the mechanisms of justice itself, even with a view to mitigating their intensity? When, by generalizing its effects and transmitting it to every level, it makes it possible to avoid its full rigour? Carceral continuity and the fusion of the prison-form make it possible to legalize, or in any case to legitimate disciplinary power, which thus avoids any element of excess or abuse it may entail.

But, conversely, the carceral pyramid gives to the power to inflict legal punishment a context in which it appears to be free of all excess and all violence. In the subtle gradation of the apparatuses of discipline and of the successive 'embeddings' that they involve, the prison does not at all represent the unleashing of a different kind of power, but simply an additional degree in the intensity of a mechanism that has continued to operate since the earliest forms of legal punishment. Between the latest institution of 'rehabilitation', where one is taken in order to avoid prison, and the prison where one is sent after a definable offence, the difference is (and must be) scarcely perceptible. There is a strict economy that has the effect of rendering as discreet as possible the singular power to punish. There is nothing in it now that recalls the former excess of sovereign power when it revenged its authority on the tortured body of those about to be executed. Prison continues, on those who are entrusted to it, a work begun elsewhere, which the whole of society pursues on each individual through innumerable mechanisms of discipline. By means of a carceral continuum, the authority that sentences infiltrates all those other authorities that supervise, transform, correct, improve. It might even be said that nothing really distinguishes them any more except the singularly 'dangerous' character of the delinquents, the gravity of their departures from normal behaviour and the necessary solemnity of the ritual. But, in its function, the power to punish is not essentially different from that of curing or educating. It receives from them, and from their lesser, smaller task, a sanction from below; but one that is no less important for that, since it is the sanction of technique and rationality. The carceral 'naturalizes' the legal power to punish, as it 'legalizes' the technical power to discipline. In thus homogenizing them, effacing what may be violent in one and arbitrary in the other, attenuating the effects of revolt that they may both arouse, thus depriving excess in either of any purpose, circulating the same calculated, mechanical and discreet methods from one to the other, the carceral makes it possible to carry out that great 'economy' of power whose formula the eighteenth century had sought, when the problem of the accumulation and useful administration of men first emerged.

By operating at every level of the social body and by mingling ceaselessly the art of rectifying and the right to punish, the universality of the carceral lowers the level from which it becomes natural and acceptable to be punished. The question is often posed as to how, before and after the Revolution, a new foundation was given to the right to punish. And no doubt the answer is to be found in the theory of the contract. But it is perhaps more important to ask the reverse question: how were people made to accept the power to punish, or quite simply, when punished, tolerate being so. The theory of the contract can only answer this question by the fiction of a juridical subject giving to others the power to exercise over him the right that he himself possesses over them. It is highly probable that the great carceral continuum, which provides a communication between the power of discipline and the power of the law, and extends without interruption from the smallest coercions to the longest penal detention, constituted the technical and real, immediately material counterpart of that chimerical granting of the right to punish.

4   With this new economy of power, the carceral system, which is its basic instrument, permitted the emergence of a new form of 'law': a mixture of legality and nature, prescription and constitution, the norm. This had a whole series of effects: the internal dislocation of the judicial power or at least of its functioning; an increasing difficulty in judging, as if one were ashamed to pass sentence; a furious desire on the part of the judges to judge, assess, diagnose, recognize the normal and abnormal and claim the honour of curing or rehabilitating. In view of this, it is useless to believe in the good or bad consciences of judges, or even of their unconscious. Their immense 'appetite for medicine' which is constantly manifested – from their appeal to psychiatric experts, to their attention to the chatter of criminology – expresses the major fact that the power they exercise has been 'denatured'; that it is at a certain level governed by laws; that at another, more fundamental level it

functions as a normative power; it is the economy of power that they exercise, and not that of their scruples or their humanism, that makes them pass 'therapeutic' sentences and recommend 'rehabilitating' periods of imprisonment. But, conversely, if the judges accept ever more reluctantly to condemn for the sake of condemning, the activity of judging has increased precisely to the extent that the normalizing power has spread. Borne along by the omnipresence of the mechanisms of discipline, basing itself on all the carceral apparatuses, it has become one of the major functions of our society. The judges of normality are present everywhere. We are in the society of the teacher–judge, the doctor–judge, the educator–judge, the 'social worker'–judge; it is on them that the universal reign of the normative is based; and each individual, wherever he may find himself, subjects to it his body, his gestures, his behaviour, his aptitudes, his achievements. The carceral network, in its compact or disseminated forms, with its systems of insertion, distribution, surveillance, observation, has been the greatest support, in modern society, of the normalizing power.

5   The carceral texture of society assures both the real capture of the body and its perpetual observation; it is, by its very nature, the apparatus of punishment that conforms most completely to the new economy of power and the instrument for the formation of knowledge that this very economy needs. Its panoptic functioning enables it to play this double role. By virtue of its methods of fixing, dividing, recording, it has been one of the simplest, crudest, also most concrete, but perhaps most indispensable conditions for the development of this immense activity of examination that has objectified human behaviour. If, after the age of 'inquisitorial' justice, we have entered the age of 'examinatory' justice, if, in an even more general way, the method of examination has been able to spread so widely throughout society, and to give rise in part to the sciences of man, one of the great instruments for this has been the multiplicity and close overlapping of the various mechanisms of incarceration. I am not saying that the human sciences emerged from the prison. But, if they have been able to be formed and to produce so many profound changes in the episteme, it is because they have been conveyed by a specific and new modality of power: a certain policy of the body, a certain way of rendering the group of men docile and useful. This policy required the involvement of definite relations of knowledge in relations of power; it called for a technique of overlapping subjection and objectification; it brought with it new procedures of individualization. The carceral network constituted one of the armatures of this power–knowledge that has made the human sciences historically possible. Knowable man (soul, individuality, consciousness, conduct, whatever it is called) is the object–effect of this analytical investment, of this domination–observation.

6   This no doubt explains the extreme solidity of the prison, that slight invention that was nevertheless decried from the outset. If it had been no more than an instrument of rejection or repression in the service of a state apparatus, it would have been easier to alter its more overt forms or to find a more acceptable substitute for it. But, rooted as it was in mechanisms and strategies of power, it could meet any attempt to transform it with a great force of inertia. One fact is characteristic: when it is a question of altering the system of imprisonment, opposition does not come from the judicial institutions alone; resistance is to be found not in the prison as penal sanction, but in the prison with all its determinations, links and extra-judicial results; in the

prison as the relay in a general network of disciplines and surveillances; in the prison as it functions in a panoptic regime. This does not mean that it cannot be altered, nor that it is once and for all indispensable to our kind of society. One may, on the contrary, cite the two processes which, in the very continuity of the processes that make the prison function, are capable of exercising considerable restraint on its use and of transforming its internal functioning. And no doubt these processes have already begun to a large degree. The first is that which reduces the utility (or increases its inconveniences) of a delinquency accommodated as a specific illegality, locked up and supervised; thus the growth of great national or international illegalities directly linked to the political and economic apparatuses (financial illegalities, information services, arms and drugs trafficking, property speculation) makes it clear that the somewhat rustic and conspicuous work force of delinquency is proving ineffective; or again, on a smaller scale, as soon as the economic levy on sexual pleasure is carried out more efficiently by the sale of contraceptives, or obliquely through publications, films or shows, the archaic hierarchy of prostitution loses much of its former usefulness. The second process is the growth of the disciplinary networks, the multiplication of their exchanges with the penal apparatus, the ever more important powers that are given them, the ever more massive transference to them of judicial functions; now, as medicine, psychology, education, public assistance, 'social work' assume an ever greater share of the powers of supervision and assessment, the penal apparatus will be able, in turn, to become medicalized, psychologized, educationalized; and by the same token that turning-point represented by the prison becomes less useful when, through the gap between its penitentiary discourse and its effect of consolidating delinquency, it articulates the penal power and the disciplinary power. In the midst of all these mechanisms of normalization, which are becoming ever more rigorous in their application, the specificity of the prison and its role as link are losing something of their purpose.

If there is an overall political issue around the prison, it is not therefore whether it is to be corrective or not; whether the judges, the psychiatrists or the sociologists are to exercise more power in it than the administrators or supervisors; it is not even whether we should have prison or something other than prison. At present, the problem lies rather in the steep rise in the use of these mechanisms of normalization and the wide-ranging powers which, through the proliferation of new disciplines, they bring with them. In 1836, a correspondent wrote to *La Phalange*:

Moralists, philosophers, legislators, flatterers of civilization, this is the plan of your Paris, neatly ordered and arranged, here is the improved plan in which all like things are gathered together. At the centre, and within a first enclosure: hospitals for all diseases, almshouses for all types of poverty, madhouses, prisons, convict-prisons for men, women and children. Around the first enclosure, barracks, court-rooms, police stations, houses for prison warders, scaffolds, houses for the executioner and his assistants. At the four corners, the Chamber of Deputies, the Chamber of Peers, the Institute and the Royal Palace. Outside, there are the various services that supply the central enclosure, commerce, with its swindlers and its bankruptcies; industry and its furious struggles; the press, with its sophisms; the gambling dens; prostitution, the people dying of hunger or wallowing in debauchery, always ready to lend an ear to the voice of the Genius of Revolutions; the heartless rich . . . Lastly the ruthless war of all against all. (*La Phalange*, 10 August 1836)

I shall stop with this anonymous text. We are now far away from the country of tortures, dotted with wheels, gibbets, gallows, pillories; we are far, too, from that dream of the reformers, less than fifty years before: the city of punishments in which a thousand small theatres would have provided an endless multicoloured representation of justice in which the punishments, meticulously produced on decorative scaffolds, would have constituted the permanent festival of the penal code. The carceral city, with its imaginary 'geo-politics', is governed by quite different principles. The extract from *La Phalange* reminds us of some of the more important ones: that at the centre of this city, and as if to hold it in place, there is, not the 'centre of power', not a network of forces, but a multiple network of diverse elements - walls, space, institution, rules, discourse; that the model of the carceral city is not, therefore, the body of the king, with the powers that emanate from it, nor the contractual meeting of wills from which a body that was both individual and collective was born, but a strategic distribution of elements of different natures and levels. That the prison is not the daughter of laws, codes or the judicial apparatus; that it is not subordinated to the court and the docile or clumsy instrument of the sentences that it hands out and of the results that it would like to achieve; that it is the court that is external and subordinate to the prison. That in the central position that it occupies, it is not alone, but linked to a whole series of 'carceral' mechanisms which seem distinct enough - since they are intended to alleviate pain, to cure, to comfort - but which all tend, like the prison, to exercise a power of normalization. That these mechanisms are applied not to transgressions against a 'central' law, but to the apparatus of production - 'commerce' and 'industry' - to a whole multiplicity of illegalities, in all their diversity of nature and origin, their specific role in profit and the different ways in which they are dealt with by the punitive mechanisms. And that ultimately what presides over all these mechanisms is not the unitary functioning of an apparatus or an institution, but the necessity of combat and the rules of strategy. That, consequently, the notions of institutions of repression, rejection, exclusion, marginalization, are not adequate to describe, at the very centre of the carceral city, the formation of the insidious leniencies, unavowable petty cruelties, small acts of cunning, calculated methods, techniques, 'sciences' that permit the fabrication of the disciplinary individual. In this central and centralized humanity, the effect and instrument of complex power relations, bodies and forces subjected by multiple mechanisms of 'incarceration', objects for discourses that are in themselves elements for this strategy, we must hear the distant roar of battle.

[. . .]

# 36

# The punitive city

## Stanley Cohen

[. . .]

## From prison to community

Our current system of deviancy control originated in those great transformations which took place from the end of the eighteenth to the beginning
of the nineteenth centuries: first the development of a centralized state
apparatus for the control of crime and the care of dependency, secondly the
increasing differentiation of the deviant and dependent into separate types
each with its own attendant corpus of 'scientific' knowledge and accredited
experts; and finally the increased segregation of deviants and dependents into
'asylums', mental hospitals, prisons, reformatories and other such closed,
purpose-built institutions for treatment and punishment. The theorists of these
transformations each place a somewhat different emphasis on just what
happened and just why it happened, but all are agreed on its essentials.[1]

The most extraordinary of these three features to explain – the other two
being, in a sense, self-evident in the development of the modern state – is the
growth of the asylum and its subsequent survival despite one and a half
centuries of failure. Any account of the current and future place of incarceration must come to terms with that original historical transformation.[2]

We are now living through what *appears* to be a reversal of this first Great
Transformation. The ideological consensus about the desirability and necessity
of the segregative asylum – questioned before but never really undermined[3] –
has been broken. The attack on prisons (and more dramatically and with more
obvious results on mental hospitals) became widespread from the mid-1960s,
was found throughout the political spectrum and was partially reflected in
such indices as declining rates of imprisonment. At the end of the eighteenth
century, asylums and prisons were places of the *last* resort; by the mid-
nineteenth century they became places of the *first* resort, the preferred
solution to problems of deviancy and dependency. By the end of the 1960s
they looked like once again becoming places of the *last* resort. The
extraordinary notion of abolition rather than mere reform became common
talk. With varying degrees of enthusiasm and actual measurable consequences, officials in Britain, the United States and some Western European
countries, became committed to the policy labelled 'decarceration': the state-
sponsored closing down of asylums, prisons and reformatories. This apparent

Abridged from 'The punitive city: notes on the dispersal of social control', *Contemporary
Crises*, 1979, 3(4): 341–63.

reversal of the Great Incarcerations of the nineteenth century was hailed as the beginning of a golden age – a form of utopianism whose ironies cannot escape anyone with an eye on history: 'There is a curious historical irony here, for the *adoption* of the asylum, whose *abolition* is now supposed to be attended with such universally beneficent consequences, aroused an almost precisely parallel set of millenial expectations among its advocates'.[4]

The irony goes even further. For just at the historical moment when every commonplace critique of 'technological' or 'post-industrial' or 'mass' society mourned the irreplaceable loss of the traditional *Gemeinschaft* community, so a new mode of deviancy control was advocated whose success rested on this very same notion of community. Indeed the decarceration movement derives its rhetoric from a much wider constituency than is implied by limited questions of how far should imprisonment be used. It touches on issues about centralization, professionalization, the rehabilitative ideal and the limits of state intervention. The current (variously labelled) 'pessimism', 'scepticism', or 'nihilism' about prisons, draws on all these wider themes.[5]

In the literature on community treatment itself,[6] two sets of assumptions are repeated with the regularity of a religious catechism. The first set is seen either as a matter of common sense, 'what everybody knows' or the irrefutable result of empirical research: (1) prisons and juvenile institutions are (in the weak version) simply ineffective – they neither successfully deter nor rehabilitate: in the strong version, they actually make things worse by strengthening criminal commitment; (2) community alternatives are much less costly and (3) they are more humane than any institution can be – prisons are cruel, brutalizing and beyond reform. Their time has come. Therefore: community alternatives 'must obviously be better', 'should at least be given a chance' or 'can't be worse'.

The second set of assumptions appeal to a number of sociological and political beliefs not as self-evident as the previous set, but taken by the believer to be just as well established: (1) theories of stigma and labelling have demonstrated that the further the deviant is processed into the system, the harder it is to return him to normal life – 'therefore' measures designed to minimize penetration into the formal system and keep the deviant in the community as long as possible are desirable; (2) the causal processes leading to most forms of deviance originate in society (family, community, school, economic system) – 'therefore' prevention and cure must lie in the community and not in artificially created agencies constructed on a model of individual intervention; (3) liberal measures, such as reformatories, the juvenile court and the whole rehabilitative model are politically suspect, whatever the benevolent motives which lie behind them. The state should be committed to be doing less harm rather than more good – 'therefore' policies such as decriminalization, diversion and decarceration should be supported.

It is the last of these beliefs which must be used to scrutinize them all – for why should community corrections itself not be subjected to the very same suspicion about benevolent reform? A large dose of such scepticism, together with a much firmer location of the new movement in overall structural and political changes, is needed for a full scale critique of community corrections. Such a critique – not the object of this paper – would have to note at least the following doubts:[7] (1) it is by no means clear, in regard to crime and delinquency at least, that decarceration has been taking place as rapidly as the ideology would have us believe; (2) it has not been established that any community alternative is more effective in reducing crime (through preventing recidivism) than traditional imprisonment; (3) nor are these new methods always dramatically cheaper; and (4) the humanitarian rationale for the move from imprisonment may be unfounded for two (opposite) reasons: (a) decarceration may indeed lead to something like non-intervention or benign neglect: services are withdrawn and deviants are left neglected or exploited by private operators: (b) alternatively, new forms of intervention result, which are often difficult to distinguish from the old institutions and reproduce in the community the very same coercive features of the system they were designed to replace.

However cogent this emergent critique might be, though, it comes from the margins of contemporary 'corrections'. Perhaps more than in any other area of social policy, crime and delinquency control has always allowed such doubts to be neutralized in the tidal wave of enthusiasm for any new 'reform'. There is little doubt that the rhetoric and ideology of community control is quite secure. And – whatever may be happening to overall rates of incarceration – most industrialized countries will continue to see a proliferation of various schemes in line with this ideology.

I shall take the term 'community control' to cover almost any form of formal social control outside the walls of traditional adult and juvenile institutions. There are two separate, but overlapping strategies: first, those various forms of intensive intervention located 'in the community': sentencing options which serve as intermediate alternatives to being sent to an institution or later options to release from institutions and, secondly, those programmes set up at some preventative, policing or pre-trial stage to divert offenders from initial or further processing by the conventional systems of justice. Behind these specific policies lies an overall commitment to almost anything which sounds like increasing community responsibility for the control of crime and delinquency.

## Blurring the boundaries

The segregated and insulated institution made the actual business of deviancy control invisible, but it did make its boundaries obvious enough. Whether prisons were built in the middle of cities, out in the remote countryside or on deserted islands, they had clear spatial boundaries to mark off the normal from the deviant. These spatial boundaries were reinforced by ceremonies of social exclusion. Those outside could wonder what went on behind the walls, those inside could think about the 'outside world'. Inside/outside, guilty/innocent, freedom/captivity, imprisoned/released – these were all meaningful distinctions.

In today's world of community corrections, these boundaries are no longer as clear. There is, we are told, a 'correctional continuum' or a 'correctional spectrum': criminals and delinquents might be found anywhere in these spaces. So fine – and at the same time so indistinct – are the gradations along the continuum, that it is by no means easy to answer such questions as where the prison ends and the community begins or just why any deviant is to be found at any particular point. Even the most dedicated spokesmen for the community treatment have some difficulty in specifying just what 'the community' is; one [official US] report confessed that the term community treatment: 'has lost all descriptive usefulness except as a code word with connotations of "advanced correctional thinking" and implied value judgements against the "locking up" and isolation of offenders'.[8]

Even the most cursory examination of the new programmes reveals that many varieties of the more or less intensive and structured 'alternatives' are virtually indistinguishable from the real thing. A great deal of energy and ingenuity is being devoted to this problem of definition: just how isolated and confining does an institution have to be before it is a prison rather than, say, a residential community facility? Luckily for us all, criminologists have got this matter well in hand and are spending a great deal of time and money on such questions. They are busy devising quantitative measures of indices such as degree of control, linkages, relationships, support – and we can soon look forward to standardized scales for assigning programmes along an institutionalization–normalization continuum.[9]

But, alas, there are not just untidy loose ends which scientific research will one day tie up. The ideology of the new movement quite deliberately and explicitly demands that boundaries should not be made too clear. The metaphor of 'crumbling walls' implies an undifferentiated open space. The main British prison reform group, the Howard League, once called for steps to 'restore the prison to the community and the community to the prison' and, less rhetorically, here is an early enthusiast for a model 'Community Correction Centre':

> The line between being 'locked up' and 'free' is purposely indistinct because it must be drawn differently for each individual. Once the client is out of Phase 1, where all clients enter and where they are all under essentially custodial control, he may be 'free' for some activities but still 'locked up' for others.[10]

There is no irony intended in using inverted commas for such words as 'free' and 'locked up' or in using such euphemisms as 'essentially custodial control'. This sort of blurring – deliberate or unintentional – may be found throughout the complicated networks of 'diversion' and 'alternatives' which are now being set up. The half-way house might serve as a good example. These agencies called variously, 'residential treatment centers', 'rehabilitation residences', 'reintegration centers' or (with the less flowery language preferred in Britain) simply 'hostels', invariably become special institutional domains themselves. They might be located in a whole range of odd settings – private houses, converted motels, the grounds of hospitals, the dormitories of university campuses or even within the walls of prisons themselves. Their programmes[11] reproduce rules – for example about security, curfew, permitted visitors, drugs – which are close to those of the institution itself. Indeed it becomes difficult to distinguish a very 'open' prison – with liberal provisions for work release, home release, outside educational programmes – from a very 'closed' half-way house. The house may be half-way *in* – for those too serious to be left at home, but not serious enough for the institution and hence a form of 'diversion' – or half-way *out* – for those who can be released from the institution but are not yet 'ready' for the open community, hence a form of 'after care'. To confuse the matter even further, the same centre is sometimes used for both these purposes, with different rules for the half-way in inmates and the half-way out inmates.

Even this blurring and confusion is not enough: one advocate[12] draws attention to the advantages of *quarter-way* houses and *three-quarter*-way houses. These 'concepts' we are told are already being used in the mental health field, but are not labelled as such in corrections. The quarter-way house deals with people who need supervision on a near permanent basis, while the three-quarter-way house is designed to care for persons in an 'acute temporary crisis needing short-term residential care and little supervision'. Then – taking the opposite tack from devising finer and finer classification schemes – other innovators argue for a multi-purpose centre: some half-way houses already serve as a parolee residence, a drop-in centre, a drug treatment programme and a non-residential walk-in centre for after-care.

The fact that many of these multi-purpose centres are directed not just at convicted offenders, but are preventative, diagnostic or screening enterprises aimed at potential, pre-delinquents, or high-risk populations, should alert us to the more important forms of blurring behind this administrative surrealism. The ideology of community treatment allows for a facile evasion of the delinquent/non-delinquent distinction. The British system of 'inter-mediate treatment' for example provides not just an intermediate possibility between sending the child away from home and leaving him in his normal home environment, but also a new way 'to make use of facilities available to children who have not been before the courts, and so to secure the treatment of "children in trouble" in the company of other children through the sharing of activities and experiences within the community'.[13] There is a deliberate attempt to evade the question of whether a rule has been actually broken. While the traditional screening mechanisms of the criminal justice system have always been influenced to a greater or lesser degree by non-offence related criteria (race, class, demeanour) the offence was at least considered. Except in the case of wrongful conviction, some law must have been broken. This is no longer clear: a delinquent may find himself in custody ('short term intensive treatment') simply because of programme failure: he has violated the norms of some other agency in the continuum – for example, by not turning up to his therapy group, 'acting out', or being uncooperative.

We are seeing, then, not just the proliferation of agencies and services, finely calibrated in terms of degree of coerciveness or intrusion or unpleasantness. The uncertainties are more profound than this: voluntary or coercive, formal or informal, locked up or free, guilty or innocent. Those apparently absurd administrative and research questions – when is a prison a prison or a community a community? is the alternative an alternative? who is half-way in and who is three-quarter-way out? – beckon to a future when it will be impossible to determine who exactly is enmeshed in the social control system – and hence subject to its jurisdiction and surveillance – at any one time.

### Thinning the mesh and widening the net

On the surface, a major ideological thrust in the move against institutions derives from a desire to limit state intervention. Whether arising from the supposed failures of the treatment model, or the legal argument about the over-reach of the law and the necessity to limit the criminal sanction, or the implicit non-interventionism of labelling theory, or a general disenchantment with paternalism, or simply the pragmatic case for easing the burdens on the system – the eventual message looked the same: the state should do less rather than more. It is ironical then – though surely the irony is too obvious even to be called this – that the major results of the new movements towards 'community' and 'diversion' have been to increase rather than decrease the *amount* of intervention directed at many groups of deviants in the system and, probably, to increase rather than decrease the total *number* who get into the system in the first place. In other words: 'alternatives' become not alternatives at all but new programmes which supplement the existing system or else expand it by attracting new populations.

I will refer to these two overlapping possibilities as 'thinning the mesh' and 'widening the net' respectively. No one who has studied the results of such historical innovations as probation and parole should be surprised by either of these effects. As Rothman, for example, comments about the early twentieth century impact of the psychiatric ideology on the criminal justice system: 'rationales and practices that initially promised to be less onerous nevertheless served to encourage the extension of state authority. The impact of the ideology was to expand intervention, not to restrict it'.[14]

The detailed processes through which the new community agencies are generating such expansion are not my concern here.[15] I will merely use the two strategies of 'alternatives' and 'diversion' to suggest how illusory is the notion that the new movement will lead to a lesser degree of formal social control.

Let us first examine community alternatives to incarceration. The key index of 'success' is not simply the proliferation of such programmes, but the question of whether they are replacing or merely providing supplementary appendages to the conventional system of incarceration. The statistical evidence is by no means easy to decipher but it is clear, both from Britain and America, that rates of incarceration – particularly in regard to juveniles – are not at all declining as rapidly as one might expect and in some spheres are even increasing. Critically – as one evaluation suggests,[16] the 'alternatives' are not, on the whole, being used for juveniles at the 'deep end' of the system, i.e. those who really would have been sent to institutions before. When the strategy is used for 'shallow end' offenders – minor or first offenders whose chances of incarceration would have been slight – then the incarceration rates will not be affected.

The exact proportions of these types are difficult to estimate: one English study of community service orders shows that only half the offenders sent would otherwise have received custodial sentences.[17] Leaving aside the question of the exact effects on the rest of the system, there is little doubt that a substantial number - perhaps the majority – of those subjected to the new programmes, will be subjected to a degree of intervention higher than they would have received under previous non-custodial options like fines, conditional discharge or ordinary probation.

What all this means is that as long as the shallow end principle is used and as long as institutions are not literally closed down (as in the much publicized Massachusetts example) there is no guarantee either that incarceration will decrease dramatically or that the system will be less interventionist overall. The conclusion of the [. . .] National Assessment of Juvenile Corrections holds true generally: although there are exceptions, 'in general as the number of community based facilities increases, the total number of youths incarcerated increases'.[18]

The paradox throughout all this is that the more benign, attractive and successful the programme is defined – especially if it uses the shallow end principle, as most do – the more it will be used and the wider it will cast its net:

> Developing and administering community programs can be a source of gratification to sincere correctional administrators and lay volunteers who believe they are 'doing good' by keeping people out of dungeons and helping them obtain social services. Judges, reluctant to send difficult children to a reformatory and equally reluctant to release them without an assurance that something will be done to prevent them from returning may be especially enthusiastic about the development of alternative dispositions.[19]

Turning now to the more explicit forms of diversion, it is once again clear that the term, like the term 'alternatives', is not quite what it implies. Diversion has been hailed as the most radical application of the non-intervention principle short of complete decriminalization. The grand rationale is to restrict the full force of the criminal justice process to more serious offences and to either eliminate or substantially minimize penetration for all others.[20] The strategy has received the greatest attention in the juvenile field: a remarkable development, because the central agency here, the juvenile courts, was *itself* the product of a reform movement aimed at 'diversion'.

Clearly, all justice systems – particularly juvenile – have always contained a substantial amount of diversion. Police discretion has been widely used to screen juveniles: either right out of the system by dropping charges, informally reprimanding or cautioning, or else informal referral to social services agencies. What has now happened, to a large degree, is that these discretionary and screening powers have been formalized and extended – and in the process, quite transformed. The net widens to include those who, if the programme had not been available would either not have been processed at all or would have been placed on options such as traditional probation. Again, the more benevolent the new agencies appear, the more will be diverted there by encouragement or coercion. And – through the blurring provided by the welfare net – this will happen to many not officially adjudicated as delinquent as well. There will be great pressure to work with parts of the population not previously 'reached'.

All this can be most clearly observed in the area of police diversion of juveniles. Where the police used to have two options – screen right out (the route for by far the *majority* of encounters) or process formally – they now have the third option of diversion into a programme. Diversion can then be used as an alternative to screening and not an alternative to processing.[21] The proportion selected will vary. British research on police juvenile liaison schemes and similar measures[22] shows a clear widening of the net and one survey of eleven Californian diversion projects suggests that only 51 per cent of clients were actually diverted from the system, with the rest receiving more processing than they would have received otherwise.[23] Another evaluation of thirty-five police departments running diversion programmes concludes:

> the meaning of 'diversion' has been shifted from 'diversion from' to 'referral to'. Ironically, one of the ramifications of this is that in contrast to some earlier cited rationales for diversion as reducing costs, caseload and the purview of the criminal justice system, diversion may in fact be extending the costs, caseload and system purview even further than had previously been the case.[24]

The key to understanding this state of affairs lies in the distinction between *traditional* or *true* diversion – removing the juvenile from the system altogether by screening out (no further treatment, no service, no follow up) – and the *new* diversion which entails screening plus programme: formal penetration is minimized by referral to programmes in the system or related to it.[25] Only traditional diversion is true diversion in the sense of diverting *from*. The new diversion diverts – for better or worse – *into* the system. Cressey and McDermott's laconic conclusion from their evaluation of one such set of programmes might apply more generally:

> If 'true' diversion occurs, the juvenile is safely out of the official realm of the juvenile justice system and he is immune from incurring the delinquent label or any of its variations – pre-delinquent, delinquent tendencies, bad guy, hard core, unreachable. Further, when he walks out of the door from the person diverting him, he is technically free to tell the diverter to go to hell. We found very little 'true' diversion in the communities studied.[26]

To conclude [. . .]: whatever the eventual pattern of the emergent social control system, it should be clear that such policies as 'alternatives' in no way represent a victory for the anti-treatment lobby or an 'application' of labelling theory. Traditional deviant populations are being processed in a different way or else new populations are being caught up in the machine. For some observers[27] all this is an index of how good theory produces bad practice: each level diverts to the next and at each level vested interests (like job security) ensure that few are diverted right out. And so the justice machine enlarges itself. This looks 'successful' in terms of the machine's own operational definition of success, but is a failure when compared to the theory from which the policy (supposedly) was derived.

Be this as it may, the new movement – in the case of crime and delinquency at least – has led to a more voracious processing of deviant populations, albeit in new settings and by professionals with different names. The machine might in some respects be getting softer, but it is not getting smaller (and probably not more efficient – but that's another story).

### Masking and disguising

The softness of the machine might also be more apparent than real. It became commonplace in historical analyses to suggest that the more benign parts of the system such as the juvenile court[28] masked their most coercive intentions and consequences. This conclusion might apply with equal force to the current strategies of diversion and alternatives. Even more than their historical antecedents, they employ a social work rather than legalistic rationale; they are committed to the principle of blurring the boundaries of social control and they use the all-purpose slogan of 'community' which cannot but sound benign.

There can be little doubt that the intentions behind the new movement and – more to the point – its end results, are often humane, compassionate and helpful. Most clients, deviants or offenders would probably prefer this new variety to the stark option of the prison. But this argument is only valid if the alternatives are real ones. The net-thinning and mesh-widening effects, though, indicate that the notion of alternatives can be misleading and mystifying. Note, for example, the curious claim that agencies like half-way houses are justified because they are just as successful in preventing crime as direct release into the community. As Greenberg notes, however, when such alternatives are presented as a condition of release from prison, 'the contrast between the brutality of the prison and the alleged humanitarianism of community corrections is beside the point, because the community institution is not used to replace the prison; instead the offender is exposed to both the prison and the community "alternatives"'.[29]

Even when the alternatives *are* real ones, it is not self-evident that they are always more humane and less stigmatizing just because, in some sense they are 'in the community'. Community agencies, for example, might use a considerable amount of more or less traditional custody and often without legal justification. As the assessment of one experiment revealed:

> When subjects failed to comply with the norms of the intensive treatment regime, or even when a program agent believes subjects might fail to comply, then, as they say in the intensive treatment circles, detention may be indicated. Both these features, and the extensive use of home placements as well, suggest that the term 'community' like the term 'intensive treatment' may come to have a very special meaning in programs designed to deliver 'intensive treatment in the community'.[30]

Such disguised detention, though, is probably not a major overall source of masking. More important is the bureaucratic generation of new treatment criteria which might allow for more unchecked coercion than at first appears. In a system with low visibility and low accountability, there is less room for such niceties as due process and legal rights. Very often, for example, 'new diversion' (minimization of penetration) occurs by deliberately avoiding due process: the client proceeds through the system on the assumption or admission of guilt. Indeed the deliberate conceptual blurring between 'diversion' and 'prevention' explicitly calls for an increase in this sort of non-legal discretion.

All this, of course, still leaves open the question of whether the end result – however mystifying some of the routes that led to it – is actually experienced as more humane and helpful by the offender. There is little evidence either way on this, beyond the rather bland common sense assumption that most offenders would prefer not to be 'locked up'. What is likely, is that deep end projects – those that are genuine alternatives to incarceration – have to make a trade-off between treatment goals (which favour the integrated community setting) and security goals which favour isolation. The trade-off under these conditions will tend to favour security – resulting in programmes which stimulate or mimic the very features of the institution they set out to replace. [. . .]

## Absorption, penetration, re-integration

The asylum represented not just isolation and confinement – like quarantining the infected – but a ritual of physical exclusion. Without the possibility of actual banishment to another society, the asylum had to serve the classic social function of scapegoating. The scapegoat of ancient legend was an animal driven to the wilderness, bearing away the sins of the community.

In the new ideology of corrections, there is no real or symbolic wilderness – just the omnipresent community into which the deviant has to be unobtrusively 'integrated' or 'reintegrated'. The blurring of social control implies both the deeper penetration of social control into the social body and the

easing of any measures of exclusion, or status degradation. For the apologists
of the new corrections, the word 're-integration' has a magic ring. Thus
Empey[31] argues that we are in the middle of a third revolution in corrections:
the first from Revenge to Restraint (in the first part of the nineteenth century),
the second from Restraint to Reformation (from the late nineteenth to the
early twentieth century) – and now from Reformation to Re-integration.
Leaving aside the historical inaccuracy of this sequence, it does not actually
tell us what this new utopia will look like.

In the most immediate sense, what is being proposed is a greater direct
involvement of the family, the school and various community agencies in the
day to day business of prevention, treatment and resocialization. This implies
something more profound than simply using more volunteers or increasing
reporting rates. It implies some sort of reversal of the presumption in positivist
criminology that the delinquent is a different and alien being. Deviance rather
is with us, woven into the fabric of social life and it must be 'brought back
home'. Parents, peers, schools, the neighbourhood, even the police should
dedicate themselves to keeping the deviant out of the formal system. He must
be absorbed back into the community and not processed by official agencies.[32]

The central role allocated to the family – part of the broader movement of
the rediscovery of the family in sociology and social policy – is a good
example of the integration ideology. Well-established methods such as foster
care, substitute homes and family placements are being extended and one
enthusiast looks forward to 'the day when middle class American families
actually wanted in large numbers to bring juvenile and pre-delinquent youths
into their homes as a service commitment'.[33] The family having a delinquent
living with them is seen as a 'remarkable correctional resource' for the future.
In Britain and Scandinavia a number of alternative systems of family
placement besides salaried foster parents have been tried – for example
'together at home', the system of intensive help in Sweden in which social
workers spend hours sharing the family's life and tasks. Alongside these
diversionary alternatives, parents and schools are also encouraged to react
sooner to early signs of trouble.

Going beyond the family setting, the stress on community absorption has
found one of its most attractive possibilities in the system of community
service orders developed in England. Under this system, offenders are
sentenced to useful supervised work in the community: helping in geriatric
wards, driving disabled people around, painting and decorating the houses of
various handicapped groups, building children's playgrounds etc. This is a
particularly attractive scheme because it appeals not just to the soft ideology
of community absorption, but the more punitive objectives of restitution and
compensation. [. . .]

### Conclusion – towards the punitive city

These emerging patterns of social control – dispersal, penetration, blurring,
absorption, widening – must be seen as no more than patterns: representations or models of what is yet to be fully constructed. Historians of social
policy can use the emergent final system to validate their reading of such
early, tentative patterns; the student of contemporary policy has no such
luxury. The largest question mark must hang over the future role of the prison

itself in the total system. The rhetoric of community control is now unassailable, but it is not yet clear how *far* the prison will be supplemented and complemented by these new forms of control.

It is, eventually, the sheer proliferation and elaboration of these other systems of control – rather than the attack on prison itself – which impresses. What is happening is a literal reproduction on a wider societal level of those astonishingly complicated systems of classification – the 'atlases of vice' – inside the nineteenth century prison. New categories and sub-categories of deviance and control are being created under our eyes. All these agencies – legal and quasi-legal, administrative and professional – are marking out their own territories of jurisdiction, competence and referral. Each set of experts produces its own 'scientific' knowledge: screening devices, diagnostic tests, treatment modalities, evaluation scales. All this creates new categories and the typifications which fill them: where there was once talk about the 'typical' prisoner, first offender or hardened recidivist, now there will be typical 'clients' of half-way houses, or community correctional centres, typical divertees or predelinquents. These creatures are then fleshed out – in papers, research proposals, official reports – with sub-systems of knowledge and new vocabularies: locking up becomes 'intensive placement', dossiers become 'anecdotal records', rewards and punishments become 'behavioural contracts'.

The enterprise justifies itself: there is hardly any point in asking about 'success' – this is not the object of the exercise. Research is done on the classification system *itself* – working out a 'continuum of community basedness', prediction tables, screening devices – and one does not ask for a classification system to 'work'. In one massive American enterprise[34] some ten Federal agencies, thirty-one task forces and ninety-three experts got together simply to study the ways of classifying various problem groups of children.

The overwhelming impression is one of bustling, almost *frenzied* activity: all these wonderful new things are being done to this same old group of troublemakers (with a few new ones allowed in). It might not be too far fetched to imagine an urban ethnographer of the future, that proverbial Martian anthropologist studying a day in the life of this strange new tribe, filing in a report something like this:[35]

Mr and Mrs Citizen, their son Joe and daughter Linda, leave their suburban home after breakfast, saying goodbye to Ron, a fifteen-year-old pre-delinquent who is living with them under the LAK (Look After a Kid) scheme. Ron will later take a bus downtown to the Community Correctional Center, where he is to be given two hours of Vocational Guidance and later tested on the Interpersonal Maturity Level Scale. Mr C. drops Joe off at the School Problems Evaluation Center from where Joe will walk to school. In his class are five children who are bussed from a local Community Home, four from a Pre-Release Facility and three, who, like Ron live with families in the neighbourhood. Linda gets off next – at the GUIDE Center (Girls Unit for Intensive Daytime Education) where she works as a Behavioural Contract Mediator. They drive past a Three-quarter-way House, a Rape Crisis Center and then a Drug Addict Cottage, where Mrs C. waves to a group of boys working in the garden. She knows them from some volunteer work she does in RODEO (Reduction of Delinquency Through Expansion of Opportunities). She gets off at a building which houses the Special Intensive Parole Unit, where she is in charge of a five-year evaluation research project on the use of the HIM (Hill Interaction Matrix) in matching group treatment to client. Mr C. finally arrives at work, but will spend his lunch hour driving around the car again as this is his duty week on patrol with TIPS (Turn in a Pusher).

Meantime, back in the ghetto. . . .

The logic of this master pattern – dispersal, penetration, spreading out – as opposed to its particular current forms, is not at all new. Its antecedents can be traced though, not to the model which its apologists cite – the idyllic pre-industrial rural community – but to a somewhat later version of social control, a version which *in theory* was an alternative to the prison. When, from the end of the eighteenth century, punishment started entering deeper into the social body, the alternative vision to the previous great concentrated spectacles of public torture, was of the dispersal of control through 'hundreds of tiny theatres of punishment'.[36] The eighteenth century reformers dreamed of dispersal and diversity but this vision of the punitive city was never to be fully realized. Instead punishment became concentrated in the coercive institution, a single uniform penalty to be varied only in length. The earlier 'projects of docility' which Foucault describes – the techniques of order, discipline and regulation developed in schools, monasteries, workshops, the army – could only serve as models. Panopticism (surveillance, discipline) began to spread: as disciplinary establishments increased, 'their mechanisms have a certain tendency to become "de-institutionalized", to emerge from the closed fortresses in which they once functioned and to circulate in a "free" state; the massive compact disciplines are broken down into flexible methods of control, which may be transferred and adapted'.[37]

This principle of 'indefinite discipline' – judgements, examinations and observations which would never end – represented the new mode of control as much as the public execution had represented the old. Only in the prison, though, could this utopia be realized in a pure, physical form. The 'new' move into the community is merely a continuation of the overall pattern established in the nineteenth century. The proliferation of new experts and professionals, the generation of specialized domains of scientific knowledge, the creation of complicated classification systems, the establishment of a network of agencies surrounding the court and the prison – all these developments marked the beginning a century ago of the widening of the 'carceral circle' or 'carceral archipelago'.

The continuous gradation of institutions then – the 'correctional continuum' – is not new. What is new is the scale of the operation and the technologies (drugs, surveillance and information gathering techniques) which facilitate the blurring and penetration which I described. Systems of medicine, social work, education, welfare take on supervisory and judicial functions, while the penal apparatus itself becomes more influenced by medicine, education, psychology.[38] This new system of subtle gradations in care, control, punishment and treatment is indeed far from the days of public execution and torture – but it is perhaps not quite as far as Foucault suggests from that early reform vision of the punitive city. The ideology of community is trying once more to increase the visibility – if not the theatricality – of social control. True, we may not know quite what is happening – treatment or punishment, public or private, locked up or free, inside or outside, voluntary or coercive – but we must know that something is happening, here, in our very own community. [. . .]

## Notes

1 G. Rusche and O. Kircheimer, *Punishment and Social Structure* (New York, Russell and Russell, 1938); M. Foucault, *Madness and Civilisation* (London, Tavistock, 1967); and *Discipline*

*and Punish: the Birth of the Prison* (London, Allen Lane, 1977); D.J. Rothman, *The Discovery of the Asylum* (Boston, Little Brown, 1971).

2 For various relevant attempts, see S. Cohen 'Prisons and the future of control systems', in M. Fitzgerald et al. (eds), *Welfare in Action* (London, Routledge, 1977), pp. 217–28; A. Scull, *Decarceration: Community Treatment and the Deviant* (London, Prentice Hall, 1977); and D. Rothman, 'Behavioural modification in total institutions: a historical overview', *Hastings Centre Report*, 5 (1975), pp. 17–24.

3 Scull, *Decarceration*, documents both the presence at the end of the nineteenth century of the equivalent of today's liberal/social scientific critique of institutions and the reasons for the failure of this earlier attack. For him, the origins of current policy lie in certain changing features of welfare capitalism. Crudely expressed: it no longer 'suits' the state to maintain segregative modes of control based on the asylum. In relative terms (and hence the appeal to fiscal conservatives) such modes become costly, while the alternative of welfare payments allowing subsistence in the community, is easier to justify and can be sold on humanitarian and scientific grounds. Scull's argument is a useful corrective to accounts purely at the level of ideas, but it places too much importance on the supposed fiscal crisis, it is less relevant to Britain than America and far less relevant for crime and delinquency than mental illness. In regard to crime and delinquency the picture is not the non-interventionist one Scull implies but – as this paper suggests – the development of parallel systems of control.

4 Ibid., p. 42.

5 See W. Gaylin et al., *Doing Good: the Limits of Benevolence* (New York, Pantheon Books, 1978) and A. Von Hirsch, *Doing Justice: the Choice of Punishments*, (New York, Hill and Wang, 1976).

6 The most informative sources in the United States would be journals such as *Crime and Delinquency* and *Federal Probation* from the mid-1960s onwards and the various publications from bodies such as the National Institute of Mental Health and, later, the Law Enforcement Assistance Administration. A representative collection of such material is G.R. Perlstein and T.R. Phelps (eds), *Alternatives to Prison: Community Based Corrections* (Pacific Palisades, CA, Goodyear Publishing, 1975). In Britain the ideology of community control has been slower and less obvious in its development, though it can be traced in various Home Office publications from the end of the 1960s. See also L. Blom-Cooper (ed.), *Progress in Penal Reform* (Oxford, Oxford University Press, 1974) and N. Tutt (ed.), *Alternative Strategies for Coping with Crime* (Oxford, Basil Blackwell, 1978).

7 Some of these may be found in Scull, *Decarceration*, and D.F. Greenberg, 'Problems in community corrections', *Issues in Criminology*, 10 (1975), pp. 1–33.

8 National Institute of Mental Health, *Community Based Correctional Programs: Models and Practices* (Washington, DC, US Government Printing Office, 1971), p. 1.

9 K.B. Coates et al., 'Social climate, extent of community linkages and quality of community linkages: the institutionalisation normalisation continuum'. Unpublished MS, Center for Criminal Justice, Harvard Law School, 1976.

10 H.B. Bradley, 'Community based treatment for young adult offenders', *Crime and Delinquency* 15(3) (1969), p. 369.

11 For a survey, see R.P. Seiter et al., *Halfway House* (Washington, DC, National Institute of Law Enforcement and Criminal Justice, LEAA, 1977).

12 V. Fox, *Community Based Corrections* (Englewood Cliffs, NJ, Prentice Hall, 1977), pp. 62–3.

13 N. Hinton, 'Intermediate treatment' in Blom-Cooper (ed.), *Penal Reform*, p. 239.

14 Rothman, 'Behavioural modification', p. 19.

15 The most exhaustive research here deals with the two Californian projects – Community Treatment and Probation Subsidy – widely hailed as exemplars of the new strategy. See, especially, P. Lerman, *Community Treatment and Social Control: a Critical Analysis of Juvenile Correctional Policy* (Chicago, University of Chicago Press, 1975) and S. Messinger, 'Confinement in the community: a selective assessment of Paul Lerman's "Community Treatment and Social Control"', *Journal of Research in Crime and Delinquency*, 13(1) (1976), pp. 82–92. Another standard Californian study of the diversion strategy is D. Cressey, and R. McDermott, *Diversion from the Juvenile Justice System* (Washington, DC, National Institute of Law Enforcement and Criminal Justice, LEAA, 1974). For two useful general evaluations of the field, see A. Rutherford, and O. Bengur, *Community Based Alternatives to Juvenile*

*Incarceration* (Washington, DC, National Institute of Law Enforcement and Criminal Justice, LEAA, 1976); A. Rutherford and R. McDermott, *Juvenile Diversion* (Washington, DC, National Institute of Law Enforcement and Criminal Justice, LEAA, 1976).

16 Rutherford and Bengur. *Community Based Alternatives.*

17 K. Pease, *Community Service Assessed in 1976.* Home Office Research Unit Study No. 35 (London, HMSO, 1977).

18 Quoted in Rutherford and Bengur, *Community Based Alternatives*, p. 30.

19 Greenberg, 'Problems in community corrections', p. 23.

20 A clear statement of this rationale and the legal problems in implementing it, is to be found in Law Reform Commission of Canada, *Working Paper No. 7: Diversion* (Ottawa, Law Reform Commission of Canada, 1975).

21 F.W. Dunford, 'Police diversion – an illusion?' *Criminology*, 15(3) (1977), pp. 335–52.

22 A. Morris, 'Diversion of juvenile offenders from the criminal justice system', in Tutt (ed.), *Coping with Crime*, pp. 50–4.

23 M. Bohnstedt, 'Answers to three questions about juvenile diversion', *Journal of Research in Crime and Delinquency*, 15(1) (1978), p. 10.

24 M.W. Klein et al., 'The explosion in police diversion programmes: evaluating the structural dimensions of a social fad', in M.W. Klein (ed.), *The Juvenile Justice System* (Beverly Hills, CA, Sage, 1976), p. 10.

25 Rutherford and McDermott, *Juvenile Diversion.*

26 Cressey and McDermott, *Diversion from the Juvenile Justice System*, pp. 3–4.

27 Rutherford and McDermott, *Juvenile Diversion*, pp. 25–6.

28 See, especially A.M. Platt, *The Child Savers: the Invention of Delinquency* (Chicago, Chicago University Press, 1969).

29 Greenberg, 'Problems in community corrections', p. 8.

30 Messinger, 'Confinement in the community', pp. 84–5.

31 L.T. Empey, *Alternatives to Incarceration* (Washington, DC, US Government Printing Office, 1967).

32 For typical statements about absorption, see R.M. Carter, 'The diversion of offenders', *Federal Probation* 36(4) (1972), pp. 31–6.

33 D. Skoler, 'Future trends in juvenile and adult community based corrections', in G.R. Perlstein and T.R. Phelps (eds), *Alternatives to Prison: Community Based Corrections* (Pacific Palisades, CA, Goodyear, 1975), p. 11.

34 N. Hobbs, *Issues in the Classification of Children* (San Francisco, Jossey Bass, 1975).

35 Strangers to the world of community corrections should be informed that all the projects named in this imaginary report are *real* and current.

36 Foucault, *Discipline and Punish*, p. 113.

37 Ibid., p. 211.

38 Ibid., p. 306.

# 37

# From the Panopticon to Disney World: the development of discipline

*Clifford D. Shearing and Philip C. Stenning*

In the literature on punishment an interesting and important debate has recently surfaced on the question of whether modern penal developments in the criminal justice system represent an extension of discipline (in the sense in which Foucault used the term) or a move away from it. In an influential article published in 1979, Cohen argued that modern penal practices provide evidence of a significant 'dispersal of social control', in which the community is increasingly being involved in its administration. He also claimed, however, that this dispersal of social control is 'merely a continuation of the overall pattern established in the nineteenth century' (p. 359), and described by Foucault, in which corporal punishment (based on the administration of pain and torture to the body) was replaced by carceral punishment (based on the exercise of sustained discipline over the soul).

In an incisive critique of Cohen's thesis, Bottoms has recently sought to show – successfully in our view – that while Cohen's conclusion that modern penal developments represent a significant dispersal of social control is correct, his conclusion that these developments are an extension of disciplinary punishment is not. Specifically, Bottoms argued that the most significant recent developments in penal practice – the greatly increased use of the fine, the growth of community service orders and the modern resort to compensation and related matters – are not essentially disciplinary in character. In making this argument, Bottoms makes the point that these new modes of punishment lack the element of 'soul-training' which is the essential hallmark of disciplinary carceral punishment. He went on to speculate that this move away from disciplinary punishment within the criminal justice system may have been made possible, and encouraged, because more effective preventative social control measures are being implemented within the general society outside the criminal justice system. This latter system, the argument goes, is increasingly being regarded only as a 'last resort' in social control, and as a result 'juridical' rather than disciplinary carceral punishments are being resorted to within it (Bottoms, 1983: 187–8, 191, 195).

Thus far, Bottoms's argument is entirely consistent with similar arguments we have made in our explanations of the implications for social control of the modern growth of private security and private control systems (Shearing and Stenning, 1983). These, we have contended, are preventative rather than punitive in character, rely heavily on strategies of disciplinary control, and

Abridged from *Perspectives in Criminal Law* (eds A. Doob and E. Greenspan), pp. 335-49. (Ontario: Canada Law Book Inc., 1985.)

make resort to the more punitively orientated public criminal justice system only as a last resort when their own strategies have failed to achieve their instrumentally conceived objectives.

Bottoms, however, went on to argue that we, too, are wrong to characterize such private control systems as disciplinary in the Foucauldian sense. This, he wrote, was because the systems we described lack the essential ingredient of discipline, which he characterized as '"the mechanics of training" upon the bodies and souls of individuals' (Bottoms, 1983: 182). Work by Mathiesen (1980, 1983), in which he characterized modern trends away from individualism as the organizing focus of social control, and towards 'surveillance of whole categories of people' as 'a change from open to hidden discipline', was criticized by Bottoms for the same reasons (Bottoms, 1983: 181–2). In both cases, he argued that the mere extension of *surveillance*, without the accompanying individualized soul-training, does not constitute 'discipline' as Foucault intended the term.

The explicit assumption which Bottoms makes in thus characterizing modern non-penal systems of social control as not 'disciplinary', is that 'discipline' necessarily involves individualized soul-training. In this essay, we shall seek to argue that the concept of 'discipline', as used by Foucault, is much broader than this, and is appropriate to describe many modern forms of social control which do not apparently have individualized soul-training as their primary organizing focus. More particularly, we shall argue that the identification of discipline with individualized soul-training reflects a failure adequately to distinguish between Foucault's generic concept of discipline and his more historically specific examination of it in the context of carceral punishment. Having made this argument, the essay will conclude with an examination of a popular modern exemplar of non-carceral disciplinary social control which, we believe, represents an important indication of what the 'social control apparatus of society is actually getting up to' (Cohen, 1979: 339).

### Discipline and carceral punishment

Central to Foucault's argument in *Discipline and Punish* is his contention that discipline as a generic form of power should be distinguished from the particular strategies through which it is expressed at any particular time.

> 'Discipline' may be identified neither with an institution nor with an apparatus; it is a type of power, a modality for its exercise, comprising a whole set of instruments, techniques, procedures, levels of application, targets; it is a 'physics' or anatomy of power, technology. (1977: 215)

This distinction between discipline, as a type of power, and its particular expression, is important for it allows for the possibility of the evolution of discipline through a series of different concrete expressions. Given this distinction it becomes apparent that carceral punishment, as exemplified in Bentham's Panopticon, should be seen as an instance of discipline that seeks compliance through individual soul-training. It is, however, only one possible expression, albeit the one that occupied Foucault's attention.

What, then, are the essential characteristics of 'discipline' as a generic concept? There can be no doubt that training of one sort or another is an objective if not an explicit element of 'discipline'. Indeed, the very derivation of the word (from the Latin *disciplina* = instruction, tuition) confirms this. The nature of such training, however, and the manner in which it is accomplished, will vary accordingly to the context in which discipline is applied. Of this we shall say more in a moment. For Foucault, there was another essential characteristic of discipline – namely, that it is a type of power that is embedded in, and dispersed through, the micro relations that constitute society. Unlike monarchical power (which is expressed through terror and torture) it is not located outside and above the social relations to be controlled but is integrated into them. As it is part of the social fabric it is everywhere, and yet it is nowhere, because it does not have an identifiable locus.

> disciplines have to bring into play the power relations, not above but inside the very texture of the multiplicity, as discretely as possible. . . . (1977: 220)

It is this embedded character that defines the Panopticon as an exemplar for discipline.

> [The Panopticon] is an important mechanism, for it automizes and disindividualizes power. Power has its principle not so much in a person as in a certain concerted distribution of bodies, surfaces, lights, gazes; in an arrangement whose internal mechanisms produce the relation in which individuals are caught up. The ceremonies, the rituals, the marks by which the sovereign's surplus power was manifested are useless. There is a machinery that assures dissymmetry, disequilibrium, difference. Consequently, it does not matter who exercises power. Any individual taken almost at random, can operate the machine. . . . (1977: 202)

The embedded nature of discipline makes it especially suitable as a preventative mode of control, as the surveillance (that is its basis) becomes part of the very relations to be controlled. Foucault illustrates this in discussing discipline in the context of the workshop:

> The discipline of the workshop, while remaining a way of enforcing respect for the regulations and authorities, of preventing thefts and losses, tends to increase aptitudes, speeds, output and therefore profits; it still exerts a moral influence over behavior, but more and more it treats actions in terms of their results, introduces bodies into a machinery, forces into an economy. (1977: 210)

It is precisely because of this embedded character of discipline that its nature varies according to the context in which it is applied, and it is for this reason that, when applied in the context of carceral punishment, one of its distinctive elements is that of individualized soul-training. This is because the context of carceral punishment (unlike that, for instance, of the factory, the hospital or the workshop) is essentially a moral one rather than a primarily instrumental one. It is perhaps because Foucault was primarily concerned to explain 'the birth of the prison' in *Discipline and Punish*, that the elements of carceral discipline have so easily come to be thought to be the fundamental elements of *all* discipline. As we shall try to illustrate, however, when applied in a context which is primarily instrumental rather than moral, the elements of discipline are significantly different.

## Instrumental and moral discipline

The three models of control that Foucault identifies (monarchical, juridical and carceral), while fundamentally different in disciplinary terms, all share a moral foundation that defines them as 'justice' systems. Foucault, in his analysis of these types of control, tended to take this feature for granted as it was common to all three models. As a result, if one works from within Foucault's framework in studying contemporary control, although one's attention will be directed towards discipline, the issue of whether the moral foundation of social control is changing will tend not to be considered. This is evident in the work of all the participants in the debate we have reviewed. Yet if contemporary control, especially as it appears in the private sector, is to be understood, it is precisely this issue (as the quotation above about disciplinary control in the work place suggests) that needs to be addressed. What makes private control different from traditional criminal justice is not its disciplinary character, which it shares with carceral control, but the challenge it offers to the moral foundation of the order-maintenance process (Shearing and Stenning, 1983).

Within criminal justice 'order' is fundamentally a moral phenomenon and its maintenance a moral process. Accordingly, social order (and its enforcement) tends to be defined in absolute terms: one proper order expressing 'natural justice'. Within criminal justice the premise that shapes order maintenance is that order is the expression of a community of morally righteous people. Thus, the criminal process is concerned with the rightness and wrongness of acts and the goodness and badness of people. It defines the boundaries of moral order by stigmatizing certain acts and persons as morally tainted (Durkheim). Its methods are indignation, retribution and redemption. Each of the models of punishment Foucault identified represents a different set of strategies for doing this.

Every aspect of the criminal process is structured and shaped by its moral, absolutist foundation. Within it, discipline is a technology of power used to achieve this moral purpose. There is no better illustration of this than the carceral regime which targets the soul, the moral centre of the human being, so as to provide for its moral reformation. Not surprisingly, therefore, individualized soul-training is the essential hallmark of carceral discipline.

Private control, in sharp contrast, rejects a moral conception of order and the control process. Private security executives, for example, not only reject, as Wilson does, the present possibility of moral reform but reject the very idea of moral reform as a basis for control. Within private control, order is conceived primarily in instrumental rather than moral terms. Order is simply the set of conditions most conducive to achieving fundamental community objectives. Thus in a business corporation, for instance, order is usually whatever maximizes profit.

In contrasting their definition of order with that of criminal justice, private control systems stress that for them 'theft' is not a moral category and consequently does not deserve, or require, a moral response. Within private control the instrumental language of profit and loss replaces the moral language of criminal justice. This is not merely terminological (different terms for the same objects) but a reconstitution of the social world. 'Loss' refers not simply to theft but includes, among other things, the cost of attempting to control theft. This redefinition has important implications for the way in which control is exercised and thus for order. For example, theft will not be subject to control if the cost of doing so is likely to be greater than the initial loss.

Where moral rhetoric appears in private control it does so not as principles that guide the order-maintenance process (as it does in judicial decision-making) but simply as a control strategy. For example, employees may be given a lecture on morality not because control is conceived of in moral terms but because it creates attitudes that are good for profit. In such a context, training, as an element of discipline, need be neither individualized nor particularly directed at the soul. Indeed, from the point of view of the evolution of discipline, perhaps the most important consequence of the shift to an instrumental focus has been the move away from a concern with individual reformation to the control of the opportunities that permit breaches of order to occur. Accordingly, within private control it is prevention through the reduction of opportunities for disorder that is the primary focus of attention (Shearing and Stenning, 1982). This directs attention away from traditional offenders to a new class of delinquents: those who create opportunities for disorder. It is thus, to use banking as an illustration, not the employee who steals who is the primary focus of the control system's attention but the teller who creates the opportunity for the theft by neglecting to secure his/her cash drawer.

This transformation of the preventative thrust within discipline has important implications for other aspects of disciplinary control. The most visible is the change in the nature of surveillance as attention shifts from the morally culpable individual to the *categories* of people who create opportunities for disorder (Mathiesen, 1983; Rule et al., 1983).

Although this focus on opportunities creates a need for mass surveillance it does not eliminate carefully pinpointed surveillance. Its purpose, however, changes; it is no longer soul-training, as such, but rather 'tuning up the machine' (of which the human operator merely constitutes one part). While such scrutiny may, for this reason, focus on individuals, it is just as likely to target system deficiencies, for instance, in the paper systems that provide for ongoing surveillance, as well as retrospective surveillance, through the paper trails that they create.

In summary, the emergence of an explicitly instrumental focus in control has changed the nature of disciplinary power while reinforcing its embedded features. Thus surveillance, while changing both its focus and its purpose, has become increasingly embedded in other structures and functions. For example, the surveillance which Oscar Newman sought to achieve through 'defensible space' is embedded both in the structure of the physical environment, as well as in the social relations it facilitates.

Finally, we may note that an instrumental focus implies a variety of orders, each reflecting the fact that different communities have different objectives. Thus, within private control systems, we find not one conception of order but many; not one societal order but many community-based orders.

### Private non-carceral discipline

In seeking to identify the carceral model, and in explicating its relationship to disciplinary control, Foucault realized that, at any point in time, the actual control mechanisms in force would reflect the influences of both established and developing forms (1977: 130). Thus in order to identify the nature and direction of these forms he turned to the ideas and projects of influential reformers. Hence his use of the Panopticon as an exemplar of the disciplinary form as expressed through carceral strategies.

This approach suggests that in seeking to understand contemporary control we should direct our attention to strategies in arenas relatively immune from the influence of the carceral model. As public sector control has been dominated over the past century by the soul-training of the carceral model we are likely to find that the control strategies within this arena will reflect a mix of both established and newer forms, so that although it will be possible to identify disciplinary initiatives, we are not likely to find exemplary instances of contemporary embedded control here. The reverse, however, is likely to be true with respect to private control systems which, because they were in decline for most of the nineteenth and the first half of the twentieth centuries, are remarkably free of carceral overtones (Spitzer and Scull, 1977; Shearing and Stenning, 1981, 1983). Their contemporary manifestations, however, display precisely the embedded features that characterize disciplinary control (Shearing and Stenning, 1982: 101). Thus, in seeking an exemplar of contemporary discipline, we turn to the private arena.

[. . .]

## Disney World: an exemplar of instrumental discipline

As the discussion to this point has indicated, research on private security has already confirmed the development of a contemporary form of discipline outside of the moral restraints of criminal justice and begun to identify some of its distinguishing features. To elucidate the notion of instrumental discipline we contrast it with moral discipline by identifying the analytic equivalents of the carceral project and the Panopticon so as to highlight the nature of the changes that have been occurring in the development of discipline. As the identification of order with profit provides the most explicit example of an instrumental order, corporate control is an appropriate equivalent to the carceral model. As the features of corporate control are highly developed in the recreational facilities operated by Disney Productions and as these facilities are so widely known (directly through visits or indirectly through media coverage and Disney advertising), Disney World, in Orlando, Florida, provides a suitable exemplar to set against the Panopticon. In order to avoid lengthy descriptions of security strategies we will draw our illustrations from consumer controls which every visitor to Disney World encounters.

The essential features of Disney's control system become apparent the moment the visitor enters Disney World. As one arrives by car one is greeted by a series of smiling young people who, with the aid of clearly visible road markings, direct one to one's parking spot, remind one to lock one's car and to remember its location and then direct one to await the rubber wheeled train that will convey visitors away from the parking lot. At the boarding location one is directed to stand safely behind guard rails and to board the train in an orderly fashion. While climbing on board one is reminded to remember the name of the parking area and the row number in which one is parked (for instance, 'Donald Duck, 1'). Once on the train one is encouraged to protect oneself from injury by keeping one's body within the bounds of the carriage and to do the same for children in one's care. Before disembarking one is told how to get from the train back to the monorail platform and where to wait for the train to the parking lot on one's return. At each transition from one stage of one's journey to the next one is wished a happy day and a 'good time' at

Disney World (this begins as one drives in and is directed by road signs to tune one's car radio to the Disney radio network).

[. . .]

It will be apparent from the above that Disney Productions is able to handle large crowds of visitors in a most orderly fashion. Potential trouble is anticipated and prevented. Opportunities for disorder are minimized by constant instruction, by physical barriers which severely limit the choice of action available and by the surveillance of omnipresent employees who detect and rectify the slightest deviation.

The vehicles that carry people between locations are an important component of the system of physical barriers. Throughout Disney World vehicles are used as barriers. This is particularly apparent in the Epcot Center, the newest Disney facility, where many exhibits are accessible only via special vehicles which automatically secure one once they begin moving.

Control strategies are embedded in both environmental features and structural relations. In both cases control structures and activities have other functions which are highlighted so that the control function is overshadowed. None the less, control is pervasive. For example, virtually every pool, fountain and flower garden serves both as an aesthetic object and to direct visitors away from, or towards, particular locations. Similarly, every Disney Productions employee, while visibly and primarily engaged in other functions, is also engaged in the maintenance of order. This integration of functions is real and not simply an appearance: beauty *is* created, safety *is* protected, employees *are* helpful. The effect is, however, to embed the control function into the 'woodwork' where its presence is unnoticed but its effects are ever present.

A critical consequence of this process of embedding control in other structures is that control becomes consensual. It is effected with the willing cooperation of those being controlled so that the controlled become, as Foucault (1977: 170) has observed, the source of their own control. Thus, for example, the batching that keeps families together provides for family unity while at the same time ensuring that parents will be available to control their children. By seeking a definition of order within Disney World that can convincingly be presented as being in the interest of visitors, order maintenance is established as a voluntary activity which allows coercion to be reduced to a minimum. Thus, adult visitors willingly submit to a variety of devices that increase the flow of consumers through Disney World, such as being corralled on the monorail platform, so as to ensure the safety of their children. Furthermore, while doing so they gratefully acknowledge the concern Disney Productions has for their family, thereby legitimating its authority, not only in the particular situation in question, but in others as well. Thus, while profit ultimately underlies the order Disney Productions seeks to maintain, it is pursued in conjunction with other objectives that will encourage the willing compliance of visitors in maintaining Disney profits. This approach to profit-making, which seeks a coincidence of corporate and individual interests (employee and consumer alike), extends beyond the control function and reflects a business philosophy to be applied to all corporate operations (Peters and Waterman).

The coercive edge of Disney's control system is seldom far from the surface, however, and becomes visible the moment the Disney-visitor consensus breaks down, that is, when a visitor attempts to exercise a choice that is incompatible with the Disney order. It is apparent in the physical barriers that forcefully prevent certain activities as well as in the action of employees who detect breaches of order. This can be illustrated by an incident that occurred during a visit to Disney World by Shearing and his daughter, during the course of which she developed a blister on her heel. To avoid further irritation she removed her shoes and proceeded to walk barefooted. They had not progressed ten yards before they were approached by a very personable security guard dressed as a Bahamian police officer, with white pith helmet and white gloves that perfectly suited the theme of the area they were moving through (so that he, at first, appeared more like a scenic prop than a security person), who informed them that walking barefoot was, 'for the safety of visitors', not permitted. [After explaining] that, given the blister, the safety of this visitor was likely to be better secured by remaining barefooted, at least on the walkways, they were informed that their safety and how best to protect it was a matter for Disney Productions to determine while they were on Disney property and that unless they complied he would be compelled to escort them out of Disney World. Shearing's daughter, on learning that failure to comply with the security guard's instruction would deprive her of the pleasures of Disney World, quickly decided that she would prefer to further injure her heel and remain on Disney property. As this example illustrates, the source of Disney Productions' power rests both in the physical coercion it can bring to bear and in its capacity to induce cooperation by depriving visitors of a resource that they value.

[. . .]

As we have hinted throughout this discussion, training is a pervasive feature of the control system of Disney Productions. It is not, however, the redemptive soul-training of the carceral project but an ever-present flow of directions for, and definitions of, order directed at every visitor. Unlike carceral training, these messages do not require detailed knowledge of the individual. They are, on the contrary, for anyone and everyone. Messages are, none the less, often conveyed to single individuals or small groups of friends and relatives. For example, in some of the newer exhibits, the vehicles that take one through swivel and turn so that one's gaze can be precisely directed. Similarly, each seat is fitted with individual sets of speakers that talk directly to one, thus permitting a seductive sense of intimacy while simultaneously imparting a uniform message.

In summary, within Disney World control is embedded, preventative, subtle, cooperative and apparently non-coercive and consensual. It focuses on categories, requires no knowledge of the individual and employs pervasive surveillance. Thus, although disciplinary, it is distinctively non-carceral. Its order is instrumental and determined by the interests of Disney Productions rather than moral and absolute. As anyone who has visited Disney World knows, it is extraordinarily effective.

## Conclusions

While this new instrumental discipline is rapidly becoming a dominant force in social control in this year, 1984, it is as different from the Orwellian totalitarian nightmare as it is from the carceral regime. Surveillance is pervasive but it is the antithesis of the blatant control of the Orwellian state: its source is not government and its vehicle is not Big Brother. The order of instrumental discipline is not the unitary order of a central state but diffuse and separate orders defined by private authorities responsible for the feudal-like domains of Disney World, condominium estates, commercial complexes and the like. Within contemporary discipline, control is as fine-grained as Orwell imagined but its features are very different.

In this auspicious year it is thus, paradoxically, not to Orwell's socialist-inspired Utopia that we must look for a picture of contemporary control but to the capitalist-inspired disciplinary model conceived of by Huxley who, in his *Brave New World*, painted a picture of consensually based control that bears a striking resemblance to the disciplinary control of Disney World and other corporate control systems. Within Huxley's imaginary world people are seduced into conformity by the pleasures offered by the drug 'soma' rather than coerced into compliance by threat of Big Brother, just as people are today seduced to conform by the pleasures of consuming the goods that corporate power has to offer.

The contrasts between morally based justice and instrumental control, carceral punishment and corporate control, the Panopticon and Disney World and Orwell's and Huxley's visions [are] succinctly captured by the novelist Beryl Bainbridge's observations about a recent journey she made retracing J.B. Priestley's celebrated trip around Britain. She notes how during his travels in 1933 the centre of the cities and towns he visited were defined by either a church or a centre of government (depicting the coalition between Church and state in the production of order that characterizes morally based regimes).

During her more recent trip one of the changes that struck her most forcibly was the transformation that had taken place in the centre of cities and towns. These were now identified not by churches or town halls, but by shopping centres; often vaulted glass-roofed structures that she found reminiscent of the cathedrals they had replaced both in their awe-inspiring architecture and in the hush that she found they sometimes created. What was worshipped in these contemporary cathedrals, she noted, was not an absolute moral order but something much more mundane: people were 'worshipping shopping' and through it, we would add, the private authorities, the order and the corporate power their worship makes possible.

# References

Bottoms, A.E. (1983) 'Neglected features of contemporary penal systems', in D. Garland and P. Young (eds), *The Power to Punish: Contemporary Penality and Social Analysis*. Atlantic Highlands, NJ: Humanities. p. 166.

Cohen, S. (1979) 'The punitive city: notes on the dispersal of social control', *Contemporary Crises*, 3(4): 339.

Foucault, M. (1977) *Discipline and Punish: the Birth of the Prison*. New York: Vintage Books.

Mathiesen, T. (1980) 'The future of social control systems – the case of Norway', *International Journal of the Sociology of Law*, 8: 149.

Mathiesen, T. (1983) 'The future of social control systems – the case of Norway', in D. Garland and P. Young (eds), *The Power to Punish: Contemporary Penality and Social Analysis*. Atlantic Highlands, NJ: Humanities. p. 130.

Newman, O. (1972) *Defensible Space: Crime Prevention through Urban Design*. New York: Macmillan.

Peters, T. and Waterman, R.H., Jr. (1982) *In Search of Excellence: Lessons from America's Best-run Companies*. New York: Warner Books.

Priestley, J.B. (1934) *English Journey: Being a Rambling but Truthful Account of What One Man*

*Saw and Heard and Felt During a Journey Through England the Autumn of the Year 1933.* London: Heinemann & Gollancz.

Rule, J.B., McAdam, D., Stearns, L. and Uglow, D. (1983) 'Documentary identification and mass surveillance in the United States', *Social Problems*, 31(2): 222.

Shearing, C.D. and Stenning P.C. (1981) 'Private security: its growth and implications', in M. Tonry and N. Morris (eds), *Crime and Justice – an Annual Review of Research*, vol. 3. Chicago: University of Chicago Press. p. 193.

Shearing, C.D. and Stenning, P.C. (1982) 'Snowflakes or good pinches? Private security's contribution to modern policing', in R. Donelan (ed.), *The Maintenance of Order in Society.* Ottawa: Canadian Police College.

Shearing, C.D. and Stenning, P.C. (1983) 'Private security: implications for social control', *Social Problems* 30(5): 493.

Spitzer, S. and Scull, A. (1977) 'Privatization and capitalist development: the case of the private police', *Social Problems*, 25(1): 18.

# 38

# The power of law

## Carol Smart

[. . .]
Foucault's concentration on the growth of the disciplinary society reflects his greater interest in the mechanisms of power than the 'old' questions of who has power. He also rejects the tendency which is apparent in the traditional formulation of power, of treating power as if it were negative, repressive and juridical. He maintains that power is creative and technical. By this it is meant that the mechanisms of power create resistances and local struggles which operate to bring about new forms of knowledge and resistance. Hence power is productive, not simply a negative sanction which stops or restricts oppositional developments. However, it is clear that although Foucault's reconceptualization of power opens new ways of understanding, it is very hard to abandon the old concept of power. Hence we not only continue to talk about power as a commodity, we also act as if it were. As Taylor (1986) has argued,

> Foucault's thesis is that, while we have not ceased talking and thinking in terms of this model (i.e. power as a system of commands and obedience), we actually live in relations of power which are quite different, and which cannot be properly described in its terms. What is wielded through the modern technologies of control is something quite different, in that it is not concerned with law but with normaliz- ation. (1986: 75)

The question that this raises is 'why do we still look to the old forms of power if they are no longer appropriate?' Interestingly, Foucault does not dismiss law and the old forms of power altogether as Taylor implies. It is, however, hard to be clear on what he has to say in this area since, by his own admission, Foucault was more interested in the mechanisms of power at its extremities (i.e. where it is least law-like) than at its core (i.e. law itself and legal institutions). He does not appear to be saying that law, and the old con- trivances of power, are no longer relevant - although he seems to argue that they will become so. Hence, we should talk of two parallel mechanisms of power which operate symbiotically, but where the old mechanism will be eventually colonized by the new.

> And I believe that in our times power is exercised simultaneously through this right and these techniques and that these techniques and these discourses, to which the disciplines give rise, invade the area of right so that the procedures of normalisation come to be ever more constantly engaged in the colonisation of those of law. (Gordon, 1980: 107)

Abridged from *Feminism and the Power of Law*, pp. 7–20. (London: Routledge, 1989.)

So Foucault sees the old power (and hence the significance of law) diminishing. I am less certain that this is happening. Rather it is possible to posit a move in the opposite direction, for example the growing legalization of everyday life from the moment of conception (i.e. increasing foetal rights) through to the legal definition of death (i.e. brain death or 'body' death). It may be that law is being colonized in some instances, but in others law may be extending its influence as I shall argue below.

We need therefore to think in terms of two parallel mechanisms of power, each with its own discourse, the discourse of rights and the discourse of normalization. Foucault tells us far more about the latter than the former, yet the former is by no means redundant (even if it is doomed to become so). This raises a number of issues. For example, what is the relationship between the two mechanisms in specific areas as opposed to broad generalities? Might we see an uneven development of this colonization of law? What does this mean for political strategy, if anything? Foucault suggests, for example, that there is little point in turning to law (the discourse of rights) as a strategy to deal with the encroachment of surveillance, since they are now symbiotically linked. I shall not answer all these questions in this chapter, but I shall explore the interface between the two mechanisms to try to give some substance to this, so far, abstract discussion. Before this I must give brief consideration to the notions of truth and knowledge.

## Truth/knowledge

In using the concept of truth Foucault does not mean 'the ensemble of truths which are to be discovered and accepted'. On the contrary, Foucault uses it to refer to 'the ensemble or rules according to which the true and the false are separated and specific effects of power attached to the true' (Gordon, 1980: 132). He is not concerned with what is considered to be the usual quest of science, namely to uncover the truth, rather he is interested in discovering how certain discourses claim to speak the truth and thus can exercise power in a society that values this notion of truth. He argues that making the claim to be a science is in fact an exercise of power because, in claiming scientificity, other knowledges are accorded less status, less value. Those knowledges which are called faith, experience, biography and so on, are ranked as lesser knowledges. They can exercise less influence, they are disqualified. Defining a field of knowledge as science is to claim that it speaks a truth which can be favourably compared to partial truths and untruths which epitomize non-scientific discourse.

Foucault does not compare the scientist's claim to truth, and hence exercise of power, with the lawyer's claim. Law does not fit into his discussion of science, knowledge and truth because, as I have pointed out, he identifies it in relation to the regime of power that predates the growth of the modern episteme. Yet I wish to argue that there are very close parallels in terms of this 'claim to truth' and the effect of power that the claim concedes. I am not saying that law attempts to call itself a science, but then it does not have to. Law has its own method, its own testing ground, its own specialized language and system of results. It may be a field of knowledge that has a lower status than those regarded as 'real' sciences, none the less it sets itself apart from other discourses in the same way that science does.

[. . .] [L]aw sets itself above other knowledges like psychology, sociology, or common sense. It claims to have the method to establish the truth of events. The main vehicle for this claim is the legal method which is taught in law schools [. . .]. A more 'public' version of this claim, however, is the criminal trial which, through the adversarial system, is thought to be a secure basis for findings of guilt and innocence. Judges and juries can come to correct legal decisions; the fact that other judges in higher courts may overrule some decisions only goes to prove that the system ultimately divines the correct view.

[. . .]

Law sets itself outside the social order, as if through the application of legal method and rigour it becomes a thing apart which can in turn reflect upon the world from which it is divorced. Consider the following quotation from Lord Denning, written when he was Master of the Rolls (i.e. head of the Court of Appeal).

> By a series of Acts of Parliament, however, starting in 1870, all the disabilities of wives in regard to property have been swept away. A married woman is now entitled to her own property and earnings, just as her husband is entitled to his. Her stocks and shares remain hers. Her wedding presents are hers. Her earnings are hers. She can deal with all property as fully as any man. . . . No longer is she dependent on her husband. She can, and does, go out to work and earn her own living. Her equality is complete. (Denning, 1980: 200)

In this conceptualization it is law that has given women quality (accepting for the moment that they do have formal equality). In this way law is taken to be outside the social body, it transcends it and acts upon it. Indeed the more it is seen as a unified discipline that responds only to its own coherent, internal logic, the more powerful it becomes. It is not simply that in this passage Denning omits to point out how many women chained themselves to railings, demonstrated and lobbied in Parliament to change the law, nor that he ignores the dramatic changes to women's economic position which occurred quite independently of law, it is rather that he constructs law as a kind of sovereign with the power to give or withhold rights. (Here we are back to Foucault's notion of the 'old' power of law.) Linked to this idea, law is constructed as a force of linear progress, a beacon to lead us out of darkness. The significance of this is not that one judge, no matter how eminent, should state this, but that this has become a commonsense approach. The idea that law has the power to right wrongs is pervasive. Just as medicine is seen as curative rather than *iatrogenic*, so law is seen as extending rights rather than creating wrongs. It is perhaps useful to coin the term *juridogenic* to apply to law as a way of conceptualizing the harm that law may generate as a consequence of its operations. [. . .] But there are two issues here. One is the idea of law as a force for good (or bad) the other is the idea of law as a force at all – both have to be subject to scrutiny. If we stop at the point of considering whether law is a force for good or bad we concede that law is a force – indeed it implies that we simply wish to redirect its purpose. If we go one step further we can begin to problematize, to challenge and even to redefine law's supposedly legitimate place in the order of things. Ultimately this is the most necessary project.

Lastly in this section on truth and knowledge, I want to consider how law extends itself beyond uttering the truth of law, to making such claims about other areas of social life. What is important about this tendency is that the framework for such utterances remains legal – and hence retains the mantle of legal power. To put it figuratively, the judge does not remove his wig when he passes comment on, for example, issues of sexual morality in rape cases. He retains the authority drawn from legal scholarship and the 'truth' of law, but he applies it to non-legal issues. This is a form of legal imperialism in which the legitimacy law claims in the field of law extends to every issue in social life. Hence Lord Denning states,

> No matter how you may dispute and argue, you cannot alter the fact that women are quite different from men. The principal task in the life of women is to bear and rear children: . . . He is physically the stronger and she the weaker. He is temperamentally the more aggressive and she the more submissive. It is he who takes the initiative and she who responds. These diversities of function and temperament lead to differences of outlook which cannot be ignored. But they are, none of them, any reason for putting women under the subjection of men. (Denning, 1980: 194)

Here Denning is articulating a Truth about the natural differences between women and men. He combines the Truth claimed by socio-biology (i.e. a 'scientific' truth) with the Truth claimed by law. He makes it clear that there is no point in argument; anyone who disagrees is, by definition, a fool. Hence the feminist position is constructed as a form of 'disqualified knowledge', while the naturalistic stance on innate gender differences acquires the status of a legal Truth. In this passage both law and biological determinism are affirmed, whilst law accredits itself with doing good.

It may be useful at this stage to summarize the main points of my argument so far. I have suggested that Foucault's analysis of power locates law as part of the *ancien régime*, that the legal discourse of rights is still a significant mode of power, but that it is being colonized by the discourses of discipline. I have suggested that whilst this formulation is persuasive, we need to look further at specific instances of the conflict between old and new contrivances of power. I have also started to consider ways in which law exercises a form of power which is parallel to the development of power associated with scientific knowledge. Although law is not a 'science' it is well able to make the same claims to truth as the sciences, and in so doing exercises a power which is not under threat. Indeed, it may be argued that law is extending its dominion in this respect as western societies become increasingly litigious and channel more and more social and economic policy through the mechanism of legal statutes. I shall now turn to consider two competing examples of the conflict between the old and the new mechanisms of power. [. . .]

## The new and old contrivances of power

As discussed above, Foucault makes frequent reference to law, or at least the form of juridical power, but he does not turn his genealogical gaze on law in the same way as he does on medicine and the human sciences. In fact one is left with an uncertainty about law whose foundations were laid before the seventeenth and eighteenth centuries and which invoke different forms of power than the more recently emergent discourses like the science of medicine (as opposed to the arts of healing). Law also predates the development of the human sciences and what Foucault terms the 'modern episteme' in which man becomes the subject of knowledge and scientific endeavour. In fact much of Foucault's genealogy de-centres law as the prime historical agent or mode of control. Rather he focuses on newly emergent forms of regulation and surveillance and constructs for us a vision of the disciplinary society in which law's place diminishes with the growth of more diverse forms of discipline. But it seems to be 'against' law that new mechanisms of power develop. As I stated above, Foucault depicts a struggle between the 'new' and the 'old' contrivances of power.

The status of law in modern societies is therefore somewhat uncertain in Foucault's account. We might think it is diminishing in significance as other modes of deploying power (i.e. through normalization) come to dominate. However, I am doubtful that law is simply being superseded, nor can we assume that it remains unchanged – a relic from pre-modern times. I shall examine these ideas in relation to law governing the personal spheres of the family and reproduction.

These areas of law coincide with parts of the social body which have been central to the growth of the disciplinary society (Donzelot, 1980; Foucault, 1979). Donzelot has discussed the growth of the alliance between the family and the medical and 'psy' professions (e.g. psychiatry, psychology and psychoanalysis) to construct the household as an intimate site of discipline. Foucault has discussed sexuality in much greater detail than reproduction but he also acknowledged that this is a site where sexuality, the medical profession and the disciplining of populations come together. Because the family can be seen to be subject to a very different modality of power it is likely to be in this area that law becomes less 'law-like' or, to put it another way, this is likely to be an area where law 'loses' the conflict between the mechanisms of discipline and the principle of right.

Of course this is an oversimplification and it is doubtful that law will simply be found to be abandoning this area of legal work to the social workers and medics. But it is possible to examine the conflict and to raise questions as to whether family issues are moving outside the domain of law, whether law retains its sovereignty, or whether law is changing the way in which it exercises power in this field, becoming more like the human sciences in the technologies of power it deploys.

I want to look at two recent instances which will illustrate these issues. The first involves a case of adoption following a surrogacy arrangement in the UK. The second, also in the UK, is a case of abortion where there was a disagreement between the pregnant woman and the putative father as to whether there should be a medical termination. It is necessary to provide a detailed description of both these cases to illustrate the point I hope to make.

*Example 1: Extending law's power through the vehicle of the 'psy' professions*

In the first case [. . .] a couple (Mr and Mrs A) had made a private arrangement with a married woman (Mrs B) that she would be inseminated with Mr A's sperm and would carry the resultant child to term and then surrender it to the commissioning couple. The surrogate mother was paid £5,000 to cover loss of earnings and other expenses. This arrangement went according to plan, and some two years later Mr and Mrs A applied to adopt the child legally with Mrs B's consent. In the UK commercial surrogacy arrangements are illegal (Surrogacy Arrangements Act 1985) and the Adoption

Act of 1958 prohibits adoption where there has been any payment of money. In cases like this English law is not at all interested in the legal question of whether a contract of this sort should be binding; this formal legal approach has never been applied to enforce contracts which could be defined as contrary to public policy. So the legal issues involved were whether this was a commercial arrangement and whether the payment of money would prohibit the legal adoption of the child. The first matter was complicated by the fact that Mrs B had written a book about her experience as a surrogate mother and had earned royalties as a consequence. However, in the event, the arrangement was not deemed to be commercial because there was no third party or agency involved, and the money that was paid was regarded as 'expenses' rather than remuneration.

The second issue was more difficult. Clearly the court had not given prior authorization for the payment to Mrs B which, under the Adoption Act, would have been the only way that such a financial exchange could have been condoned. So the judge argued that the courts had the power to give this authorization retrospectively. It was, however, only possible to construct this argument by reference to a criterion outside the coherence of the strict legal parameters of the case. This criterion was 'the best interests of the child'.

[. . .]

The history of the idea of children as a specific category of persons with special needs has been traced (Ariès, 1979) and it is clearly part of the growth of the human sciences – especially biology, medicine and the 'psy' professions. As statute law extended itself more and more to cover family matters and children (e.g. legislation covering child labour, divorce, domestic violence, age of marriage and consent) so it encroached upon those areas of special concern to the emergent 'psy' professions. It is not correct to depict this historical development in terms of law being 'challenged' by the new discourses; rather law attempts to extend its sovereignty over areas constructed by the discourses of the human sciences as significant to the disciplining of the social body. But law extended its legitimacy by embracing the objects of this discourse. For example, as the medical profession constructed homosexuality as a perversion ultimately in need of treatment, so the law extended its powers over homosexual activity. As children were identified as a special category of great importance to the regulation of populations (through 'proper' socialization, education, health matters etc.) so the law extended its 'protection' of children by introducing legislation on the age of consent, procurement, incest and so on. So we can see a form of cooperation rather than conflict and a process by which law extends its influence into more and more 'personal' or 'private' areas of life. In this respect law is most definitely exercising a mode of disciplinary regulation. With each of these moves law incorporated the terms of the discourses of the human sciences and, I would argue, extended its exercise of power to include the new technologies identified by Foucault. Hence law retains its 'old' power, namely the ability to extend rights, whilst exercising new contrivances of power in the form of surveillance and modes of discipline.

*Example 2: Law's power overshadowed by medical discourse*

The second case to which I shall refer is C v S (*The Times' Law Report*, 25 February 1987). This case shows the relationship between law and medicine in a rather different light, but it is also important for the way in which the adjudication concentrated on 'medical' issues rather than issues of competing rights.

This case was one where two students had had a brief relationship resulting in the disputed pregnancy. The young woman at the time of the case coming to court was between 18 and 21 weeks pregnant. But she had taken the 'morning after pill' and, not believing herself to be pregnant, she had undergone medical treatment in the form of examination by X-ray. She had also been taking anti-depressants. Her former lover was a member of an anti-abortion campaigning group and on discovering her intention to have a medical termination he attempted to use the law to prevent her.

In the UK, medical abortion is available under the 1967 Abortion Act in which the procedure is made available if two doctors have certified that the continuance of the pregnancy would involve greater risk to the life of the pregnant woman, or of injury to her physical or mental health, than if the pregnancy were terminated. However, this legislation is vulnerable to earlier legislation which Parliament has not revoked. In particular the Offences Against the Person Act 1861 (section 58) which makes it an offence to induce a miscarriage, and the Infant Life Preservation Act 1929 (section 1) which provides that 'any person who, with intent to destroy the life of a child capable of being born alive, by any wilful act causes a child to die before it has an existence independent of its mother, shall be guilty of a felony' (see Kingdom 1985a, 1985b).

This case was brought under the 1929 Act, it being argued that, with the advances made by medical science, the 18–20 week old foetus was capable of being born alive. So the case was not, in legal terms, about whether the putative father had a *right* of veto or a *right* to fatherhood, but about a medical matter of the viability of a foetus of 18–20 weeks. This strategy was partly based on the fact that there had already been a case in which a husband had tried to prevent his wife having an abortion on the grounds of his *right* to be consulted over a medical procedure affecting his wife. He had lost the case and C v S would not have proceeded very far on the same grounds given that the putative father was not married to the pregnant woman and was therefore without the common law rights of married men in general. The interesting difference between these two cases is that the first relied on the question of rights whilst the second relied on the scientific status of medical knowledge. So the putative father in the second case was not appealing to law's traditional jurisdiction in terms of its power to allocate rights, but to law in the shadow of changing and increasingly powerful medical knowledge.

I use the term 'in the shadow' because in this case the law has a different relationship to medicine than in the case of adoption cited above. In this case medical opinion agreed that, whilst the foetus showed real signs of life, it could not breathe independently nor with the help of a ventilator. The Court of Appeal therefore judged that the foetus was not capable of being born alive under the Act. But the Court went further and quoted the words of the President of the Family Division in a previous case to the effect that,

> not only would it be a bold and brave judge . . . who would seek to interfere with the discretion of doctors acting under the Abortion Act 1967, but I think he would be a really foolish judge . . . (Paton v British Pregnancy Advisory Service Trustees (1979) QB 276: 282)

In this case we see law deferring to medical knowledge/power. In Foucault's terms we can see the 'principle of right', giving way to the 'mechanisms of discipline'. Unlike the adoption cases, questions of the viability of foetuses have remained within the medical sphere, subject to scientific criteria, whilst questions of the interests of children have been historically formulated in a much wider fashion. Had the putative father in this case been able to construct his arguments in terms of the best interests of children, or a father's right to have a say in the best interests of his future biological offspring, the outcome of the case might have been very different.

However, it is not my purpose here to speculate on this, rather it is my intention to show that we cannot easily read off from an individual case the nature of the law/medicine debate because the respective power of these different discourses varies. In some instances we may see a coalition, in others a conflict and we cannot assume a pattern or clear signposts which will point us to an inevitable future. Our vision of these issues will perhaps only become clear retrospectively, or after more detailed analysis of similar cases. However, it might be unwise to assume that law and the traditional 'principle of right' should cease to be a focus of concern. It would seem that the rights discourse still has political purchase and there is a growing tendency to resort to law for remedies which are couched in terms of rights. It should be borne in mind that it matters a great deal *who* is making an appeal to the 'principle of right' before we assume that all such appeals are fruitless. [. . .] [T]he traditional mode of power responds rapidly to such appeals by men who are attempting to re-establish patriarchal authority in the family (see also Smart, 1989). We should also be alert to the way in which law can transform appeals couched in the discourse of welfare into issues of rights – hence reasserting law's traditional dominion over the matter. One example of this is the question of access to children by fathers after divorce. In this case the idea of parental rights has diminished as a valid appeal to make to law, but the claim for access has been substantiated by the 'psy' discourses which maintain that it is in the child's best interests to see his/her father. The courts have accepted this, but have reconceptualized the issue into one of rights. Hence the law argues that access is the inalienable *right* of the child. Once defined as a right the law can deploy its traditional powers to defend this right (even to the extent of obliging a child to exercise his/her rights against his or her will). *This transformation of power conflicts into the language of rights enables law to exercise power rather than abdicating control to the 'psy' professions and the mechanisms of discipline.*

The fact that law may fail to provide remedies (except in a very narrow sense) is immaterial. Law is now the accepted mechanism for resolving social and individual problems and conflicts from the theft of a bottle of milk to industrial conflict and genetic engineering. In this context law's colonization by the mechanisms of discipline should be seen in a new light rather than in terms of a form of power which is withering away. There is indeed a struggle going on, but at the same time law is extending its terrain in every direction. [. . .]

## References

Ariès, P. (1979) *Centuries of Childhood*. Harmondsworth: Penguin.
Denning, Lord (1980) *The Due Process of Law*. London: Butterworth.
Donzelot, J. (1980) *The Policing of Families*. London: Hutchinson.

Foucault, M. (1979) *Discipline and Punish*. New York: Vintage Books.

Kingdom, E. (1985a) 'Legal recognition of a woman's right to choose', in J. Brophy and C. Smart (eds), *Women in Law*. London: Routledge.

Kingdom E. (1985b) 'The sexual politics of sterilisation', *Journal of Law and Society*, 12(1): 19–34.

Gordon, C. (1980) *Michel Foucault: Power/Knowledge*. Brighton: Harvester Press.

Smart, C. and Sevenhuijsen, S. (eds) (1989) *Child Custody and the Politics of Gender*. London: Routledge.

Taylor, C. (1986) 'Foucault on freedom and truth', in D. Couzens Hoy (ed.), *Foucault: a Critical Reader*. Oxford: Blackwell.

# 39

# Reintegrative shaming

## John Braithwaite

[. . .]

It would seem that sanctions imposed by relatives, friends or a personally relevant collectivity have more effect on criminal behavior than sanctions imposed by a remote legal authority. I will argue that this is because repute in the eyes of close acquaintances matters more to people than the opinions or actions of criminal justice officials. As Blau (1964: 20) points out: 'a person who is attracted to others is interested in proving himself attractive to them, for his ability to associate with them and reap the benefits expected from the association is contingent on their finding him an attractive associate and thus wanting to interact with him'.

A British Government Social Survey asked youths to rank what they saw as the most important consequences of arrest. While only 10 per cent said 'the punishment I might get' was the most important consequence of arrest, 55 per cent said either 'What my family' or 'my girlfriend' would think about it. Another 12 per cent ranked 'the publicity or shame of having to appear in court' as the most serious consequence of arrest, and this was ranked as a more serious consequence on average than 'the punishment I might get' (Zimring and Hawkins, 1973: 192). There is clearly a need for more empirical work to ascertain whether the following conclusion is too sweeping, but Tittle would seem to speak for the current state of this literature when he says:

> social control as a general process seems to be rooted almost completely in informal sanctioning. Perceptions of formal sanction probabilities or severities do not appear to have much of an effect, and those effects that are evident turn out to be dependent upon perceptions of informal sanctions. (Tittle, 1980: 214)

Only a small proportion of the informal sanctions which prevent crime are coupled with formal sanctions, so this literature in a sense understates the importance of informal sanctions. These studies are also by no means tests of the theory of reintegrative shaming [. . .] but they certainly suggest that we are looking in the right place for an explanation of crime. To quote Tittle (1980: 198) again, they suggest that 'to the extent that individuals are deterred from deviance by fear, the fear that is relevant is most likely to be that their deviance will evoke some respect or status loss among acquaintances or in the community as a whole'. In the rational weighting of the costs and benefits of crime, loss of respect weighs more heavily for most of us than formal punishment. Yet in learning theory terms this rational weighing results from

Abridged from *Crime, Shame and Reintegration*, pp. 69–83. (Cambridge: Cambridge University Press, 1989.)

the operant conditioning part of learning. There is also the much more important effect of consciences which may be classically conditioned by shame [. . .].

A related reading of the deterrence literature is that it shows it is not the formal punitive features of social control that matter, but rather its informal moralizing features. The surprising findings of a classic field experiment by Schwartz and Orleans (1967) has fostered such a reading. Taxpayers were interviewed during the month prior to the filing of income tax returns, with one randomly selected group exposed to an interview stressing the penalties for income tax evasion, the other to an interview stressing the moral reasons for tax compliance. Whereas the moral appeal led to a significant increase in the actual tax paid, the deterrent threat was associated with no significant increase in tax paid compared to a control group.

## Beyond deterrence, beyond operant conditioning: conscience and shaming

Jackson Toby (1964: 333) suggests that deterrence is irrelevant 'to the bulk of the population who have introjected the moral norms of society'. People comply with the law most of the time not through fear of punishment, or even fear of shaming, but because criminal behavior is simply abhorrent to them. Most serious crimes are unthinkable to most people; these people engage in no rational weighing of the costs and benefits of crime before deciding whether to comply with the law. Shaming, we will argue, is critical to understanding why most serious crime is unthinkable to most of us.

The unthinkableness of crime is a manifestation of our conscience or superego, whatever we want to call it depending on our psychological theoretical preferences. [. . .] We will leave it to the psychologists to debate how much the acquisition and generalization of conscience is a conditioning or a cognitive process. The point is that conscience is acquired.

For adolescents and adults, conscience is a much more powerful weapon to control misbehavior than punishment. In the wider society, it is no longer logistically possible, as it is in the nursery, for arrangements to be made for punishment to hang over the heads of persons whenever temptation to break the rules is put in their path. Happily, conscience more than compensates for absence of formal control. For a well-socialized individual, conscience delivers an anxiety response to punish each and every involvement in crime – a more systematic punishment than haphazard enforcement by the police. Unlike any punishment handed down by the courts, the anxiety response happens without delay, indeed punishment by anxiety precedes the rewards obtained from the crime, while any punishment by law will follow long after the reward. For most of us, punishment by our own conscience is therefore a much more potent threat than punishment by the criminal justice system.

Shaming is critical as the societal process that underwrites the family process of building consciences in children. Just as the insurance company cannot do business without the underwriter, the family could not develop young consciences in the cultural vacuum which would be left without societal practices of shaming. Shaming is an important child-rearing practice in itself; it is an extremely valuable tool in the hands of a responsible loving parent. However, as children's morality develops, as socialization moves from building responsiveness to external controls to responsiveness to internal controls, direct forms of shaming become less important than induction: appealing to the child's affection or respect for others, appealing to the child's own standards of right and wrong. [. . .]

However, the external controls must still be there in the background. If the maturation of conscience proceeds as it should, direct forms of shaming, and even more so punishment, are resorted to less and less. But there are times when conscience fails all of us, and we need a refresher course in the consequences of a compromised conscience. In this backstop role, shaming has a great advantage over formal punishment. Shaming is more pregnant with symbolic content than punishment. Punishment is a denial of confidence in the morality of the offender by reducing norm compliance to a crude cost–benefit calculation; shaming can be a reaffirmation of the morality of the offender by expressing personal disappointment that the offender should do something so out of character, and, if the shaming is reintegrative, by expressing personal satisfaction in seeing the character of the offender restored. Punishment erects barriers between the offender and punisher through transforming the relationship into one of power assertion and injury; shaming produces a greater interconnectedness between the parties, albeit a painful one, an interconnectedness which can produce the repulsion of stigmatization or the establishment of a potentially more positive relationship following reintegration. Punishment is often shameful and shaming usually punishes. But whereas punishment gets its symbolic content only from its denunciatory association with shaming, shaming is pure symbolic content.

Nevertheless, just as shaming is needed when conscience fails, punishment is needed when offenders are beyond being shamed. Unfortunately, however, the shameless, the remorseless, those who are beyond conditioning by shame are also likely to be those beyond conditioning by punishment – that is, psychopaths (consider, for example, the work of Mednick on conditionability and psychopathy – which would seem equally relevant to conditioning by fear of shame or fear of formal punishment (Mednick and Christiansen, 1977; Wilson and Herrnstein, 1985: 198–204)). The evidence is that punishment is a very ineffective ultimate backstop with people who have developed beyond the control techniques which were effective when they were infants. This is the problem with behavior modification (based on either rewards or punishment) for rehabilitating offenders. Offenders will play the game by reverting to pre-adolescent responsiveness to reward–cost social control because this is the way they can make their life most comfortable. But when they leave the institution they will return to behaving like the adults they are in an adult world in which punishment contingencies for indulging deviant conduct are remote.

The conscience-building effects of shaming that give it superiority over control strategies based simply on changing the rewards and costs of crime are enhanced by the participatory nature of shaming. Whereas an actual punishment will only be administered by one person or a limited number of criminal justice officials, the shaming associated with punishment may involve almost all of the members of a community. Thus, in the following passage, when Znaniecki refers to 'punishment', he really means the denunciation or shaming associated with the punishment:

Regardless of whether punishment really does deter future violation of the law or not, it seems to significantly reinforce agreement and solidarity among those who actively or vicariously participate in meting it out . . . Opposing the misdemeanours of other people increases the conformity of those administering the punishment, thus leading to the maintenance of the systems in which they participate. (Znaniecki, 1971: 604)

Participation in expressions of abhorrence toward the criminal acts of others is part of what makes crime an abhorrent choice for us ourselves to make. [. . .]

When we shame ourselves, that is when we feel pangs of conscience, we take the role of the other, treating ourselves as an object worthy of shame (Mead, 1934; Shott, 1979). We learn to do this by participating with others in shaming criminals and evil-doers. Internal control is a social product of external control. Self-regulation can displace social control by an external agent only when control has been internalized through the prior existence of external control in the culture.

Cultures like that of Japan, which shame reintegratively, follow shaming ceremonies with ceremonies of repentance and reacceptance. The nice advantage such cultures get in conscience building is two ceremonies instead of one, but, more critically, confirmation of the moral order from two very different quarters – both from those affronted and from him who caused the affront. The moral order derives a very special kind of credibility when even he who has breached it openly comes out and affirms the evil of the breach.

This is achieved by what Goffman (1971: 113) calls disassociation:

An apology is a gesture through which an individual splits himself into two parts, the part that is guilty of an offense and the part that disassociates itself from the delict and affirms a belief in the offended rule.

In cultures like that of Japan which practise disassociation, the vilification of the self that misbehaved by the repentant self can be much more savage than would be safe with vilification by other persons: 'he can overstate or overplay the case against himself, thereby giving others the task of cutting the self-derogation short' (Goffman, 1971: 113).
[. . .]

In summary then, shame operates at two levels to effect social control. First, it deters criminal behavior because social approval of significant others is something we do not like to lose. Second, and more importantly, both shaming and repentance build consciences which internally deter criminal behavior even in the absence of any external shaming associated with an offense. Shaming brings into existence two very different kinds of punishers – social disapproval and pangs of conscience.

[. . .] Community-wide shaming is necessary because most crimes are not experienced within the average household. Children need to learn about the evil of murder, rape, car theft and environmental pollution offenses through condemnation of the local butcher or the far away image on the television screen. But the shaming of the local offender known personally to children in the neighborhood is especially important, because the wrongdoing and the shaming are so vivid as to leave a lasting impression.

Much shaming in the socialization of children is of course vicarious, through stories. Because they are not so vivid as real-life incidents of shaming, they are not so powerful. Yet they are necessary because so many types of misbehavior will not occur in the family or the neighborhood. A culture without stories for children in which morals are clearly drawn and evil deeds clearly identified would be a culture which failed the moral development of its children. Because human beings are story-telling animals, they get much of their identity from answers to the question 'Of what stories do I find myself a part?' 'Deprive children of stories and you leave them unscripted, anxious stutterers in their actions as in their words' (MacIntyre, 1984: 138).

Essentially, societal processes of shaming do three things:

1 They give content to a day-to-day socialization of children which occurs mainly through induction. As we have just seen, shaming supplies the morals which build consciences. The evil of acts beyond the immediate experience of children is more effectively communicated by shaming than by pure reasoning.

2 Societal incidents of shaming remind parents of the wide range of evils about which they must moralize with their children. Parents do not have to keep a checklist of crimes, a curriculum of sins, to ˙ ˙ ᷄uss with their offspring. In a society where shaming is important, ᷄ᷓ ᷆ incidents of shaming will trigger vicarious shaming within t̂ ᷆ so that the criminal code is eventually more or less automatical₋, ᷀ᷢᷓed. Thus, the child will one day observe condemnation of someone who has committed rape, and will ask a parent or other older person about the basis of this wrongdoing, or will piece the story together from a series of such incidents. Of course societies which shame only half-heartedly run a risk that the full curriculum of crimes will not be covered. Both this point and the last one could be summarized in another way by saying that public shaming puts pressure on parents, teachers and neighbors to ensure that they engage in private shaming which is sufficiently systematic.

3 Societal shaming in considerable measure takes over from parental socialization once children move away from the influence of the family and the school. Put another way, shaming generalizes beyond childhood principles learnt during the early years of life.

This third principle is about the 'criminal law as a moral eye-opener' as Andenaes (1974: 116–17) calls it. As a child, I may have learnt the principle that killing is wrong, but when I leave the familiar surroundings of the family to work in the unfamiliar environment of a nuclear power plant, I am taught by a nuclear safety regulatory system that to breach certain safety laws can cost lives, and so persons who breach them are treated with a comparable level of shame. The principle that illegal killing is shameful is generalized. To the extent that genuine shame is not directed against those who defy the safety rules, however, I am liable to take them much less seriously. Unfortunately, societal shaming processes often do fail to generalize to organizational crime.

Recent years in some Western societies have seen more effective shaming directed at certain kinds of offenses – drunk driving, occupational health and safety and environmental offenses, and political corruption. [. . .] This shaming has for many adults integrated new categories of wrongdoing (for which they had not been socialized as children) into the moral frameworks pre-existing from their childhood.

While most citizens are aware of the content of most criminal laws, knowledge of what the law requires of citizens in detail can be enhanced by cases of public shaming. Through shaming directed at new legal frontiers, feminists in many countries have clarified for citizens just what sexual harassment, rape within marriage, and employment discrimination mean. Social change is increasingly rapid, particularly in the face of burgeoning technologies which require new moralities of nuclear, environmental and consumer safety, responsible use of new technologies of information exchange and electronic funds transfer, ethical exploitation of new institutions such as futures exchanges, and so on. Shaming is thus particularly vital in sustaining a contemporarily relevant legal and moral order.

[. . .]

## The problem of discontinuity in socialization practices

The most fundamental problem of socialization in modern societies is that as children mature in the family we gradually wean them from control by punishment to shaming and reasoned appeals to internal controls. The transition from family to school involves a partial reversion back to greater reliance on formal punishment for social control. The further transition to social control on the streets, at discos and pubs by the police is an almost total reversion to the punishment model. A discontinuity with the developmental pattern set in the family is established by the other major socializing institutions for adolescents – the school and the police.

[. . .] Japanese society handles this discontinuity much better than Western societies by having a criminal justice system (and a school system) much more orientated to catalysing internal controls than ours. Japanese police, prosecutors and courts rely heavily on guilt-induction and shaming as alternatives to punishment. If appeals to shame produce expressions of guilt, repentance and a will to seek reunification and forgiveness from loved ones (and/or the victim), this is regarded as the best result by all actors in the drama of criminal justice. The Japanese phenomena of neighborhood police, reintegrative shaming at work and school as alternatives to formal punishment processes, have two effects. First, they put social control back into the hands of significant others, where it can be most effective. Second, they soften some of the discontinuity between the increasing trust to inner controls of family life and the shock of a reversion to external control in the wide world. Just as the evidence shows that aggression and delinquency is the reaction to excessive use of punishment and power assertion as the control strategy within the family, we might expect rebellion against a demeaning punitiveness on the street to be all the more acute when families have eschewed authoritarianism in favor of authoritativeness.

[. . .]

In short, societies which replace much of their punitive social control with shaming and reintegrative appeals to the better nature of people will be societies with less crime. These societies will do better at easing the crushing discontinuity between the shift away from punitive control in home life and the inevitable reversion to heavier reliance on punitive control in the wider society.

[. . .]

## References

Andenaes, J. (1974) *Punishment and Deterrence*. Ann Arbor: University of Michigan Press.

Blau, P.M. (1964) *Exchange and Power in Social Life*. New York: Wiley.

Goffman, E. (1971) *Relations in Public*. New York: Basic Books.

MacIntyre, A. (1984) 'The virtues, the unity of a human life and the concept of a tradition', in M. Sandel (ed.), *Liberalism and Its Critics*. Oxford: Basil Blackwell.

Mead, G.H. (1934) *Mind, Self and Society*. Chicago: University of Chicago Press.

Mednick, S. and Christiansen, K.O. (1977) *Biosocial Bases of Criminal Behavior*. New York: Gardner Press.

Schwartz, R.D. and Orleans, S. (1967) 'On legal sanctions', *University of Chicago Law Review*, 34: 274–300.

Shott, S. (1979) 'Emotion and social life: a symbolic interactionist's analysis', *American Journal of Sociology*, 84: 1317–34.

Tittle, C.R. (1980) *Sanctions and Social Deviance*. New York: Praeger.

Toby, J. (1964) 'Is punishment necessary?' *Journal of Criminal Law, Criminology and Political Science*, 55: 332–7.

Wilson, J.Q. and Herrnstein, R. (1985) *Crime and Human Nature*. New York: Simon and Schuster.

Zimring, F.E. and Hawkins, G.J. (1973) *Deterrence: the Legal Threat in Crime Control*. Chicago: University of Chicago Press.

Znaniecki, F. (1971) *Nauki o Kulturze*. Warsaw: PWN.

# PART SIX
# WITHIN AND BEYOND
# CRIMINOLOGY

---

# Introduction

The readings in this section map the shifts, displacements and diverse debates that constituted critical criminology in the 1980s and early 1990s. As will have been gathered from previous readings, critical criminology attempted to deconstruct and decentre mainstream criminology. However, in the 1980s and 1990s it is critical criminology that is in turmoil and crisis and some would argue on the verge of implosion. As we shall see, long-term conceptual displacements, devastating political dislocations and fundamental paradigmatic convulsions and fractures, challenge and dispute the most solid and meaningful of critical criminology's convictions, assumptions, rationales and parameters.

We start with Jock Young's (1986) clarion call for a left realist criminology that is imaginative, sophisticated and above all policy-relevant. The essential requirement for the Left, according to Young, is to generate a rigorous criminological theory which takes crime seriously by addressing the problem of conventional criminality and producing effective crime control policies. To make realism the fundamental marker of radical criminology, a sustained attack was launched to discredit virtually every aspect of radical criminology's original idealistic and utopian imaginary. Perhaps even more significantly in the long run, left realism deliberately turned away from the wider theoretical debates about postmodernism that were engulfing the wider academy in the 1980s because they were not research-relevant or policy-focused.

Carol Smart's (1990) forceful and elegant article poses a stark question: what has criminology, of any kind, got to offer feminism in the 1990s? In answering it, she takes the left realists to task for choosing to anchor themselves within a criminology which remains tied to a flawed and discredited positivist paradigm. Young, like the founding forefathers, still believes that he can objectively uncover both the causes of and solutions to 'crime'. As a consequence, realist criminology is in a dilemma: it cannot give up on the notion of 'crime' because it would mean looking beyond criminology but in so doing it condemns itself to working within a 'weak thought' discipline. It is this 'reality' that leads Smart to suggest that feminists should abandon the arid, monolithic and totalizing world of criminology altogether and relocate themselves wholeheartedly within wider more open theoretical debates, particularly those emanating from postmodernism and feminism. If they do not, they will remain marginal within criminology and perhaps more seriously risk losing contact with broader eclectic developments in feminist discourse. Maureen Cain's (1990) stringent analysis also exhorts feminist criminologists to situate themselves beyond the essentially narrow conceptual boundaries of traditional and indeed radical criminological thinking. For her there is an urgent need for feminists to constitute a fully post-criminological transgressive perspective that consciously stands 'outside' of criminology. It needs to (i) prioritize questions about women not crime (ii) think seriously about gender and (iii) stress reflexivity, de-construction and re-construction.

Pat Carlen (1992), after detailing its strengths, criticizes left realism for its positivistic, essentializing and deterministic tendencies. But she has even more severe reservations about the theoretical and political implications of the perspectives championed by feminists such as Smart and Cain. In particular she attacks what she describes as their overly theoretical, separatist and gender-centric tendencies. For her those feminists who advocate these approaches are taking the easy way out. She goes on to lay out an extensive feminist realist criminological agenda which involves the de-construction and re-theorization of the problematic relation between 'women and crime' and the development of policies and campaigns which aim to increase criminal justice for women. Overall, she suggests that it is crucial and perfectly possible for feminists to continue to work within as well as against criminology.

Alan Hunt (1991) believes that there is an urgent need for critical criminology to respond in a measured manner to postmodern theorizing. He recognizes that much is at stake in this debate and that the outcome will have profound consequences for the future of critical criminology. He believes that we must give serious consideration to the trenchant postmodern critique of reason, progress, truth, master-narratives and the positivist, mechanistic, linear, predictive, empiricist, rational-logical suppositions of modern science.

Stan Cohen (1993), in the course of his important discussion of human rights and crimes of the state, poses some very uncomfortable questions for both the left realists and the postmodernists. He notes how the realists devoted their efforts to analysing the state of crime and downplayed the criminological and political significance of the crimes of the state. With one or two notable exceptions, critical criminologists have been noticeably silent on the genocide, ethnic cleansing, extra-judicial killings and gross violations of human rights that scarred many parts of the world in the 1980s and 1990s. But as Cohen argues, if nothing else, the concepts of radical and indeed conventional criminology could have been employed to analyse and explain these atrocities. This did not happen and it was human rights campaigners rather than criminologists who spoke for and remembered the victims of these criminal events and demanded that the world take these crimes seriously. Cohen also expresses concern about the political implications of uncritically embracing the postmodernist turn because it is, for example, quite capable of asserting that we have no way of knowing if any of these atrocities ever happened.

Richard Ericson and Kevin Carriere (1994) remind us that it is not just in criminology where fragmentation and blurring is taking place. These are academy-wide processes. There will be criminologists who seek comfort and security in the old truths and those who would re-impose order upon criminology, attempting to police its boundaries against intellectual intruders and punish transgressors. There will be others who will continue to seek technocratic salvation in the patronage of policy-makers by promising to re-orient criminology into an even more relevant control science in future. They hope eventually to be accepted and acknowledged as the real criminologists.

Yet others will continue to have a love/hate relationship with the subject and believe that it is important and intellectually profitable to work within and against criminology and sharpen and extend the criminological 'gaze'. There is likely to be an overall division between those who have invested heavily in existing paradigms and the 'Others' who welcome the final unravelling and fragmentation of criminology and the intellectual insecurity, risk, uncertainty, diversity, reflexivity and plurality this brings in its wake. They are likely to be those marginalized, decentred, unrepresented, muted and denied by the criminological discourse. For outsiders, as Ericson and Carriere suggest, looking beyond the limited horizons of all criminologies is not the problem that it is for those who perceive themselves to be insiders.

# 40

# The failure of criminology: the need for a radical realism

## Jock Young

[. . .]

A silent revolution has occurred in conventional criminology in the United States and in Great Britain. The demise of positivism and social democratic ways of reforming crime has been rapid. A few perceptive commentators have noted the sea-change in the orthodox centre of criminology but the extent of the paradigm shift has been scarcely analysed, or its likely impact understood.

The first sighting of realignment in Western criminology was in a perceptive article written in 1977 by Tony Platt and Paul Takagi entitled 'Intellectuals for law and order' (Platt and Takagi, 1981). They grouped together writers such as Ernest van den Haag, James Q. Wilson and Norval Morris and noted how they represented the demise of 'liberal', social democratic ways of understanding crime and prisons in the United States. 'Intellectuals for law and order are not a criminological fad', they write, but 'a decisive influence in criminology' (Platt and Takagi, 1981: 54). Developing this line of argument, Donald Cressey writes:

> The tragedy is in the tendency of modern criminologists to drop the search for causes and to join the politicians rather than develop better ideas about why crime flourishes, for example, these criminologists Wilson, and van den Haag, Ehrlich, Fogel, Morris and Hawkins – and hundreds of others – seem satisfied with a technological criminology whose main concern is for showing policy-makers how to repress criminals and criminal justice work more efficiently, [and he adds:] If more and more criminologists respond – and they seem to be doing so – criminology will eventually have only 'handcuffs 1a' orientation. (Cressey, 1978)

There is an unfortunate tendency to conflate these various thinkers together as if they were politically similar. But van den Haag is very much a traditional conservative whereas Morris is a 'J.S. Mill' type of liberal and Wilson differs explicitly from both of them. Such a confusion makes it difficult to understand the particular purchase which writers such as James Q. Wilson in the United States and Ron Clarke in Britain have had on the new administrative criminology and their ability to mobilize writers of various positions in support for a broad policy. The basis of this is what all these writers have in common, namely:

1   An antagonism to the notion of crime being determined by social circumstances – 'the smothering of sociological criminology' as Cressey puts it.

Abridged from *Confronting Crime* (eds R. Matthews and J. Young), pp. 9–30. (London: Sage, 1986.)

2   A lack of interest in aetiology. As Platt and Takagi note: '[they] are basically uninterested in the causes of crime. For them, it's a side issue, a distraction and a waste of their valuable time' (Platt and Takagi, 1981: 45). The historic research programme of criminology into causes and the possibilities of rehabilitation is thus abandoned.
3   A belief in human choice in the criminal act.
4   An advocacy of deterrence.

The key figure in this shift is James Q. Wilson in his role as a theoretician, as author of the bestselling book *Thinking About Crime* and as an adviser to the Reagan administration. His central problem and starting-point is the aetiological crisis of social democratic positivist theory and practice:

> If in 1960 one had been asked what steps society might take to prevent a sharp increase in the crime rate, one might well have answered that crime could best be curtailed by reducing poverty, increasing educational attainment, eliminating dilapidated housing, encouraging community organization, and providing troubled or delinquent youth with counseling services . . . .
>
> Early in the decade of the 1960s, this country began the longest sustained period of prosperity since World War II, much of it fueled, as we later realized, by a semi-war economy. A great array of programs aimed at the young, the poor, and the deprived were mounted. Though these efforts were not made primarily out of a desire to reduce crime, they were wholly consistent with - indeed, in their aggregate money levels, wildly exceeded - the policy prescription that a thoughtful citizen worried about crime would have offered at the beginning of the decade.
>
> Crime soared. It did not just increase a little; it rose at a faster rate and to higher levels than at any time since the 1930s and, in some categories, to higher levels than any experienced in this century.
>
> It all began in about 1963. That was the year, to over-dramatize a bit, that a decade began to fall apart. (Wilson, 1975: 3–4)

What then can be done about crime? Wilson does not rule out that crime may be caused by psychological factors or by the breakdown of family structure. But he argues that there is little that public policy can do in this region. He adamantly rules out the option of reducing crime by improving social conditions. In terms of this interpretation of the aetiological crises – the amelioration of social conditions has resulted in an exponential rise in crime rather than its decline. Thus reform on any level is discarded and with it the notion that the reduction of crime can be achieved by an increase in social justice. But there are other factors that policy can manipulate and it is to these that Wilson turns his attention.

Although the poor commit crime more than the rich, he notes that only a small minority of the poor ever commit crimes. People obviously, then, have a choice in the matter; furthermore, these moral choices can be affected by the circumstances decreed by governments. And here he focuses in on the jugular of liberal thinking about crime and punishment:

> If objective conditions are used to explain crime, spokesmen who use poverty as an explanation of crime should, by the force of their own logic, be prepared to consider the capacity of society to deter crime by raising the risks of crime. But they rarely do. Indeed, those who use poverty as an explanation are largely among the ranks of those who vehemently deny that crime can be deterred. (Wilson, 1975: xiv. See also Van den Haag, 1975: 84–90).

The goal of social policy must be to build up effective deterrents to crime. The problem is not to be solved, he argues, by the conservative measures of draconian punishments but rather by an increase of police effectiveness; the certainty of punishment, not its severity, is his key to government action. Thus Wilson differentiates his view from both conservatives and 'liberal'/ social democrats. He advocates punishment but punishment which is appropriate and effective. He sees the informal controls of community as eventually more important than the formal, but that in areas where community has broken down and there is a high incidence of crime, formal control through policing can regenerate the natural regulative functions of the community (the influential Wilson–Kelling hypothesis, see Wilson and Kelling, 1982).

This intellectual current is immensely influential on policy-making in the United States. Thus, the working party set up in the United States in the early years of the Reagan administration under the chairmanship of Wilson gave a low priority, amongst other things, to 'the aetiology of delinquency and a high rating to work in the area of the effects of community cohesiveness and policing for controlling crime' (see Trasler, 1984; Wilson, 1982).

A similar 'social control' theory of crime has been dominant in Britain at the Home Office Research Unit in the recent period particularly influenced by their major theoretician Ron Clarke (see Clarke, 1980). Here, as with Wilson, causal theories of crime came under caution as unproven or impractical (Clarke calls them disposition theories). Situational factors, however, are eminently manipulable. The focus should, therefore, be on making the opportunities for crime more difficult through target hardening, reducing the opportunities for crime and increasing the risks of being caught. This represents a major shift in emphasis against the dispositional bias in almost all previous criminologies.

This move to administrative criminology (or varieties of 'control theory' as Downes and Rock, 1982, would have it) represents the re-emergence of neo-classicist theory on a grand scale. The classicist theory of Beccaria and Bentham had many defects, among them a uniform notion of the impact of the various deterrent devices legislated to control crime (see Rutter and Giller, 1983: 261–2). By introducing concepts of differential risk and opportunity as variables which can be varied by policy-makers and police on a territorial basis, they add a considerable refinement to this model of control. [. . .]

## Left idealism: the loss of a criminology

I have detailed elsewhere the fundamental characteristics of left idealism (Lea and Young, 1984; Young, 1979). Suffice it to say that the tenets of left idealism are simple and familiar to all of us. Crime is seen to occur amongst working-class people as an inevitable result of their poverty, the criminal sees through the inequitable nature of present day society and crime itself is an attempt – however clumsily and ill-thought out – to redress this balance. There is little need to have complex explanations for working-class crime. Its causes are obvious and to blame the poor for their criminality is to blame the victim, to point moral accusations at those whose very actions are a result of their being social casualties. In contrast, the real crime on which we should focus is that of the ruling class: the police, the corporations and the state agencies. This causes real problems for the mass of people, unlike working-class crime which is seen as minor, involving petty theft and occasional violence, of little impact to the working-class community. If the causes of working-class crime are obviously poverty, the causes of upper-class crime are equally obvious: the natural cupidity and power-seeking of the powerful as they enact out the dictates of capital. Criminal law in this context is a direct expression of the ruling class; it is concerned with the protection of their property and the consolidation of their political power. The 'real' function of policing is political rather than the control of crime *per se*; it is social order rather than crime control which is the *raison d'être* of the police.

[. . .]

## The convergence between left idealism and administrative criminology

I have noted that the anomaly which traditional positivist criminology confronted was what I have termed the aetiological crisis; that is, a rapidly rising crime rate despite the increase in all the circumstances which were supposed to decrease crime. This was coupled by a crisis in rehabilitation – the palpable failure of the prison system despite decades of penal 'reform'. With the passing of the 1960s the new administrative criminology concluded that, given that affluence itself had led to crime, it was social control which was the only variable worth focusing upon. On the other hand, left idealism forgot about the affluent period altogether and found the correlation between crime and the recession too obvious to merit a discussion of aetiology. If administrative criminology side-stepped the aetiological crisis, left idealism conveniently forgot about it. Both, from their own political perspective, saw social control as the major focus of the study, both were remarkably un-sophisticated in their analysis of control within the wider society – and anyway were attempting the impossible, to explain the crime control whilst ignoring the causes of crime itself - the other half of the equation.

In a way, such a convergence suggests a stasis in criminological theory. And, of course, this is precisely what has occurred over the past ten years. But, as I have tried to indicate, theory is very much influenced by changes in empirical data and in social and political developments. And it is in this direction, particularly in the phenomenal rise of criminal victimization studies, that we must look for the motor forces which begin to force criminology back to theory.

The empirical anomalies arising from both radical and conventional victim-ology were a major spur to the formation of realist criminology. Paradoxically, findings which nestled so easily with administrative criminology caused conceptual abrasions with left idealism. Thus, as the crisis of aetiology waned, the problem of the victim became predominant.

## The nature of left realism

The basic defect of pathology and of its romantic opposite is that both yield concepts that are untrue to the phenomenon and which thus fail to illuminate it. Pathology reckons without the patent tenability and durability of deviant enterprise, and without the subjective capacity of man to create novelty and manage diversity. Romance, as always, obscures the seamier and more mundane aspects of the world. It obscures the stress that may underlie resilience. (Matza, 1969: 44)

The central tenet of left realism is to reflect the reality of crime, that is in its origins, its nature and its impact. This involves a rejection of tendencies to romanticize crime or to pathologize it, to analyse solely from the point of view of the administration of crime or the criminal actor, to underestimate crime or to exaggerate it. And our understanding of methodology, our interpretation of the statistics, our notions of aetiology follow from this. Most importantly, it is realism which informs our notion of practice: in answering what can be done about the problems of crime and social control.

It is with this in mind that I have mapped out the fundamental principles of left realism

[. . .]

> It is unrealistic to suggest that the problem of crime like mugging is merely the problem of mis-categorization and concomitant moral panics. If we choose to embrace this liberal position, we leave the political arena open to conservative campaigns for law and order – for, however exaggerated and distorted the arguments conservatives may marshal, the reality of crime in the streets *can be* the reality of human suffering and personal disaster. (Young, 1975: 89)

To be realistic about crime as a problem is not an easy task. We are caught between two currents, one which would grotesquely exaggerate the problems of crime, another covering a wide swathe of political opinion that may seriously underestimate the extent of the problem. Crime is a staple of news in the Western mass media and police fiction a major genre of television drama. We have detailed elsewhere the structured distortion of images of crime, victimization and policing which occur in the mass media (see Cohen and Young, 1981). It is a commonplace of criminological research that most violence is between acquaintances and is intra-class and intra-racial. Yet the media abound with images of the dangerous stranger. On television we see folk monsters who are psychopathic killers or serial murderers yet offenders who even remotely fit these caricatures are extremely rare. The police are portrayed as engaged in an extremely scientific investigative policy with high clear-up rates and exciting denouements although the criminologist knows that this is far from the humdrum nature of reality. Furthermore, it grossly conceals the true relationship between police and public in the process of detection, namely that there is an extremely high degree of dependence of the police on public reporting and witnessing of crime.

The nature of crime, of victimization and of policing is thus systematically distorted in the mass media. And it is undoubtedly true that such a barrage of misinformation has its effect – although perhaps scarcely in such a one-to-one way that is sometimes suggested. For example, a typical category of violence in Britain is a man battering his wife. But this is rarely represented in the mass media – instead we have numerous examples of professional criminals engaged in violent crime – a quantitatively minor problem when compared to domestic violence. So presumably the husband can watch criminal violence on television and not see himself there. His offence does not exist as a category of media censure. People watching depictions of burglary presumably get an impression of threats of violence, sophisticated adult criminals and scenes of desecrated homes. But this is of course not at all the normal burglary – which is typically amateurish and carried out by an adolescent boy. When people come home to find their house broken into there is no one there and their fantasies about the dangerous intruder are left to run riot. Sometimes the consequences of such fantastic images of criminals are tragic. For example, people buy large guard dogs to protect themselves. Yet the one most likely to commit violence is the man of the house against his wife, and there are many more relatives – usually children – killed and injured by dogs than by burglars!

In the recent period there has been an alliance between liberals (often involved in the new administrative criminology) and left idealists which evokes the very mirror image of the mass media. The chance of being criminally injured, however slightly, the British Crime Survey tells us, is once in a hundred years (Hough and Mayhew, 1983) and such a Home Office view is readily echoed by left idealists who inform us that crime is, by and large, a minor problem and indeed the fear of crime is more of a problem than crime itself. Thus, they would argue, undue fear of crime provides popular support for conservative law and order campaigns and allows the build-up of further police powers whose repressive aim is political dissent rather than crime. For radicals to enter into the discourse of law and order is further to legitimize it. Furthermore, such a stance maintains that fear of crime has not only ideological consequences, it has material effects on the community itself. For to give credence to the fear of crime is to divide the community – to encourage racism, fester splits between the 'respectable' and 'non-respectable' working class and between youths and adults. More subtly, by emptying the streets particularly at night, it actually breaks down the system of informal controls which usually discourage crime.

Realism must navigate between these two poles; it must neither succumb to hysteria nor relapse into a critical denial of the severity of crime as a problem. It must be fiercely sceptical of official statistics and control institutions without taking the posture of a blanket rejection of all figures or, indeed, the very possibility of reform.

Realism necessitates an accurate victimology. It must counterpoise this against those liberal and idealist criminologies, on the one side, which play down victimization or even bluntly state that the 'real' victim is the offender and, on the other, those conservatives who celebrate moral panic and see violence and robbery as ubiquitous on our streets.

To do this involves mapping out who is at risk and what precise effect crime has on their lives. This moves beyond the invocation of the global risk rates of the average citizen. All too often this serves to conceal the actual severity of crime amongst significant sections of the population whilst providing a fake statistical backdrop for the discussion of 'irrational' fears.

A radical victimology notes two key elements of criminal victimization. First, that crime is focused both geographically and socially on the most vulnerable sections of the community. Secondly, that the impact of victimization is a product of risk rate and vulnerability. Average risk rates across a city ignore such a focusing and imply that equal crimes impact equally. As it is, the most vulnerable are not only more affected by crime, they also have the highest risk rates.

Realism must also trace accurately the relationship between victim and offender. Crime is not an activity of latter day Robin Hoods – the vast majority of working-class crime is directed within the working class. It is intra-class *not* inter-class in its nature. Similarly, despite the mass media predilection for focusing on inter-racial crime it is overwhelmingly intra-racial. Crimes of violence, for example, are by and large one poor person hitting another poor person – and in almost half of these instances it is a man hitting his wife or lover.

This is not to deny the impact of crimes of the powerful or indeed of the social problems created by capitalism which are perfectly legal. Rather, left realism notes that the working class is a victim of crime from all directions. It notes that the more vulnerable a person is economically and socially the more likely it is that *both* working-class and white-collar crime will occur against them; that one sort of crime tends to compound another, as does one social problem another. Furthermore, it notes that crime is a potent symbol of the antisocial nature of capitalism and is the most immediate way in which people experience other problems, such as unemployment or competitive individualism.

Realism starts from problems as people experience them. It takes seriously the complaints of women [with regard to] the dangers of being in public places at night, it takes note of the fears of the elderly with regard to burglary, it acknowledges the widespread occurrence of domestic violence and racist attacks. It does not ignore the fears of the vulnerable nor recontextualize them out of existence by putting them into a perspective which abounds with abstractions such as the 'average citizen' bereft of class or gender. It is only too aware of the systematic concealment and ignorance of crimes against the least powerful. Yet it does not take these fears at face value – it pinpoints their rational kernel but it is also aware of the forces towards irrationality.

Realism is not empiricism. Crime and deviance are prime sites of moral anxiety and tension in a society which is fraught with real inequalities and injustices. Criminals can quite easily become folk devils onto which are projected such feelings of unfairness. But there is a rational core to the fear of crime just as there is a rational core to the anxieties which distort it. Realism argues with popular consciousness in its attempts to separate out reality from fantasy. But it does not deny that crime is a problem. Indeed, if there were no rational core the media would have no power of leverage to the public consciousness. Crime becomes a metaphor but it is a metaphor rooted in reality.

When one examines anxiety about crime, one often finds a great deal more rationality than is commonly accorded to the public. Thus, frequently a glaring discrepancy has been claimed between the high fear of crime of women and their low risk rates. Recent research, particularly by feminist victimologists, has shown that this is often a mere artefact of a low reporting of sexual attacks to interviewers – a position reversed when sympathetic women are used in the survey team (see Hall, 1985; Hanmer and Saunders, 1984; Russell, 1982). Similarly, it is often suggested that fear of crime is somehow a petit bourgeois or upper middle-class phenomenon despite the lower risk rates of the more wealthy. Yet the Merseyside Crime Survey, for example, showed a close correspondence between risk rate and the prioritization of crime as a problem, with the working class having far higher risk rates *and* estimation of the importance of crime as a problem. Indeed, they saw crime as the second problem after unemployment whereas in the middle-class suburbs only 13 per cent of people rated crime as a major problem (see Kinsey et al., 1986). Similarly, Richard Sparks and his colleagues found that working-class people and blacks rated property crimes more seriously than middle-class people and whites (Sparks et al., 1977). Those affected by crime and those most vulnerable are the most concerned about crime.

Of course, there is a fantastic element in the conception of crime. The images of the identity of the criminal and his mode of operation are, as we have seen, highly distorted. And undoubtedly *fear displacement* occurs, where real anxieties about one type of crime are projected on another, as does *tunnel vision*, where only certain sorts of crime are feared, but the evidence for a substantial infrastructure of rationality is considerable.

The emergence of a left realist position in crime has occurred in the last five years. This has involved criminologists in Britain, Canada, the United States and Australia. In particular, the Crime and Justice Collective in California have devoted a large amount of space in their journal for a far-ranging discussion on the need for a left-wing programme on crime control (see e.g., *Crime and Social Justice*, Summer, 1981). There have been also violent denunciations, as the English journalist Martin Kettle put it:

> For their pains the [realists] have been denounced with extraordinary ferocity from the left, sometimes in an almost paranoid manner. To take crime seriously, to take fear of crime seriously and, worst of all, to take police reform seriously, is seen by the fundamentalists as the ultimate betrayal and deviation. (Kettle, 1984: 367)

This, apart, the basis of a widespread support for a realist position has already been made. What remains now is the task of creating a realist *criminology*. For although the left idealist denial of crime is increasingly being rejected, the tasks of radical criminology still remain. That is, to create an adequate explanation of crime, victimization and the reaction of the state. And this is all the more important given that the new administrative criminology has abdicated all such responsibility and indeed shares some convergence with left idealism.

[. . .]

## Conclusion

This article has argued for the need for a systematic programme within radical criminology which should have theoretical, research and policy components. We must develop a realist theory which adequately encompasses the scope of the criminal act. That is, it must deal with both macro- and micro-levels, with the causes of criminal action and social reaction, and with the triangular inter-relationship between offender, victim and the state. It must learn from past theory, take up again the debates between the three strands of criminological theory and attempt to bring them together within a radical rubric. It must stand for theory in a time when criminology has all but abandoned theory. It must rescue the action of causality whilst stressing both the specificity of generalization and the existence of human choice and value in any equation of criminality.

On a research level we must develop theoretically grounded empirical work against the current of atheoretical empiricism. The expansion of radical victimology in the area of victimization surveys is paramount but concern should also be made with regard to developments in qualitative research and ethnography (see West, 1984). The development of sophisticated statistical analysis (see for example Box and Hale, 1986; Greenberg, 1984; Melossi, 1985) should not be anathema to the radical criminologist nor should quantitative and qualitative work be seen as alternatives from which the radical must obviously choose. Both methods, as long as they are based in theory, complement and enrich each other.

In terms of practical policy we must combat impossibilism: whether it is the impossibility of reform, the ineluctable nature of a rising crime rate or the inevitable failure of rehabilitation. It is time for us to *compete* in policy terms, to get out of the ghetto of impossibilism. Orthodox criminology with its inability to question the political and its abandonment of aetiology is hopelessly unable to generate workable policies. All commentators are united about the inevitability of a rising crime rate. Left idealists think it cannot be halted because without a profound social transformation nothing can be done; the new administrative criminologists have given up the ghost of doing anything but the most superficial containment job. Let us state quite categorically that the major task of radical criminology is to seek a solution to the problem of crime and that of a socialist policy is substantially to reduce the crime rate. And the same is true of rehabilitation. Left idealists think that it is at best a con-trick, indeed argue that unapologetic punishment would at least be less mystifying to the offender. The new administrative criminologists seek to construct a system of punishment and surveillance which discards rehabilitation and replaces it with a social behaviourism worthy of the management of white rats in laboratory cages. They both deny the moral nature of crime, that choice is always made in varying determining circumstances and that the denial of responsibility fundamentally misunderstands the reality of the criminal act. As socialists it is important to stress that most working class crime is intra-class, that mugging, wife battering, burglary and child abuse are actions which cannot be morally absolved in the flux of determinacy. The offender should be ashamed, he/she should feel morally responsible within the limits of circumstance and rehabilitation is truly *impossible* without this moral dimension.

Crime is of importance politically because unchecked it divides the working class community and is materially and morally the basis of disorganization: the loss of political control. It is also a potential unifier – a realistic issue, *amongst others*, for recreating community.

Bertram Gross, in a perceptive article originally published in the American magazine *The Nation*, wrote: 'on crime, more than on most matters, the left seems bereft of ideas' (Gross, 1982: 51). He is completely correct, of course, in terms of there being a lack of any developed strategy amongst socialists for dealing with crime. I have tried to show, however, that it was the prevalence – though often implicit and frequently ill-thought [out] – of left idealist ideas which, in fact, directly resulted in the neglect of crime. There is now a growing consensus amongst radical criminologists that crime really is a problem for the working class, women, ethnic minorities: for all the most vulnerable members of capitalist societies, and that something must be done about it. But to recognize the reality of crime as a problem is only the first stage of the business. A fully blown theory of crime must relate to the contradictory reality of the phenomenon as must any strategy for combating it. And it must analyse how working class attitudes to crime are not merely the result of false ideas derived from the mass media and such like but have a rational basis in one moment of a contradictory and wrongly contextualized reality.

In a recent diatribe against radical criminology Carl Klockars remarked: 'Imagination is one thing, criminology another' (Klockars, 1980: 93). It is true that recent criminology has been characterized by a chronic lack of imagination – although I scarcely think that this was what Klockars lamented by his disparaging remark. Many of us were attracted to the discipline because of its theoretical verve, because of the centrality of the study of disorder to understanding society, because of the flair of its practitioners and the tremendous human interest of the subject. Indeed many of the major debates in the social sciences in the 1960s and 1970s focused quite naturally around deviance and social control. And this is as it should be – as it has been throughout history both in social science and in literature – both in mass media and the arts. What is needed now is an intellectual and political imagination which can comprehend the way in which we learn about order through the investigation of disorder. The paradox of the textbook in orthodox criminology is that it takes that which is of great human interest and transmits it into the dullest of 'facts'. I challenge anyone to read one of the conventional journals from cover to cover without having a desperate wish to fall asleep. Research grants come and research grants go and people are gainfully employed but crime remains, indeed it grows and nothing they do seems able to do anything about it. But is it so surprising that such a grotesquely eviscerated discipline should be so ineffective? For the one-dimensional discourse that constitutes orthodox criminology does not even know its own name. It is often unaware of the sociological and philosophical assumptions behind it. James Q. Wilson, for example, has become one of the most influential and significant of the new administrative criminologists. Yet his work and its proposals have scarcely been examined outside of the most perfunctory empiricist discussions. The discipline is redolent with a scientism which does not realize that its relationship with its object of study is more metaphysical than realistic, an apolitical recital of facts, more facts and even more facts [and] then does not want to acknowledge that it is profoundly political, a paradigm that sees its salvation in the latest statistical innovation rather than in any ability to engage with the actual reality of the world. It is ironic that it is precisely in orthodox criminology, where practitioners and researchers are extremely politically constrained, that they write as if crime and criminology were little to do with politics. Radical criminology, by stressing the political nature of crime and social censure, and the philosophical and social underpinnings of the various criminologies is able immediately to take such problems aboard. The key virtue of realist criminology is the central weakness of its administrative opponent.

We are privileged to work in one of the most central, exciting and enigmatic fields of study. It is the very staple of the mass media, a major focus of much day to day public gossip, speculation and debate. And this is as it should be. But during the past decade the subject has been eviscerated, talk of theory, causality and justice has all but disappeared and what is central to human concern has been relegated to the margins. It is time for us to go back to the drawing boards, time to regain our acquaintanceship with theory, to dispel amnesia about the past and adequately comprehend the present. This is the central task of left realist criminology: we will need more than a modicum of imagination and scientific ability to achieve it.

# References

Box, S. and Hale, C. (1986) 'Unemployment, crime and imprisonment, and the enduring problem of prison overcrowding', in R. Matthews and J. Young (eds), *Confronting Crime*. London: Sage.

Clarke, R. (1980) 'Situational crime prevention: theory and practice', *British Journal of Criminology*, 20(2): 136–47.

Cohen, S. and Young, J. (1981) *The Manufacture of News*, rev. edn. London: Constable/Beverly Hills, CA: Sage.

Cressey, D. (1978) 'Criminological theory, social science, and the repression of crime', *Criminology*, 16: 171–91.

Downes, D. and Rock, P. (1982) *Understanding Deviance*. Oxford: Clarendon Press.

Greenberg, D.F. (1984) 'Age and crime: in search of sociology'. Mimeo.

Gross, B. (1982) 'Some anticrime proposals for Progressives', *Crime and Social Justice*, Summer, 51–4.

Hall, R.E. (1985) *Ask Any Woman – a London Enquiry into Rape and Sexual Assault*. Bristol: Falling Wall Press.

Hanmer, J. and Saunders, S. (1984) *Well-Founded Fears: a Community Study of Violence to Women*. London: Hutchinson.

Hough, M. and Mayhew, P. (1983) *The British Crime Survey: First Report*. London: Home Office Research and Planning Unit.

Kettle, M. (1984) 'The police and the Left', *New Society*, 70(1146): 366–7.

Kinsey, R., Lea, J. and Young, J. (1986) *Losing the Fight Against Crime*. Oxford: Blackwell.

Klockars, C. (1980) 'The contemporary crisis of Marxist criminology', in J. Incardi (ed.), *Radical Criminology: the Coming Crisis*, Beverly Hills, CA: Sage.

Lea, J. and Young, J. (1984) *What is to be Done About Law and Order?* Harmondsworth: Penguin.

Matza, D. (1969) *Becoming Deviant*. Englewood Cliffs, NJ: Prentice Hall.

Melossi, D. (1985) 'Punishment and social action', in S.C. McNall (ed.), *Current Perspectives in Social Theory*. Greenwich, CT: JAI Press.

Platt, T. and Takagi, P. (1981) 'Intellectuals for law and order: a critique of the New Realists', in T. Platt and P. Takagi (eds), *Crime and Social Justice*. London: Macmillan.

Russell, D. (1982) *Rape in Marriage*. New York: Macmillan.

Rutter, M. and Giller, H. (1983) *Juvenile Delinquency*. Harmondsworth: Penguin Books.

Sparks, R., Genn, H. and Dodd, D. (1977) *Surveying Victims: a Study of the Measurement of Criminal Victimisation*. Chichester: Wiley.

Trasler, G. (1984) *Crime and Criminal Justice Research in the United States*, Home Office Research Bulletin, 18, HMSO.

Van den Haag, E. (1975) *Punishing Criminals*. New York: Basic Books.

West, G. (1984) 'Phenomenon and form', in L. Barton and S. Walker (eds), *Educational Research and Social Crisis*. London: Croom Helm.

Wilson, J.Q. (1975) *Thinking About Crime*. New York: Vintage.

Wilson, J.Q. (1982) *Report and Recommendations of the Ad Hoc Committee on the Future of Criminal Justice Research*. Washington, DC: National Institute of Justice.

Wilson, J.Q. and Kelling, G. (1982) 'Broken Windows', *The Atlantic Monthly*, March, pp. 29–38.

Young, J. (1975) 'Working class criminology', in I. Taylor, P. Walton and J. Young (eds), *Critical Criminology*. London: Routledge and Kegan Paul.

Young, J. (1979) 'Left idealism, reformism and beyond: from New Criminology to Marxism', in B. Fine et al. (eds), *Capitalism and the Rule of Law: From Deviancy Theory to Marxism*. London: Hutchinson.

# 41

# Feminist approaches to criminology or postmodern woman meets atavistic man

*Carol Smart*

[. . .]

It is a story that has been told many times, although most effectively in *The New Criminology* (Taylor et al., 1973) that criminology is an applied discipline which searches for the causes of crime in order to eradicate the problem. Admittedly, criminology as a subject embraces much more than this. For example, it tends to focus also on the operations of the criminal justice system, the relationship between the police and communities or systems of punishment. However, such topics fit just as easily under the rubric of the sociology of law or even philosophy. What is unique about criminology, indeed its defining characteristic, is the central question of the *causes* of crime and the ultimate focus of the 'offender' rather than on mechanisms of discipline and regulation which go beyond the limits of the field of crime. It is this defining characteristic with which I wish to take issue here. Arguably, it is this which creates a kind of vortex in this area of intellectual endeavour. It is the ultimate question against which criminology is judged. Can the causes of crime be identified and explained? Moreover, once identified, can they be modified?

Criminologies of the traditional schools have been unashamedly inter-ventionist in aim if not always in practice. This goal was criticized by the radical criminologists of the 1970s for being oppressive, conservative and narrowly partisan (that is, on the side of the state and/or powerful). Moreover, the radicals argued that the traditional criminologists had, in any case, got their theories wrong. Crime, it was argued, could not be explained by chromosomal imbalance, hereditary factors, working-class membership, racial difference, intelligence and so on. So, among the many errors of traditional criminology, the two main ones to be identified were an inherent conser-vatism and inadequate theorization. The repudiation of these errors was condensed into the most critically damning term of abuse – positivist. To be positivist embodied everything that was bad. Positivism, like functionalism, had to be sought out, exposed and eliminated. Now, in some respects I would agree with this; but the problem we face is whether critical criminologies or the more recent left realist criminologies have transcended the problem of positivism or whether they have merely projected it on to their political opponents while assuming that they themselves are untainted.

I would argue that positivism is misconstrued if its main problem is seen as

Abridged from *Feminist Perspectives in Criminology* (eds A. Morris and L. Gelsthorpe), pp. 71–84. (Milton Keynes: Open University Press, 1990.)

its connection to a conservative politics or a biological determinism. The problem of positivism is arguably less transparent than this and lies in the basic presumption that we can establish a verifiable knowledge or truth about events: in particular, that we can establish a causal explanation which will in turn provide us with objective methods for intervening in the events defined as problematic. Given this formulation, positivism may be, at the level of political orientation, either socialist or reactionary. The problem of positivism is, therefore, not redeemed by the espousal of left politics. Positivism poses an epistemological problem; it is not a simple problem of party membership.

It is this problem of epistemology which has begun to attract the attention of feminist scholarship (the postmodern woman of my title). Feminism is now raising significant questions about the status and power of knowledge (Harding, 1986; Weedon, 1987) and formulating challenges to modes of totalizing or grand theorizing which impose a uniformity of perspective and ignore the immense diversity of subjectivities of women and men. This has in turn led to a questioning of whether 'scientific' work can ever provide a basis for intervention as positivism would presuppose. This is not to argue that intervention is inevitably undesirable or impossible, but rather to challenge the modernist assumption that, once we have the theory ('master' narrative, (Kellner, 1988)) which will explain all forms of social behaviour, we will also know what to do and that the rightness of this 'doing' will be verifiable and transparent.

### The continuing search for the theory, the cause and the solution

It is useful to concentrate on the work of Jock Young as a main exponent of left realism in criminology. His work is particularly significant because, unlike many other left thinkers, he has remained inside criminology and, while acknowledging many of the problems of his earlier stance in critical criminology, has sustained a commitment to the core element of the subject. That is to say he addresses the question of the causes of crime and the associated problems of attempting to devise policies to reduce crime. For example, he states:

> It is time for us to *compete* in policy terms . . . the major task of radical criminology is to seek a solution to the problem of crime and that of a socialist policy is to substantially reduce the crime rate. (1986: 28, emphasis in the original)

This is compelling stuff but it is precisely what I want to argue is problematic about the new forms of radical criminology for feminism. It might be useful initially to outline Young's position before highlighting some of the problems it poses.

As part of his call for a left realist criminology, Young (1986) constructs a version of the recent history of post-war criminology. He sees it as a series of crises and failures (and in this respect we are at one). He points to the positivist heritage of post-war criminology in Britain which, in his account, amounts to a faith in medicine and cure and/or a reliance on biologically determinist explanations of crime. He sees the influence of North American criminology in a positive light, [. . .] and then turns to the work of the 'new criminologists' in Britain who constructed a political paradigm in which to reappraise criminal behaviour. He is, however, critical of the idealism of this work and interprets it as the 'seedbed' of more radical work to come rather than a real challenge to mainstream orthodoxy or an adequate account in and of itself.

The failures of the criminological enterprise overall which Young identifies are twofold. The first is the failure 'really' to explain criminal behaviour. The theories are always flawed either ontologically or politically. The second is the failure to solve the problem of crime or even to stem its rise. These are not two separate failures, however, as the failure to stop crime is 'proof' of the failure of the theories to explain the causes of crime. [. . .] It is through this linkage between theory and policy that the positivism of the left realists comes to light. The problem is not that there is a commitment to reducing the misery to which crime is often wedded, nor is the problem that socialists (and feminists) want policies which are less punitive and oppressive. The problem is that science is held to have the answer if only it is scientific enough. Here is revealed the faith in the totalizing theory, the 'master' narrative which will eventually – when sufficient scales have fallen from our eyes or sufficient connections have been made – allow us to see things for what they really are.

To return to Young's story, we pick up the unfolding of criminology at the point of intervention by the new criminologists. Young points out that while this intervention may have excited the academic criminologists there was simultaneously another revolution in mainstream criminology. This revolution was the transformation of traditional criminology from a discipline concerned with causes and cures to one concerned with administrative efficiency and methods of containment. Young argues that mainstream criminology has given up the search for causes, the goal of the meta-narrative of criminal causation. It has gone wholeheartedly over to the state and merely provides techniques of control and manipulation. Again it is important to highlight the linkages in Young's argument. On the one hand, he is critical of what he calls administrative criminology because it has become (even more transparently?) an extension of the state (or a disciplinary mechanism). But the reason for this is identified as the abandonment of the search for the causes (a search which was, according to Young, in any case misdirected). The thesis, therefore, is that to abandon the search for the causes is to become prey to reactionary forces. This, it seems to me, is to ignore completely the debates which have been going on within sociology and cultural theory about the problems of grand and totalizing theories. And such ideas are coming not from the right but precisely from the subjects which such theoretical enterprises have subjugated, that is, lesbians and gays, black women and men, Asian women and men, feminists and so on. I shall briefly consider aspects of this debate before returning to the specific problem of feminism in criminology.

## The debate over postmodernism

There is now a considerable literature on postmodernism and a number of scholars are particularly concerned to explore the consequences of this development for sociology (Bauman, 1988; Kellner, 1988; Smart, 1989) and for feminism (Fraser and Nicholson, 1988; Harding, 1986; Weedon, 1987). The concept of postmodernism derives from outside the social sciences, from the fields of architecture and art (Rose, 1988). Bauman (1988) argues that we should not assume that postmodernism is simply another word for post-industrialism or post-capitalism. It has a specific meaning and a specific significance, especially for a discipline like sociology (and by extension criminology), one which challenges the very existence of such an enterprise. Postmodernism refers to a mode of thinking which threatens to overturn the basic premises of modernism within which sociology has been nurtured.

Briefly, the modern age has been identified by Foucault (1973) as beginning at the start of the nineteenth century. The rise of modernity marks the eclipsing of Classical thought and, most importantly, heralds the centring of the conception of 'man' as the knowing actor who is author of his own actions and knowledge (that is, the liberal subject) and who simultaneously becomes the object of (human) scientific enquiry. Modernism is, however, more than the moment in which the human subject is constituted and transformed. It is a world view, a way of seeing and interpreting, a science which holds the promise that it can reveal the truth about human behaviour. The human sciences, at the moment of constituting the human subject, make her knowable – a site of investigation. What secrets there are will succumb to better knowledge, more rigorous methodologies, or more accurate typologizing. Implicit in the modernist paradigm is the idea that there is progress. What we do not know now, we will know tomorrow. It presumes that it is only a matter of time before science can explain all from the broad sweep of societal change to the motivations of the child molester. And because progress is presumed to be good and inevitable, science inevitably serves progress. Knowledge becomes nothing if it is not knowledge for something. Knowledge must be applied or applicable – even if we do not know how to apply it now, there is the hope that one day we will find a use for it (space travel did after all justify itself for we do now have non-stick frying pans).

Modernity has now become associated with some of the most deep-seated intellectual problems of the end of the twentieth century. It is seen as synonymous with racism, sexism, Euro-centredness and the attempt to reduce cultural and sexual differences to one dominant set of values and knowledge. Modernism is the intellectual mode of Western thought which has been identified as male or phallogocentric (for example, by Duchen, 1986 and Gilligan, 1982) and as white or Eurocentric (for example, by Dixon, 1976 and Harding, 1987). It is also seen as an exhausted mode, one which has failed to live up to its promise and which is losing credibility. As Bauman argues:

> Nobody but the most rabid of the diehards believes today that the western mode of life, either the actual one or one idealized ('utopianized') in the intellectual mode has more than a sporting chance of ever becoming universal . . . The search for the universal standards has suddenly become gratuitous . . . Impracticality erodes interest. The task of establishing universal standards of truth, morality, taste does not seem that much important. (1988: 220-1)

Clinging to modernist thought, in this account, is not only antediluvian; it is also politically suspect. It presumes that sociology (which for brevity's sake I shall take to include criminology in this section) as a way of knowing the world is superior, more objective, more truthful than other knowledges. However, it is easier said than done to shake off the grip of a way of knowing which is almost all one knows. In turn, this reflects a dilemma which has always plagued sociology. If we say we do not know (in the modernist sense) then we seem to be succumbing to the forces of the right who have always said we knew nothing – or, at least, that we were good for nothing.

The irony is, as Bauman (1988) points out, that we are damned if we do and also if we do not. He points to the way in which sociology has little choice but to recognize the failure of its originating paradigm. On the one hand, doubts cannot be wished away and we cannot pretend that sociology produces the goods that the post-war welfare state required of it. On the other hand, governments already know this. We cannot keep it a secret. State funding of sociological research is already much reduced and what will be funded is narrowly restricted to meet governmental aims. It may have been possible in the past to claim that more money was necessary or that a larger study was imperative before conclusions could be drawn but now we know (and they know) that conclusions, in the sense of final definitive statements, cannot be drawn. The point is whether we argue that all the studies that have been carried out to date have been inadequate or whether we reappraise the very idea that we will find solutions. Young, for example, is scathing about a major study carried out on 400 schoolboys by West (1969). He points out that this was one of the largest and most expensive pieces of criminological work to be carried out in Britain. Yet, he argues disparagingly, it could only come up with a link between delinquency and poverty and no real causes. For Young the problem is the intellectual bankruptcy of the positivist paradigm. From where I stand he is right, but, as I shall argue below, the problem is that he locates himself inside exactly the same paradigm.

## The vortex that is criminology

It is, then, interesting that Young acknowledges many of the problems outlined above, although he does not do so from a postmodern stance. Rather he is situated inside the modernist problematic itself. He acknowledges that mainstream criminology has given up the search for causes and the 'master' narrative. He also recognizes the power of governments to diminish an academic enterprise which they no longer have use for. Hence, to keep their jobs, criminologists have had to give up promising the solutions and knuckle down to oiling the wheels. He is rightly critical of this, but, rather than seeing the broad implications of this development, these criminolo*gists* are depicted as capitalist lackeys while criminolog*y* as an enterprise can be saved from such political impurity by a reassertion of a modernist faith. While applauding Young's resistance to the logic of the market which has infected much of criminology (and sociology), I am doubtful that a backward looking, almost nostalgic, *cri de coeur* for the theory that will answer everything is very convincing. Yet Young can see nothing positive in challenging the modernist mode of thought; he only sees capitulation. The way to resist is apparently to proclaim that suffering is real and that we still need a 'scientific' solution for it.

In so doing Young claims the moral high ground for the realists, since to contradict the intellectual content of the argument appears to be a denial of misery and a negation of the very constituencies for whom he now speaks. So, let me make it plain that the challenge to modernist thought, with its positivist overtones which are apparent in criminology, does not entail a denial of poverty, inequality, repression, racism, sexual violence and so on. Rather it denies that the intellectual can divine the answer to these through the demand for more scientific activity and bigger and better theories.

The problem which faces criminology is not insignificant, however, and, arguably, its dilemma is even more fundamental than that facing sociology. The whole *raison d'être* of criminology is that it addresses crime. It categorizes a vast range of activities and treats them as if they were all subject to the same laws – whether laws of human behaviour, genetic inheritance, economic rationality, development or the like. The argument within criminology has always been between those who give primacy to one form of explanation rather than another. The thing that criminology cannot do is deconstruct crime. It cannot locate rape or child sexual abuse in the domain of sexuality or theft in the domain of economic activity or drug use in the domain of health. To do so would be to abandon criminology to sociology; but more importantly it would involve abandoning the idea of a unified problem which requires a unified response – at least, at the theoretical level. However, left realist criminology does not seem prepared for this: see, for example, Young, 1986: 27–8.

## Feminist intervention into criminology

[. . .] the core enterprise of criminology is profoundly problematic. However, it is important to acknowledge that it is not just criminology which is inevitably challenged by the more general reappraisal of modernist thinking. My argument is not that criminology alone is vulnerable to the question of whether or not such a knowledge project is tenable. But criminology does occupy a particularly significant position in this debate because both traditional and realist criminological thinking are especially wedded to the positivist paradigm of modernism. This makes it particularly important for feminist work to challenge the core of criminology and to avoid isolation from some of the major theoretical and political questions which are engaging feminist scholarship elsewhere. It might, therefore, be useful to consider schematically a range of feminist contributions to criminology to see the extent to which feminism has resisted or succumbed to the vortex.

### Feminist empiricism

Sandra Harding (1986, 1987) has provided a useful conceptual framework for mapping the development of feminist thought in the social sciences. She refers to feminist empiricism, standpoint feminism and postmodern feminism. By feminist empiricism she means that work which has criticized the claims to objectivity made by mainstream social science. Feminist empiricism points out that what has passed for science is in fact the world perceived from the perspective of men, what looks like objectivity is really sexism and that the kinds of questions social science has traditionally asked have systematically excluded women and the interests of women. Feminist empiricism, therefore, claims that a truly objective science would not be androcentric but would take account of both genders. What is required under this model is that social scientists live up to their proclaimed codes of objectivity. Under this schema, empirical practice is critiqued but empiricism remains intact. Such a perspective is not particularly threatening to the established order. It facilitates the study of female offenders to fill the gaps in existing knowledge; men can go on studying men and the relevances of men as long as they acknowledge that it is men and not humanity they are addressing.

In criminology there has been a growth in the study of female offenders (for example, Carlen, 1988; Eaton, 1986; Heidensohn, 1985). It would be unjust to suggest that these have merely followed the basic tenets of mainstream empirical work, but a motivating element in all of these has been to do studies on women. But, as Dorothy Smith pointed out in 1973, to direct research at women without revising traditional assumptions about methodology and epistemology can result in making women a mere addendum to the main project of studying men. It also leaves unchallenged the way men are studied.

Harding sees a radical potential in feminist empiricism, however. She argues that the fact that feminists identify different areas for study (for example, wife abuse rather than delinquency) has brought a whole range of new issues on to the agenda. It is also the case that feminists who subscribe to empiricism have challenged the way we arrive at the goal of objective knowledge. Hence different kinds of methods are espoused, note is taken of the power relationship between researcher and researched and so on (Stanley and Wise, 1983). The move towards ethnographic research is an example of this (although this is not, of course, peculiar to feminist work).

It is perhaps important at this stage to differentiate between empiricism and empirical work. Harding's categories refer to epistemological stances rather than practices (although the two are not unrelated). Empiricism is a stance which proclaims the possibility of objective and true knowledge which can be arrived at and tested against clearly identified procedures. Mainstream criminology, having followed these tenets, claimed to have discovered valid truths about women's criminal behaviour (and, of course, men's). The initial reaction of feminism to this claim was to reinterpret this truth as a patriarchal lie. It was argued that the methods used had been tainted with bias and so the outcome was inevitably faulty (Smart, 1986). This left open the presumption that the methods could be retained if the biases were removed because the ideal of a true or real science was posited as the alternative to the biased one.

Empirical research does not have to be attached to empiricism, however. To engage with women, to interview them, to document their oral histories, to participate with them, does not automatically mean that one upholds the ideal of empiricism. To be critical of empiricism is not to reject empirical work *per se*. However, some of the empirical studies, generated under the goal of collecting more knowledge about women, which feminist empiricism engendered presented a different sort of problem for the project of a feminist criminology.

This problem was the thorny question of discrimination. The early feminist contributions did not only challenge the objectivity of criminological thought; they challenged the idea of an objective judiciary and criminal justice system. Hence there grew up a major preoccupation with revealing the truth or otherwise of equality before the law in a range of empirical studies. Some studies seemed to find that the police or courts treated women and girls more leniently than men and boys. Others found the opposite. Then there were discoveries that much depended on the nature of the offence or the length of previous record or whether the offender was married or not (see, for example, Farrington and Morris, 1983). As Gelsthorpe (1986) has pointed out, the search for straightforward sexism was more difficult than anyone imagined at first. It was, of course, a false trail in as much as it was anticipated that forms of oppression (whether sexual or racial or other) could be identified in a few simple criteria which could then be established (or not) in following a ritual procedure. So in this respect the (with the benefit of hindsight) overly simplistic approach of early feminist work in this field has created an obstacle to further developments.

The other drawback to this type of research is the one which has been highlighted by MacKinnon (1987). She argues that any approach which focuses on equality and inequality always presumes that the norm is men. Hence studies of the criminal justice system always compare the treatment of women with men and men remain the standard against which all are judged. This has led to two problems. The first arouses a facile, yet widespread, reaction that if one has the audacity to compare women to men in circumstances where men are more favourably treated, then in those instances where they are treated less favourably one must, *ipso facto*, also be requiring the standard of treatment for women to be reduced. Hence, in comparing how the courts treat men and women, the response is inevitably the threat that if women want equality they must have it in full and so some feminists want women to be sent in their droves to dirty, violent and overcrowded prisons for long periods of time. This is what Lahey (1985) has called 'equality with a vengeance'.

The second problem goes beyond the transparent difficulties of treating women as if they were men to the level of the symbolic. Basically the equality paradigm always reaffirms the centrality of men. Men continue to constitute the norm, the unproblematic, the natural social actor. Women are thus always seen as interlopers into a world already organized by others. This has been well established in areas like employment law where the equality argument has been seen unintentionally to reproduce men as the ideal employees, with women struggling to make the grade (Kenney, 1986). Underlying such an approach in any case is the presumption that law is fundamentally a neutral object inside a liberal regime, thus wholly misconstruing the nature of power and the power of law (Smart, 1989). Law does not stand outside gender relations and adjudicate upon them. Law is part of these relations and is always already gendered in its principles and practices. We cannot separate out one practice – called discrimination – and ask for it to cease to be gendered as it would be a meaningless request. This is not to say we cannot object to certain principles and practices but we need to think carefully before we continue to sustain a conceptual framework which either prioritizes men as the norm, or assumes that genderlessness (or gender-blindness) is either possible or desirable.

*Standpoint feminism*

The second category identified by Harding is standpoint feminism. The epistemological basis of this form of feminist knowledge is experience. However, not just any experience is deemed to be equally valuable or valid. *Feminist* experience is achieved through a struggle against oppression; it is, therefore, argued to be more complete and less distorted than the perspective of the ruling group of men. A feminist standpoint then is not just the experience of women, but of women *reflexively* engaged in struggle (intellectual and political). In this process it is argued that a more accurate or fuller version of reality is achieved. This stance does not divide knowledge from values and politics but sees knowledge arising from engagement.

Arguably, standpoint feminism does not feature strongly in feminist criminology except in quite specific areas of concern like rape, sexual assault and wife abuse. It is undoubtedly the influence of feminists engaged at a political level with these forms of oppression that has begun to transform some areas of criminological thinking. Hence the work of Rape Crisis Centres [. . .] has been vital in proffering an alternative 'truth' about rape and women's experience of the criminal justice system. However, as far as mainstream criminology is concerned we should perhaps not be too optimistic about this since the accounts provided by such organizations have only been partially accepted and, even then, as a consequence of substantiation by more orthodox accounts (Blair, 1985; Chambers and Millar, 1983).

Taking experience as a starting-point and testing ground has only made a partial entry into criminology and, interestingly, where it has entered has been in the domain of left realism. It is here we find the resort to experience (that is, women's experience of crime) a constant referent and justification. Women's fear of rape and violence is used in this context to argue that rape and violence must be treated as serious problems. The question that this poses is whether we now have a feminist realist criminology or whether left realism (and consequently criminology as a whole) has been revitalized by the energies and concerns of a politically active women's movement. If we consider texts like *Well-Founded Fear* (Hanmer and Saunders, 1984) or *Leaving Violent Men* (Binney et al., 1981), we find that the motivating drive is the desire to let women's experiences be told. These experiences are not meant to stand alongside the experiences of the police or violent men; they represent the expression of subjugation which will replace the dominant account. Hanmer and Saunders outline methodological procedures for tapping into this experience and produce what Harding has referred to as a 'successor science'. As she argues, 'the adoption of this standpoint is fundamentally a moral and political act of commitment to understanding the world from the perspective of the socially subjugated' (1986: 149). In fact, it goes beyond this as the researchers, as feminists, also inhabit the world of the socially subjugated. It is not an act of empathy as such but a shared knowledge.

The real issue remains unresolved, however. For while feminist work is generating another sort of knowledge (for example, other ways of accounting for violence), feminist work which fits under the umbrella of left realist criminology does not embrace the full scope of what Young has called for. [. . .] This is because standpoint feminism has not taken masculinity as a focus of investigation. Precisely because standpoint feminism in this area has arisen from a grassroots concern to protect women and to reveal the victimization of women, it has not been sympathetic to the study of masculinity(ies). Indeed, it would argue that we have heard enough from that quarter and that any attempt by feminists to turn their attention away from women is to neglect the very real problems that women still face. So the feminist realists (if we can use this term for the sake of argument) are on quite a different trajectory from the left realists. It may be convenient to the Left to support the work of feminists in this area but it is unclear to me where this unholy 'alliance' is going analytically. Like the protracted debate about the marriage of Marxism and feminism, we may find that this alliance ends in annulment.

*Feminist postmodernism*

It would be a mistake to depict feminist postmodernism as the third stage or synthesis of feminist empiricism and standpoint feminism. Feminist post-modernism does not try to resolve the problems of other positions; rather it starts from a different place and proceeds in other directions. Much post-modern analysis is rooted in philosophy and aesthetics (Fekete, 1988; Lyotard, 1986; Rorty, 1985) but in the case of feminism it started in political practice. It began with the separate demises of sisterhood and of Marxism.

By the demise of sisterhood, I mean the realization that women were not all white, middle-class and of Anglo-Saxon, Protestant extract. Feminism resisted this realization by invoking notions of womanhood as a core essence to unite women (under the leadership of the said white, middle-class and Protestant women). However, black feminists, lesbian feminists, Third World feminists, aboriginal feminists and many others simply refused to swallow the story. To put it simply, they knew power when they saw it exercised. Feminism had to abandon its early framework and to start to look for other ways of thinking which did not subjugate other subjectivities. But at the same time, feminism came to recognize that individual women did not have unitary selves. Debates over sexuality, pornography and desire began to undo the idea of the true self and gave way to notions of fractured subjectivities. These developments were much influenced by the work of Foucault and psychoanalytic theory but they cannot be dismissed simply as a 'fad' because the recognition of the inadequacy of the feminist paradigm was not imposed by the intellectuals but arose out of a series of painful struggles for understanding combined with a progressive political stance.

The other key element in this development was the demise of Marxism as a rigorously policed grid of analysis, adherence to which had meant the promise of the total explanation or master narrative. Again, feminist practice revealed the inadequacy of the grand theoretical project of Marxism quite early in the second wave. But the struggle to retain the paradigm lasted much longer. None the less it is now realized that we cannot keep adding bits of Marxist orthodoxy to try to explain all the awkward silences. While many Marxian values may be retained, the idea and the promise of the totalizing theory have gradually loosened their grip.

The core element of feminist postmodernism is the rejection of the one reality which arises from 'the falsely universalizing perspective of the master' (Harding, 1987: 188). But unlike standpoint feminism it does not seek to impose a different unitary reality. Rather it refers to subjugated knowledges, which tell different stories and have different specificities. Thus the aim of feminism ceases to be the establishment of the feminist truth and becomes the deconstruction of truth and analysis of the power effects which claims to truth entail. So there is a shift away from treating knowledge as ultimately objective or, at least, the final standard and hence able to reveal the concealed truth, towards recognizing that knowledge is part of power and that power is ubiquitous. Feminist knowledge, therefore, becomes part of a multiplicity of resistances. Take, for example, feminist interventions in the area of rape. This is an area which I have explored in detail elsewhere (Smart, 1989) but for the sake of this discussion I wish to rely on the work of Woodhull (1988). Woodhull, in an article on sexuality and Foucault, argues against a traditional feminist mode of explanation for rape. She concentrates on Brownmiller's

(1975) approach which seeks to explain rape in terms of the physiological differences between men and women. Woodhull's argument is that in explaining rape in this way, Brownmiller puts sex and biology outside the social, as preceding all power relations. What is missing is an understanding of how sexual difference and the meanings of different bits of bodies are constructed. Woodhull argues:

> If we are seriously to come to terms with rape, we must explain how the vagina comes to be coded – and experienced – as a place of emptiness and vulnerability, the penis as a weapon, and intercourse as violation, rather than naturalize these processes through references to 'basic' physiology. (1988: 171)

So it becomes a concern of feminism to explore how women's bodies have become saturated with (hetero)sex, how codes of sexualized meaning are reproduced and sustained and to begin (or continue) the deconstruction of these meanings.

This is just one example of how postmodernism is influencing feminist practice (for others, see Diamond and Quinby, 1988; Fraser and Nicholson, 1988; Jardine, 1985; Weedon, 1987) and it is clear that the ramifications of the epistemological crisis of modernism are far from being fully mapped or exhaustively considered as yet. We are in no position to judge what shapes feminism will take in the next decade or so. However, it might be interesting to consider, albeit prematurely, what all this means for criminology.

## Concluding remarks

It is a feature of postmodernism that questions posed within a modernist frame are turned about. So, for a long time, we have been asking 'what does feminism have to contribute to criminology (or sociology)?'. Feminism has been knocking at the door of established disciplines hoping to be let in on equal terms. These established disciplines have largely looked down their noses (metaphorically speaking) and found feminism wanting. Feminism has been required to become more objective, more substantive, more scientific, more anything before a grudging entry could be granted. But now the established disciplines are themselves looking rather insecure (Bauman, 1988) and, as the door is opening, we must ask whether feminism really does want to enter.

Perhaps it is now apt to rephrase the traditional question to read 'what has criminology got to offer feminism?' Feminism is now a broadly based scholarship and political practice. Its concerns range from questions of philosophy to representations to engagement; it is, therefore, no longer in the supplicant position of an Olivia Twist. On the contrary, we have already seen that a lot of feminist work has revitalized radical criminology. It might be that criminology needs feminism more than the converse. Of course, many criminologists, especially the traditional variety, will find this preposterous; but perhaps they had better look to who their students are and who their students are reading.

It is clear that if mainstream criminology remains unchanged it will follow the path that Young has outlined into greater and greater complicity with mechanisms of discipline. However, the path of radical criminology seems wedded to the modernist enterprise and is, as yet, unaffected by the epistemological sea-changes which have touched feminism and other discourses. Under such circumstances, it is very hard to see what criminology has to offer to feminism.

## References

Bauman, Z. (1988) 'Is there a postmodern sociology?', *Theory, Culture and Society*, 5(2/3): 217–38.

Binney, V., Harknell, G. and Nixon, J. (1981) *Leaving Violent Men: a Study of Refuges and Housing for Battered Women*. Leeds: Women's Aid Federation.

Blair, I. (1985) *Investigating Rape: a New Approach for the Police*. London: Croom Helm.

Brownmiller, S. (1975) *Against Our Will: Men, Women and Rape*. London: Secker and Warburg.

Carlen, P. (1988) *Women, Crime and Poverty*. Milton Keynes: Open University Press.

Chambers, G. and Millar, A. (1983) *Investigating Sexual Assault*. Scottish Office Social Research Study. Edinburgh: HMSO.

Diamond, I. and Quinby, L. (eds) (1988) *Feminism and Foucault*. Boston, MA: Northeastern University Press.

Dixon, V. (1976) 'World views and research methodology', in L. King, V. Dixon and W. Nobles (eds), *African Philosophy: Assumptions and Paradigms for Research on Black Persons*. Los Angeles: Fanon Centre.

Duchen, C. (1986) *Feminism in France*. London: Routledge.

Eaton, M. (1986) *Justice for Women? Family, Court and Social Control*. Milton Keynes: Open University Press.

Farrington, D. and Morris, A. (1983) 'Sex, sentencing and reconviction', *British Journal of Criminology*, 23(3): 229–48.

Fekete, J. (1988) *Life After Postmodernism*. London: Macmillan.

Foucault, M. (1973) *The Order of Things*. New York: Vintage Books.

Fraser, N. and Nicholson, L. (1988) 'Social criticism without philosophy: an encounter between feminism and postmodernism', *Theory, Culture and Society*, 5(2/3): 373–94.

Gelsthorpe, L. (1986) 'Towards a sceptical look at sexism', *International Journal of the Sociology of Law*. 14(2): 125–52.

Gilligan, C. (1982) *In a Different Voice*. London: Harvard University Press.

Hanmer, J. and Saunders, S. (1984) *Well-Founded Fear: a Community Study of Violence to Women*. London: Hutchinson.

Harding, S. (ed.) (1986) *The Science Question in Feminism*. Milton Keynes: Open University Press.

Harding, S. (ed.) (1987) *Feminism and Methodology*. Milton Keynes: Open University Press.

Heidensohn, F. (1985) *Women and Crime*. Basingstoke: Macmillan.

Jardine, A. (1985) *Gynsis*. London: Cornell University Press.

Kellner, D. (1988) 'Postmodernism as social theory: some challenges and problems', *Theory, Culture and Society*, 5(2/3): 239–70.

Kenney, S.J. (1986) 'Reproductive hazards in the workplace: the law and sexual difference', *International Journal of the Sociology of Law*, 14(3/4): 393–444.

Lahey, K. (1985) '. . . until women themselves have been told all that they have to tell . . .' *Osgood Hall Law Journal*, 23(3): 519–41.

Lyotard, J. (1986) *The Postmodern Condition*. Manchester: Manchester University Press.

MacKinnon, C. (1987) *Feminism Unmodified: Discourses on Life and Law*. Cambridge, MA: Harvard University Press.

Rorty, R. (1985) 'Habermas and Lyotard on postmodernity', in R. Bernstein (ed.), *Habermas and Modernity*. Cambridge: Polity.

Rose, G. (1988) 'Architecture to philosophy – the postmodern complicity', *Theory, Culture and Society*, 5(2/3): 357–72.

Smart, C. (1986) 'Feminism and law: some problems of analysis and strategy', *International Journal of the Sociology of Law*, 14(1): 109–23.

Smart, C. (1989) *Feminism and the Power of Law*. London: Routledge.

Smith, D. (1973) 'Women's perspective as a radical critique of sociology', *Sociological Inquiry*, 14(1): 7–13.

Stanley, L. and Wise, S. (1983) *Breaking Out: Feminist Consciousness and Feminist Research*. London: Routledge.

Taylor, I., Walton, P. and Young, J. (1973) *The New Criminology*. London: Routledge.

Weedon, C. (1987) *Feminist Practice and Poststructuralist Theory*. Oxford: Basil Blackwell.

West, D. (1969) *Present Conduct and Future Delinquency*. London: Heinemann.

Woodhull, W. (1988) 'Sexuality, power and the question of rape', in I. Diamond and L. Quinby (eds), *Feminism and Foucault*. Boston: Northeastern University Press.

Young, J. (1986) 'The failure of criminology: the need for a radical realism', in R. Matthews and J. Young (eds) *Confronting Crime*. London: Sage.

42

# Towards transgression: new directions in feminist criminology

*Maureen Cain*

[. . .]

Before constructing my specific and personal agenda I will describe the three strategies which together constitute a transgressive criminology. The three strategies are reflexivity, de-construction and re-construction. The example I use to elucidate these strategies is the policing of the sexuality of girls and women.

Everyone who comes into contact with women, including girls and young men themselves, seems to be preoccupied with female sexuality and with a range of gender approved ways of behaving. Certainly police officers (Eaton, 1986; Gelsthorpe, 1986) court officials and workers in carceral institutions are (for example, Carlen, 1983; Ferrari-Bravo and Arcidiacono, 1989; Kersten, 1989). It is all very well to describe this as a male hegemony, which sees their sexual difference as the primary (master?) characteristic of women, to which all others are subordinate. The trouble is that feminist researchers have often seemed themselves to fall victim of the same male hegemony, so much does their work appear to be preoccupied with their subjects' sexuality, as opposed, for example, to their industry, their spirituality, or the good times they have together.

A strategy of *reflexivity* enables us to see that this is both correct and totally insufficient. We have to take the real concerns of girls and women seriously, and they are concerned about their relationships with men (see, for example, Lees, 1986, 1989). Working-class girls are being entirely realistic when they recognize that their life chances are related to their ability to secure a good wage earner as a mate, and all women who do not couple will be vulnerable to systematic denigration of their lifestyle. There are real rewards for conventional living, and real penalties for eschewing it. It is therefore necessary for researchers to recognize these realities and the discourse of sexually appropriate behaviour which expresses and constitutes them. But we have also to get beyond what Lorraine Hansberry, in discussing realist drama, described as 'photographing the garbage can' (1969: 236) and distance ourselves from the dominant and limiting discourse even while we deploy it. This recognition of a discourse as being 'only' a discourse is the *strategy of reflexivity*.

The quotation marks round 'only' indicate that discourses are one aspect of reality, and others might argue the whole of it. Wherever one stands in the

Abridged from *International Journal of the Sociology of Law*, 1990, 18(1): 1–18.

grand debates of this sociological age, it is clear that discourses can be used to authorize and justify painful and even penal practices, and that sometimes the use of language can constitute a pain in itself (cf. Lees, 1986, 1989). It is necessary, therefore, not only to recognize the discourse but also to examine its internal (il)logic, and the ways and sites in which it is deployed. This is the *strategy of de-construction*.

Thirdly, there is a growing body of evidence that some girls and some women, some times, become aware of a discrepancy between the discourse and themselves, between who they are and who they feel themselves to be. The work of Lees (1986) on girls' views of marriage and future plans reveals this. Their mothers, they said, were tired and bored, but marriage for them would be different because . . . More often, though, the discrepancy lacks a conventional language of expression. In some inchoate way girls and women fleetingly grasp that they are not who they are told they are (Maquieira, 1989). They go to church to sing this loss of a never recognized possibility; or they go mad (Brown and Harris, 1978; Laing and Esterson, 1960; Mathiesen, 1980); or they 'achieve' psychic congruity, resignation and compliance.

Girls and women, then, are vulnerable to a common sense of near absolute pervasiveness, in terms of which they are constituted and continually reconstitute themselves and each other. Living this common sense can be an arduous and painful experience. So the third aspect of a transgressive criminology involves helping girls and women to get outside or beyond this discourse, and to get beyond it with impunity. Here is a double transgression. The purpose of transgressing criminology is to enable women and girls to transgress the binding web of co-man sense. This is the *strategy of re-construction*. It is the only way to get beyond the denial which I argue is the common lot of woman kind (Cain, 1989: 17).

## Studying women

Reflexivity, de-construction, and re-construction all necessitate the study of women, and in particular, *women only* studies. This has to be the first item on an agenda for a transgressive criminology. The case rests in part on the negative argument that women do not need to be compared with men in order to exist, in part on the positive, re-constructive argument which I have already begun above.

The negative argument goes back to De Beauvoir (1949). It is that everywhere woman is defined as that which is not man. In her inception she is different, as far as our pervasive male co-man sense is concerned. In her inception, therefore, she does not exist for herself or as herself but only as what she is not. Any consideration of women and men together, in a comparative way, runs the risk of re-creating this non-existence. While acknowledging exceptions (Kersten, 1989), it must also be noted that the question immanently posed by male–female comparison as an investigative structure is how are women different. But in order to re-construct it is necessary to ask instead *who* are women, and how do they become who they are. This is not a simple question, because of hegemony and because of real female variation.

Hegemony as a concept implies not just a shared sense, but a process of transmitting it; the processes indeed whereby a mode of thought and speech becomes shared not only by men but amongst women too. Women, of course, have struggled against hegemony since before the concept was available to them. Hegemony is the reason why women have insisted on 'women only' spaces. Only in such spaces could a new language to capture their own incapable-of-being-thought-about experiences be brought to consciousness in a supportive process of giving these experiences voice and (re)cognition. This making it possible to speak the unspeakable is difficult, because each new naming is a creative invention and an emotional release. Harding (1983) has used the example of sexual harassment to explore this.

Sexual harassment can be said to be a very recent object in the world. But women had to be uncomfortable in work relationships *before* it was possible for sexual harassment to be invented. How frighteningly uncertain women must have been before they could know or 'recognize' and therefore confidently *have* that experience. Am I immature because I can't handle it? Am I a bad sport? Does it happen to other women? Does it mean that I'm particularly attractive or that I'm not worth caring for 'properly'? Indeed, but worse, women could not be certain of the experience they had had unless other women supported them. Men could always say that the woman had misunderstood, and that the misunderstanding was proof of her preoccupation with sex. So the invention of sexual harassment even amongst women was probably embarrassing, a socially and emotionally risky business. Maybe that is why girls dare have, and need, only one confidante, rather than a 'peer group'. Speaking the unspeakable is both difficult and dangerous.

In the same way, inventing domestic violence, rediscovering or admitting to incest, coping with being called a slag or drag (Lees, 1986, 1989) require the political environment which only a group of women talking, working and laughing together can provide. What a powerful thing it is, when women talk to women!

All this must seem a far cry from 'criminology'. Well, it is and it isn't. These concerns are totally irrelevant to the traditional criminological discourse. But they are integral to the transgressive discourse. Let me reiterate.

I have argued that 'women only' spaces are needed for women's unspeakable 'experiences' to be captured, experienced, named and tamed. I argue further that it is the task of the transgressive criminologist to facilitate that process. It is the task of feminists, including but not exclusively academic feminists whatever their sub-discipline, to help in the creative business of formulating the real but not experienced relationships in which women are constituted and enmeshed. Just as a name can only be found or is most likely to be found in 'women only' settings, so in research the male voices may need to be silenced in order for a *quite different* female discourse, which is *not* the flip side of a male one, to emerge and/or to be heard. Not only will this destroy hegemony but it will also reveal variation amongst women, who have learned resistance to gynogenizing theories whether men or women perpetrate them (Stanley and Wise, 1983).

So a transgressive feminist criminology will give 'women only' studies a central place, and will do this for both political and theoretical reasons.

Furthermore, in order to enhance our knowledge of our rich variety, comparative work between groups of women may be undertaken. So we shall gain insights from a female standpoint which enable theoretically and politically more valuable formulations of female conformity and criminality to be developed. Studying women as women, and comparing different groups of women, rather than women and men, takes off the blinkers of the male-as-yardstick and male common sense, so that *new* thoughts can come into the social and criminological worlds.

## Starting from outside

Starting from women's experiences, and helping women to formulate and re-formulate these experiences, means starting somewhere beyond the boundaries of criminological discourse. It is in this way that 'women only' studies are transgressive, but the point is a general one: *it is a defining characteristic of transgressive criminology that it starts from outside criminological discourse.*

Feminist criminology must explore the total lives of women, and there are no tools in existing criminological theory with which to do this. This necessity was made apparent by the impossibility of staying within the discourse discovered by feminists exploring penal processes, female criminality, or women as victims. It simply has not proved possible to make adequate sense of what is going on in these three areas of concern by starting from inside criminological discourse. Only by starting from outside, with the social construction of gender, or with women's experiences of their total lives, or with the structure of the domestic space, can we begin to make sense of what is going on. Feminist criminology must now start from outside. Together we have tried all the intra-discursive starting points and they have led us round in criminological circles. Feminist criminology must transgress those discursive boundaries, but if it does, in what sense is it a criminology?

First let me say that the practical humanitarian concerns which most of us have about what goes on in police stations, courts and penal (correctional) institutions are entirely legitimate. This is an important collection of state agencies which can impact severely upon people's lives. They are not more important than other agencies, but they are undeniably worthy of study and worthy of our political or reformist zeal.

What transgressive criminology involves, however, is displacing the traditional criminological discourse about these practices, and asking instead some questions which in their very formulation connect these practices with the rest of the lives of the people passing through as staff or offenders, questions which are thus concrete and specific but which also make possible abstract formulations and therefore comparisons and generalizations.

What is necessary is to look at these practices and sites and to enquire 'How is gender constituted in these sites? How do these sites and modes of constitution of gender connect with other sites and modes; what are the effects of these practices for women, for men, and for human self-fulfilment?' Feminist transgressive criminology would therefore start with a large question, and then move in on the sites and practices which have typically been the province of criminology.

Traditional criminology, however, starts with the sites and practices which are 'given' to it by the criminal law and its administration (Garland, 1985). Thus while traditional criminology, whether in conservative, liberal, or radical guise, has always been concerned with social class, for example, it has rarely posed class relations and their constitution and re-constitution as its central question: rather it has seen class as impinging on what goes on in its area of central concern.

Similarly in the case of gender, feminists are concerned with the relationships governing and governed by a discourse which is not particular to crimes, criminals, victims of crime, courts, or penal or welfare sites. We are concerned with the complex ways in which these discursive practices and the sites of their constitution and of their expression interlock or are independent.

Transgressive criminologists do then share a set of social concerns and knowledge of a body of literature with 'regular' criminologists, whether conventional or radical. But our questions are about *women*, not about crime. And should crime, law and criminal justice institutions ever turn out to be of little importance to our central questions, we would probably stop being criminologists.

## Studying men

This extra-criminological problematic, and these central questions about women, require that when we do consider crime, law and criminal justice institutions we can and must re-introduce men. There are two reasons for this apparent paradox.

First, gender is a relational concept. Men exist as male in and as their relationship with women; women exist as female in and as their relationship with men. We shall fall into essentialism if we exclude men from our analyses, even though we may wish to exclude them from much of our field research.

Secondly, women are constituted in their absence in sites occupied by men. Nowhere is this more apparent than in the criminal process, where most police and most judges and most lawyers are men. As Eaton in particular has shown (1986), the absent woman looms very large in discussions about how men should be treated by other men. Her guiding hand, her controlling influence, her provision of home 'n hearth – or the absence of these things – profoundly influence decision-making. And this discourse, which may keep men out of prison, also keeps women in their societally allotted place.

Lastly, however, we must study men because the most consistent and dramatic finding from Lombroso to postmodern criminology is not that most criminals are working-class – a fact which has received continuous theoretical attention from all perspectives – but that *most criminals are and always have been men*. Yet so great has been the gender-blindness of criminological discourse that men as males have never been the objects of the criminological gaze. Instead of asking how the social construction of maleness connects with this astonishing and world-wide result, with this hugely unexplained finding, criminology has asked why it is that women do not offend. It is as if even the criminogenic properties of maleness were normal compared with the cheerful and resigned conformity of women! This happens because criminological discourse cannot think gender: indeed, it cannot really think extra-correctional practices at all. So the criminological gaze does not see maleness: it cannot see or speak gender at all.

This is another reason why feminists must transgress criminology itself in order to understand men and women as offenders, victims, defendants and prisoners. For starting with a non-essentialist concept of gender means starting outside criminology, as it also means moving into the sites with which criminology is concerned, where men in all their taken-for-granted maleness preponderate.

A transgressive criminology, then, must take on board the vexed question of what in the social construction of maleness is so profoundly criminogenic: why do males so disproportionately turn out to be criminals?

## Reflexivity and self-help

Clarke (1985) and also the new realists have pointed out that social workers and the staff of correction agencies cannot simply be written off as yet more agents of social control. Most of them, after all, go into the job because they want to help the unfortunate. And almost all of them will have been trained since the 1960s revolution in criminology. Nonetheless critical criminologists have not been at all clear as to what their stance in relation to practitioners should be. Practitioners themselves now debate how feminism may influence their practice (Harris, 1987). The transgressive approach gives us some clues as to how we might develop an approach which helps practitioners to help the people delivered into their care. We must find ways of listening to these practitioners so that we can help them to be reflexive and to de-construct and re-construct their discourses and the practices in which they are enshrined. This applies not just to their professional and occupational discourses, but also to commonsensical discourses of gender and criminality, the good, the normal and the bad which underpin them.

Let me give you two examples of such studies very briefly. The first is a study by Gabriella Ferrari-Bravo and Caterina Arcidiacono. It was decided by the Italian government that their institutions for young people should go co-ed. As an experimental beginning they picked an institution noted for its liberal mixed sex staff. The day the girls arrived a banner was slung over the road reading 'welcome women'. The girls settled down in their quarters and mixed freely during the day, forming attachments and looking after the sewing and other small needs of the boys who were the objects of their affections. But two things went wrong. First, the girls objected to female staff, and secondly, they or some of them, were the ringleaders in a prison revolt, effectively a sit-in in the common parts of the building.

To cut a long story short, the prison officials decided when the girls complained about staff that they naturally needed father and/or authority figures. Later after the revolt, the agreed interpretation of that event was that the presence of the girls was understandably unsettling the boys.

The authors – two feminist psychologists who worked in the prison throughout the period – listened more carefully to what the girls were saying. On staffing they noted that women staff had a lower status, were seen as 'less' by colleagues. The girls were actually claiming staff of equal clout with the boys. Yet the staff common sense about themselves prevented this from being understood, and the girls themselves were not able to express it except in terms of individual manifestations of hostility.

As regards the revolt, the authors argue that what went wrong lay outside the prison, in the discourse of 'women' in terms of which the girls were ostensibly welcomed, and the practical taken-for-granted subordination of women in everyday life. To the prison officials a mirror image of this everyday stratification inside the prison constituted integration. To the rebels, and, more consciously to the researchers, true integration was only achieved in the moment of the revolt itself, and for the girls the ultimate crushing obscenity – more physically destructive because they could not comprehend or formulate or counter what was wrong with it – the ultimate obscenity was that their resistance was seen as confirming the discursively constructed femininity against which they were rebelling.

My second example is Joachim Kersten's work on both male and female institutions. He was observing in part with the eye of an experienced feminist, his wife, and used theories of gendering to sensitize him to what was happening to the boys. He writes of the taboo of homosexuality – a fear not quite so deeply entrenched discursively as that of being uncoupled is for girls, but none the less affecting all institutional practices (and note that the fears are asymmetrical: they are not mirror images of each other). Thus physical expressions of affection and concern were taboo; necessary caring activities (cooking and cleaning) were carried out instrumentally as 'blitzes'; physical contacts in sport and in fighting were ritualized. Emotionally wretched children were taught not to speak of their feelings. Neither in female nor in these male institutions could the staff hear the discourse of gender deployed in their activities. Yet they genuinely wanted to help the children, as did the liberal progressive staff of the Italian institution.

This suggests an immediate political practice. Training sessions for institutional staff could be organized by feminist transgressive criminologists who should first listen carefully to the way the staff see their work and secondly help them to reflect upon the assumptions embedded in their routines. Reflection and de-construction, followed by working with the staff and their clients (at this stage) to identify alternatives is the prescription. It is an arduous and unspectacular one, but it is a contribution that feminist criminologists can (and perhaps should) make in their role as the creative thinkers of transgressive criminology.

Annie Hudson (1989) has argued that social workers too must transform their own practice before they can be useful to girls, in particular, who are in their care. Young people spot an hypocrisy very fast, and will not stomach, for example, talk of democracy from those locked in to hierarchic structures and their associated status games. The message from Hudson is put your own house in order first, and it is a message which applies as keenly to academics as to corrections practitioners. Let us first, then, transform our own practice where we can, as we advise and encourage others about transforming theirs.

The fourth item on the transgressive agenda then argues that the contradiction between control images and help images expresses a reality, for the most progressive helpers hold their charges in place in terms of their common sense assumptions. We therefore need more reflexive research and more self-examination, and in particular an examination of our most fundamental assumptions about crime, about gender, about how it is 'natural' and therefore good for people to be. Because it is those assumptions which are inscribed even in our own most progressive practices, and it is these assumptions which may in themselves be criminogenic for boys and men and schizophrenogenic for girls and women.

### Women and politics

One assumption of the argument so far is that transgressive criminology is inescapably political. Whether we interpret our role as passive interpretation or as active assistance to offenders, victims and members of the helping professions, we are attempting to change the ways in which people think and act, and to change them in favour of women.

The fifth and final item on my transgressive agenda is therefore that we make an active effort to learn from other women who have engaged in political struggle. Coming from the Caribbean as I now do it is impossible not to be aware that women's politics is profoundly inventive. Women's political inventions are polycentric, diverse, original and apt. This is all the more reason why women should keep a record of what we have done, and analyse as best we can what works in one setting rather than another and why. We also need to explore how, and how effectively, these activities have been censured and policed (Young, 1988; 1990). And most particularly, we must record those forms of resistance to censure and policing which have been effective. This construction of an analytic dossier of women's political struggles, repression and resistance will have a morale function, will save us from continually having to re-invent the wheel, and will drive the creative political enterprise which has brought us this far. It is one more task of feminists doing transgressive criminology to develop this dossier.

Those are the theoretical and political reasons why a dossier of women's political struggles is important. There are two others. First, women's contribution to popular politics has been as hidden from history as their contributions in other spheres. Reddock (1988) has begun to uncover their role in the labour struggles which rocked the Caribbean in the 1930s. Krakovitch (1988) has made clear the contribution of women to the slave uprising in Martinique in 1870. These contributions have been written out of the history of the oppressed, as the history of the oppressed itself has frequently been obscured or distorted. Again, a double loss.

Secondly we should quite simply celebrate the joyful creativity with which women resist. And I think this would be a good note on which to end [. . .] Let us celebrate the mothers of Jamaica and Tobago who, after Emancipation in 1838, precipitated an acute labour shortage as they one by one refused to let their children – no longer slaves – be apprenticed to the planters (Craig, 1988; Mair, 1986). At moments like these the distinction between private and public spheres is revealed as a sham.

And let us celebrate too the women of Greenham Common in England, not just for the ways in which they braved and outfaced abuse and censure, [. . .] not just for their endurance of a five-year-long demonstration (so far), but for that special lightness and laughter of protest which embroiders, decorates with flowers, and knits the perimeter wire of an unwanted USAF nuclear missile base (Young, 1990).

Transgressive criminology must not always be serious or it will miss the point of women's struggle. . . .

## References

Brown, G. and Harris, T. (1978) *The Social Origins of Depression: a Study of Disorder in Women*. London: Tavistock.

Cain, M. (ed.) (1989) *Growing Up Good: Policing of Girls in Europe*. London: Sage.

Carlen, P. (1983) *Women's Imprisonment*. London: Routledge.

Clarke, J. (1985) 'Whose justice? The politics of judicial control', *International Journal of the Sociology of Law*, 13(4): 407–21.

Craig, S. (1988) 'Social reconstruction after slavery: the case of Tobago'. Unpublished talk to a Department of Sociology Seminar, University of the West Indies, St Augustine.

De Beauvoir, S. (1949) *Le Deuxième Sexe*. Gallimard: Paris.

Eaton, M. (1986) *Justice for Women? Family, Court, and Social Control*. Milton Keynes: Open University Press.

Ferrari-Bravo, G. and Arcidiacono, C. (1989) 'Relations between staff and girls in an Italian juvenile prison', in M. Cain (ed.), *Growing Up Good*. London: Sage.

Garland, D. (1985) *Punishment and Welfare: a History of Penal Strategies*. Aldershot: Gower.

Gelsthorpe, L. (1986) 'Towards a sceptical look at feminism', *International Journal of the Sociology of Law*, 14(2): 125–52.

Hancock, L. (1980) 'The myth that females are treated more leniently than males in the juvenile justice system', *Australia and New Zealand Journal of Sociology*, 16(3): 4–13.

Hanmer, J. and Stanko, E. (1985) 'Stripping away the rhetoric of protection: violence to women, law and the state', *International Journal of the Sociology of Law*, 13(4): 357–74.

Hansberry, L. (1969) *To Be Young, Gifted, and Black*. New York: Signet.

Harding, S. (1983) 'Why has the sex-gender structure become visible only now?', in S. Harding and M. Hintikka (eds), *Discovering Reality*. Boston, MA: D. Reidel.

Harris, M. (1987) 'Moving into the new millennium: towards a feminist vision of justice', *The Prison Journal*, 67(2): 160–76.

Hudson, A. (1989) 'Troublesome girls: towards alternative definitions and policies', in M. Cain (ed.), *Growing Up Good*. London: Sage.

Kersten, J. (1989) 'The institutional control of girls and boys: an attempt at a gender-specific approach', in M. Cain (ed.), *Growing Up Good*.London: Sage.

Krakovitch, O. (1988) 'The part played by women in the uprising in the South of Martinique in September 1870', *International Journal of the Sociology of Law*, 16(2): 185–201.

Laing, R. and Esterson, A. (1960) *Sanity, Madness, and the Family*. Harmondsworth: Penguin.

Lees, S. (1986) *Losing Out: Sexuality and Adolescent Girls*. London: Hutchinson.

Lees, S. (1989) 'Learning to love: sexual reputation, morality, and the social control of girls', in M. Cain (ed.), *Growing Up Good*. London: Sage.

Mair, L. (1986) 'Women Field Workers in Jamaica During Slavery'. The Elsa Goveia Memorial Lecture. Department of History, University of the West Indies, Mona, Jamaica.

Maquieira, V. (1989) 'Girls, boys, and the discourse of identity: growing up in Madrid', in M. Cain (ed.), *Growing Up Good*. London: Sage.

Mathiesen, T. (1980) *Law, Society, and Political Action: Towards a Strategy Under Late Capitalism*. London: Academic Press.

Reddock, R. (1988) *Elma Francois: the NWCSA and the Workers' Struggle for Change in the Caribbean in the 1930s*. London and Port of Spain: New Beacon Books.

Stanley, L. and Wise, S. (1983) *Breaking Out*. London: Routledge.

Young, A. (1988) '"Wild Women": the censure of the suffragette movement', *International Journal of the Sociology of Law*, 16(3): 279–93.

Young, A. (1990) *Representations of Deviance: Femininity and Dissent at Greenham Common*. London: Routledge.

# 43

# Criminal women and criminal justice: the limits to, and potential of, feminist and left realist perspectives

*Pat Carlen*

[. . .]

Although left realists have specified a number of theoretical tenets concerning the left realist approach to thinking about crime, it is often difficult to work out exactly why they have termed their programme 'realist'. One difficulty stems from their conflation of a political programme with a set of theoretical assumptions which do not emanate from either the philosophical realism of, say, Karl Popper or the sociological realism of, for instance, Emile Durkheim. Another results from their juxtaposition of their own left 'realist' theories to those which they call left 'idealist' and where 'idealist' is not being used in its usual sense to refer to theories which *explain* the present by reference to some not yet realized ideal, but merely to condemn theories which would not, according to the realists, lead to any realizable programmes of crime control.

And it may be because they do not clearly define and distinguish 'realism as theory' and 'realism as politics' that left realists produce theoretical propositions which appear positivistic and essentialist as well as a penal politics which can appear to be marred by opportunism, populism and moralism.

## Realism, idealism and common sense

Whereas the realism of Durkheim (1964) and Popper (1972) was aimed at subverting common sense, left realists appear to call for a theory of crime that will fit the facts of crime as popularly conceived of in common sense (cf. Jones et al., 1986: 3–4). Hence the often uncritical use of the victim survey.

## The essentialism of crime as a unifier

One of the strongest attacks on left realism has been that it is essentialist (Hogg, 1988: 32), that it attributes to the common sense phenomenon 'crime' – a phenomenon that consists of many different types of law-breaking and many different modes of criminalization – a unitary existence known to all people of good will and common sense. In other words, there is an easily recognizable reality 'out there', known as crime, that can be understood through empirical investigation and in its own terms.

In answer to the foregoing criticisms Young (1987) has claimed that far from

Abridged from *Issues in Realist Criminology* (eds R. Matthews and J. Young), pp. 51–69. (London: Sage, 1992.)

being essentialist, left realists aim to 'deconstruct' the crime phenomenon. However, it turns out that by 'deconstruct' he means that the common sense 'crime' is broken down into small substantive dimensions for analysis – but not an analysis which might subvert the common sense meaning. Indeed, once the common sense meaning is denied it is unlikely that the new explanation will have popular appeal!

## The essentialism of criminology as a unifier

Because they portray crime as a unitary concept it follows that left realists idealize 'criminology' as a unitary discipline rather than as an organizational site for the investigation of law-breaking and ciminalization. Linked with this thrust towards the unification of theory and politics is the left realist criticism that other theories are 'partial' – that explanations fail in so far as they are not symmetrical, that is, in so far as they do not provide the same explanations for social action and reaction. Yet one of the greatest contributions of 1960s interactionism was the insistence that law-breaking and criminalization are two separate processes, each requiring entirely different explanations (Kitsuse and Cicourel, 1963). Furthermore, and as I have argued elsewhere (Carlen, 1980), a deconstructionist position assumes that:

> the theoretical relationships between the criminal law, juridical relations, criminaliz-ation processes and lawbreaking are embedded in asymmetrical practices and discourses. These discourses are 'neither mirror images of each other nor reducible one to the other'. 'Today' as Foucault points out, 'criminal justice functions and justifies itself . . . only by perpetual reference to something other than itself, by its unceasing reinscription in non-judicial systems' (Foucault, 1977: 22) . . . [the preconditions and effects of] criminal law, juridical relationships and criminalization processes are asymmetrical to each other. Once they are inscribed within and around notions like morality, freedom, guilt and retribution . . . they fragment into ironic icons of juridical relations . . . [the] effect [of which] is dispersed *not* in criminological but in economic, religious or political discourse. (Carlen, 1980: 16)

Deconstructionist approaches to questions of women and crime can no more be confined within the parameters of a populist criminology than they can be solely and indissolubly tied to the concerns of feminism or the concepts of a 'feminist' theory. For deconstructionism – whether in 'criminology' or in 'feminism' – has constantly to say 'No' to the conditions of its own existence.

## Left realists' idealistic and moralistic notions of responsibility

Seeing all previous explanations of crime as being deterministic, left realists insist that individuals must take responsibility for their crimes; they operate within the simplistic free will versus determinism dichotomy. In reply to the crude 'social conditions cause crime' claim, they answer that individuals choose to commit crime. They appear to think that deterministic (sociological?) explanations of law-breaking alienate from a leftist politics those working-class people who, though living in less-than-ideal conditions, do *not* commit crime. Yet can such a simplistic dichotomy be justified on either theoretical or political grounds? Of course *'people choose to act, sometimes criminally*, [but] *they do not do so under conditions of their own choosing*. Their choice makes them responsible, but the conditions make the choice comprehensible. These conditions, social and economic, contribute to crime because they constrain, limit or narrow the choices available' (Box, 1987: 29, emphasis in original).

Furthermore, is it either logical or justifiable for left realists to use an anti-social rhetoric of individualism in the furtherance of socialist political ends? I think not. And this crude invocation of free will seems to me to be the worst example of the theoretical bad faith which results from attempting to fashion a theory in the service of a politics. By attempting to appeal to an electorate via populist and individualist conceptions of criminality, left realism loses an opportunity to show how individualized problems of criminal justice are also problems of social justice in general. To follow their example when posing questions of women and crime would be to make it impossible to assume that the experiences of 'women as a status group' have any ideological, economic and political preconditions which are distinctly different to the experiences of 'men as a status group'.

*The need for a principled idealism to counter the impossibilism of left idealism and the opportunistic tendency of left realism*

A major concern of left realism (and one which I totally support) has been to counter the 'impossibilism' of left idealist theories which claim that nothing can be done about crime until there is a fundamental change in the present exploitative class relations constitutive of capitalism. Yet a refusal to abandon the space of politics should not also entail an abandonment of a principled theoretical commitment to calling into question all already-known explanations of crime, including those developed under the auspices of socialism, feminism and/or left realism. The task of theory is to produce new knowledge; a task of politics is to calculate how, when and if new knowledge can be used to change balances of power and induce desired social change. Principled commitment to an open-ended deconstructionist theoretical programme, plus political commitment to sets of collectivist (feminist and/or socialist) ideals or aspirations is required to help ensure that theoretical production and political practice are neither opportunistically conflated nor opportunistically reduced, the one to serve the other. Which is why I am reluctant to endorse the more conflationary and/or reductionist theoretical and political claims of both feminism and left realism when they invoke either a politics to justify their theories or, conversely, a theoretical position to guarantee the rectitude of their politics and/or policy interventions.

## Against theoreticist, libertarian, separatist and gender-centric tendencies in recent feminist writings on women's law-breaking and criminal justice

Given my very strong reservations about certain aspects of left realist theorizing, it may seem perverse of me now to state that at the time of writing (August 1990) I feel, on balance, more sympathetic towards the general political project of left realist criminologists than I do towards the theoreticist, libertarian, separatist and gender-centric tendencies inherent (sometimes separately and sometimes combined) in some recent feminist writings on women, crime and criminology. In particular, I take issue with the anti-criminology stance of Smart (1990) and the implication that anyone taking a policy-oriented approach is at worst engaged in social 'engineering' or, at best, a committed do-gooding fool unaware of the risk-taking involved in working on the contradictions between theoretical knowledge and political strategy

(Frigon, 1990; Smart, 1990). I will now, therefore, make a few observations as to why I believe that certain tendencies in the writings of some feminists on women and crime are neither particularly original nor in the interests of either the minority of women who break the law or that even smaller minority who are imprisoned.

## *The theoreticist tendency*

The theoreticist tendency (which is anti-policy, anti-problem orientation) in the prescriptions of feminist anti-criminologists is most marked in the work of Smart (1989a, 1990). It seems to stem from two major fears: one, that to focus on an empirical referent like crime which has pre-given ideological and institutional meaning entails an essentialist trap from which there is no escape; second, that radical ideas or strategies used in the service of the state are necessarily subverted by administrators whose aims are far from those of the women's movement.

First I will address the problem of the empirical referent. [. . .] [F]ear of the ideological and already institutionalized meanings of the empirical referent is not new among social scientists or political theorists attempting radical critique. Yet the very task of theory is to engage in a struggle for power over the 'meaning of things' (including all material and ideological constructs). The purpose is to produce new meanings which will empower. Now certainly there is no reason why theoretical work should not be valuable *in itself* and certainly no reason why any theorist should *also* engage in political intervention. Yet I would not have expected theorists with an explicit political orientation such as 'feminist' or 'socialist' to inveigh against the suggestion that the theoretical product might at least in part both inform their analyses and empower their own political programme. Of course, there is usually a loss of theoretical rigour (and virtue?) when theories are put at the service of politics. But so what? The non-stop self-conscious elaboration of theoretical 'positions' unrelated to their possible analytic usefulness is in my opinion a peculiarly sterile practice, and a surprising one for those committed to the openness of deconstructionism. The purpose of deconstructing a logic (or anything else) is to find out what makes it work – and then to create new knowledge from the bricolage of the old.

The second fear – of the incorporation and subversion of radical critique and product – is related to the first and has likewise perennially exercised the minds of radical political groups. Yet unless one believes in the possibility of an end to ideology (and, incidentally, to knowledge) such incorporation and subversion needs to be recognized as a necessary part of political struggle without which there would be ideological closure. At the political level, too, it should be remembered that the state is not monolithic, that feminists also work in state agencies (cf. Cain, 1990) and that they continually ruminate about the meanings of their jobs. Furthermore, and as left realists repeatedly remind us, too great a fear of 'incorporation' can eventually lead to a paralysis of action, marginalization and, ultimately a state of powerlessness whence it is difficult to regain ground lost to the enemy.

## *The 'libertarian' tendency*

The libertarian tendency of some feminist writing on crime also repeats the libertarian tendencies of the left idealists of the early 1970s. It implies that women's law-breaking should not be treated as being problematic either for the law-breakers themselves or their victims (Frigon, 1990; Smart, 1989b); that feminist theorists should not put forward policy proposals on the grounds that they might reduce crime as such proposals smack of 'social engineering' (Smart, 1989b); and that women law-breakers should alone have privileged audience concerning the meaning of their crimes and the appropriate social response to them (Frigon, 1990).

First let me give an example which illustrates both the 'privileging' of subjects' understanding and the fear of 'social engineering'. In reviewing *Women, Crime and Poverty* (Carlen, 1988), Frigon wrote: 'Since 20 out of 39 women have committed drug-related offences, Carlen devotes some time to the subject. Her discussion is interesting but when she talks about the "expensive demands of *destructive* lifestyles involving heroin . . ." (emphasis added, p. 44), the reader can feel uncomfortable with this kind of language that can suggest a judgement' (Frigon, 1990: 226). Sadly, the language in this context was intended as literal description. Women with drink or drug addictions often choke to death on their own vomit, commit suicide or die of a drugs overdose. Others have Aids as a result of either sharing needles or engaging in prostitution to fund their habits. Sleeping rough, nursing bleeding sores and suffering withdrawal symptoms are not particularly life-enhancing processes either. Not one woman of the many I have known with addictions has celebrated her addictive state; many have themselves referred to 'destructive lifestyles', 'abusing my body' and 'killing myself'.

Yet what if the language had intentionally conveyed a judgement? I myself can see no reason whatsoever why a theorist should not also make judgements, as to more or less desirable states of affairs – so long as she does not conflate her analyses with her judgements and imply that there is a one-to-one relationship between the two. Certainly in *Women, Crime and Poverty* I make several judgements (on the state of women's prisons, on recent welfare legislation, on Mrs Thatcher, etc.). An academic squeamishness concerning the real problems of women in crime and on drugs is a return to one of the less acceptable faces of 1960s romanticism and idealism. It certainly is not helpful to the development of progressive policies aimed at reducing the further suffering incurred by women in trouble who turn to drugs or drink to relieve their pain and misery.

A second facet of what I have called the 'libertarian tendency' is the glorification by some writers of the notion that feminists should 'let women speak for themselves' or that researchers should 'listen to women'. Now I have no objection to the injunction that social researchers should take seriously people's understanding of their own situations. But what is distinctly 'feminist' about this, and why should such a strategy only involve women? The really difficult question is to decide what status and space to attribute to subjects' understandings of their own situation. My own solution is to quote people verbatim to such an extent that their own voices *are* heard. At the same time I also make my own (usually different) theoretical perspective sufficiently explicit to alert readers to the fact that these extracts have been *chosen* by me to illustrate a particular point. Ultimately, of course, everybody and nobody speaks for herself. The tendency towards an empiricist realism which is immanent in some of the writings of both left realist criminologists and libertarian feminists is not a progressive one.

*The separatist tendency*

The separatist tendency in feminist writings on crime is usually signalled by the lavish use of 'malestream' (instead of mainstream) and other crypto-logically unsatisfying neologisms or puns. Again, Frigon (1990) provides a good example when she complains that control theory is a 'mainstream and/or malestream theory in criminology. To fit women, or more correctly gender, in that mould is therefore problematic.' Now, gender isn't a custard or jelly and theory is not a mould. But positivistic notions that words and theories are like custard *do* ignore all of the more sophisticated theoretical advances that have been made this century concerning the attribution of meanings to words and statements. Given the revolutionary work of Saussure, Foucault and Derrida it is a pity that separatist feminists continue to imply that words, theories and concepts are forever tied to their sites of origin and essentially engendered by their authors. The repeated implication by some feminists that concepts are always already-gendered should offend theoretical, political and even what (in the tradition of the genre) Maureen Cain (1989, 1990) would call 'co-man' (!) sense.

*The gender-centric tendency*

In fact, Cain's recent writings (1989, 1990) actually eschew separatism. They do, however, contain a tendency towards gender-centrism, as do the works of Smart (1989a, 1989b). My own perspective inclines towards a political realism similar to that of the left realists and, as I have repeatedly said, is not shaken by fear of any essential power of the empirical referent.

Women (as a group) in the penal system are a striking example of what Laffargue and Godefroy (1989) have referred to as the '"hard core" of repression' whose criminalization has been overdetermined by the threefold effects of sexism, racism and the class injustices of an increasingly repressive state. Because explanations of racism, class structure and gender structure are not reducible one to another, [. . .] it is likely that people wishing to engage in criminological work which may have some theoretical, policy or campaigning pay-off in relation to women's crimes and women's imprisonment, will not wish to rely solely on the insights of feminism into gender structure when mounting their investigations. This is not to assert that there is no need for studies and theories which privilege gender as the major explanatory concept – indeed the need for such studies is urgent. It is to warn against a theoretical imperialism which might result in the theoretical closure which self-styled 'transgressive' (Cain, 1989, 1990) and anti-criminologists (Smart, 1990) fear.

**An agenda for the realization of some attainable ideals both in the deconstruction and theorization of 'women and crime' questions; and in the development of policies aimed at righting some of the wrongs encountered by women law-breakers in the criminal justice and penal systems**

*Academic agenda*

Detailed empirical investigation of both the context (that is, economic, ideological and political conditions) in which women break the law and of their subsequent careers through the welfare, criminal justice and penal systems (cf. Carlen, 1988). Detailed empirical investigation of the ideological discourses within which women's law-breaking is known (cf. Allen, 1987; Carlen, 1983; Worrall, 1990). Deconstruction of what is 'already known' about women law-breakers via a 'bricolage' of concepts appropriated from a variety of theoretical discourses to inform answers to questions about the four main features of women's law-breaking and imprisonment in Britain, the United States and Canada, namely:

1 that women's crimes are predominantly the crimes of the powerless;
2 that disproportionate numbers of women from ethnic minority groups are imprisoned;
3 that typifications of conventional femininity play a major role in the decision whether or not to imprison women;
4 that the majority of women appear to be law-abiding and when in trouble are much more likely to be in receipt of medical, psychiatric or welfare regulation than caught up in the machinery of criminal justice.

The construction of a feminist jurisprudence which in assuming (and empirically documenting the ways in which) (a) women's experiences are different from men's and (b) the criminal law affects and protects women differently from men, might be advocated as one jurisprudential paradigm (among others) which could inform campaigning strategies and policy recommendations. The establishment of women's law as a special area of study not just as an optional subject but as a component of all compulsory subjects. (See Stang-Dahl, 1986, for an account of the lead in this direction given by the Institute of Women's Law at the University of Oslo where women's law has already been fully integrated into the degree scheme of the Faculty of Law.)

The dissolution of 'women and criminal justice' questions within an interrogation of women and social justice in general. The development of more sophisticated models of the relationships between culpability, responsibility and accountability in societies where class relationships, racism and gender discrimination call into question the very general concept of social justice which must underpin the more specific concept of criminal justice.

*Campaigning and policy agenda*

Any campaigning and policy agenda might (ideally) be comprised of: (a) fundamental aims; (b) general strategies; (c) short-term achievable goals for the relief of women presently bearing the brunt of both gender-discrimination and racist gender-discrimination in the criminal justice and penal systems; and (d) long-term programmes that, although not achievable under present political conditions, can be argued for on the basis of a deconstructionist analysis of present penal discourses and practices.

*Fundamental aims*  To ensure that the penal regulation of female law-breakers does not increase their oppression as unconventional women, as black people and as poverty-stricken defendants still further; and to ensure that the penal regulation of law-breaking men is not such that it brutalizes them and makes them behave even more violently or oppressively towards women in the future.

*General strategies*  *Remedial action* to redress the present wrongs of women in the criminal justice and penal systems; *resistance* to penal or other regulatory measures based on essentialized stereotypes of gender; and *democratic exploration* of the many different possible modes of living and learning in a variety of all-female (and, for women who want them, mixed) half-way houses, accommodation schemes and self-help groups (Carlen, 1990).

*Short-term achievable goals*  The monitoring and (remedying) of sexist and racist–sexist practices within the welfare, criminal justice and penal systems; development of feasible non-custodial programmes for women which recognize that women's social responsibilities and resources are usually different from men's; proper medical provision (especially well-women clinics) for physically and mentally ill women in trouble or in custody; the setting of minimum standards for all prison establishments and the closure of all institutions not conforming to those standards; and rejection of any justification for the discriminatory treatment of women in the penal system which invokes the relatively few numbers of women prisoners as just cause of their less favourable treatment.

*Long-term programmes which, though idealistic, need to be adhered to and worked on, to counter the conservative compromises based on pragmatism and opportunism which usually have to be made in order to achieve short-term goals*  Whatever compromises are made in the name of realist politics, campaigners should not abandon the pursuit of long-term goals (even if, under present political arrangements they are idealistic – for example, the virtual abolition of women's imprisonment, Carlen, 1990). Nor should theorists abdicate (in the name of democracy) their responsibility perpetually to question existent forms of knowledge (including 'feminism' and 'realism'). Of course campaigners will have to be prepared to live with, and work on, the contradictions between the actions required for attainment of short-term goals and the principles to be held to in the construction of new forms of justice. Likewise, theorists will have to work on the contradiction that ideological knowledge (or the already-known) is a necessary constituent of new knowledge. But these tensions are essential elements of any politics or theory which is against closure and committed to being open-ended. The concomitant implication for theorists is that they should forever be intent on seeking that loss of authorship which, in the production and recognition of new knowledge, would render the *politically* important significance of 'feminist' and 'realist' irrelevant.

## References

Allen, H. (1987) *Justice Unbalanced*. Milton Keynes: Open University Press.
Box, S. (1987) *Recession, Crime and Punishment*. London: Tavistock.
Cain, M. (1989) *Growing Up Good*. London: Sage.
Cain, M. (1990) 'Towards transgression: new directions in feminist criminology', in *International Journal of the Sociology of Law*, 18(1): 1–18.
Carlen, P. (1980) 'Radical criminology, penal politics and the rule of law', in P. Carlen and M. Collison (eds), *Radical Issues in Criminology*. Oxford: Martin Robertson.
Carlen, P. (1983) *Women's Imprisonment: a Study in Social Control*. London: Routledge and Kegan Paul.
Carlen, P. (1988) *Women, Crime and Poverty*. Milton Keynes: Open University Press.
Carlen, P. (1990) *Alternatives to Women's Imprisonment*. Buckingham: Open University Press.

Durkheim, E. (1964) *Rules of Sociological Method*. New York: Free Press.

Foucault, M. (1977) *Discipline and Punish*. London: Allen Lane.

Frigon, S. (1990) 'Review of P. Carlen, *Women, Crime and Poverty*', *International Journal of the Sociology of Law*, 18(2): 225–9.

Hogg, R. (1988) 'Taking crime seriously: left realism and Australian criminology', in M. Findlay and R. Hogg (eds), *Understanding Crime and Criminal Justice*. Sydney: The Law Book Company. pp. 24–51.

Jones, T., MacLean, B. and Young, J. (1986) *The Islington Crime Survey*. Aldershot: Gower.

Kitsuse, J. and Cicourel, A. (1963) 'A note on the use of official statistics', *Social Problems*, 11: 131–9.

Laffargue, B. and Godefroy, T. (1989) 'Economic cycles and punishment: unemployment and imprisonment. A times series study. France, 1920–1985', *Contemporary Crises*, 13(4): 371–404.

Popper, K. (1972) *Objective Knowledge*. Oxford: Oxford University Press.

Smart, C. (1989a) *Feminism and the Power of Law*. London: Routledge.

Smart, C. (1989b) 'Review of *Women, Crime and Poverty* by Pat Carlen', *Journal of Law and Society*, 16(4): 521–4.

Smart, C. (1990) 'Feminist approaches to criminology, or postmodern woman meets atavistic man', in L. Gelsthorpe and A. Morris, *Feminist Perspectives in Criminology*. London: Routledge and Kegan Paul.

Stang-Dahl, T. (1986) *Women's Law: Methods, Problems, Values*. Norway: University of Oslo.

Worrall, A. (1990) *Offending Women*. London: Routledge.

Young, J. (1986) 'The failure of criminology: the need for a radical realism', in R. Matthews and J. Young (eds), *Confronting Crime*. London: Sage.

Young, J. (1987) 'The tasks of a realist criminology', *Contemporary Crises*, II(4): 337–56.

44

# Postmodernism and critical criminology

*Alan Hunt*

[. . .]

What is this thing called postmodernism? I take postmodernism to be the embracing of a judgement that we have traversed a significant divide between the modernism of the early twentieth century and the postmodern reality of the late twentieth century. The most significant step in forming the post-modernism perspective is the inference that if the old world has passed then its problems have become redundant. It is not simply that a new set of questions should replace a prior set; the radical self-conception of post-modernism arises from its claim that we must break with the kind of 'big' questions which have traditionally motivated the intellectual projects of the previous epoch. It is not so much that modernism arrived at the wrong answers, but that its questions were unanswerable; they have been too broad, too abstract, riddled with a distinctive mix of naive humanism, an un-warranted faith in science and an over-optimistic view of the capacity of language to capture and share knowledge. Two key texts may be taken as embodying the core of postmodernism; Jean-François Lyotard *The Postmodern Condition: a Report on Knowledge*, (1984); and Michel Foucault's essays and interviews in *Power/Knowledge* (1980).

Neither a simple espousal nor a rejection of postmodernism is adequate; rather I will contend that there are valuable elements in the postmodernist perspective which can contribute to progressive thinking, but which need to be separated from its negative dimensions. Lest this sounds too even-handed it is as well to make clear that what I reject is most of the general perspective that constitutes postmodernism and what is recommended for retention are some useful, yet partial, insights. To situate the postmodernist challenge it is important to recognize the complex interconnection between the intellectual and political strands which it incorporates. The suggestion to be explored is that postmodernism involves two distinguishable elements. At its most general level postmodernism is a critique of the rationalism of Enlightenment thought. Postmodernism's more specific features revolve around reactions against socialist thought and Marxism in particular. The emergence of a specifically Left postmodernism has been one of the expressions of the 'crisis of Marxism'.

Postmodernism's starting-point is a critique of the Enlightenment as a failed rationalist project which has run its time but which continues to encumber contemporary thought with illusions of a rational route to knowledge, a faith in science and in progress. The radical core of postmodernism lies in its mission of shedding the illusions of the Enlightenment. The political ambiguity

Abridged from *New Directions in Critical Criminology* (eds B.D. Maclean and D. Milanovic), pp. 79–95. (Vancouver: Collective Press, 1991.)

of postmodernism lies in its insistence that our received and familiar dichotomy between Left and Right is itself a product of Enlightenment thought and that contemporary Left theoretical and political positions, especially Marxism, are deeply inscribed with the illusions of the Enlightenment. This is how postmodernism comes to claim progressive credentials whilst devoting much of its energy to the critique of erstwhile Left positions. Postmodernism has a pronounced tendency to be absolutist in its judgements. Most noticeably it adopts a decidedly one-dimensional and almost wholly negative view of the Enlightenment and of the modern world. Postmodernist authors present us with an unhelpful and, I suggest, avoidable dichotomy between the wholesale endorsement of some classical version of the Enlightenment project and its complete abandonment. We are presented with a stark choice between the Enlightenment and postmodernism; significantly no intermediate positions are considered.

Modernity and enlightenment are much more complex, ambiguous and nuanced than this one-dimensional view permits. Marshall Berman captures the ambiguity of modernism. 'From Marx's and Dostoevsky's time to our own, it has been impossible to grasp and embrace the modern world's potentialities without loathing and fighting against some of its most palpable realities'. Whereas the intellectual giants of the nineteenth century were simultaneously enthusiasts for and enemies of modernity, their postmodernist successors have 'lurched far more toward rigid polarities and flat totalizations. Modernity is either embraced with a blind and uncritical enthusiasm, or else condemned with neo-Olympian remoteness and contempt; in either case it is conceived as a closed monolith'.

I want to suggest that we should adopt a more dispassionate view of the substance of postmodernism by separating its content from its general intellectual mood. At root postmodernism is grounded in a profound disenchantment with modernity. There is a very specific reason why many progressive intellectuals have come to adopt this disenchantment as their own. Whether in disillusionment with contemporary socialism since the events of 1968 (symbolized by the May events in Paris and the invasion of Czechoslovakia in August) or with the swing to the Right during the 1980s, it is not surprising that postmodernism has had its attractions for progressives.

Whilst I empathize with postmodernism's critique of instrumental reason, scientism, the cult of progress and much more associated with the Enlightenment, I also want to affirm that the central project of social emancipation remains unrealized. In very different ways both Edward Thompson and Jürgen Habermas articulate the view that modern liberalism has lost the will to pursue this goal and that [its] realization has fallen to contemporary socialism; this in turn underlines my view that socialism must engage with and draw significantly from liberalism in order to fulfil this objective. It is for these reasons that I am unhappy with the general intellectual and political mood of postmodernism.

In the discourse of the Enlightenment, law and crime play the role of what Foucault termed a 'total history' in that it came to be conceived as constituting the overall form or principle of a civilization; indeed law becomes the very personification of civilization. In this role law is attributed a teleological self-conception combining four projects; that of totality (the rational organization and ordering of a whole society), unity (the sovereignty of the nation state), civilization (the supersession of a dangerous and unordered past – law versus self-help). And finally the project of 'the subject' (the constitution of the legal subject as citizen, and citizen as legal subject endowed with self-responsibility and legal liability).

In challenging the Enlightenment's conception of law, postmodernism joins with and supplements other strands of critical theory. Its general thrust is to displace and decentre the privileged position accorded to 'the Law'. Post-modernism challenges the four interconnected projects assigned to law. It denies totality by stressing plurality and particularity of social life. It denies unity, emphasizing instead the diversity of social life. Postmodernism questions civilization by exposing its suppression or silencing of the expelled voices of the insane, women or colonial peoples. And most famously, postmodernism displaces and decentres the sovereign subject.

The second challenge involves a rejection of the philosophical and epistemological presuppositions of both liberal legalism and of critical perspectives. In its most general form postmodernism is anti-foundational in the sense that it denies the possibility of either philosophy or social theory providing any epistemological guarantees for knowledge claims. This anti-foundationalism, epitomized by Foucault's critique of the human sciences, insists that the epistemological postures of any discipline are resultant of the play of relations of power. In general, postmodernism announces the end of theory whilst paradoxically insinuating an alternative 'non-theory theory'. This is nowhere more evident than in Foucault's displacement of Marxism's concern with the complex connection between state, class and power by an (under-theorized) new 'disciplinary' society in which capitalism, quietly, disappears. Let me make clear that the modern forms of power and discipline present major challenges for contemporary critical scholars; I certainly don't take the view that Marxism has (or has ever had) 'all the answers'. But before embracing postmodernism too enthusiastically, we need to take cognizance of precisely what it is that is thrown out.

Not only are there problems in finding appropriate ways of posing the issues in dispute, but there is just as big a difficulty in deciding what the political implications of intellectual positions are. One dimension of the dilemma of the progressive intellectual is: How do we decide what is progressive? There is nothing to be gained by bemoaning the loss of the old certainties. These apparent certainties were themselves the result of an ossification of the political thought of both the Left and the Right. That postmodernism has challenged and disrupted the process of political evaluation is one of its significant contributions. But the inherent limitation of the politics of postmodernism is a lack of clarity about the political consequences of its characteristic positions.

The most distinctive feature of the politics of postmodernism is the suspicion of any strategy of large scale political change since these tend to be premised upon 'privileged agents', such as 'the state' or 'the working class', and were posed in terms of totalities (e.g. capitalism). The alternative to macro-politics is the politics of localism. But it is difficult to understand just how such a view of politics can provide any challenge to the institutionalized structures of power and inequality which characterize modern society. It follows directly from the Foucauldian thesis that 'power is everywhere' that politics must also be everywhere. There is an obvious sense in which this is true, but a more important sense in which it is misleading, since it fails to take account of the fact that local politics are not autonomous realms, but that states, legal institutions and political parties intervene in and to hegemonize local struggles and resistances. It is important to my case to stress that I do not seek to disapprove of or to denigrate local politics. Indeed the stress on local politics has been an important part of the rethinking of progressive politics during recent years. But I do challenge the simple substitution of micro- for macro-politics. Postmodernism has a tendency to adopt a wilful self-limitation and onus to disempower itself from undertaking more than the most fragmentary analysis. There are profoundly important questions about the relationship between local and state politics. Among the questions that need to be explored are: to what extent can local politics succeed without at the same time engaging with the multifaceted forms of social oppression? Under what conditions is it possible to achieve concerted action and alliances effective at the level of the state? Unless these questions are explored, the powerless are doomed forever to engage in an endless series of single-issue struggles. It is not that such struggles are unimportant. They are the starting-point of action and empowerment, but unless they find appropriate forms of articulation at the national or international level, they may remain locked into a vicious circle of a reformism that can never achieve their most significant goals.

A second and linked strand within the politics of postmodernism is organized around a strong commitment to a model of an ideal political practice which is participatory. The roots of this configuration involve a sharp reaction against the traditional categories of socialist politics; the working class, political parties and the struggle for state power have no place in postmodernist politics. What is sketched is an odd mixture of Foucault's conception of a politics which is directed to bringing into play 'an insurrection of subjugated knowledges'. Such influences do not constitute a political programme nor even an agenda. Rather, they serve to sketch out the parameters of a potential political space whose major characteristic is precisely its marked departures from traditional progressive politics. True to the project of redrawing the map of politics and culture embodied in postmodernism, this 'new politics' defies and seeks to break out of the old categories of Left and Right.

The source of the attraction of postmodernism lies in all those aspects of the human condition in which we are no longer as certain as we used to be that things are better today than they were yesterday. The deep significance of the inexorable rise of environmentalism is [that] precisely that which has been the key evidence of the universality of progress, namely, the species' ability to control and subordinate nature, is now the source of the greatest collective danger. There is another, and explicitly political, side to contemporary doubts about progress. The parallel political transformations of the twentieth century, socialism (in both its Communist and Social-Democratic forms) and anti-colonialism have failed to produce societies which offer much encouragement to the progressive commitment to remaking the world. When the cake comes out of the political oven, it has persistently failed to live up to its promise.

If the Left is committed to change, but unhappy with its results, and less confident about progress, then it appears that progressives have no alternative but to take the postmodernist challenge seriously. If the engagement with postmodernism is to be fruitful (not simply oppositional) then it is necessary to concede that postmodernism does present a challenge to the normal progressivist embrace of science, rationality and progress. It, perhaps, reduces the shock of embracing postmodernism to recognize that much recent progressive thought has already taken on board many of the characteristic themes of postmodernism, but has done so without embracing its more cataclysmic manifestations. Thus, for example, the commitment to any linear, let alone unilinear, conception of progress has long since been abandoned. But this does not imply that the rejection of progress has been replaced by a radical relativism. Similarly, the faith in narrowly conceived positivistic methods of 'science' has long been left behind, but again this has not involved the abandonment of the idea that it is possible to compare competing knowledge claims and to make judgements as to which is 'better'. It is sufficient that we specify the context in which our judgements are made and the standpoint which we occupy for our judgements to be grounded and thus avoid the slide to ethical relativism.

Progressive thought has similarly taken important strides towards connecting such grounded conceptions of knowledge with the source and mobilization of power. The most revealing measure of this shift is that it finds expression in the across-the-board influence of Michel Foucault. But, as I have suggested above, it is necessary to redress the over-reaction against orthodox Marxism which led Foucault to simply substitute a prioritization of local politics for state politics. Much contemporary scholarship quite correctly emphasizes the plurality of the forms of discipline and control, but this should not lead to a neglect of the central importance of the state. A more developed account of the inter-penetration of the macro- and micro-levels is needed.

There is, then, much of value that has emerged during the engagement with postmodernism. But the deeper problem remains of the negative face, and indeed it is the most visible face, of postmodernism. It is precisely because the pervasive issues surrounding law and crime seem so intractable that progressive scholarship has been so deeply, almost passionately, affected by the general mood of self-doubt, failure and impossibilism that has been the most distinctive manifestation of postmodernism.

It is still possible to face our age and its problems without relapsing into the pessimism that is the final resting place of relativism, nihilism and of postmodernism once its radical guise is stripped away. If the engagement with postmodernism, and the big fear which it has engendered, has brought us nearer to this understanding, then it has played its part.

### References

Foucault, M. (1980) *Power/Knowledge* (C. Gordon, ed.). Brighton: Harvester Press.
Lyotard, J.F. (1984) *The Postmodern Condition*. Minneapolis, MN: University of Minnesota Press.

# 45

# Human rights and crimes of the state: the culture of denial

*Stanley Cohen*

[. . .]

It would be ludicrous to claim that Western criminology over the past decades has completely ignored the subject of state crime or the broader discourse of human rights. [. . .] [T]he subject has often been raised and then its implications conveniently repressed. This is a process strangely reminiscent of my substantive interest in the sociology of denial: how information is known but its implications are not acknowledged.

The first significant confrontation with the subject came in the early phase of radical criminology in the late 1960s. That favourite debate of the times – 'who are the *real* criminals?' – naturally turned attention from street crime to white-collar/corporate crime and then to the wider notion of 'crimes of the powerful'. The particular context of the Vietnam War, pushed our slogans ('Hey, hey LBJ! How many kids have you killed today?') explicitly in the direction of 'crimes of the state'.

In criminology, this sentiment was expressed in the much cited paper by the Schwendingers (1970) entitled 'Defenders of order or guardians of human rights?'. Looking back at this text, it appears a missed opportunity to deal with the core issues of state crime.

Quite rightly, the Schwendingers saw themselves going in the same direction, but a step further than Sutherland by invoking the criterion of *social injury* to define crime. In the case of white-collar crime, this mandated us to go beyond criminal law into the areas of civil and administrative law. The Schwendingers then noted that if Sutherland had consistently followed what they rightly call his 'ethical' rather than legal categorization, he should also have arrived at those other socially injurious actions which are not defined as either criminal or civil law violations. So far, so good. But their argument then goes awry.

First, they cite as examples of other socially injurious action (their only examples) 'genocide and economic exploitation'. Now, besides the fact that these are hardly morally equivalent categories, genocide is crucially different from economic exploitation. It is recognized in current political discourse as crime by the state; it is clearly illegal by internal state laws; and since the Nuremberg Judgements and the 1948 UN Convention Against Genocide, it is a 'crime' according to international law. Genocide belongs to the same conceptual universe as 'war crimes' and 'crimes against humanity'. By any

Abridged from *Australian and New Zealand Journal of Criminology*, 1993, 26(2): 97–115.

known criteria, genocide is more self-evidently criminal than economic exploitation.

The Schwendingers make no such distinctions nor try to establish the criminality of human rights violations. Instead they launch into a moral crusade against imperialistic war, racism, sexism and economic exploitation. We might agree with their ideology and we might even use the term 'crime' rhetorically to describe racism, sexism and economic exploitation. This type of 1960s rhetoric indeed anticipates the current third and fourth generation 'social rights'. A more restricted and literal use of the concept 'state crime', however, is both more defensible and useful. If we come from the discourse of human rights, this covers what is known in the jargon (for once, not euphemistic) as 'gross' violations of human rights – genocide, mass political killings, state terrorism, torture, disappearances. If we come from the discourse of criminology, we are talking about clear criminal offences – murder, rape, espionage, kidnapping, assault.

I don't want to get into definitional quibbles. Enough to say that the extension of criminology into the terrain of state crimes can be justified without our object of study becoming simply everything we might not like at the time. Let us see what happened after that mid-1960s to mid-1970s phase when questions about state crimes and human rights were placed on the criminological agenda by the radicals.

What mostly happened was that the human rights connection became lost. In the discourse of critical criminology, the putative connection between crime and politics took two different directions, both quite removed from the idea of state crime.

The first was the short-lived notion of the criminal as proto-revolutionary actor and the extension of this to all forms of deviance. This whole enterprise – referred to as the 'politicization of deviance' – was soon abandoned and eventually denounced as naive, romantic and sentimental. The second connection – which turned out the more productive – was the focus on the criminalizing power of the state. This led to the whole revisionist discourse on the sociology of law, social control and punishment that has remained so salient and powerful.

But neither direction leads anywhere near towards talking about state crimes. The subject simply faded away from criminological view in the mid-1970s to mid-1980s. By the time left realist criminology appeared, we [had moved] entirely from 'crimes of the state' back to the 'state of crime'. Today, the subject has re-appeared from two contexts, one *external* to the discipline, the other *internal*.

The *external* context is the incremental growth of the international human rights movement itself. Emerging from the United Nations Charter and the great declarations and conventions of the next decade, from international governmental organizations such as UNESCO and the Council of Europe, from fledgling pressure groups such as Amnesty International to the vast current list of national and international non-governmental organizations, the human rights movement has become a major institutional force. Pushed by the rhetorical use of 'human rights' by the Carter Administration about Latin America and its critique of the Soviet Union, the ideal of human rights took on a powerful life of its own. It has become a secular religion.

This discourse, of course, is very dense, complex and contradictory [. . .] 'Human Rights' has become a slogan raised from most extraordinary different directions. Progressive forces and organizations like Amnesty can enlist famous rock stars to perform in defence of international human rights. Right wing pressure groups in the USA can unseat politicians and defeat Supreme Court nominations by invoking the human rights of the unborn foetus. Civil liberties groups defend pornography on the grounds of freedom of speech and the women's movement attacks this freedom as an assault on the human rights of women. Nations with the most appalling record of state violence and terror can self-righteously join together in the UN to condemn other nations for their human rights violations. Some human rights activists are awarded the Nobel Peace Prize, others are jailed, tortured, have disappeared or been assassinated. The human rights of one group are held sacred, the rights of another totally ignored . . . and so on.

But whatever the concept of human rights means, it has become a dominant narrative. Arguably, with the so-called death of the old meta-narratives of Marxism, liberalism and the Cold War, human rights will become *the* normative political language of the future. I have no time to go into its conceptual ambiguities – the difference between civil and human rights, the relationship between political and human rights work, the tension between universalism and cultural relativism. Nor can I raise the numerous policy issues of policing, enforcement and international law. One of the most salient issues for criminologists, raised dramatically by the current horrors in the former Yugoslavia, is the long-proposed establishment of an international criminal tribunal.

So this is one way – from the outside – that criminologists as citizens who read the news, must have become aware of the subject of human rights violations and crimes of the state. Not that you know about this awareness if you just read criminological texts. There is, however, one *internal* way in which the subject has been registered in criminology. This is through the growth of victimology.

There are many obvious echoes of human rights issues in victimological literature – whether in the feminist debate about female victims of male sexualized violence; in talking about children and children's rights; in the concern about victims of corporate crime, ecological abuse, etc. Some students (Karmen, 1990) find these echoes only in 'radical' rather than 'conservative' or 'liberal' victimology. The conservative tendency is concerned with victims of street crime, making offenders accountable, encouraging self reliance and advocating retributive justice. The liberal tendency includes white-collar crime, is concerned with making the victim 'whole' and advocates restitution and reconciliation. Only the radical tendency extends to all forms of human suffering and sees law and the criminal justice system as implicated in this suffering.

This distinction, though, between conservative, liberal and radical tendencies, is not always clear. And in the context of one crucial subject – what happens to state criminals such as torturers after democratization or a change in regime – the distinction breaks down altogether. Here, it is the 'radicals' who call for punishment and retributive justice, while it is the 'conservatives' who invoke ideals such as reconciliation to call for impunity.

In any event, these external and internal inputs are slowly making their way into criminology. In the mainstream, this can be seen in recent standard textbooks which explicitly deal with the subject of state crime, and others which consider the human rights definition of crime.

In the radical stream, there is Barak's recent (1991) volume *Crimes By the Capitalist State*. The editor makes a strong case for including state criminality in the field of criminology – both on the grounds that the consequences of state crimes are more widespread and destructive than traditional crime and because this would be a logical extension of the already accepted move into the field of white-collar crime. The overall tone of the volume, though, is too redolent of the 1960s debates: general ideas about discrimination and abuse of political and economic power, the focus only on capitalism and the disproportionate attention on worldwide low intensity warfare by the USA (CIA, counter-insurgency etc.).

Despite this recent interest, major gaps in the criminological discourse remain.

(a) First, there is little understanding that a major source of criminalization at national and international levels draws on the rhetoric of human rights. Significant waves of moral enterprise and criminalization over the last decade are derived not from the old middle-class morality, the Protestant ethic nor the interests of corporate capitalism, but from the feminist, ecological and human rights movements. A major part of criminology is supposed to be the study of law making – criminalization – but we pay little attention to the driving force behind so many new laws: the demand for protection from 'abuses of power'. The radical slogans of the 1960s have become the commonplace of any government and inter-government forum. Alongside our standard research on domestic legislatures and ministries of justice, we should see what our foreign ministries are doing – at the Council of Europe, the United Nations, etc.

(b) Another important defect in recent literature is its American focus. It is pre-occupied with 'exposures' – of the CIA (e.g. drug running in Vietnam), FBI surveillance methods, the global drug wars, international arms dealing, etc. This results in a certain ethnocentrism, but also allows the derivative subjects (political economy, globalization, state propaganda, illegal clandestine operations, counter-intelligence) to be denied as being 'normal politics' (like the white-collar crime issue allowed the denial of 'normal business'). For my purposes here, I want to stress not the politicality of the subject but its criminality. For this, we don't need theories of the state, we need merely to pick up the latest Amnesty Annual Report.

(c) If we have missed something about law making, we have ignored even more the facts of victimization. Again, there is a ritualistic acknowledgement of the damage, harm and violence that are the obvious consequences of state crime – and then we return to easier topics. It is as if we don't want to face these facts; as if – to anticipate the substance of the second part of [this chapter] – we have denied their implications. I am aware that phrases such as 'crimes of the twentieth century' sound bombastic – but for vast populations of the world, this is a fair characterization of those 'gross violations of human rights': genocide, mass political killings, disappearances, torture, rape by agents of state.

This terrible record is known but (as I will show) simultaneously not known. Take genocides and mass political killings only: the Turkish genocide of at least a million Armenians; the Holocaust against six million Jews and the hundreds of thousands of political opponents, gypsies and others; the millions killed under Stalin's regime; the tribal and religious massacres in Burundi, Bengal and Paraguay; the mass political killings in East Timor and Uganda;

the 'autogenocide' in Cambodia; the 'ethnic cleansing' in Bosnia; the death squads and disappearances in Argentina, Guatemala, El Salvador. Or take torture – a practice supposedly eradicated from Europe by the beginning of the nineteenth century and now routinely used in two-thirds of the world.

To add up the deaths, injuries and destruction from all these sources and then compare this to the cumulative results of homicide, assault, property crime and sexual crime in even the highest crime countries of the world, is too tendentious an exercise, too insulting to the intelligence. One cannot calibrate human suffering in this way.

But criminologists do, after all, talk about offence 'seriousness'. The standard literature in this area – and allied debates on culpability, harm, responsibility and the 'just deserts' model – already compares street crime with white-collar crime. A current important contribution (von Hirsch and Jareborg, 1991) tries to gauge criminal harm by using a 'living-standard analysis'. Von Hirsch and his colleague have argued ingeniously that criminal acts can be ranked by a complicated scale of 'degrees of intrusion' on different kinds of legally protected interests: physical integrity; material support and amenity; freedom from humiliation; privacy and autonomy.

What von Hirsch calls 'interests' are strikingly close to what are also called 'human rights'. His examples, however, come only from the standard criminological terrain of citizen against citizen. Including corporate crime would extend the list to (business) organizations against citizen. This is certainly an interesting and worthwhile exercise. It allows, for example, the ranking of forcible rape by a stranger as very grave because this is so demeaning and gross an attack against the 'freedom from humiliation' interest; therefore rape at gun point becomes more serious than armed robbery; date rape comes lower on the cumulative scale on grounds that threat to bodily safety is eliminated, and so on.

But neither crimes of state nor the wider category of 'political crime' are mentioned. There is no logical reason why the identity of the offender should be assumed to be fixed as citizen against citizen, rather than state agent against citizen when talking about, say, murder, assault or rape. In fact, there are good *moral* reasons why any grading of seriousness should take this into account – in particular, the fact that the very agent responsible for upholding law, is actually responsible for the crime. And there is a good *empirical* reason: that for large parts of the world's population, state agents (or paramilitary groups, vigilantes or terrorists) are the normal violators of your 'legally protected interests'.

I don't want to oversimplify the many conceptual objections and obstacles that criminologists will legitimately raise to my glib appeal to include state crime in our frame of reference. Most such objections fall under two categories.

First, there are the equivalent arguments to those used in the field of corporate crime – that the state is not an actor and that individual criminal responsibility cannot be identified. For corporate crime, this objection has been disposed of often enough, most recently (and to my mind convincingly) by Braithwaite and Fisse (1990). The corporation engages in rational goal-seeking behaviour; it can act; it can have intentions; it can commit crimes. This is just as (though more complicatedly) true for the state.

The second objection (again paralleled from Sutherland onwards in the case of corporate crime) is that the resultant action is not 'really' crime. Here, the counter-arguments are complicated and come from a number of different directions: (i) an appeal to international law and conventions on such concepts as 'war crimes' or 'crimes against humanity'; (ii) a demonstration that these acts are illegal by domestic criminal law and fit all criteria of 'crime'; (iii) and even if the acts in question are legal by internal state jurisdiction, then the question arises of how this legal legitimation occurs. We have to remember (perhaps by inscribing this on our consciousness each morning) that state crimes are not just the unlicensed terror of totalitarian or fascist regimes, police states, dictatorships or military juntas. And in even the most extreme of these regimes, such as Nazi Germany, the discourse of legality is used (Muller, 1991).

One of the clearest and most eloquent texts for understanding these symbiotic issues of responsibility and criminality, is the 1985 trial in Argentina of the former military junta members responsible for the mass killings, atrocities, disappearances of the 'dirty war'. Reports of this trial (e.g. by Amnesty International) should be on all criminology reading lists.

The reasons why we don't make these connections are less logical than epistemological. The political discourse of the atrocity is, as I will soon show, designed to hide its presence from awareness. This is not a matter of secrecy, in the sense of lack of access to information, but an unwillingness to confront anomalous or disturbing information. Take the example of torture. Democratic-type societies – the French in Algeria (Maran, 1989); the British in Northern Ireland; the Israelis in the Occupied Territories (Cohen, 1991) – could all proclaim their adherence to international conventions and domestic laws against torture. This called for a complex discourse of denial that what they were doing constituted torture. No, it was something else, 'special procedures' or 'moderate physical pressure'. So something happened – but it was not illegal. In more totalitarian societies (with no accountability, no free press, no independent judiciary) denial is simpler – you do it, but say you do not. Nothing happened.

The standard vocabulary of official (government) denial weaves its way – at times simultaneously, at times sequentially – through a complete spiral of denial. First you try 'it didn't happen'. There was no massacre, no one was tortured. But then the media, human rights organizations and victims show that it does happen: here are the graves; we have the photos; look at the autopsy reports. So you have to say that what happened was not what it looks to be but really something else: a 'transfer of population', 'collateral damage', 'self-defence'. And then – the crucial subtext – what happened anyway was completely justified – protecting national security, part of the war against terrorism. So:

- It doesn't happen here.
- If it does, 'it' is something else.
- Even if it is what you say it is, it is justified.

Faced with this spiral of denial, criminologists may not be expected to respond very differently from ordinary citizens. But the debate is only a little more complex and dramatic than debates about whether white-collar crime is really crime. I say more 'dramatic' because we are forced back not just to questions about what is normal business, but what is the normal state. Take, for example, the question of jurisdiction and punishment. Precisely because we expect so little from domestic and international law as sanctions against gross state crimes (against our own or other citizens), we seldom frame human rights violations in criminal terms. Talking about the limitations in the 1948 UN Convention Against Genocide and in the UN Charter itself, the anthropologist Leo Kuper remarks with characteristic irony that an unstated assumption of the international discourse is that:

> the sovereign territorial state claims, as an integral part of its sovereignty, the right to commit genocide or engage in genocidal massacres against people under its rule, and that the United Nations for all practical purposes, defends this right. (Kuper, 1981: 161)

Obviously, this is very complex territory – more complex that I can even hint at here – and it is understandable why mainstream criminology is reluctant to become too immersed in these debates. Their absence in 'left realist' criminology is stranger to explain. After all, the ontological base here is a realist philosophy which starts with harm, victimization, seriousness, suffering and supposed indifference to all this by the adolescent left idealism of the 1960s.

I will return to some possible explanations for this blindsight. On one level, this is nothing more sinister than a Western ethnocentrism preoccupied with its own national concerns and secure in the great achievement of liberal capitalism; the separation of crime from the state. On another more interesting level, this stems from the universal tendency to see only what is convenient to see.

## The culture of denial

Let me now turn to my substantive topic – denial. How did I get to this subject?

During the decade in which I have lived in Israel, but especially the past five years of the *intifada* (the uprising of Palestinians in the Occupied Territories), I have been puzzled by the apparent lack of overt reaction (dissent, criticism, protest) in just those sectors of Israeli society [which] one would expect to be reacting more. In the face of clear information about what's going on – escalating levels of violence and repression, beatings, torture, daily humiliations, collective punishment (curfews, house demolition, deportations), death-squad-type killings by army undercover units – the level of shame, outrage and protest is not psychologically or morally appropriate.

Of course there are no objective scales of psychological or moral 'appropriateness'. But many observers, inside and outside the country, have sensed that this part of the public should find [things] more disturbing and be prepared to act accordingly.

Remember that I am talking not about that clear majority of the population who support these measures and would not object to even more severe repression. My object of study is the minority: the enlightened, educated middle class, responsive to messages of peace and co-existence, first to condemn human rights violations everywhere else in the world.

Note that unlike most societies where gross human rights violations occur, the facts are both private and public knowledge. Nearly everyone has direct personal knowledge, especially from army service. These are not conscripts or mercenary soldiers drawn from the underclass; everybody serves (including the middle class liberals) or has a husband, son, cousin or neighbour in reserve duty. There is a relatively open press, liberal in tone, which regularly and clearly exposes what is happening in the Occupied Territories. No one – least of all the group which interests me – can say those terrible (though, as I will show, complicated) words 'I didn't know'.

It is way beyond my scope to discuss the special reasons in Israel for denial, passivity or indifference. These are part of a complex political history – of being Jewish, of Zionism, of fear and insecurity. I mention this case only because it led me to comparisons, to looking for similarities and differences in other societies. I went back to my experience of growing up in apartheid South Africa. More fatefully, I turned to the emblematic events of this century: the Holocaust 'texts' about the good Germans who knew what was happening; the lawyers and doctors who colluded; the ordinary people who passed by the concentration camps every day and claimed not to know what was happening; the politicians in Europe and America who did not believe what they were told. Then from this one historical event, I went to the contemporary horrors reported every day in the mass media and documented by human rights reports – about Bosnia, Peru, Guatemala, Burma, Uganda . . .

All this – and the relevant social scientific literature – led me back to versions of the same universal question. This is not Milgram's famous question of how ordinary people will behave in terrible ways, but rather how ordinary, even good people, will not react appropriately to knowledge of the terrible. Why, when faced by knowledge of others' suffering and pain – particularly the suffering and pain resulting from what are called 'human rights violations' – does 'reaction' so often take the form of denial, avoidance, passivity, indifference, rationalization or collusion?

I have mentioned the official state discourse: the pure denials (it didn't happen, they are lying, the media are biased, the world community is just picking on us) and the pure justifications (deterrence, self-defence, national security, ideology, information gathering). But my concern is not the actor but rather (back, in a curious way, to labelling theory!) the audience. In the triangle of human suffering so familiar to criminologists – the victim, to whom things are done; the perpetrator, who is actively causing the suffering; the observer who sees and knows – my interest lies in this third corner: the audience, the observers, the bystanders.

For my purposes here, I want to consider a specific group of observers – not those whose avoidance derives from (crudely speaking) their *support* for the action. If they see nothing morally wrong or emotionally disturbing in what is happening, why should they do anything? In this sense, their denial or passivity is 'easy' to explain. My interest is more in the subgroup who are ideologically predisposed to be against what is happening, to be disturbed by what they know. How do they react to their knowledge of the terrible?

Before presenting some lines of enquiry into this subject, let me note an important distinction which I won't have time to follow through. In talking about the denial of atrocities or human rights violations, there is a world of difference between reacting to your own government's actions as distinct from what might be happening in a distant country. My response, say, as an Australian, to newspaper revelations about the treatment of Aborigines in custody, follows different lines from my response to sitting in Melbourne and reading a human rights report about death squads in El Salvador.

[. . .] First, I will list some of the more useful bodies of literature which deal – directly, but more often obliquely – with the general phenomenon of denial. Then I will give a preliminary classification of the major forms of denial. Finally, I will note a few questions from my fieldwork on human rights organizations. Through interviews, analysis of publications, educational material advertisements and campaign evaluations, I am trying to understand how human rights messages are disseminated and received.

This last part of the work is a study in communication. The *sender* is the international human rights community (directly or through the mass media). The *audience* is our real and metaphorical bystanders. The *message* is something like this (to quote from an actual Amnesty International advert in Britain in 1991):

*Brazil has solved the Problem of how to keep kids off the street. Kill Them.*

What bodies of literature might be of relevance?

### 1 *The psychology of denial*

Orthodox psychoanalysis sees denial as an unconscious defence mechanism for coping with guilt and other disturbing psychic realities. Freud originally distinguished between 'repression' which applies to defences against internal instinctual demands and 'denial' (or what he called 'disavowal') which applies to defences against the claims of external reality.

With a few exceptions, pure psychoanalytic theory has paid much less attention to denial in this sense than repression (but see Edelstein, 1989). We have to look in the more applied fields of psychoanalysis (or its derivatives) for studies about the denial of external information. This yields a mass of useful material. There is the rich literature on the denial of knowledge about fatal disease (especially cancer and more recently, AIDS) affecting self or loved ones. More familiar to criminologists, there is the literature on family violence and pathology: spouse abuse, child abuse, incest etc. The concept of denial is standard to describe a mother's reaction on 'discovering' that her husband had been sexually abusing their daughter for many years: 'I didn't notice anything'. In this case, the concept implies that in fact the mother did 'know' – how could she not have? – but that this knowledge was too unbearable to confront.

The subject of denial has also been dealt with by cognitive psychology and information theory. Of particular interest is the 'denial paradox': in order to use the term 'denial' to describe a person's statement 'I didn't know', you have to assume that he or she knew or knows about what it is he or she claims not to know (otherwise the term 'denial' is inappropriate).

Cognitive psychologists have used the language of information processing, selective perception, filtering, attention span etc., to understand the phenomenon of how we notice and simultaneously do not notice (Goleman, 1985). Some have even argued that the neurological phenomenon of 'blindsight' suggests a startling possibility: that one part of the mind may know just what it is doing, while the part that supposedly knows, remains oblivious of this.

We are all familiar, from basic social psychology, with the notion of cognitive bias: the selection of information to fit existing perceptual frames. At the extreme, information which is too threatening to absorb is shut out altogether. The mind somehow grasps what is going on, but rushes a protective filter into place, steering information away from what threatens. Information slips into a kind of 'black hole of the mind' – a blind zone of blocked attention and self-deception. Attention is thus diverted from facts or their meaning. Thus, the 'vital lies' sustained by family members about violence, incest, sexual abuse, infidelity, unhappiness. Lies continue unrevealed, covered up by the family's silence, collusion, alibis and conspiracies (Goleman, 1985).

Similar processes have been well documented outside both the social psychology laboratory and intimate settings like the family. The litany by observers of atrocities is all too familiar: 'we didn't see anything', 'no one told us', 'it looked different at the time'.

In addition to psychoanalytical and cognitive theory, there is also the tradition in philosophical psychology concerned with questions of self-knowledge and self-deception. The Sartrean notion of 'bad faith' is of particular interest in implying – contrary to psychoanalytical theory – that the denial is indeed conscious.

## 2 Bystanders and rescuers

Another body of literature more obviously relevant (and more familiar to criminologists) derives from the victimological focus on the bystander. The classic 'bystander effect' has become a cliché: how witnesses to a crime will somehow disassociate themselves from what is happening and not help the victim. The prototype is the famous Kitty Genovese case. (One night in New York in 1964, a young woman, Kitty Genovese, was savagely assaulted in the street just before reaching her apartment. Her assailant attacked her over a period of forty minutes while she struggled, battered and screaming, to reach her apartment. Her screams and calls for help were heard by at least 38 neighbours who, from their own windows saw or heard her struggle. No one intervened directly or by calling the police. Eventually a patrol car arrived – too late to save her life.)

Studies of the bystander effect (Sheleff, 1978) suggest that intervention is less likely to occur under three conditions:

1  *Diffusion of responsibility* – so many others are watching, why should I be the one to intervene? Besides, it's none of my business.
2  *Inability to identify with the victim* – even if I see someone as a victim, I won't act if I cannot sympathize or emphathize with their suffering. We help our family, friends, nation, in-group – not those excluded from our moral universe (*Journal of Social Issues*, 1990). In fact, those who are outside out moral universe may be blamed for their predicament (the common experience of women victims of sexual violence). If full responsibility is laid on the political out-group (they provoked us, they had it coming), this releases you from your obligation to respond.
3  *Inability to conceive of effective intervention* – even if you do not erect barriers of denial, even if you feel genuine moral or psychological unease ('I feel so awful about what's going on in Bosnia', 'I just can't get those

pictures from Somalia out of my mind'), this will not necessarily result in intervention. Observers will not act if they do not know what to do, if they feel powerless and helpless themselves, if they don't see any reward in helping, or if they fear punishment if they help.

These processes are of obvious relevance to my work on human rights violations. There are immediate and literal 'bystanders': all massacres, disappearances and atrocities have their witnesses. And there are also metaphorical bystanders; remember the reader looking at the Amnesty adverts about street kids being killed in Brazil or dissidents being tortured in Turkey: Is this really my problem? Can I identify with these victims? What can I do about it anyway?

The obverse of the bystander effect has generated its own special discourse. Just as interesting as the social bases of indifference, are the conditions under which people are aroused to intervene – often at great personal cost and risk. There is a vast ranging literature here: experimental studies on the social psychology of altruism and pro-social behaviour; the sociology of charity and philanthropy; philosophical and economic discussions of altruism (notably attempts to reconcile the phenomenon to rational choice theory); historical studies of helping, rescuing, altruism, the Good Samaritan. The best known of this work deals with rescuers of Jews in Nazi Europe (Oliner and Oliner, 1988).

## 3   Neutralization theory

More familiar ground to criminologists is the body of literature known as 'motivational accounts' or 'vocabulary of motives' theory. The application of this theory in Sykes and Matza's (1957) 'techniques of neutralization' paper is a criminological classic. [. . .]

The theory assumes that motivational accounts which actors (offenders) give of their (deviant) behaviour must be acceptable to their audience (or audiences). Moreover, accounts are not just *post facto* improvisations, but are drawn upon in advance from the cultural pool of motivational vocabularies available to actors and observers (and honoured by systems of legality and morality). Remember Sykes and Matza's original list; each technique of neutralization is a way of denying the moral bind of the law and the blame attached to the offence: denial of injury ('no one got hurt'); denial of victim ('they started it'; 'it's all their fault'); denial of responsibility ('I didn't mean to do it', 'they made me do it'); condemnation of the condemners ('they are just as bad') and appeal to higher loyalties (friends, gang, family, neighbourhood).

Something very strange happens if we apply this list not to the techniques for denying or neutralizing conventional delinquency but to human rights violations and state crimes. For Sykes and Matza's point was precisely that delinquents are *not* 'political' in the sense implied by subcultural theory; that is, they are not committed to an alternative value system nor do they withdraw legitimacy from conventional values. The necessity for verbal neutralization shows precisely the continuing bind of conventional values.

But exactly the same techniques appear in the manifestly political discourse of human rights violations – whether in collective political trials (note, for example, the Nuremberg trials or the Argentinian junta trial) or official government responses to human rights reports (a genre which I am studying) or media debates about war crimes and human rights abuses. I will return soon to 'literal denial', that first twist of the denial spiral which I identified earlier (it didn't happen, it can't happen here, they are all liars). Neutralization comes into play when you acknowledge (admit) that something happened – but either refuse to accept the category of acts to which it is assigned ('crime' or 'massacre') or present it as morally justified. Here are the original neutralization techniques, with corresponding examples from the realm of human rights violations.

- *Denial of injury* – they exaggerate, they don't feel it, they are used to violence, see what they do to each other.
- *Denial of victim* – they started it, look what they've done to us; they are the terrorists, we are just defending ourselves, we are the real victims.
- *Denial of responsibility* – here, instead of the criminal versions of psychological incapacity or diminished responsibility (I didn't know what I was doing. I blacked out, etc.) we find a denial of individual moral responsibility on the grounds of obedience: I was following orders, only doing my duty, just a cog in the machine. (For individual offenders like the ordinary soldier, this is the most pervasive and powerful of all denial systems).
- *Condemnation of the condemners* – here, the politics are obviously more explicit than in the original delinquency context. Instead of condemning the police for being corrupt and biased or teachers for being hypocrites, we have the vast discourse of official denial used by the modern state to protect its public image: the whole world is picking on us; they are using double standards to judge us; it's worse elsewhere (Syria, Iraq, Guatemala or wherever is convenient to name); they are condemning us only because of their anti-semitism (the Israeli version), their hostility to Islam (the Arab version), their racism and cultural imperialism in imposing Western values (all Third World tyrannies).
- *Appeal to higher loyalty* – the original subdued 'ideology' is now total and self-righteous justification. The appeal to the army, the nation, the *volk*, the sacred mission, the higher cause – whether the revolution, 'history', the purity of Islam, Zionism, the defence of the free world or state security. As the tragic events of the last few years show, despite the end of the cold war, the end of history and the decline of meta narratives, there is no shortage of 'higher loyalties', old and new.

Let us remember the implications of accounts theory for our subject. Built into the offender's action, is the knowledge that certain accounts will be accepted. Soldiers on trial for, say, killing a peaceful demonstrator, can offer the account of 'obeying orders' because this will be honoured by the legal system and the wider public. This honouring is, of course, not a simple matter: Were the orders clear? Did the soldier suspect that the order was illegal? Where in the chain of command did the order originate from? These, and other ambiguities, make up the stuff of legal, moral and political discourses of denial.

I have no time here to apply each of these theoretical frameworks – psychoanalysis, cognitive psychology, bystander theory, motivational accounts etc. – to my case study of reactions to knowledge of human rights violations and state crimes. (There are obviously also many other relevant fields: political socialization and mobilization, mass media analysis, collective memory). For illustration only, let me list some elementary forms of denial which these theories might illuminate.

I will distinguish three forms of denial, each of which operates at (i) the individual or psychic level and (ii) at the organized, political, collective or official level.

## 1 Denial of the past

At the individual level, there are the complex psychic mechanisms which allow us to 'forget' unpleasant, threatening or terrible information. Memories of what we have done or seen or known are selected out and filtered.

At the collective level, there are the organized attempts to cover up the record of past atrocities. The most dramatic and successful example in the modern era is the eighty years of organized denial by successive Turkish governments of the 1915–17 genocide against the Armenians – in which some one and half million people lost their lives (Hovanissian, 1986). This denial has been sustained by deliberate propaganda, lying and cover-ups, forging of documents, suppression of archives and bribing of scholars. The West, especially the USA, has colluded by not referring to the massacres in the UN, ignoring memorial ceremonies and by surrendering to Turkish pressure in NATO and other arenas of strategic cooperation.

The less successful example, of course, is the so-called 'revisionist' history of holocaust of European Jews, dismissed as a 'hoax' or a 'myth'.

At both levels, we can approach the process of denial through its opposite: the attempt to recover or uncover the past. At the individual level, the entire psychoanalytic procedure itself is a massive onslaught on individual denial and self-deception. At the political level, there is the opening of collective memory, the painful coming to terms with the past, the literal and metaphorical digging up of graves when regimes change and try to exorcise their history.

## 2 Literal denial

Here we enter the grey area sketched out by psychoanalysis and cognitive theory. In what senses can we be said to 'know' about something we profess not to know about? If we do shut something out of knowledge, is this unconscious or conscious? Under what conditions (for example, information overload or desensitization) is such denial likely to take place?

There are many different versions of literal denial, some of which appear to be wholly individual, others which are clearly structured by the massive resources of the state. We didn't know, we didn't see anything, it couldn't have happened without us knowing (or it could have happened without us knowing). Or: things like this can't happen here, people like us don't do things like this. Or: you can't believe the source of your knowledge: – victims, sympathizers, human rights monitors, journalists are biased, partial or ignorant.

The psychological ambiguities of 'literal denial' and their political implications are nicely illustrated by the psychoanalyst John Steiner's reinterpretation of the Oedipus drama (Steiner, 1985, 1990).

The standard version of the legend is a tragedy in which Oedipus is a victim of fate who bravely pursues the truth. At the beginning he does not know the truth (that he has killed his father, that he had sexual relations with his mother); at the end he does. This is taken as a paradigm for the therapeutic process itself: the patient in analysis to whom, gradually and painfully, the secrets of the unconscious are revealed. But alongside this version, Steiner shows, Sophocles also conveys a quite different message in the original drama: the message is that the main characters in the play must have been aware of the identity of Oedipus and realized that he had committed patricide and incest. There is a deliberate ambiguity throughout the text about the nature of this awareness – just how much did each character know? Each of the participants (including Oedipus himself) and especially the various court officials, had (good) different reasons for denying their knowledge, for staging a cover-up. The Oedipus story is not at all about the discovery of truth, but the denial of truth – a cover-up like Watergate, Iran Contra. Thus the question: how much did Nixon or Bush 'know'?

The ambiguity about how conscious or unconscious our knowledge is, how much we are aware of what we say we are unaware, is nicely captured in Steiner's title 'Turning a Blind Eye'. This suggests the possibility of *simultaneously* knowing and not knowing. We are not talking about the simple lie or fraud where facts are accessible but lead to a conclusion which is knowingly evaded. This, of course, is standard in the organized government cover-up: bodies are burnt, evidence is concealed, officials are given detailed instructions on how to lie. Rather, we are talking about the more common situation where 'we are vaguely aware that we choose not to look at the facts without being conscious of what it is we are evading' (Steiner, 1985: 61).

### 3 Implicatory denial

The forms of denial that we conceptualize as excuses, justifications, rationalizations or neutralizations, do not assert that the event did not happen. They seek to negotiate or impose a different construction of the event from what might appear the case. At the individual level, you know and admit to what you have done, seen or heard about. At the organized level, the event is also registered but is subjected to cultural reconstruction (for example, through euphemistic, technical or legalistic terminology). The point is to deny the implications – psychological and moral – of what is known. The common linguistic structure is 'yes, but'. Yes, detainees are being tortured but there is no other way to obtain information. Yes, Bosnian women are being raped, but what can a mere individual thousands of miles away do about it?

'Denial of Responsibility', as I noted earlier, is one of the most common forms of implicatory denial. The sociology of 'crimes of obedience' has received sustained attention, notably by Kelman and Hamilton (1989). The anatomy of obedience and conformity – the frightening degree to which ordinary people are willing to inflict great psychological and physical harm to others – was originally revealed by Milgram's famous experiment. Kelman and Hamilton begin from history rather than a university laboratory: the famous case of Lieutenant Calley and the My Lai massacre during the Vietnam War in May 1968 when a platoon of American soldiers massacred some 400 civilians. From this case and other 'guilt free' or 'sanctioned' massacres, they extract a rather stable set of conditions under which crimes of obedience will occur.

1 *Authorization*: when acts are ordered, encouraged, or tacitly approved by those in authority, then normal moral principles are replaced by the duty to obey.

2 *Routinization*: the first step is often difficult, but when you pass the initial moral and psychological barrier, then the pressure to continue is powerful. You become involved without considering the implications; it's all in a day's work. This tendency is re-inforced by special vocabularies and euphemisms ('surgical strike') or a simple sense of routine. (Asked about what he thought he was doing, Calley replied in one of the most chilling sentences of all times: 'It was no big deal').

3 *Dehumanization*: when the qualities of being human are deprived from the other, then the usual principles of morality do not apply. The enemy is described as animals, monsters, gooks, sub-humans. A whole language excludes them from your shared moral universe.

The conditions under which perpetrators behave can be translated into the very bystander rationalizations which allow the action in the first place and then deny its implications afterwards. As Kelman and Hamilton show in their analysis of successive public opinion surveys (in which people were asked both to imagine how they would react to a My Lai situation themselves and to judge the actual perpetrators), obedience and authorization are powerful justifications. And observers as well as offenders are subject to desensitization (the bombardment by horror stories from the media to a point that you cannot absorb them any more and they are no longer 'news') and dehumanization.

My research on human rights organizations (national and international) deals with their attempts to overcome these barriers of denial. What is the difference between working in your own country and trying to arouse an international audience in distant and different places? What messages work best in mobilizing public action (whether going to a demonstration, donating money or joining an organization like Amnesty International)? Does focusing on a country work better than raising an issue (such as torture or the death penalty)? And which countries or which issues? Are some techniques of confronting denial - for example, inducing guilt or representing the horrors more vividly - counter-productive? Is there competition for the human rights message within the same audiences (for example, from the environmental movement)? . . .

## Conclusion

[. . .]

Instead of a conclusion, let me instead end with two footnotes. One raises - dare I say - some meta-theoretical issues; the other introduces a little optimism into an otherwise bleak story.

### Meta theory

I mentioned the strange neglect of these issues by new realist criminologists and suggested that what is at stake is their sense of reality. But 'reality' is not a word used too easily these days - or if used, only politically correct in inverted commas. This is the legacy of post-structuralism, deconstructionism and postmodernism. There are a number of trends in postmodernist theory which – usually unwittingly – impinge on the human rights discourse. Let me mention a few such meta issues:

First, there is the question of moral relativism. This is the familiar claim – now supposedly finally vindicated – that if there is no universal, foundational base for morality (the death of meta-narratives), then it is impossible to stake out universal values (such as those enshrined in human rights standards). Then comes the derivative claim that such values and standards are Western, ethnocentric, individualistic, alien and imposed.

Now, whatever the historical record, this claim has some strange political implications. The standard and age-old government denials of the applicability of international human rights norms – we are different, we face special problems, the world doesn't understand us – now acquire a new philosophical dignity. And further, the condemners are condemned for being ethnocentric and imperialist.

A similar problem comes from the assertion that local struggles for human rights lose their meaning because they are informed by the very universal foundations and master narratives now so thoroughly discredited or tarnished. This is again a complex debate; I side with those who argue that no amount of deconstructive scepticism should deny the force with which we defend these values. It is surely a bizarre sight for Western progressives to be telling human rights activists from the Third World or Eastern Europe that their struggle is, after all, not worth the candle.

A second problem is posed by the proclaimed end of history. This is the current round of the old 'end of ideology' game: the collapse of international socialism finally proving the triumph of Western democratic capitalism. Besides the poverty of the case itself, it can make little sense for those still living between death squads, famine, disease and violence. For them, history is not over. But even if one meta narrative has won and there is nothing left for 'history' in the industrialized world, then how does this world react to what is happening elsewhere? Why – if not because of racism, selfishness, greed, and the type of denial I've talked about – do the victors not devote more resources to achieve these values elsewhere?

A third postmodernist theme is even more directly relevant to my subject here – and potentially even more destructive. This is the attack on all modes of rational enquiry which work with positivist categories of reality. The human rights movement can live without absolute, foundational values. But it cannot live with a theory which denies any way of knowing what has really happened. All of us who carried the anti-positivist banners of the 1960s are responsible for the emergent epistemological circus.

[. . .] On 29 March 1991, shortly after the cessation of hostilities in the Gulf War – just as thousands were lying dead and maimed in Iraq, the country's infra-structure deliberately destroyed by savage bombing, the Kurds abandoned to their fate – the high priest of postmodernism, Jean Baudrillard, published an article entitled 'The Gulf War Has Not Taken Place' (Baudrillard, 1991b). The 'true belligerents' he argued, are those who thrive on the ideology of the truth of this war.

He was only being consistent with an article he wrote a few days before the war (Baudrillard, 1991a) in which he predicted that it would never happen. The war existed only as a figment of media simulation, of imaginary scenarios that exceeded all limits of real world facticity. The war, Baudrillard had solemnly declared, was strictly unthinkable except as an exchange of threats so exorbitant that it would guarantee that the event would not take place. The 'thing' would happen only in the minds of its audience, as an extension of the video games imagery which had filled our screens during the long build up. Dependent as we all were – prime time viewers as well as generals – on these computer generated images, we might as well drop all self-deluding distinctions between screen events and 'reality'.

Given this 'prediction', it was unlikely that Baudrillard would be proved wrong if the war really did break out. So indeed the 'war' – a free floating signifier, devoid of referential bearing – did not happen. To complain that he was caught out by events only shows our theoretical naïveté, our nostalgia for the old truth-telling discourses.

What does one make of all this? I take my cue from Christopher Norris (1992), who has devoted a splendid polemical book to attacking Baudrillard's theses on the Gulf War. Norris is by no means a philistine critic or an unregenerated 'positivist'. He is the author of altogether sympathetic studies of Derrida and deconstructionism. And he concedes that Baudrillard makes some shrewd observations about how the war was presented by its managers and the media: the meaningless statistical data to create a illusory sense of factual reporting, the absurd claims about 'precision targeting', and 'clever bombs' to convince us that the mass destruction of civilian lives were either not happening (literal denial) or were accidental (denial of responsibility).

But Norris is now appalled by the precious nonsense to which the fashionable tracks of postmodernism have led. What disturbs him is how seriously these ideas were taken, 'to the point where Baudrillard can deliver his ludicrous theses on the Gulf War without fear of subsequent exposure as a charlatan or of finding these theses resoundingly disconfirmed by the course of real-world events' (Norris, 1992: 17).

It is beyond my scope and competence to consider Norris's explanation for how these ideas emerged and just where they lost their plausibility. He places particular importance on the curious ascendancy of literary theory as a paradigm for other areas of study. There is the bland assumption that because every text involves some kind of narrative interest, therefore there is no way to distinguish factual, historical or documentary material on the one hand from fictive, imaginary or simulated material on the other. With no possible access to truth or historical record, we are asked, Norris shows, to inhabit a realm of unanchored persuasive utterances where rhetoric goes all the way down and where nothing could count as an argument against what the media or governments would have us currently believe.

This re-definition of history finds strange echoes, as Norris notes, among the right wing revisionist historians of the holocaust, 'those for whom it clearly comes as good news that past events can only be interpreted according to present consensus values, or ideas of what currently and contingently counts as "good in the way of belief"' (Norris, 1992: 21). In the case of current events, like the Gulf War, we are left with no resources to deal with the obvious contradictions between official propaganda and personal witness (for example, about the bombing of the Amiriyah civilian air raid shelter). The cult following of these ideas by some intellectuals reflects, as Norris suggests, their lack of desire to make any political judgement, their cynical acquiescence in the war. If the war was so unreal, so completely beyond our competence to judge as informed observers, then we can say nothing to challenge the official (media sponsored) version of events.

My point in raising this example is simple. If the Turkish government can deny that the Armenian genocide happened; if revisionist historians and neo-Nazis deny that the Holocaust took place; if powerful states all around the world today can systematically deny the systematic violations of human rights they are carrying out – then we know that we're in bad shape. But we're in even worse shape when the intellectual *avant garde* invent a form of denial so profound, that serious people – including progressives – will have to debate whether the Gulf War actually took place or not.

*Acknowledgement*

I promised a more optimistic second footnote. This is not to cheer you up, but just to be honest. Denial has it opposites. What has to be understood are the conditions under which denial does not occur, in which the truth (even if this concept is disappearing down the postmodern black hole) is acknowledged, not just its existence but its moral implications.

After all, in the Milgram experiment, somewhere around 30 per cent of the subjects (depending on the conditions) did not push the button. In Kelman and Hamilton's public opinion surveys, again another 30 per cent would not obey orders to shoot innocent women and children. In the middle of even the most grotesque of state crimes, such as genocide, there are extraordinary tales of courage, rescuing and resistance. Acts of altruism, compassion and pro-social behaviour are woven into the social fabric. Above all, there is the whole human rights movement itself, which over the last three decades has mobilized an extraordinary number of people into wholly selfless behaviour to alleviate the suffering of others – whether by giving money, writing to a prisoner of conscience or joining a campaign.

In my initial interviews with human rights organizations, I was surprised to hear a sense of optimism. Yes, there are some people (referred to in the trade as the 'ostriches') who do not want to know. But most organizations were certain that their potential pool has not been reached. I mentioned to one of my interviewees the cynical notion of 'compassion fatigue' – that people are just too tired to respond, they can't bear seeing any more pictures of the homeless in the streets, victims of AIDS, children starving in Somalia, refugees in Bosnia. Her response was that the concept was a journalistic invention; what there is, is media fatigue.

This is where we return to the state of hyper-reality which postmodernist theories have so well exposed. The question is right open: Will the type of manipulation and simulation seen in the Gulf War dominate, creating indeed a culture of denial? Or can we conceive of a flow of information which will allow people to acknowledge reality and act accordingly?

This might seem a pretentious question for us humble criminologists to consider, but I hope that you will allow me to get away with it.

**References**

Barak, G. (ed.) (1991) *Crimes by the Capitalist State: an Introduction to State Criminality*. Albany: State University of New York Press.
Baudrillard, J. (1991a) 'The Reality Gulf', *Guardian*, 11 January.
Baudrillard, J. (1991b) 'La guerre du Golfe n'a pas eu lieu', *Libération*, 29 March.
Braithwaite, J. and Fisse, B. (1990) 'On the plausibility of corporate crime theory', in W.

Laufer and F. Adler (eds), *Advances in Criminological Theory*, vol. II. New Brunswick, NJ: Transaction Books.

Cohen, S. (1991) 'Talking about torture in Israel', *Tikkun*, 6(6): 22–30, 89–90.

Edelstein, E.L. et al. (eds) (1989) *Denial: a Clarification of Concepts and Research*. New York: Plenum Press.

Goleman, D. (1985) *Vital Lies, Simple Truths: On the Psychology of Self Deception*. New York: Simon and Schuster.

Hovanissian, R.G. (ed.) (1986) *The Armenian Genocide in Perspective*. New Brunswick, NJ: Transaction Books.

Karmen, A. (1990) *Crime Victims: an Introduction to Victimology*. California: Brooks Cole.

Kelman, H.C. and Hamilton, V.L. (1989) *Crimes of Obedience*. New Haven, CT: Yale University Press.

Kuper, L. (1981) *Genocide*. Harmondsworth: Penguin Books.

Maran, R. (1989) *Torture: the Role of Ideology in the French-Algerian War*. New York: Praeger.

Muller, I. (1991) *Hitler's Justice: the Courts of the Third Reich*. Cambridge, MA: Harvard University Press.

Norris, C. (1992) *Uncritical Theory: Postmodernism, Intellectuals and the Gulf War*. London: Lawrence and Wishart.

Oliner, S. and Oliner, P. (1988) *The Altruistic Personality: Rescuers of Jews in Nazi Europe*. New York: Free Press.

Schwendinger, H. and Schwendinger, J. (1970) 'Defenders of order or guardians of human rights', *Issues in Criminology*, 7: 72–81.

Sheleff, L. (1978) *The Bystander*, Lexington, MA.

Steiner, J. (1985) 'Turning a blind eye: the cover up for Oedipus', *International Review of Psycho-Analysis*, 12: 161–72.

Steiner, J. (1990) 'The retreat from truth to omnipotence in Sophocles' *Oedipus at Colonus*', *International Review of Psycho-Analysis*, 17: 227–37.

Sykes, G. and Matza, D. (1957) 'Techniques of neutralization: a theory of delinquency', *American Sociology Review*, 22: 664–70.

von Hirsch, A. and Jareborg, N. (1991) 'Gauging criminal harm: a living-standard analysis', *Oxford Journal of Legal Studies*, II(1): 1–38.

# 46

# The fragmentation of criminology

*Richard Ericson and Kevin Carriere*

[. . .]

The fragmentation of academic literatures and the blurring of disciplinary boundaries is occurring across modern science (Capra, 1976; Giddens, 1987; Lyotard, 1984). Marcus (1986: 166) has declared: 'In anthropology and all other human sciences at the moment, "high" theoretical discourse – the body of ideas that authoritatively unify a field – is in disarray.' As the boundaries of modern science dissipate, and as interdisciplinary fields become ascendant, many academics experience vertigo.

> A conceptual revolution in the humanities and social sciences has given new vigor to inquiries about cultural studies in a variety of fields over the past twenty years, but that ongoing revolution leaves investigators with no stable ground on which to stand. A dizzying succession of new methods and theories has shattered disciplinary paradigms, forced scholars to engage in bold departures from their own training, to become 'specialists' in fields with few acknowledged experts and few firm standards of evidence and argument. My own inquiries have often left me between fields – too historical for the sociologists, too sociological for the linguists, and too linguistic and too sociological for the historians. (Lipsitz, 1990: vii–ix)

Within the academy, responses to the fragmentation of criminology vary. Some scholars who are cited by criminologists, but who do not see criminology as their field, simply ignore the issue. Criminologists who are disillusioned by the very thing that constitutes the field, namely its multidisciplinary and fragmented character, offer essentialist solutions. The essentialist solutions include treating criminology as an effective politics of crime control, or as a branch of a particular master discipline, or as a unified critical practice. Each of these essentialist solutions ignores the fact that the

> search for final solutions to questions about truth, rationality and knowledge could lead to the 'freezing over of culture' and the 'dehumanization of human beings' . . . the Platonic quest for a final, rational justified consensus based on access to an eternal Truth is actually a manifestation of what Nietzsche called a 'craving for metaphysical comfort': the desire to close off inquiry, to calcify a privileged set of descriptions, and to 'escape our humanity' by becoming properly programmed machines. (Guignon and Hylery, 1990: 339)

Most criminologists respond to fragmentation by identifying their discipline and their selves with the template of the criminal law institution. They join with those working within that institution to produce a discourse about crime and its regulation. This response entails patrolling the boundaries of their institution to police what other knowledges or forms of expertise will be

---

Abridged from *The Futures of Criminology* (ed. D. Nelken), pp. 89–109. (London: Sage, 1994.)

allowed as they fit their discourse. Driven by practical questions, practices and power relations of those working within the criminal law institution, this criminology begins with questions of reform and improvement – What is faulty? How can it be corrected? How can it be made more efficient? – rather than questions arising from problems and academic puzzles derived from scholarly literature. This criminology of applied knowledge and social necessity (Rock, 1988) has always been dominant, but it has become predominant in the past decade through versions of what constitutes an effective politics of crime control.

In the form of right realism, academic criminology becomes synonymous with the institution of criminal law and the effective politics of crime control favoured by those who control that institution at a given time and place (Wilson and Herrnstein, 1985). Such efforts to make criminology the institutional voice of criminal law create all sorts of analytical problems. For example, agencies that participate in the criminal law institution, such as the police, tend to be essentialized as criminal law enforcers, which leads analysts to neglect other aspects of police work including their participation in many other institutions (for example Sherman, 1992; Sherman et al., 1989). Moreover, the ways in which crime and its regulation are constituted by, and constitute, other institutions and their subject populations are ignored by those whose criminology does not go beyond the discourse of the criminal law institution.

Right realism arose in the United States as a political strategy for addressing the urban decay and underclass produced by the very conservative forces with which it identifies. Grounded in assumptions of consensus and unified interest, right realism is oriented to all right-thinking people who believe that the criminal law institution is there to protect their persons and property through strong measures of general deterrence, specific deterrence and incapacitation. It sympathizes with the propertied, in particular with trying to prevent their reserves of peace and prosperity from becoming preserves fortified to the hilt against the desperate urban poor (see the descriptions by Davis, 1990: ch 4; Reich, 1991). Their criminology is the ideological and technological arm of a criminal law institution left with too much of the burden for shoring up the spatial, material and social 'disorder and decline' (Skogan, 1990). Their preferred technologies include, for example, longitudinal studies that identify the criminal other and justify his or her differential treatment (for example, Farrington et al., 1986); and, they also include research that is meant to assist in the calibration of the 'scale of punishment' (Zimring and Hawkins, 1990), where prison is taken for granted as *the* response to crime and the refinement of penal technique is the only puzzle left.

While right realism defines itself with a conservative world view, left realism arose in the United Kingdom as a political strategy for challenging the law and order politics of the Conservative government (Lea and Young, 1984; Young, 1986, 1988a). As Michalowski (1991: 30) has pointed out, left realism was also born through a critique of two academic traditions in criminology: the cultural school, concerned with moral panics and other symbolic aspects of crime (Cohen, 1972; Hall et al., 1978); and, Marxist approaches, concerned with the plight of criminals (Taylor et al., 1973). Identifying with the consumers of criminal justice, especially crime victims who are poor and otherwise disadvantaged, left realism asks how the criminal justice system can meet their needs more adequately. In contrast to right realists who believe that the police are already in touch with essential community interests, left realists challenge state definitions by documenting community interests through victimization and fear of crime surveys. Survey data are treated as indicative of essential community interests. They are used as a template for rationalizing formal policing practices, and for making the police more accountable to the urban poor and other minorities.

Left realists focus almost exclusively on those who suffer most in criminal victimization and yet have the fewest resources to defend themselves or to seek compensation (for example, Jones et al., 1986; Young, 1988b). Part of a wider politics of 'community', the central concern is state responsibility for the just distribution of risks through security measures such as social insurance and protective services (Young, 1988a; see generally Burchell et al., 1991). Led by criminologists who appeared more radical in the 1970s, left realists have adjusted to a 1980s and 1990s 'realism' that really entails joining the ranks of those who take a pragmatic, piecemeal, administrative approach to the field on behalf of particular interests.

Between these extremes of what constitutes an effective politics of crime control is a liberal approach that both Right and Left Realists see as unrealistic. This approach is embodied in the academy in some departments of criminal justice (for example, Ashworth, 1988; Griffiths and Verdun-Jones, 1989). This form of criminology is essentially concerned with the just administration of criminal law conceived in terms of due process of law, and efficiency and humaneness in its administration. Various knowledges are assessed, and the technologies associated with those knowledges are selected, in terms of whether they meet the due process, efficiency and humaneness parameters of the criminal justice institution.

Criminologists who commit themselves to one of these three positions on the politics of crime control typically defend their position vehemently, which includes heaping scorn on opposing positions that are not politically correct. The result, at least among those committed to criminology as an effective politics of crime control, is a field that is not only fragmented but fractured. Meanwhile, criminologists driven by an effective politics of crime control are scorned in turn by those who feel such work is not significant academically because it does not take its lead from core theoretical puzzles of a master discipline. Academic purists argue that there is no scholarly benefit from research that begins with questions of pragmatic penal technique and reform. To accept pragmatic control questions as the first principle of enquiry is to concede that criminology is as Foucault (1977) depicted it in his harshest criticisms: a technology for the suppression and management of crime, conservative in character and devoid of serious intellectual content. In support of their stance, academic purists point to cases where the most significant intellectual breakthroughs derive from master disciplines 'outside' of criminology.

Academics who speak from a master discipline 'outside' of criminology essentialize the field as being synonymous with the theoretical puzzles and preferred methodologies of their discipline. While such a stance is taken, for example, by historians, psychologists, political scientists, semioticians and philosophers, it is exemplified in recent statements of sociologists.

John Hagan (1989) proselytizes 'structural criminology'. [. . .] Criminology is neither other academic disciplines nor an effective politics of crime control. Criminology is his brand of positivistic sociology.

If sociology is the scientific study of social relations, then the approach outlined in this volume is not only a structural criminology, but a sociological criminology as well. The sociological tradition has long been ascendant in criminology [see Gibbons, 1979], but today is under attack. The attack comes on the one hand from those who see criminology as its own 'fully autonomous discipline' [for example Thomas, 1984], and on the other hand from those in other disciplines [for example Wilson, 1975] who believe their own or some grander combination of disciplines provides a better approach to the study of crime and delinquency. The structural approach outlined in this volume is inherently opposed to the separation of criminology from sociology, arguing instead that the structural foundations of sociology make its explanatory role necessary for an understanding of crime and delinquency. The policy analysis of crime leaves off where the sociological study of crime and delinquency began. Sociologists, it seems, may still be uniquely suited to pursue the causes of these behaviours regarded by others as disreputable. (Hagan, 1989: 257-8)

Hagan attempts to disqualify or render subservient alternative methods and disciplines. He does so through the use of metaphors of war such as 'attack' (cf. McGaw, 1991), which are aimed at securing his ontological terrain. The activities of 'discontents' are characterized as subsidiary, unreasonable or ex-centric. In the face of such academic essentialism and imperialism, Foucault (1980: 565) asked rhetorically: 'Should the actual question not be what forms of knowledge do you want to disqualify, if you ask me "is it science"?'. Positivists such as Hagan 'find themselves treating as their object what is in fact their condition of possibility' (Foucault, 1972: 364).

Clifford Shearing (1989) argues that criminology is essentially concerned with the sociological problem of order. Any criminology that focuses on crime is political because crime itself is a political rather than technical construct. Therefore, not only are those who take one of the three positions on an effective politics of crime control dismissed as politically rather than academically motivated, so too are sociologists such as Hagan who focus their analysis on the causes of and social reaction to crime. Against 'crime-ology', Shearing is for 'internally driven agendas and boundaries' (1989: 172) of his discipline. With the sociological problem of order as his agenda, Shearing draws boundaries which reduce and essentialize criminology to sociology, and a rather traditional sociology at that.

It is our failure to translate our theoretical insights and the practices they promote into a disciplinary definition that has produced the straight-jacket of crime-ology. It is because we have allowed ourselves, in our definition of our discipline, to remain so closely tied to the 'natural attitude' that pervades practical political and policy discourse, that we have created barriers, perhaps the appropriate metaphor would be a prison, that has stifled the development of our discipline. . . . The struggle over order, the activity that seeks to guarantee it, and the activity that resists the realization of this guarantee, either in part or in whole, is the phenomenon that gives unity to criminological research and teaching. Ordering both includes crime-ology and goes beyond it in precisely the way that work in our discipline in fact does . . . [I]t is not crime that is our central topic but the struggle around order and the products it produces, among which are crime and criminal justice. Only then will criminology truly reflect its beginnings and the vision that inspired it. (Shearing, 1989: 173, 176, 178)

Shearing and Hagan are typical of criminologists who yearn for order in the field. It comes as no surprise that what 'truly reflects' the tradition of criminology turns out to be a truth derived from their own master discipline.

Fragmentation within the field also results in a sense of dis-ease for some academics who operate under the broad rubric of 'critical' or 'radical' criminology. Despite the fact that the hegemony of Marxism has faded, and it no longer enjoys a monopoly as *the* voice of *the* Left (Laclau and Mouffe, 1985), some criminologists are still trying to forge unification among critical forces. For example, in a [. . .] book entitled *New Directions in Critical Criminology*, the editors argue that perspectives as diverse as left realism, feminism, postmodernism and peacemaking should be viewed as complementary (MacLean and Milovanovic, 1991: 1). This statement is made despite the fact that some of the contributors to this collection recognize the difficulties associated with such a position. The final article in this collection, entitled 'The future of critical criminology', asserts that the term '"critical criminology" is a metaphor for those of us who work in a common tradition with common goals' (Schwartz, 1991: 119). Such attempts to unify the field betray a nostalgia for the Enlightenment fantasy of the pursuit of freedom through the collection and synthesis of truth, as well as the Marxist fantasy of a united revolutionary class. From any Realist perspective, there is no consideration of the possibility that scientific and technical knowledge may not be cumulative: 'At most, what is debated is the form that accumulation takes – some picture it as regular, continuous, others as periodic, discontinuous and conflictual' (Lyotard, 1984: 7).

In their attempts to impose an artificial order and unity upon the field, academic essentialists proceed by criticizing the truths of their opponents as being reductionist and essentialist. Ironically, they then advance an alternative that is itself reductionist and essentialist. This paradox can be avoided, however, if criminologists stop worrying about discipline and order in the field and start celebrating its fragmented character. The only problem with the fragmentation of criminology is criminologists who fret about it. Problems arise when criminologists essentialize the field within their preferred template of political and/or academic correctness.

The drive to essentialize is itself a worthy topic for research. For example, Rabinow (1986: 253) suggests research on the 'micropolitics of knowledge in the academy'. A reflexive criminology must be sensitive to the immediate political conditions and institutional contexts that encourage essentialism.

> Asking whether longer, dispersive, multi-authored texts would yield tenure might seem petty. But those are the dimensions of power relations to which Nietzsche exhorted us to be scrupulously attentive. The taboo against specifying them is much greater than the strictures against denouncing colonialism . . . Just as there was formerly a discursive knot preventing discussion of exactly those field practices that defined the authority of the anthropologist, which has now been untied (Rabinow, 1977), so, too, the micropractices of the academy might well do with some scrutiny. (Rabinow, 1986: 253)

Fragmentation is endemic to the human sciences because of their particular place in the modern *episteme* (Foucault, 1972: esp. 344–87). Foucault situates the development of the human sciences within the context of other scientific discourses on life, labour and language. Arguing that the title of human 'sciences' is a misnomer, he says:

> what renders them possible, in fact, is a certain situation of vicinity with regard to biology, economics and philology (or linguistics); they exist only in so far as they dwell side by side with those sciences – or rather beneath them, in the space of their projections . . . the configuration that defines their positivity and gives them roots in the modern *episteme* at the same time makes it impossible for them to be sciences. (Foucault, 1972: 366)

For Foucault, the precarious status of the human sciences on the landscape of the modern *episteme* makes the blurring of disciplinary boundaries and interdisciplinary dialogue inevitable.

> [H]ence the frequent difficulty in fixing limits, not merely between the objects, but also between the methods proper to psychology, sociology, and the analysis of literature and myth . . . In this way all of the human sciences interlock and can always be used to interpret one another: their frontiers become blurred, intermediary and composite disciplines multiply endlessly, and in the end their proper object may even disappear altogether. (Foucault, 1972: 357–8)

Criminology has the same theoretical ambitions as the disciplines that constitute it and are constituted by it. It is therefore no surprise that important theoretical breakthroughs occur in conjunction with other disciplines. A few recent developments are illustrative.

Foucault's interest in the institutional basis of historical memory has an affinity with Nietzsche's passionate plea for us to 'remember' the role of institutions in mediating history through 'the will to tradition, to authority, to centuries long responsibility, to solidarity between succeeding generations backwards and forwards in infinitum' (Nietzsche, 1968 [1889]: 93). In turn, Foucault's work has, of course, penetrated and transformed the boundaries between a wide range of academic disciplines and fields, including criminology.

Literary studies are influencing criminology. For example, following Burke (1989), Gusfield (1981) and Wagner-Pacifici (1986) have used literary theory to analyse public culture discourse about crime and criminals. The law-as-literature field has shown similar cross-fertilization among disciplines (Posner, 1990), as has the study of how law criminalizes and regulates writing and other forms of representation (Stewart, 1991).

Historians, political scientists and sociologists have converged on questions about how institutions and their authorities imprint social reality, and thereby constitute their identities, ideologies and authority, through discourses and practices of crime and punishment (Gladstone et al., 1991).This has led to changes in each discipline. Historians have become more sensitive to wider questions in social and political theory, while sociologists and political scientists have better anchorage for understanding the institutions and reform processes that are the objects of their enquiries.

At the same time criminology helps to make clear that there are distinct differences among and within academic disciplines. Academic disciplines cannot be entirely folded into one another and made a single entity. This consideration is related to the point that there are limits to any given body of knowledge and its ways of knowing. Criminology tells us a great deal about the limited character and methodologies of particular disciplines.

In the light of the above considerations, the fragmentation of criminological literature and the blurring of disciplinary boundaries cannot be thought of as representing an acute phase that must be endured until the field can be properly diagnosed and corrected. Rather, the fragmentation of criminology is a chronic condition. While the growth in the academy and in its myriad discourses and communications media mean that criminology has become more fragmented, this merely represents an accentuation of what has always been the case.

If a criminologist takes this view, he or she also lets go of the belief that academic consensus is possible or desirable, since all narratives of crime can never be united. An ultimate vision of truth and synthesis of knowledge is fantasy. The truths that constitute scientific knowledge can no longer be thought of as individual pieces of a puzzle to be put together to form a whole. While a celebration of fragmentation is not limited to those who write from a postmodernist position, Lyotard's conclusion to *The Postmodern Condition* is exemplary. In the face of unifying meta-narratives such as science and Marxism, he says:

> We have paid a high enough price for the nostalgia of the whole and the one, for the reconciliation of the concept and the sensible, of the transparent and the communicable experience. Under the general demand for slackening and for appeasement, we can hear the mutterings of the desire for a return of terror, for the realization of the fantasy to seize reality. The answer is: Let us wage war on totality; let us be witness to the unpresentable; let us activate the differences and save the honour of the name. (Lyotard, 1984: 81–2)

When fragmentation is viewed as the norm, a situation of reverse onus is created. Concern shifts from the problem of fragmentation in criminology to those who view the fragmentation of criminology to be a problem. Pluralism is no longer viewed as indicative of a crisis of knowledge. The analytical eye becomes focused instead on those wishing to unify and essentialize the field, and to silence antagonistic voices (Cheal, 1990). There must be an interrogation of any authoritative claims over what is reputable.

A fragmented criminology does not lack direction. To portray criminology as lacking in direction is disrespectful of the interested parties – often ex-centrics such as the poor, women, blacks and gays – who have resisted and forced a wider range of political issues and methodologies onto academic agendas (Hutcheon, 1989: esp. 57–73). The fragmentation of criminology can be viewed as indicative of the collapse of conservative orthodoxies which were previously more successful at imposing a relatively monolithic order upon the field. Scholars can enjoy using the fragments to create mosaics. For example, Butler (1990) says that her analytical strategy in the area of gender deviance is based on a desire

> to affirm those positions on the critical boundaries of disciplinary life. The point is not to stay marginal, but to participate in whatever network of marginal zones is spawned from other disciplinary centers and which, together, constitute a multiple displacement of those authorities. The complexity of gender requires an interdisciplinary and postdisciplinary set of discourses in order to resist the domestication of gender studies or women studies within the academy and to radicalize the notion of feminist critique. (Butler, 1990: xiii)

It is peculiar indeed to still find criminologists who essentialize the field in the ways discussed above. To be other than highly reflexive can only lead to frustration and a narrowness of focus. Perhaps it is their tendency to be insufficiently reflexive in a highly reflexive world that leads some criminologists to question the relevance of a lot of criminology, and to retreat into either a narrow political concern or a single discipline that they believe will finally allow mastery.

Ethnocentric in terms of discipline and political position, many criminologists persist in believing that what they do is most central and worthwhile, while other approaches are worn, unproductive, or simply wrongheaded. As is characteristic of all forms of ethnocentrism, they experience dis-ease about disciplinary boundaries that are blurred or disintegrating. This heightens their anxiety about the value of their own projects and the distinctiveness of their own academic identity. They react by trying to essentialize criminology into a more unified, even singular project, and to proselytize in terms of that project. Of course their efforts intensify and proliferate the very thing they are trying to avoid, that is an acute sense that the field is coming apart. The only viable *academic* sensibility is to encourage people to let their minds wander, to travel intellectually across the boundaries and frontiers and perhaps never return to them. It is connections with myriad cultures of knowledge that are crucial for the vitality of criminology.

# References

Ashworth, A. (1988) 'Criminal justice and the criminal process', in P. Rock (ed.), *A History of British Criminology*. Oxford: Oxford University Press.

Burchell, G., Gordon, C. and Miller, P. (eds) (1991) *The Foucault Effect: Studies in Governmentality*. Chicago, IL: University of Chicago Press.

Burke, K. (1989) *On Symbols and Society*. Chicago, IL: University of Chicago Press.

Butler, J. (1990) *Gender Trouble: Feminism and the Subversion of Identity*. New York: Routledge.

Capra, F. (1976) *The Turning Point: Science, Society and the Rising Culture*. New York: Simon and Schuster.

Cheal, D. (1990) 'Authority and incredulity: sociology between modernism and postmodernism', *Canadian Journal of Sociology*, 15(2): 129–48.

Cohen, S. (1972) *Folk Devils and Moral Panics*. London: Paladin.

Davis, M. (1990) *City of Quartz*, London: Verso.

Farrington, D., Ohlin, L. and Wilson, J. (1986) *Understanding and Controlling Crime*. Berlin: Springer-Verlag.

Foucault, M. (1972) *The Order of Things: an Archaeology of the Human Sciences*. New York: Random House.

Foucault, M. (1977) *Discipline and Punish: the Birth of the Prison*. New York: Pantheon.

Foucault, M. (1980) 'Debat avec Michel Foucault', in M. Perrot (ed.), *L'impossible Prison: Recherche sur le système pénitentiaire au XIX siècle*. Paris: Seuil.

Gibbons, D. (1979) *The Criminological Enterprise*. Englewood Cliffs, NJ: Prentice-Hall.

Giddens, A. (1987) *Social Theory and Modern Sociology*. Cambridge: Polity.

Gladstone, J., Ericson, R. and Shearing, C. (eds) (1991) *Criminology: a Reader's Guide*. Toronto: Centre of Criminology, University of Toronto.

Griffiths, C. and Verdun-Jones, S. (1989) *Canadian Criminal Justice*. Toronto: Butterworths.

Guignon, C. and Hylery, D. (1990) 'Biting the bullet: Rorty on private and public morality', in A. Malachowski (ed.), *Reading Rorty*. Cambridge, MA: Blackwell.

Gusfield, J. (1981) *The Culture of Public Problems*. Chicago, IL: University of Chicago Press.

Hagan, J. (1989) *Structural Criminology*, Cambridge: Polity.

Hall, S., Critcher, C., Jefferson, T., Clarke, J. and Roberts, B. (1978) *Policing the Crisis*. London: Macmillan.

Hutcheon, L. (1989) *A Poetics of Postmodernism: History, Theory, Fiction*. New York: Routledge.

Jones, T., MacLean, B. and Young, J. (1986) *The Islington Crime Survey*. Aldershot: Gower.

Laclau, E. and Mouffe, C. (1985) *Hegemony and Socialist Strategy: Towards a Radical Democratic Politics*. Thetford: Thetford Press.

Lea, J. and Young, J. (1984) *What is to be done about Law and Order*. London: Penguin.

Lipsitz, G. (1990) *Time Passages: Collective Memory and American Popular Culture*. Minneapolis, MN: University of Minnesota Press.

Lyotard, J.-F. (1984) *The Postmodern Condition: a Report on Knowledge*. Minneapolis, MN: University of Minnesota Press.

McGaw, D. (1991) 'Governing metaphors: the war on drugs', *American Journal of Semiotics*, 8: 53–74.

MacLean, B. and Milovanovic, D. (1991) 'On critical criminology', in B. MacLean and D. Milovanovic (eds), *New Directions in Critical Criminology*. Vancouver: The Collective Press.

Marcus, G. (1986) 'Contemporary problems of ethnography in the modern world system', in J. Clifford and G. Marcus (eds), *Writing Culture: the Poetics and Politics of Ethnography*. Berkeley, CA: University of California Press.

Michalowski, R. (1991) 'Niggers, welfare scum, and homeless assholes: the problems of idealism, consciousness and context in Left Realism', in B. Maclean and D. Milovanovic (eds), *New Directions in Critical Criminology*. Vancouver: The Collective Press.

Nietzsche, F. (1968 [1889]) *Twilight of the Idols*. London: Penguin.

Posner, R. (1990) *Law as Literature*. Cambridge, MA: Harvard University Press.

Rabinow, P. (1977) *Reflections on Fieldwork in Morocco*. Berkeley, CA: University of California Press.

Rabinow, P. (1986) 'Representations are social facts: modernity and postmodernity in anthropology', in J. Clifford and G. Marcus (eds), *Writing Culture: the Poetics and Politics of Ethnography*. Berkeley, CA: University of California Press.

Reich, R. (1991) 'Secession of the successful', *New York Times Magazine*, 20 January.

Rock, P. (1988) 'The present state of criminology in Britain', in P. Rock (ed.), *A History of British Criminology*. Oxford: Oxford University Press.

Schwartz, M. (1991) 'The future of critical criminology', in B. MacLean and D. Milovanovic (eds), *New Directions in Critical Criminology*. Vancouver: The Collective Press.

Shearing, C. (1989) 'Decriminalizing criminology: reflections on the literal and tropological meaning of the term', *Canadian Journal of Criminology*, 31: 169–78.

Sherman, L. (1992) 'Attacking crime: policing and crime control', in M. Tonry and N. Morris (eds), *Modern Policing*. Chicago, IL: University of Chicago Press.

Sherman, L., Gartin, P. and Buerger, M. (1989) 'Hot spots of predatory crime: routine activities and the criminology of place', *Criminology*, 27: 27–55.

Skogan, W. (1990) *Disorder and Decline*. New York: Free Press.

Stewart, S. (1991) *Crimes of Writing*. New York: Oxford University Press.

Taylor, I., Walton, P. and Young, J. (1973) *The New Criminology*. New York: Harper and Row.

Thomas, C. (1984) 'From the editor's desk', *Criminology*, 22: 467–71.

Wagner-Pacifici, R. (1986) *The Moro Morality Play: Terrorism as Social Drama*. Chicago, IL: University of Chicago Press.

Wilson, J. (1975) *Thinking About Crime*. New York: Basic Books.

Wilson, J. and Herrnstein, R. (1985) *Crime and Human Nature*. New York: Simon and Schuster.

Young, J. (1986) 'The failure of criminology: the need for radical realism', in R. Matthews and J. Young (eds), *Confronting Crime*. London: Sage.

Young, J. (1988a) *Realist Criminology*. London: Sage.

Young, J. (1988b) 'Risk of crime and fear of crime: a realist critique of survey based assumptions', in M. Maguire and J. Ponting (eds), *Victims of Crime: a New Deal*. Milton Keynes: Open University Press.

Zimring, F. and Hawkins, G. (1990) *The Scale of Imprisonment*. Chicago, IL: University of Chicago Press.

# Index